EVOLUTION AND THE GENETICS OF POPULATIONS

EVOLUTION AND THE GENETICS OF POPULATIONS
A Treatise in Three Volumes

VOLUME 2
THE THEORY OF GENE FREQUENCIES

Sewall Wright

THE UNIVERSITY OF CHICAGO PRESS
CHICAGO AND LONDON

Standard Book Number: 226–91050–4

Library of Congress Catalog Card Number: 67–25533

THE UNIVERSITY OF CHICAGO PRESS, CHICAGO 60637

The University of Chicago Press, Ltd., London

Published 1969

Printed in the United States of America

To my wife Louise

CONTENTS

CHAPTER 1

Introduction

Volume 1 of this treatise was concerned with the genetic and biometric foundations on which population genetics must be built. Since the emphasis here is to be on higher organisms, most emphasis will be placed on diploids, but some attention must be given to the haploid phase, to sex-linked loci, and to polysomic loci and polyploids. Equational segregation will in general be taken for granted, but the consequences of unequal segregation will be discussed briefly. Linkage must be given considerable attention. Recurrent mutation, typically at rates of the order of 10^{-5} per generation or less, giving rise to an enormous number of different alleles (at least at the molecular level), will be taken as one of the basic phenomena.

Chromosome aberration as a factor in evolution will be largely deferred until volume 3, because it does not lend itself well to either determinate or stochastic mathematical treatment, to which volume 2 is to be devoted. Differences in cytoplasmic heredity will be discussed only briefly, because of their great diversity of modes and our relatively imperfect present understanding of them.

The relations of genes to characters of the organisms and ultimately to selection were discussed at considerable length in volume 1 and will be of primary importance in the present volume. The consequences of the various kinds of selection will in general be worked out for different degrees of dominance. Diverse patterns of factor interaction will be considered, with special attention to the consequences of selection directed toward an intermediate optimum.

The biometric principles discussed in volume 1 will be assumed throughout. Of primary importance is the theory of compound variables. It will in general be assumed that the distributions of quantitatively varying characters are normal on an appropriate scale. The modes of treatment of point variables and threshold characters are also, however, of major importance.

Path analysis, which was discussed at considerable length, will be made use of in many connections, especially in dealing with inbreeding, assortative mating, and other aspects of population structure.

Finally, the multiple factor theory of quantitative variability, discussed at length near the end of volume 1, will be basic to a large part of the present volume.

CHAPTER 2

Genotypic Frequencies under Random Mating

Single Autosomal Locus

Yule (1902) showed that after the first generation of a cross $(AA \times aa)$, the composition of a population with respect to a pair of Mendelian alleles remains indefinitely 25% AA:50% Aa:25% aa under random mating in the absence of disturbing factors. Castle (1903) worked out the binomial square distributions for other gene frequencies. Weinberg (1908) and Hardy (1908) independently expressed this in more general form, and Weinberg carried the generalization to the case of multiple alleles.

Consider a population of haploid organisms which is classified according to the frequencies (q_i) of the alleles (A_i) at locus A. The array of gene frequencies can be written

$$(2.1) \qquad q_1 A_1 + q_2 A_2 + \cdots + q_k A_k.$$

If the population is self-contained (no immigration), if each gene always duplicates according to its kind (no mutation), and if the probabilities of duplication and loss are the same for all alleles (no selection), this array of gene frequencies may be expected to remain the same because of the symmetry of the Mendelian mechanism, except for accidents of sampling, the effects of which are slight in a large population and indeterminate in direction.

The situation is not altered if at times there is conjugation to form diploid zygotes which later undergo equational reduction to form cells in which the properties of the alleles have not been modified by association in the diploid phase.

Random mating in the diploid phase implies random combination of the alleles. Thus, consider an autosomal locus A and the array of females $\sum_j \sum_i f_{ij(F)} A_i A_j$ and of males $\sum_j \sum_i f_{ij(M)} A_i A_j$ in which the frequencies, $f_{ij(F)}$ and $f_{ij(M)}$, are not necessarily the same. The frequencies of the various sorts of matings are given by expansion of the product of these arrays. The frequency of any class of homozygous offspring, for example of A_1A_1 with frequency $f_{11(o)}$, can easily be written, letting subscript x represent collectively all alleles of A_1:

$$(2.2) \quad f_{11(o)} = f_{11(F)}f_{11(M)} + 0.5f_{11(F)}f_{1x(M)} + 0.5f_{1x(F)}f_{11(M)} + 0.25f_{1x(F)}f_{1x(M)}.$$

The frequency of A_1 in the eggs produced by the females is $q_{1(F)} = f_{11(F)} + 0.5f_{1x(F)}$, and similarly in the sperms of the males, $q_{1(M)} = f_{11(M)} + 0.5f_{1x(M)}$. Thus:

$$(2.3) \qquad\qquad f_{11(o)} = q_{1(F)}q_{1(M)},$$

as expected from random combination of the gene frequencies in the parental gametes.

By classifying the parents according to any two specified alleles, for example A_1 and A_2, and letting y represent collectively all other alleles, it can similarly be shown that random mating yields the proportion of heterozygotes, A_1A_2, expected by random union of gametes.

$$(2.4) \qquad\qquad f_{12(o)} = q_{1(F)}q_{2(M)} + q_{1(M)}q_{2(F)}.$$

Under the above conditions, the zygote frequencies are the same in sons and daughters, and the gene frequencies of their gametes are the averages of the corresponding gene frequencies in the parental gametes.

$$(2.5) \quad q_{1(o)} = f_{11(o)} + 0.5f_{1x(o)} = q_{1(F)}q_{1(M)} + 0.5[q_{1(F)}q_{x(M)} + q_{x(F)}q_{1(M)}],$$
$$q_{1(o)} = 0.5[q_{1(F)} + q_{1(M)}]$$

since

$$(q_{1(F)} + q_{x(F)}) = (q_{1(M)} + q_{x(M)}) = 1.$$

It is to be noted that if a population is started from unequal numbers of males and females, the effective gene frequency is not that which would be obtained from the individuals, disregarding sex, but is the average of those calculated separately for the sexes, as of course is to be expected since each offspring has just one father and one mother, irrespective of the numbers of males and females in the parental population.

Dropping subscripts (F) and (M) where $q_{1(F)} = q_{1(M)}$, the gametic arrays of both sexes of the offspring are $\sum q_i A_i$ and the zygotes of their randombred progeny may be written as the product of these arrays:

$$(2.6) \qquad (q_1A_1 + q_2A_2 + \cdots + q_KA_K)^2 = \sum_j \sum_i q_iq_jA_iA_j.$$

Since the array of frequencies in the gametes of those individuals remains unchanged from the preceding generation, $\sum q_i A_i$, the zygotic array after another generation of random mating is still the same, and this continues as long as random mating is continued (and there are no disturbing factors). This array is usually known as the Hardy–Weinberg distribution.

Two Autosomal Loci

Weinberg (1909) noted that in a random breeding population, the alleles in two loci approach random combination asymptotically, in contrast with the immediate attainment of equilibrium in the loci separately. The mode of approach was given by Robbins (1918) from analysis of the full gametic and zygotic arrays. It will be convenient for what follows to derive his results by path analysis (Wright 1933b).

Assume random mating and the same gene frequencies in males and females at each of two autosomal loci, A_1 and B_1. This means starting from the offspring generation if the foundation males and females differed in gene frequencies.

The departure from random combination in the gametes may be measured by the correlations with respect to the values (which may be arbitrary) assigned to the alleles at each locus. The symbols for the genes will be used for their values.

$$\bar{A} = \sum (q_i A_i) \qquad\qquad \sigma_A{}^2 = \sum [q_i(A_i - \bar{A})^2]$$
$$\bar{B} = \sum (q_j B_j) \qquad\qquad \sigma_B{}^2 = \sum [q_j(B_j - \bar{B})^2]$$
$$r_{AB} = [\sum \sum f_{ij} A_i B_j - \bar{A}\bar{B}]/\sigma_A \sigma_B$$

If there is random combination $f_{ij} = q_i q_j$:

(2.7) $$r_{AB} = \left\{ \sum \left[q_i A_i \sum (q_j B_j) \right] - \bar{A}\bar{B} \right\} \Big/ \sigma_A \sigma_B = 0.$$

The form which this correlation takes if there are only pairs of alleles $(A, a;\ B, b)$ or if any one allele is opposed to all others collectively, is as follows, assigning values 0 and 1 to the alleles at each locus:

(2.8)

	b	B	
A	f_{Ab}	f_{AB}	q_A
a	f_{ab}	f_{aB}	p_A
	p_B	q_B	1

$$\bar{A} = q_A = f_{Ab} + f_{AB}, \qquad \sigma_A = \sqrt{(p_A q_A)}$$
$$\bar{B} = q_B = f_{AB} + f_{aB}, \qquad \sigma_B = \sqrt{(p_B q_B)}$$
$$r_{AB} = \frac{f_{AB} - q_A q_B}{\sqrt{(p_A q_A p_B q_B)}} = \frac{f_{AB} f_{ab} - f_{Ab} f_{aB}}{\sqrt{(p_A q_A p_B q_B)}}$$

If $r_{AB} \neq 0$ in the general case, its value after a generation can be found from Figure 2.1, in which A_F and B_F are variables representing respectively the A and B loci in ova, and A_M and B_M, similarly, are variables representing the loci in the sperms. The variables $(AA)_F$ and $(BB)_F$ represent the female zygotes as sums of gametic values and $(AA)_M$ and $(BB)_M$ represent the male

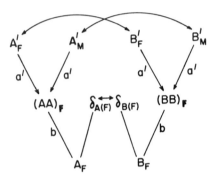

FIG. 2.1. Path diagram for two linked autosomal loci (redrawn from Wright 1933*b*, Fig. 1).

zygotes. The correlations between ultimate factors differ in general in males and females because of differences in the amounts of recombination (c_F in oogenesis, c_M in spermatogenesis).

There is equal and complete determination of the zygote scores for each locus, by the scores of the uniting gametes. Since the latter are uncorrelated under random mating, the path coefficients relating zygote to parental gametes must have the value $a' = \sqrt{0.5}$ from the equation $2a'^2 = 1$ that expresses complete determination by two equal contributions.

For each locus the correlation of zygote with one of the gametes derived from it must be the same as that of this zygote with one of the gametes that contributed to it, assuming that there has been no mutation or selection, since the gene is in either instance a random choice from the two in the zygote. Because there is only one connecting path in both cases, $a' = b = \sqrt{0.5}$. The compound path coefficient, connecting gametes in successive generations, is thus $ba' = 0.5$, a result that is obviously correct from the consideration that there is a probability of identity of 0.5 and the same probability of a merely random relationship:

$$r_{AA'} = 0.5(1) + 0.5(0) = 0.5.$$

Since A_F is derived from $(AA)_F$ (with score $A_F' + A_M'$) by random sampling, the residual factor δA_F may be chosen so as to be independent of $(AA)_F$. Its score must be proportional to $(A_F' - A_M')$ to satisfy this condition. Similarly, δB_F must be proportional to $(B_F' - B_M')$. The signs of these expressions are, however, indeterminate. If A_F and B_F refer to the same gamete, δA_F and δB_F involve the same sampling process (that of meiosis) and are correlated with each other unless there is random assortment. The path coefficient relating A_F to δA_F must be $\sqrt{(1 - b^2)} = \pm \sqrt{0.5}$ to represent complete determination of A_F by $(AA)_F$ and δA_F. This also follows from the formula for δA_F. Similarly, that relating B_F to δB_F is also $\pm \sqrt{0.5}$. The correlation between δA_F with δB_F must be calculated indirectly because of the indeterminacy of the signs of these coefficients.

Let $g_F = 0.5 r_{\delta_{A(F)} \, \delta_{B(F)}}$ be the contribution to $r_{AB(F)}$ due to linkage. If there is random assortment, then $g_F | (c_F = c_M = 0.5) = 0$.

$$(2.9) \qquad r_{AB(F)} | (c_F = c_M = 0.5) = (ba')^2 [r'_{AB(F)} + r'_{AB(M)}] = 0.5 \tilde{r}'_{AB}.$$

If there is no recombination, then $r_{AB(F)} | (c_F = c_M = 0) = \tilde{r}'_{AB}$. But $r_{AB(F)} = (ba')^2 (r'_{AB(F)} + r'_{AB(M)}) + g_F = (0.5) \tilde{r}'_{AB} + g_F$. Thus

$$(2.10) \qquad g_F | (c_F = c_M = 0) = 0.5 \tilde{r}'_{AB}.$$

If there were random assortment with frequency x and complete linkage with frequency $1 - x$, the frequency of recombinant gametes c_F would be $0.5x$, giving $x = 2c_F$. The resulting value of g_F is thus

$$(2.11) \qquad g_F = [(2c_F) \times 0 + (1 - 2c_F)0.5 \tilde{r}'_{AB}] = 0.5(1 - 2c_F)\tilde{r}'_{AB},$$

and $r_{AB(F)} = 0.5 \tilde{r}'_{AB} + g_F = (1 - c_F)\tilde{r}'_{AB}$. Similarly, $g_M = 0.5(1 - 2c_M)\tilde{r}'_{AB}$, and $r_{AB(M)} = 0.5 \tilde{r}'_{AB} + g_M = (1 - c_M)\tilde{r}'_{AB}$.

$$(2.12) \qquad \tilde{r}_{AB} = 0.5[r_{AB(F)} + r_{AB(M)}] = (1 - \bar{c})\tilde{r}'_{AB},$$

where

$$\bar{c} = 0.5(c_F + c_M).$$

Thus the correlation between A and B, and hence the deviation of their joint frequency from equilibrium, falls off at the rate $\bar{c}$ per generation, as found by Robbins. This is irrespective of the number of alleles.

Let $D = f_{AB} - q_A q_B$:

$$(2.13) \qquad D_n = (1 - \bar{c})^{n-1} D_1,$$

where n relates to generation number. Thus the deviation of f_{AB} from random combination is halved in each generation if $\bar{c} = 0.5$ (random assortment). In general, half of the deviation is lost when $(1 - \bar{c})^n = 0.5$, giving $n = \log_e 0.5 / \log_e (1 - \bar{c}) = -0.693/[-\bar{c} + (1/2)\bar{c}^2 - (1/3\bar{c})^3 + \cdots]$, or approximately $0.693/\bar{c}$ if $\bar{c}$ is small.

The half period is 6.6 generations if $\bar{c} = 0.10$, as with 20% recombination in Drosophila females, 0% in males. It is 69 generations if $\bar{c} = 0.01$ and 693 generations if $\bar{c} = 0.001$.

If the effects of the genes on the characters determined by A and B are additive, the genetic correlation between the characters is given by

$0.5(r_{AB(F)} + r_{AB(M)}) = \bar{r}_{AB}$. This would fall off as above. If not additive, the relations would be more complicated, but the rate of falling-off would usually be of the same order.

It is often suggested that an observed correlation between characters in a population may be due to linkage. This may well be true in an F_2 population or in one of recent origin from a cross between strains that differed in both characters. It is not likely, however, if the population has been breeding substantially at random for hundreds of generations—even if linkage is of the order observed between pseudoalleles in higher organisms—unless there is severe selection against the rare combinations.

Multiple Autosomal Loci

The treatment of the changing relations among three or more loci requires a more elaborate method than path analysis. A general analysis was first given by Geiringer (1944, 1948). Since the algebra is rather extensive, we will give a full analysis only for three loci and merely indicate the mode of analysis for larger numbers. For a fuller treatment Geiringer's papers should be consulted.

First it may be well to give an example to show that random association in all pairs of loci does not at all imply random association in the set as a whole. In the following case, in which all gene frequencies are 0.50, A is combined at random with B and with C, which are combined at random with each other, but there is obviously not random combination among the three loci as a group.

ABC	0	aBC	0.25
ABc	0.25	aBc	0
AbC	0.25	abC	0
Abc	0	abc	0.25

The following symbolism will be used for the patterns of segregation of the four kinds of triple heterozygotes in the three locus case, with a particular allele at each opposed by all others.

	Zygotes			
Gametes	$\dfrac{ABC}{abc}$	$\dfrac{Abc}{aBC}$	$\dfrac{ABc}{abC}$	$\dfrac{AbC}{aBc}$
$ABC + abc$	l_{123}	$l_{1.23}$	$l_{12.3}$	$l_{1.2.3}$
$Abc\ + aBC$	$l_{1.23}$	l_{123}	$l_{1.2.3}$	$l_{12.3}$
$ABc\ + abC$	$l_{12.3}$	$l_{1.2.3}$	l_{123}	$l_{1.23}$
$AbC + aBc$	$l_{1.2.3}$	$l_{12.3}$	$l_{1.23}$	l_{123}
Total	1	1	1	1

A chromosome with ABC may be derived from individuals of the population in eight different ways, if the maternal (F) and paternal (M) chromosomes are distinguished. The dashes in the formulas may be filled by any allele at the locus indicated by position.

from $\dfrac{(ABC)M}{(---)F}$ or $\dfrac{(---)M}{(ABC)F}$ as a noncrossover,

from $\dfrac{(A--)M}{(-BC)F}$ or $\dfrac{(-BC)M}{(A--)F}$ by crossing over between A and B,

from $\dfrac{(AB-)M}{(--C)F}$ or $\dfrac{(--C)M}{(AB-)F}$ by crossing over between B and C,

from $\dfrac{(A-C)M}{(-B-)F}$ or $\dfrac{(-B-)M}{(A-C)F}$ by double crossing over.

Note that the same parent may enter into more than one category (e.g., $(ABC)M/(ABC)F$ can provide (ABC) in all eight ways). The eight types of contributions from females of the preceding generation to the frequency of chromosome (ABC) are as follows:

$$(2.14)\quad\begin{aligned}
f_{ABC(F)} = {}& l_{123(F)}[0.5f'_{ABC(F)} + 0.5f'_{ABC(M)}] \\
& + l_{1.23(F)}[0.5q'_{A(F)}f'_{BC(M)} + 0.5q'_{A(M)}f'_{BC(F)}] \\
& + l_{12.3(F)}[0.5q'_{C(F)}f'_{AB(M)} + 0.5q'_{C(M)}f'_{AB(F)}] \\
& + l_{1.2.3(F)}[0.5q'_{B(F)}f'_{AC(M)} + 0.5q'_{B(M)}q'_{AC(F)}].
\end{aligned}$$

The formula for $f_{ABC(M)}$ differs only in substitution of M for F in the l's. It will be assumed that the frequencies of chromosome types are the same in males and females as expected after one generation of random mating. The gene frequencies become the same in this generation and remain constant. By using $l = 0.5(l_F + l_M)$, $q = 0.5(q_F + q_M)$, $f_{BC} = 0.5(f_{BC(F)} + f_{BC(M)})$, etc., subscripts F and M may be dropped.

It will now be convenient to use subscripts such as (n), $(n-1)$, $(n-2)$, etc., instead of primes for generations:

$$f_{ABC(n)} = l_{123}f_{ABC(n-1)} + l_{1.23}q_A f_{BC(n-1)} + l_{12.3}q_C f_{AB(n-1)} \\
+ l_{1.2.3}q_B f_{AC(n-1)};$$

$$l_{123}f_{ABC(n-1)} = l_{123}^2 f_{ABC(n-2)} + l_{123}[l_{1.23}q_A f_{BC(n-2)} + l_{12.3}q_C f_{AB(n-2)} \\
+ l_{1.2.3}q_B f_{AC(n-2)}];$$

$$l_{123}^2 f_{ABC(n-2)} = l_{123}^3 f_{ABC(n-3)} + l_{123}^2[l_{1.23}q_A f_{BC(n-3)} + l_{12.3}q_C f_{AB(n-3)} \\
+ l_{1.2.3}q_B f_{AC(n-3)}].$$

By continuing this process down to $l_{123}^{n-2} f_{ABC(2)}$ and substituting in the first equation above:

$$f_{ABC(n)} = l_{123}^{n-1} f_{ABC(1)} + l_{1.23} q_A [f_{BC(n-1)} + l_{123} f_{BC(n-2)} + \cdots + l_{123}^{n-2} f_{BC(1)}]$$

(2.15)
$$+ l_{12.3} q_C [f_{AB(n-1)} + l_{123} f_{AB(n-2)} + \cdots + l_{123}^{n-2} f_{AB(1)}]$$

$$+ l_{1.2.3} q_B [f_{AC(n-1)} + l_{123} f_{AC(n-2)} + \cdots + l_{123}^{n-2} f_{AC(1)}].$$

Using l_{23} for $l_{1.23} + l_{123}$, the proportion of noncrossovers from BC/bc, $f_{BC(n-1)} = q_B q_C + l_{23}^{n-2} D_{BC(1)}$ from (2.13), where $D_{BC(1)} = f_{BC(1)} - q_B q_C$. The second term on the right in (2.15) can be now written

$$l_{1.23} \{ q_A q_B q_C [1 + l_{123} + \cdots + l_{123}^{n-2}] + D_{BC(1)} q_A (l_{23}^{n-2} + l_{123} l_{23}^{n-3} + \cdots + l_{123}^{n-2}) \}$$

$$= l_{1.23} \left\{ q_A q_B q_C \left[\frac{1 - l_{123}^{n-1}}{1 - l_{123}} \right] + D_{BC(1)} q_A l_{23}^{n-2} \left[1 - \left(\frac{l_{123}}{l_{23}} \right)^{n-1} \right] \Big/ \left[1 - \frac{l_{123}}{l_{23}} \right] \right\}$$

$$= l_{1.23} q_A q_B q_C \left[\frac{1 - l_{123}^{n-1}}{1 - l_{123}} \right] + D_{BC(1)} q_A [l_{23}^{n-1} - l_{123}^{n-1}].$$

The other terms can be written similarly, giving

$$f_{ABC(n)} = l_{123}^{n-1} f_{ABC(1)} + q_A q_B q_C (l_{1.23} + l_{12.3} + l_{1.2.3})[1 - l_{123}^{n-1}]/[1 - l_{123}]$$

(2.16)
$$+ q_A D_{BC(1)} (l_{23}^{n-1} - l_{123}^{n-1}) + q_B D_{AC(1)} (l_{13}^{n-1} - l_{123}^{n-1})$$

$$+ q_C D_{AB(1)} (l_{12}^{n-1} - l_{123}^{n-1}),$$

in which $(l_{1.23} + l_{12.3} + l_{1.2.3})$ is cancelled by $(1 - l_{123})$.

The limiting value of $f_{ABC(\infty)} = q_A q_B q_C$ as expected. Writing $D_{ABC} (= f_{ABC} - q_A q_B q_C)$ for the deviation of f_{ABC} from its limiting value:

(2.17)
$$D_{ABC(n)} = l_{123}^{n-1} D_{ABC(1)} + (l_{23}^{n-1} - l_{123}^{n-1}) q_A D_{BC(1)}$$

$$+ (l_{13}^{n-1} - l_{123}^{n-1}) q_B D_{AC(1)} + (l_{12}^{n-1} - l_{123}^{n-1}) q_C D_{AB(1)}.$$

Analogous expressions can be written for other chromosomes by the appropriate substitutions. Note that $D_{AB} = D_{ab} = -D_{Ab} = -D_{aB}$.

Similar procedures can be followed with larger numbers of loci. If recombination is the same in oogenesis and spermatogenesis so that expressions such as $0.5[f'_{AB(F)} f'_{CD(M)} + f'_{AB(M)} f'_{CD(F)}]$ can be reduced to $f'_{AB} f'_{CD}$, there is no essential complication in reducing to averages. If, however, this is not the case, such expressions cannot be simplified, and the analysis becomes more complicated. The expressions for eggs and sperms can, however, be averaged, and this is also true of the l's. The symbolism $\langle f_{AB} f_{CD} \rangle$ will be used for $0.5[f_{AB(F)} f_{CD(M)} + f_{AB(M)} f_{CD(F)}]$. In the four-locus case, the same procedure as in the three-locus case leads to the following:

$f_{ABCD(n-1)}$

$$
\begin{aligned}
&= l_{1234}^{n-1} f_{ABCD(1)} + l_{1.234} q_A [f_{BCD(n-1)} + l_{1234} f_{BCD(n-2)} + \cdots + l_{1234}^{n-2} f_{BCD(1)}] \\
&\quad + l_{12.34}[\langle f_{AB} f_{CD}\rangle_{n-1} + l_{1234}\langle f_{AB} f_{CD}\rangle_{n-2} + \cdots + l_{1234}^{n-2}\langle f_{AB} f_{CD}\rangle_1] \\
&\quad + l_{123.4} q_D [f_{ABC(n-1)} + l_{1234} f_{ABC(n-2)} + \cdots + l_{1234}^{n-2} f_{ABC(1)}] \\
(2.18) &\quad + l_{1.2.34} q_B [f_{ACD(n-1)} + l_{1234} f_{ACD(n-2)} + \cdots + l_{1234}^{n-2} f_{ACD(1)}] \\
&\quad + l_{1.23.4}[\langle f_{AD} f_{BC}\rangle_{n-1} + l_{1234}\langle f_{AD} f_{BC}\rangle_{n-2} + \cdots + l_{1234}^{n-2}\langle f_{AD} f_{BC}\rangle_1] \\
&\quad + l_{12.3.4} q_C [f_{ABD(n-1)} + l_{1234} f_{ABD(n-2)} + \cdots + l_{1234}^{n-2} f_{ABD(1)}] \\
&\quad + l_{1.2.3.4}[\langle f_{AC} f_{BD}\rangle_{n-1} + l_{1234}\langle f_{AC} f_{BD}\rangle_{n-2} + \cdots + l_{1234}^{n-2}\langle f_{AC} f_{BD}\rangle_1]
\end{aligned}
$$

As n becomes indefinitely large, the first term disappears and all of the others approach the form $l_x q_A q_B q_C q_D [1 + l_{1234} + l_{1234}^2 + \cdots]$. Thus

$$
\begin{aligned}
(2.19) \quad f_{ABCD(\infty)} &= (1 - l_{1234}) q_A q_B q_C q_D (1 + l_{1234} + l_{1234}^2 + \cdots) \\
&= q_A q_B q_C q_D .
\end{aligned}
$$

Similarly, with five or any larger number of loci, there is equilibrium, not surprisingly, only when the frequencies are combined at random.

The way in which a gene, carried initially between two others, disentangles itself from the association in the long run under random mating is illustrated (Table 2.1) in the symmetrical three-locus case $(q_A = q_B = q_C = 1/2)$. There is considerable simplification, since $D_{ABC(n)} = D_{abc(n)}$ and $D_{ABC} = q_A D_{BC} + q_B D_{AC} + q_C D_{AB}$ in this case.

$$
(2.20) \qquad D_{ABC(n)} = 0.5[l_{23}^{n-1} D_{BC(1)} + l_{13}^{n-1} D_{AC(1)} + l_{12}^{n-1} D_{AB(1)}].
$$

The frequencies of all eight types of gametes are close to equality after 50 generations with 10% recombination, but more than 500 generations are required for the same degree of approach with 1% recombination.

Sex-linked Loci

In dealing with sex linkage, it is convenient to assume that the males are XY and the females XX with respect to sex chromosomes. Primes will be used to indicate preceding generations. Males derive their X chromosomes only from their mothers, while females derive theirs with equal probabilities from both parents. Females must be given double weight in averaging gene frequencies because they furnish twice as many X chromosomes as males:

$$
\begin{aligned}
q_M &= q_F', \\
(2.21) \qquad q_F &= 0.5(q_F' + q_M'), \\
\bar{q} &= (1/3)(2q_F + q_M) = (1/3)(2q_F' + q_M') = \bar{q}'.
\end{aligned}
$$

TABLE 2.1. Frequencies by generations of the various kinds of gametes on starting from ABC/abc and assuming 10% or 1% recombination between adjacent loci and no double crossing over.

	FROM ABC/abc $c_{AB} = c_{BC} = 0.10$ $c_{AC} = 0.20$			FROM ABC/abc $c_{AB} = c_{BC} = 0.01$ $c_{AC} = 0.02$		
GENERATION	ABC abc	Abc aBC ABc abC	AbC aBc	ABC abc	Abc aBC ABc abC	aBc aBc
0	0.4000	0.0500	0.0000	0.4900	0.0050	0.0000
1	.3650	.0650	.0050	.4852	.0074	.00005
2	.3350	.0770	.0110	.4804	.0098	.0001
5	.2677	.1004	.0315	.4664	.0165	.0005
10	.2028	.1169	.0633	.4446	.0270	.0015
20	.1502	.1241	.1015	.4055	.0449	.0047
50	.1260	.1250	.1240	.3169	.0813	.0205
100	.1250	.1250	.1250	.2306	.1091	.0512
200	.1250	.1250	.1250	.1599	.1229	.0943
500	.1250	.1250	.1250	.1266	.1250	.1234
1000	0.1250	0.1250	0.1250	0.1250	0.1250	0.1250

$$(2.22) \qquad \begin{aligned} (q_F - \bar{q}) &= -0.5(q_F' - \bar{q}), \\ (q_M - \bar{q}) &= -0.5(q_M' - \bar{q}). \end{aligned}$$

Thus deviation in either sex from $\bar{q}$, as defined above, is followed in the next generation by half as great a deviation in the opposite direction (Jennings 1916). There is a rapid oscillatory approach to equilibrium at $\bar{q}$. The zygotic arrays at equilibrium are $(\sum q_i X_i)^2$ in females but $(\sum q_i X_i)Y$ in males.

Two Sex-linked Loci

For two sex-linked loci, the path diagrams for males and females are radically different (Figure 2.2). Apart from this, the mode of analysis is the same as with autosomal loci (Wright 1933a).

$$(2.23) \qquad \begin{aligned} r_{AB(M)} &= r'_{AB(F)}, \\ r_{AB(F)} &= 0.25[r'_{AB(F)} + r'_{AB(M)}] + g, \\ &= 0.25[r'_{AB(F)} + r''_{AB(F)}] + g, \\ r_{AB(F)}|(c = 0) &= 0.5[r'_{AB(F)} + r''_{AB(F)}], \\ r_{AB(F)}|(c = 0.5) &= 0.25[r'_{AB(F)} + r''_{AB(F)}], \\ r_{AB(F)} &= 0.5(1 - c)[r'_{AB(F)} + r''_{AB(F)}]. \end{aligned}$$

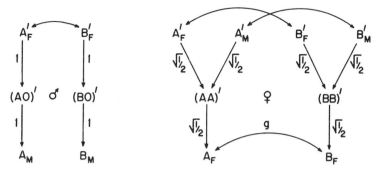

FIG. 2.2. Path diagrams for two sex-linked loci (redrawn from Wright 1933*b*, Figs. 2,3).

The limiting ratio of $r_{AB(F)}$ in successive generations can be found by putting $\lambda = r_{AB(F)}/r'_{AB(F)} = r'_{AB(F)}/r''_{AB(F)}$:

$$\lambda^2 - 0.5(1 - c)(\lambda + 1) = 0,$$

$$\lambda = 0.25(1 - c) + \left(\frac{9 - 5c}{12}\right)\sqrt{\left[1 - \left(\frac{4c}{9 - 5c}\right)^2\right]} \approx 1 - \frac{2c}{3}\left[1 + \frac{c}{9 - 5c}\right].$$

The rate of approach $(1 - \lambda)$ is thus approximately $2c/3$ per generation instead of c as with pairs of autosomal loci.

Autosomal and Sex-linked Loci

From Figure 2.3:

(2.25) $r_{AB(M)} = 0.5r'_{AB(F)},$

$r_{AB(F)} = 0.25[r'_{AB(F)} + r'_{AB(M)}] = 0.125[2r'_{AB(F)} + r''_{AB(F)}].$

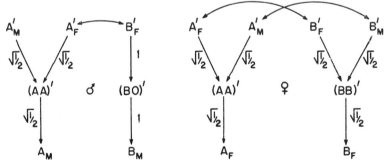

FIG. 2.3. Path diagrams for autosomal and sex-linked loci (redrawn from Wright 1933*b*, Figs. 4,5).

Putting $\lambda = r_{AB(F)}/r'_{AB(F)} = r'_{AB(F)}/r''_{AB(F)}$:

(2.26)
$$8\lambda^2 - 2\lambda - 1 = 0$$
$$\lambda = 0.5$$

Thus an autosomal and a sex-linked locus go halfway toward equilibrium in each generation as in the case of two autosomal loci in different chromosomes (Wright 1933a).

Equilibrium at a Polysomic Locus

This case also can be dealt with conveniently by path analysis (Figure 2.4). The genes that enter into the same gamete (for example G_1') may be correlated with each other (v'), but the gametes (G_1', G_2') that unite to form the zygote (Z') are uncorrelated in accordance with the assumption of panmixia. It is again assumed that arbitrary scores are assigned each allele and that G' and Z' are scored as sums. Z' is completely determined by the scores of its $2k$ genes (if a $2k$-ploid or $2k$-somic). Letting a' represent a compound path coefficient relating Z' to one of its component genes, and b that relating one of those in a gamete produced by Z', to Z', we may write the equation expressing complete determination, ($\sum^{2k} p_{Z'A'}r_{Z'A'} = 1$):

$$2ka'\{a'[1 + (k - 1)v']\} = 1;$$

(2.27)
$$a' = \sqrt{\left\{\frac{1}{2k[1 + (k - 1)v']}\right\}}.$$

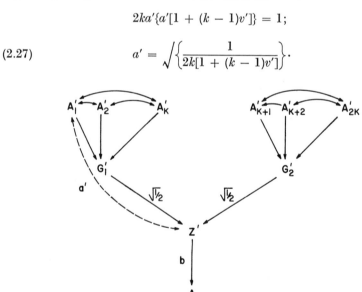

FIG. 2.4. Path diagram for a polysomic locus

If there is no mutation, immigration, or selection, $r_{AZ'} = r_{Z'A'}$ since A is merely a random one of the same genes, A', of which Z' is composed.

$$(2.28) \qquad b = a'[1 + (k - 1)v'] = \sqrt{\left[\frac{1 + (k - 1)v'}{2k}\right]}.$$

Thus $ba' = 1/2k$ irrespective of v', as is of course to be expected. The correlation, f, between two different genes of the same zygote is

$$f = \frac{(k - 1)v + k(0)}{2k - 1} = \frac{(k - 1)v}{2k - 1}.$$

Assume that there is a probability, e, that two different genes in G' trace to the same gene a generation back by double reduction.

$$(2.29) \qquad v = e(1) + (1 - e)f' = e + (1 - e)\frac{(k - 1)v'}{2k - 1}.$$

Correlation v approaches a limiting value, v_∞, which may be found by equating v and v'.

$$(2.30) \qquad v_\infty = \frac{(2k - 1)e}{k + (k - 1)e}.$$

Thus if $e = 0$, then $v_\infty = 0$ (gene completely linked to centromere). If $e = 1/(4k - 1)$, then $v_\infty = 1/(2k + 1)$ (gene duplicants assorted at random).

Consider the nature of the correlation v if the genes are assigned the values $A = 1, a = 0$ with frequency array $[qA + (1 - q)a]$ and the array of pairs as $[xAA + yAa + zaa]$.

	a	A	
A	$y/2$	x	q
a	z	$y/2$	p
	p	q	1

The mean of the gene frequency array is q and its standard deviation $\sqrt{(pq)}$ where $p = 1 - q$. By the product moment formula:

$$v = (x - q^2)/pq, \qquad \text{giving} \qquad v = 1 - y/(2pq).$$

Thus

$$y = 2pq(1 - v).$$

$$y_\infty = 2pq(1 - v_\infty) = 2pq[k(1 - e)]/[k + (k - 1)e],$$

$$(2.31) \qquad x = q - 0.5y, \quad x_\infty = (1 - v_\infty)q^2 + v_\infty q,$$

$$z = p - 0.5y, \quad z_\infty = (1 - v_\infty)p^2 + v_\infty p.$$

The mode of approach to the limiting values is the question of most interest. It is the same for x, y, z, and v. Let

$$\lambda = \frac{y - y_\infty}{y' - y_\infty} = \frac{v_\infty - v}{v_\infty - v'} = \frac{(k-1)(1-e)}{2k-1}.$$

If $k = 1$ (disomic), $\lambda = 0$;

If $k = 2$ (tetrasomic), $\lambda = (1-e)/3$;

If $k = 3$ (hexasomic), $\lambda = [2(1-e)]/5$;

If $k = 4$ (octosomic), $\lambda = [3(1-e)]/7$.

Since v_∞ is a function merely of k and e, it is the same for all modes of dichotomizing the set of alleles. Let A_1 and A_2 be two of the alleles. At equilibrium:

$$f_{11} = (1 - v_\infty)q_1{}^2 + v_\infty q_1;$$
$$f_{22} = (1 - v_\infty)q_2{}^2 + v_\infty q_2.$$

Alleles A_1 and A_2 may be grouped together as if one, A_{12}, with frequency $(q_1 + q_2)$:

$$f_{12\ 12} = (1 - v_\infty)(q_1 + q_2)^2 + v_\infty(q_1 + q_2).$$

But

$$f_{12\ 12} = f_{11} + f_{22} + f_{12}.$$

Thus

$$f_{12} = 2(1 - v_\infty)q_1 q_2.$$

If arbitrary values are assigned to all of the alleles, $\bar{A} = \sum (q_i A_i)$,

$\sigma_A{}^2 = \sum (q_i A_i{}^2) - \bar{A}^2.$

$$r_{ij} = \left[\sum_j \sum_i (f_{ij} A_i A_j) - \bar{A}^2 \right] / \sigma_A{}^2;$$

(2.32) $$= \left\{ (1 - v_\infty) \sum \left[q_i A_i \left(\sum q_j A_j \right) \right] + v_\infty \sum q_i A_i{}^2 - \bar{A}^2 \right\} / \sigma_A{}^2;$$

$$= v_\infty.$$

Thus the correlation between two representatives of a locus in gametes, at equilibrium, is the same for any set of arbitrary values assigned the alleles, as well as for any dichotomy (or other cleavage) of the alleles, as implied by the derivation from path analysis.

If there is no double reduction, v_∞ becomes 0 for all types of polyploids and the ratio of successive terms becomes $(k - 1)/(2k - 1)$, and thus $1/3$ in tetraploids, $2/5$ in hexaploids, and $3/7$ in octoploids; and the distribution of frequencies in gametes becomes $[\sum q_i A_i]^k$ and in zygotes $(\sum q_i A_i)^{2k}$ in agreement with Haldane (1930c).

For tetrasomics with double reduction, the frequencies of gamete types at equilibrium are merely those of f_{ii} and f_{ij}, already given. The array at equilibrium is thus

$$
\begin{aligned}
\text{(2.33)} \quad & (1 - v_\infty) \sum \sum [q_i q_j A_i A_j] + v_\infty \sum q_i A_i{}^2 \\
& = \left[2(1 - e) \sum \sum (q_i q_j A_i A_j) + 3e \sum q_i A_i{}^2 \right] / (2 + e).
\end{aligned}
$$

The deviation from equilibrium, $D_n = [(1 - e)/3]^n D_0$, falls off very rapidly. The subject has been discussed in terms of the full gametic and zygotic arrays by Fisher (1947), Fisher and Mather (1943), Geiringer (1948a, 1949a,b), and Bennett (1954). The distribution of gametic types in hexaploids in the presence of double reduction given by Geiringer is considerably more complicated than her result with tetrasomics, with which the results derived above agree.

Two Polysomic Loci

In Figure 2.5:

c = proportion of recombination of A and B in pairs drawn from zygote.

r = correlation between A and B of same chromosome.

s = correlation between A and B in different chromosomes of same gamete.

t = correlation between A and B in different gametes from same zygote.

u = correlation between A and B in mated individuals (here $u = 0$).

v = correlation between two A's in same gamete as before.

w = correlation between two A's in uniting gametes (here $w = 0$).

g and h are contributions to r and s, respectively, due to linkage.

Recalling that $p_{AA'} = 1/(2k)$:

$$
\text{(2.34)} \quad t = \left(\frac{1}{2k} \right)^2 \left\{ 2k[r' + (k - 1)s'] \right\} = \left(\frac{1}{2k} \right) [r' + (k - 1)s'].
$$

The contribution g to r because of assortment in the same reduction division can be calculated as for diploids. If there is random assortment $c = (2k - 1)/2k$, $g = 0$ and $r = t = [1/(2k)][r' + (k - 1)s']$. If there is complete linkage $(c = 0)$, then $r = r' = t + g$ and $g = r' - t$.

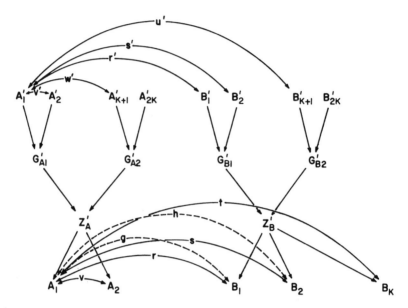

FIG. 2.5. Path diagram for two polysomic loci

Recombination at rate c is equivalent to random assortment with frequency $2kc/(2k - 1)$ and complete linkage with frequency $[1 - 2kc/(2k - 1)]$.

$$g = \left(1 - \frac{2kc}{2k - 1}\right)(r' - t),$$

$$r = t + g = \left[1 - \frac{2kc}{2k - 1}\right]r' + \frac{2kc}{2k - 1}t,$$

$$= (1 - c)r' + \left(\frac{k - 1}{2k - 1}\right)cs'.$$

Similarly,

$$s = t + h.$$

If there is random assortment, $h = 0$ and $s = t$. If there is complete linkage,

$$s = \frac{1}{2k - 1}[(k - 1)s' + ku'], \quad h = \frac{k - 1}{2k - 1}s' - t. \qquad (u' = 0)$$

In general,

$$h = \left[1 - \frac{2kc}{2k-1}\right]\left[\frac{k-1}{2k-1}s' - t\right],$$

$$s = t + h = \left(\frac{c}{2k-1}\right)r' + \frac{k-1}{2k-1}\left[1 - \frac{c}{2k-1}\right]s'.$$

If $k = 1$ (disomic):

s does not exist,

$$r = (1 - c)r' \quad \text{as before,}$$
$$t = (1/2)r'.$$

If $k = 2$ (tetrasomic):

$$r = (1 - c)r' + (1/3)cs',$$
$$s = (1/3)cr' + (1/3)[1 - (1/3)c]s',$$
$$t = (1/4)r' + (1/4)s'.$$

If $k = 3$ (hexasomic):

$$r = (1 - c)r' + (2/5)cs',$$
$$s = (1/5)cr' + (2/5)[1 - (1/5)c]s',$$
$$t = (1/6)r' + (1/3)s'.$$

If $k = 4$ (octosomic):

$$r = (1 - c)r' + (3/7)cs',$$
$$s = (1/7)cr' + (3/7)[1 - (1/7)c]s',$$
$$t = (1/8)r' + (3/8)s'.$$

The deviations from random combination of A and B may be expected to approach a uniform rate of decrease. This rate may be found from the characteristic equation of the recurrence equations for r and s. The larger root is the pertinent one. Let C_1, C_2, C_3, and C_4 be the coefficients; let $r = C_1 r' + C_2 s'$ and $s = C_3 r' + C_4 s'$ and λ the ratio of successive values:

$$\begin{vmatrix} C_1 - \lambda & C_2 \\ C_3 & C_4 - \lambda \end{vmatrix} = 0,$$

$$(C_1 - \lambda)(C_4 - \lambda) - C_2 C_3 = 0,$$

$$\lambda^2 - (C_1 + C_4)\lambda + (C_1 C_4 - C_2 C_3) = 0,$$

$$\lambda = (1/2)\{(C_1 + C_4) + \sqrt{[(C_1 - C_4)^2 + 4C_2 C_3]}\} \approx C_1 + \frac{C_2 C_3}{C_1 - C_4}$$

if $(C_1 - C_4)^2$ is much larger than $4C_2C_3$. Substituting the values of C_1, C_2, C_3, and C_4:

$$\lambda \approx (1 - c) + \frac{(k - 1)c^2}{k(2k - 1) - (4k^2 - 5k + 2)c}.$$

The rate $(1 - \lambda)$ at which the deviation from random combination falls off is thus approximately c if c is small, for all polysomics (exactly in disomics), but if $c = 0.5$ it becomes $(2k - 1)/(6k - 4)$. These apply irrespective of the number of alleles.

The frequency of any type of chromosome in a tetrasomic can be determined from the correlation $r = (f_{AB} - q_A q_B)/\sqrt{(p_A q_A p_B q_B)}$ between loci A and B in the same chromosome.

$$r\sqrt{(p_A q_A p_B q_B)} = f_{AB} - q_A q_B = -(f_{Ab} - q_A p_B) = -(f_{aB} - p_A q_B)$$
$$= f_{ab} - p_A p_B,$$

$$f_{AB} = q_A q_B + r\sqrt{(p_A q_A p_B p_B)},$$
$$f_{Ab} = q_A p_B - r\sqrt{(p_A q_A p_B q_B)},$$
$$f_{aB} = p_A q_B - r\sqrt{(p_A q_A p_B q_B)},$$
$$f_{ab} = p_A p_B + r\sqrt{(p_A q_A p_B p_B)}.$$

Similarly, the frequency of association of a gene of locus A with one of locus B in another chromosome of the same gamete can be determined from the correlation $s = (f_{A/B} - q_A q_B)/\sqrt{(p_A q_A p_B q_B)}$. The formulas for $f_{A/B}$, etc., are the same as the corresponding ones above except for substitution of s for r.

The frequencies of chromosome types in higher polysomics require more information than can be obtained from the correlations between pairs of genes. Analysis in terms of chromosome types has been given by Bennett (1953, 1954) for hexasomics as well as tetrasomics, following a mode of treatment of linkage theory for polyploids presented by Fisher (1947). Crow (1954b) has simplified the rather complicated forms given by Bennett.

The Field of Gene Frequencies

The momentary state of a random breeding population may be described by its array of gene frequencies, with qualifications to be considered later. It is often convenient to think of this array as located in a geometric field. Any given array may be represented as a point in a closed system located so that the lengths of perpendiculars to the boundaries (lines if two dimensions, areas if three dimensions, solids if four dimensions) are proportional to the frequencies (Wright 1960a).

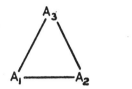

 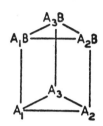 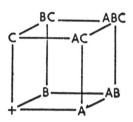

FIG. 2.6. Gene frequency systems with two or three independent frequencies (top and bottom rows respectively) (Wright 1960a, Figs. 1–5).

There are two possible two-dimensional systems, Figures 2.6a, 2.6b.

Figure 2.6a: $(p_1 A_1 + p_2 A_2 + p_3 A_3)$, $\sum p = 1$, equilateral triangle of unit height.

Figure 2.6b: $[(1 - p)a + pA][(1 - q)b + qB]$ square of unit height.

There are three possible three-dimensional systems, Figures 2.6c, 2.6d, and 2.6e.

Figure 2.6c: $(p_1 A_1 + p_2 A_2 + p_3 A_3 + p_4 A_4)$, $\sum p = 1$, regular tetrahedron of unit height.

Figure 2.6d: $(p_1 A_1 + p_2 A_2 + p_3 A_3)[(1 - q)b + qB]$, $\sum p = 1$, triangular prism of unit height with equilateral triangles of unit height at top and at bottom.

Figure 2.6e: $[(1 - p)a + pA][(1 - q)b + qB][(1 - r)c + rC]$, cube of unit height.

More extensive systems can be represented by networks that bring out the relations much less completely. There are five four-dimensional systems. The bounding solids (degenerate systems in which one gene is absent) can be recognized in Figure 2.7, but not all simultaneously. It cannot be brought out adequately that these have no internal points in common and that the locations of nondegenerate systems are not included in any of them. Lines

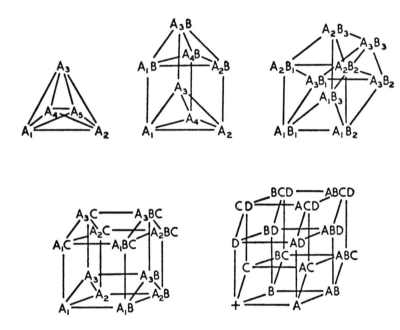

FIG. 2.7. Gene frequency systems with four independent frequencies (Wright 1960*a*, Figs. 6–10).

representing the gene frequencies must be perpendicular to *all* lines in the solid boundary to which they are dropped:

Figure 2.7a: $(p_1A_1 + p_2A_2 + p_3A_3 + p_4A_4 + p_5A_5)$, $\sum p = 1$. This four-dimensional system is bounded by five regular tetrahedra.

Figure 2.7b: $(p_1A_1 + p_2A_2 + p_3A_3 + p_4A_4)[(1 - q)b + qB]$, $\sum p = 1$. This four-dimensional figure is bounded by two regular tetrahedra (top and bottom) and four regular prisms. The p's are measured by perpendiculars to the latter, the q's to the former.

Figure 2.7c: $(p_1A_1 + p_2A_2 + p_3A_3)(q_1B_1 + q_2B_2 + q_3B_3)$, $\sum p = 1$, $\sum q = 1$. This system is bounded by six triangular prisms. The p's are measured by perpendiculars to the three that lack A_1, A_2, and A_3, respectively, and the q's by the perpendiculars to the three that lack B_1, B_2, and B_3, respectively.

Figure 2.7d: $(p_1A_1 + p_2A_2 + p_3A_3)[(1 - q)b + qB][(1 - q)c + qC]$, $\sum p = 1$. This system is bounded by three cubes and four triangular prisms.

Figure 2.7e: $[(1 - p)a + pA][(1 - q)b + qB][(1 - r)c + rC][(1 - s)d + sD]$. This is a regular four-dimensional coordinate system with sides of unit length. There are eight bounding cubes.

Four alleles at each of a dozen loci constitute a rather modest "gene pool" for a single character. It requires only $36(= 12 \times 3)$ independent variables (q's) to describe the set of gene frequencies. The number of different potential genotypes is, however, a million million (10 combinations at each of 12 loci). Systems involving four alleles at each of 100 loci involve 300 independent gene frequencies, but imply the possibility of enormously more genotypes (10^{100}) than there are elementary particles in the visible universe.

CHAPTER 3

Systematic Change of Gene Frequency: Single Loci

Such evolutionary processes as mutation, immigration, selection, and inbreeding seem at first sight to be so different in nature that quantitative comparisons of effects would be impossible. They may, however, be brought under a common viewpoint by measuring each by its effect on gene frequency much as physical phenomena of the most diverse sorts may be reduced to a common quantitative basis by measuring their capacities to do work.

The persistence of gene frequencies discussed in the preceding chapter is not due to a true equilibrium but merely to the absence of disturbing processes. The slightest disturbance may be expected to produce changes that have no tendency to revert.

Mutation Pressure

In small or even in moderately large laboratory populations, followed for only a few generations, the occurrence of a mutation appears to be a unique, unpredictable event. In a population numbered in the millions, or even in a much smaller one, considered over thousands of generations, a particular type of mutation is likely to recur many times. Rates of the order of 10^{-5} to 10^{-6} per generation have been found to be characteristic of observable mutations in organisms as diverse as maize, Drosophila species, and man.

One may think of a certain type of recurrent mutation as exerting a pressure on the frequency of the mutant gene. Let Δq represent the amount of change per generation and u and v the rates from and to the gene in question (Wright 1931).

(3.1) $$\Delta q = v(1 - q) - uq.$$

If these are the only disturbing processes a true equilibrium is reached at the frequency at which $\Delta q = 0$. Let $\hat{q}$ be the equilibrium frequency.

(3.2) $$\hat{q} = v/(u + v),$$

(3.3) $$\Delta q = -(u + v)(q - \hat{q}).$$

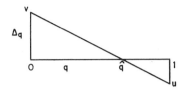

FIG. 3.1. Δq (exaggerated) under reversible mutation (redrawn from Wright 1940b, Fig. 1).

This is a stable equilibrium since any deviation from $\hat{q}$ tends to be reduced. A graphic representation with exaggerated ordinates is given in Figure 3.1.

The total amount of change after any given number of generations is easily found. The subscripts here indicate generation.

$$q_1 - \hat{q} = [1 - (u + v)](q_0 - \hat{q}),$$

(3.4) $\quad\quad q_2 - \hat{q} = [1 - (u + v)](q_1 - \hat{q}),$

$$q_n - \hat{q} = [1 - (u + v)]^n(q_0 - \hat{q})$$

This sort of calculation applies only if there are discrete generations. In many cases, generations overlap so that it is convenient to think of change as occurring continuously. If time (t) is measured in average intervals between generations, Δq may be replaced approximately by the time derivative of q.

$$\frac{dq}{dt} = -(u + v)(q - \hat{q}),$$

(3.5) $\quad\quad \int \frac{dq}{q - \hat{q}} = -(u + v) \int dt,$

$$\log (q - \hat{q}) = \log (q_0 - \hat{q}) - (u + v)t,$$

$$q - \hat{q} = e^{-(u + v)t}(q_0 - \hat{q}).$$

Since $e^{-(u+v)t}$ is approximately $[1 - (u + v)]^t$ if u and v are small, the expectation for n average generations agrees approximately with that for n discrete generations.

Multiple alleles have usually been found at loci that have been studied intensively. Let u_{ix} be the rate of mutation from A_i to A_x, using subscripts here to distinguish alleles (Wright 1949b, 1955).

(3.6) $\quad\quad \Delta q_x = \sum (u_{ix}q_i) - \left(\sum u_{xi}\right)q_x.$

Determination of the equilibrium point requires solution of $(k - 1)$ independent equations of the type $\Delta q_i = 0$ if there are k alleles, noting that $\sum^k \Delta q_i = 0$. For three alleles:

$$
\begin{aligned}
\hat{q}_1 &= (u_2 u_3 - u_{23} u_{32})/D, \\
\hat{q}_2 &= (u_3 u_1 - u_{31} u_{13})/D, \\
\hat{q}_3 &= (u_1 u_2 - u_{12} u_{21})/D,
\end{aligned}
$$

(3.7)

in which the denominator D is the sum of the numerators.

With four alleles:

(3.8)
$$
\hat{q}_1 = \begin{vmatrix} u_2 & -u_{32} & -u_{42} \\ -u_{23} & u_3 & -u_{43} \\ -u_{24} & -u_{34} & u_4 \end{vmatrix} / D.
$$

The values are analogous for larger numbers of alleles. With an unlimited number of alleles, there are, of course, no equilibrium frequencies. There is continuing evolution at each locus.

It is probably true that most recurrence rates for point mutations refer to classes of alleles with more or less similar effects rather than to single ones, from the standpoint of complete DNA composition. It is sometimes convenient, moreover, to oppose a given allele or group of alleles to all of the rest, in the formula $\Delta q = v(1 - q) - uq$, but it must be recognized that v (and also u, if q is the frequency of a group) are variables dependent on the gradually changing composition of the arrays of alleles to which they pertain.

Conversions and Recombination

So far it has been assumed that the rate of mutation from one allele to another is independent of the array of gene or zygote frequencies. A class of mutations known as conversions occurs, however, only in heterozygotes and has been interpreted as due to rearrangements of the components of a complex locus by a highly localized double exchange.

Even ordinary recombination may indeed be treated as a sort of mutation (Wright 1952a; Kimura 1956c). Let f_{AB}, f_{Ab}, f_{aB}, and f_{ab} be the frequencies of "alleles" AB, Ab, aB, and ab, respectively, and assume random union of gametes. Let c be the average proportion of recombination in double heterozygotes. Then, letting $D = (f_{AB} f_{ab} - f_{Ab} f_{aB})$, measure the departure from random combination:

$$
\begin{aligned}
\Delta f_{AB} &= \Delta f_{ab} = -cD, \\
\Delta f_{Ab} &= \Delta f_{aB} = cD.
\end{aligned}
$$

The value of D after a generation is, as noted earlier (2.13):

$$(3.9) \quad (f_{AB} - cD)(f_{ab} - cD) - (f_{Ab} + cD)(f_{aB} + cD) = (1 - c)D.$$

Chromosome Aberrations

Chromosome aberrations may be treated as gene mutations insofar as they segregate in simple Mendelian fashion. Those that affect a particular locus under consideration may be treated as alleles at this locus. Thus rates of occurrence of deficiencies at such a locus may be treated as recurrence rates of the same mutation, even if not identical with respect to deficiencies at other loci. If, on the other hand, the full effect of a chromosome aberration is being considered and it is of a type that depends on two independent breaks for its origin, exact recurrence would ordinarily be so rare that each mutation must be treated as a unique event.

An aberration that brings about a change in the number of segregating entities (polysomy, polyploidy) brings about a change in the pattern of segregation and thus must be dealt with as a process supplementary to the evolution of gene frequency systems within a given segregation pattern.

Immigration Pressure

Natural species are often composed of subspecies that differ conspicuously except in the zones of intergradation, and these are likely to be subdivided into local races with marked statistical differences and so on in hierarchic fashion to ones with only slight statistical differences. The ultimate unit is the more or less completely isolated local population or deme (Gilmour and Gregor 1939) within which breeding may usually be treated as occurring at random. It is very unusual for a whole species to consist of a single deme.

The attempt to develop a precise mathematical theory of population genetics for such a complex entity as a typical species is hardly practicable. Much of the mathematical discussion in this book is thus restricted to the deme.

The effective size of a deme is often so small that the recurrence rates of mutations are likely to be negligibly small even over considerable periods of time. On the other hand, immigration of individuals from other demes, followed by crossbreeding, must nearly always be a very important factor in their histories.

Let m_o be the observed proportion of the population of a deme replaced per generation from outside and Q_o the observed frequency of a given gene in the immigrants in contrast with q for the same gene within the deme (Wright 1931):

(3.10) $$\Delta q = -m_o(q - Q_o).$$

It may, however, be desirable to express this in terms of the average gene frequency Q of the species as a whole. The actual immigrants, coming largely from neighboring demes, would ordinarily differ little in gene frequency from the deme in question. If their deviation is only 1% of the deviation of this deme from that of the species as a whole, effective m would be only 1% of the observed percentage of immigration.

In general:

(3.11) $$m = m_o\left(\frac{q - Q_o}{q - Q}\right).$$

It may be noted that while m_o is necessarily the same for all loci, this need not be true of the effective values. Nevertheless, it is a convenient approximation to treat m as uniform except where consequences of nonuniformity are under consideration.

Equation (3.10) is a linear equation which may be written in a form analogous to the equation for mutation pressure:

(3.12) $$\Delta q = mQ(1 - q) - m(1 - Q)q.$$

This may be combined with mutation pressure in dealing with a pair of alleles:

(3.13)
$$\Delta q = (mQ + v)(1 - q) - [m(1 - Q) + u]q$$
$$\Delta q = -(m + u + v)(q - \hat{q}), \qquad \hat{q} = (mQ + v)/(m + u + v).$$

In most cases, however, m would be so much greater than $(u + v)$ that the latter can be ignored in dealing with demes.

Selection Pressure in General

Selection is here defined as any process in a population that alters gene frequency in a directed fashion without change of the genetic material (mutation) or introduction from without (immigration). Thus there can be no selection unless more than one allele is present. Change in gene frequency from selection, $(\Delta q)_s$, is thus zero if $q = 0$ or $q = 1$, and if these values are possible its formula must include $q(1 - q)$ as a factor and be at least quadratic in contrast with the linear formulas for changes in gene frequency from recurrent mutation and immigration.

As thus defined, selection includes many diverse processes. It includes gametic and zygotic selection or, in plants, gametophytic and sporophytic selection. It may depend on differences in mortality or in tendency to emigrate up to and in some cases beyond the reproductive age, on differences in onset and duration of reproductive capacity, on success in mating, and on fecundity. Many cases can be dealt with fairly adequately by assigning constant selective values (relative or absolute) under given conditions to genes or one locus genotypes (assumed in this chapter), or to multiple factor genotypes (next chapter), but in general selection is a function of the set of gene frequencies (chapter 5). This is obviously true if there is selective mating among genotypes or if selection depends on social interactions of any other sort, but it is probably always true to some extent. A case that would be of major importance, if common, is that in which there is unequal segregation in heterozygotes (meiotic drive, Sandler and Novitski 1957). This will be dealt with in this chapter.

As implied above, selective values, both relative and absolute, are functions of the environmental conditions. They are also functions of population density. Sex differences and the occurrence of selection at more than one stage of the life cycle introduce other complications in mathematical analysis. It is evident that any attempt at complete mathematical formulation must ordinarily lead to extreme complexity and that simplifying assumptions are necessary in order to obtain an understanding of the essential effects of each complication.

Castle (1903) worked out the effect of continued elimination of recessives and Norton (in Punnett 1915) calculated the number of generations required to change the frequencies of mutations, dominant or recessive, with certain selective advantages over type, by specified amounts. More comprehensive studies of the effects of selection under diverse assumptions were presented by Haldane in a series of papers in the 1920's and 1930's, summarized in book form in 1932.

Haldane gave his results in terms of the ratio (u) of the frequency of the mutant gene to that of the type gene. For many purposes, it is more convenient to deal symmetrically with gene frequencies (q). My formulas (Wright 1931) may be translated into frequency ratios by the relations $q = u/(1 + u)$, $\Delta q = \Delta u/(1 + u)^2$, and the reverse transformation may be made by means of the relations $u = q/(1 - q)$, $\Delta u = \Delta q/(1 - q)^2$.

Genic Selection

The formulas for genic selection to be considered in this section apply not only to selection among monoploid organisms such as bacteria and many algae, but to the gametes and gametophytes of diploid organisms. Let w_x be the reproductive value (in general a variable) of a given gene relative to that for a suitable standard (usually one of the alleles) over a period of a full generation. For a gamete or gametophyte this must take account of differences in viability, productivity, etc., of the zygotes that carry this gene, giving full weight to homozygotes and half weight to heterozygotes. The change in frequency from one generation to the next is

$$(3.14) \qquad \Delta q_x = (w_x/\bar{w})q_x - q_x = q_x(w_x - \bar{w})/\bar{w},$$

where $\bar{w}(= \sum w_i q_i)$ is the average of the reproductive values for all alleles.

It is often more convenient to express this in terms of selective differences by writing $1 + s_x$ in place of w_x.

$$(3.15) \qquad \Delta q_x = q_x(s_x - \bar{s})/(1 + \bar{s}).$$

With slight selective differences, the denominator may be treated as one and dropped without serious error.

If there are only two alleles, with reproductive values $1 + s$ and 1, respectively, $\bar{s} = sq$, and

$$(3.16) \qquad \Delta q = sq(1 - q)/(1 + sq) \approx sq(1 - q).$$

If s is a constant, the approximate formula is the simplest possible that is compatible with $\Delta q = 0$ for both $q = 0$ and $q = 1$.

In some connections it is desirable to deal with absolute rates of increase (or decrease) and absolute reproductive values. These will be represented by capital letters. The absolute rate of increase of the population per generation $(\Delta N/N)$ is $\bar{S} = \bar{W} - 1$ under a given array of genes at other loci and of environmental conditions. The formulas for Δq_x are the same as above after substituting W and S for w and s but the denominators cannot be treated as unity if the population is rapidly changing in size even though the differences among the alleles in the locus under consideration are very small.

The model used above applies exactly only to populations with discrete generations. If the population is changing continuously because of overlapping generations, it is more appropriate to express rate of change as the time derivative of q, instead of as a finite difference, Δq. Haldane (1927a) showed that if time is measured in average generation lengths, the difference is slight. Fisher (1930a) based a formulation for a continuous population on Lotka's equation (Lotka 1925):

$$(3.17) \qquad \int_0^\infty e^{-mx} l_x b_x \, dx = 1,$$

in which l_x is the proportion of survival to age x, b_x is the birth rate at age x, and m, which Fisher called the Malthusian parameter, measures the momentary growth rate of the population. It can be applied to particular genes by proper averaging of the individuals that carry it.

If the absolute reproductive value of a gene for a small fraction of a generation is $(1 + m \, \Delta t)$ in a continuous population, that for a period equal to an average generation is $(1 + m \, \Delta t)^{1/\Delta t}$, which becomes e^m with infinitesimal Δt. Thus e^m corresponds to W, and m to $\log_e W$ if this period is treated as if it were a discrete generation. The change of gene frequency in the interval Δt may be written:

(3.18)
$$\Delta q = q\left(\frac{1 + m \, \Delta t}{1 + \bar{m} \, \Delta t}\right) - q = q\left(\frac{m - \bar{m}}{1 + \bar{m} \, \Delta t}\right) \Delta t,$$

leading to

(3.19)
$$\frac{dq}{dt} = q(m - \bar{m}).$$

This is similar in form to the discrete formula $\Delta q = q(S - \bar{S})/(1 + \bar{S})$ except for the denominator (Kimura 1958). Thus we can pass from the discrete formula to the corresponding continuous one merely by dropping the denominator $\overline{W} \, (= 1 + \bar{S})$ in the former and replacing S by m with a change in meaning that is often slight. There is no difference in a static population.

Constant Selective Values of Locus Genotypes

Pairs of autosomal alleles.—In this section, selective values are assigned locus genotypes instead of genes. Mating is assumed to be at random.

	Zygote	Frequency (f)	Value (W)	$\dfrac{df}{dq}$
	A_1A_1	q^2	$1 + S_{11}$	$2q$
(3.20)	A_1A_2	$2q(1 - q)$	$1 + S_{12}$	$2(1 - 2q)$
	A_2A_2	$(1 - q)^2$	$1 + S_{22}$	$-2(1 - q)$
		1		0

The most direct method of calculating Δq is to subtract the frequency of A_1 before from that after selection, noting that $\overline{W} = \sum Wf = 1 + q^2 S_{11} + 2q(1 - q)S_{12} + (1 - q)^2 S_{22}$.

(3.21)
$$\Delta q = \frac{q^2(1 + S_{11}) + q(1 - q)(1 + S_{12})}{\overline{W}} - q$$
$$= q(1 - q)[qS_{11} + (1 - 2q)S_{12} - (1 - q)S_{22}]/\overline{W}.$$

Δq can also be found from formula (3.14):

$$W_1 = [q^2(1 + S_{11}) + q(1 - q)(1 + S_{12})]/q$$
$$= 1 + qS_{11} + (1 - q)S_{12},$$

$$W_2 = [q(1 - q)(1 + S_{12}) + (1 - q)^2(1 + S_{22})]/(1 - q)$$
$$= 1 + qS_{12} + (1 - q)S_{22},$$

$$\overline{W} = qW_1 + (1 - q)W_2,$$

(3.22)
$$\Delta q = q(W_1 - \overline{W})/\overline{W}$$
$$= q(1 - q)[qS_{11} + (1 - 2q)S_{12} - (1 - q)S_{22}]/\overline{W}.$$

By using the values of the differential coefficients in the last column of (3.20) above, it may be seen that (Wright 1942, 1949b):

(3.23)
$$\Delta q = q(1 - q) \sum \left(W \frac{df}{dq} \right) \Big/ 2\overline{W}.$$

If, as assumed in this chapter, the W's for zygotes are constant (Wright 1935, 1937):

(3.24)
$$\Delta q = q(1 - q) \frac{d\overline{W}}{dq} \Big/ 2\overline{W}.$$

Criticisms of this formula by Fisher (1941) were based on misinterpretations which have been discussed elsewhere (Wright 1964).

For consideration of dominance effects, it is convenient to use relative selective values. These are here assumed to be constant.

	f	w
AA	q^2	$1 + s_2$
(3.25) Aa	$2q(1 - q)$	$1 + s_1$
aa	$(1 - q)^2$	1

$$\bar{w} = 1 + 2s_1 q(1 - q) + s_2 q^2$$

$$\frac{d\bar{w}}{dq} = 2s_1(1 - 2q) + 2s_2 q$$

(3.26)
$$\Delta q = q(1 - q)[s_1 + (s_2 - 2s_1)q]/\overline{W}.$$

If the heterozygotes are exactly intermediate ($s_2 = 2s_1$),

(3.27)
$$\Delta q = s_1 q(1 - q)/(1 + 2s_1 q).$$

If the heterozygote is at the geometric mean of the homozygotes,

$$w_2 = (1 + s_1)^2, \qquad \bar{w} = (1 + s_1 q)^2, \qquad \frac{d\bar{w}}{dq} = 2s_1(1 + s_1 q),$$

(3.28)
$$\Delta q = s_1 q(1 - q)/(1 + s_1 q).$$

This is exactly equivalent to a constant selective advantage, s, of gene A (formula [3.16]). There is, however, no appreciable difference between formulas (3.27) and (3.28) if s_1 is small, and the formulas may both be written $\Delta q = s_1 q(1 - q)$. Returning to formula (3.26):
If $s_1 = hs_2$,

$$\Delta q = s_2 q(1 - q)[h + (1 - 2h)q]/\{1 + s_2 q[2h + (1 - 2h)q]\}. \tag{3.29}$$

If $h = 1$ (A dominant),

$$\Delta q = s_2 q(1 - q)^2/[1 + s_2 q(2 - q)]. \tag{3.30}$$

If $h = 0$ (A recessive),

$$\Delta q = s_2 q^2(1 - q)/[1 + s_2 q^2]. \tag{3.31}$$

The denominators may again be dropped for small selective differences.

These formulas (Wright 1931) are equivalent to those given by Haldane (1924–27) in terms of the gene frequency ratios $q/(1 - q)$.

Formula (3.26) can be applied to heterotic loci (given first by Fisher 1922). It is usually more convenient, however, to take the heterozygote as standard in this case (Wright 1931).

(3.32)

	f	w	
A_1A_1	q^2	$1 - s$	$\bar{w} = 1 - sq^2 - t(1 - q)^2$
A_1A_2	$2q(1 - q)$	1	
A_2A_2	$(1 - q)^2$	$1 - t$	$\dfrac{d\bar{w}}{dq} = 2[t - (s + t)q]$

$$\Delta q = q(1 - q)[t - (s + t)q]/\bar{w}. \tag{3.33}$$

Equilibrium Frequencies

A favorable allele progresses toward fixation ($q = 1$), and an unfavorable one toward extinction ($q = 0$) along courses that can be approximated by substituting the time derivative for Δq and integrating. If, however, change in frequency from selection is opposed by recurrent mutation in the opposite direction, there must be an equilibrium frequency at which the opposed pressures balance.

It will be assumed here that the effect of selection is so much greater than that of mutation that the equilibrium frequency is close to one for a favorable gene and very small for an unfavorable one, making it unnecessary in either case to take account of reverse mutation.

For an unfavorable gene it is convenient to take the selective value of heterozygotes as $1 - s_1$, and of homozygotes as $1 - s_2$ relative to 1 for the favorable homozygote. If the disadvantage of the heterozygote is just half that of the homozygote ($s_2 = 2s_1$):

(3.34) $$\Delta q = v(1 - q) - s_1 q(1 - q) = 0,$$

(3.35) $$\hat{q} = v/s_1$$

where $\hat{q}$ is the equilibrium frequency.

If s_1 is much larger than v, the selective value of the rare homozygote usually makes little difference.

(3.36) $$\Delta q = v(1 - q) - q(1 - q)[s_1 + (s_2 - 2s_1)q],$$

(3.37) $$(2s_1 - s_2)q^2 - s_1 q + v = 0,$$

(3.38) $$\hat{q} = [s_1 - \sqrt{(s_1{}^2 - 8s_1 v + 4s_2 v)}]/[2(2s_1 - s_2)],$$

(3.39) $$\hat{q} \approx v/s_1 \quad \text{if} \quad s_1{}^2 > |4v(2s_1 - s_2)|.$$

Thus the equilibrium point is substantially the same over a wide range.

For a completely recessive, deleterious mutation ($s_1 = 0$),

(3.40) $$\Delta q = v(1 - q) - s_2 q^2 (1 - q) = 0,$$

(3.41) $$\hat{q} = \sqrt{(v/s_2)}.$$

The equilibrium value is much higher than in the preceding case because selection operates only against the very rare homozygotes.

For a favorable mutation, and returning to $1 + s_1$ and $1 + s_2$ as the selective values of the heterozygous and homozygous mutant, respectively, similar analysis leads $\hat{q} = 1 - u/(s_2 - s_1)$ as the equilibrium point over a wide range and $\hat{q} = 1 - \sqrt{(u/s)}$ if the mutant is completely dominant ($s_1 = s_2$). Figure 3.2 shows values of Δq (exaggerated) under semidominance, $u = 0.01s$, $\hat{q} = 0.99$, and complete dominance, $\hat{q} = 0.90$.

For heterotic loci, equation (3.33) can be written

(3.42) $$\Delta q = -(s + t)q(1 - q)(q - \hat{q})/\bar{w} \qquad \text{where} \qquad \hat{q} = \frac{t}{(s + t)}.$$

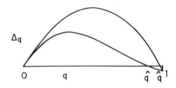

FIG. 3.2. Δq (exaggerated) under favorable selection, opposed by mutation pressure. Case of semidominance (upper) and of complete dominance (lower).

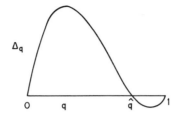

FIG. 3.3. Δq (exaggerated) under heterotic selection

The negative relation to deviations of q from equilibrium, if s and t are both positive, shows that equilibrium is stable (Figure 3.3). If both s and t are negative (heterozygote at a disadvantage to both homozygotes) there is a point of unstable equilibrium at $q = t/(s + t)$.

On introducing mutation pressure in one direction or the other,

$$(3.43) \qquad \hat{q} \approx \frac{t}{s + t} + \frac{v}{t} \qquad \text{or} \qquad \hat{q} \approx \frac{t}{s + t} - \frac{u}{s}.$$

Thus if the mutation rate in either direction is small in comparison with the selective disadvantages of the homozygotes there is only a slight displacement of the equilibrium value.

Mean Selective Value: Haldane's Principle

Haldane (1937b) pointed out a property of the mean selective value of a population at equilibrium between adverse selection and recurrent mutation that at first sight seems rather surprising, viz., that this value is independent of the severity of the selection.

If the heterozygote is exactly intermediate ($s_2 = 2s_1$), so that $\hat{q} = v/s_1$ and $\hat{w} = 1 - 2s_1\hat{q}$, it follows at once that

$$(3.44) \qquad \hat{w} = 1 - 2v,$$

a value independent of selection. It was noted above that these values of $\hat{q}$ and $\hat{w}$ hold approximately over a wide range of values of s_1 and s_2. For a completely recessive deleterious mutation, $\hat{q} = \sqrt{(v/s_2)}$,

$$(3.45) \qquad \hat{w} = 1 - s_2\hat{q}^2 = 1 - v,$$

and the depression is still independent of selection though the amount is only half as great as when the heterozygote has an appreciable deleterious effect.

The essential equivalence of all deleterious mutations from trivial to lethal, in effect on mean selective value at equilibrium, led to the concept of "genetic load" (Muller 1950; Morton *et al.* 1956). Discussion will be deferred to volume 3.

This principle does not, of course, apply at all to equilibrium due to a favorable heterotic effect of the heterozygous mutant.

Returning to the cases in which it does apply, it is important to recognize (from the formulas for Δq) that severity of selection has a great deal to do with the rate at which the above equilibrium values are approached. The evolutionary aspect is discussed in volume 3.

Selection and Immigration

The joint effects of selection and immigration are especially important in evolutionary theory. For an exactly intermediate heterozygote,

$$(3.46) \qquad \Delta q = sq(1 - q) - m(q - Q).$$

The equilibrium value is readily obtained from the quadratic equation, $\Delta q = 0$. Figure 3.4 shows Δq (exaggerated) for $Q = 0.64$, $m = 0.05$, and $s = -0.05, -0.01, 0, +0.01$, and $+0.05$, left to right.

The situation is most readily grasped from the following approximate values (Wright 1931). Note that s is here treated as negative for unfavorable selection.

	$\lvert s \rvert \gg m$	$\lvert s \rvert = m$	$\lvert s \rvert \ll m$
Favorable selection ($s > 0$)	$1 - \dfrac{m}{s}(1 - Q)$	$\sqrt{Q}$	$Q\left[1 + \dfrac{s}{m}(1 - Q)\right]$
(3.47) Unfavorable selection ($s < 0$)	$\dfrac{mQ}{(-s)}$	$1 - \sqrt{(1 - Q)}$	$Q\left[1 - \dfrac{(-s)}{m}(1 - Q)\right]$

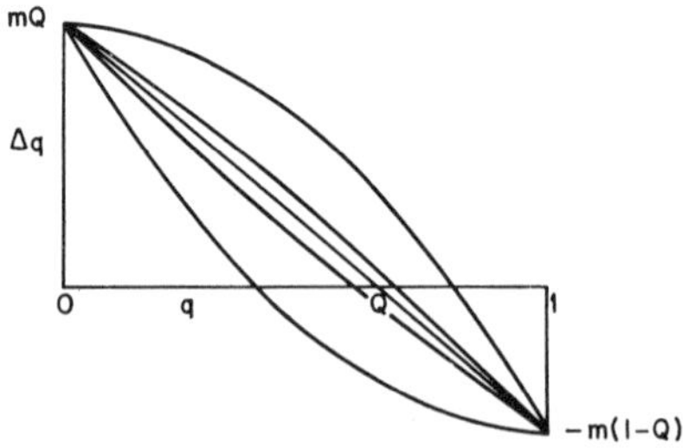

Fig. 3.4. Δq (exaggerated) under various selection pressures, all with semi-dominance, opposed by immigration pressure.

With relatively strong favorable selection the gene is almost fixed, and with relatively strong unfavorable selection it is almost lost, while with relatively weak selection the equilibrium point is slightly above or slightly below the mean gene frequency of the immigrants, according to the sign of s, all of which are, of course, as expected.

More generally:

$$(3.48) \qquad \Delta q = [s_1 + (s_2 - 2s_1)q]q(1 - q) - m(q - Q).$$

The equilibrium value of q for any particular case is readily obtained from the cubic equation, $\Delta q = 0$. Approximate solutions can readily be obtained in the cases of relatively very strong and relatively very weak selection. In the following it is assumed that the gene does not approach closely to complete dominance or recessiveness and is not heterotic.

	$\lvert s_2 - s_1 \rvert \gg m$	$\lvert s_2 - s_1 \rvert \ll m$
Favorable selection $s_2 > s_1 > 0$	$1 - \dfrac{m(1 - Q)}{s_2 - s_1}$	$Q\left\{1 + \left[\dfrac{s_1 + (s_2 - 2s_1)Q}{m}\right](1 - Q)\right\}$
(3.49) Unfavorable selection $s_2 < s_1 < 0$	$\dfrac{mQ}{(-s_1)}$	$Q\left\{1 + \left[\dfrac{s_1 + (s_2 - 2s_1)Q}{m}\right](1 - Q)\right\}$

These approximate formulas apply also however to a recessive gene ($s_1 = 0$) with relatively very strong favorable selection, and apply to a dominant gene ($s_1 = s_2$) with relatively very strong unfavorable selection.

	$\lvert s_2 \rvert \gg m$	$\lvert s_2 \rvert \ll m$
Favorable recessive $s_2 > 0, s_1 = 0$	$1 - (m/s_2)(1 - Q)$	$Q[1 + (s_2/m)Q(1 - Q)]$
(3.50) Unfavorable recessive $s_2 < 0, s_1 = 0$	$\sqrt{(mQ/-s_2)}$	$Q[1 + (s_2/m)Q(1 - Q)]$
Favorable dominant $s_2 > 0, s_1 = s_2$	$1 - \sqrt{[(m/s_2)(1 - Q)]}$	$Q[1 + (s_2/m)(1 - Q)^2]$
Unfavorable dominant $s_2 < 0, s_1 = s_2$	$mQ/(-s_2)$	$Q[1 + (s_2/m)(1 - Q)^2]$

For a heterotic locus, both selection and immigration tend to produce intermediate equilibrium values, and the resultant is a compromise. It is again most convenient to take the selective value of the heterozygote as standard and let s be the selective disadvantage of the homozygote of the gene in question and t that of the other homozygote.

(3.51) $$\Delta q = q(1 - q)[t - (s + t)q] - m(q - Q).$$

The value of $\hat{q}$ in particular cases may be readily calculated. Following are approximate values in which equilibrium deviates only slightly from values due to immigration or selection alone, $\hat{q} = Q + x$ or $\hat{q} = [t/(s + t)] + x$:

(3.52)

$$|s|, |t| \ll m \qquad Q\left\{1 + \frac{[t - (s + t)Q]}{m}[1 - Q]\right\}$$

$$|s|, |t| \gg m \qquad \frac{t}{s + t} - \frac{m[t - (s + t)Q]}{st + m(s + t)}$$

Multiple Alleles

The formulas for change of gene frequency under selection may easily be extended to systems of multiple alleles, since any group of alleles may be treated formally as if one. Let A_x be a particular allele with frequency q_x, mean selective value W_x, and let A_i, A_j be any other alleles (frequencies q_i, q_j). Double subscripts will be used in symbols for frequencies (f) and selective values (W) of zygotes. Random mating continues to be assumed.

(3.53)
$$W_x = [W_{xx}f_{xx} + 0.5 \sum (W_{xi}f_{xi})]/q_x \qquad (i \neq x),$$
$$= q_x W_{xx} + \sum (q_i W_{xi})$$

(3.54) $$\overline{W} = q_x^2 W_{xx} + 2q_x \sum (q_i W_{xi}) + \sum_j \sum_i (q_i q_j W_{ij}) \qquad (i, j \neq x),$$

(3.55)
$$\Delta q_x = q_x(W_x - \overline{W})/\overline{W}$$
$$= q_x[q_x(1 - q_x)W_{xx} + (1 - 2q_x) \sum (q_i W_{xi}) - \sum \sum (q_i q_j W_{ij})]/\overline{W}.$$

This may be put in a form that brings out the relation of Δq to the "surface" $\overline{W}$ that will be useful later, by expressing the frequencies of alleles other than A_x as fractions (c_{ix}) of $(1 - q_x)$ (Wright 1949b).

(3.56) $$q_i = c_{ix}(1 - q_x),$$

(3.57) $$\frac{\partial q_i}{\partial q_x} = -c_{ix} = \frac{-q_i}{1 - q_x},$$

$$\Delta q_x = q_x(1 - q_x)[q_x W_{xx} + (1 - 2q_x) \sum (c_{ix} W_{xi})$$

$$- (1 - q_x) \sum \sum (c_{ix} c_{jx} W_{ij})]/\overline{W}$$

(3.58)
$$= q_x(1 - q_x)\left\{\frac{W_{xx}}{2}\frac{\partial q_x^2}{\partial q_x} + \sum\left[\frac{W_{xi}}{\partial q_x}\frac{\partial(2q_x q_i)}{\partial q_x}\right]\right.$$

$$\left. + \sum\sum\left[\frac{W_{ij}}{2}\frac{\partial(2q_i q_j)}{\partial q_x}\right]\right\} / \overline{W}$$

$$= q_x(1 - q_x) \sum \left[W \frac{\partial f}{\partial q_x}\right] \Big/ 2\overline{W}.$$

In this last formula summation includes all genotypes.

If the genotypic selective values (W's) are constant, as assumed in this chapter

(3.59)
$$\Delta q_x = q_x(1 - q_x)\frac{\partial \overline{W}}{\partial q_x}\Big/ 2\overline{W}.$$

These are the same as formulas (3.23) and (3.24), except that they involve partial differentiation (under the above convention) instead of total differentiation. As brought out in Figure 3.5 for three alleles, the partial differentiation formula (3.57) measures rate of change in q_i relative to change in q_x as the position of the set of gene frequencies moves directly toward fixation of A_x. The partial derivative in (3.59) is the slope of the surface $\overline{W}$ in this direction in which the ratios of the frequencies of other alleles to each other does not change.

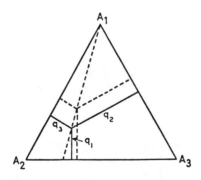

FIG. 3.5. System of three alleles. Gene frequencies q_2 and q_3 are treated as constant fractions of $(1 - q_1)$ so that $\partial q_2/\partial q_1 = -q_2/(1 - q_1)$ and $\partial q_3/\partial q_1 = -q_3/(1 - q_1)$. These partial derivatives measure the rates of changes of q_2 and q_3, respectively, relative to q_1, as the population moves toward fixation of A_1 (upper corner) (Wright 1960a, Fig. 11).

Any gene frequency (q_x) ceases to change, not only if $q_x = 0$ or $q_x = 1$ but also if the above slope is zero. A set of gene frequencies at which all Δq's are equal to zero for the latter reason is of special interest and, as earlier, is referred to as an equilibrium point.

From equation (3.55), $W_x = \overline{W}$ at equilibrium. Thus the following equations (from 3.53) must be satisfied at this point, assuming k alleles.

$$
\begin{aligned}
W_{11}\hat{q}_1 + W_{12}\hat{q}_2 + \cdots + W_{1k}\hat{q}_k &= \overline{W}, \\
W_{12}\hat{q}_1 + W_{22}\hat{q}_2 + \cdots + W_{2k}\hat{q}_k &= \overline{W}, \\
&\cdots\cdots\cdots\cdots\cdots\cdots\cdots\cdots \\
W_{1k}\hat{q}_1 + W_{2k}\hat{q}_2 + \cdots + W_{kk}\hat{q}_k &= \overline{W}.
\end{aligned}
$$
(3.60)

On dividing by $\overline{W}$, these give a system of k simultaneous linear equations for the variables $\hat{q}_i/\overline{W}$, which may be solved by Cramer's rule. Letting D be the common denominator (the determinant of the matrix of W_{ij}'s) and D_i the numerators (the determinant of the same matrix with numeral 1 substituted in the ith column), $\hat{q}_i/\overline{W} = D_i/D$. In the 3-allele case,

$$
(3.61) \qquad D_1 = \begin{vmatrix} 1 & W_{12} & W_{13} \\ 1 & W_{22} & W_{23} \\ 1 & W_{23} & W_{33} \end{vmatrix}, \qquad D_2 = \begin{vmatrix} W_{11} & 1 & W_{13} \\ W_{12} & 1 & W_{23} \\ W_{13} & 1 & W_{33} \end{vmatrix},
$$

$$
D_3 = \begin{vmatrix} W_{11} & W_{12} & 1 \\ W_{12} & W_{22} & 1 \\ W_{13} & W_{23} & 1 \end{vmatrix}.
$$

Then

$$
(3.62) \qquad \hat{q}_1 = D_1 \Big/ \sum D_i, \qquad \hat{q}_2 = D_2 \Big/ \sum D_i, \qquad \hat{q}_3 = D_3 \Big/ \sum D_i,
$$

since $\sum \hat{q}_i = 1$.

The solution was given in expanded form by Wright and Dobzhansky (1946). The following equivalent expressions are convenient:

$$
\begin{aligned}
D_1 &= (W_{12} - W_{22})(W_{31} - W_{33}) - (W_{12} - W_{23})(W_{31} - W_{23}), \\
(3.63) \quad D_2 &= (W_{23} - W_{33})(W_{12} - W_{11}) - (W_{23} - W_{31})(W_{12} - W_{31}), \\
D_3 &= (W_{31} - W_{11})(W_{23} - W_{22}) - (W_{31} - W_{12})(W_{23} - W_{12}).
\end{aligned}
$$

There can be only one solution of the set of linear equations and thus only one (if any) equilibrium point with all alleles present, however many there may be. Such an equilibrium exists if all D_i's are of the same sign, since all $\hat{q}$'s must be between 0 and 1. If one or more are zero and the rest are of the same sign the alleles corresponding to the former are absent, but all slopes at the point are zero.

If all D's are zero, solution is indeterminate. In the case of three alleles there is either a ridge or trough of uniform $\overline{W}$ on the surface $\overline{W}$.

With D's of different signs, there is no point on the surface at which all slopes are zero. There may, however, be selective pits, peaks, or saddle points at margins or corners at which the slopes relative to absent alleles are not zero.

The calculus provides criteria for determining whether an equilibrium point is at a maximum or minimum value of $\overline{W}$ or neither (e.g., a saddle point). For this purpose, the k gene frequencies, subject to the condition $\sum^{k} q_i = 1$, may be reduced to $(k - 1)$ independent variables by the substitution $q_k = 1 - q_1 - q_2 - q_{k-1}$ in the formula (3.54) for $\overline{W}$. The tests depend on the values of the second derivatives, which are readily found to be as follows. Note that these partial derivatives are of a wholly different nature from those of formula (3.57).

(3.64)
$$\frac{\partial^2 \overline{W}}{\partial q_i{}^2} = 2(W_{ii} - 2W_{ik} + W_{kk});$$
$$\frac{\partial^2 \overline{W}}{\partial q_i\, \partial q_j} = 2(W_{ij} - W_{ik} - W_{jk} + W_{kk}).$$

On approaching a maximum along any line, the slope passes from positive toward zero (at the maximum) and on continuing becomes negative. The slope of the slope is thus negative throughout, and $\partial^2 \overline{W}/\partial q_i{}^2 < 0$ for all q_i's. The opposite is true of a minimum, so that all $\partial^2 \overline{W}/\partial q_i{}^2 > 0$ in this case. There are not sufficient criteria, however, since even though $\partial^2 \overline{W}/\partial q_i{}^2$ and $\partial^2 \overline{W}/\partial q_j{}^2$ are of the same sign there may be intermediate lines of approach to an equilibrium point along which the slope of the slope is of opposite sign. If this is true, the slope relative to q_i through a line a little below the equilibrium point relative to q_j is very different from that through a line a little above the equilibrium point $(\partial^2 \overline{W}_i/\partial q_i\, \partial q_j$ large in absolute value) contrary to the case at a maximum or minimum. The criterion for either a maximum or minimum is that

(3.65)
$$\frac{\partial^2 \overline{W}}{\partial q_i{}^2} \frac{\partial^2 \overline{W}}{\partial q_j} > \left(\frac{\partial^2 \overline{W}}{\partial q_i\, \partial q_j}\right)^2.$$

At this point it is convenient to use t_{ii} for $\partial^2 \overline{W}/\partial q_i{}^2$ and t_{ij} for $\partial^2 \overline{W}/\partial q_i\, \partial q_j$ (essentially following Kimura 1956b). With this terminology, the criteria considered so far are as follows:

(1) All D_i's of the same sign for any equilibrium of all alleles.

(2) All $\begin{vmatrix} t_{ii} & t_{ij} \\ t_{ij} & t_{jj} \end{vmatrix} > 0$ for either a maximum or minimum.

$$(3) \begin{cases} \text{All } t_{ii} < 0 \text{ for maximum.} \\ \text{All } t_{ii} > 0 \text{ for minimum.} \end{cases}$$

If t_{ii} is negative and (2) holds, t_{jj} must also be negative. Thus these two criteria are sufficient to demonstrate a maximum, and similarly (2) and $t_{ii} > 0$ are sufficient to demonstrate a minimum if there are only two independent variables (as with three alleles).

If there are three independent variables (as with four alleles) there is an additional requirement:

$$(3.66) \qquad \begin{vmatrix} t_{11} & t_{12} & t_{13} \\ t_{12} & t_{22} & t_{23} \\ t_{13} & t_{23} & t_{33} \end{vmatrix}$$

must be less than zero for a maximum; greater than zero for a minimum.

Hence it may be seen that if

$$\begin{vmatrix} t_{11} & t_{12} \\ t_{12} & t_{22} \end{vmatrix} > 0,$$

it is implied that

$$\begin{vmatrix} t_{11} & t_{13} \\ t_{13} & t_{33} \end{vmatrix} > 0$$

and

$$\begin{vmatrix} t_{22} & t_{23} \\ t_{23} & t_{33} \end{vmatrix} > 0,$$

and further that $t_{33} < 0$ in the case of a maximum, $t_{33} > 0$ in the case of a minimum. Thus the three criteria

$$(3.67) \qquad t_{11} < 0, \qquad \begin{vmatrix} t_{11} & t_{12} \\ t_{12} & t_{22} \end{vmatrix} > 0, \qquad \begin{vmatrix} t_{11} & t_{12} & t_{13} \\ t_{12} & t_{22} & t_{23} \\ t_{13} & t_{22} & t_{33} \end{vmatrix} < 0$$

are all that are necessary and are sufficient for a maximum; for a minimum the sign must be reversed in the first and last cases.

With still large numbers of independent variables

$$(3.68) \qquad (-1)^n \begin{vmatrix} t_{11} & t_{12} \cdots t_{1n} \\ t_{12} & t_{22} \cdots t_{2n} \\ \cdots\cdots\cdots\cdots \\ t_{1n} & t_{2n} \cdots t_{nn} \end{vmatrix} > 0$$

for a maximum for each n up to the number of variables.

These are the conditions as given by Kimura (1956b). He notes that the determinant of the highest t matrix is equal to $\sum D_i$ as can easily be verified in the three-allele case. Essentially similar results have been given by Penrose et al. (1956) and Mandel (1959).

For a minimum, all of the successive determinants of the t matrices must be positive.

A special case of considerable interest is that in which all heterozygotes are alike in selective value and are superior to all of the homozygotes (Wright and Dobzhansky 1946).

Let $w_{ij} = 1$, $w_{ii} = 1 - s_{ii}$, etc., using relative selective values.

$$(3.69) \qquad \bar{w} = 1 - \sum s_{ii}q_i^2,$$

$$(3.70) \qquad \Delta q_x = q_x[\sum s_{ii}q_i^2 - s_{xx}q_x]/\bar{w}.$$

At equilibrium $s_{xx}q_x = \sum s_{ii}q_i^2$ is the same for all alleles

$$(3.71) \qquad \hat{q}_x = (1/s_{xx})/\sum (1/s_{ii}).$$

It is fairly obvious and easily verified that equilibrium is stable ($\bar{w}$ maximum).

The formula arrived at in the case of two heterotic alleles, $\hat{q} = t/(s + t) = (1/s)/(1/s + 1/t)$, is a special case.

If the heterozygotes all have the same selective value but are at a disadvantage with respect to all homozygotes, the signs of s_{ii}, etc., must be reversed. The same formulas as above refer to a position of unstable equilibrium ($\bar{w}$ minimum). In this case, each fixed homozygote corresponds to a selective peak, which is not at a maximum of $\bar{w}$ in the mathematical sense (nonzero slope). Although there can never be more than one equilibrium point at which all alleles are present (such as the minimum in the preceding case) there may be as many selective peaks as there are alleles.

If it is the k homozygotes that all have the same selective value, but the heterozygotes are either all superior or all inferior, the situation is more complicated. Consider the case in which the selective values of the homozygotes are taken as the standard and all heterozygotes have the value $1 + s$ except one, A_1A_2, with value $1 + t$ (Wright 1949b):

$$(3.72) \qquad \bar{w} = \left[1 + s\left(1 - \sum^k q_i^2\right) + 2(t - s)q_1q_2\right],$$

$$(3.73) \qquad \Delta q_1 = q_1\left[s\left(\sum^k q_i^2 - q_1\right) - (t - s)(2q_1q_2 - q_2)\right]\Big/\bar{w},$$

(3.74) $\Delta q_3 = q_3 \left[s \left(\sum_{i}^{k} q_i^2 - q_3 \right) - (t - s)2q_1 q_2 \right] \bigg/ \bar{w},$

(3.75) $\hat{q}_1 = \hat{q}_2 = s/[ks - (k - 2)(t - s)]$ if $0 < t < 2s,$

(3.76) $\hat{q}_3 = \hat{q}_k = (2s - t)/[ks - (k - 2)(t - s)]$ if $0 < t < 2s.$

All alleles are maintained in equilibrium if t is between 0 and $2s$. If t is negative, equilibrium is unstable: either A_1 or A_2 is eliminated according to the initial conditions. If t is greater than $2s$, all alleles other than A_1 and A_2 tend to be eliminated.

A situation of considerable importance may occur in the common case in which superiority of the heterozygote $A_1 A_2$ maintains a population in a heterallelic state. A mutation, A_3, may occur that combines the favorable effects of A_1 and A_2 and if fixed would produce a population superior to the previous heterallelic one (Haldane 1937b).

The condition for establishment of A_3, as far as selection is concerned, is that Δq_3 be positive from its first appearance. Dropping terms in q_3^2 and q_3^3 as negligible, we have:

(3.77) $\Delta q_3 = q_3[\hat{q}_1 s_{13} + \hat{q}_2 s_{23} - \hat{q}_1^2 s_{11} - 2\hat{q}_1 \hat{q}_2 s_{12} - \hat{q}_2^2 s_{22}] > 0.$

Putting

$$s = s_{12} - s_{11} \quad \text{and} \quad t = s_{12} - s_{22}, \quad \hat{q}_1 = \frac{t}{s + t}, \quad \text{and} \quad \hat{q}_2 = \frac{s}{s + t}:$$

$$\frac{t}{s + t} s_{13} + \frac{s}{s + t} s_{23} - \frac{1}{(s + t)^2} [t^2(s_{12} - s) + 2sts_{12} + s^2(s_{12} - t)] > 0,$$

$$ts_{13} + ss_{23} - (s + t)s_{12} + st > 0,$$

$$\frac{s_{13}}{s} + \frac{s_{23}}{t} - \frac{s_{12}}{s} - \frac{s_{12}}{t} + 1 > 0,$$

$$\frac{s_{13} - s_{11}}{s} + \frac{s_{23} - s_{22}}{t} - \frac{s_{12} - s_{11}}{s} - \frac{s_{12} - s_{22}}{t} + 1 > 0.$$

Replacing s and t:

(3.78) $$\frac{s_{13} - s_{11}}{s_{12} - s_{11}} + \frac{s_{23} - s_{22}}{s_{12} - s_{22}} > 1.$$

The first term is the ratio of the selective advantage of the new heterozygote $A_1 A_3$ to that of the old heterozygote, $A_1 A_2$, both relative to $A_1 A_1$. The second term is analogous for the other new heterozygote, relative to $A_2 A_2$. In the symmetrical case ($w_{22} = w_{11}$, $w_{23} = w_{13}$) the condition for establishment of A_3 is that the new heterozygotes have more than half the selective advantage over the homozygotes as the old heterozygote (Wright 1956). The selective value of the new homozygote A_3A_3 does not enter into the conditions for establishment of A_3 in the population but does, of course, with respect to fixation. It must be at least equal to that of both the new heterozygotes for this to occur. This subject has been discussed from a somewhat different viewpoint by Bodmer and Parsons (1960).

An analysis of the types of equilibrium possible in the three-allele case is instructive (equation [3.63]). Let values be assigned to D_1, D_2, and D_3 (and hence to q_1, q_2, and q_3), to w_{11}, w_{12}, and w_{22}, and solve for w_{13}, w_{23}, and w_{33}. C is a function of these known quantities:

$$w_{13} - w_{23} = \frac{D_1}{D_3}(w_{12} - w_{11}) + \frac{D_2}{D_3}(w_{22} - w_{12}) = C,$$

(3.79) $w_{13} = [w_{12}^2 - w_{11}w_{22} + D_3 + C(w_{12} - w_{11})]/(2w_{12} - w_{11} - w_{22}),$

(3.80)
$$w_{23} = [w_{12}^2 - w_{11}w_{22} + D_3 + C(w_{22} - w_{12})]/(2w_{12} - w_{11} - w_{22}),$$
$$w_{33} = w_{13} + [C(w_{12} - w_{23}) + D_1]/(w_{22} - w_{12})$$

or

$$w_{33} = w_{23} + [C(w_{12} - w_{13}) - D_2]/(w_{12} - w_{11}).$$

Taking $w_{11} = 1$ as standard, $w_{12} = 1 + s_{12}$, $w_{22} = 1 + s_{22}$, and considering the case of equilibrium at the central point $D_1 = D_2 = D_3 = D$, $\hat{q}_1 = \hat{q}_2 = \hat{q}_3 = 1/3$, in which case $C = s_{22}$:

(3.82)
$$s_{13} = (s_{12}^2 + s_{12}s_{22} + D)/(2s_{12} - s_{22}),$$
$$s_{23} = s_{13} - s_{22},$$
$$s_{33} = s_{12} - s_{23}.$$

Another case of interest is that of a marginal equilibrium, $D_1 = 0$, $D_2 = D_3 = D$, $\hat{q}_1 = 0$, $\hat{q}_2 = \hat{q}_3 = 1/2$, in which case $C = s_{22} - s_{12}$:

(3.83)
$$s_{13} = (s_{12}s_{22} + D)/(2s_{12} - s_{22}),$$
$$s_{23} = s_{13} - s_{22} + s_{12},$$
$$s_{33} = s_{22}.$$

Table 3.1 and Figure 3.6 illustrate the nature of the surface $\bar{w}$ in three-allele cases with exactly central equilibrium ($D_1 = D_2 = D_3 = D$), taking $w_{11} = 1$, $w_{22} = 1.03$ but varying w_{12} from 0.99 to 1.04 by steps of 0.01. There is no central equilibrium point if the heterozygote A_1A_2 is exactly intermediate ($w_{12} = 1.015$), since s_{13} and s_{23} become infinite if $2s_{12} - s_{22} = 0$ in equation (3.82). Four values of D are compared (0.0015, 0, -0.0005, and -0.0015). Table 3.1 gives the values deduced for w_{13}, w_{23}, and w_{33}, the locations and mean selective values of the marginal equilibrium points when a

given allele is absent, and finally the mean selective value at the central
equilibrium point at which $\hat{q}_1 = \hat{q}_2 = \hat{q}_3 = 1/3$. The nature of the surface in
each case may be inferred from comparison of these selective values.

Such a comparison is facilitated by representing the sets of gene frequencies
by points in an equilateral triangle with A_1A_1 in lower left corner, A_2A_2 in
lower right, and A_3A_3 at the top so that q_1 is the perpendicular distance from

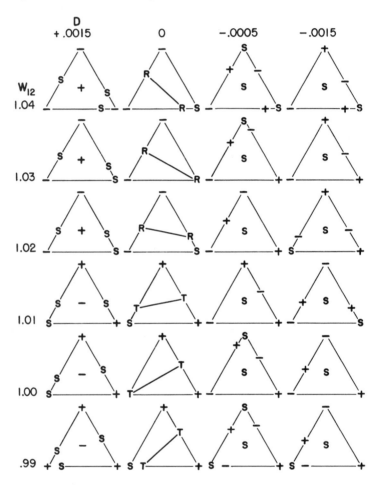

FIG. 3.6. Patterns of $\overline{W}$ with three alleles and equilibrium at equal gene frequencies (center). $W_{11} = 1$, $W_{22} = 1.03$, but W_{12} varies from 0.99 to 1.04
(rows) and D varies in the columns. The values of W_{13}, W_{23}, and W_{33} that are
implied are given in Table 3.1. Peaks are represented by $+$, saddles by S, pits by
$-$, a ridge by R-R, and a trough by T-T.

the upper right side, q_2 that from the upper left side, and q_3 that from the base. The 24 cases in Table 3.1 are represented in this way in Figure 3.6. The upper three rows are those in which w_{12} is above the average of w_{11} and w_{22}, and the lower three rows are those in which it is below. A point toward which gene frequencies move from all directions (a selective peak) is indicated by $+$. One from which there may be movement in any direction (a selective pit) is indicated by $-$. A point toward which there is movement from some directions but from which there is movement in others (a selective saddle point) is indicated by S. Level selective ridges are indicated by $R - R$ and level troughs by $T - T$.

There is a peak at the center only if $2s_{12} > s_{22}$ and D is positive (illustrated in the upper three triangles, first column). It is interesting to note than an allele, A_1, that would be lost if a certain other one, A_3, were absent, may be retained in equilibrium if this allele is present (second and third in column 1).

The central point becomes merely a point in a level ridge if $D = 0$ (upper three triangles in the second column) and becomes a saddle point if D is negative (columns 3 and 4). There are peaks, saddles, and pits in margins and corners that shift in position with changes in w_{12} and D. The direction of movement between adjacent saddles may be determined from Table 3.1.

The patterns in the lower three rows of figures are reversed from those in the upper three rows ($+$ for $-$, $-$ for $+$, T-T for R-R, but S for S) on comparing the top triangle of one with the bottom triangle in the same column in the other, next to top with next to bottom, third with fourth, and reversing the right and left lower corners of the triangles. Thus for $2s_{12} < s_{22}$ there can be central pits only if D is positive (first column of Figure 3.6). The central point is in a trough if D is zero and $2s_{12} < s_{22}$ (second column). If, however, D is negative there is a central saddle point whether $2s_{12}$ is less or greater than s_{22}.

Polysomy

It has been noted earlier that the equilibrium zygotic distribution in the case of a $2k$-somic is according to the expansion of $[(1 - q)A_2 + qA_1]^{2k}$ in the absence of double reduction, but equilibrium is not reached in one generation of random mating after a deviation, if k is greater than one (pp. 16, 17). The deviation falls off rapidly, however:

$$D_n = \left(\frac{k - 1}{2k - 1}\right)^n D_0.$$

With double reduction at rate e, the approach to equilibrium is even more rapid:

$$D_n = \left[\frac{(k - 1)(1 - e)}{2k - 1}\right]^n D_0,$$

TABLE 3.1. Selective values in three-allele cases with equilibrium at center, $D_1 = D_2 = D_3 = D$, taking $w_{11} = 1$ and $w_{22} = 1.03$ in all cases, but variation of w_{12} from 0.99 to 1.04 for four values of D. The values deduced for w_{13}, w_{23}, and w_{33}, the location and selective value of marginal equilibria for $\hat{q}_3 = 0$, $q_2 = 0$, and $q_1 = 0$, and the selective value for $\hat{q}_1 = \hat{q}_2 = \hat{q}_3 = \frac{1}{3}$ are given.

w_{12}	w_{13}	$w_{22}=1.03$ w_{23}	w_{33}	$q_3=0$ $\hat{q}_1=1-\hat{q}_2$ $\hat{q}_2$	$\hat{w}_{1-2}$	$q_2=0$ $\hat{q}_1=1-\hat{q}_3$ $\hat{q}_3$	$\hat{w}_{1-3}$	$q_1=0$ $\hat{q}_2=1-\hat{q}_3$ $\hat{q}_3$	$\hat{w}_{2-3}$	$\hat{q}_1=\hat{q}_2=\hat{q}_3=\frac{1}{3}$ $\hat{w}_{1-2-3}$
D = +0.0015										
1.04	1.086	1.056	0.984	0.80	1.032	0.457	1.039	0.265	1.037	1.042
1.03	1.11	1.08	0.95	—	—	.407	1.045	.278	1.044	1.047
1.02	1.25	1.22	0.80	—	—	.357	1.089	.312	1.089	1.090
1.01	0.81	0.78	1.23	—	—	.312	0.941	.357	0.941	0.940
1.00	0.95	0.92	1.08	—	—	.278	0.986	.407	0.985	0.983
0.99	0.974	0.944	1.046	0.20	0.998	0.265	0.993	0.457	0.991	0.988
D = 0										
1.04	1.056	1.026	1.014	0.80	1.032	0.571	1.032	—	—	1.032
1.03	1.06	1.03	1.00	—	—	.500	1.030	—	—	1.030
1.02	1.10	1.07	0.95	—	—	.400	1.040	0.250	1.040	1.040
1.01	0.96	0.93	1.08	—	—	.250	0.990	.400	0.990	0.990
1.00	1.00	0.97	1.03	—	—	—	—	.500	1.000	1.000
0.99	1.004	0.974	1.016	0.20	0.998	—	—	0.571	0.998	0.998
D = -0.0005										
1.04	1.046	1.016	1.024	0.80	1.032	0.677	1.031	0.636	1.021	1.029
1.03	1.043	1.013	1.017	—	—	.619	1.027	.833	1.016	1.024
1.02	1.05	1.02	1.00	—	—	.500	1.025	—	—	1.023
1.01	1.01	0.98	1.03	—	—	—	—	.500	1.005	1.006
1.00	1.017	0.987	1.013	—	—	.833	1.014	.619	1.003	1.005
0.99	1.014	0.984	1.006	0.20	0.998	.636	1.009	0.677	0.999	1.001
D = -0.0015										
1.04	1.026	0.996	1.044	0.80	1.032	—	—	0.415	1.016	1.022
1.03	1.01	0.98	1.05	—	—	—	—	.417	1.009	1.013
1.02	0.95	0.92	1.10	—	—	0.250	0.988	.379	0.987	0.990
1.01	1.11	1.08	0.93	—	—	.379	1.042	0.250	1.043	1.040
1.00	1.05	1.02	0.98	—	—	.417	1.021	—	—	1.016
0.99	1.034	1.004	0.986	0.20	0.998	0.415	1.014	—	—	1.008

but as noted the distribution at equilibrium is more complicated. Only the case of no double reduction and such small selective differences that there is never appreciable deviation from equilibrium will be considered here.

Zygote	f	w	$\dfrac{(w-1)}{2k}\dfrac{df}{dq}$
A_1^{2k}	q^{2k}	$1+s_{2k}$	$s_{2k}q^{2k-1}$
$A_1^{2k-1}A_2$	$2kq^{2k-1}(1-q)$	$1+s_{2k-1}$	$s_{2k-1}q^{2k-2}[(2k(1-q)-1]$
$A_1^{2k-2}A_2^{2}$	$\dfrac{2k(2k-1)}{2!}q^{2k-2}(1-q)^2$	$1+s_{2k-2}$	$\dfrac{2k-1}{2!}s_{2k-2}q^{2k-3}(1-q)$ $\times[2k(1-q)-2]$
—	—	—	—
—	—	—	—
$A_1^{2k-r}A_2^{r}$	$\binom{2k}{r}q^{2k-r}(1-q)^r$	$1+s_{2k-r}$	$\dfrac{1}{2k}\binom{2k}{r}s_{2k-r}q^{2k-r-1}$ $\times(1-q)^{r-1}[2k(1-q)-r]$
—	—	—	—
—	—	—	—
$A_1A_2^{2k-1}$	$2kq(1-q)^{2k-1}$	$1+s_1$	$s_1(1-q)^{2k-2}[1-2kq]$
A_2^{2k}	$(1-q)^{2k}$	$1+s_0$	$-s_0(1-q)^{2k-1}$

(3.84)

Note that $\sum f = 0$ and $\sum (df/dq) = 0$.

$$(3.85)\quad \bar{w} = 1 + s_{2k}q^{2k} + 2ks_{2k-1}q^{2k-1}(1-q)$$
$$+ \frac{2k(2k-1)}{2!}s_{2k-2}q^{2k-2}(1-q)^2 + \cdots.$$

The value of q in the offspring, $q_{(o)}$, is as follows:

$$q_{(o)} = \left[q + s_{2k}q^{2k} + (2k-1)s_{2k-1}q^{2k-1}(1-q) \right.$$
$$\left. + \frac{(2k-1)(2k-2)}{2!}s_{2k-2}q^{2k-2}(1-q)^2 + \cdots \right]\Big/ \bar{w}.$$

The change in gene frequency is given by

$$\Delta q = (q_0 - q);$$

$$\Delta q = \frac{q(1-q)}{\bar{w}}\left\{ s_{2k}q^{2k-1} + s_{2k-1}q^{2k-2}[2k(1-q)-1] \right.$$

$$(3.86)\quad \left. + \frac{2k-1}{2!}s_{2k-2}q^{2k-3}(1-q)[2k(1-q)-2]\cdots \right\};$$

$$\Delta q = q(1-q)\sum w\frac{df}{dq}\Big/ 2k\bar{w}.$$

This agrees with the previous results for diploids ($k = 1$) and haploids ($k = 1/2$). If it is assumed that the w's are constant (Wright, 1938), as throughout the present chapter,

$$(3.87) \qquad \Delta q = q(1 - q) \frac{d\bar{w}}{dq} \bigg/ 2k\bar{w}.$$

This formula can be extended to multiple alleles with the same convention with respect to differentiation as in diploids.

Unequal Selection in Males and Females

Up to this point, constant selective values have been assumed for each sort of zygote, irrespective of sex. Selection, however, frequently operates differently on males (M) and females (F). If this is the case, the zygotic frequencies after random fertilization are according to the expansion $[q_e A_1 + (1 - q_e)A_2][q_s A_1 + (1 - q_s)A_2]$ where q_e and q_s are the frequencies in eggs and sperms respectively (Wright and Dobzhansky 1946).

	Zygote	f	w_F	w_M
	A_1A_1	$q_e q_s$	$1 - s_{11}$	$1 - t_{11}$
(3.88)	A_1A_2	$q_e(1 - q_s) + q_s(1 - q_e)$	$1 - s_{12}$	$1 - t_{12}$
	A_2A_2	$(1 - q_e)(1 - q_s)$	1	1

$$(3.89) \qquad \begin{aligned} \bar{w}_F &= 1 - s_{12}(q_e + q_s) + (2s_{12} - s_{11})q_e q_s \\ \bar{w}_M &= 1 - t_{12}(q_e + q_s) + (2t_{12} - t_{11})q_e q_s \end{aligned}$$

$$(3.90) \qquad \begin{aligned} q_{e(o)} &= [0.5(1 - s_{12})(q_e + q_s) + (s_{12} - s_{11})q_e q_s]/\bar{w}_F \\ q_{s(o)} &= [0.5(1 - t_{12})(q_e + q_s) + (t_{12} - t_{11})q_e q_s]/\bar{w}_M \end{aligned}$$

The composition of the population may be found generation after generation.

The restricted conditions for equilibrium with complete dominance of the same allele in both sexes ($s_{12} = t_{12} = 0$) but selection in opposed directions, s_{11} (favorable) $> t_{11} > s_{11}/(1 + 2s_{11})$, were given by Haldane (1961). There is always a position of stable equilibrium if there is more than semidominance of the allele favorable in each case, where selection in opposite directions in the sexes causes overdominance on the average. Equilibrium with overdominance in one sex, dominance in the other, has been dealt with by Li (1963).

If the selective differences between the sexes are not great, a close approximation may be obtained by using $w = 0.5(w_F + w_M)$ and $q = 0.5(q_e + q_s)$ in each case as if there were no sex differences (Wright and Dobzhansky 1946). Let $q_e = q + \delta q$, $q_s = q - \delta q$, $w_F = w + \delta w$, and $w_M = w - \delta w$.

Selective values

Zygote	f	w_F	w_M	w
A_1A_1	$q^2 - \delta^2 q$	$w_{11} + \delta w_{11}$	$w_{11} - \delta w_{11}$	w_{11}
(3.91) A_1A_2	$2q(1-q) + 2\delta^2 q$	$w_{12} + \delta w_{12}$	$w_{12} - \delta w_{12}$	w_{12}
A_2A_2	$(1-q)^2 - \delta^2 q$	$w_{22} + \delta w_{22}$	$w_{22} - \delta w_{22}$	w_{22}

Following are the values in the next generation, after some reduction:

$$(3.92) \quad \begin{aligned} q_{(o)} &= \{(q^2 - \delta^2 q)[\bar{w}w_{11} - \delta w_{11}\,\delta\bar{w}] \\ &\quad + [q(1-q) + \delta^2 q][\bar{w}w_{12} - \delta w_{12}\,\delta\bar{w}]\}/(\bar{w}^2 - \delta^2\bar{w}) \\ \delta q_{(o)} &= \{(q^2 - \delta^2 q)[\bar{w}\,\delta w_{11} - w_{11}\,\delta\bar{w}] \\ &\quad + [q(1-q) + \delta^2 q][\bar{w}\,\delta w_{12} - w_{12}\,\delta\bar{w}]\}/(\bar{w}^2 - \delta^2\bar{w}). \end{aligned}$$

The above expression for $q_{(o)}$ differs from $[q^2 w_{11} + q(1-q)w_{12}]/\bar{w}$ only by terms that are of the second degree with respect to sex differences.

As an illustration of these results consider the case of a sex-limited lethal.

Zygote	f	w_e	w_s
aa	$q_e q_s$	1	0
(3.93) Aa	$q_e + q_s - 2q_e q_s$	1	1
AA	$(1 - q_e)(1 - q_s)$	1	1

$$(3.94) \quad \begin{aligned} q_{e(o)} &= 0.5(q_e + q_s) \\ q_{s(o)} &= [0.5(q_e + q_s) - q_e q_s]/(1 - q_e q_s) \end{aligned}$$

Approximate	f	$\bar{w}$
aa	q^2	0.5
(3.95) Aa	$2q(1-q)$	1
AA	$(1-q)^2$	1

$$(3.96) \quad \begin{aligned} \bar{w} &= 1 - 0.5q^2 \\ q_{(o)} &= (q - 0.5q^2)/(1 - 0.5q^2) \end{aligned}$$

$$(3.97) \quad \Delta q = -0.5q^2(1-q)/(1 - 0.5q^2)$$

In the former case, the minimum value of q is 0.75. The solid line in Figure 3.7 shows how q falls off in the course of 20 generations. The broken line shows how q falls off from 0.75 if the selective value of aa is taken as the average of that in males and females. The difference is not very great, considering the extreme selective difference in the sexes. It would be negligible for most purposes if the sex differences were only moderately great.

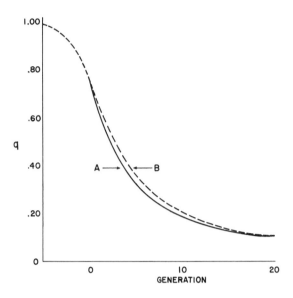

FIG. 3.7. Curve A represents the course of change in the frequency of a gene which acts as a recessive lethal in males but is neutral in females. Curve B is that for a gene that is selected against equally in both sexes with intermediate intensity ($s = 0.5$).

These points are illustrated in the case of a heterotic locus in the reference above.

Sex Linkage

It was shown in equations (2.22) that any deviation from equilibrium in the gene frequencies in either sex, under sex linkage, is halved in the next generation of random mating with reversal of sign. The course of selection may thus be expected to be somewhat complicated. In the following, gene frequencies of alleles A_1 and A_2 are represented by q_e and p_e ($= 1 - q_e$), respectively, and similarly in sperms except that the subscript is s. The zygotic frequencies below are in terms of the gametic frequencies of the preceding generation.

	Females	f	w	Males	f	w
	A_1A_1	$q_e q_s$	w_{11}	$A_1 Y$	q_e	w_1
(3.98)	A_1A_2	$q_e p_s + p_e q_s$	w_{12}	$A_2 Y$	p_e	w_2
	A_2A_2	$p_e p_s$	w_{22}			

The gene frequencies in the gametes of the progeny are as follows:

$$q_{e(o)} = [w_{11}q_eq_s + 0.5w_{12}(q_ep_s + p_eq_s)]/D_e,$$
$$p_{e(o)} = [w_{22}p_ep_s + 0.5w_{12}(q_ep_s + p_eq_s)]/D_e,$$
(3.99) $$D_e = w_{11}q_eq_s + w_{12}(q_ep_s + p_eq_s) + w_{22}p_ep_s,$$
$$q_{s(o)} = w_1q_e/[w_1q_e + w_2p_e],$$
$$p_{s(o)} = w_2p_e/[w_1q_e + w_2p_e].$$

These formulas permit calculation of q_e and q_s generation after generation. If an equilibrium is approached the values of q_e and q_s may be found by equating $q_{e(o)}$ to q_e and $q_{s(o)}$ to q_s, giving an equation of the type $aq_e^2 - (a + b)q_e + b = 0$, pertinent solution b/a.

(3.100) $$\hat{q}_e = \frac{w_{22}w_2 - 0.5w_{12}(w_1 + w_2)}{w_{11}w_1 - w_{12}(w_1 + w_2) + w_{22}w_2}, \qquad \hat{q}_s = \frac{w_1\hat{q}_e}{w_1\hat{q}_e + w_2\hat{p}_e}.$$

Haldane (1924a, 1926) first gave the rate of change of the gene frequency ratio for sex linkage, and Haldane and Jayakar (1964) gave the condition for equilibrium. The condition implied by $\hat{q}_e$ and $\hat{p}_e$ from (3.98), $0.5w_{12}(w_1 + w_2)$ greater than either $w_{22}w_2$ or $w_{11}w_1$, agrees with their result.

Much simpler approximate formulas may be obtained if the selective differences among genotypes are so small that their frequencies may be assumed without serious error to be continuously in equilibrium (Wright 1939b).

	Female	f	w	Male	f	w
	A_1A_1	q^2	$1 - s_{11}$	A_1Y	q	$1 - s_1$
(3.101)	A_1A_2	$2q(1 - q)$	$1 - s_{12}$	A_2Y	$1 - q$	1
	A_2A_2	$(1 - q)^2$	1			

$$\bar{w}_e = 1 - 2s_{12}q + (2s_{12} - s_{11})q^2, \qquad \bar{w}_s = 1 - s_1q, \quad .$$

(3.102) $$\Delta q_e = -q(1 - q)[s_{12} - (2s_{12} - s_{11})q]/\bar{w}_e = q(1 - q)\frac{d\bar{w}_e}{dq}\bigg/2\bar{w}_e,$$

$$\Delta q_s = -q(1 - q)s_1/\bar{w}_s = q(1 - q)\frac{d\bar{w}_s}{dq}\bigg/\bar{w}_s,$$

(3.103)
$$\Delta q = (2/3)\,\Delta q_e + (1/3)\,\Delta q_s$$
$$= (1/3)q(1 - q)\frac{d}{dq}(\log \bar{w}_e + \log \bar{w}_s).$$

The general formula

$$\Delta q = q(1 - q)\frac{d \log \bar{w}}{dq}\bigg/2k,$$

applies approximately to sex linkage if k is treated as 3/4.

On introducing a weak mutation pressure in opposition to that due to selection:

$$(3.104) \quad \Delta q \approx v(1 - q) - (1/3)q(1 - q)[2s_{12} - (4s_{12} - 2s_{11})q + s_1];$$

$$(3.105) \quad \hat{q} \approx \frac{3v}{2s_{12} + s_1}.$$

Thus for a deleterious recessive in which $s_{12} = 0$ there is equilibrium at approximately $3v/s_1$.

Compound Selection

So far selection has been treated as if it were a single process. Most actual populations, however, are subject to many kinds of selection, and genes may act pleiotropically on more than one. The partial selective values of the genotypes at such a locus are not likely to be wholly parallel and may deviate in opposite directions (Wright and Kerr 1954; Haldane 1961; Haldane and Jayakar 1963).

In most such populations, genotypic frequencies and hence gene frequencies can be determined directly only after there has been selection of some sort (e.g., that from differential prenatal mortality), but before selection is complete (e.g., that from differential productivity). Such genotypic frequencies are not Hardy–Weinberg frequencies and do not permit determination of Δq as a function of q unless they are divided by the partial selective values that have changed them from their initial values. These considerations point to practical difficulties in applying the theory to the analysis of actual populations, subject to strong selection. Experimental determination of the various components of selection is necessary.

For theoretical consideration, it is well to start from the gene frequencies in the fertilized eggs. Let $W_V (= 1 + S_V)$ and $W_P (= 1 + S_P)$ be absolute partial selective values with respect to two aspects of selective value, here taken to be viability and productivity respectively. The total selective value is the product, $W = W_V W_P$, with selection coefficient of the type $(S_V + S_P + S_V S_P)$ or approximately $(S_V + S_P)$ if the partial coefficients are small.

If there is parallelism in direction in such partial selective values as W_V and W_P, the degree of dominance exhibited by W is a weighted average of those exhibited by the components. If, however, the factors deviate in opposite directions, the situation is more complicated. Assume here that there is a tendency toward dominance of each favorable effect so that the coefficients h_V and h_P, which describe the heterozygous effects as fractions of the homozygous effects, are small.

$$
\begin{array}{lccc}
 & W_V & W_P & W \\
A_1A_1 & 1 - S_V & 1 & 1 - S_V \\
(3.106)\quad A_1A_2 & 1 - h_V S_P & 1 - h_P S_P & 1 - h_V S_V - h_P S_P + h_V h_P S_V S_P \\
A_2A_2 & 1 & 1 - S_P & 1 - S_P
\end{array}
$$

In this case, the heterozygote may have an overall advantage over each homozygote. If, on the other hand, there is enough tendency toward dominance of unfavorable effects, the heterozygote is at an overall disadvantage. The former case seems clearly to be the more usual situation, and this has long been a favored interpretation of heterosis (East 1936).

Overall selective value may be analyzable in many ways other than that indicated above. One allele may be more favorable under certain seasonal conditions, the other under the alternative ones. Assume that condition X occurs in the proportion P, and condition Y in proportion $(1 - P)$.

$$
\begin{array}{lccc}
 & W_X & W_Y & W \\
 & \text{Weight } P & \text{Weight } (1 - P) & \\
A_1A_1 & 1 - S_X & 1 & (1 - S_X)^P \\
(3.107)\quad A_1A_2 & 1 - h_X S_X & 1 - h_Y S_Y & (1 - h_X S_X)^P (1 - h_Y S_Y)^{1-P} \\
A_2A_2 & 1 & 1 - S_Y & (1 - S_Y)^{1-P}
\end{array}
$$

The locus is heterotic if there is sufficient dominance of each allele when favorable.

Another common situation is that in which there are two different environments within the range of the species, in one of which A_1 is more favorable, while A_2 is more favorable in the other. Assume that these two environments, X and Y, occur in the proportion P and $(1 - P)$ respectively. It is assumed that the genotypes are distributed at random.

$$
\begin{array}{lccc}
 & W_X & W_Y & W \\
 & \text{Weight } P & \text{Weight } (1 - P) & \\
A_1A_1 & 1 - S_X & 1 & 1 - P S_X \\
(3.108)\quad A_1A_2 & 1 - h_X S_X & 1 - h_Y S_Y & 1 - P h_X S_X - (1 - P) h_Y S_Y \\
A_2A_2 & 1 & 1 - S_Y & 1 - (1 - P) S_Y
\end{array}
$$

Under the above assumptions, the overall selective value is the weighted average of the partial values instead of the product, but again the locus may be heterotic if the h's are small enough.

The situation is more complicated if the individuals have a choice of environments, since then their distribution becomes a function of gene frequency. This implies that selective value is such a function, a situation that is the subject of chapter 5.

A locus may have effects on both haploid and diploid phases of the reproductive cycle. The gene frequency in the haploid *before* selection is that which is considered.

	Haploid			Diploid	
Gene	f	W	Genotype	f	W
A_1	q_1	W_1	A_1A_1	$W_1^2 q_1^2$	W_{11}
A_2	q_2	W_2	A_1A_2	$2W_1W_2q_1q_2$	W_{12}
			A_2A_2	$W_2^2 q_2^2$	W_{22}

(3.109)

	Haploid
Gene	f
A_1	$[W_1^2 W_{11} q_1^2 + W_1 W_2 W_{12} q_1 q_2]/\overline{W}$
A_2	$[W_2^2 W_{22} q_2^2 + W_1 W_2 W_{12} q_1 q_2]/\overline{W}$

$$\overline{W} = W_1^2 W_{11} q_1^2 + 2W_1 W_2 W_{12} q_1 q_2 + W_2^2 W_{22} q_2^2$$

$$(3.110) \quad \Delta q_1 = q_1(1 - q_1)[W_1^2 W_{11} q_1 + W_1 W_2 W_{12}(1 - 2q_1)$$
$$- W_2^2 W_{22}(1 - q_1)]/\overline{W}$$

$$(3.111) \qquad = q_1(1 - q_1)\frac{d\overline{W}}{dq_1}\Big/ 2\overline{W}$$

The form is the same with respect to q as with ordinary zygotic selection but the constants are more complicated.

There is equilibrium from these selective processes if the values of q_1 and q_2 from solution of $\Delta q_1 = 0$, $\Delta q_2 = 0$, are both positive. Equilibrium is stable if $2W_1 W_2 W_{12} - W_1^2 W_{11} - W_2^2 W_{22}$ is positive.

$$(3.112) \quad \Delta q_1 = -[2W_1 W_2 W_{12} - W_1^2 W_{11} - W_2^2 W_{22}]q_1(1 - q_1)(q_1 - \hat{q}_1),$$

where

$$(3.113) \quad \hat{q}_1 = W_2(W_1 W_{12} - W_2 W_{22})/[2W_1 W_2 W_{12} - W_1^2 W_{11} - W_2^2 W_{22}].$$

The relation among the selective values in the two phases at equilibrium may be indicated by taking those for A_2 and A_1A_2 as the standards of reference ($W_2 = 1$, $W_{12} = 1$) and writing $R = \hat{q}_1/(1 - \hat{q}_1)$.

$$W_{22} = (1 - R)W_1 + RW_1^2 W_{11}.$$

Figure 3.8 indicates the equilibrium states for values of W_{11} and W_{22} taking the relative selective value of A_1 as 0.9. The line $W_{22} = W_1 = 0.9$ is that along which $\hat{q}_1 = 0$ and the line $W_{11} = 1/W_1 = 1.11$ is that along which $\hat{q}_1 = 1$. These lines divide the field into four quadrants which do not correspond to the four quadrants given by the broken lines, $W_{22} = 1$, $W_{11} = 1$,

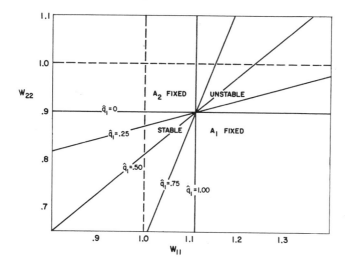

FIG. 3.8. Equilibrium states $\hat{q}$ (on solid lines) where there is selection in both the haploid phase ($W_1 = 0.9 \ W_2$) and the diploid phase (any W_{11} and W_{22} relative to $W_{12} = 1$). The broken lines bound the quadrants in the absence of haploid selection.

which indicate the equilibrium state in the absence of haploid selection ($W_1 = 1$). The lower left quadrant in each case is that of stable equilibrium, the lower right that of fixation of A_1, the upper left that of fixation of A_2, and the upper right that of unstable equilibrium, A_1 or A_2 becoming fixed according to the position of (q_1, q_2) with respect to ($\hat{q}_1$, $\hat{q}_2$) for the given selective values. It is to be noted that haploid selection results in equilibrium in a region ($1 \le W_{11} < 1/W_1$, $W_{22} < W_1$) in which A_1 would be fixed in its absence, and there is another region ($W_{11} < 1$, $W_1 \le W_{22} < 1$) in which haploid selection upsets the equilibrium which occurs in its absence and fixes A_2.

Maternal Inheritance

Characters are frequently affected by the genotype of the mother, and sometimes they are wholly determined by this. A case of the latter, dependent on a single pair of alleles, is assumed in the following table. It is assumed that the parental genotypes are in the array ($xAA + 2yAa + zaa$) with selective values of the progeny of females of these genotypes in the ratio $(1 + s_2):(1 + s_1):1$.

Parental Genotypes		Genotypic Frequencies of Offspring		
♀	♂	AA	Aa	aa
AA	AA	$x^2(1 + s_2)$		
	Aa	$xy(1 + s_2)$	$xy(1 + s_2)$	
	aa		$xz(1 + s_2)$	
(3.114) Aa	AA	$xy(1 + s_1)$	$xy(1 + s_1)$	
	Aa	$y^2(1 + s_1)$	$2y^2(1 + s_1)$	$y^2(1 + s_1)$
	aa		$yz(1 + s_1)$	$yz(1 + s_1)$
aa	AA	xz		
	Aa		yz	yz
	aa			z^2

Noting that the array of gene frequencies in the parental generation $(x + y)A + (y + z)a$ can be written $qA + (1 - q)a$, the zygotic frequencies in the offspring generation are:

$$x_{(o)} = [q^2 + (s_2xq + s_1yq)]/\overline{W},$$
$$2y_{(o)} = [2q(1 - q) + s_2x(1 - q) + s_1y]/\overline{W},$$
$$z_{(o)} = [(1 - q)^2 + s_1y(1 - q)]/\overline{W},$$

where

(3.115) $$\overline{W} = 1 + s_2x + 2s_1y.$$

The composition of the population can be calculated step by step. The gene frequencies in the offspring generation, $q_{(o)} = (x_{(o)} + y_{(o)})$, $1 - q_{(o)} = (y_{(o)} + z_{(o)})$, are:

(3.116) $$q_{(o)} = q + s_2x\left(\frac{1 + q}{2}\right) + s_1y\left(\frac{1 + 2q}{2}\right)\Big/\overline{W},$$

$$1 - q_{(o)} = \left[1 - q + s_2x\left(\frac{1 - q}{2}\right) + s_1y\left(\frac{3 - 2q}{2}\right)\right]\Big/\overline{W}.$$

Change of gene frequency is as follows:

(3.117) $$\Delta q = q_{(o)} - q = \left[s_2x\left(\frac{1 - q}{2}\right) + s_1y\left(\frac{1 - 2q}{2}\right)\right]\Big/\overline{W}.$$

If the selective differences are small, this can be expressed wholly in terms of q by assuming that $x = q^2$, $2y = 2q(1 - q)$, and $z = (1 - q)^2$.

(3.118) $$\overline{W} = 1 + s_2q^2 + 2s_1q(1 - q),$$

(3.119) $$\Delta q \approx \frac{q(1-q)}{2}[q(s_2 - 2s_1) + s_1]/\overline{W}.$$

This is just half the value that would hold if the same selective values applied directly to the offspring genotypes.

If the character is determined in part by the genotype of the mother and in part by that of the individual, it may be assumed that change of gene frequency is intermediate between one half and the full value under exclusive determination by the latter in the same or opposite direction, according to the portions of the variance determined by each. Stable equilibrium is possible if in opposite directions.

Meiotic Drive

One of the basic postulates of population genetics is that heterozygotes produce equal numbers of gametes with respect to the two alleles which they carry and that any inequality in apparent segregation ratio is due to preceding gametic or zygotic selection. Like most biological principles, however, there are exceptions. As noted, Sandler and Novitski (1957) coined the term "meiotic drive" for the resulting evolutionary process.

They pointed out that the effect is the same as that from competition among the gametes of heterozygotes and thus indistinguishable without cytologic evidence. No distinction will be made in the following discussion of the peculiar form of selection that arises from either process. It is unlikely in either case that there would be the same irregularity in segregation ratio among eggs and sperms. The former is represented by $k_e A_1 : (1 - k_e)A_2$ and the latter by $k_s A_1 : (1 - k_s)A_2$. It is assumed that the locus in question may also have effects on zygotic selection.

	Genotype	Zygotes f	W	W_{1e}	W_{2e}	W_{1s}	W_{2s}
	A_1A_1	$q_e q_s$	W_{11}	1	—	1	—
(3.120)	A_1A_2	$q_e(1-q_s)+q_s(1-q_e)$	W_{12}	k_e	$1-k_e$	k_s	$1-k_s$
	A_2A_2	$(1-q_s)(1-q_e)$	W_{22}	—	1	—	1

(3.121)
$$\overline{W} = W_{11}q_e q_s + W_{12}[q_e + q_s - 2q_e q_s]$$
$$+ W_{22}[1 - q_e - q_s + q_e q_s]$$

(3.122)
$$q_{e(o)} = [W_{11}q_e q_s + W_{12}k_e(q_e + q_s - 2q_e q_s)]/\overline{W}$$
$$q_{s(o)} = [W_{11}q_e q_s + W_{12}k_s(q_e + q_s - 2q_e q_s)]/\overline{W}$$

The composition of the population may be found generation after generation by application of these two formulas.

There is, of course, simplification if there is equal meiotic drive in both sexes ($k_e = k_s = k$, $q_e = q_s = q$). Even if not equal but not very different, a close approximation can be obtained by taking k as $0.5(k_e + k_s)$:

$$(3.123) \quad \overline{W} = W_{11}q^2 + 2W_{12}q(1 - q) + W_{22}(1 - q)^2,$$

$$(3.124) \quad \Delta q = -q(1 - q)[q(2W_{12} - W_{11} - W_{22}) - (2kW_{12} - W_{22})]/\overline{W}.$$

This is in the same form as for ordinary zygotic selection except that the coefficients are different functions of the W's. For this reason the differential formula is more complicated:

$$(3.125) \quad \Delta q = q(1 - q)\frac{d}{dq}[\overline{W} - 2(1 - 2k)W_{12}q]/2\overline{W}.$$

If there is equilibrium the values are as follows:

$$(3.126) \quad \hat{q}_1 = \frac{2kW_{12} - W_{22}}{2W_{12} - W_{11} - W_{22}}, \quad \hat{q}_2 = \frac{2(1 - k)W_{12} - W_{11}}{2W_{12} - W_{11} - W_{22}}.$$

Taking the selective value of A_1A_2 as standard ($W_{12} = 1$) and letting $R = \hat{q}_1/\hat{q}_2$:

$$(3.127) \quad W_{22} = 2k - 2R(1 - k) + RW_{11}$$

at equilibrium.

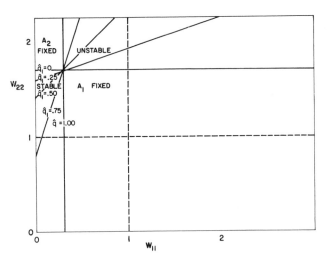

FIG. 3.9. Equilibrium states $\hat{q}$ (on solid lines) with any W_{11} and W_{22}, $W_{12} = 1$ and equal meiotic drive in both sexes ($k = 0.85$). The broken lines bound the quadrants in the absence of meiotic drive.

Figure 3.9 shows values of q for given W_{11} and W_{22} and $k = 0.85$. The field is divided into quadrants by the lines $W_{22} = 2k$, along which $\hat{q}_1 = 0$ and $W_{11} = 2(1 - k)$, along which $\hat{q}_1 = 1$. There is stable equilibrium in the lower left, unstable equilibrium in the upper right, fixation of A_1 in the lower right, and fixation of A_2 in the upper left. The broken lines $W_{11} = 1$, $W_{22} = 1$ define the corresponding quadrants in the absence of meiotic drive.

There is simplification in spite of differences between the sexes in the important case in which one of the homozygotes is lethal. It will be assumed that $W_{11} = 0$ and that the selective value of A_2A_2 is taken as standard.

It may be seen from equation (3.122) that the ratio $\varphi = q_s/q_e$ becomes constant ($\varphi = k_s/k_e$) if $W_{11} = 0$. On substituting $q_s = \varphi q_e$ in the equation for $q_{e(o)}$, it becomes possible to solve for Δq_e ($= q_{e(o)} - q_e$). Hiraizumi, Sandler, and Crow (1960) followed essentially this procedure except that they solved for change in the gene frequency ratio: $\Psi = (1 - q_s)/q_s$. The solution for Δq_e is as follows:

(3.128) $\quad q_{e(o)} = W_{12}k_e[q_e(1 + \varphi) - 2\varphi q_e{}^2]/\{W_{12}[q_e(1 + \varphi) - 2\varphi q_e{}^2]$
$$+ [1 - q_e(1 + \varphi) + \varphi q_e{}^2]\};$$

(3.129) $\quad \Delta q_e = q_e\{q_e{}^2\varphi(2W_{12} - 1) - q_e[(1 + \varphi)(W_{12} - 1) + 2\varphi W_{12}k_e]$
$$+ [(1 + \varphi)W_{12}k_e - 1]\}/\overline{W}.$$

In this case $(1 - q_e)$ is not a factor of Δq_e, but q_e cannot approach the value 1 if A_1A_1 is lethal.

Under certain circumstances there may be equilibrium. The value of q_e may be found by putting Δq_e equal to zero and solving.

Figure 3.10 shows the relation of k_s to W_{12} and q_e, at equilibrium assuming that there is no meiotic drive in oogenesis ($k_e = 0.5$). The values of k_s have been calculated from the equation (3.130) (derived from equation [3.129]).

(3.130) $\quad k_s = [2 - W_{12} + 2(W_{12} - 1)\hat{q}_e]/[2W_{12} - 4(2W_{12} - 1)\hat{q}_e(1 - \hat{q}_e)].$

The case of no zygotic selection of A_1A_2 and A_2A_2 but lethality of A_1A_1 is of special interest and is relatively simple:

(3.131) $\quad \Delta q_e = q_e\{q_e{}^2\varphi - q_e(2\varphi k_e) + [(1 + \varphi)k_e - 1]\}/\overline{W};$

(3.132) $\quad \hat{q}_e = k_e - \sqrt{[k_e(1 - k_e)(1 - k_s)/k_s]}.$

If, in addition, $k_e = 0.5$, $\hat{q}_e = 0.5\{1 - \sqrt{[(1 - k_s)/k_s]}\}$. This solution was given by Bruck (1957) in an analysis of the case of the house mouse in which most wild populations had been found by Dunn (1957) to be carrying an allele, t^x, lethal when homozygous but segregating in great excess (k_s up to 0.95) in sperms of $+t^x$ males. Segregation is normal in the females ($k_e = 0.5$).

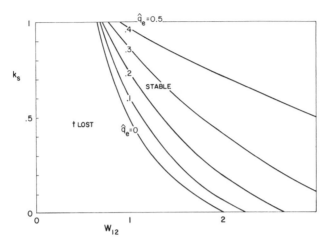

FIG. 3.10. Equilibrium values $\hat{q}_e$, assuming lethality of tt ($W_{11} = 0$), any W_{12}, $W_{22} = 1$, where there is unequal segregation in males ($k_s = 0$ to 1) but equal segregation in females ($k_e = 0.5$), as with t alleles of mice.

In this case, there is evidence that competition rather than meiotic drive in the strict sense is responsible.

The effect of "sex ratio" genes in several species of Drosophila is another case in which there is unequal segregation. Males A_1Y with this gene produce almost 100% X-bearing sperms. It will be assumed for simplicity that they produce 100% daughters. The formulation (3.98) for ordinary sex linkage can be used except that the sex ratio allele A_1 must be given double weight. Let q_e be the frequency of this gene in females after selection and hence in eggs; and let q_s be that in males after selection.

That in X-bearing sperms is $2q_s/(1 + q_s)$. The relative frequencies in offspring and the relative selective values are as follows, taking those of A_1A_2 and A_2Y as standard:

	Females	f	w	Males	f	w
	A_1A_1	$2q_eq_s$	w_{11}	A_1Y	q_e	w_1
(3.133)	A_2A_1	$2(1 - q_e)q_s$	1	A_2Y	$1 - q_e$	1
	A_1A_2	$q_e(1 - q_s)$	1			
	A_2A_2	$(1 - q_e)(1 - q_s)$	w_{22}			

(3.134) $q_{e(o)} = 0.5q_e + q_s + (q_eq_s)(2w_{11} - 1.5)/\bar{w}_e$,

(3.135) $\bar{w}_e = w_{22} + q_e[1 - w_{22}] + q_s[2 - w_{22}] + q_eq_s[2w_{11} - 3 + w_{22}]$,

(3.136) $q_{s(o)} = w_1 q_e / \bar{w}_s$,

(3.137) $\bar{w}_s = 1 + (w_1 - 1)q_e$,

(3.138) $\Delta q_e = \{0.5 q_e + q_s + q_e q_s [2w_{11} - 1.5] - q_e \bar{w}_e\}/\bar{w}_e$,

(3.139) $\Delta q_s = \{w_1 q_e - q_s[1 + (w_1 - 1)q_e]\}/\bar{w}_s$.

At equilibrium,

(3.140) $\hat{q}_s = w_1 \hat{q}_e / [1 + (w_1 - 1)q_e]$.

On substituting $\hat{q}_e$ for q_e and the above value of $\hat{q}_s$ for q_s in (3.138) and putting $\Delta q_e = 0$, the equation for solution of q_e is found to be

(3.141) $\hat{q}_e{}^2[2w_1(1 - w_{11}) + 1 - w_{22}] - \hat{q}_e[w_1(3 - 2w_{11}) + 1.5 - 2w_{22}]$
$$+ [w_1 + 0.5 - w_{22}] = 0.$$

This is of the form $aq^2 - (a + b)q + b$, $\hat{q} = 1$, or b/a. The pertinent solution is thus:

(3.142) $\hat{q}_e = (w_1 + 0.5 - w_{22})/[2w_1(1 - w_{11}) + 1 - w_{22}]$.

In Figure 3.11, it is assumed that there is no selection in males apart from the nonequational segregation of A_1, $w_1 = 1$. In this case:

(3.143) $\hat{q}_s = \hat{q}_e$,

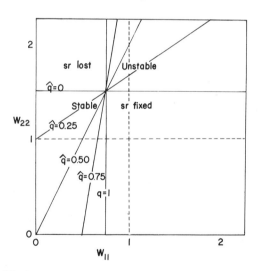

FIG. 3.11. Equilibrium states $\hat{q}$ (in solid lines) of sex ratio gene, A_1, with various selective values, W_{11}, W_{22} ($W_{12} = 1$) in females, but no selective difference in males except that $A_1 Y$ males produce only daughters. The broken lines bound the quadrants in the absence of the sex ratio effect.

(3.144) $\hat{q}_e = (3 - 2w_{22})/(6 - 4w_{11} - 2w_{22})$.

Values of w_{22}, associated with given values of w_{11} and q_e, have been calculated by the formula

(3.145) $w_{22} = [3(1 - 2\hat{q}_e) + 4w_{11}\hat{q}_e]/2(1 - q_e)$.

There is stable equilibrium in the lower left quadrant, unstable in the upper right, loss of the sex ratio gene A_1 in the upper left, and extinction of the population in the lower right under the assumption that A_1Y males have no sons. The broken lines show the corresponding quadrants (fixation of A_1 instead of extinction in the lower right) under ordinary sex linkage with the same selective values.

CHAPTER 4

Selection in Interaction Systems

The treatment of selection in the preceding chapter was based on the assignment of values to the genotypes at single loci. Selection, however, necessarily applies to the organism as a whole and thus to the effects of the entire gene system, rather than to single genes. In dealing with evolution, the primary emphasis should thus be placed on the effects of selection in the presence of interaction systems.

It was shown in chapter 2 that under random mating the genotypes at all loci tend to be combined at random in the long run, in spite of linkage. If, however, there is interaction among loci with respect to selection, this tendency is disturbed and, as also shown in chapter 2, there is not immediate recovery even for genes in different chromosomes. The result is that genotypic frequencies approach an equilibrium that departs more or less from that of random combination.

This departure will, however, be shown to be slight if the amounts of recombination are of a higher order of magnitude than the interactive aspect of selection. It is desirable to begin with the simple limiting case in which random combination is assumed. The first studies of selection in interaction systems seem to have been those of Haldane (1927a, 1931b). A different model will be used here.

Selection under Random Combination

General Formulas

According to the preceding chapter the rate of change of frequency of one (A_x) of a series of alleles at a locus that acts additively with all others is given exactly by formula (3.58), provided that the frequencies of the other alleles are expressed as fractions of $1 - q_x$ so that $\partial q_i/\partial q_x = -q_i/(1 - q_x)$.

$$(4.1) \qquad \Delta q_x = q_x(1 - q_x) \sum_{ij} \left[W_{ij} \frac{\partial f_{ij}}{\partial q_x} \right] \bigg/ 2\overline{W}$$

where summation includes all genotypes A_iA_j (frequency f_{ij}) at the A locus.

Passing now to cases in which there are interaction effects with respect to selective value, subscript k will be used for the portion of the total genotype due to genes at these other loci. The mean selective value of the population is

$$(4.2) \qquad \overline{W} = \sum_{ijk} f_{ij:k} W_{ij:k}.$$

Under the assumption of random combination:

$$(4.3) \qquad f_{ij:k} = f_{ij} f_k,$$

$$(4.4) \qquad \overline{W} = \sum_{ij} \left[f_{ij} \sum_{k} (f_k W_{ij:k}) \right] = \sum_{ij} f_{ij} \overline{W}_{ij}.$$

Since $\overline{W}_{ij}$ is constant for given $A_i A_j$ and a given set of frequencies at other loci, the formula for Δq_x with constant selective values for all genotypes at the A locus may be applied (Wright 1942, 1955):

$$\Delta q_x = q_x(1 - q_x) \sum_{ijk} \left[W_{ij:k} \frac{\partial f_{ij:k}}{\partial q_x} \right] \Big/ 2\overline{W} \qquad \text{(all sets at other loci),}$$

$$(4.5)$$

$$\Delta q_x = q_x (1 - q_x) \sum \left[W \frac{\partial f}{\partial q_x} \right] \Big/ 2\overline{W},$$

where $W \; (= W_{ij:k})$ and $f \; (= f_{ij:k})$ apply to the total genotypes of the interaction system in question.

If, as will be assumed in the rest of this chapter, the selective values of these total genotypes are independent of q_x (Wright 1935, 1937):

$$(4.6) \qquad \Delta q_x = q_x(1 - q_x) \frac{\partial \overline{W}}{\partial q_x} \Big/ 2\overline{W} = 0.5 q_x(1 - q_x) \frac{\partial \log \overline{W}}{\partial q_x}.$$

It should be emphasized that these formulas are necessarily concerned directly only with interaction with respect to selective value. The first application (Wright 1935) was to cases in which there is an intermediate optimum in a quantitatively varying character, determined by multiple additive factors. This implies interaction of the most extreme sort with respect to selective value, although none with respect to the underlying character.

It is obvious that numerical application is practicable only for simple models—those that involve few loci or, if many, patterns of dominance and interaction that can be expressed in simple mathematical forms. Even so, the use of such models and consideration of the formula itself permit important deductions on the nature of the evolutionary process.

Simple Examples

As a simple example, consider two pairs of alleles, with complete dominance in each case. The selective values are assumed to be sufficiently small, and linkage, if any, sufficiently loose that the formula (4.6), based on random combination, is adequate (Wright 1939b).

	Genotype	f	w
	$A-B-$	$(1 - p^2)(1 - q^2)$	1
	$A-bb$	$(1 - p^2)q^2$	$1 + s$
(4.7)	$aaB-$	$p^2(1 - q^2)$	$1 + r$
	$aabb$	p^2q^2	$1 + t$

$$(4.8) \qquad \bar{w} = 1 + rp^2(1 - q^2) + s(1 - p^2)q^2 + tp^2q^2$$

$$(4.9) \qquad \frac{\partial \bar{w}}{\partial p} = 2p[r - (r + s - t)q^2],$$

$$(4.10) \qquad \Delta p = p^2(1 - p)[r - (r + s - t)q^2]/\bar{w},$$

$$(4.11) \qquad \frac{\partial \bar{w}}{\partial q} = 2q[s - (r + s - t)p^2],$$

$$(4.12) \qquad \Delta q = q^2(1 - q)[s - (r + s - t)p^2]/\bar{w}.$$

The condition for complete independence is $(1 + t) = (1 + r)(1 + s)$, which implies multiplicative selective values. In this case:

$$(4.13) \qquad \bar{w} = (1 + rp^2)(1 + sq^2),$$

$$(4.14) \qquad \frac{\partial \bar{w}}{\partial p} = 2rp(1 + sq^2), \qquad \Delta p = rp^2(1 - p)/(1 + rp^2),$$

$$(4.15) \qquad \frac{\partial \bar{w}}{\partial q} = 2sq(1 + rp^2), \qquad \Delta q = sq^2(1 - q)/(1 + sq^2).$$

If the selective differences are so small that $\bar{w}$ in the denominator of the general formula may be treated as unity, the condition for independence is additivity of selective values ($t = r + s$).

The rates of change of the gene frequencies in all of the familiar patterns of two-factor interaction with dominance can be obtained at once from the above formula. Thus with a favorable recessive, aa, made more favorable by a specific recessive modifier in $aabb$, $s = 0$, and there is a 12:3:1 F_2 ratio.

$$(4.16) \qquad \Delta p = p^2(1 - p)[(t - r)q^2 + r]/\bar{w},$$

(4.17) $\Delta q = q^2(1 - q)[(t - r)p^2]/\bar{w}$.

If the mutations a and b are initially rare, the rate of increase of the latter lags far behind that of the former. If only the double recessive is at an advantage over type ($r = 0$ as well as $s = 0$), with therefore a 15:1 F_2 ratio, the rates of increase of both mutations vary at first as the product of the squares of two small quantities and thus both are exceedingly small and nil unless both are simultaneously present. With a 15:1 ratio in which, on the other hand, either of two dominant mutations is at an advantage over the double recessive type, progress at first is rapid but fixation of one stops the increase in frequency of the other. In the types of interaction represented by the common 9:3:4 and 9:7 F_2 ratios with favorable double dominant, initial progress from type $aabb$ is of course much more rapid than is that of a favorable double recessive in the cases discussed above.

There is equilibrium with all four genes present if the values of r, s, and t are such that $\hat{p} (= \sqrt{[s/(r + s - t)]})$ and $\hat{q} (= \sqrt{[r/(r + s - t)]})$ are both between 0 and 1. Obviously r, s, and the quantity $(r + s - t)$ must all be of the same sign, and thus $t < r$ and $t < s$ if both r and s are positive; $t > r$ and $t > s$ if both r and s are negative, or in other words, $A-B-$ and $aabb$ must both have lower, or both have higher, selective values than either of the other genotypes. The point $(\hat{p}, \hat{q})$ if it exists must be a saddle point. The formal test for its nature is the same as that discussed in the case of multiple alleles:

$$\frac{\partial^2 \bar{w}}{\partial p^2} = 0, \qquad \frac{\partial^2 \bar{w}}{\partial q^2} = 0, \qquad \frac{\partial^2 \bar{w}}{\partial p\, \partial q} = -4\sqrt{(rs)}.$$

Thus

$$\left(\frac{\partial^2 \bar{w}}{\partial p^2}\right)\left(\frac{\partial^2 \bar{w}}{\partial q^2}\right) - \left(\frac{\partial^2 \bar{w}}{\partial p\, \partial q}\right)^2 = -16rs.$$

Since this is necessarily negative, $(\hat{p}, \hat{q})$ cannot be either a maximum or a minimum.

In the special case of Figure 4.1, $AABB$ and $aabb$ are two "selective peaks" in the surface of mean selective values. The sets of gene frequencies at selective peaks have been described as "harmonious," and those at "selective pits" (such as those of $AAbb$ and $aaBB$ in the present case) as "disharmonious" (Wright 1932). In this example these sets are homallelic at both loci, but this is not necessarily true. The term "coadaptive system" (Dobzhansky and Wallace 1953) is also applicable to selective peaks. Since there tends, by definition, to be return to a selective peak after any slight deviation, it has the property defined by Lerner (1954) as "genetic homeostasis" as far

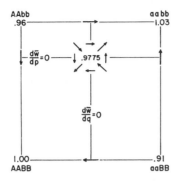

FIG. 4.1. Field of gene frequencies for two interacting dominant genes showing peak values of $\overline{W}$ at (0, 0) and (1, 1), pits at (0, 1) and (1, 0), and a saddle where $\partial \overline{W}/\partial p$ and $\partial \overline{W}/\partial q$ intersect. Arrows show trajectories.

as selection is concerned. It should be noted, however, that the point to which the population actually returns is the resultant of all directed pressures and thus includes those of recurrent mutation and immigration as well as selection, and it is to this equilibrium point that the term genetic homeostasis most properly applies.

The Pleiotropic Threshold

A case in which the selective differential is so small that there is no question that deviation from random combination may be ignored is that of modifiers of the dominance of recurrent *deleterious* mutations. Fisher (1928) proposed the theory that the prevailing recessiveness of such mutations is due to selection of modifiers that cause the heterozygotes to resemble wild type but have no effect on homozygous wild type. The effect on the very unfavorable but very rare homozygous mutants is largely irrelevant. We will here assume that the modifier M is semidominant, and that it shifts the relative selective value of the heterozygous mutant, Aa, by the proportion x of its deviation from wild type AA. The selective value of the homozygous mutant $(1 - s)$ is taken as constant. The original degree of dominance of the heterozygote is measured by h.

Genotype	Frequency	AA $(1 - p)^2$	Aa $2p(1 - p)$	aa p^2
MM	q^2	1	$1 - hs(1 - x)$	$1 - s$
Mm	$2q(1 - q)$	1	$1 - hs(1 - 0.5x)$	$1 - s$
mm	$(1 - q)^2$	1	$1 - hs$	$1 - s$

(4.18) $\bar{w} = 1 - 2hsp(1 - xq) - sp^2[1 - 2h + 2hxq].$

The intensity of selection against a is as follows:

(4.19) $\dfrac{\partial \bar{w}}{2\partial p} = -hs(1 - xq) - sp[1 - 2h + 2hxq].$

This is approximately

(4.20) $\dfrac{\partial \bar{w}}{2\partial p} \approx -hs(1 - xq)$

if p is small.

(4.21) $\Delta p \approx u_{Aa}(1 - p) - hsp(1 - p)(1 - xq),$

where u_{Aa} is the rate of mutation from A to a.

(4.22) $\hat{p} \approx u_{Aa}/[hs(1 - xq)].$

The intensity of selection for M is as follows:

(4.23) $\dfrac{\partial \bar{w}}{2\partial q} = hsxp(1 - p).$

On substitution of $\hat{p}$ for p this becomes

(4.24) $\dfrac{\partial \bar{w}}{2\partial q} \approx xu_{Aa}/(1 - xq).$

This agrees essentially, with Fisher's estimate, the smallness of which he stressed (1928) as illustrating the important effects which may follow from exceedingly weak but long-continued action of selection. How weak this is may be seen from the reasonable case in which the selection intensity for a modifier that shifts the heterozygote 10% of the way toward complete dominance over a deleterious mutation recurring at the rate 10^{-6} per generation is only about 10^{-7}.

I criticized this hypothesis on the basis that practically all modifiers of the heterozygote would be expected to have also some effect in homozygous wild type which would take precedence because of the greater frequency of the latter (Wright 1929a,b). Assume that Mm adds the amount t, and MM the amount $2t$ to the relative selective values, and thus the term $2tq$ to $\bar{w}$. The values of Δp and $\hat{p}$ are unaffected.

(4.25) $\Delta q \approx q(1 - q)\{t + xu_{Aa}/(1 - xq)\}.$

If t is positive and of higher order than xu_{Aa}, the modifier becomes fixed at practically the usual rate, $tq(1 - q)$, and thus largely irrespective of whether mutation of A to a has ever occurred. If t is negative and of higher order than xu_{Aa}, the modifier is soon lost, or is held at a low frequency if mutation from m to M recurs at a usual rate.

If the modifier is itself dominant and brings about complete dominance of wild type by itself, as I (1929a) assumed in order to take the case most favorable to Fisher's hypothesis, the selection intensity from this cause comes out approximately $2u_{Aa}/(1 - q)$ until the modifier approaches fixation. Fisher (1934) maintained that the selection intensity "increases without limit as the dominant modifier becomes more and more numerous." Ewens (1965a,b) showed, however, that this is incorrect where proper allowance is made for the resulting change in the frequency of the wild type gene and that actually the selective intensity for the modifier, after rising to a small multiple of the mutation rate, approaches zero as q approaches one. This point does not arise at all if the modifier is not completely dominant and does not bring about complete dominance by itself when fixed.

Haldane (1930b), Plunkett (1932), and Muller (1932) also criticized Fisher's hypothesis as not allowing for the virtually certain effect in one way or another of modifiers on homozygous wild type. There has been much discussion since, much of which has been invalidated by the persistent confusion by Fisher and others between the question at issue and the wholly different one of the evolution of dominance of *favorable* mutations to which these criticisms were stated from the first not to apply.

It is not the purpose to go here into the complicated general problem of dominance. The particular case of recurrent deleterious mutations raised by Fisher (1928) is discussed here as an illustration of the important principle of the pleiotropic threshold (Wright 1956). A major contribution of a gene to selective intensity acts somewhat as a threshold below which pleiotropic contributions of lower order of magnitude do not control the direction of change of gene frequency, however long they may operate.

A statement made by Mather (1954) in another connection than Fisher's hypothesis, agrees with my view.

In the first place, as I have pointed out, both above and in earlier writings, the response of a gene difference to selection must depend on its total effect on the phenotype as this is translated into fitness. The response of a gene difference having a major as well as minor effects will therefore depend chiefly on the major effect. In so far as this effect is large and specific, it will not be replaceable and the difference will not respond to selection in a way characteristic of a member of a polygenic system. Its polygenic contribution is therefore incidental and for selection, indecisive.

Nonrandom Combination in Centripetal Selection

The Optimum Model: Two Loci

At this point, it will be well to consider the conditions under which deviations from random combination become important. We begin with a simple, two-factor model of the very important case in which the optimum is at the mean (M) (Wright 1945a, 1952a). Additive effects, including semidominance, are assumed. Capitals are used to indicate plus factors rather than dominance.

Genotype	Grade of Character	Selective Value w
$AABB$	$M + 2\alpha$	$1 - t$
$AABb, AaBB$	$M + \alpha$	$1 - s$
$AAbb, aaBB$ $\Big\}$ $AaBb$	M	1
$Aabb, aaBb$	$M - \alpha$	$1 - s$
$aabb$	$M - 2\alpha$	$1 - t$

Homallelic $AAbb$ and $aaBB$ are both at the intermediate optimum and thus at separate "selective peaks" $(1, 0)$ and $(0, 1)$ with respect to the gene frequencies p and q at the two loci. The extremes, $aabb$ and $AABB$, are in selective pits $(0, 0)$ and $(1, 1)$, respectively. There is metastable equilibrium at the saddle $(0.5, 0.5)$. The balance between selection, favoring gametes Ab and aB, and recombination (rate c) can be isolated from change in gene frequency by considering the situation at metastable equilibrium in a population so large that the accidents of sampling that would upset it and ultimately bring about fixation of Ab or aB may be ignored.

The equations expressing the lack of change in the frequencies f_{Ab} and f_{aB} of the balanced gametes and in the frequencies f_{AB} and f_{ab} of the unbalanced gametes can easily be written from a table of uniting gametes. Let $x = f_{Ab} = f_{aB}$ and $y = f_{AB} = f_{ab} = 0.5 - x$:

$$(4.26) \quad \begin{aligned} x &= [cy^2 + 2(1 - s)xy + (2 - c)x^2]/\bar{w} \\ &= [(c/4) + (1 - c - s)x + 2sx^2]/\bar{w}, \end{aligned}$$

$$(4.27) \quad y = [(2 - c - t)y^2 + 2(1 - s)xy + cx^2]/\bar{w},$$

$$(4.28) \quad \begin{aligned} \bar{w} &= 2[(2 - t)y^2 + 4(1 - s)xy + 2x^2] \\ &= 1 - (t/2) - (4s - 2t)x + (8s - 2t)x^2. \end{aligned}$$

On equating the values of x in successive generations, as above,

$$(4.29) \quad 8(4s - t)x^3 - 8(3s - t)x^2 + 2(2s - t + 2c)x - c = 0.$$

This can readily be solved for any assumed values of s and t.

In most cases it is to be expected that selective value will fall off disproportionately with deviation from the optimum. The most convenient assumption is that it falls off as the square of the deviation. In the present case this implies $t = 4s$, under which the equation reduces to a quadratic.

$$(4.30) \qquad 8sx^2 - 4(s - c)x - c = 0,$$

$$(4.31) \qquad x = f_{Ab} = f_{aB} = [(s - c) + \sqrt{(s^2 + c^2)}]/4s,$$

$$(4.32) \qquad y = f_{AB} = f_{ab} = [(s + c) - \sqrt{(s^2 + c^2)}]/4s,$$

$$(4.33) \qquad D = x^2 - y^2 = [\sqrt{(s^2 + c^2)} - c]/4s,$$

$$(4.34) \qquad \bar{w} = 1 - 2s(1 - 2x) = 1 - 4sy.$$

If $s = c$, then $x = 0.25\sqrt{2} = 0.3535$, $y = 0.1465$, and $D = 0.1035$. There is considerable departure from random combination in the population but not enough to make the unbalanced chromosomes rare. Unbalanced chromosomes are kept at really small frequencies only if $c/(2s)$ is very small in which case $x \approx 0.5[1 - c/(2s)]$ and the value of D approaches its limiting value 0.25. If, on the other hand, s is much smaller than c, the value of x approaches $0.25[1 + s/(2c)]$, and the deviation from random combination usually becomes negligible, $D = s/(8c)$. It should be noted, however, that there is some departure from random combination even if the two loci are in different chromosomes but the amount is negligible for small selective differences, $D = s/4$, $x = 0.25(1 + s)$. A number of cases are given in Table 4.1.

TABLE 4.1. Gametic frequencies at (0.5, 0.5)

	$s \gg c$	$s = 100c$	$s = 10c$	$s = c$	$s = 0.1c$	$s \ll c$
$f_{Ab} = f_{aB}$	$0.50-$	0.4975	0.4762	0.3535	0.2625	$0.25+$
$f_{AB} = f_{ab}$	$0+$	0.0025	0.0238	0.1465	0.2375	$0.25-$
D	$0.25-$	0.2475	0.2262	0.1035	0.0125	$0+$
$\bar{w}$ at (0.5, 0.5)	$1-c$	$1 - 0.01s$	$1 - 0.095s$	$1 - 0.586s$	$1 - 0.950s$	$1-s$

The field of *gametic* frequencies is three-dimensional and can be represented as an equilateral tetrahedron (Fig. 4.2) with $\bar{w} = 1$ at the corners at which $f_{Ab} = 1$ or $f_{aB} = 1$; with $\bar{w} = 1 - 4s$ at the corners at which $f_{AB} = 1$ or $f_{ab} = 1$; but with $\bar{w} = 1 - 2s$ halfway between. Halfway between corners representing gametes that differ in only one gene, $\bar{w} = 1 - 1.5s$. At the equilibrium point at which all gametes are present, $\bar{w} = 1 - 4sy$, which varies from nearly $1 - s$ if s is much less than c, to nearly $1 - c$ if $s \gg c$. This is always a saddle point (unless $c = 0$). The effect of increased linkage, assuming a given set of selective values, is to make this saddle shallower.

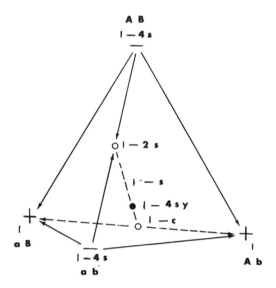

FIG. 4.2. Tetrahedral field of gametic frequencies for two-locus optimum model. The mean selective values are shown at various points.

The field of *gene* frequencies (Fig. 4.3) gives a less complete representation of the situation, since $\bar{w}$ may take different values for the same pairs of gene frequencies. For example, in a population made up of the four homozygotes in equal numbers, $\bar{w} = 1 - 2s$. In the next generation, with no change in gametic frequencies and with s very small, $\bar{w}$ becomes $1 - s$ and remains the same under random recombination as long as the set remains at $(0.5, 0.5)$. With linkage, it rises to $1 - 4sy$, the maximum value for this point. In such a model as Figure 4.3, it is to be assumed that the surface $\bar{w}$ is that of the maximum values of $\bar{w}$ for the set of gene frequencies to which it pertains.

In the limiting case in which $s/(2c)$ is so small that random combination may be assumed:

(4.35) $\bar{w} = 1 - 2s(2 - 3q_A - 3q_B + q_A{}^2 + 4q_Aq_B + q_B{}^2)$,

(4.36) $\Delta q_A = -2sq_A(1 - q_A)[q_A + 2q_B - 1.5]$.

There is a ridge of high values of $\bar{w}$ connecting the peak at $(0, 1)$ with that at $(1, 0)$, defined by $q_B = (1 - q_A)$. Along this ridge:

(4.37) $\bar{w} = 1 - 4sq_A(1 - q_A)$,

(4.38) $\Delta q_A = 2sq_A(1 - q_A)(q_A - 0.5)$

from 4.36 (not 4.37).

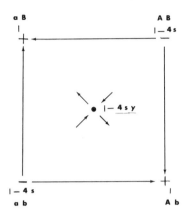

FIG. 4.3. Field of gene frequencies corresponding to the gametic frequencies of Figure 4.2.

Equilibrium at $(0.5, 0.5)$ is of course unstable. It may, however, be converted into a point of stable equilibrium by rather small pressures toward equilibrium. Thus if there is reversible mutation at the rate u in each direction, the rate of change of gene frequency due to this is $u(1 - q_A) - uq_A = u(1 - 2q_A)$. The rate of change of q_A for points along the above ridge is

$$(4.39) \qquad \Delta q_A = -2[u - sq_A(1 - q_A)][q_A - 0.5].$$

Assuming the same rates of mutation, Δq_B is analogous. Thus there is stable equilibrium if $u > 0.25s$ in this case.

With seriously nonrandom combination because of large $s/(2c)$, it was noted above that $\bar{w} = 1 - 4sy$ with y at the saddle declining from 0.25 to 0 as $s/(2c)$ is increased. The instability of equilibrium at this point may be overcome by smaller mutation rates with such increase.

Instability may, of course, be very easily overcome by small rates of immigration from surrounding areas in which $q_A = 1/2$ and $q_B = 1/2$. It may also be overcome by small amounts of pleiotropic heterosis at these loci.

If h_1 is added to the selective value of Aa, and h_2 to that of Bb, the array of selective values at $(1/2, 1/2)$ is as follows:

	aa	Aa	AA
BB	1	$1 - s + h_1$	$1 - t$
Bb	$1 - s + h_2$	$1 + h_1 + h_2$	$1 - s + h_2$
bb	$1 - t$	$1 - s + h_1$	1

$$(4.40) \quad \bar{w} = [1 - (t/2) + 0.5(h_1 + h_2)] - [4s - 2t]x + [8s - 2t]x^2.$$

This is the same as before (4.28) except for the addition of $0.5(h_1 + h_2)$. The equation to be solved for the frequency of the balanced gametes is

(4.41)
$$8(4s - t)x^3 - 8(3s - t)x^2 + 2[2s - t + 2c(1 + h_1 + h_2)]x \\ - c[1 + h_1 + h_2].$$

This is the same as before (4.29) except that c is multiplied by $(1 + h_1 + h_2)$. Thus the effect on gene frequencies must be exactly the same as if linkage were relaxed by the amount indicated (Wright 1952a).

Bodmer and Parsons (1962) arrived at essentially the same equation (for $h_1 = h_2$) from a different viewpoint. Their equation was in the terms of our $y = 0.5 - x$ and they used α for $2h$, β for $s - h$, and γ for t. Parsons (1963a) gives a number of graphs that show the gene frequencies if there is stable equilibrium for various assumed values of the coefficients.

If $t = 4s$, the term in x^3 disappears as before and the solution for the gene frequencies given above differs merely as stated. Since the depression of the saddle is $4sy$ it is converted into a maximum if $h_1 + h_2 > 8sy$.

It is evident that only one of the loci need be heterotic to give this sort of result. If $h_2 = 0$, there is stable equilibrium if $h_1 > 8sy$.

A selective advantage, on the average, of the middle of the range over both extremes may either be phenotypic as in the pure optimum model ($h_1 = h_2 = 0$) or due to heterotic loci ($s = t = 0$) or a mixture. A. Robertson (1956) and Latter (1959) have compared the consequences of the two pure models. They emphasize especially the point that in a multifactorial case selection tends to bring about homallelism at all loci (or all but one, Wright 1935) in the optimum model, whereas it tends to maintain heterallelism at all loci in the pure heterotic model. As noted above, however, the selection pressure in the neighborhood of the optimum in the former is usually so slight that low immigration pressure and even mutation pressure are likely to maintain strong heterallelism at many loci, at least in nature. The commonest situation is probably a mixture. There can be little doubt that extremes are usually at a selective disadvantage in nature, as such, but that heterotic loci are also fairly common, though probably much less common than heterotic chromosomes.

Three Loci

We will consider next the case of selection toward the optimum at the midrange of a character determined additively by three pairs of alleles $(A, a; B, b; C, c)$ all semidominant and with equal differential effects of the plus factors (capitals). It will again be assumed that selective value falls off according to the square of the deviation from the optimum (Wright 1965a).

Plus Factors	Grade	w
6	$M + 3\alpha$	$1 - 9s$
5	$M + 2\alpha$	$1 - 4s$
4	$M + \alpha$	$1 - s$
3	M	1
2	$M - \alpha$	$1 - s$
1	$M - 2\alpha$	$1 - 4s$
0	$M - 3\alpha$	$1 - 9s$

Let c_1 and c_2 be the amounts of recombination in the two regions $A - B$ and $B - C$, and let that between A and C be $c_1 + c_2 - 2d$, with d the amount of double crossing over. Because of symmetry, a metastable equilibrium point is to be expected at some set of gametic frequencies at which complementary gametes are equally frequent (and thus $q_A = q_B = q_C = 0.5$). Let f_1 be the frequency of AbC and aBc in such sets, f_2 that of ABc and abC, f_3 that of Abc and aBC, and f_4 that of ABC and abc. The frequencies in the generation following one in which complementary gametes are equally frequent, but not necessarily at equilibrium, are shown below, letting $E = (f_1 + f_4)^2 - (f_2 + f_3)^2 - 2s(f_1 f_4 - f_2 f_3)$. (An error of sign in E in the original paper is here corrected.)

$$f_1 = \{f_1 - 0.5c_1(f_1 - f_2)[1 - 2s(f_3 + f_4)]$$
$$-0.5c_2(f_1 - f_3)[1 - 2s(f_2 + f_4)] - 0.5sf_1 - 4sf_1 f_4 + dE\}/\bar{w},$$
$$f_2 = \{f_2 + 0.5c_1(f_1 - f_2)[1 - 2s(f_3 + f_4)]$$
(4.42)
$$-0.5c_2(f_2 - f_4)[1 - 2s(f_1 + f_3)] - 0.5sf_2 - 4sf_2 f_4 - dE\}/\bar{w},$$
$$f_3 = \{f_3 - 0.5c_1(f_3 - f_4)[1 - 2s(f_1 + f_2)]$$
$$+ 0.5c_2(f_1 - f_3)[1 - 2s(f_2 + f_4)] - 0.5sf_3 - 4sf_3 f_4 - dE\}/\bar{w},$$
$$f_4 = \{f_4 + 0.5c_1(f_3 - f_4)[1 - 2s(f_1 + f_2)]$$
$$+ 0.5c_2(f_2 - f_4)[1 - 2s(f_1 + f_3)] - 2.5sf_4 - 4sf_4^2 + dE\}/\bar{w}.$$

The mean selective value $\bar{w}$ may be found by adding these equations, since $f_1 + f_2 + f_3 + f_4 = 0.5$.

(4.43)
$$\bar{w} = 1 - 0.5s - 8sf_4.$$

Little is lost for our purpose by assuming that the loci are equally spaced ($c_2 = c_1 = c$) and thus that $f_3 = f_2$ at equilibrium. The first and third equations above may conveniently be expressed in terms of f_2 and f_4, then

(4.44)
$$E = 2sf_4^2 - (s - 4sf_2)f_4 + 2sf_2^2 - 2f_2 + 0.25:$$

TABLE 4.2. Gametic frequencies at equilibrium (metastable) at (0.5, 0.5, 0.5), where selective value falls off as the square of the deviation from the optimum ($w = 1 - s$ at unit deviation) in the case of three equally spaced loci (c = recombination between adjacent loci). No double crossing over.

GAMETES	$s = 0.10$						$s = 0.01$		$s = 0$
	$c = 0.0005$	$c = 0.0010$	$c = 0.005$	$c = 0.010$	$c = 0.05$	$c = 0.10$	$c = 0.05$	$c = 0.10$	
AbC, aBc	0.2051	0.2049	0.2030	0.2008	0.1863	0.1737	0.1429	0.1339	0.125
Abc, aBC	.1473	.1472	.1468	.1463	.1427	.1394	.1296	.1278	.125
ABc, abC	.1473	.1472	.1468	.1463	.1427	.1394	.1296	.1278	.125
ABC, abc	.00034	.00068	.0034	.0066	.0283	.0475	.0979	.1105	.125
AB, ab	.1476	.1479	.1502	.1529	.1710	.1869	.2275	.2383	.250
AC, ac	0.2054	0.2055	0.2064	0.2075	0.2147	0.2212	0.2408	0.2443	0.250

$$f_4{}^2[4s + 2cs] - f_4[2s + c + cs] + f_2f_4(8s + 8cs)$$

$$+ 6csf_2{}^2 - (3c + cs)f_2 + 0.5c - dE = 0,$$

(4.45)

$$f_4{}^2[4s - 2cs] - f_4[2s + c - cs]$$

$$+ 2csf_2{}^2 + (c - cs)f_2 + dE = 0.$$

These may be solved by trial and error. Some examples are given in Table 4.2 in which double crossing over is assumed to be absent ($d = 0$). The results for given s/c, but with s and c smaller than in Table 4.2, differ only slightly.

The value $s = 0.10$ is almost the maximum under the system considered, since $AABBCC$ and $aabbcc$ are lethal ($w = 1 - 9s = 0$ if $s = 0.1111$). The cases with $s = 0.10$ thus illustrate the amount of nonrandom combination under very strong selection and moderate to very close linkage. The only types of gametes that are infrequent even in the most extreme cases are ABC and abc. The two bottom rows give the frequencies of unbalanced pairs of genes on disregarding the third. These frequencies are much greater than if there were no other locus affecting the character (as in Table 4.1).

As in the two-factor case, the equilibrium point becomes stable with sufficient reversible mutation, recurrent immigration, or pleiotropic heterotic effect. If h is added to the selective values of each single heterozygote, $2h$ to those of each double heterozygote, and $3h$ to that of the triple heterozygotes, the mean selective value of the population at the equilibrium point is increased by $1.5h$. The saddle disappears if $h = (1/3)s(1 + 16f_4)$, which lies between $(1/3)s$ and s. There is a peak at $(0.5, 0.5, 0.5)$ if h is larger than this. It has been shown that for values of h up to a point that gives a shallow selective peak, equations (4.42) hold approximately if c is replaced by $c(1 + 2.5h)$ (Wright 1965a).

Table 4.3 gives some results for cases in which at least one of the loci (M) is in a different chromosome from the others so that double crossing over must be taken into account. Taking c as the amount of recombination between loci A and B, and 0.5 as that between both A and M and B and M, then $d = 0.5(1 - c)$ is the amount of double crossing over.

Where A and B are closely linked and there is strong selection, there is almost as much deviation from random combination of A and B as if they were the only heterallelic loci that affected the character, as may be seen by comparing the frequencies in the next to last row of Table 4.3 with those having the same ratio (s/c) in Table 4.1. The comparable figures in Table 4.2 are very much in contrast.

Where all three loci are in different chromosomes ($c = 0.50$), all kinds of gametes except ABM and abm are equally frequent.

TABLE 4.3. Same as Table 4.2 except that locus M, m is in a different chromosome from A, a and B, b, and double crossing over $d = 0.5(1 - c)$ must be taken into account.

GAMETES	$s = 0.10$				$s = 0.01$			$s = 0$
	$c = 0.001$	$c = 0.01$	$c = 0.10$	$c = 0.50$	$c = 0.01$	$c = 0.10$	$c = 0.50$	
$Ab:m, aB:M$	0.2486	0.2363	0.1712	0.1357	0.1760	0.1311	0.1262	0.125
$Ab:M, aB:m$	.2486	.2363	.1712	.1357	.1760	.1311	.1262	.125
$AB:m, ab:M$	.0017	.0162	.0937	.1357	.0755	.1212	.1262	.125
$AB:M, ab:m$	.0012	.0112	.0639	.0930	.0725	.1165	.1213	.125
AB, ab	.0029	.0274	.1576	.2287	.1480	.2377	.2475	.250
AM, am	0.2498	0.2475	0.2351	0.2287	0.2485	0.2476	0.2475	0.250

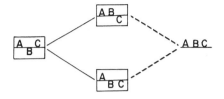

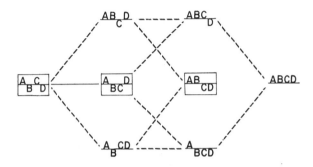

FIG. 4.4. The four kinds of triple heterozygotes (above) and the eight kinds of quadruple heterozygotes (below) with connections to show which are derivable from each other by single crossing over. Only plus alleles are represented. Those which are most balanced (2/1 above, 2/2 below) are in boxes with directly connecting lines solid (new but expected to appear in *Japanese Journal of Genetics*, 1969).

Four Loci

We may go on to the case of a character determined additively by four pairs of alleles (A, a; B, b; C, c; D, d), all semidominant and equal in contribution of the plus factors (capitals), again assuming that selective value falls off as the square of the deviation from the optimum ($w = 1$ with four plus factors, $w = 1 - s$ with three or five, $w = 1 - 4s$ with two or six, $w = 1 - 9s$ with one or seven, and $w = 1 - 16s$ for *aabbccdd* and *AABBCCDD*). It will be assumed that the amount of recombination (c) is so low that there are no double or triple crossovers. Figure 4.4*b* shows the eight possible quadruple heterozygotes with lines connecting those whose chromosomes can be derived from each other by single crossovers, in comparison with a similar diagram for the four possible triple heterozygotes (4.4*a*).

At metastable equilibrium, all gene frequencies are the same (0.5), and complementary gametes are also equally frequent. The most unbalanced and hence least frequent are *ABCD* and *abcd*. There are three kinds of quadruple heterozygotes composed of balanced gametes. Of these, $AbCd/aBcD$ and $AbcD/aBCd$ can each give rise to gametes of the other by single crossovers. These two pairs of gametes should be almost equally frequent. The former pair, being farther from the more unbalanced gametes in terms of numbers of crossovers, should be slightly more numerous. The other pair of complementary balanced gametes, $ABcd$ and $abCD$, can only be derived from the others through unbalanced gametes and are only one step from the most unbalanced ones. They may be expected to be rather infrequent. The following symbols will be used for the 16 gametic frequencies, grouping similar ones.

Balanced Gametes	Frequency	Unbalanced Gametes	Frequency
$AbCd, aBcD$	f_1	$ABcD, abCd, AbCD, aBcd$	f_4
$AbcD, aBCd$	f_2	$ABCd, abcD, Abcd, aBCD$	f_5
$ABcd, abCD$	f_3	$ABCD, abcd$	f_6

$$2f_1 + 2f_2 + 2f_3 + 4f_4 + 4f_5 + 2f_6 = 1.$$

After making up a table of zygotes, showing the kinds of gametes produced without crossing over or by single crossing over, and the proportions, a table can be made in which are entered the contributions of each kind of zygote to each gamete frequency, taking account of their selective values. The proportion of each noncrossover is $(1 - 3c)/2$ if the terminal loci are both heterozygous, $(1 - 2c)/2$ if loci two apart are both heterozygous but one of the terminal ones is homozygous, and $(1 - c)/2$ if only two adjacent loci are heterozygous. The frequency of a crossover gamete is $c/2$ if the crossover is between adjacent heterozygous loci, c if a single homozygous locus intervenes between two heterozygous ones, and $3c/2$ if only the terminal loci are heterozygous.

The terms in the contributions of zygotes that do not involve c reduce easily to simple form. Those that involve c but not s are given vertically for each gene frequency, in Table 4.4.

These can also be reduced to fairly simple form as shown in equations (4.46).

The terms involving cs are shown in Table 4.5, again vertically, but must be so small under the assumed conditions that they need not be used. The assumption of no double crossing over implies that c is small, and the requirement that the selective values $(1 - 16s)$ not be negative restricts s to values not greater than 0.0625. Moreover, all of the contributions involve frequencies f_4, f_5, or f_6, which are expected to be small where there is appreciable deviation from random combination.

SELECTION IN INTERACTION SYSTEMS

TABLE 4.4. The coefficients of the c-terms (vertically) in the contributions of classes of zygotes to gametic frequencies.

	f_1	f_2	f_3	$2f_4$	$2f_5$	f_6	Total
$f_1{}^2$	-3	$+1$	0	$+2$	0	0	0
f_1f_2	-2	-2	0	$+2$	$+2$	0	0
f_1f_3	-4	0	-4	$+6$	$+2$	0	0
f_1f_4	-4	$+2$	$+2$	-2	$+2$	0	0
f_1f_5	-6	$+4$	0	$+6$	-6	$+2$	0
f_1f_6	-4	0	0	$+4$	$+4$	-4	0
$f_2{}^2$	$+1$	-3	0	0	$+2$	0	0
f_2f_3	0	-4	-4	$+4$	$+4$	0	0
f_2f_4	$+4$	-6	$+2$	-6	$+6$	0	0
f_2f_5	$+2$	-4	0	$+2$	-2	$+2$	0
f_2f_6	0	-4	0	$+2$	$+6$	-4	0
$f_3{}^2$	0	0	-3	$+2$	0	$+1$	0
f_3f_4	$+2$	0	-4	-2	$+2$	$+2$	0
f_3f_5	0	$+2$	-6	$+6$	-6	$+4$	0
f_3f_6	0	0	-2	$+2$	$+2$	-2	0
$f_4{}^2$	$+5$	$+1$	$+5$	-14	$+2$	$+1$	0
f_4f_5	$+6$	$+6$	$+6$	-12	-12	$+6$	0
f_4f_6	$+2$	0	$+4$	-6	$+6$	-6	0
$f_5{}^2$	$+1$	$+5$	$+1$	$+2$	-14	$+5$	0
f_5f_6	0	$+2$	$+2$	$+2$	-2	-4	0
$f_6{}^2$	0	0	$+1$	0	$+2$	-3	0

The equilibrium equations, on omitting the cs-terms, are:

$$f_1 = [f_1 - 4sf_1z + c(f_4 - 2f_1 + x^2)]/\bar{w},$$
$$f_2 = [f_2 - 4sf_2z + c(f_5 - 2f_2 + x^2)]/\bar{w},$$
(4.46)
$$f_3 = [f_3 - 4sf_3z + c(f_4 - 2f_3 + y^2)]/\bar{w},$$
$$2f_4 = [2f_4 - 2sf_4(4z + 1) + c(f_1 + f_3 - 4f_4 + 2xy)]/\bar{w},$$
$$2f_5 = [2f_5 - 2sf_5(4z + 1) + c(f_2 + f_6 - 4f_5 + 2xy)]/\bar{w},$$
$$f_6 = [f_6 - 4sf_6(z + 1) + c(f_5 - 2f_6 + y^2)]/\bar{w},$$

where $x = (f_1 + f_2 + f_4 + f_5)$ and $y = (f_3 + f_4 + f_5 + f_6)$, so that $x + y = 0.5$ and $z = (f_4 + f_5 + 2f_6)$.

As shown in Table 4.4, the sum of the c-terms is zero, which may be verified from equations (4.46). Since the sum of the cs-terms is also zero, as shown in Table 4.5, the total for the full equations is exactly $(0.5 - 4sz)/\bar{w} = 0.5$, and

(4.47) $$\bar{w} = 1 - 8sz = 1 - 8s(f_4 + f_5 + 2f_6).$$

TABLE 4.5. The coefficients of the cs-terms (vertical) in the contributions of classes of zygotes to gametic frequencies.

	f_1	f_2	f_3	$2f_4$	$2f_5$	f_6	Total
$f_1 f_4$	+4	−2	−2	+2	−2	0	0
$f_1 f_5$	+6	−4	0	−6	+6	−2	0
$f_2 f_4$	−4	+6	−2	+6	−6	0	0
$f_2 f_5$	−2	+4	0	−2	+2	−2	0
$f_3 f_4$	−2	0	+4	+2	−2	−2	0
$f_3 f_5$	0	−2	+6	−6	+6	−4	0
$f_4{}^2$	0	−4	0	+8	0	−4	0
$f_4 f_5$	−16	0	−8	+24	+24	−24	0
$f_5{}^2$	0	−12	0	0	+24	−12	0
$f_1 f_6$	+16	0	0	−16	−16	+16	0
$f_2 f_6$	0	+16	0	−8	−24	+16	0
$f_3 f_6$	0	0	+8	−8	−8	+8	0
$f_4 f_6$	−2	0	−4	+6	−6	+6	0
$f_5 f_6$	0	−2	−2	−2	+2	+4	0

On substituting this in equations (4.46), the terms free from both s and c cancel, so that the equations can be solved for the ratio $s/c = R$ as long as the cs-terms are negligible:

$$
\begin{aligned}
f_1 &= (2f_1 - f_4 - x^2)/4Rz, \\
f_2 &= (2f_2 - f_5 - x^2)/4Rz, \\
f_3 &= (2f_3 - f_4 - y^2)/4Rz, \\
f_4 &= (f_1 + f_3 - 4f_4 + 2xy)/2R(1 - 4z), \\
f_5 &= (f_2 + f_6 - 4f_5 + 2xy)/2R(1 - 4z), \\
f_6 &= (f_5 - 2f_6 + y^2)/4R(1 - z).
\end{aligned}
$$

(4.48)

Solution of these simultaneous quadratic equations is facilitated by use of the following easily derived relations:

$$
\begin{aligned}
(f_4 - f_5) &= 2Rf_6/[(2 - 4Rz)(R + 2 - 4Rz) - 1], \\
(f_3 - f_6) &= [(f_4 - f_5) + 4Rf_6]/(2 - 4Rz), \\
(f_1 - f_2) &= [(f_4 - f_5)/(2 - 4Rz)].
\end{aligned}
$$

(4.49)

Table 4.6 gives the equilibrium frequency for each kind of gamete with various values of s/c, assuming that s and c are so small that sc is less than about 0.001.

Again there is relatively little deviation from random combination if s/c is as great as 0.1. Somewhat unexpectedly, the balanced gametes $ABcd$ and $abCD$ are slightly less frequent for $s/c = 0.1$ than the unbalanced ones that

TABLE 4.6. Gametic frequencies at equilibrium (metastable) at (0.5, 0.5, 0.5, 0.5), where selective value falls off as the square of the deviation from the optimum ($w = 1 - s$ at unit deviation) in the case of four equally spaced equivalent loci (recombination between adjacent loci c). No double crossing over.

Gametes	Frequency	$s/c = 100$	10	1	0.1	0
$AbCd,\ aBcD$	f_1	0.24688	0.2200	0.1086	0.0693	0.0625
$AbcD,\ aBCd$	f_2	.24687	.2194	.1006	.0674	.0625
$ABcd,\ abCD$	f_3	.00126	.0131	.0638	.0634	.0625
$ABcD,\ abCd$	f_4	.00125	.0121	.0588	.0640	.0625
$AbCD,\ aBcd$	f_4	.00125	.0121	.0588	.0640	.0625
$ABCd,\ abcD$	f_5	.00124	.0115	.0472	.0605	.0625
$Abcd,\ aBCD$	f_5	.00124	.0115	.0472	.0605	.0625
$ABCD,\ abcd$	f_6	.000003	.0003	.0150	.0509	.0625
$AB,\ ab,\ CD,\ cd$		.00375	.0370	.1848	.2385	.2500
$BC,\ bc$		.24936	.2427	.2100	.2393	.2500
$AC,\ ac,\ BD,\ bd$		.24937	.2439	.2296	.2447	.2500
$AD,\ ad$		0.24937	0.2439	0.2332	0.2463	0.2500

are only one step from $AbCd$ and $aBcD$, the only instance in the table of an inversion of the order indicated by subscripts of the f's. There is considerable deviation from random combination if $s/c = 1$, but even the most unbalanced gametes are not uncommon (24% of their frequency under random combination). If $s/c = 10$, however, the balanced pairs $AbCd$, $aBcD$, and $AbcD$, $aBCd$ which are almost equally frequent make up nearly 88% of all gametes. Gametes $ABCD$ and $abcd$ are very uncommon (0.0003) while all of the other ten kinds have about the same frequency, 0.0115 to 0.0131. This pattern is exaggerated if $s/c = 100$. As a result, there is almost random combination of all pairs of loci, in these cases, except for adjacent terminal loci, which show strong repulsion linkage if s/c is as great as 10.

As with two or three loci, the equilibrium at equal gene frequencies becomes stable with sufficiently high rates of symmetrically reversible mutation, immigration from the rest of the species if average gene frequencies are 0.50 or there are sufficient pleiotropic heterotic effects. If there are pleiotropic bonuses at the four loci averaging $\bar{h}$, then $\bar{w}$ is increased by $2\bar{h}$. There is stable equilibrium if $\bar{h} > 4s(f_4 + f_5 + 2f_6)$.

Five to Eight Loci

The gamete frequencies for more than four equivalent, equally spaced loci and selective value falling off from the mean according to the square of the deviation have not been worked out, but some idea of the relative frequencies

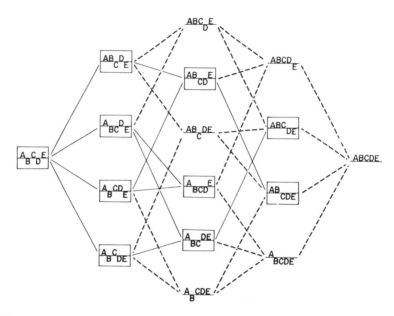

FIG. 4.5. The 16 kinds of quintuple heterozygotes arranged as in Figure 4.4

can be obtained from diagrams in which zygotes, heterozygous in all respects (and thus balanced), are connected, if derivable from each other by single crossovers. This is done for groups of five and six loci in Figures 4.5 and 4.6. As in Figure 4.4, the heterozygotes composed of gametes that are balanced (6 loci), or balanced as much as possible (5 loci), are enclosed in boxes and connected by heavy lines. It may be assumed that there is enough pleiotropic heterosis to give stable equilibrium with all gene frequencies 0.5.

With five loci, all such heterozygotes are connected (in contrast with one of the four-locus cases and several of the six-locus cases). Thus all of the gametes with two or three plus factors are probably fairly common even where the s/c ratio is high, but the more unbalanced ones are all undoubtedly held to low frequencies, under this condition. While the array of fivefold heterozygotes and their connections is far from giving all the information necessary for determination of the relative frequencies of the various balanced gametes, they give an important sample of the information in this case in which all gene frequencies are 0.5 at equilibrium. The following symbols will be used for the frequencies of each kind of nearly balanced five locus gamete, designated as in Figure 4.4 by the plus factors only.

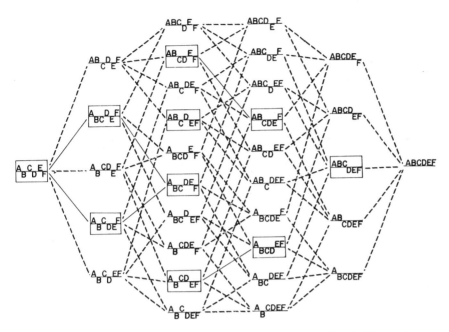

FIG. 4.6. The 32 kinds of sextuple heterozygotes arranged as in Figure 4.4

	Frequency	Gamete	Frequency
ACE, BD	f_1	AE, BCD	f_4
$AD, BCE; ACD, BE$	f_2	$ABE, CD; ADE, BC$	f_5
$ABD, CE; AC, BDE$	f_3	$ABC, DE; AB, CDE$	f_6

There can be no doubt that f_1 (gametes of a quintuple heterozygote connected with four others that produce nearly balanced gametes) is the largest, f_2 is next, and f_6 is the smallest of these. The order among the others is not wholly clear.

The question of most interest is which if any pairs of loci tend to be retained almost wholly in repulsion with high s/c, recalling that none were, with three closely linked loci, but that the terminal pairs were, with four loci. The seriously unbalanced gametes are undoubtedly all very rare with high s/c and need not be considered. The contributions to coupling and repulsion of each pair of loci from the six frequency classes above are shown in Table 4.7. The ratio of couplings to repulsions is in all cases 4 to 6, indicating that even with very high s/c, coupling gametes are fairly common in all cases.

However, f_6 is undoubtedly much the smallest under this condition. On omitting it, it appears that coupling is probably least frequent with two adjacent terminal loci (AB, DE) in a closely linked group of five, especially since neither f_1 nor f_2 is represented. For all other pairs coupling must be common.

TABLE 4.7. Main contributions to the frequencies of coupling and repulsion of pairs of loci from a group of five closely linked loci $ABCDE$, assuming very strong selection.

		f_1	f_2	f_3	f_4	f_5	f_6	f_1 to f_6	f_1 to f_5
AB, DE	coupling			1		1	2	4	2
	repulsion	1	2	1	1	1		6	6
BC, CD	coupling			1	1	1	1	4	3
	repulsion	1	1	2		1	1	6	5
AC, CE	coupling	1	1	1			1	4	3
	repulsion		1	1	1	2	1	6	5
BD	coupling	1		2	1			4	4
	repulsion		2			2	2	6	4
AD, BE	coupling		2	1		1		4	4
	repulsion	1		1	1	1	2	6	4
AE	coupling	1			1	2		4	4
	repulsion		2	2			2	6	4

The case of six linked loci under the postulated condition is represented in Figure 4.6 by the 32 balanced heterozygotes with connections showing which are derivable from each other by single crossing over. Those that produce balanced gametes are, as in Figures 4.4 and 4.5, enclosed in boxes. They fall into five disconnected groups. The frequencies of the balanced gametes will be designated as follows:

Gamete	Frequency	Gamete	Frequency
ACE, BDF	f_1	ABE, CDF; ACD, BEF	f_4
ADF, BCE; ACF, BDE	f_2	ABF, CDE; AEF, BCD	f_5
		ABD, CEF	f_6
ADE, BCF	f_3	ABC, DEF	f_7

Here f_1, f_2, and f_3, in this order, are clearly the largest. With very high s/c, frequencies f_4 to f_7 pertaining to gametes which are related to the first group only through unbalanced gametes are undoubtedly much less.

Again the point of most interest is the rarity of coupling between pairs of loci in the group. The contributions of the above frequencies are shown in Table 4.8. The ratio of number of contributions of coupling to those of repulsion is again 4 to 6 for all pairs, but in this case those from frequency classes f_4 to f_7 must, as noted above, be severely discounted if s/c is high. Considering only frequencies f_1, f_2, f_3, it appears that coupling would be rare (at equilibrium) with respect to terminal pairs of loci (AB, EF) and the middle pair, CD, the former probably being slightly less frequent ($f_4 + f_5 > f_6 + f_7$). For all other pairs coupling must be common.

The analogous seven-locus case somewhat resembles the cases of three and five loci at metastable equilibrium. There are 64 balanced heterozygotes of which 35 come from union of a gamete with four plus factors with one with three. All of the latter are connected with one or more of the others by single crossovers, the number of connections ranging from one ($ABCDefg/abcdEFG$ and $ABCdefg/abcDEFG$) to six ($AbCdEfG/aBcDeFg$). The ratio of repulsion to coupling is 20:15 for all pairs of loci but if the 15 which are probably the

TABLE 4.8. Main contributions to the frequencies of coupling and repulsion of pairs of loci from a group of six closely linked loci $ABCDEF$, assuming strong selection.

Loci		f_1	f_2	f_3	f_4	f_5	f_6	f_7	f_1 to f_7	f_1 to f_3
AB, EF	coupling				1	1	1	1	4	0
	repulsion	1	2	1	1	1			6	4
BC, DE	coupling		1	1		1		1	4	2
	repulsion	1	1		2	1	1		6	2
CD	coupling				2	2			4	0
	repulsion	1	2	1			1	1	6	4
AC, DF	coupling	1	1		1			1	4	2
	repulsion		1	1	1	2	1		6	2
BD, CE	coupling	1	1			1	1		4	2
	repulsion		1	1	2	1		1	6	2
AD, CF	coupling		1	1	1		1		4	2
	repulsion	1	1		1	2		1	6	2
BE	coupling		2		2				4	2
	repulsion	1		1		2	1	1	6	2
AE, BF	coupling	1		1	1	1			4	2
	repulsion		2		1	1	1	1	6	2
AF	coupling		2			2			4	2
	repulsion	1		1	2		1	1	6	2

least common are omitted the ratios are 16:4 for the terminal pairs AB and FG, 14:6 for CD and DE, 12:8 for BC, EF, AC, CD, and EG, and 10:10 for all others. Thus coupling gametes may be expected to become somewhat low in frequency in some cases, especially AB and FG, with high s/c, but never to become very rare.

The analogous eight-locus case has 128 balanced heterozygotes. As with the cases of four and six loci, there is a small isolated group, here eight of those with balanced gametes, which may be expected to become much more frequent with high s/c than all others. These range from $AbCdEfGh/aBcDeFgH$ to $AbcDEfgH/aBCdeFGh$. Each is connected to three of the others by single crossovers while none is connected with any other zygote derived from complementary balanced gametes. The ratio of repulsion to coupling is 8:0.

TABLE 4.9. Frequencies at equilibrium of coupling of two genes, located at various positions in a sequence of equivalent segregating loci, equally spaced (except for M, m), under selection according to the symmetrical optimum model, with various values of s/c. The segregating loci other than the pair in question are in parentheses. (M, m) is in a different chromosome from AB. There are symmetrical cases starting from the other end of each linkage system.

No. Loci	Order	s/c				
		100	10	1	0.1	0
2	$A\ B$	0.0025	0.0238	0.1465	0.2375	0.25
3	$A\ B$; (M, m)	.0029	.0274	.1480	.2377	.25
4	$A\ B\ (C, c)\ (D, d)$	.0038	.0370	.1848	.2385	.25
6	$A\ B\ (C, c)\ (D, d)\ (E, e)$ (F, f)	0+	low	medium	.25−	.25
6	$(A, a)\ (B, b)\ C\ D\ (E, e)$ (F, f)	0+	,,	,,	.25−	.25
8	$A\ B\ (C, c)\ (D, d)\ (E, e)$ $(F, f)\ (G, g)\ (H, h)$	0+	,,	,,	.25−	.25
8	$(A, a)\ (B, b)\ C\ D\ (E, e)$ $(F, f)\ (G, g)\ (H, h)$	0+	,,	,,	.25−	.25
3	$A\ B\ (C, c)$	.1479	.1529	.1869	.2383	.25
5	$A\ B\ (C, c)\ (D, d)\ (E, e)$	medium	medium	high	.25−	.25
7	$A\ B\ (C, c)\ (D, d)\ (E, e)$ $(F, f)\ (G, g)$	,,	,,	,,	.25−	.25
3	$A\ (B, b)\ C$	.2055	.2075	.2212	.2443	.25
4	$(A, a)\ B\ C\ (D, d)$	.2494	.2427	.2100	.2393	.25
4	$A\ (B, b)\ C\ (D, d)$	.2494	.2439	.2296	.2447	.25
4	$A\ (B, b)\ (C, c)\ D$	.2494	.2439	.2332	.2463	.25
5–8	Other types than above	0.25−	0.25−	0.25−	0.25−	0.25

for terminal pairs AB, GH, and the pairs at two steps from these, CD and EF, while for all other pairs the ratio is 4:4. Coupling may thus be expected to become rare with high s/c in only the above four pairs.

Table 4.9 shows how the equilibrium frequency of coupling of two genes depends, under the conditions discussed here, on their positions in the series of linked segregating loci and the value of s/c for adjacent loci.

The first general conclusion is that there is not much departure from random combination of pairs of loci if s/c (for adjacent loci) is as small as 0.1. The second is that gametes showing coupling of two genes become really rare with high s/c only if they are largely isolated from other similar segregating loci, AB and AB; (M, m), or are at one end of a tightly linked group consisting of an even number of equivalent segregating loci (as found with four, six, or eight loci), or are separated from each end by an even number of such loci (as found in sets of six or eight loci). In a linkage system with an odd number of such loci (here three, five, or seven) the frequency of coupling gametes with respect to any two loci never becomes really low but is lowest for a terminal pair.

In drawing conclusions from these cases, it must be borne in mind that they deal only with segregating loci with equivalent effects. Ones with much smaller effects than the others could presumably be present without affecting much the conclusions based on the major factors. The loci are, moreover, assumed to be equally spaced except in the case AB; (M, m) in which M, m has 50% recombination with the others. Presumably loci rather widely removed from the others in the same linkage system would have an effect intermediate between equal spacing and presence in a different chromosome. The striking difference between odd and even numbers of linked loci would no doubt be much blurred by inequalities in effect or spacing.

Intrachromosomal Balance

These results bear on a thesis advanced by Mather (1941) to the effect that natural selection directed toward the mean of a quantitatively varying character ("stabilizing selection") tends to build up an alternation of plus and minus factors along chromosomes taking account of dominance in heterozygotes. He illustrated "internal balance" and "relational balance" as follows (Mather 1943):

		Relational
Internal Balance		Balance
Homozygotes		Heterozygotes
$A^+b^-C^+d^-$	$a^-B^+c^-D^+$	$A^+b^-C^+d^-$
$\overline{A^+b^-C^+d^-}$	$\overline{a^-B^+c^-D^+}$	$\overline{a^-B^+c^-D^+}$
$+\ -\ +\ -$	$-\ +\ -\ +$	$+\ +\ +\ +$
good		poor

Internal Balance Homozygotes		Relational Balance Heterozygotes
$\dfrac{A^+b^+C^+d^+}{A^+b^+C^+d^+}$	$\dfrac{a^-B^-c^-D^-}{a^-B^-c^-D^-}$	$\dfrac{A^+b^+C^+d^+}{a^-B^-c^-D^-}$
$+\;+\;+\;+$	$-\;-\;-\;-$	$+\;-\;+\;-$
poor		good

He argued that balance evolves in the minimizing of overt variability while maximizing potential variability.

It appears that both kinds of balance can occur only if all dominant alleles are assembled with internal balance in one kind of chromosome, all recessives in another, giving heterozygotes $A^+B^-C^+D^-/a^-b^+c^-d^+$. Mather's assumption that complete dominance is characteristic of allelic "polygenes" seems to have been based on Fisher's (1928) theory of a strong general tendency toward evolution of dominance by selection of specific modifiers of heterozygotes.

The theory of the evolution of dominance of the prevailing allele over recurrent deleterious mutations would hardly be pertinent here even if valid, which, as brought out earlier, it rather clearly is not. Also not pertinent is the physiological bias toward dominance of genes with highly active products over more or less inactive alleles. The undoubted effectiveness of strong unidirectional selection in bringing about dominance of the favored allele of a pair with major differential effect in cases in which the heterozygote is intermediate in spite of the above bias is obviously not pertinent. We are concerned here with minor effects on quantitatively varying characters which have presumably been subject in the main to centripetal selection. There seems to be no clear theoretical reason and no good evidence for complete dominance of either allele as the rule. With intermediacy the rule, the two kinds of balance, if present at all, would tend to be associated.

The analysis presented here indicates that departures from random combination are not great where the selective disadvantage, s, at one step from the optimum is of lower order than the amount of recombination, c, between adjacent loci. With a high ratio s/c the frequency of completely unbalanced gametes does, indeed, become small but there is little build up of a strict alternation of plus and minus effects. With respect to pairs of loci, within tightly linked groups, there is a considerable tendency to excess repulsion of the two at either end of a long series of equivalent loci (four or more). The value of s is, however, likely to be so small in nature that this is not likely to apply except in very tightly linked systems.

These conclusions have no bearing on the likelihood of a delayed advance under strong artificial directional selection in a population derived from a few individuals. Even if there are no important deviations from random combination above the level of pseudoalleles, a small sample may well happen to have only complementary chromosome blocks, $+ -$ and $- +$, on which even strong directional selection has little effect until a crossover, $+ +$ or $- -$, occurs after long delay.

Mather emphasized the effect of "balance" in reducing variability. There is, indeed, drastic reduction if s is of the same order as c or greater. Table 4.10 shows the genotypic variances implied by gametic frequencies with two, three, or four equivalent, equally spaced loci. With two or four loci, the variance approaches zero as s/c increases but approaches 0.5 with three loci, in which a genotype with the mean value toward which selection is directed must be heterozygous at least at one locus.

TABLE 4.10. The genotypic variance from the gametic frequencies at metastable equilibrium with two, three, or four equivalent equally spaced loci, assigning unit value to each plus factor and assuming no losses from differential viability.

Loci		100	10	1	0.1	0
AB	Table 4.1	0.0100	0.0952	0.5860	0.9500	1.0
ABC	Table 4.2	0.5056	0.5528	0.8800	1.3840	1.5
$ABCD$	Table 4.6	0.0200	0.1941	1.0880	1.8101	2.0

Nonrandom Combination: General Two-Factor Case

Interactive Selection

In the preceding examples, the deviations from random combination have been related to the ratio s/c in a particular pattern of selection. For more general treatment, it becomes necessary to use measures of interactive selection (s_I) and its relation to recombination. This has been done only for two-locus cases.

In haploids, the measure of two-factor interactive selection is simple. The absence of interaction implies that $(w_{AB} - w_{ab}) = (w_{Ab} - w_{ab}) + (w_{aB} - w_{ab})$, so that the deviation is given by

$$(4.50) \qquad s_I = w_{AB} - w_{Ab} - w_{aB} + w_{ab}.$$

Four such statistics are required in diploids, one for each kind of gamete (Kojima and Kelleher 1961).

$$(4.51) \qquad s_{I(AB)} = w_{AB/AB} - w_{AB/Ab} - w_{AB/aB} + w_{AB/ab}$$

$(s_{I(Ab)}, s_{I(aB)}, \text{ and } s_{I(ab)} \text{ are analogous})$.

The average amount of interactive selection is thus:

(4.52) $\qquad \bar{s}_I = f_{AB}s_{I(AB)} + f_{Ab}s_{I(Ab)} + f_{aB}s_{I(aB)} + f_{ab}s_{I(ab)}.$

In the two-factor optimum model to which (4.29) applies:

$$s_{I(AB)} = s_{I(ab)} = 2s - t,$$

(4.53) $\qquad s_{I(Ab)} = s_{I(aB)} = -2s,$

$$\bar{s}_I = (f_{AB} + f_{ab})(2s - t) - (f_{Ab} + f_{aB})2s.$$

If $t = 4s$, then $s_I = -2s$ is uniform.

These measures of interactive selection are relative to the standard adopted for the w's. For purposes of comparison of different two-factor cases it is convenient to take the selective value of the double heterozygote as standard and use $K = \bar{s}_I/cw_{AaBb}$ as the index of the relation of interactive selection to recombination.

Change of Gametic Frequencies

The general formulas for rates of change of gametic frequencies allowing for nonrandom combination for two pairs of alleles in continuously reproducing populations were given by Kimura (1956b). The corresponding formulas in terms of discrete generations were given by Lewontin and Kojima (1960).

If there were no recombination, the situation would be the same as for a set of four alleles, AB, Ab, aB, and ab. The effect of recombination (chapter 2) may be added to the Δf's for these alleles. It is assumed that the w's are constants and that the selective differences are small enough that the order of occurrence of the selective and recombinational components may be ignored.

$$\Delta f_{AB} = [f_{AB}(w_{AB} - \bar{w}) - cDw_{AaBb}]/\bar{w} \qquad (D = f_{AB}f_{ab} - f_{Ab}f_{aB}),$$

(4.54) $\quad \Delta f_{Ab} = [f_{Ab}(w_{Ab} - \bar{w}) + cDw_{AaBb}]/\bar{w},$

$\qquad \Delta f_{aB} = [f_{aB}(w_{aB} - \bar{w}) + cDw_{AaBb}]/\bar{w},$

$\qquad \Delta f_{ab} = [f_{ab}(w_{ab} - \bar{w}) - cDw_{AaBb}]/\bar{w},$

where

(4.55) $\qquad w_{AB} = f_{AB}w_{AB/AB} + f_{Ab}w_{AB/Ab} + f_{aB}w_{AB/aB} + f_{ab}w_{AB/ab}$

$$(w_{Ab}, w_{aB}, \text{ and } w_{ab} \text{ are analogous}),$$

and

(4.56) $\qquad \bar{w} = f_{AB}w_{AB} + f_{Ab}w_{Ab} + f_{aB}w_{aB} + f_{ab}w_{ab}.$

If the selective values of the cis and trans double heterozygotes differ, the recombinational term was found by Bodmer and Parsons (1962) to be $cD_w/\bar{w}$, in which $D_w = f_{AB}f_{ab}w_{AB/ab} - f_{Ab}f_{aB}w_{Ab/aB}$. There is not likely to be a difference except in the case of pseudoalleles.

Equations (4.54) can be reduced to three by expressing one gametic frequency in terms of the others ($f_{AB} = 1 - f_{Ab} - f_{aB} - f_{ab}$). The equilibrium points can be found by equating these equations to zero and solving as three simultaneous cubic equations.

It may be seen that solutions for interaction systems involving multiple alleles and more than two loci, comparable to (4.6), but allowing for nonrandom combination, are likely to be rather formidable.

Some Special Cases

Kimura (1956c) gave the following simple example. It will be assumed that s and t are both positive.

	aa	Aa	AA
BB	$1 - s$	$1 + t$	$1 + s$
Bb	1	$1 + t$	1
bb	$1 + s$	$1 + t$	$1 - s$

Here $s_1 = s$ is constant. If there were no departure from random combination, $\bar{w} = 1 + s(1 - 2p)(1 - 2q) + 2tp(1 - p)$. There would always be a saddle at $(0.5, 0.5)$ and ultimate fixation of BB or of bb. There would be ultimate fixation of $AABB$ or of $aabb$ if $t \leq s$, but continued polymorphism at the A locus if $t > s$. On taking account of nonrandom combination, Kimura showed that there could be a selective peak at $(0.5, 0.5)$ under sufficiently close linkage, sufficiently small s, and sufficiently large t. The extreme case is that of complete linkage of A and B under which there is obviously polymorphism of AB, ab if $t > s$. He showed that mechanisms reducing crossing over, such as inversions, are favored by selection and tend to be established under the above conditions. This case illustrates the possibility of a qualitative difference in the course of evolution from that expected under the assumption of random combination.

Lewontin and Kojima (1960) investigated the following system:

	aa	Aa	AA
BB	1	$1 + s_1$	1
Bb	$1 + s_2$	$1 + s_3$	$1 + s_2$
bb	1	$1 + s_1$	1

We will restrict consideration here to cases in which none of the selection coefficients is negative and s_3 is the largest, which insures the existence of a selective peak at $(0.5, 0.5)$. The amount of interactive selection is not uniform, $s_{I(AB)} = s_{I(ab)} = -s_{I(Ab)} = -s_{I(aB)} = s_3 - s_1 - s_2$. Let $K_1 = (s_3 - s_1 - s_2)/c(1 + s_3)$. It was shown that there is random combination at the selective peak (all gametic frequencies 0.25) in spite of the presence of interaction if $K_1 \leq 4$. If, however, $K > 4$, equilibrium is reached only with departure from random combination.

$$(4.57) \qquad \begin{aligned} f_{AB} &= f_{ab} = 0.25 \{1 \pm \sqrt{[1 - (4/K_1)]}\}, \\ f_{Ab} &= f_{aB} = 0.5 - f_{AB}. \end{aligned}$$

This can occur only if c is less than 0.25 even if s_3 is enormously greater than s_1 and s_2 and in general requires that c be rather small. In the example given by the authors, $s_1 = 0.5$, $s_2 = 1.5$, and $s_3 = 3$ giving $K_1 = 0.25/c$ under which there is random combination if $c \geq 0.0625$, but departure from this if there is closer linkage. If $c = 0.05$, so that $K_1 = 5$, then $f_{AB} = f_{ab} = 0.362$ or 0.138, and $f_{Ab} = f_{aB} = 0.138$ or 0.362 at equilibrium. The mean selective value at this point, 0.58, is not much greater than its value 0.5625 if all gene frequencies were equal.

Felsenstein (1965) considered the effect of linkage on unidirectional selection involving two pairs of alleles, the genotypic selective values of which rise nonlinearly toward a selective peak at one extreme ($AABB$). He found that if the selective values rise disproportionately in comparison with additive genotypic values, so that the slopes are increasing and $\bar{s}_I$ is positive, the departure from random combination, D, is positive, and vice versa. With positive D, close linkage increases the rate of change of gene frequencies, whereas with negative D, close linkage decreases it. He showed that truncation selection of a constant percentage of a population operating on additive phenotypic effects generates negative departures from random combination, and thus less response under close than under loose linkage.

There have been many studies of the course of evolution of specified interaction systems by means of electronic computers. Fraser (1958, 1960) studied diverse multifactorial systems including those in which selection against both extremes operated among loci with various kinds of interactions. These experiments illustrated the possibility of simulating the results of certain selection experiments. Fraser and Burnell (1967) have made computer studies of models in which selective values decline according to various powers of the deviation from the optimum in connection with inversion polymorphisms.

Martin and Cockerham (1960) simulated unidirectional selection in multifactorial systems. Close linkage was found to reduce the rate of response, a result which has been interpreted by Felsenstein (1965) by extension of his two-factor analysis.

Lewontin (1963, 1964a,b), has made computer studies of systems involving nonadditivity in both selection and heterosis, and also of ones involving selection toward an intermediate optimum. The former included asymmetrical two-locus heterotic models, supplementing the symmetrical ones of Lewontin and Kojima (1960) referred to above, and five-locus heterotic models. The latter included two- and five-locus optimum models. In the asymmetric two-factor heterotic models there were departures from random combination at equilibrium even with $c = 0.50$, but they were slight unless linkage was rather close. There were pairs of solutions which were asymmetrical in contrast with those in the symmetrical model. In the five-locus heterotic models (symmetrical) there were again departures from random combination only with rather close linkage, but given this, a fairly extensive region of the linkage system could be maintained in a large proportion of the gametes. He studied a five-locus case with near dominance on the primary scale ($aa = 0$, $Aa = 0.9$, $AA = 1.0$), optimum 4.5 not far below the upper limit $S = 5$ and selective disadvantage proportional to the square of the deviation from this ($w = 1 - 0.048(S - 4.5)^2$ where S is the primary grade). He showed that there is stable equilibrium in contrast with the usual metastable equilibrium under selection toward an intermediate optimum. He found very little effect of linkage for recombination greater than 0.05 and not much for $c = 0.01$. This cannot be compared directly with the symmetrical cases discussed earlier, but there is general agreement that linkage must be very close even with strong selection, giving near lethality at one extreme, to cause deviation from random combination.

Jain and Allard (1965) made computer studies of a number of two-locus models of selection toward an intermediate optimum. One of these showed that one of two models that I had used to illustrate a combination of such selection with heterosis which yielded two heterallelic selective peaks, under the assumption of random combination, was left with only one such peak on making allowance for the departure from random combination. We will return to this case later. They arrived at different conclusions from Kojima's (1959b) on the conditions for stable equilibrium under uncomplicated optimizing selection, but in this were shown to be incorrect by Singh and Lewontin (1966). This case also will be considered later.

In another paper Jain and Allard (1966) presented extensive computer studies of a great variety of two-locus cases, including heterotic models, models with intermediate optimum, mixtures of these, and models with mixed under- and overdominance. The effects of inbreeding on the results were considered for the first time.

Finally, we will refer to a detailed and very instructive study by Kojima (1965) of the dynamics of certain two-factor systems with varied patterns of interaction and various amounts of recombination. A measure of rate of evolutionary change followed wavelike patterns of decreases and increases which took on widely different characters with change in the amount of recombination. There was usually rapid early increase in selective value (if this was low at first) followed by slow approach to the limiting value, but in some cases there were actual declines over many generations, contrary to the invariable rise under random combination. "The totality of the findings is quite complex and gives a hopeless impression that no simple principles may be in sight for adequate evolutionary prediction of multiple locus systems."

Quasi-equilibrium

Kimura (1965b) has shown that the ratio $R = f_{AB}f_{ab}/f_{Ab}f_{aB}$ approaches constancy, "quasi-equilibrium," during the evolution of systems under widely occurring conditions. It is convenient to use symbols that make R greater than one as far as practicable. From equation (4.54):

$$\Delta \log R \approx \frac{\Delta f_{AB}}{f_{AB}} - \frac{\Delta f_{Ab}}{f_{Ab}} - \frac{\Delta f_{aB}}{f_{aB}} + \frac{\Delta f_{ab}}{f_{ab}},$$

$$\bar{w} \, \Delta \log R \approx [w_{AB} - w_{Ab} - w_{aB} + w_{ab}]$$

(4.58)
$$- cDw_{AaBb}\left(\frac{1}{f_{AB}} + \frac{1}{f_{Ab}} + \frac{1}{f_{aB}} + \frac{1}{f_{ab}}\right),$$

$$\bar{w} \, \Delta \log R \approx \bar{s}_I - cw_{AaBb}f_{Ab}f_{aB}(R - 1)\left(\frac{1}{f_{AB}} + \frac{1}{f_{Ab}} + \frac{1}{f_{aB}} + \frac{1}{f_{ab}}\right).$$

Kimura showed that with small selective differences and loose, if any, linkage, R changes so little in a single generation that $\bar{w} \, \Delta \log R$ may be treated as zero to obtain a useful approximate result. He gave a number of examples, calculated through hundreds of generations by electronic computer, in which R approached constancy. He also illustrated the failure of the principle where moderately great interactive selection is associated with very tight linkage and R increased without limit as fixation of one of the genotypes was approached.

It is convenient to let $x = R - 1$, and as before use $K = \bar{s}_I/cw_{AaBb}$ as the index that expresses the relation between interactive selection and recombination where the term $\bar{w} \, \Delta \log R$ is negligible.

(4.59) $x^2(f_{Ab} + f_{aB}) + x(1 - K) - K = 0.$

If $\bar{w} \, \Delta \log R$ is not negligible in comparison with $\bar{s}_I$ it is possible to make provisional estimates and redefine K as $(\bar{s}_I - \bar{w} \, \Delta \log R)/c W_{AaBb}$ in the iteration process of solution.

$$(4.60) \quad x = \{\sqrt{[(1 - K)^2 + 4K(f_{Ab} + f_{aB})]} - (1 - K)\}/[2(f_{Ab} + f_{aB})].$$

If K is always small, x is approximately $K/(1 - K)$, R is never much larger than one and is sufficiently uniform that $\bar{w} \, \Delta \log R$ is unimportant, and there is consequently quasi-equilibrium in Kimura's sense. But even if K approaches one, and R becomes indefinitely large as AB or ab approaches fixation, there may be quasi-equilibrium in a broader sense.

The Surface of Mean Selective Values

As noted earlier, the system of gametic frequencies for pairs of alleles can be represented by points in an equilateral tetrahedron of unit height, to each of which a mean selective value can be assigned. Assuming that gametic frequencies change only slowly and K is not too large, there is a surface within this space, bounded by the edges ab–Ab, Ab–AB, AB–aB, and aB–ab on which $\bar{w} \, \Delta \log R$ is less than for points on each side. Populations reaching this surface move along it in quasi-equilibrium, in a broad sense, even though R may change greatly with the changes in the set of gene frequencies (Wright 1967).

If there is symmetry of the selective values about the line of equal frequencies of genes B and A ($q = p$), the gametic frequencies and the mean selective values along this line can readily be calculated. We will consider cases in which the selective peak or peaks are on this line. These values, in conjunction with those of homallelic $AAbb$ and $aaBB$, indicate fairly well the nature of the surface.

If $q = p$ then $f_{aB} = f_{Ab}, f_{AB} = p - f_{Ab}$, and $f_{ab} = 1 - p - f_{Ab}$.

$$(4.61) \qquad R = 1 + x = (p - f_{Ab})(1 - p - f_{Ab})/f_{Ab}^2,$$

$$(4.62) \qquad x f_{Ab}^2 + f_{Ab} - p(1 - p) = 0,$$

$$(4.63) \qquad f_{Ab} = \{\sqrt{[1 + 4p(1 - p)x]} - 1\}/2x,$$

$$(4.64) \qquad R - 1 = x = \{\sqrt{[(1 - K)^2 + 8K f_{Ab}]} - (1 - K)\}/4f_{Ab}$$

$$\text{(from (4.60)).}$$

The gametic frequencies, the values of K (if not constant), of R and of $\bar{w}$ can be found by iteration of equations (4.63), (4.52) if necessary, and (4.64) for each desired value of $q = p$ for systems with given selective values, w, and given amounts of recombination, for comparison with those given under the assumption of random combination ($R = 1$).

The following systems of constant genotypic values (*aabb* at lower left, *AABB* at upper right) will be considered.

I ($\bar{s}_I = 0.20$)

0.6	0.9	1
0.9	1	0.9
1	0.9	0.6

II ($\bar{s}_I = 0.20$)

0.6	1.1	1
1.1	1.4	1.1
1	1.1	0.6

III ($\bar{s}_I = 0.15$)

0.75	1	1.10
0.95	1.05	1
1	0.95	0.75

IV

1	1	1
1	1.25	1
1	1	1

V

0.81	1	0.97
1	1.03	1
0.97	1	0.81

VI

0.64	1	0.96
1	1.05	1
0.94	1	0.64

VII ($\bar{s}_I = 0.25$)

1	1.50	2
1	1.25	1.50
1	1	1

Case I, symmetrical about both diagonals, is of the sort in which there is an optimum at the midpoint of the phenotypic scale, discussed earlier (4.30), but here with exchange of B and b. Case II is the same except for a bonus (0.2) for heterosis at each locus. Case III is somewhat like Case I except that the selective peaks are unequal. In each of these three cases, the interactive selection is uniform. Case IV is a simple example of nonadditive heterosis. The interactive selection is variable (± 0.25 in the four corners), so that $\bar{s}_I$ must be calculated for each p in the iteration process. It is a special case of the type discussed by Lewontin and Kojima (1960). Cases V and VI were cases presented previously (Wright 1960a) to illustrate the possibility of two selective peaks that may be heterallelic at both loci. In both, s_I varies. In VII, as in the cases considered by Felsenstein (1965), mean selective value rises toward one extreme, but does so nonlinearly. Interactive selection is uniform.

Calculations for $c = 0.5$ and 0.2 were made, first treating $\bar{w} \, \Delta \log R$ as negligible. Having estimated R for each value of p, at intervals of 0.1, this

TABLE 4.11. Ratio of the term $\bar{w} \, \Delta \log R$ to $\bar{s}_I$

	$c = 0.5$			$c = 0.2$		
Case	$\sum\|\bar{w} \, \Delta \log R\|$	$\sum\|\bar{s}_I\|$	Ratio	$\sum\|\bar{w} \, \Delta \log R\|$	$\sum\|\bar{s}_I\|$	Ratio
I	0.012	1.80	0.007	0.058	1.80	0.032
II	.006	1.80	.004	.054	1.80	.030
III	.004	1.35	.003	.027	1.35	.020
IV	.043	0.62	.068	.129	0.66	.193
V	.002	0.51	.031	.004	0.49	.009
VI	.005	0.97	.005	0.014	0.91	0.015
VII	0.060	2.25	0.027	—	—	—

term was estimated in each case from the formula $\bar{w}\,\Delta p[(d \log R)/dp]$ in which

(4.65) $\bar{w}\,\Delta p = [f_{AB}w_{AB} + f_{Ab}w_{Ab} - p\bar{w}].$

The sums of the nine absolute estimates of $\bar{w}\,\Delta \log R$ and of $\bar{s}_I$ and the ratios are given in Table 4.11. The largest ratios are in Case IV but involve only trivial deviation of $\bar{w}$ from its value under random combination. Of more interest is Case I with relatively large deviations of $\bar{w}$. Recalculations were made in these cases using $K = (\bar{s}_I - \bar{w}\,\Delta \log R)/cW_{AaBb}$. The changes were trivial except for R in a few cases.

Tables 4.12 and 4.13 give the quantities indicated in the headings, using the recalculations where made.

Figure 4.7 shows the values of $\bar{w}$ for $c = 0.5$, 0.2, and 0 in Cases I to VI in solid lines, for comparison with those under the assumption of random combination (broken lines). The latter are all outside the range of true values ($c = 0.5$ to $c = 0$) except at the extreme values of p, and at $p = 0.5$ in Case IV.

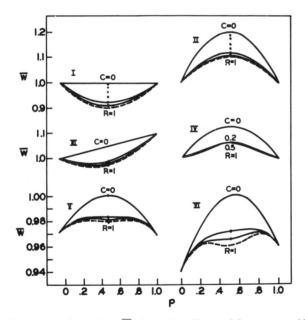

FIG. 4.7. Mean selective value $\overline{W}$ along the diagonal between $aabb$ and $AABB$ on the surface of $\overline{W}$'s, in six two-factor interaction systems described in the text. Cases of random combination ($R = 1$), of recombination rates, $c = 0.50$, $c = 0.20$, and $c = 0$.

TABLE 4.12. Data on the quasi-equilibrium surfaces of mean selective value, $\bar{w}$, in six cases of interacting loci, $R = 1$, $c = 0.5$, 0.2, or 0.

CASE	p	f_{Ab}	$R = 1$			$c = 0.5$				$c = 0.2$				$c = 0$
			$q = p$, $\bar{w}$	Δp	$q = 1 - p$, $\bar{w}$	f_{Ab}	$\bar{w}$	R	K	f_{Ab}	$\bar{w}$	R	K	$f_{Ab} = 0$, $\bar{w}$
I	0	0	1.000	0	0.600	0	1.000	1.67	0.400	0	1.000	∞	1.000	1.000
	0.1	0.09	0.964	−0.0075	0.708	0.086	0.966	1.57	.400	0.077	0.969	3.24	1.000	1.000
	0.2	.16	0.936	−.0103	0.792	.148	0.941	1.53	.400	.129	0.948	2.84	1.000	1.000
	0.3	.21	0.916	−.0092	0.852	.192	0.923	1.50	.400	.164	0.935	2.70	1.000	1.000
	0.4	.24	0.904	−.0053	0.888	.217	0.913	1.49	.400	.184	0.926	2.64	1.000	1.000
	0.5	.25	0.900	0	0.900	.225	0.910	1.49	.400	.191	0.924	2.62	1.000	1.000
II	0	0	1.000	0	0.600	0	1.000	1.40	.286	0	1.000	2.50	0.714	1.000
	0.1	.09	1.036	+.0069	0.780	.087	1.037	1.37	.286	.081	1.040	2.40	0.714	1.072
	0.2	.16	1.064	+.0090	0.920	.152	1.067	1.35	.286	.138	1.073	2.17	0.714	1.128
	0.3	.21	1.084	+.0077	1.020	.197	1.089	1.34	.286	.177	1.097	2.07	0.714	1.168
	0.4	.24	1.096	+.0044	1.080	.223	1.103	1.33	.286	.199	1.112	2.03	0.714	1.192
	0.5	.25	1.100	0	1.100	.232	1.107	1.33	.286	.207	1.117	2.01	0.714	1.200
III	0	0	1.000	0	0.750	0	1.000	1.40	.286	0	1.000	2.50	0.714	1.000
	0.1	.09	0.983	−.0032	0.831	.087	0.984	1.37	.286	.081	0.986	2.40	0.714	1.010
	0.2	.16	0.972	−.0033	0.894	.152	0.974	1.35	.286	.138	0.979	2.17	0.714	1.020
	0.3	.21	0.967	−.0011	0.939	.197	0.971	1.34	.286	.177	0.977	2.07	0.714	1.030
	0.4	.24	0.968	+.0025	0.966	.223	0.973	1.33	.286	.199	0.980	2.03	0.714	1.040
	0.5	.25	0.975	+.0063	0.975	.232	0.980	1.33	.286	.207	0.988	2.01	0.714	1.050
	0.6	.24	0.988	+.0097	0.966	.223	0.993	1.33	.286	.199	1.000	2.03	0.714	1.060
	0.7	.21	1.007	+.0115	0.939	.197	1.011	1.34	.286	.177	1.017	2.07	0.714	1.070
	0.8	.16	1.032	+.0109	0.894	.152	1.034	1.35	.286	.138	1.039	2.17	0.714	1.080
	0.9	.09	1.063	+.0072	0.831	.087	1.064	1.37	.286	.081	1.066	2.40	0.714	1.090
	1.0	0	1.100	0	0.750	0	1.100	1.40	.286	0	1.100	2.50	0.714	1.100

CASE	R = 1					c = 0.5				c = 0.2				c = 0 ($f_{Ab}=0$)
	p	f_{Ab}	$q=\dfrac{p}{\bar w}$	Δp	$q=\dfrac{1-p}{\bar w}$	f_{Ab}	$\bar w$	R	K	f_{Ab}	$\bar w$	R	K	$\bar w$
IV	0	0	1.000	0	1.000	0	1.000	1.67	.400	0	1.000	∞	1.000	1.000
	0.1	.09	1.008	+.0032	1.008	.087	1.009	1.34	.268	.081	1.011	2.43	0.723	1.045
	0.2	.16	1.026	+.0075	1.026	.156	1.026	1.18	.164	.145	1.029	1.73	0.513	1.080
	0.3	.21	1.044	+.0084	1.044	.206	1.044	1.08	.080	.196	1.045	1.35	0.295	1.105
	0.4	.24	1.058	+.0054	1.058	.239	1.058	1.02	.022	.235	1.058	1.09	0.088	1.120
	0.5	.25	1.063	0	1.063	.250	1.063	1.00	0	.250	1.063	1.00	0	1.125
V	0	0	0.970	0	0.810	0	0.970	1.00	0	0	0.970	1.00	0	0.970
	0.1	.09	0.978	+.0011	0.876	.090	0.978	1.06	.056	.089	0.978	1.16	0.138	0.981
	0.2	.16	0.981	+.0004	0.923	.157	0.981	1.11	.098	.153	0.982	1.28	0.238	0.989
	0.3	.21	0.981	−.0003	0.955	.204	0.982	1.14	.127	.196	0.983	1.36	0.305	0.995
	0.4	.24	0.980	−.0004	0.974	.232	0.982	1.16	.144	.220	0.983	1.41	0.342	0.999
	0.5	.25	0.980	0	0.980	.241	0.981	1.16	.149	.228	0.983	1.42	0.354	1.000
VI	0	0	0.940	0	0.640	0	0.940	0.98	−.019	0	0.940	0.95	−0.048	0.940
	0.1	.09	0.956	+.0024	0.765	.089	0.956	1.10	.090	.088	0.957	1.27	0.222	0.960
	0.2	.16	0.962	+.0009	0.855	.155	0.963	1.19	.172	.148	0.964	1.54	0.409	0.976
	0.3	.21	0.962	−.0005	0.915	.200	0.965	1.26	.228	.185	0.968	1.72	0.528	0.988
	0.4	.24	0.961	−.0005	0.950	.225	0.966	1.30	.262	.206	0.971	1.81	0.598	0.996
	0.5	.25	0.961	0	0.961	.233	0.966	1.32	.275	.212	0.972	1.85	0.625	1.000
	0.6	.24	0.963	+.0019	0.950	.224	0.968	1.31	.269	.205	0.973	1.84	0.614	1.000
	0.7	.21	0.967	+.0021	0.915	.199	0.970	1.28	.243	.184	0.974	1.78	0.562	0.996
	0.8	.16	0.970	+.0008	0.853	.155	0.971	1.22	.194	.146	0.973	1.64	0.461	0.988
	0.9	0.09	0.970	−0.0010	0.765	0.089	0.970	1.13	.120	0.087	0.970	1.38	0.295	0.976
	1.0	0	0.960	0	0.640	0	0.960	1.02	0.019	0	0.960	1.05	0.048	0.960

TABLE 4.13. Data on the quasi-equilibrium surface of mean selective value, $\bar{w}$, in Case VII for $R = 1$, $c = 0.5$, and $c = 0$.

		R = 1				c = 0.5			c = 0
		$q = p$		$q = 1 - p$					$f_{Ab} = 0$
p	f_{Ab}	$\bar{w}$	Δp	$\bar{w}$	f_{Ab}	$\bar{w}$	R	K	$\bar{w}$
0	0	1.000	0	1.000	0	1.000	1.67	0.400	1.000
0.1	0.09	1.010	+0.0045	1.090	0.086	1.012	1.57	.400	1.055
0.2	.16	1.040	+.0160	1.160	.148	1.046	1.53	.400	1.120
0.3	.21	1.090	+.0318	1.210	.192	1.099	1.50	.400	1.195
0.4	.24	1.160	+.0493	1.240	.217	1.172	1.49	.400	1.280
0.5	.25	1.250	+.0666	1.250	.225	1.262	1.49	.400	1.375
0.6	.24	1.360	+.0828	1.240	.217	1.372	1.49	.400	1.480
0.7	.21	1.490	+.0967	1.210	.197	1.499	1.50	.400	1.595
0.8	.16	1.640	+.1085	1.160	.148	1.646	1.53	.400	1.720
0.9	0.09	1.810	+0.1178	1.090	0.086	1.812	1.57	.400	1.855
1.0	0	2.000	0	1.000	0	2.000	1.67	0.400	2.000

In Cases I to III, the curves represent $\bar{w}$ along a ridge on the quasi-equilibrium surface ($aabb$ to $AABB$) between deep depressions at $AAbb$ and $aaBB$. The curves for $c = 0.5$ differ little from the approximation shown by the broken line. That for the curve on the surface at right angles to this, passing through the same value at $(0.5, 0.5)$, can differ little from the approximation. Even with $c = 0.2$ there is rough approximation. The values for $\bar{w}$ at $q = p = 0.5$, $c = 0.10$, 0.05, 0.02, and 0.01 are shown by dots in Cases I and II (formula (4.31).

In Case IV, the true curves, even for $c = 0.2$, differ very little from the approximation, there being no difference at $(0.5, 0.5)$.

Case V has the smallest selective differences and the least interactive selection on the average. The shallow saddle between heterallelic peaks is, however, close to the threshold, and disappears, by coalescence of the peaks, if $c = 0.2$ (but not if $c = 0.5$). Case VI, with unequal peaks, is even more sensitive, in spite of greater selective differences. There is loss of the saddle even if $c = 0.50$, as brought out in the computer study by Jain and Allard (1965), referred to earlier. The saddle would persist, however, if selective differences from W_{AaBb} were less than one third as great.

In Case VII, the deviation of $\bar{w}$, $c = 0.5$, from that under random combination would be barely perceptible in a figure of the scale of the others in spite of the large uniform value of K (0.40).

In all of these cases, the calculation of $\bar{w}$ under the assumption of random combination ($R = 1$) gives a good first-order approximation to the nature of the quasi-equilibrium surface for $c = 0.5$, except where a feature is close to the threshold. From the results for $c = 0.2$, it appears that rough approximations can be obtained up to values of K of at least 0.5, and that allowance for deviations from random combination is hardly necessary for this purpose where K is 0.05 or less.

The concept of a multidimensional "surface" of mean selective values on which a population moves toward the immediately controlling peak (except as diverted by the other systematic pressures, recurrent mutation, and immigration, and by random processes) was developed (Wright 1932) for natural populations, assumed to have been breeding according to the same system long enough that there is divergence from random combination only as forced by interactive selection.

A cross between two inbred lines is likely to have a selective value higher than the nearest peak on the equilibrium surface. The randomly bred descendants will thus move *down* toward the latter. Because of this sort of situation, Moran (1964) has drawn the conclusion indicated by the title of his paper, "The Nonexistence of Adaptive Topographies." This, however, was based on a misunderstanding of the concept.

The concept of a surface of mean selective values is of most value where the selective differences are small and there is fairly free recombination. For example, a population which starts with equal frequencies of the four kinds of gametes in Case III and thus with $\bar{w}$ at the midpoint of the curve for $R = 1$ ($\bar{w} = 0.9750$) would rise at once by 0.0035 with an increase of gene frequency of 0.0063. Recombination, if $c = 0.5$, would pull $\bar{w}$ halfway back, to rise further by selection in the next generation and so on. Very soon the course would be practically along the curve for $c = 0.5$. Even if $c = 0.2$, it would not require many generations. If the initial population is $(0.5AB + 0.5ab)$ with $\bar{w} = 1.05$ (midpoint of the curve for $c = 0$), recombination at the rate $c = 0.5$ would pull it down to the midpoint of curve $R = 1$, whence it would rise toward the curve $c = 0.5$, as in the other case. With $c = 0.2$, it would descend toward the same curve fairly rapidly. If, on the other hand, $c = 0.01$, the approach toward the appropriate curve from the midpoint of either that for $c = 0.5$ or $c = 0$ would be so slow that fixation of AB would approach completion by courses so different throughout from the curve for $c = 0.01$ that the concept of a quasi-equilibrium surface would be of little significance.

Centripetal Selection under Random Combination

General Formulas

It has been frequently emphasized (Fisher 1930a; Wright 1931, 1935; Haldane 1932b) that the most important kind of interaction system in connection with evolutionary processes in nature is probably that implied by selection directed toward an intermediate optimum close to the mean. Special cases of this sort of selection have been used in preceding sections. The conclusion that the deviations from random combination are negligible if the relation, $K = \bar{s}_I/cw_{AaBb}$, between interactive selection and recombination in the two-factor case, is less than about 0.05, and usually unimportant at considerably larger values, taken in conjunction with the smallness of the selective differences between alleles in an array of multifactorial genotypes with an intermediate optimum, warrants the ignoring of nonrandom combination in exploring more difficult questions about this important system than are practicable by exact analysis. It will continue to be assumed for simplicity that selective value falls off as the square of the deviation from the optimum, V_o.

$$(4.66) \quad \begin{aligned} \bar{w} &= 1 - s(V - V_o)^2 = 1 - s[(V - \bar{V}) + (\bar{V} - V_o)]^2, \\ \bar{w} &= 1 - s[\sigma_V^2 + (\bar{V} - V_o)^2]. \end{aligned}$$

The frequencies and contributions of a typical locus to the additive scale are assumed to be as follows, using subscripts here to designate loci instead of alleles.

(4.67)

	Frequency	Contribution
A_iA_i	q_i^2	$(1 + x)\alpha_i$
A_ia_i	$2q_i(1 - q_i)$	α_i
a_ia_i	$(1 - q_i)^2$	0

$$(4.68) \quad \bar{V}_i = [2q_i - q_i^2(1 - x_i)]\alpha_i,$$

$$(4.69) \quad \sigma_{V_i}^2 = [q_i^2(1 + x)^2 + 2q_i(1 - q_i) - 4q_i^2 + 4q_i^3(1 - x_i) \\ - q_i^4(1 - x_i)^2]\alpha_i^2.$$

The mean and variance on the additive scale are the sums of these expressions over all loci.

$$(4.70) \quad \bar{w} = 1 - s\left[\sum_i \{[q_i^2(1 + x_i)^2 + 2q_i(1 - q_i) - 4q_i^2 + 4q_i^3(1 - x_i) \\ - q_i^4(1 - x_i)^2]\alpha_i^2\} + (\bar{V} - V_o)^2\right].$$

The subscript will be omitted in referring to a particular locus.

$$(4.71) \quad \frac{\partial \bar{w}}{\partial q} = -2s\{[q(1 + x)^2 + 1 - 6q + 6q^2(1 - x) \\ - 2q^3(1 - x)^2]\alpha^2 + 2(\bar{V} - V_o)[1 - q(1 - x)]\alpha\},$$

$$(4.72) \quad \Delta q = q(1 - q)\frac{\partial \bar{w}}{\partial q}\Big/ 2\bar{w}.$$

These formulas are too complicated to permit ready generalization. The case of exactly intermediate heterozygotes ($x_i = 1$) (on scale V) will be considered first.

(4.73) $\qquad \bar{V} = 2 \sum q_i \alpha_i,$

(4.74) $\qquad \sigma_V^2 = 2 \sum_i q_i(1 - q_i)\alpha_i^2,$

(4.75) $\qquad \bar{w} = 1 - s\left[\sum_i [2q_i(1 - q_i)\alpha_i^2] + \left[2 \sum q_i \alpha_i - V_0\right]^2\right],$

(4.76) $\qquad \dfrac{\partial \bar{w}}{\partial q} = -2s\left\{(1 - 2q)\alpha^2 + 2\alpha\left(2 \sum q_i \alpha_i - V_0\right)\right\},$

(4.77) $\qquad \Delta q = -sq(1 - q)\left[(1 - 2q)\alpha^2 + 2\alpha\left(\sum q_i \alpha_i - V_0\right)\right]/\bar{w}.$

Differences in Genetic Contributions

This applies to systems with any number of heterallelic loci. It will be convenient to consider the effects of differences in the contribution to scale V of two loci. Let α and $k\alpha$ be the contributions of A_1 and A_2, express the optimum $r(1 + k)\alpha$ as a multiple of the midrange $(1 + k)\alpha$ and let p and q be the gene frequencies q_1 and q_2, to avoid subscripts.

(4.78) $\qquad \bar{V} = 2(p + kq)\alpha,$

(4.79) $\qquad \sigma_V^2 = 2[p(1 - p) + k^2 q(1 - q)]\alpha^2,$

(4.80) $\qquad \bar{w} = 1 - s\{2p(1 - p) + 2k^2 q(1 - q) + [(2p + 2kq) - r(1 + k)]^2\}\alpha^2,$

(4.81) $\qquad \dfrac{\partial \bar{w}}{\partial p} = -s[4p + 8kq + 2 - 4r(1 + k)]\alpha^2,$

(4.82) $\qquad \dfrac{\partial \bar{w}}{\partial q} = -s[8kp + 4k^2 q + 2k^2 - 4kr(1 + k)]\alpha^2,$

(4.83) $\qquad \dfrac{\partial^2 \bar{w}}{\partial p^2} = -4s\alpha^2, \qquad \dfrac{\partial^2 \bar{w}}{\partial q^2} = -4sk^2\alpha^2, \qquad \dfrac{\partial^2 \bar{w}}{\partial p\,\partial q} = -8sk\alpha^2,$

(4.84) $\qquad \left(\dfrac{\partial^2 \bar{w}}{\partial p^2}\right)\left(\dfrac{\partial^2 \bar{w}}{\partial q^2}\right) - \left(\dfrac{\partial^2 \bar{w}}{\partial p\,\partial q}\right)^2 = -48s^2 k^2 \alpha^4.$

Since this criterion is always negative there can be no maximum or minimum with both loci heterallelic. If there is equilibrium in any case, it must be at a saddle point. Let

$$\frac{\partial \bar{w}}{\partial p} = 0, \qquad \frac{\partial \bar{w}}{\partial q} = 0:$$

(4.85) $\hat{p} = [1 - 2k + 2y]/6, \qquad \hat{q} = [k - 2 + 2y]/6k,$

where $y = r(1 + k)$.

If the optimum is at the middle ($r = 1$) there is a saddle point at $(0.5, 0.5)$ irrespective of the relative contributions of the two loci. If these contributions are equal ($k = 1$), there is a saddle point for positions of the optimum between $V_0 = 0.5\alpha$ to $V_0 = 3.5\alpha$; the total range being $V = 0$ to $V = 4\alpha$. The values of p and q with equal contributions shift from almost zero to almost one within the above range of values of the optimum. If the contributions are unequal ($k < 1$) the range of positions of the optimum that permit a saddle point is more restricted. There is approach to restriction to the position $V_0 = \alpha$ as k becomes indefinitely small. These relations are indicated in Table 4.14.

TABLE 4.14. Frequencies $\hat{p}$ and $\hat{q}$ at the saddle point in the case of two genes which make contributions α and $k\alpha$ respectively on the underlying scale, 0 to $2(1 + k)\alpha$, while selective value falls off according to the square of the deviation from the optimum at $r(1 + k)\alpha$.

	$k = 0$		$k = 0.20$		$k = 0.50$		$k = 1.00$	
r	$\hat{p}$	$\hat{q}$	$\hat{p}$	$\hat{q}$	$\hat{p}$	$\hat{q}$	$\hat{p}$	$\hat{q}$
1.75	—	—	—	—	—	—	1.000	1.000
1.50	—	—	—	—	0.750	1.000	0.833	0.833
1.25	—	—	0.600	1.000	0.625	0.750	0.667	0.667
1.00	0.500	0.500	0.500	0.500	0.500	0.500	0.500	0.500
0.75	—	—	0.400	0	0.375	0.250	0.333	0.333
0.50	—	—	—	—	0.250	0	0.167	0.167
0.25	—	—	—	—	—	—	0	0

Number of Selective Peaks

Since equilibrium with two loci is necessarily unstable in systems of the sort considered here, one at least of the loci may be expected to become fixed sooner or later (apart from mutation or immigration).

If more than two loci are heterallelic, all or all but one ultimately become fixed. With many loci there are, in general, many genotypes at or near the optimum that constitute selective peaks. With an even number (n) of loci with equivalent effects and optimum at the midrange, the number of peaks is $n!/[(n/2)!]^2$: thus 6 with 4 loci, 20 with 6 loci, 70 with 8 loci, etc. With an odd number of loci the possible number of peaks is

$$n! \bigg/ \left[\left(\frac{n-1}{2}\right)!\right]^2 :$$

thus 6 with 3 loci, 30 with 5 loci, 140 with 7 loci, etc. The number of peaks tends to be reduced if there is asymmetry but is likely to be large in any case of quantitative variability due to numerous loci kept heterallelic by recurrent mutation or immigration. These peaks are at the same or nearly the same level of $\bar{w}$ if selection depends solely on distance from the optimum. Pleiotropy, however, while tending to reduce the number of peaks, may cause those that persist to be at very different levels. The evolutionary significance of a system of multiple selective peaks at various levels separated by shallow saddles will be discussed later.

The consequences of multiple alleles on the optimum model will be considered here only with respect to the possible number of selective peaks. It will be assumed that on the underlying scale all gene effects are additive, that alleles have uniformly graded effects, the same at all loci, and that the optimum is at the middle of the range. Under these assumptions the selective peaks all have the same value of $\bar{w}$ with respect to the character under consideration. Peak genotypes may be homozygous at all loci or heterozygous at one but only one locus (Wright 1935).

To illustrate the mode of calculation, consider the case of five alleles at each of three loci. The contributions at loci will be indicated by the subscripts 0, 1, 2, 3, and 4. The optimum total contribution is thus 12. Only one of the permutations among the loci (A, B, C) is represented. There are five homozygous types with various numbers of permutations among the loci, making 19 in all that would be stable in the presence of low rates of immigration. Peaks that are heterallelic at one locus may be found by replacing 3, 3 by 4, 2; 2, 2 by 4, 0 or 3, 1; 1, 1 by 2, 0. There are 54 of these, allowing for permutations.

Homallelic Peaks		Heterallelic Peaks	
Type	Permutations	Type	Permutations
A_4A_4 B_2B_2 C_0C_0	6	A_4A_4 B_4B_0 C_0C_0	6
		A_4A_4 B_3B_1 C_0C_0	6
A_4A_4 B_1B_1 C_1C_1	3	A_4A_4 B_2B_0 C_1C_1	6
A_3A_3 B_3B_3 C_0C_0	3	A_4A_2 B_3B_3 C_0C_0	6
		A_4A_2 B_2B_2 C_1C_1	6
A_3A_3 B_2B_2 C_1C_1	6	A_3A_3 B_4B_0 C_1C_1	6
		A_3A_3 B_3B_1 C_1C_1	6
		A_3A_3 B_2B_2 C_2C_0	6
A_2A_2 B_2B_2 C_2C_2	1	A_4A_0 B_2B_2 C_2C_2	3
		A_3A_1 B_2B_2 C_2C_2	3
	19		54

Table 4.15 shows the number of selective peaks according to the number of loci and number of alleles, both up to five. Those which are in nearly homallelic populations are shown before the dash; those which are strongly heterallelic at one locus, after the dash (Wright 1965a).

TABLE 4.15. Number of selective peaks in a system with various numbers of equivalent loci, and with alleles with effects in arithmetic series, assuming an optimum at the midpoint of the range (Wright 1965a).

No. of Loci	2	3	4	5
1	0–1	1–1	0–2	1–2
2	2–0	3–2	4–4	5–8
3	0–6	7–9	0–42	19–54
4	6–0	19–28	44–96	85–296
5	0–30	51–95	0–840	381–1650

It may be seen that the possible number of selective peaks increases rapidly with the number of loci and of alleles. The actual number for a given number of loci and alleles would no doubt usually be much less, because of irregularities in the effect on the character in question and in pleiotropic effects on other characters that take precedence.

On the other hand, on considering all characters, interlocked by pleiotropic effects, the total number of selective peaks would usually be enormous. Most sufficiently isolated populations would be expected to differ more or less in their controlling peaks. In the system as a whole, pleiotropy would insure that the peaks differ more or less in their selective values, thus giving the basis for interdeme selection.

Reinforcing Dominance

This section will be concerned with all degrees of dominance in effect on the character from exact intermediacy of heterozygotes ($x = 1$ in (4.86)), the only case considered up to this point, to complete dominance of one allele ($x = 0$), and with all degrees of overdominance up to pure overdominance ($x = -1$). It should be noted that overdominance in this respect is a wholly different matter from the heterosis with respect to selective value discussed earlier. Discussion will, however, be restricted to pairs of alleles with equal effects on the underlying scale including degree of dominance, except that both the case in which the dominants act in the same direction, and that in which they act in opposite directions, will be considered. The former has been termed reinforcing dominance and the latter oppositional dominance by

Mather (1949). The interactive selection will be assumed to be so slight that the differential formula for Δq may be used. This was done by Kojima (1959a,b) in a study of reinforcing dominance and, as here, an optimum from which selective value falls off according to the square of the deviation.

In the case of reinforcing dominance the effects of the two loci on the underlying additive character, V, and on selective value, w, will be represented as follows. The grade of $aabb$ is taken as the base, α as the contribution of the heterozygote, and $(1 + x)\alpha$ as the contribution of the positive homozygote. The grade of the optimum is taken as $y\alpha$. For simplicity, however, this analysis will be given in terms of $\alpha = 1$, with optimum y.

$$V$$

	aa	Aa	AA
BB	$1 + x$	$2 + x$	$2 + 2x$
Bb	1	2	$2 + x$
bb	0	1	$1 + x$

(4.86) $\qquad w = 1 - s(V - y)^2$

The gene frequencies of A and B will be represented by p and q, respectively.

(4.87) $\quad \bar{V} = 2(p + q) - (1 - x)(p^2 + q^2),$

(4.88)
$$\bar{w} = 1 - s\{2(p + q) + [(1 + x)^2 - 6](p^2 + q^2) \\ + 4(1 - x)(p^3 + q^3) - (1 - x)^2(p^4 + q^4) + (\bar{V} - y)^2\}.$$

The nature of the surface of selective values, $\bar{w}$, can be indicated by plotting the lines along which $\partial\bar{w}/\partial p = 0$ and $\partial\bar{w}/\partial q = 0$ on a gene frequency diagram, q vs. p.

(4.89) $\quad \dfrac{1}{s}\dfrac{\partial\bar{w}}{\partial p} = 4y - 8q - 2 + 4(1 - x)q^2$
$$+ \{(6 + 2x - 4y)(1 - x) - 4[1 - (1 - x)q]^2\}p.$$

Putting $\partial\bar{w}/\partial p = 0$:

(4.90)
$$p = [2q - (1 - x)q^2 - (y - 0.5)]/\{0.5(1 - x)(3 + x - 2y) \\ - [1 - (1 - x)q]^2\}.$$

Because of symmetry with respect to p and q, $\partial\bar{w}/\partial q$ and q (in terms of p for $\partial\bar{w}/\partial q = 0$) are given by exchanging p and q.

These are the lines along which the population trajectories are respectively vertical and horizontal. They are symmetrical about the axis $q = p$. Many, but not all, of the intersections, defining points of equilibrium, not necessarily stable, are along this axis and thus easily determined.

Equilibria that are not on this axis may be found from the simultaneous equations $(\partial\bar{w}/\partial p) - (\partial\bar{w}/\partial q) = 0$ and $p(\partial\bar{w}/\partial p) - q(\partial\bar{w}/\partial q) = 0$, both of which contain the factor $p - q$. Removal of this leaves two equations in $(\hat{p} + \hat{q})$ and $\hat{p}\hat{q}$ that permit determination of $\hat{p}$ and $\hat{q}$ at the required intersections.

(4.91)
$$2(1 - x)^2(\hat{p}\hat{q}) - 2(1 - x)(\hat{p} + \hat{q})$$
$$+ [5 - 2x - x^2 - 2y(1 - x)] = 0,$$
$$2(1 - x)\ (\hat{p}\hat{q}) + [1 - 2x - x^2 - 2y(1 - x)](\hat{p} + \hat{q})$$
$$+ (2y - 1) = 0.$$

Figure 4.8 shows representative gene frequency diagrams. The columns pertain to given values of x. The values of y in rows are varied in order to increase the number of patterns shown.

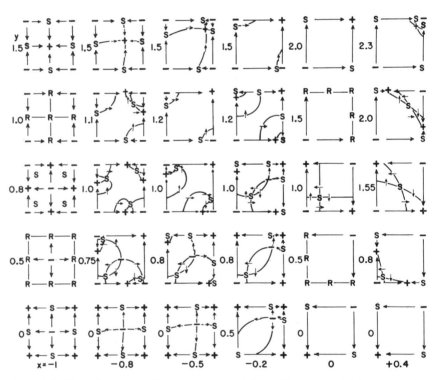

FIG. 4.8. Gene frequency diagrams (q vs. p) for optimum models based on two equivalent genes, each with reinforcing dominance, at various values of x (deviation from complete dominance) and y (deviation of optimum from midrange), showing selective peaks ($+$), saddles (S), pits ($-$), ridges (R-R), and trajectories.

In these diagrams, $+$ refers to positions toward which the population tends to move from all directions, $-$ to positions from which it tends to move in all directions, and S (saddle) to positions toward which it tends to move from some directions while tending to move away in others. R–R refers to a ridge and T–T to a trough. These symbols are applied to margins and corners, assuming small amounts of mutation or immigration, as well as to the interiors. The directions of the trajectories along the margins are obvious. The direction along the line $\partial \bar{w}/\partial p = 0$ in the adjacent interior is the same as along the neighboring margin. The situation is analogous for trajectories along the line $\partial \bar{w}/\partial q = 0$. The four directions around an intersection (at which directions reverse), define the nature of the equilibrium, which can also be found from the conventional criteria in terms of second derivatives.

The value of y that is associated with given x and an equilibrium at which $\hat{p} = \hat{q}$ can be found by putting $q = p$ in (4.89) and putting $\partial \bar{w}/\partial p$ equal to 0 and solving for y.

$$(4.92) \quad y = \{[\hat{p} + 2\hat{p}^3]x^2 + [2\hat{p} + 6\hat{p}^2 - 4\hat{p}^3]x \\ + [1 + 3\hat{p} - 6\hat{p}^2 + 2\hat{p}^3]\}/2[1 - (1 - x)\hat{p}].$$

Conversely, the values of $p = q$ for given x and y may be found from the cubic equation in $\hat{p}$ on putting $q = p$ in either slope equation.

$$(4.93) \quad 2(1 - x)^2\hat{p}^3 - 6(1 - x)\hat{p}^2 + [6 - (1 - x)(3 + x - 2y)]\hat{p} \\ + [1 - 2y] = 0.$$

Figure 4.9 shows the locations with respect to x and y of these equilibrium points. Thirteen regions (A to M) are bounded by heavy lines, excluding a few narrow transitional ones. Lighter solid lines show positions of two-factor maxima, according to values of $\hat{p}$ ($= \hat{q}$) at intervals of 0.10. Broken lines similarly show positions of two-factor saddles, and dotted lines those of two-factor minima. Two-factor minima for $\hat{p} = \hat{q} = 0.49$ and $\hat{p} = \hat{q} = 0.48$ are shown by dotted lines in regions H, G, and E.

There is a triangle including regions J, K, G, and H in which there are two saddles that are not shown because they are not on the axis $\hat{q} = \hat{p}$. There is a narrow region between B and C in which there are two peaks, not on this axis, as well as a saddle that is on it. Thus with $x = 0.4$, $y = 2.140$ in region B, the only interior equilibrium point is a saddle, $\hat{p} = \hat{q} = 0.7967$, but if $y = 2.145$ there are two peaks, $\hat{p} = 0.6064$, $\hat{q} = 0.9412$ and the converse, in region C, as well as a saddle $\hat{p} = \hat{q} = 0.7991$. If $y = 2.150$, in typical region C, the three equilibria merge into a single peak $\hat{p} = \hat{q} = 0.8016$. Region C, characterized by a peak in which both loci are heterallelic, was discovered by

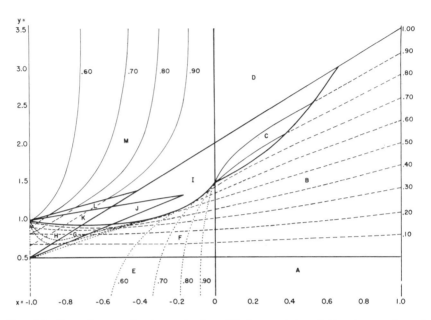

FIG. 4.9. Gene frequencies ($q = p$) of equilibrium points relative to x and y of Figure 4.8. Light solid lines for peaks, broken lines for saddles, and dotted lines for pits. Major types of patterns (A to M) are bounded by heavy lines. In the triangle including regions G, H, J, K, there are paired equilibria not on the diagonal $q = p$.

Kojima (1959b), with whose results the present conclusions fully agree after transformation of the parameters.

The complicated situation where there is overdominance in the same direction in both loci on the primary scale may best be appreciated by comparing Figures 4.8, 4.9, and 4.10. Region I has no interior equilibrium point of any sort.

The numbers and kinds of selective peaks in various regions (combining or subdividing some of those in Figure 4.9) are shown in Figure 4.10. The empirical boundaries $B|C$, $L|M$, $L|K$, and $I|J$ of Figure 4.9 reappear. The other boundaries are those at which a marginal maximum just reaches a corner. These would not be affected by allowance for nonrandom combination, since this has no effect on $\bar{w}$ along a margin. These boundaries are the lines $y = 0.5$, $y = 1 + 0.5x$, $y = 1.5 + x$, and $y = 2 + 1.5x$. The lines themselves go with the region below in the first and third of these, but above in the second and fourth, where $x > 0$. The opposite is true for all boun-

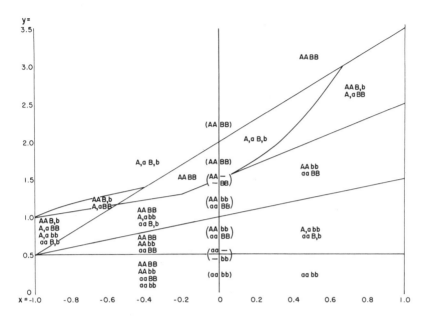

Fig. 4.10. Kinds of selective peaks, including marginal peaks, in the regions of Figure 4.9, combining or subdividing in some cases.

daries where $x < 0$. The nature of the peaks for complete dominance ($x = 0$) is given in parentheses.

Oppositional Dominance

The pattern of underlying grades, V, for pairs of alleles with equal opposite effects will be represented as follows:

$$
\begin{array}{c}
V \\
\begin{array}{cccc}
 & aa & Aa & AA \\
MM & -(1 + x) & -x & 0 \\
Mm & -1 & 0 & x \qquad w = 1 - s(V - y)^2 \\
mm & 0 & 1 & 1 + x
\end{array}
\end{array}
$$

(4.94)

The frequencies of gene A (positive effect) and of gene M (negative effect) will be represented by p and q, respectively.

(4.95) $\overline{V} = 2(p - q) - (1 - x)(p^2 - q^2),$

(4.96)
$$
\begin{aligned}
\bar{w} = 1 - s\{2(p + q) + [(1 + x)^2 - 6](p^2 + q^2) \\
+ 4(1 - x)(p^3 + q^3) - (1 - x)^2(p^4 + q^4) + (\overline{V} - y)^2\}.
\end{aligned}
$$

Note that (4.96) is the same as (4.88) as long as $\overline{V}$ is not expanded.

(4.97) $\dfrac{1}{s}\dfrac{\partial \bar{w}}{\partial p} = [1 - (1 - x)p][4y + 8q - 2 - 4(1 - x)q^2] - 2x(1 + x)p.$

Putting $\partial \bar{w}/\partial p = 0$:

(4.98) $p = [2q - (1 - x)q^2 + (y - 0.5)]/\{(1 - x)y + 0.5(1 + x)^2$
$- [1 - (1 - x)q]^2\},$

(4.99) $\dfrac{1}{s}\dfrac{\partial \bar{w}}{\partial q} = [1 - (1 - x)q][8p - 4y - 2 - 4(1 - x)p^2] - 2x(1 + x)q.$

Putting $\partial \bar{w}/\partial q = 0$:

(4.100) $q = [2p - (1 - x)p^2 - (y + 0.5)]/\{0.5(1 + x)^2 - (1 - x)y$
$- [1 - (1 - x)p]^2\}.$

These are not symmetrical about the axis $q = p$ unless $y = 0$. The value of $\hat{q}$ associated with $\hat{p}$ at given x and y is the same as that for $\hat{p}$ at the same x but at $-y$. Figure 4.11 shows the lines of vertical and horizontal trajectories, the various kinds of equilibria: $+$, S, and $-$, and ridges R–R and

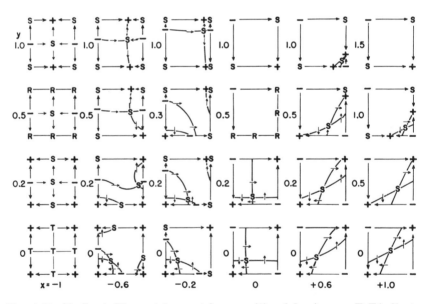

FIG. 4.11. Similar to Figure 4.8 except for oppositional dominance. T-T indicates a trough.

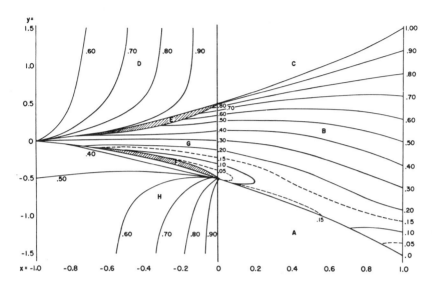

FIG. 4.12. Similar to Figure 4.9 except for oppositional dominance. All of the lines in this figure, including broken lines for gene frequencies 0.05 and 0.15, refer to saddles. The only regions in which there are no saddles are A, C, E, and F.

troughs T–T, in a number of cases in which x varies from −1 to +1 and y ≥ 0. For negative y it is merely necessary to exchange p and q.

The case of semidominance (x = 1) could have been included in Figure 4.8 except that because of the difference in scales it would be necessary to add the number 2 to the values of y in Figure 4.11 and rotate so as to exchange q and (1 − q).

With pure overdominance (x = −1) there is always a central saddle except in the case y = 0 in which two troughs p = 0.5, q = 0.5 intersect in the center.

The lines in Figure 4.12 show the two-factor equilibrium values of p for values of x and y. The corresponding equilibrium values of q are, as noted, those for p with the same x but with −y. All of the lines in this figure refer to two-factor saddles. The only regions in which there are no two-factor saddles are at the extremes if x ≥ 0 (regions A and C), at x = −1, y = 0 as noted above, and two narrow cross-hatched regions E and F.

Figure 4.13 shows the selective peaks in the same way as in Figure 4.10. All are either wholly homallelic or heterallelic at only one locus. The boundaries of regions are all determined here by the values of y at which the

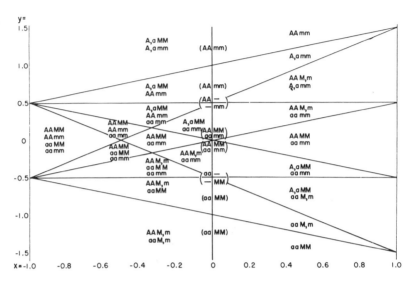

FIG. 4.13. Similar to Figure 4.10 except for oppositional dominance

slopes disappear at the corners and thus are independent of whether there is or is not random combination. They consist of eight lines, four radiating from $x = -1$, $y = 0.5$: $y = -(0.5 + x)$, $y = -0.5x$, $y = 0.5$, and $y = (1 + 0.5x)$, and the four mirror images of these about $x = -1$, $y = -0.5$: $y = (0.5 + x)$, $y = 0.5x$, $y = -0.5$, and $y = -(1 + 0.5x)$. In both groups, the first and third from the bottom belong in the region below if $x > 0$, above if $x > 0$, and the opposite is true of the second and fourth from the bottom in both groups.

With either reinforcing or oppositional dominance, selection toward a sufficiently extreme optimum leads to the same end results as if there were constant selective values at each locus proportional to the V's of the arrays of (4.86) and (4.94), respectively.

The midrange for centripetal reinforcing dominance is the line $y = 1 + x$ if there is partial to complete dominance, but $y = 1$ if there is overdominance (on the underlying scale). There are two or more selective peaks for optima at all points along these lines. These peaks are separated by shallow saddles except for about $x = -0.3$ to -0.5. There are indeed only two regions within the outer boundaries that have only one peak (C and upper I), and both are at considerable distances from the midrange.

For centripetal oppositional dominance, the midrange is at $y = 0$. There are two or more selective peaks, separated by shallow saddles along its whole

SELECTION IN INTERACTION SYSTEMS

length, and this applies for considerable distances on each side except for the absence of two-factor saddles in regions E and F.

The prevailing pattern for selection directed toward an optimum near the middle of the range of variability is thus the occurrence of multiple selective peaks separated by shallow saddles.

An important conclusion from the present chapter is that in dealing with selection in interaction systems, deviations from random combination are negligible, for most purposes, if the amount of interactive selection is of lower order than that of recombination. Where not negligible, such deviations are most important for isolated pairs of loci that are subject to the same sort of selection and, next to this, for the terminal pairs in a chain of four or more closely linked loci. The concept of a surface of selective values on which sets of frequencies of interacting genes tend to move and come to equilibrium under the pressures of selection has been developed, making allowance for deviations from random combination if necessary. Another important concept is the pleiotropic threshold. A low selection pressure based on a particular differential effect of alleles is, in general, ineffective if there is a pleiotropic effect, subject to selection pressure of a higher order. Especial attention has been paid to selection directed toward an intermediate optimum under which there are usually multiple selective peaks. Near which of these a population tends to reach equilibrium depends on its past history.

CHAPTER 5

Frequency Dependent Selective Values

The constancy of relative selective values, assumed in the preceding chapters, should often be a good approximation where selection is based on competition in biological efficiency or in meeting the challenge of the external environment, including relations with other species. Where, on the other hand, selection depends on interactions among members of the same species, relative selective values may be expected to be affected by the genotypic frequencies. The consequences of this situation are the topics which will be considered in this chapter.

General Formulas

As noted in chapter 3, the absolute as well as the relative selective values are of interest. It may be recalled that the absolute selective value, W_i, of one of the genotypes in a system of loci that is under consideration under given conditions of environment and residual loci is measured by the ratio of its absolute number of representatives, N_i, to that in the preceding generation, N_i'. Thus $W_i = N_i/N_i'$ and $\overline{W} - 1$ is the rate of population growth under the specified conditions. Absolute selective value W_i may be a function of genotypic frequencies even where the relative selective value w_i is not, and in general W_i and w_i may be different functions.

To avoid serious mathematical complications, selection coefficients will be assumed to be small. The analysis of concrete cases that involve strong selection pressures requires a detailed consideration of all the aspects peculiar to each that preclude general treatment.

As brought out in chapter 4, the general formula for rate of increase of gene frequency is approximately $\Delta q = 0.5q(1 - q) \sum [(w/\bar{w})(\partial f/\partial q)]$, where selective differences are sufficiently small in relation to recombination rates to permit the assumption of random combination. Since w_i is the ratio of the corresponding relative selective value to that of an arbitrarily chosen standard, $W_i/\overline{W}_i = w_i/\bar{w}_i$, and $W/\overline{W}$ may be substituted for $w/\bar{w}$ in the above formula.

The discussion in the preceding chapters was restricted to cases in which the w's are independent of genotypic frequencies so that the term $\sum [(w/\bar{w})(\partial f/\partial q)]$ could be written $(1/\bar{w})(\partial \bar{w}/\partial q) = (\partial \log \bar{w}/\partial q)$ or practically $(\partial \bar{w}/\partial q)$ if selective differences are small. In either case, the set of formulas for the Δq's has the important property that these show by their form that within their range of approximate validity the set of gene frequencies tends to move up the gradient of the "surface" $\log \bar{w}$ (or practically $\bar{w}$), except as qualified by the positive factor, $0.5q(1 - q)$, and thus tends to approach a "peak" in this surface which is either a maximum at which $\partial \bar{w}/\partial q_i = 0$ for all q's, or is as close to a maximum as permitted by limiting gene frequencies ($q = 0$ or $q = 1$) at one or more loci.

This property is lost if the w's are not constant. It would be useful if the term $\sum [(w/\bar{w})(\partial f/\partial q)]$ could be written as the slope of some more general surface, $F(w/\bar{w})$ or $F(W/\overline{W})$, which thus would determine the course of evolution of the system in the same way that $\log \bar{w}$ determines it in cases in which the w's are constant, i.e., $\Delta q = 0.5q(1 - q)[\partial F(W/\overline{W})/\partial q]$.

The function $F(W/\overline{W})$ always exists in cases in which only one pair of alleles is under consideration in a panmictic population in which $W/\overline{W}$ can be expressed as a function of the single parameter, q, that is involved in the genotypic frequencies. On the other hand, it exists only in certain types of cases if there are more than two alleles or there are interacting loci (Wright 1955).

Important among these is one in which the rate of growth of the population as a whole is affected by the presence of one or more genotypes according to some function, Ψ, of their frequencies, since this function cancels in the ratio $W/\overline{W}$ (Wright 1949b, 1964).

More generally, to meet the requirement that $\int \sum (W_i/\overline{W})(\partial f_i/\partial q_{Ij}) \, dq_{Ij}$ yield the same expression, $F(W/\overline{W})$, with all gene frequencies, q_{Ij}, each W_i must be a function, $\chi(f_i)$, of its frequency f_i so that the formula reduces to $\int \sum \{\chi(f_i)/\sum [f_i\chi(f_i)]\} \, df_i$. The formulas are apt to be rather awkward unless the selection coefficients are so small that they may be ignored in $\overline{W}$ in the denominator in obtaining an approximation. The resort to an approximation is of little significance, however, in the cases considered here, since the differential formula is itself an approximation which is only valid if the non-additive aspects of the selection coefficients are of considerably lower order than the amounts of recombination (Wright 1960a, 1964).

The expression $F(W/\overline{W})$ will be called the fitness function, since its rate of change in time $dF(W/\overline{W})/dt$ agrees with what Fisher (1930) called the rate of increase of fitness in his "fundamental theorem of natural selection."

The term internal selective value (V_I) was defined (Wright 1955) as $\int [\sum W_T(\partial f_T/\partial q_{Ai})] \, dq_{Ai}$ in which T refers to total genotype and A_i to a particular allele at a particular locus. This was contrasted with the selective value in relation to other populations (external selective value, V_E) of which $\overline{W}$ is usually the most important factor. V_I (or $F(W)$ Wright 1964) differs from $F(W/\overline{W})$ in not incorporating $\overline{W}$. Theoretically, however, $F(W/\overline{W})$ (or V, Wright 1960a) is more appropriately called the fitness function and will be used here in spite of restriction to approximate values in most multifactorial cases.

Frequency dependent selection has been discussed with other mathematical models by Haldane (1932b), Li (1955a,b, 1967), Lewontin (1958), Haldane and Jayakar (1963b), and Clarke and O'Donald (1964).

Some One-Factor Examples

In the following, one allele is assumed to be completely dominant. Absolute selective values are used, noting that functional relations are chosen here for mathematical simplicity rather than for maximum appropriateness to actual cases.

	Genotype	f	W	$\dfrac{df}{dq}$
(5.1)	$A-$	$1 - q^2$	$k_1[1 + s_1(1 - q^2)]$	$-2q$
	aa	q^2	$k_2[1 + s_2 q^2]$	$2q$

(5.2) $\overline{W} = k_1(1 + s_1) - [k_1(1 + 2s_1) - k_2]q^2 + (k_1 s_1 + k_2 s_2)q^4$

(5.3) $\dfrac{d\overline{W}}{dq} = 2q[(k_2 - k_1 - 2k_1 s_1) + 2(k_1 s_1 + k_2 s_2)q^2],$

(5.4)
$$\sum \left[(W/\overline{W})\frac{df}{dq} \right] = 2q[(k_2 - k_1 - k_1 s_1) + (k_1 s_1 + k_2 s_2)q^2]/\overline{W}$$
$$= \frac{dF(W/\overline{W})}{dq}.$$

There is some simplification if $k_2 = k_1 = k$.

(5.5) $\overline{W} = k[(1 + s_1) - 2s_1 q^2 + (s_1 + s_2)q^4],$

(5.6) $\dfrac{d\overline{W}}{dq} = 4kq[(s_1 + s_2)q^2 - s_1],$

(5.7) $\dfrac{dF(W/\overline{W})}{dq} = 2kq[(s_1 + s_2)q^2 - s_1]/\overline{W} = \dfrac{d\overline{W}}{dq}\Big/ 2\overline{W},$

(5.8) $\Delta q = kq^2(1 - q)[(s_1 + s_2)q^2 - s_1]/\overline{W}.$

Treating $\overline{W}$ in the denominator as k and using C as an arbitrary constant:

(5.9) $F(W/\overline{W}) \approx C - s_1 q^2 + (1/2)(s_1 + s_2)q^4.$

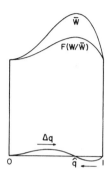

Fig. 5.1. Comparison of $\overline{W}$ and $F(w/\overline{w})$, relative to q, based on the set (5.1) with selective advantage of rarity. Δq is also shown.

In this case, approximate $F(W/\overline{W})$ differs from $\overline{W}$ in its variable part, merely in having a slope $1/(2k)$ times as great (Fig. 5.1).

There is an equilibrium point at $\hat{q} = \sqrt{[s_1/(s_1 + s_2)]}$ if $s_1/(s_1 + s_2)$ falls between 0 and 1. It is stable if both s_1 and s_2 are negative, i.e., if the selective value of each genotype falls off from its maximum value in proportion to its abundance. The growth rate $(\overline{W} - 1)$ is maximum at this same value in the case considered here $(k_2 = k_1)$, but this is not true if k_1 and k_2 differ.

This kind of equilibrium, based on selective advantage of rarity, may occur in a population which lives in a heterogeneous environment in which one genotype is at an advantage in some places and the other elsewhere, and all local selective values are related negatively to population density. It occurs in pure form where there is no net selective advantage of heterozygosis and where mating is at random in spite of the heterogeneity which, if associated with partial isolation, would tend to bring about a balance in each locality between selection and immigration. All of these tendencies may, of course, be operating simultaneously.

The occurrence of local differences in direction of selection within a random breeding population does not in itself tend to give equilibrium. Assume random dispersion of offspring and let c_i be the weighting factor for the ith niche after such dispersion but before selection. Assume absolute selective values $W_{AA(i)}$, $W_{Aa(i)}$, and $W_{aa(i)}$ for the indicated genotypes in this niche. The mean selective value for the population is then $\overline{W} = [\sum (c_i W_{AA(i)})]q^2 + [\sum (c_i W_{Aa(i)})]2q(1 - q) + [\sum (c_i W_{aa(i)})](1 - q)^2$. Since the coefficients are constants for the given set of niches and selective values, this is merely the kind of selection discussed in chapter 3. Whichever allele is at a net selective disadvantage tends toward extinction unless there is a net superiority of the heterozygote over both homozygotes. This differs from the treatment given by Levene (1953) who averaged the Δq's for the niches, based on selective values relative to the heterozygotes and weighting factors based on number of survivors. It is, however, the total population which is breeding at random, and the weighting factors should be independent of the selection process.

If the selective value in each niche is affected by changes in density brought about by differential mortality of genotypes, the situation is different. A favorable effect of low density, especially on the better adapted genotype, would result in a negative relation of the total selective values of the genotypes to overall frequency as in the model. An equilibrium in gene frequency will tend to be established in spite of random mating and absence of mobility of the offspring after random dispersion (as in plants).

The operation of the process is more obvious if the offspring, after random mating, tend to search out favorable niches, but again they must be subject to adverse effects of overcrowding to bring about the negative relation between gene frequency and net selective value on which equilibrium depends (Wright and Dobzhansky 1946; Wright 1949b, 1955). Other examples of this process will be given later and the joint results in the presence of heterozygous superiority will be considered.

Returning to the model, it can also represent cases in which there is selective advantage in excess abundance (in conformity to the majority). For this, both s_1 and s_2 must be positive. There is unstable equilibrium of $\hat{q} = \sqrt{[s_1/(s_1 + s_2)]}$, with runaway fixation of whichever genotype is in excess. If s_1 and s_2 differ in sign, there is, of course, a trend toward fixation of the favored genotype from any initial gene frequency.

The selective advantage or disadvantage of excess abundance in a heterogeneous environment need not change linearly. The following case (Wright 1955) in which the selection coefficient varies inversely with the corresponding genotypic frequency, makes an interesting comparison.

Genotype	f	W	$\dfrac{df}{dq}$

(5.10)

$A-$	$1 - q^2$	$k[1 + s_1/(1 - q^2)]$	$-2q$
aa	q^2	$k[1 + s_2/q^2]$	$+2q$

$$\text{(5.11)} \qquad \overline{W} = k[1 + s_1 + s_2],$$

$$\text{(5.12)} \qquad \frac{d\overline{W}}{dq} = 0,$$

$$\text{(5.13)} \qquad \sum \left[(W/\overline{W}) \frac{df}{dq} \right] = q \left[\frac{2s_2}{q^2} - \frac{2s_1}{1 - q^2} \right] \bigg/ (1 + s_1 + s_2),$$

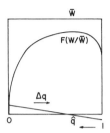

FIG. 5.2. Comparison of $\overline{W}$ and $F(w/\bar{w})$, relative to q, based on the set (5.10) with a different sort of selective advantage of rarity from 5.1. Δq is also shown.

$$(5.14) \quad F(W/\overline{W}) = C + [s_2 \log q^2 + s_1 \log (1 - q^2)]/(1 + s_1 + s_2),$$

$$(5.15) \qquad \Delta q = q^2(1 - q)\left[\frac{s_2}{q^2} - \frac{s_1}{(1 - q^2)}\right]\Big/(1 + s_1 + s_2).$$

In this case $\overline{W}$ and $F(W/\overline{W})$ are very different, since rate of population growth $(\overline{W} - 1)$ is the same at all gene frequencies, while the fitness function $F(W/\overline{W})$ has a maximum at $\hat{q} = \sqrt{[s_2/(s_1 + s_2)]}$ if both s_1 and s_2 are positive (Fig. 5.2), a minimum at this point if both are negative, or a high point at one extreme or the other if s_1 and s_2 differ in sign.

This case would apply roughly (except near the extremes) to a panmictic population in an environment that is fairly homogeneous except for very small portions of the range in which the individuals of one or the other genotype do exceedingly well unless they are overcrowded.

Diverse Fitness Functions

Population Size Unaffected by Selection

It is quite possible for even strong selection to have no appreciable effect on population size. Reproduction may for example be restricted to a limited number of "territories" and thus may be independent of the selection that determines which individuals occupy these territories. Where there is not territoriality, there may be other factors that regulate population size independently of the selection that determines which individuals reproduce (Wright 1949b).

The simplest case is that in which $W_i = kw_i/\bar{w}$ so that $\overline{W} = k$.

	Genotype	f	w	W	$\dfrac{df}{dq}$
(5.16)	$A-$	$1 - q^2$	1	$k[1/(1 + sq^2)]$	$-2q$
	aa	q^2	$1 + s$	$k[(1 + s)/(1 + sq^2)]$	$2q$

(5.17)
$$\bar{w} = 1 + sq^2, \qquad \overline{W} = k,$$

(5.18)
$$\frac{d\bar{w}}{dq} = 2sq, \qquad \frac{d\overline{W}}{dq} = 0,$$

(5.19)
$$\sum (W/\overline{W})\frac{df}{dq} = \frac{2sq}{1 + sq^2},$$

(5.20)
$$F(W/\overline{W}) = C + \log(1 + sq^2) \approx C + sq^2,$$

(5.21)
$$\Delta q = sq^2(1 - q)/(1 + sq^2) \approx sq^2(1 - q).$$

The rate Δq is, of course, the same as that derived directly from the constant *relative* selective values, but the variable "fitness," $F(W/\overline{W})$, is very different from the constant mean selective value, $\overline{W}$ (Fig. 5.3).

General Effects on Population Growth

The preceding example is a special case of the situation in which all W's involve a common function, Ψ, of some or all of the genotypic frequencies.

(5.22)
$$W_i = w_i\Psi, \qquad \overline{W} = \bar{w}\Psi,$$

(5.23)
$$F(W/\overline{W}) = F(w/\bar{w}) = \int \sum (w/\bar{w})\frac{\partial f}{\partial q}\, dq.$$

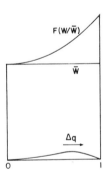

FIG. 5.3. Comparison of $\overline{W}$ and $F(w/\bar{w})$ relative to q, based on the set (5.16) with differences in relative but not absolute selective values. This is selection that does not affect population size. Δq is also shown.

The set of gene frequencies reaches stability at a peak value of $F(w/\bar{w})$ if the latter exists, but the rate of population growth reaches a peak at the peak value $\bar{w}\Psi - 1$, which may be wholly different. It is quite possible for "fitness" as measured by $F(w/\bar{w})$ to be increasing while the population is tending toward extinction.

In the following example A_2 is a mutation from A_1 that at any given time is disadvantageous to individuals that carry it, although these individuals have a general favorable effect on the growth of the population (assuming s and t to be positive [Wright 1949b]).

Genic selective values will be assumed.

Gene	f	W	w	$\dfrac{df}{dq}$
A_1	$1 - q$	$k(1 + tq)$	1	-1
A_2	q	$k(1 + tq)(1 - s)$	$1 - s$	$+1$

(5.24)

$$(5.25) \qquad \bar{w} = 1 - sq,$$

$$(5.26) \qquad \overline{W} = k(1 + tq)(1 - sq),$$

$$(5.27) \qquad \sum (W/\overline{W})\frac{df}{dq} = \sum (w/\bar{w})\frac{df}{dq} = \frac{d \log \bar{w}}{dq} = -s/\bar{w};$$

$$(5.28) \qquad F(W/\overline{W}) = C + \log (1 - sq),$$

$$(5.29) \qquad \Delta q = -sq(1 - q)/(1 - sq).$$

Since Δq is negative, the socially favorable gene A_2 cannot be established in a large panmictic population, except insofar as recurrent mutation or migration maintains it at a low frequency. Yet if t is equal to or greater than $s/(1 - 2s)$, $\overline{W}$ would be maximum if A_2 were fixed. If k is less than 1, the population tends toward extinction as the individually fitter gene A_1 increases in frequency.

Conversely, if s and t are both negative, A_2 is advantageous to the individuals that carry it although these individuals are causing general damage to the population. A_2 tends to be fixed even though the population may be tending toward extinction if the general deleterious effect is large enough (Fig. 5.4).

In both cases, the fitness of the individuals and that of the population are negatively related. Similarily, interaction systems may have general deleterious or beneficial effects on the population. Following is a simple example in which genotypes carrying AB with semidominance of both genes have a general deleterious effect if t is positive, a beneficial effect if t is

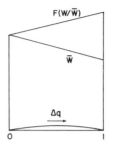

FIG. 5.4. Comparison of $\overline{W}$ and $F(w/\bar{w})$ relative to q, based on the set (5.24). The gene is advantageous to its carriers (rising $F(w/\bar{w})$) but these are injurious to the population (falling $\overline{W}$). Δq is also shown.

negative but AB also has a specific selective advantage or disadvantage indicated by the coefficient s.

	Gamete	f	W	w	$\dfrac{\partial f}{\partial p}$	$\dfrac{\partial f}{\partial q}$
	AB	pq	$k(1-tpq)(1+s)$	$1+s$	q	p
(5.30)	Ab	$p(1-q)$	$k(1-tpq)$	1	$1-q$	$-p$
	aB	$(1-p)q$	$k(1-tpq)$	1	$-q$	$1-p$
	ab	$(1-p)(1-q)$	$k(1-tpq)$	1	$-(1-q)$	$-(1-p)$

(5.31) $\bar{w} = 1 + spq,$

(5.32) $\overline{W} = k(1 - tpq)(1 + spq),$

(5.33) $\displaystyle\sum (W/\overline{W})\,\frac{\partial f}{\partial p} = sq/(1 + spq),$

(5.34)
$$F(W/\overline{W}) = C + \int \frac{sq}{1 + spq}\,dp = C + \int \frac{sp}{1 + spq}\,dq$$
$$= C + \log(1 + spq) \approx C + spq,$$

(5.35)
$$\Delta p = sp(1 - p)q/(1 + spq),$$
$$\Delta q = spq(1 - q)/(1 + spq).$$

If s is positive, AB tends to fixation (Fig. 5.5a), yet if t is also positive and greater than s (Fig. 5.5b), there is maximum population growth if either A or B is lost. If s is negative, either A or B tends to be fixed, depending on the initial set of gene frequencies, yet if t is also negative and absolutely greater than s there is maximum population growth with AB fixed.

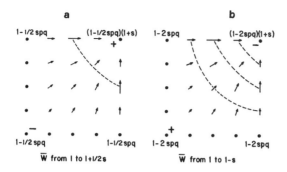

FIG. 5.5. Two-factor gene frequency diagrams based on the set (5.30) showing corner values and contours of $\overline{W}$, and trajectories. Combination AB is advantageous to its carriers but these are injurious to the population. This injury is too slight in 5.5a (left) to prevent rise in $\overline{W}$, but with a fourfold increase in 5.5b (right) the population moves to low $\overline{W}$ (Fig. 5.5b redrawn from Wright 1964, Fig. 16, by permission, University of Wisconsin Press, © 1964 by the Regents of The University of Wisconsin).

Whether there is any way in which a species can be protected from parasitic genotypes that may arise within it or whether there is any way in which a species may evolve characters that are adaptive for it as a whole, although deleterious to the individuals that carry them, are important questions in evolutionary theory.

Pleiotropic Selective Effects

This section is concerned with genes that have two kinds of specific selective effects, ones that are reflected in the growth of the population and ones that are not. We will consider first a case of genic selection with effects in opposite directions.

	Gene	f	W	$\dfrac{df}{dq}$
(5.36)	A_1	$1-q$	$k\left[\dfrac{1}{1+sq}\right]$	-1
	A_2	q	$k\left[\dfrac{1+s}{1+sq}-t\right]$	$+1$

$$(5.37) \qquad \overline{W} = k[1 - tq],$$

$$(5.38) \qquad \frac{d\overline{W}}{dq} = -kt,$$

$$\sum (W/\overline{W}) \frac{df}{dq} = \frac{s}{(1 + sq)(1 - tq)} - \frac{t}{(1 - tq)}$$

(5.39)

$$= \frac{1}{s + t} \left[\frac{s^2}{1 + sq} - \frac{t^2}{1 - tq} \right],$$

(5.40)

$$F(W/\overline{W}) = C + \left(\frac{s}{s + t} \right) \log (1 + sq) + \left(\frac{t}{s + t} \right) \log (1 - tq)$$

$$\approx C + (s - t)q - (1/2)[s^2 - st + t^2]q^2,$$

(5.41)

$$\Delta q = \frac{q (1 - q)}{s + t} \left[\frac{s^2}{1 + sq} - \frac{t^2}{1 - tq} \right]$$

$$\approx q(1 - q)[(s - t) - (s^2 - st + t^2)q].$$

General formulas can easily be given for pairs of alleles where

$$W_i = k \left[\frac{1 + s_i}{1 + \bar{s}} + t_i \right]$$

and $\bar{s}$ and $\bar{t}$ are so small that $1 + \bar{s}$ and $1 + \bar{t}$ may be treated as one in the denominator of $\sum (W/\overline{W})(df/dq)$.

Let

$$W_i = k \left[\frac{1 + s_i}{1 + \bar{s}} + t_i \right].$$

(5.42)

$$\overline{W} = k[1 + \bar{t}],$$

(5.43)

$$\frac{d\overline{W}}{dq} = k \frac{d\bar{t}}{dq},$$

(5.44)

$$\sum (W/\overline{W}) \frac{df}{dq} = \frac{1}{(1 + \bar{s})(1 + \bar{t})} \frac{d\bar{s}}{dq} + \frac{1}{(1 + \bar{t})} \frac{d\bar{t}}{dq} \approx \frac{d\bar{s}}{dq} + \frac{d\bar{t}}{dq},$$

(5.45)

$$F(W/\overline{W}) \approx C + \bar{s} + \bar{t},$$

(5.46)

$$\Delta q \approx q(1 - q) \left[\frac{d\bar{s}}{dq} + \frac{d\bar{t}}{dq} \right].$$

The genic case (5.41) agrees if terms involving second and higher powers of the selection coefficients are dropped, and t is negative.

Figure 5.6 gives three two-allele cases in which $s_1 = 0$, $s_2 = 2a$ and $t_1 = 0$, $t_2 = 0$, $-a$, or $-4a$. In the first, there is fixation of A_2 in spite of constancy of $\overline{W}$. In the second, there is less rapid fixation of A_2, while $\overline{W}$ is declining; in the third, A_2 is disappearing as $\overline{W}$ rapidly declines.

In Figure 5.7 the same situations with respect to the A locus are complicated by a second, additive, pair of alleles $s_1 = 0$, $s_2 = a$, and $t_1 = 0$,

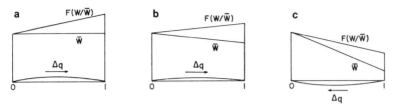

FIG. 5.6. Comparisons of $\overline{W}$ and $F(w/\overline{w})$ relative to q from equations (5.42) and (5.45), with three values of t_2: from left to right 0 in 5.6a, $-a$ in 5.6b, and $-4a$ in 5.6c. In this case, the genes have two kinds of effect, one reflected in growth of the population, the other (parameter t) not. Δq is also shown.

$t_2 = 0$, $-a/2$, or $-2a$. The broken lines represent contours in the surface of mean selective values $\overline{W}$, while the arrows indicate trajectories $(\Delta p, \Delta q)$ governed by the surface of fitness functions $F(W/\overline{W})$.

Selective Value a Function of the Genotypic Frequency

If either the absolute or relative selective values of genotypes vary solely as functions of their own frequencies, an approximate fitness function, $F(W/\overline{W})$, can be calculated irrespective of the number of loci or number of alleles at each (Wright 1960a).
Let

(5.47)
$$W_i = \chi(f_i).$$
$$\overline{W} = \sum [f_i \chi(f_i)].$$

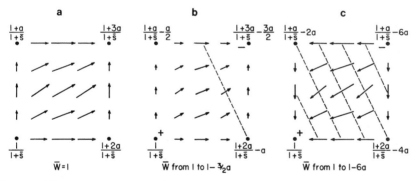

FIG. 5.7. The same situations as in Figure 5.6 with respect to gene A, complicated by additive effects with respect to B which are half as great. Corner values of $\overline{W}$ (all equal to one in 5.7a at left) and contours. Trajectories are shown for three values of the t's.

Assume that $\chi(f_i)$ can be expanded in a power series.

(5.48) $W_i = 1 + s_{i1}f_i + s_{i2}f_i^2 + s_{i3}f_i^3 + \cdots,$

(5.49) $\overline{W} = 1 + \sum s_{i1}f_i^2 + \sum s_{i2}f_i^3 + \sum s_{i3}f_i^4 + \cdots.$

It will be assumed that the selection coefficients are so small that $\bar{w}$ may be treated as one in the formula for $F(w/\bar{w})$.

(5.50) $F(W/\overline{W}) = F(w/\bar{w}) \approx \int \sum \chi(f_i)\,df_i$

(5.51) $\approx C + (1/2) \sum s_{i1}f_i^2 + (1/3) \sum s_{i2}f_i^3$
$$+ (1/4) \sum s_{i3}f_i^4 + \cdots.$$

Thus if a term in $\chi(f_i)$ is $s_{in}f_i^n$, the corresponding terms in $\overline{W}$ and $F(W/\overline{W})$ are $\sum (s_{in}f_i^{n+1})$ and $[1/(n+1)] \sum (s_{in}f_i^{n+1})$ respectively (except that if a term of the type $t_i f_i^{-1}$ is used in W_i, this leads to $\sum t_i$ and $\sum (t_i \log f_i)$ in $\overline{W}$ and $F(W/\overline{W})$ respectively). Apart from this, it may be seen that if the total selection coefficients $s_i = (W_i - 1)$ are all multiples of the same single power of f_i, then

$$F(W/\overline{W}) = \frac{1}{n+1} \int \frac{d\overline{W}}{\overline{W}} = C + \frac{1}{n+1} \log(\overline{W})$$

approximately.

The following case of multiple alleles with variable genic selective values is a simple example. It may be noted that the zygotic selective values are not functions of the zygotic frequencies in this case but merely of the genic frequencies, whether the former are additive or multiplicative (cf. Wright 1949b).

	Gene	f	w	$\partial f/\partial q_1$
	A_1	q_1	$1 + s_1 q_1$	1
(5.52)	A_2	q_2	$1 + s_2 q_2$	$-q_2/(1-q_1)$
	A_3	q_3	$1 + s_3 q_3$	$-q_3/(1-q_1)$

(5.53) $\bar{w} = 1 + \sum s_i q_i^2,$

(5.54) $\dfrac{\partial \bar{w}}{\partial q_x} = 2\big[s_x q_x - \sum s_i q_i^2\big]/(1 - q_x),$

(5.55) $\sum (w/\bar{w}) \dfrac{\partial f}{\partial q_x} = \big[s_x q_x - \sum s_i q_i^2\big]/(1 - q_x)\bar{w} = \dfrac{1}{2\bar{w}}\left(\dfrac{\partial \bar{w}}{\partial q_x}\right);$

(5.56) $F(w/\bar{w}) = C + 0.5 \log \bar{w} \approx C + 0.5 \sum s_i q_i^2$ (if all s's are small).

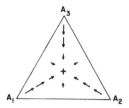

FIG. 5.8. Frequency diagram for three alleles, based on the set (5.52), showing trajectories under equal, negative, frequency dependent selection intensities, directed toward the center, which is a peak for both $F(w/\bar{w})$ and $\overline{W}$.

Differentiation of equations (5.56) yield equation 5.55, exactly or approximately on treating q's other than q_x as multiples of $(1 - q_x)$.

$$(5.57) \qquad \Delta q_x = q_x\left[s_x q_x - \sum s_i q_i^2\right]/\bar{w}.$$

The variable portion of $F(w/\bar{w})$ is just half that of $\bar{w}$ in the approximation used for the former. If $\overline{W} = k\bar{w}$, the variable portion of $F(W/\overline{W})$ is $1/(2k)$ times that of $\overline{W}$ to the same approximation. Selection thus carries the set of gene frequencies to the point at which population growth is maximum. There is an equilibrium point where each $\hat{q}_x = (1/s_x)/\sum (1/s_i)$ if all s's are of the same sign. This is unstable with selective peaks at fixation of each allele if the selection coefficients are positive but stable if all are negative (Fig. 5.8).

The case in which selection coefficients vary inversely, as the gene frequencies, is again of interest.

	Gene	f	w	$\partial f/\partial q_1$
	A_1	q_1	$1 + (s_1/q_1)$	1
(5.58)	A_2	q_2	$1 + (s_2/q_2)$	$-q_2/(1 - q_1)$
	A_3	q_3	$1 + (s_3/q_3)$	$-q_3/(1 - q_1)$

$$(5.59) \qquad \bar{w} = 1 + \sum s_i,$$

$$(5.60) \qquad \frac{\partial \bar{w}}{\partial q} = 0,$$

$$(5.61) \qquad \sum \left[(w/\bar{w})\frac{\partial f}{\partial q_x}\right] = \left[s_x - \left(\sum s_i\right)q_x\right]/\left(1 + \sum s_i\right)q_x(1 - q_x),$$

$$(5.62) \qquad F(w/\bar{w}) = C + \frac{\sum (s_i \log q_i)}{1 + \sum s_i}.$$

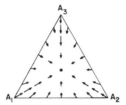

FIG. 5.9. Frequency diagrams for three alleles based on the set (5.58), showing trajectories under equal, negative, selective values with a different kind of frequency dependence from Figure 5.8. In this case, $\overline{W} = 1$ throughout, but again there is a peak for $F(w/\bar{w})$ at the center toward which the population moves.

Differentiation of equation (5.62) yields equation (5.61).

$$(5.63) \qquad \Delta q_x = \left[s_x - \left(\sum s_i \right) q_x \right] \Big/ \left(1 + \sum s_i \right),$$

$$(5.64) \qquad \hat{q}_x = s_x \Big/ \sum s_i \qquad \text{(if all } s\text{'s of same sign).}$$

The formula for Δq above violates the rule that $q(1 - q)$ should be a factor. The model breaks down, however, in the neighborhood of $q = 0$ because of the indefinitely great selection coefficients that it indicates. Throughout the rest of the range Δq is related linearly to gene frequencies as in the cases of mutation and immigration pressures.

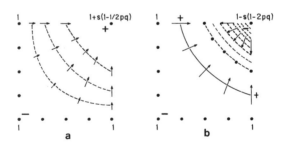

FIG. 5.10. Two-factor gene frequency diagrams based on the set (5.65), showing corner values and contours of $\overline{W}$. Combination AB is subject to selective advantage of rarity. In 5.10a (left), this aspect is so slight that AB is always at an advantage and tends to fixation. In 5.10b (right) the frequency dependent parameter is four times as great and there is equilibrium along a contour of $\overline{W}$ (ridge) between a contour of high $\overline{W}$ and the low value of $\overline{W}$ at homallelic AB (Fig. 5.10b redrawn from Wright 1960, Fig. 17).

An interesting feature is that the mean selective value $\bar{w}$ is constant (throughout the range of validity) while the fitness function $F(w/\bar{w})$ has a maximum if all selection coefficients are positive and a minimum if all are negative. As in the preceding case, there is approach to stable equilibrium if there is selective advantage in rarity (Fig. 5.9), but a runaway process toward fixation of one of the alleles if there is selective advantage in abundance. The sort of situation in nature to which this model would apply is analogous to that discussed in the two-allele case in which the selection coefficients varied as the reciprocals of the genotypic frequencies.

The significant genotypes may be multifactorial. Figure 5.10 gives examples in a two-locus case in which the selective value of only one of the four haploid combinations is a function of its frequency.

	Genotype	f	w	$\dfrac{\partial f}{\partial p}$
	AB	pq	$1 + s - tpq$	q
(5.65)	Ab	$p(1 - q)$	1	$1 - q$
	aB	$(1 - p)q$	1	$-q$
	ab	$(1 - p)(1 - q)$	1	$-(1 - q)$

$$(5.66) \qquad \bar{w} = 1 + spq - tp^2q^2,$$

$$(5.67) \qquad \frac{\partial \bar{w}}{\partial p} = q[s - 2tpq],$$

$$(5.68) \qquad \sum (w/\bar{w})\frac{\partial f}{\partial p} = (sq - tpq^2)/(1 + spq - tp^2q^2),$$

$$(5.69) \quad F(w/\bar{w}) = C + \frac{1}{\lambda_2 - \lambda_1}[\lambda_2 \log(pq - \lambda_1) - \lambda_1 \log(\lambda_2 - pq)]$$

where

$$\lambda_1 = [s - \sqrt{(s^2 + 4t)}]/2t \qquad \lambda_2 = [s + \sqrt{(s^2 + 4t)}]/2t;$$

$$(5.70) \qquad F(w/\bar{w}) \approx C + pq[s - 0.5tpq] \qquad \text{(if very small } s \text{ and } t),$$

$$(5.71) \qquad \begin{aligned} \Delta p &= p(1 - p)q(s - tpq)/\bar{w}, \\ \Delta q &= pq(1 - q)(s - tpq)/\bar{w}. \end{aligned}$$

Since $\Delta q/\Delta p = (1 - q)/(1 - p)$ the set of gene frequencies always moves in a line directly toward or away from $(1, 1)$ (fixation of AB). In Figure 5.10a, with $t = 0.5s$, the trajectories are always directed toward this point which is also the maximum for $\bar{w}$ (and thus of maximum growth rate for the population if W is a multiple of w). In Figure 5.10b, however, with, $t = 2s$

there is maximum population growth in a ridge in the surface $\bar{w}$ along the line $pq = 0.25$. The trajectories cross this and stop at a ridge in the surface, $F(w/\bar{w})$, along the line $pq = 0.5$ (line of dots). The broken lines represent contours of $\bar{w}$.

Joint Effects of Heterozygosis and Rarity

Since gene frequencies may be maintained at intermediate values either by heterosis or by selective advantage of rarity, it is of interest to consider the joint effects of those two mechanisms of equilibrium. Following is a simple example and the special case of it in which the heterozygotes are always exactly intermediate.

	Genotype	f	w	$\dfrac{df}{dq}$	Special Case of w $t_1 = t_2 = -(s_1 + s_2)$
	A_1A_1	q^2	$1 + s_1 + t_1 q$	$2q$	$1 + s_1 - (s_1 + s_2)q$
(5.72)	A_1A_2	$2q(1 - q)$	1	$2(1 - 2q)$	1
	A_2A_2	$(1 - q)^2$	$1 + s_2 + t_2(1 - q)$	$-2(1 - q)$	$1 - s_1 + (s_1 + s_2)q$

$$(5.73) \qquad \bar{w} = 1 + s_1 q^2 + s_2(1 - q)^2 + t_1 q^3 + t_2(1 - q)^3.$$

Letting $t_1 = t_2$ for simplicity (elimination of term in q^3):

$$(5.74) \qquad \bar{w} = 1 + (s_2 + t) - (2s_2 + 3t)q + (s_1 + s_2 + 3t)q^2,$$

$$(5.75) \qquad \frac{d\bar{w}}{dq} = -(2s_2 + 3t) + 2(s_1 + s_2 + 3t)q,$$

$$(5.76) \qquad \sum \left[(w/\bar{w}) \frac{df}{dq} \right] = [-2(s_2 + t) + 2(s_1 + s_2 + 2t)q]/\bar{w},$$

$$(5.77) \qquad F(w/\bar{w}) \approx C + [-2(s_2 + t)q + (s_1 + s_2 + 2t)q^2]$$
$$\text{(if very small } s_1, s_2, \text{ and } t),$$

$$(5.78) \qquad \Delta q = q(1 - q)[-(s_2 + t) + (s_1 + s_2 + 2t)q]/\bar{w},$$

$$(5.79) \qquad \hat{q} = \frac{s_2 + t}{s_1 + s_2 + 2t}.$$

There is stable equilibrium if $(s_1 + t)$ and $(s_2 + t)$ are both negative, unstable if both are positive.

In the special case, $t = -(s_1 + s_2)$ (considered by Wright and Dobzhansky 1946), the heterozygotes are always exactly intermediate, so that heterosis is absent. There is stable equilibrium, $\hat{q} = s_1/(s_1 + s_2)$, if both s_1

and s_2 are positive. Table 5.1 compares such a case ($s_1 = 0.902$, $s_2 = 0.386$) with that of a heterotic locus ($w_{11} = 0.70$, $w_{12} = 1$, $w_{22} = 0.30$) which has the same equilibrium value, $\hat{q} = 0.70$, and the same slope in the neighborhood of this value (Fig. 5.11).

These cases were used to illustrate two very different possible interpretations of an experiment in which flies (Drosophila pseudoobscura) with different inversion patterns of chromosome III (Standard and Chiricahua) competed in population cages (Wright and Dobzhansky 1946). Equilibrium

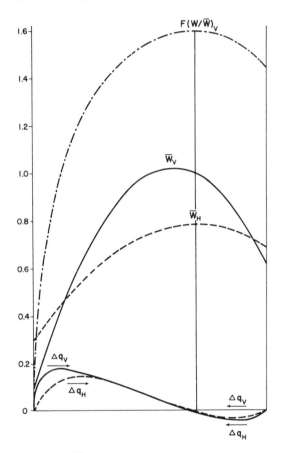

FIG. 5.11. Comparison of $\overline{W}_v$ and $F(w/\bar{w})_v$, based on the special case of set (5.72) in which there is selective advantage in rarity and an intermediate heterozygote, with $\overline{W}_H$ for a heterotic locus with equilibrium at the same point ($\hat{q} = 0.70$) as for $F(w/\bar{w})_v$. The curves for Δq_v and Δq_H are closely similar at intermediate gene frequencies.

TABLE 5.1. Comparison of case in which W's vary with gene frequency but there is no heterosis $(w_{11} = 1.902 - 1.288q; \ w_{12} = 1; \ w_{22} = 0.10 + 1.288q)$ with a case of constant selective disadvantage of both homozygotes (Wright and Dobzhansky 1946).

	w_V's Vary							w_H CONSTANT
	$q = 0$	0.10	0.30	0.50	0.70	0.90	1.00	
A_1A_1	1.90	1.77	1.51	1.26	1.00	0.74	0.61	0.70
A_1A_2	1.00	1.00	1.00	1.00	1.00	1.00	1.00	1.00
A_2A_2	0.10	0.23	0.49	0.74	1.00	1.26	1.39	0.30

was reached from both directions at $q_{ST} = 0.70$ at rates that could be interpreted equally well by either hypothesis. The virtual coincidence of Δq_V (w's vary as indicated) and Δq_H (constant heterosis) is shown in Figure 5.11. The mean selective value $\overline{W}_H$ is maximum at $\hat{q} = 0.70$, but $\overline{W}_V$ is maximum at $q = 0.60$. Between 0.60 and 0.70, selection reduces the mean selective value of the population in this case, but necessarily increases "fitness" $(F(w/\bar{w})_V)$ in Fisher's sense up to its maximum at $\hat{q} = 0.70$. In this figure $F(w/\bar{w})_V$ is estimated by subtracting the sums of the negative slopes $\Delta F(w/\bar{w})_V/\Delta q$ from the arbitrary value 1.00 at $\hat{q} = 0.70$.

(5.80) $\bar{w}_V = 1 - (0.902 - 1.288q)(1 - 2q)$,

(5.81) $\Delta q_V = q(1 - q)[0.902 - 1.288q]/\bar{w}_V$,

(5.82) $0.05 \dfrac{dF(w/\bar{w})_V}{dq} = 0.05 \sum (w/\bar{w}_V) \dfrac{df}{dq} = 0.1[0.902 - 1.288q]/\bar{w}_V$,

(5.83) $\bar{w}_H = 1 - 0.30q^2 - 0.70(1 - q)^2$,

(5.84) $\Delta q_H = q(1 - q)(0.70 - q)/\bar{w}_H$.

It is to be noted that in the general case in which both kinds of selection occur, there may be instability at an intermediate gene frequency in spite of heterozygous advantage and stability in spite of heterozygous disadvantage. Lewontin (1958) has discussed more complicated cases of opposition between overdominance and selective advantage of rarity. The subject has been further elaborated by Haldane and Jayakar (1963b).

Cases with No Fitness Function

As brought out earlier, there can be no fitness function $F(W/\overline{W}) = \int \sum (W_i/\overline{W})(\partial f_i/\partial q) \, dq$ if there are multiple alleles or multiple loci unless the selective values, W_i, of all genotypes are expressible as functions exclusively of their own genotypes, apart from general effects on the whole population, cancelled in the ratio $W_i/\overline{W}$. Thus there are indefinitely many conditions in which no fitness function exists and these probably include most actual cases in nature, although it is probable also that there are usually models with a fitness function that give reasonably good approximations. We will consider only some models without fitness functions which, though implausible as representations of natural situations, indicate in extreme form some of the complications that may occur.

The three-allele case shown in Figure 5.12 illustrates the possibility of cyclic changes in gene frequency (Wright 1949b). Genic selection, essentially equivalent to semidominance, is assumed for simplicity.

	Gene	f	w	$\dfrac{\partial f}{\partial q_1}$
	A_1	q_1	$1 + sq_1 + tq_2$	1
(5.85)	A_2	q_2	$1 + sq_2 + tq_3$	$-q_2/(1 - q_1)$
	A_3	q_3	$1 + sq_3 + tq_1$	$-q_3/(1 - q_1)$

$$(5.86) \qquad \bar{w} = 1 + (t/2) + [s - (t/2)] \sum q_i^2,$$

$$(5.87) \quad \sum (w_i/\bar{w}) \frac{\partial f}{\partial q_1} = \frac{1}{1 - q_1} \{sq_1 + t[q_2 - 0.5] - [s - (t/2)] \sum q_i^2\}/\bar{w},$$

$$(5.88) \qquad \Delta q_1 = q_1 \{sq_1 + t[q_2 - 0.5] - [s - (t/2)] \sum q_i^2\}/\bar{w}.$$

This reduces to the symmetrical case of 5.52 if $t = 0$. In this case there is equilibrium at $\hat{q}_1 = \hat{q}_2 = \hat{q}_3 = 1/3$, stable if s is negative, unstable if s is positive. There is a selective peak at this point in the former case, a selective pit in the latter.

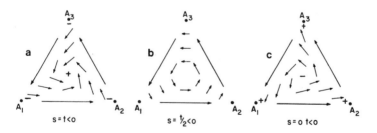

Fig. 5.12. Frequency diagram for three alleles, based on the set (5.85) with cyclic selective values that yield no fitness function. According to the parameters there is spiral convergence (5.12a, left), cyclic movement (5.12b, middle), or spiral divergence (5.12c, right).

If, however, $t < 0$, the set of gene frequencies tends to move in a counter-clockwise spiral. This ultimately approaches the center if s and t are equal and negative as shown in Figure 5.12a. There is approach to circular movement about the center on a level surface ($\bar{w} = 1 + t/2$) if $s = t/2$ is negative and infinitesimal, but divergent spiral movement if finite, in spite of the level surface (Fig. 5.12b). If s is less strongly negative than $t/2$ or is zero (Fig. 5.12c) or positive (t negative in either case), there is spiral movement away from a central pit, leading to fixation of one or other allele. With positive t, movement is clockwise.

The discrepancy between direction of movement and the characters of the surface $\bar{w}$ becomes more pronounced with zygotic selection, complicated by overdominance (h added to the selective values of the heterozygotes).

$$(5.89) \qquad \bar{w} = 1 + t + h + (2s - h - t) \sum q^2,$$

$$(5.90) \qquad \Delta q_1 = q_1\{2(s - h)q_1 + t(2q_2 - 1) - [2(s - h) - t] \sum q^2\}/2\bar{w}, \text{ etc.}$$

	$\bar{w}$	Movement
If $h > 2s - t$	central peak	inward spiral
$h = 2s - t$	level	inward spiral
$2s - t > h > s - t/2$	central pit	inward spiral
$h = s - t/2$	central pit	cyclic motion
$h < s - t/2$	central pit	outward spiral

Only in the first and last cases is the direction of movement in conformity with the slope of $\bar{w}$.

Similar cases can readily be devised with two interacting loci. Figure 5.13 illustrates such a case in which the surface of mean selective values is level and the set of gene frequencies moves cyclically about the center if the selection coefficient is infinitesimal, in an outward spiral if finite. Other cases analogous to those above can be obtained by introducing two selection coefficients, s and t, with various relative values.

There is a very different situation if the selective values of gametes are functions exclusively of the frequencies of the complementary gametes in a two-locus case.

	Gamete	f	w
	AB	pq	$1 + s_{11}(1 - p)(1 - q)$
	Ab	$p(1 - q)$	$1 + s_{10}(1 - p)q$
(5.91)	aB	$(1 - p)q$	$1 + s_{01}p(1 - q)$
	ab	$(1 - p)(1 - q)$	$1 + s_{00}pq$

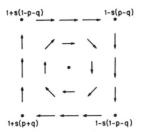

FIG. 5.13. A two-factor gene frequency diagram with cyclic selective values and parameters chosen to give cyclic movement (redrawn from Wright 1964, Fig. 19, by permission, University of Wisconsin Press, © 1964 by the Regents of The University of Wisconsin).

$$(5.92) \qquad \bar{w} = 1 + \left(\sum s\right)p(1 - p)q(1 - q),$$

$$(5.93) \qquad \frac{\partial \bar{w}}{\partial p} = \left(\sum s\right)(1 - 2p)q(1 - q),$$

$$(5.94) \qquad \sum (w/\bar{w}) \frac{\partial f}{\partial p} = q(1 - q)\left[(s_{11} + s_{10}) - \left(\sum s\right)p\right]/\bar{w},$$

$$\sum (w/\bar{w}) \frac{\partial f}{\partial q} = p(1 - p)\left[(s_{11} + s_{01}) - \left(\sum s\right)q\right]/\bar{w},$$

$$(5.95) \qquad \Delta p = p(1 - p)q(1 - q)\left[(s_{11} + s_{10}) - \left(\sum s\right)p\right]/\bar{w},$$

$$\Delta q = p(1 - p)q(1 - q)\left[(s_{11} + s_{01}) - \left(\sum s\right)q\right]/\bar{w}.$$

The surface $\bar{w}$ is level if $\sum s = 0$, has a central peak if $\sum s > 0$, and has a central pit if $\sum s < 0$.

The fitness function $F(w/\bar{w})$ does not exist, but it would be possible to define a different fitness function $F'(w/\bar{w})$ that controls changes in gene frequency in a somewhat similar way.

$$(5.96) \quad F'(w/\bar{w}) = (s_{11} + s_{10})p + (s_{11} + s_{01})q - (1/2)(\sum s)(p^2 + q^2),$$

$$(5.97) \qquad \Delta p = p(1 - p)q(1 - q) \frac{\partial F'(w/\bar{w})}{\partial p}\bigg/ \bar{w}$$

$$\Delta q = p(1 - p)q(1 - q) \frac{\partial F'(w/\bar{w})}{\partial q}\bigg/ \bar{w}.$$

Here the set of gene frequencies moves up the gradient of $F'(w/\bar{w})$ qualified by the positive factor $p(1 - p)q(1 - q)$. There is no movement if any one of the four genes is fixed.

The special case $s_{10} = s_{01} = 0$ is that in which there is a special relation, mutually beneficial if both $s = s_{11}$ and $t = s_{00}$ are positive, mutually deleterious if both are negative, and that of predator-prey if of opposite sign.

(5.98) $$\bar{w} = 1 + (s + t)p(1 - p)q(1 - q),$$

(5.99) $$F'(w/\bar{w}) = s(p + q) - 0.5(s + t)(p^2 + q^2)/\bar{w},$$

(5.100) $$\Delta p = p(1 - p)q(1 - q)[s - (s + t)p]/\bar{w}$$
$$\Delta q = p(1 - p)q(1 - q)[s - (s + t)q]/\bar{w},$$

(5.101) $$\hat{p} = \hat{q} = s/(s + t).$$

The case of level $\bar{w}$ (no effect on growth), s positive, $t = -s$, is shown in Figure 5.14. The trajectories of gene frequencies are exactly parallel, in marked contrast to the cyclic movements in Figure 5.13, and tend toward fixation of either A or B. With s still positive but $s + t$ negative, there is a central pit in the surface $\bar{w}$ (minimum population growth at $(0.5, 0.5)$). The trajectories tend, as before, toward fixation of A or B but diverge from parallelism. With $(s + t)$ positive, there is a central peak in $\bar{w}$ (maximum population growth at $(0.5, 0.5)$). The trajectories converge toward fixation of A or B if t is not positive, but if positive converge toward the point $[s/(s + t), s/(s + t)]$.

Special Cases

There are many cases which require special treatment because of peculiarities in the relation of selection to the generations.

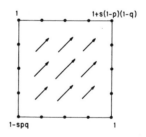

FIG. 5.14. A two-factor gene frequency diagram based on the set (5.91) ($\overline{W} = 1$), with no fitness function $F(w/\bar{w})$ as defined, though a different one can be devised. The trajectories are parallel and either A or B tends to be fixed (redrawn from Wright 1960, Fig. 15).

Intrabrood Selection

An important special case of variable selection coefficients is that of selection within broods. Such competition, although determining which members of a brood survive, may have no effect on the number of survivors or the growth of the population. This case was analyzed by Haldane (1924, 1932b) and from a somewhat different standpoint by Wright (1949b). An inversion of certain symbols in the latter was later corrected (Wright 1955). The w's in Table 5.2 refer to relative selective values within broods, not in the total population, and are assumed to be constants.

The relative selective values of the three genotypes in the total population are given by the sums of the three offspring columns each divided by the appropriate frequency, f, before selection (q_1^2, $2q_1q_2$, or q_2^2). Their mean, $\bar{w} = \sum fw = 1$, implies no effect of the selection on population growth.

$$\Delta q_1 = 0.5q_1(1 - q_1) \sum \left[(w/\bar{w}) \frac{df}{dq} \right]$$

$$(5.102) \qquad = q_1(1 - q_1)\left[q_1^2 \left(\frac{w_{11} - w_{12}}{w_{11} + w_{12}} \right) + 2q_1q_2 \left(\frac{w_{11} - w_{22}}{w_{11} + 2w_{12} + w_{22}} \right) \right.$$

$$\left. + q_2^2 \left(\frac{w_{12} - w_{22}}{w_{12} + w_{22}} \right) \right].$$

Let $w_{11} = 1 + s_{11}$, $w_{12} = 1 + s_{12}$, $w_{22} = 1 + s_{22}$ in which the s's refer to intrabrood selective values.

$$\Delta q_1 = q_1(1 - q_1)\left\{ q_1^2 \left[\frac{s_{11} - s_{12}}{2 + (s_{11} + s_{12})} \right] \right.$$

$$(5.103)$$

$$\left. + 2q_1q_2 \left[\frac{s_{11} - s_{22}}{4 + (s_{11} + 2s_{12} + s_{22})} \right] + q_2^2 \left[\frac{s_{12} - s_{22}}{2 + (s_{12} + s_{22})} \right] \right\}.$$

If the intrabrood selective differentials are small,

$$(5.104) \qquad \Delta q_1 \approx 0.5q_1(1 - q_1)[(s_{11} - 2s_{12} + s_{22})q_1 - (s_{22} - s_{12})].$$

This is the same as if there were constant selective differentials of half the assigned values applied to competition in a panmictic population as a whole instead of within broods.

Self-incompatibility Alleles

The self-incompatibility mechanism of many flowering plants in which there is failure of pollen tube growth on a style in which either of the alleles is that of the pollen grain presents an interesting case in which selection is a function of gene frequency. The smallest possible number of alleles for persistence is three.

TABLE 5.2. Frequencies of offspring in relation to parental matings after intrabrood selection (Wright 1955).

PARENTS	FREQUENCY	OFFSPRING AFTER SELECTION		
		A_1A_1	A_1A_2	A_2A_2
$A_1A_1 \times A_1A_1$	q_1^4	q_1^4		
$A_1A_1 \times A_1A_2$	$4q_1^3q_2$	$2q_1^3q_2[2w_{11}/(w_{11}+w_{12})]$	$2q_1^3q_2[2w_{12}/(w_{11}+w_{12})]$	
$A_1A_1 \times A_2A_2$	$2q_1^2q_2^2$		$2q_1^2q_2^2$	
$A_1A_2 \times A_1A_2$	$4q_1^2q_2^2$	$q_1^2q_2^2[4w_{11}/(w_{11}+2w_{12}+w_{22})]$	$q_1^2q_2^2[4w_{12}/(w_{11}+2w_{12}+w_{22})]$	$q_1^2q_2^2[4w_{22}/(w_{11}+2w_{12}+w_{22})]$
$A_1A_2 \times A_2A_2$	$4q_1q_2^3$		$2q_1q_2^3[2w_{12}/(w_{12}+w_{22})]$	$2q_1q_2^3[2w_{22}/(w_{12}+w_{22})]$
$A_2A_2 \times A_2A_2$	q_2^4			q_2^4

Parent		Offspring		
Ovule	Pollen	S_1S_2	S_1S_3	S_2S_3
S_1S_2	S_3	0.0	0.50	0.50
(5.105) S_1S_3	S_2	0.50	0.0	0.50
S_2S_3	S_1	0.50	0.50	0.0

This mode of inheritance does not lead to an exact formula for rate of change of gene frequency. The following approximate method was used by the present author (1939a).

Self-incompatibility alleles with frequencies $q_1, q_2, \ldots, q_n$ are assumed such that $\sum q = 1$ in a population of N diploid individuals. The frequencies of zygotes containing one of these (S_x) must be $2q_x$ since all are heterozygotes. The frequency of functioning S_x female gametes is q_x, assuming no differential selection. The frequency of functioning S_x pollen grains is not in general the same. By hypothesis, S_x pollen has no chance of functioning on the styles of zygotes containing S_x but has a better than average chance in zygotes that lack S_x, frequency $(1 - 2q_x)$, since each zygote of this class inhibits pollen of two of the other kinds. Assume that on non-S_x styles the ratio of successful S_x pollen grains to successful ones of the other types is as $q_x : R(1 - q_x)$. The total frequency of functioning S_x pollen is then $q_x(1 - 2q_x)/[q_x + R(1 - q_x)]$. The average frequency of functioning S_x gametes is $q_x(1 - q_x)(1 + R)/2[q_x + R(1 - q_x)]$, and the change from the previous generation is therefore:

$$(5.106) \qquad \Delta q = \frac{q(1 - q)(1 + R)}{2[q + R(1 - q)]} - q = \frac{q}{2}\left[\frac{(1 - R) - q(3 - R)}{R + q(1 - R)}\right].$$

If $n = 3$, R is obviously zero and Δq reduces to $-(3/2)[q - 1/3]$ exactly. Note that in this case the deviation of q from $\hat{q} = 1/3$ goes in the next generation to half its value in the opposite direction. There is a rapid oscillatory approach to equality of the frequencies of the three alleles. Otherwise R varies among the alleles but approaches uniformity either as the number of alleles increases or as their frequencies cluster more closely about the equilibrium point. It was assumed that an adequate approximation could be obtained by assuming constancy of R. Where this is valid, the gene frequency at which $\Delta q = 0$ is given by $\hat{q} = (1 - R)/(3 - R)$. This led to the equivalent approximate formula.

$$(5.107) \qquad \Delta q = -\frac{q(q - \hat{q})}{1 - 3\hat{q} + 2\hat{q}q}.$$

The term $2\hat{q}q$ is so small with large n that the estimate would be little changed by replacing it by $2\hat{q}^2$ giving the more convenient formula (Wright 1960b).

(5.108)
$$\Delta q = -\frac{q(q - \hat{q})}{(1 - \hat{q})(1 - 2\hat{q})}.$$

There is, of course, no difficulty in calculating the exact change in gene frequency due to self-incompatibility if the set of zygotic frequencies f_{ij} is given. In the following, the summation relates to all pairs of alleles S_i, S_j of the one considered S_x.

(5.109)
$$\Delta q_x = -\frac{q_x}{2}\left[1 - \sum\left(\frac{f_{ij}}{1 - q_i - q_j}\right)\right].$$

Fisher (1958) criticized the method described above and used this latter approach. He held that a good approximation for Δq could be obtained by replacing q_i and q_j by the equilibrium value $\hat{q}$. If this is done (5.109) reduces to the following, noting that $\sum f_{ij} = 1 - 2q_x$:

(5.110)
$$\Delta q_x = -\frac{q(q - \hat{q})}{1 - 2\hat{q}}.$$

This differs from (5.108) only in lacking the factor $(1 - \hat{q})$ in the denominator. As noted above, (5.106) reduces to the exact formula if $n = 3$. Formulas (5.108) and (5.110) are both far from accurate in this case, but this is of little importance since the gene frequencies are not allowed to deviate appreciably from $1/3$ in any population of appreciable size. The inaccuracies of all of the formulas become more important if $n = 4$ but decrease in importance as n increases.

TABLE 5.3. The gene frequencies from the zygote distribution $[0.04S_1S_2 + 0.05S_1S_3 + 0.11S_1S_4 + 0.11S_2S_3 + 0.25S_2S_4 + 0.44S_3S_4]$, the exact change in gene frequency in the next generation (5.109) and estimates based on 5.107, 5.110, and 5.108, respectively. The bottom row gives rms (the square root of the mean-squared deviation from exact Δq) for each of set of estimates.

Gene Frequencies	Change of Gene Frequency (Δq)			
	Exact (5.109)	(5.107)	(5.110)	(5.108)
$\hat{q}$	—	0.27786	0.295	0.295
$q_1 = 0.10$	$+0.0656$	$+0.0838$	$+0.0500$	$+0.0714$
$q_2 = 0.20$	$+0.0770$	$+0.0592$	$+0.0500$	$+0.0714$
$q_3 = 0.30$	-0.0147	-0.0181	0	0
$q_4 = 0.40$	-0.1279	-0.1249	-0.1000	-0.1428
rms	—	0.0129	0.0222	0.0112

It is interesting to compare the three estimates (5.107), (5.110), and (5.108) with exact values of Δq for representative sets of zygotic frequencies. An example is shown in Table 5.3.

The equilibrium frequency, $\hat{q}$, comes from the equation $\sum (\Delta q) = 0$. It is given by $\hat{q} = \sum q^2$ in (5.110) and (5.108) but requires solution of a polynomial in (5.107).

The square roots (rms) of the mean square differences from the exact values of Δq are given as a basis for judgment of the closeness of approximation.

Four widely different sets of zygote frequencies were tested in the case of four alleles and four also in the case of five. The details, including the zygotic distribution, are given in Wright (1960b). A summary in terms of the gene frequencies and the square roots of the mean square deviations from the exact changes in gene frequencies based on the zygotic distributions is given in Table 5.4.

TABLE 5.4. Gene frequencies from eight zygote distributions and the values of rms derived from the estimates of Δq given by formulas 5.107 (Wright 1939a), 5.110 (Fisher 1958), and 5.108 (Wright 1960b), respectively.

Four Alleles				(5.107)	(5.110)	(5.108)
a	0.10	0.25	0.25	0.40	0.0132	0.0156	0.0094
b	.10	.20	.30	.40	.0129	.0222	.0112
c	.10	.30	.30	.30	.0129	.0053	.0035
d	0.20	0.20	0.20	0.40	0.0023	0.0139	0.0105
Five Alleles					(5.107)	(5.110)	(5.108)
e	0.05	0.20	0.20	0.20	0.35	0.0051	0.0096	0.0026
f	.15	.20	.20	.20	.25	.0007	.0026	.0003
g	.10	.10	.20	.30	.30	.0043	.0094	.0020
h	0.11	0.11	0.22	0.22	0.34	0.0038	0.0091	0.0016

The distributions are not, of course, equilibrium distributions which take account of random fluctuations due to sampling at any specifiable sizes of population, and $\hat{q}$ is thus not a permanent constant. The last two (c, d) with four alleles are those that differ most from equilibrium.

It may be seen that in all but one of the cases (d), formula (5.108), has the smallest deviations. In this case (5.107) is the best and (5.110) the worst. Equation (5.107) is next to the best in all of the others except (c). It is clear that by this empirical test (5.108) is much the best, (5.107) is next, and (5.110) is the least satisfactory. It is to be noted that the superiority of

(5.108) over (5.107) and thus over (5.110) is relatively greater for $n = 5$ than for $n = 4$, and that the errors (especially in (5.108)) tend to be less with the larger number of alleles as expected. Thus in spite of its lack of completely logical derivation, (5.108) seems to give the best approximate estimates of change of gene frequency for more than three alleles (at which, as noted, (5.107) is exact).

Maternal-Fetal Interaction

Determination of offspring phenotype by the genetic constitution of the mother has been considered in a previous chapter. The present will deal with the occasional determination of maternal antibodies by antigens of the fetus, derived from the father, followed by disastrous effects on later off-spring, with the same antigen. The erythroblastosis in man in the offspring of rh negative mother but Rh father was the first example. Only a simple model will be considered that does not attempt to take account of all the factors involved in a full interpretation.

Assume that genotypes RR, Rr, and rr occur in a given generation in the frequencies $X:2Y:Z$, respectively, with selective elimination of Rr off-spring of rr mothers RR fathers to the extent t, and Rr offspring of $rr \times Rr$ to the extent s. Because of this elimination of heterozygotes the frequency, ZY, of Rr individuals is expected to be somewhat less than $2q(1 - q)$ where $q = (Y + Z)$ is the gene frequency of r. This case was analyzed by Haldane (1942). (See Table 5.5.)

In the offspring generation:

$$(5.111) \qquad \begin{aligned} X_1 &= (1 - q)^2/\bar{w}, \\ 2Y_1 &= [2q(1 - q) - tXZ - sYZ]/\bar{w}, \\ Z_1 &= q^2/\bar{w}, \\ \bar{w} &= 1 - tXZ - sYZ. \end{aligned}$$

The composition of the population can be calculated step by step. The gene frequencies in the offspring generation are $q_1 = (Y_1 + Z_1)$, $1 - q_1 = (X_1 + Y_1)$.

$$(5.112) \qquad \begin{aligned} q_1 &= [q - (t/2)XZ - (s/2)YZ]/\bar{w}, \\ 1 - q_1 &= [1 - q - (t/2)XZ - (s/2)YZ]/\bar{w}. \end{aligned}$$

Change of gene frequency is given by $\Delta q = q_1 - q$.

$$(5.113) \qquad \Delta q = (tX + sY)Z[q - 0.5]/\bar{w}.$$

Thus there is no change if $\hat{q} = 1/2$, but the equilibrium is unstable.

TABLE 5.5. Frequencies of surviving offspring from the various types of matings of R,r genotypes.

PARENTAL GENOTYPES		OFFSPRING		
♀	♂	RR	Rr	rr
RR	RR	X^2		
	Rr	XY	XY	
	rr		XZ	
Rr	RR	XY	XY	
	Rr	Y^2	$2Y^2$	Y^2
	rr		YZ	YZ
rr	RR		$XZ(1-t)$	
	Rr		$YZ(1-s)$	YZ
	rr			Z^2

If t and s are both small, the approximate rate can be determined by putting $X = (1 - q)^2$, $2Y = 2q(1 - q)$, and $Z = q^2$ and substituting, or by using the differential formula.

		f	w	$\dfrac{df}{dq}$
	RR	$(1 - q)^2$	1	$-2(1 - q)$
(5.114)	Rr	$2q(1 - q)$	$1 - (q/2)[t - (t - s)q]$	$2(1 - 2q)$
	rr	q^2	1	$2q$

$$(5.115) \qquad \bar{w} = 1 - q^2(1 - q)[t - (t - s)q],$$

$$(5.116) \qquad \sum \left[(w/\bar{w}) \frac{df}{dq} \right] = 2q[q - 0.5][t - (t - s)q]/\bar{w},$$

$$(5.117) \qquad \Delta q = q^2(1 - q)[q - 0.5][t - (t - s)q]/\bar{w}.$$

The unstable equilibrium at $\hat{q} = 1/2$ may again be noted.

Among white Americans and in western Europe, the frequency of rr is about 15%–16% and thus q is about 0.40. The proportion of affected births would be about $q^2(1 - q) = 0.16 \times 0.60 = 0.096$ if both s and t were equal to one. Actually the proportion affected is only about 0.005, indicating that s and t, if equal, are only about 0.05, justifying the above approximation. Actually s is considerably less than t. Since only half the children from $rr \times Rr$ are Rr, the immunization of the mother is likely to be delayed.

Selective Mating

The term selective mating may be used in two senses. Mating may be selective with respect to which individuals mate at all or with respect to choice of mates.

In the first case, the theory differs in no way from that for selective mortality or selective emigration. There are merely different relative selective values for the various genotypes to be applied as factors to their relative frequencies as fertilized eggs along with the relative selective values in other respects.

Selective mating in the second sense need not be associated with any changes in gene frequency and thus is not a form of selection at all, as the term is used here. Such mating is termed assortative mating and is measured by the phenotypic correlation between mates which may be negative (disassortative) as well as positive. Assortative mating that does not involve change of gene frequency will be discussed in chapter 11.

A combination of the two kinds of selective mating is, however, common. Thus it is often found in experiments with Drosophila that recessive males mate disproportionately less often with type females than with recessive females. The comparison with the results of uniform discrimination against such mutant types can be brought out most simply by considering cases in which the selective disadvantages are so slight that the deviations from the Hardy–Weinberg frequencies due to selective mating may be ignored.

Assume gene arrays $[(1 - p)A + pa]$ and a selection disadvantage of s for matings of aa males with $A-$ females and of t with aa females. The approximate relative frequencies of the various types of matings are as follows:

		AA	Aa	aa	Mated Males
	AA	$\dfrac{(1-q)^4}{1-sq^2}$	$\dfrac{2q(1-q)^3}{1-sq^2}$	$\dfrac{q^2(1-q)^2}{1-tq^2}$	$\dfrac{(1-q)^2[1-tq^2-(s-t)q^4]}{(1-sq^2)(1-tq^2)}$
(5.118)	Aa	$\dfrac{2q(1-q)^3}{1-sq^2}$	$\dfrac{4q^2(1-q)^2}{1-sq^2}$	$\dfrac{2q^3(1-q)}{1-tq^2}$	$\dfrac{2q(1-q)[1-tq^2-(s-t)q^4]}{(1-sq^2)(1-tq^2)}$
	aa	$\dfrac{(1-s)q^2(1-q)^2}{1-sq^2}$	$\dfrac{2(1-s)q^3(1-q)}{1-sq^2}$	$\dfrac{(1-t)q^4}{1-tq^2}$	$\dfrac{q^2[1-s+(s-2t+st)q^2-(s-t)q^4]}{(1-sq^2)(1-tq^2)}$
Mated Females	$(1-q)^2$		$2q(1-q)$	q^2	1

The array of genotypes among the offspring is as follows:

$$AA \qquad \frac{(1-q)^2}{1-sq^2}$$

(5.119)

$$Aa \qquad q(1-q)\left[\frac{2-q-sq}{1-sq^2} + \frac{q}{1-tq^2}\right]$$

$$aa \qquad q^2\left[\frac{(1-q)(1-sq)}{1-sq^2} + \frac{q(1-tq)}{1-tq^2}\right].$$

These yield the following gene frequencies:

$$
(5.120) \quad
\begin{array}{ll}
A & (1 - q)\left[\dfrac{2 - q^2 - sq^2}{2(1 - sq^2)} + \dfrac{q^2}{2(1 - tq^2)}\right] \\[2ex]
a & q\left[\dfrac{2 - q(1 + s) - q^2(1 + s) + 2sq^3}{2(1 - sq^2)} + \dfrac{q(1 + q - 2tq^2)}{2(1 - tq^2)}\right].
\end{array}
$$

$$
(5.121) \quad
\begin{aligned}
\Delta q &= -\left(\frac{q^2}{2}\right)(1 - q)[s - (s - t + st)q^2]/(1 - sq^2)(1 - tq^2) \\[1ex]
&\approx -\frac{q^2}{2}(1 - q)[s - (s - t)q^2].
\end{aligned}
$$

If recessive males are discriminated against only by dominant females $(t = 0)$, then $\Delta q \approx - (sq^2/2)(1 - q)(1 - q^2)$. The rate of decrease of recessive genes is proportional to the percentage of dominant females $(1 - q^2)$ as expected, and if recessives are rare, approach the same value $-(sq^2/2)(1 - q)$ as if there were equal discrimination by all females $(t = s)$, which, as expected, is about half the rate from a selective disadvantage, s, for both recessive males and females.

A similar analysis for the case under sex-linked heredity in which the recessive males are discriminated against to a slight extent, s, by dominant females and to a slight extent, t, by recessive females yields:

$$
(5.122) \quad
\begin{aligned}
\Delta q &= (1/3)q(1 - q)[-s + stq + (s - t)q^2]/(1 - sq)(1 - tq) \\[1ex]
&\approx (1/3)q(1 - q)[-s + (s - t)q^2].
\end{aligned}
$$

If $t = s$, the rate, $-(s/3)q(1 - q)$, is that of uniform selective disadvantage against recessive males (chap. 3). If $t = 0$, the factor $(1 - q^2)$ introduces the expected proportionality to the dominant females.

Selection of Quantitative Variability

This section is concerned with unidirectional selection of quantitatively varying characters. It will be well to consider this first from a purely empirical standpoint. It is assumed that because of numerous largely independent factors, genetic and environmental, the distribution may be treated as normal with mean, M, and standard deviation, σ. There is a regression, $b_{o\bar{p}}$, of the grades of offspring on the average deviation of their parents. The deviation, ΔM_o, of the mean of the offspring of parents selected to have an average deviation of $\Delta M_{\bar{p}}$ is:

$$
(5.123) \quad \Delta M_o = b_{o\bar{p}}\, \Delta M_{\bar{p}}.
$$

In artificial selection, there is usually an attempt to select a proportion, p, at the desired extreme, to be parents. This determines a truncation point at $M + t$ in the distribution or at $x = t/\sigma$ on the corresponding unit normal curve.

$$(5.124) \qquad p = \frac{1}{\sqrt{(2\pi)}} \int_{t/\sigma}^{\infty} e^{-0.5x^2}\, dx,$$

$$(5.125) \qquad \Delta M_{\bar{p}} = (z/p)\sigma \qquad\qquad (z \text{ is ordinate at } x = t/\sigma),$$

$$(5.126) \qquad \Delta M_o = b_{o\bar{p}}(z/p)\sigma.$$

Table 5.6 relates t/σ and z/p to p. There is not likely to be sharp truncation under natural selection, but $\Delta M_{\bar{p}}$ may be considered to correspond to a certain effective value of $(z/p)\sigma$.

TABLE 5.6. Values of p and z/p at various values of t/σ.

t/σ	p	z/p	t/σ	p	z/p	t/σ	p	z/p
-3.09	0.999	0.0034	-0.524	0.70	0.497	0.842	0.20	1.400
-2.326	.99	.0269	-0.253	.60	0.644	1.282	.10	1.755
-1.645	.95	.1086	0.000	.50	0.798	1.645	.05	2.063
-1.282	.90	.1950	0.253	.40	0.960	2.326	.01	2.665
-0.842	0.80	0.3500	0.524	.30	1.159	3.090	0.001	3.367

Haldane (1932b) went into the effect of selection on an equal mixture of two clones, which differ in their means but which overlap extensively because of nongenetic variabilities that are not necessarily the same.

	Frequency	Mean	Variance
Clone 2	q	$M_2 = M_1 + \alpha$	$\sigma_2{}^2 = \sigma_1{}^2 + \beta$
Clone 1	$1-q$	M_1	$\sigma_1{}^2$
Total	1	$M = (1-q)M_1 + qM_2$	$\sigma^2 = (1-q)\sigma_1{}^2 + q\sigma_2{}^2 + q(1-q)\alpha^2$

From these

$$(5.127) \qquad \begin{aligned} M_2 &= M + (1-q)\alpha, \\ M_1 &= M - q\alpha; \end{aligned}$$

$$(5.128) \qquad \begin{aligned} \sigma_2{}^2 &= \sigma^2 + (1-q)\beta - q(1-q)\alpha^2, \\ \sigma_1{}^2 &= \sigma^2 - q\beta - q(1-q)\alpha^2. \end{aligned}$$

The truncation point, $M + t$, deviates from M_2 and M_1, respectively, by:

$$(5.129) \qquad \begin{aligned} t_2 &= t - (1-q)\alpha, \\ t_1 &= t + q\alpha. \end{aligned}$$

The standard deviations are approximately as follows, dropping terms in α^2/σ^2 as negligibly small if α/σ is small:

(5.130)
$$\sigma_2 \approx \sigma[1 + (1 - q)\beta/(2\sigma^2)],$$
$$\sigma_1 \approx \sigma[1 - q\beta/(2\sigma^2)];$$

(5.131)
$$t_2/\sigma_2 \approx \frac{t}{\sigma} - \frac{(1 - q)[\alpha + t\beta/(2\sigma^2)]}{\sigma},$$
$$t_1/\sigma_1 \approx \frac{t}{\sigma} + \frac{q[\alpha + t\beta/(2\sigma^2)]}{\sigma}.$$

The proportions of the two clones retained as parents are approximately as follows:

(5.132)
$$p_2 = \frac{1}{\sqrt{(2\pi)}} \int_{t_2/\sigma_2}^{\infty} e^{-0/5x^2}\, dx \approx p + (1 - q)[\alpha + t\beta/(2\sigma^2)](z/\sigma),$$
$$p_1 = \frac{1}{\sqrt{(2\pi)}} \int_{t_1/\sigma_1}^{\infty} e^{-0/5x^2}\, dx \approx p - q[\alpha + t\beta/(2\sigma^2)](z/\sigma).$$

Note that $qp_2 + (1 - q)p_1 = p$.

(5.133)
$$\Delta q = \frac{qp_2}{p} - q \approx q(1 - q)[\alpha + t\beta/(2\sigma^2)]z/(p\sigma).$$

An interesting paradox, noted by Haldane, is that if the clone with *smaller* mean (M_1 if α is positive) has the larger standard deviation, selection of sufficiently extreme parents *increases* its frequency. The condition is that t be greater than $2\alpha\sigma^2/(-\beta)$, β being by hypothesis of opposite sign to α. Here, Δq is negative. With smaller or negative t, it becomes positive until, with very strongly negative t, $[(t/\sigma)z]$ approaches zero and there is no selection.

Extension can be made to a pair of alleles in a panmictic population where the genotypes make only small contributions to the total variability.

(5.134)

Genotype	Contribution to Mean	Residual Variance
AA	$\alpha_1 + \alpha_2$	$\sigma_{aa}^2 + \beta_1 + \beta_2$
Aa	α_1	$\sigma_{aa}^2 + \beta_1$
aa	0	σ_{aa}^2

Assume that the means and residual variances can be written as follows:

(5.135)

Genotype	Frequency	Mean	Variance
AA	q^2	$M + (1 - q)^2 x_2$	$\sigma^2 + (1 - q)^2 y_2$
Aa	$2q(1 - q)$	$M + q(1 - q)x_1$	$\sigma^2 + q(1 - q)y_1$
aa	$(1 - q)^2$	$M + q^2 x_0$	$\sigma^2 + q^2 y_0$
Total	1	M	σ^2

The following equations can be written with respect to the x's:

$$x_2 + 2x_1 + x_0 = 0,$$

(5.136) $\quad M_{AA} - M_{Aa} = (1-q)^2 x_2 - q(1-q)x_1 = \alpha_2,$

$$M_{Aa} - M_{aa} = q(1-q)x_1 - q^2 x_0 = \alpha_1.$$

The solutions are:

$$x_2 = [(1-q)\alpha_1 + (1+q)\alpha_2]/(1-q),$$

(5.137) $\quad x_1 = [(1-q)^2\alpha_1 - q^2\alpha_2]/q(1-q),$

$$x_0 = -[(2-q)\alpha_1 + q\alpha_2]/q.$$

Exactly parallel equations can be written for the y's in terms of β_1 and β_2.

$$\frac{t_{AA}}{\sigma_{AA}} \approx \frac{t - (1-q)^2 x_2}{\sigma[1 + (1-q)^2 y_2/(2\sigma^2)]} \approx \frac{t}{\sigma} - \frac{(1-q)^2[x_2 + ty_2/(2\sigma^2)]}{\sigma},$$

(5.138) $\quad \dfrac{t_{Aa}}{\sigma_{Aa}} \approx \dfrac{t - q(1-q)x_1}{\sigma[1 + q(1-q)y_1/(2\sigma^2)]} \approx \dfrac{t}{\sigma} - \dfrac{q(1-q)[x_1 + ty_1/(2\sigma^2)]}{\sigma},$

$$\frac{t_{aa}}{\sigma_{aa}} \approx \frac{t - q^2 x_0}{\sigma[1 + q^2 y_0/(2\sigma^2)]} \approx \frac{t}{\sigma} - \frac{q^2[x_0 + ty_0/(2\sigma^2)]}{\sigma};$$

$$p_{AA} \approx p + (1-q)^2[x_2 + ty_2/(2\sigma^2)](z/\sigma),$$

(5.139) $\quad p_{Aa} \approx p + q(1-q)[x_1 + ty_1/(2\sigma^2)](z/\sigma),$

$$p_{aa} \approx p + q^2[x_0 + ty_0/(2\sigma^2)](z/\sigma).$$

On substituting the values of the x's in terms of α's and of y's in terms of β's.

(5.140) $\quad p_A = q p_{AA} + (1-q)p_{Aa} = p - (1-q)\{(1-q)\alpha_1 + q\alpha_2$
$$+ [(1-q)\beta_1 + q\beta_2]t/(2\sigma^2)\}z/\sigma,$$

(5.141) $\quad \Delta q = \dfrac{p_A q}{p} - q = q(1-q)\{(1-q)\alpha_1 + q\alpha_2$
$$+ [(1-q)\beta_1 + q\beta_2]t/(2\sigma^2)\}z/p\sigma.$$

This becomes the same as (5.133) if $\alpha_2 = \alpha_1$, $\beta_2 = \beta_1$.

Consider first the case in which there are no differences in the means ($\alpha_1 = 0$, $\alpha_2 = 0$). If also $\beta_1 = 0$, $\beta_2 = 0$ there is, of course, no selection ($\Delta q = 0$). This is also true, irrespective of the values of the β's if just half the population is retained ($t/\sigma = 0$). If less than half the population is retained ($t/\sigma > 0$), there are four cases to consider: (1) The quantity $[(1-q)\beta_1 + q\beta_2]$ is positive for all q's between 0 and 1, in which case A approaches fixation ($\Delta q > 0$). (2) The quantity $[(1-q)\beta_1 + q\beta_2]$ is negative for all q's between 0 and 1, in which case a approaches fixation ($\Delta q < 0$). (3) There is stable equilibrium if $\beta_1 > 0$, $\beta_2 < 0$. (4) There is metastable equilibrium if $\beta_1 < 0$, $\beta_2 > 0$, and runaway change in q toward 0 below and toward 1 above.

If more than half the population is retained $(t/\sigma < 0)$, the situation in cases (1) and (2) is reversed and the same is true of cases (3) and (4).

The equilibrium point in cases (3) and (4) is given by

$$(5.142) \qquad \hat{q} = \beta_1/(\beta_1 - \beta_2).$$

If there are differences in the means and $[(1 - q)\alpha_1 + q\alpha_2]$ is positive for all values of q between 0 and 1, a tendency toward fixation of A is superimposed on the effects of the differences in variability. Similarly a tendency toward fixation of a is superimposed if $[(1 - q)\alpha_1 + q\alpha_2]$ is negative for all values of q between 0 and 1. If there is overdominance, $\alpha_1 > 0$, $\alpha_2 < 0$, a tendency toward stable equilibrium is superimposed, and if $\alpha_1 < 0$, $\alpha_2 > 0$, a tendency toward a runaway process is superimposed. These may be overcome by the situation with respect to variability. The general formula for the equilibrium point, stable or unstable, if it exists, is rather complicated.

$$(5.143) \qquad \hat{q} = [\alpha_1 + \beta_1 t/(2\sigma^2)]/[(\alpha_1 - \alpha_2) + (\beta_1 - \beta_2)t/(2\sigma^2)].$$

It may be noted, however, that it depends solely on the means if just half the population is retained $(t = 0)$.

The way in which selection at one locus effects that at another may be brought out by comparing the selection pressures from a certain overall intensity of selection, on any one of a considerable number of genes that have equal semidominant effects (each α) and equal frequencies (q_1) with selection on the same system, supplemented by a major semidominant factor, effect $k\alpha$, frequency q_2.

With only the n minor factors and nongenetic variance σ_E^2:

$$(5.144) \qquad \sigma_a^2 = 2n\alpha^2 q_1(1 - q_1) + \sigma_E^2,$$

$$(5.145) \qquad \begin{aligned} \Delta q_{1(a)} &= (z/p)q_1(1 - q_1)(\alpha/\sigma) \\ &= (z/p)q_1(1 - q_1)/\sqrt{[2nq_1(1 - q_1) + \sigma_E^2/\alpha^2]}. \end{aligned}$$

In the presence of the major factor:

$$(5.146) \qquad \sigma_b^2 = 2n\alpha^2 q_1(1 - q_1) + 2k^2\alpha^2 q_2(1 - q_2) + \sigma_E^2,$$

$$(5.147) \quad \Delta q_{1(b)} = (z/p)q_1(1 - q_1)/\sqrt{[2nq_1(1 - q_1) + 2k^2 q_2(1 - q_2) + \sigma_E^2/\alpha^2]},$$

$$(5.148) \quad \Delta q_{2(b)} = (z/p)kq_2(1 - q_2)/\sqrt{[2nq_1(1 - q_1) + 2k^2 q_2(1 - q_2) + \sigma_E^2/\alpha^2]}.$$

If the gene frequencies at the time of comparison are the same (as immediately after a cross between strains differing in all respects ($q_1 = q_2 = 0.50$), $\Delta q_2 = k \, \Delta q_1$. As selection proceeds, the more rapid approach of the major factor to fixation reduces the term $q_2(1 - q_2)$ and the ratio $\Delta q_2/\Delta q_1$ declines. Conversely, on starting from initial gene frequencies below 0.50, the ratio would rise at first. The main point here, however, is the effect of presence of the major factor on Δq_1. There is little effect if the variance is largely nongenetic. If wholly genetic, however, the ratio becomes $\sqrt{[n/(n + k^2)]}$ (if $q_2 = q_1$), which may be much less than in the absence of the major factor.

The value of $\Delta q_{1(a)}$ under complete determination by heredity $\Delta q_{1(a)} = (z/p)\sqrt{[q(1 - q)/2n]}$ implies a rather different course of evolution than where there is predominant nongenetic variability, approximately $(z/p)q(1 - q)(\alpha/\sigma_E)$. There is a more rapid rise from low frequencies and less tapering as fixation is approached. The course is much affected in any case if there is a mixture of major and minor factors, if initial gene frequencies are different, or if there is a mixture of genes with different degrees of dominance. General discussion of this topic will be deferred to volume 3.

The discussion in this section has been applied primarily to artificial selection of a particular quantitative character in cases in which natural selection is very slight. Under natural selection all characters contribute to the mean selective value $\bar{w}$. For application to natural selection, the α's and β's must be in terms of the contributions of the genes in question to the mean and variance of total selective value and can never really be constant, contrary to the assumption in chapter 3. In the simple case of semidominance for which the formula $\Delta q = sq(1 - q)$ with constant s was derived, the actual value of s is $(z/p)(\alpha/\sigma)$, which varies inversely with the standard deviation of selective values for all loci irrespective of the characters affected. There cannot be many loci with large momentary selection coefficients, s, in a natural population that is being selected simultaneously in many respects.

There have been other treatments of truncation selection. Griffing (1960a,b, 1962) has developed an elaborate theory that takes account of factor interaction and linkage.

Equilibrium Surfaces

It has been assumed so far in this chapter that interactive selection is so small compared with the amount of recombination that deviations from random combination may be ignored. Such deviations can, however, be allowed for, if necessary, in the same way as in chapter 4 for constant genotypic selective values. The simplest example is that in which competition between genotypes has no effect on the size of the population. Here $F(w/\bar{w}) = \bar{w}$ if the w's are constant. All of the "surfaces" dealt with in chapter 4 may be considered under the above condition as referring to $F(w/\bar{w})$, as well as to $\bar{w}$, but $\overline{W}$ becomes level (a horizontal line between $aabb$ and $AABB$ on the graphs).

Another sort of case (A) is that in which the absolute productivities of all genotypes are subject to the same function Ψ of particular genotypic frequencies, $W_i = w_i \Psi$. Assume that the relative selective values in case VII in chapter 4 are all multiplied by the factor $\Psi = (1 - f_{A,B})$ where $f_{A,B}$ is the frequency of genotypes carrying AB, giving full weight to $AABB$, half to $AABb$ and $AaBB$, and one fourth to $AaBb$.

$$f_{A,B} = f_{AB}^2 + f_{AB}(f_{Ab} + f_{aB}) + 0.5(f_{AB}f_{ab} + f_{Ab}f_{aB}),$$
$$(5.149) \quad f_{A,B} = f_{AB} - 0.5(f_{AB}f_{ab} - f_{Ab}f_{aB}),$$
$$f_{A,B} = pq \quad \text{if} \quad R = 1.$$

The selective values, w and W, are as follows, with $aabb$ in lower left and $AABB$ in upper right.

w (Case A)

1	1.5	2
1	1.25	1.5
1	1	1

W (Case A)

$(1 - f_{A,B})$	$1.5(1 - f_{A,B})$	$2(1 - f_{A,B})$
$(1 - f_{A,B})$	$1.25(1 - f_{A,B})$	$1.5(1 - f_{A,B})$
$(1 - f_{A,B})$	$(1 - f_{A,B})$	$(1 - f_{A,B})$

Table 5.7 gives the values for $\overline{W}$, $F(w/\bar{w})$, and other quantities under random combination ($R = 1$), in the absence of linkage ($c = 0.5$), and with complete linkage ($c = 0$). The curves for $F(w/\bar{w})$ and $\overline{W}$ are compared in Figure 5.15. The selective peak for $F(w/\bar{w})$ is at $p = q = 1$ at which its value is two while that of $\overline{W}$ is zero. The selective peak for $\overline{W}$ (value 1) is at the other extreme, $p = q = 0$. In a panmictic population, the type of individual that has an advantage in competition tends toward fixation (peak of $F(w/\bar{w})$) while the population on which it is having a severe deleterious effect is tending to extinction ($\overline{W} = 0$).

Case B is one in which the quasi-equilibrium surfaces of $F(w/\bar{w})$ and $\overline{W}$ differ, but not to such an extreme extent. Defining $f_{A,B}$ as above, $\overline{W}$ is here assumed to be proportional to $\bar{w}$, but $F(w/\bar{w})$ is not.

w (Case B)

1	$1 + 0.5(s - tf_{A,B})$	$1 + (s - tf_{A,B})$
1	$1 + 0.25(s - tf_{A,B})$	$1 + 0.5(s - tf_{A,B})$
1	1	1

If

$$(5.150) \quad R = 1, \quad \text{then} \quad f_{A,B} = pq, \quad \bar{w} = 1 + pq(s - tpq):$$

TABLE 5.7. Data on the quasi-equilibrium surfaces of mean absolute selective value ($\bar{W}$) and of the fitness function $F(w/\bar{w})$ in two cases of frequency dependent interaction, $R = 1$, $c = 0.5$, and $c = 0$ (Wright 1967).

		$R = 1$, $q = p$			$R = 1$, $q = 1 - p$			$c = 0.5$, $q = p$					$c = 0$, $q = p$	
CASE	p	f_{Ab}	$\bar{W}$	$F(w/\bar{w})$	Δp	$\bar{W}$	$F(w/\bar{w})$	f_{Ab}	$\bar{W}$	$F(w/\bar{w})$	R	k	$\bar{W}$	$F(w/\bar{w})$
A	0	0	1.000	1.000	0	1.000	1.000	0	1.000	1.000	1.67	0.400	1.000	1.000
	0.1	0.09	1.000	1.010	0.0045	0.992	1.090	.086	1.000	1.012	1.57	.400	0.997	1.055
	0.2	.16	0.998	1.040	.0160	0.974	1.160	.148	0.998	1.046	1.53	.400	0.986	1.120
	0.3	.21	0.992	1.090	.0318	0.956	1.210	.192	0.990	1.099	1.50	.400	0.962	1.195
	0.4	.24	0.974	1.160	.0493	0.942	1.240	.217	0.971	1.172	1.49	.400	0.922	1.280
	0.5	.25	0.938	1.250	.0666	0.938	1.250	.225	0.931	1.262	1.49	.400	0.859	1.375
	0.6	.24	0.870	1.360	.0828	0.942	1.240	.217	0.862	1.372	1.49	.400	0.770	1.480
	0.7	.21	0.760	1.490	.0967	0.956	1.210	.192	0.751	1.499	1.50	.400	0.646	1.595
	0.8	.16	0.590	1.640	.1085	0.974	1.160	.148	0.583	1.646	1.53	.400	0.482	1.720
	0.9	.09	0.344	1.810	.1178	0.992	1.090	.086	0.340	1.812	1.57	.400	0.269	1.855
	1.0	0	0	2.000	0	1.000	1.000	0	0	2.000	1.67	.400	0	2.000
B	0	0	1.000	1.000	0	1.000	1.000	0	1	—	1.67	.400	1.000	1.000
	0.1	.09	1.010	1.010	.0041	1.074	1.079	.086	1.012	—	1.56	.396	1.054	1.053
	0.2	.16	1.037	1.038	.0142	1.109	1.127	.149	1.042	—	1.50	.381	1.108	1.110
	0.3	.21	1.074	1.079	.0241	1.122	1.155	.194	1.079	—	1.43	.354	1.160	1.168
	0.4	.24	1.109	1.127	.0294	1.125	1.170	.222	1.112	—	1.37	.313	1.190	1.222
	0.5	.25	1.125	1.174	.0278	1.125	1.174	.234	1.125	—	1.29	.255	1.188	1.269
	0.6	.24	1.101	1.213	.0183	1.122	1.170	.230	1.099	—	1.18	.172	1.134	1.305
	0.7	.21	1.010	1.231	.0015	1.109	1.155	.209	1.009	—	1.02	.015	1.012	1.321
	0.8	.16	0.821	1.209	-0.0218	1.074	1.127	.165	0.825	—	0.81	-.226	0.726	1.302
	0.9	0.09	0.498	1.089	-0.0504	1.074	1.079	0.093	0.501	—	0.67	-.456	0.470	1.204
	1.0	0	0	$-\infty$	0	1.000	1.000	0	0	—	0.60	-0.667	0	$-\infty$

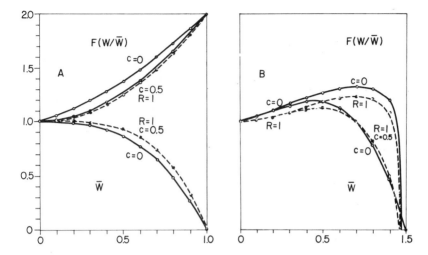

FIG. 5.15. Comparisons of the surfaces of $F(w/\bar{w})$ and $\overline{W}$ along the diagonal between $aabb$ and $AABB$ with random combination ($R = 1$) and with no linkage ($c = 0.5$) or complete linkage ($c = 0$) in two cases of frequency dependent selection. In that at the left, the relative selective values are as in case VII in chapter 4, but the absolute values are multiplied by a common factor $\psi = 1 - f_{A,B}$ while that at the right is one in which the surfaces $F(w/\bar{w})$ and $\overline{W}$ differ less radically, as described in the text.

$$(5.151) \quad F(w/\bar{w}) = \int \sum (w/\bar{w}) \frac{\partial f}{\partial p}\, dp = \int \frac{q(s - tpq)}{1 + spq - tp^2q^2}\, dp,$$

$$(5.152) \quad F(w/\bar{w}) = C + \frac{1}{\lambda_2 - \lambda_1} [\lambda_2 \log (pq - \lambda_1) - \lambda_1 \log (\lambda_2 - pq)],$$

where

$$(5.153) \quad \begin{aligned} &\lambda_1 = [s - \sqrt{(s^2 + 4t)}]/2t, \qquad \lambda_2 = [s + \sqrt{(s^2 + 4t)}]/2t, \\ &\Delta p = 0.5p(1 - p)q(s - tpq)/\bar{w}. \end{aligned}$$

If

$$(5.154) \quad s = 1, \qquad t = 2, \qquad \bar{w} = 1 + pq(1 - 2pq):$$

$$(5.155) \quad F(w/\bar{w}) = 1 + (1/3) \log (1 - pq) + (2/3) \log (1 + 2pq).$$

The nature of the surface along both diagonals under the assumption of random combination is indicated by the data in Table 5.7 and Figure 5.15. The values of $\overline{W}$ for $c = 0.5$ are also given in Table 5.7 but do not differ enough from those under random combinations to be distinguishable in

Figure 5.15, although there is appreciable deviation of the frequencies from random combination. The values for both $\overline{W}$ and $F(w/\bar{w})$, the latter calculated from the slopes, are given for $c = 0$, $p = q$ in both table 5.7 and Figure 5.15.

The peaks of the surfaces for intrademe selection ($F(w/\bar{w})$) and interdeme selection ($\overline{W}$) differ much less than in the preceding case. With $R = 1$, that for $F(w/\bar{w})$ comes at $q = p = \sqrt{0.5} = 0.707$ and cannot differ appreciably with any value of c between 0 and 0.5, while that for $\overline{W}$ with $R = 1$ comes at $q = p = 0.50$ and can be only slightly less with values of c down to 0.

Selective Value a Function of Population Density

The selective values of genotypes are as already noted undoubtedly often affected by the density of the population. Only a very simple case will be considered here, that in which the selective values of a pair of alleles vary as a linear function of density (N) (Wright 1960a).

	Gene	f	W
(5.156)	A	q	$1 + s_1 - t_1 N$
	a	$1 - q$	$1 - s_0 + t_0 N$

$$(5.157) \qquad \overline{W} = 1 - (s_0 - t_0 N) + [(s_0 + s_1) - (t_0 + t_1)N]q,$$

$$(5.158) \qquad \Delta q = q(1 - q)[(s_0 + s_1) - (t_0 + t_1)N]/\overline{W}.$$

There is a critical value of N at $(s_0 + s_1)/(t_0 + t_1)$. Selection tends to keep the population close to fixation of A as long as density is below this value but to bring about loss of A if this value is passed, and vice versa.

It was assumed above that changes in density are not themselves functions of the frequency at this locus. But the rate of population growth depends on the mean absolute selective value of the genome as a whole ($\overline{W}_T$) under given environmental conditions, $\Delta N/N = \overline{W}_T - 1$. If the extreme assumption is made that W_T depends only on the locus in question:

$$(5.159) \qquad \Delta N/N = [(s_0 + s_1) - (t_0 + t_1)N]q - (s_0 - t_0 N).$$

Thus the selective values vary with gene frequency in a complicated way. Nevertheless,

$$\Delta q = q(1 - q) \sum \left(W \frac{\partial f}{\partial q} \right) \bigg/ \overline{W}$$

gives (5.158).

If the density N, at which $\Delta N/N = 0$ for $q = 1$ is less than that at which $\Delta q = 0$, $(s_0/t_0) > (s_1/t_1)$, the density and fixation of A tends to be maintained and to be restored after wide deviations in N and q. If, however, N

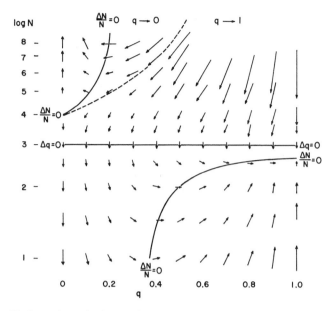

FIG. 5.16. Trajectories relative to log N and q in a special case in which the selective values are a function of population density (N) and rate of change of density depends wholly on the gene in question ($\Delta N/N = \overline{W} - 1$), as described in the text.

and q are above a certain functional relation, there is a runaway loss of A and an increase of N until the latter is dampened by some process not here considered.

Figure 5.16 illustrates this situation in a special case. N is to be taken as the density in a small unit area rather than as an absolute number. Its logarithm is plotted against gene frequency.

Gene	f	W
A	q	$1.02 - 0.0075N$
a	$1 - q$	$0.99 + 0.0025N$

$$\overline{W} = 1 - (0.01 - 0.0025N) + (0.03 - 0.01N)q,$$

$$\frac{\Delta N}{N} = (0.03 - 0.01N)q - (0.01 - 0.0025N),$$

$$\Delta q \approx q(1 - q)[0.03 - 0.01N].$$

Since $\Delta q = 0$ if $N = 3$ and this is larger than the value of N ($= 2.667$) at which $\Delta N/N = 0$ for $q = 1$, the condition for stable N at 2.667 is met.

The arrows indicate trajectories of the system log N, q. All sets to the right and below the broken line ultimately reach fixation of A at $N = 2.667$, while all sets to the left and above this line ultimately reach fixation of a at an indefinitely large value of N. It may be seen that populations with density as great as 8 and gene frequency q as small as 0.5 decline rapidly in both number and gene frequency, but at some value below $N = 2.667$, q begins to rise and later N rises to the equilibrium value at $q = 1$.

If $\Delta N/N = 0$ for $q = 1$ at a greater value of N than that at which $\Delta q = 0$ (for all N's), there is no equilibrium value of N. At first N declines in association with decline of q if both N and q are sufficiently large or N declines and q rises if both are sufficiently small, but ultimately there is a runaway process of increasing N as q approaches 0. The condition is that $(s_O/t_O) < (s_1/t_1)$.

CHAPTER 6

Selection and Cytoplasmic Heredity

General Formulas

Although the number of cases of non-Mendelian heredity that have been studied is now large, they still appear to play a very minor role in the variability of most characters. Since the modes of transmission are highly diverse (vol. 1, chap. 4), and often not understood, it has not seemed practicable to discuss more than a few examples.

The effect of selection on the frequencies of alternative cytoplasmic factors that are transmitted regularly and exclusively by the female parent is, of course, the same as for clones or for a semidominant gene in a diploid population. With selective advantage, s, of the factor with frequency q, the rate of change of the latter is

$$(6.1) \qquad \Delta q = sq(1 - q)/\bar{w}.$$

Similarly, if there is mutation of the favorable to the unfavorable alternative at the rate v per generation, there is equilibrium at approximately

$$(6.2) \qquad \hat{q} = v/s.$$

Actual cases are apt to be more complicated. There may be a number of entities of the alternative sorts, apportioned more or less at random at cell division. Apparent "mutation" of the character may depend on chance segregation of these alternatives to the daughter cells. There is a stochastic process which will be discussed later in connection with gene frequencies in small populations. Some chlorophyl variegations have been interpreted in this way but without general acceptance. Perhaps the clearest case is that of the mutation of normal yeast to a type which lacks respiratory enzymes and which in consequence produces small colonies in the presence of oxygen (Ephrussi 1953).

Nucleo-cytoplasmic Incompatibility

An important class of cases is that in which there is incompatibility between a certain genome and a certain kind of cytoplasm. Watson and Caspari (1960) worked out the dynamics where there are different degrees of pollen sterility of a recessive in two alternative cytoplasms each transmitted regularly in the female line. The discussion here will be largely restricted to the relatively simple case of the type of pollen sterility found in flax by Gairdner (1929) in which it occurred in descendants of a cross between two strains, "tall" $(T)ff$ and "procumbent" $(P)FF$, whenever there was segregation of ff in a plant which traced to procumbent in the straight female line. The formulation here' will be of the sort used elsewhere in this book rather than that used by Watson and Caspari.

Under the assumption that all ovules are fertilized, there is no tendency for the frequencies of the two kinds of cytoplasm in the array $[(1 - s)(T) + s(P)]$ to change in a panmictic population. The gene frequencies may differ in the two cytoplasms initially but the origin of half of the genes of the oogonia from the pollen in each generation insures rapid approach to identity of gene frequencies in the cytoplasms. This being the case the dynamics soon become essentially the same as that of unequal selection in the sexes, discussed in chapter 3.

It will be assumed here that the ovule array has become $[(1 - q_o)F + q_of]$ in both cytoplasms. The frequency array in the pollen $[(1 - q_p)F + q_pf]$ is different because of the pollen sterility of $(P)ff$, if this is present. Random pollination gives the product array in the offspring. Thus their ovule array is $[(1 - \bar{q})F + \bar{q}f]$ where $\bar{q} = 0.5(q_o + q_p)$. The absence of pollen from those of composition $(P)ff$ implies the pollen array:

$$\frac{(1 - \bar{q})}{1 - sq_oq_p} F + \frac{\bar{q} - sq_oq_p}{1 - sq_oq_p} f.$$

On averaging the frequencies in ovules and pollen, the change in mean gene frequency comes out:

$$(6.3) \qquad \Delta\bar{q} = \frac{2\bar{q} - s(1 - \bar{q})q_oq_p}{2(1 - sq_oq_p)} - \bar{q} = -\frac{s(1 - \bar{q})q_oq_p}{2(1 - sq_oq_p)}.$$

An approximation can be obtained by averaging the selection coefficients of the sexes, giving $s/2$ for that against ff, $\bar{w} = 1 - 0.5s\bar{q}^2$, and $\Delta\bar{q} = -s\bar{q}^2(1 - \bar{q})/2\bar{w}$. This does not differ appreciably from equation (6.3) if q_o and q_p have become fairly small or the procumbent cytoplasm is rare.

Table 6.1 shows the values of q_o, q_p, $\bar{q}$, and $\Delta\bar{q}$ for ten generations on starting from $(P)Ff$ derivable by crossing $(P)FF \times (T)ff$. Here $s = 1$ and

TABLE 6.1. Frequency of gene f in ovules (q_o), pollen (q_p), and average, $\bar{q}$; and change, $\Delta\bar{q}$, to the next generation of gene f, starting from F_1 of the cross $P(FF) \times T(ff)$ and assuming pollen sterility of $(P)ff$.

	q_o	q_p	$\bar{q}$	$\Delta\bar{q}$
0	0.5000	0.5000	0.5000	0.0833
1	.5000	.3333	.4167	.0583
2	.4167	.3000	.3583	.0458
3	.3583	.2667	.3125	.0363
4	.3125	.2399	.2762	.0293
5	.2762	.2175	.2469	.0241
6	.2469	.1987	.2228	.0200
7	.2228	.1827	.2027	.0169
8	.2027	.1689	.1858	.0144
9	.1858	.1570	.1714	.0124
10	0.1714	0.1465	0.1589	0.0108

$q_o = q_p = 0.5$ at first. On starting from the array $[(1 - s)(T) + s(P)]$ the rate of decrease of the frequency of f would be s times as great.

The results differ only in rate in the case of pollen sterility due to conjunction of a cytoplasmic factor and any sort of genome. There would be no selective effect on the frequencies of alternative cytoplasms if all ovules are equally likely to be fertilized, whereas the gene or gene system that is involved would be selected against as long as any male steriles are produced.

Grun and Aubertin (1965) have found considerable numbers of dominant (In) as well as recessive genes that give male sterility with specific cytoplasms $[In^s]$, and also dominant restorers of normal male fertility, in particular cases among South American species of *Solanum*. In a mixed population with the proportion p of the sensitive cytoplasm, and q for the frequency of sensitive gene, in this case the dominant allele, the array of eggs produced in the offspring generation is $[(1 - \bar{q})in + \bar{q}In]$. Plants with $[In^s]$ cytoplasm produce pollen only if of genotype $in\ in$. The pollen array is

$$[(1 - \bar{q} + 0.5p\bar{q})in + (\bar{q} - 0.5p\bar{q})In]$$

(6.4) $$\Delta q = -0.5p\bar{q}.$$

On starting from the cross $[In^s]in\ in \times [in^n]In\ In$, all F_1's are pollen sterile. In a population starting from fertilization of these by in pollen, gene In is lost at the rate of 50% per generation. With an equal mixture of reciprocal crosses the rate of loss is half as great.

The authors held that mutations in cytoplasm and gene could establish partial isolation between populations where there was limited diffusion. This was investigated by Caspari, Watson, and Smith (1966), by a computer study. Since they considered the case in which a gene causing self-sterility in an incompatible cytoplasm is recessive, I will return to the symbolism used with the strains of flax. They assumed three populations $I = (T)ff$, $III = (P)FF$, and II an equal mixture of reciprocal F_1's. With no migration, populations I and III remained constant, while II retained 50% of both cytoplasms but eliminated gene f, as expected from the theory. With equal migration into II from I and III, but with no back migration, the computer study showed equal persistence of both cytoplasms in II, but attainment of a balance between immigration and the tendency to lose f, which was different in the two cytoplasms. Population II was assumed to consist in each genera-tion of m immigrants from each of the others and thus $(1 - 2m)$ from random mating of the preceding generation, where m was 20%, 10%, or 5% in three tests.

TABLE 6.2. Proportion of allele f in the two cytoplasms at equilibrium in population II at three levels of immigration (Caspari, Watson, and Smith 1966).

m	Generations	Frequency of f in	
		(T)	(P)
20%	10	0.6244	0.3384
10%	20	0.5157	0.3491
5%	40	0.4032	0.3121

In another computer series, II was assumed to derive 20% per generation from both I and III, but the latter each derived 5% from II. In 100 genera-tions, all three populations had reached practically the same composition. The cytoplasms were about 50% of each sort and f was approaching elimina-tion in all, the frequencies in I and III differing very little from II with 90.8% FF, 9.0% Ff, and 0.2% ff. There was no indication of an isolating effect on the male sterility.

In a final series, asymmetrical migration was assumed: 10% of II from I, none back; 30% of II from III, 10% back. Population I of course remained constant, $(T)ff$. Cytoplasm (P) gradually decreased in frequency in the others (more rapidly in II). The frequency of f fell off at first from initial 50% in both cytoplasms but more rapidly in (P) than in (T). Later, as (T) increased in frequency because of migration from I, gene f rose in frequency in association, and more in II than in III. The results were reported at

TABLE 6.3. Proportions of two cytoplasms and of gene f in populations II and III under asymmetrical migration, 10% of II from I, none back, 30% of II from III, 10% back (Caspari, Watson, and Smith 1966).

Population	Generation	(T)	f in (T)	(P)	f in (P)
I	—	1.000	1.000	0	
II	0	0.500	0.500	0.500	0.500
	50	0.742	0.473	0.258	0.405
	100	0.910	0.600	0.090	0.559
III	0	0	0	1.000	1.000
	50	0.674	0.317	0.326	0.308
	100	0.886	0.489	0.114	0.484

generations 50 and 100. It appears that the end result would be 100% $(T)ff$ in all three populations.

Complete sterility or lethality due to conjunction of a cytoplasmic factor and some genome would result in selection against both in a mixed population.

Two populations which had developed different cytoplasms and different genomes, which reciprocally yield completely sterile or lethal F_1's on meeting, would of course be completely isolated genetically. If, however, the pertinent genes are recessive there would merely be rapid elimination of the foreign cytoplasms within the two strains because of backcrossing, very slight selection against the introgressive recessive genes as long as their frequencies were low, and no selection against independently segregating ones not involved in the incompatibility.

An interesting special case is that of unidirectional incompatibility of crosses between many local strains of mosquitoes, but bidirectional incompatibility in others, all morphologically Culex pipiens. One case, analyzed with great thoroughness by Laven (1959), was between a North German strain from Hamburg (Ha), and a South German one from Oggelshausen (Og). The cross Og ♀ × Ha ♂ gave only inviable embryos (apart from some 0.2% parthenogenetic Og daughters) while Ha ♀ × Og ♂ offspring were of normal viability. Laven backcrossed the latter for 60 consecutive generations, achieving homozygosis of all three Og chromosomes as far as could be determined from genetic markers; yet males still produced only inviable embryos on mating with Og females. He interpreted this as indicating transmission along the straight female line of an Ha factor, presumably cytoplasmic, to sons as well as daughters, which caused the sperms of the former to be incompatible with Og-carrying eggs. On the other hand, the Og factor in sperms of Og males does not give incompatibility with Ha-carrying eggs.

Laven noted that a single mutation to the *Ha* factor in a female of an *Og* population would ultimately completely displace the *Og* factor because of the unidirectional sterility and that the occurrence of a different mutation in another *Og* population which similarly displaced the *Og* factor might be reciprocally incompatible with *Ha*, established in the first population, and thus bring about genetic isolation of these two populations.

TABLE 6.4. Rise in frequency of *Ha* in one generation p_1 from initial p_0 and number of generations for fixation. Frequency of associated gene *C* after one and many generations in *Ha* cytoplasm, (q), and altogether, pq.

FREQUENCY OF *Ha*		GENERA- TION	FREQUENCY OF C IN (*Ha*)			OVERALL FREQUENCY OF *C*		
p_0	p_1	$p = 1$	q_0	q_1	q	$p_0 q_0$	$p_1 q_1$	pq
0.900	0.989	3	1	0.950	0.945	0.900	0.940	0.945
.500	.667	5	1	.750	.574	.500	.500	.574
.400	.526	7	1	.700	.426	.400	.368	.426
.300	.380	7	1	.650	.255	.300	.247	.255
.200	.238	10	1	.600	.089	.200	.108	.089
0.100	0.110	15	1	0.550	0.003	0.100	0.060	0.003

In a mixed population with low frequency of (*Ha*), frequency rises slowly at first but later rather rapidly to 100% (15 generations if $p_0 = 10\%$). The frequency of gene *C* initially associated with *Ha* falls off rapidly from crosses with initially numerous (*Og*)cc individuals and is almost wholly displaced in a few generations. It is not wholly displaced, however, even if initial p_0 was as low as 10%. The overall frequency of *C* declines from an initially low value.

If the initial frequency of (*Ha*) is 36% it requires only 7 generations to reach 100%, but the frequency of gene *C* within (*Ha*) declines from 100% to 36% at the end. The overall frequency of *C* starting from 36% ends at the same frequency but only after declining to 31.1% by the second generation.

If (*Ha*) has a high initial frequency, it reaches 100% very soon and the frequency of *C* within it, or overall, declines relatively little.

Og cytoplasm may have a selective advantage over *Ha* cytoplasm that counterbalances the tendency to elimination. If this is measured by s and the initial frequency of *Ha* is greater than $s/(1 + s)$, *Og* will still be eliminated but if less it is *Ha* that is eliminated.

The evolutionary significance of this case has been discussed by Caspari and Watson (1959) as well as by Laven.

CHAPTER 7

Inbreeding

It has long been known that close inbreeding has effects on populations that are independent of those of selection. Various ways of dealing with mating systems for the purpose of comparison were devised before the attempt to give a Mendelian interpretation.

Pearl (1917) devised a "coefficient of inbreeding" based on the ratio of actual to maximum possible number of different ancestors in the ancestral generations, and designed to be independent of any theory of heredity, including the Mendelian. In accomplishing this, however, it yielded the same value for systems of mating, known to give very different results experimentally. Figure 7.1 compares three systems in which there are just four ancestors in all generations from the grandparents back to the beginning. The first (double-first-cousin mating) is a system of rather close inbreeding which tends to bring about the fixation of some random combination of genes and reduction in vigor. In the second, the individuals in question are the products of a cross between two independent lines that have long been maintained under brother-sister mating. Such crossbreds exhibit much heterosis. The third, the system under which most hybrid corn has been produced, brings together four self-fertilized lines. In such lines, heterozygosis is lost about three times as rapidly as under brother-sister mating. The four-strain hybrids are extraordinarily vigorous.

Pearl recognized this difficulty and attempted to supplement his inbreeding coefficient by one designed to bring out the proportion due to relationship between the parents. There was no assurance, however, that it did this in a way that was quantitatively related to experimental results.

Self-fertilization

The Mendelian theory had already been applied by Mendel himself (1866) to the case of continued self-fertilization. In this case it is immediately obvious that initiation of exclusive self-fertilization in a population of diploids is followed by a 50% reduction of the amount of heterozygosis per generation

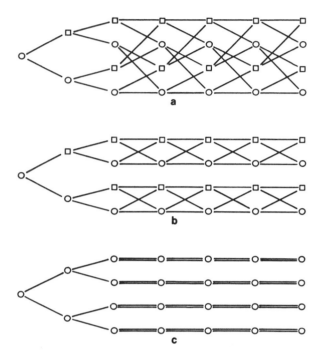

FIG. 7.1. Comparison of three mating systems in which individuals have four ancestors in each of many generations back of the parents: a (top) double-first-cousin mating, b (middle) cross between sib-mated lines, c (bottom) double crosses from four self-fertilized lines (Wright 1951, Fig. 1, reprinted by permission, Cambridge University Press).

at all loci since homozygotes produce only their own kind and heterozygotes produce only 50% of their kind. This leads in ten generations to a reduction of the initial amount to 0.1%.

The situation is more complicated at polysomic loci. Haldane (1930c) represented the symmetrical case in tetraploids as

$$p_n A^4 : q_n A^3 a : r_n A^2 a^2 : q_n A a^3 : p_n a^4,$$

where $2p_n + 2q_n + r_n = 1$. Disregarding double reduction, he showed that:

$$p_{n+1} = p_n + (1/4)q_n + (1/36)r_n,$$

(7.1) $$q_{n+1} = (1/2)q_n + (2/9)r_n,$$

$$r_{n+1} = (1/2)q_n + (1/2)r_n;$$

(7.2) $z_{n+1} = (5/6)z_n$ where $z_n = (3q_n + 2r_n)$.

For hexaploids, $p_n A^6 : q_n A^5 a : r_n A^4 a^2 : s_n A^3 a^3 : r_n A^2 a^4 : q_n A a^5 : p_n a^6$.

$$p_{n+1} = p_n + (1/4)q_n + (1/25)r_n + (1/400)s_n,$$

(7.3)
$$q_{n+1} = \quad (1/2)q_n + (6/25)r_n + (9/200)s_n,$$
$$r_{n+1} = \quad (1/4)q_n + (12/25)r_n + (99/400)s_n,$$
$$s_{n+1} = \quad (12/25)r_n + (41/100)s_n;$$

(7.4) $$z_{n+1} = (9/10)z_n \quad \text{where} \quad z_n = (10q_n + 16r_n + 9s_n).$$

After a few generations, the declining frequencies of each type of hetero-zygote approximate a geometric series whose successive terms are in the ratio $5:6$ in the case of tetraploids and $9:10$ in hexaploids.

Analysis from Matrix of Mating Types

The first attempt at mathematical analysis of the effects of brother-sister mating was that of Pearl (1913) who pointed out that the cross $AA \times aa$, giving 100% heterozygotes in F_1, gives 50% in both F_2 and F_3. He erro-neously concluded that no further change occurs. This was independently challenged by Jennings (1914) and Fish (1914) whose papers, however, followed a correction by Pearl himself (1914). My own first encounter with this sort of problem was in assisting Fish in his analysis.

The method followed was to make a table of the proportions of matings of each type that would be made at random among the offspring of each type (see Table 7.1).

The proportions of the various types of mating in successive generations could easily be calculated from any initial array, and from these the successive amounts of heterozygosis. For lines derived from a cross ($p = q$ and $s = t$) this led to the series 1, 1/2, 2/4, 3/8, 5/16, 8/32, 13/64, etc. in which each numerator is the sum of the two preceding numerators (Fibonacci series) if the denominator is doubled in each generation.

Path analysis (Wright 1921), devised for a wholly different purpose, was found to give the same result more simply and to be much more capable of extension to systems of mating in general. Before considering this, however, it will be desirable to go briefly into a development of the mating-type method that considerably extended its scope.

Bartlett and Haldane (1934) showed that on excluding the fixed offspring matings ($AA \times AA$, $aa \times aa$) from the matrix (Table 7.1), the characteristic equation of its determinant gave the general solution for any generation:

$$\begin{pmatrix} -\lambda & 0 & 0 & 1/8 \\ 0 & 1/2 - \lambda & 0 & 1/4 \\ 0 & 0 & 1/2 - \lambda & 1/4 \\ 0 & 1/4 & 1/4 & 1/4 - \lambda \end{pmatrix} = 0;$$

TABLE 7.1. Matrix of parental and offspring matings under brother-sister mating.

OFFSPRING MATINGS		PARENTAL MATINGS					
Genotypes	Frequency	$AA \times AA$	$aa \times aa$	$AA \times aa$	$AA \times Aa$	$Aa \times aa$	$Aa \times Aa$
$AA \times AA$	$p_{n+1} =$	p			$+ (1/4)s$		$+ (1/16)u$
$aa \times aa$	$q_{n+1} =$		q			$+ (1/4)t$	$+ (1/16)u$
$AA \times aa$	$r_{n+1} =$						$+ (1/8)u$
$AA \times Aa$	$s_{n+1} =$				$(1/2)s$		$+ (1/4)u$
$Aa \times aa$	$t_{n+1} =$					$(1/2)t$	$+ (1/4)u$
$Aa \times Aa$	$u_{n+1} =$			r	$+ (1/4)s$	$+ (1/4)t$	$+ (1/4)u$
Total	$1 =$	p	$+ \quad q$	$+ \quad r$	$+ \quad s$	$+ \quad t$	$+ \quad u$

(7.5)

(7.6) $\lambda^4 - (5/4)\lambda^3 + (1/4)\lambda^2 + (1/8)\lambda - (1/32) = 0.$

The roots are $\lambda_1 = (1/4)[1 + \sqrt{5}], \lambda_2 = (1/2), \lambda_3 = (1/4), \lambda_4 = (1/4)[1 - \sqrt{5}]$.

In such a system, $r_n = a_1\lambda_1{}^n + a_2\lambda_2{}^n + a_3\lambda_3{}^n + a_4\lambda_4{}^n$, and similarly with s, t, and u where the a's are constants that depend on the initial conditions. The mode of determining the a's was discussed by Haldane (1937a) in connection with sib mating with four alleles. In this paper he combined matings of similar type, giving a 6×6 determinant. In a later paper (1955), he noted that there actually are 55 kinds of matings, which, however, involved only two additional roots different from those above, $-1/8$ and $-1/4$.

In Bartlett and Haldane's 1934 paper, this method was applied to sib mating at a tetrasomic locus. They obtained $\lambda_1 = 0.92356$ as the largest root of the octic characteristic equation (2 alleles). In 1935 they worked out the consequences of forced heterozygosis at a linked locus in systems with one to three individuals, a subject discussed in chapter 10.

An elaborate exposition of this method and application to sib mating in diploids and tetraploids, double-first-cousin mating, and other simple systems, all but one of which had been worked out previously, was presented by Fisher (1949). Since his widely used book makes no reference to previous treatments of the subject (including much more complicated cases) and thus may have led some to suppose that these were unsound, it may be well to note that his method was essentially identical with that of Bartlett and Haldane and his results for λ were all the same as ones previously obtained by others (cf. Lush 1950) except that he analyzed the case of parent-offspring mating in tetraploids for the first time.

The Fixation Index F

In a panmictic population, there is no correlation between homologous genes of uniting gametes relative to the gene frequencies in the whole population. On splitting up into small lines which breed within themselves, a correlation between uniting gametes is to be expected. This suggests description of population structure in general and the effects of inbreeding in particular by means of the correlations expected under Mendelian heredity. This point of view makes the method of analyzing correlations by path analysis available (cf. chap. 2).

Consider first a pair of autosomal genes with the frequency array $(1 - q)a + qA$. Let y be the proportion of heterozygotes. The pattern of union of gametes may be presented in the form of a 2×2 correlations table (Table 7.2). It will be assumed that this is symmetrical. The values assigned alleles

TABLE 7.2

G_2 G_1	a	A	Total	
A	$y/2$	$q - y/2$	q	$\bar{G} = q$
a	$1 - q - y/2$	$y/2$	$1 - q$	$\sigma_G^2 = q(1 - q)$
Total	$1 - q$	q	1	

are irrelevant but are most conveniently taken as 0 and 1 for a and A, respectively.

(7.7) $$r_{12} = [q - y/2 - q^2]/[q(1 - q)] = 1 - y/y_0,$$

where

$$y_0 = 2q(1 - q).$$

If there is panmixia, $y = y_0 = 2q(1 - q)$ and $r_{12} = 0$. If there is complete fixation in all lines but the same gene frequency and thus the array $(1 - q)aa + qAA$, then $y = 0$, $r_{12} = 1$. If there are only heterozygotes, as in a balanced lethal population, $y = 1$, $q = 1/2$, $r_{12} = -1$. The symbol F (fixation index) is used for this correlation between uniting gametes. It was used first (in the form f, Wright 1921) in studies of inbreeding and of assortative mating (for $q = 1/2$). Later (Wright 1922a,b) it was given for any q, and the proposal was made that it be used in a narrower sense as a "coefficient of inbreeding." It should be clear from the context whether F is being used in the broad or narrow sense.

It is often convenient to use a single symbol for the amount of heterozygosis relative to that in the foundation stock, $y/y_0 = 1 - F$. The symbol P, "panmictic index," will be used for this purpose (Wright 1951).

A symbol α, proposed by Bernstein (1930) is identical in meaning with F.

Table 7.3 compares the composition of a panmictic population $P = 1$, $F = 0$ at the left, a population with the same gene frequencies but one in which all subpopulations are completely fixed ($P = 0$, $F = 1$) at the right, and three algebraically equivalent expressions for an intermediate case, with the same gene frequencies. The first of the latter is in terms of deviations from panmixia, the third in terms of deviations from complete fixation of each subpopulation, and the middle one is a weighted average.

Inbreeding Relative to a Foundation Stock

As brought out in chapter 2, the arbitrary assignment of additive values to the representatives of a locus permits use of path analysis in dealing with

TABLE 7.3. The frequencies of zygotes from a pair of alleles under (1) panmixia, (2) an intermediate degree of inbreeding, and (3) complete fixation without change of gene frequency. The intermediate condition is expressed in three equivalent ways in terms of the inbreeding coefficient F and the panmictic index P ($= 1 - F$) (Wright 1951).

Genotype	(1) PANMIXIA ($r = 0$) Frequency	INTERMEDIATE ($r = F$)			(3) COMPLETE FIXATION ($r = 1$) Frequency
		(2a) Deviation from Panmixia Frequency	(2b) Weighted Average Frequency	(2c) Deviation from Fixation Frequency	
AA	q^2	$q^2 \quad + Fq(1-q)$	$Pq^2 \quad + Fq$	$q \qquad -Pq(1-q)$	q
Aa	$2q(1-q)$	$2q(1-q) - 2Fq(1-q)$	$2Pq(1-q)$	$2Pq(1-q)$	
aa	$(1-q)^2$	$(1-q)^2 + Fq(1-q)$	$P(1-q)^2 + F(1-q)$	$(1-q) - Pq(1-q)$	$(1-q)$
	1	$1 \qquad 0$	$P + F = 1$	$1 \qquad 0$	1

Consider the case of an autosomal disomic locus. Let $a = p_{ZG}$ be coefficient relating a zygote (as the sum of gametic values) to the genes that unite to produce it. Let $b = p_{GZ'}$ be the path co-lating a gene in a gamete to the zygote that produced it. The zygote is a compound variable, but is transitive with respect to gametes that are drawn from it at random. Let F be the correlation between uniting genes. Primes are used here and later to indicate preceding generations.

Since Z is determined equally by the component genes (Fig. 7.2),

$$a_1 = a_2 = a.$$

The correlation between zygote and one of these genes may be seen to be as follows, on tracing the connecting paths:

$$r_{ZG_1} = r_{ZG_2} = a + aF.$$

The equation expressing complete determination is:

$$\sum p_{ZG} r_{ZG} = 2a^2 + 2a^2 F = 1.$$

Thus

(7.8) $$a = \sqrt{\frac{1}{2(1 + F)}}.$$

Assuming that there is no intervening selection, the correlation between zygote, Z', and one of the randomly segregating genes, G, must be the same as that between such zygotes and one of the genes that united to produce it.

(7.9) $$r_{GZ'} = b = r_{Z'G'} = a'(1 + F') = \sqrt{[0.5(1 + F')]}.$$

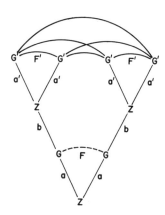

FIG. 7.2. Path diagram for autosomal heredity (redrawn from Wright 1921, I, Fig. 1).

Note that the compound path coefficient ba' relating a gene in one generation to one in the preceding always has the value 0.5, irrespective of the amount of inbreeding. This reflects the fact that there is an even chance that the gene G is identical with G', by descent, recalling the relation between a path regression and the corresponding probability, discussed in volume 1, chapter 13.

Let A be a common ancestor to which two genes such as G_1 and G_2 trace through wholly independent paths and thus through two different gametes. The coefficients relating these to the zygote A have the value $b_A = \sqrt{[0.5(1 + F_A)]}$, where F_A is the inbreeding coefficient of A.

Assume that there are n zygotes in the compound path $G_1 - A - G_2$. The contribution of this path to F is thus $0.5^{n-1}b_A^2 = 0.5^n(1 + F_A)$.

Genes G_1 and G_2 may be connected by other compound paths of this sort (paths that do not pass through any zygote more than once). Thus:

$$(7.10) \qquad F = \sum [0.5^n(1 + F_A)]$$

where the summation is with respect to all such paths (Wright 1922a).

The symbol F is to be interpreted as the correlation between pairs of homologous genes in the class of uniting gametes that trace in the way indicated by the pedigree to the foundation stock, relative to the array of genes at any neutral locus in this stock. It has, of course, no relevance to loci that are homallelic. When F is derived in this way it may be referred to as pedigree F.

The relativity referred to above has sometimes been overlooked or misinterpreted (Fisher 1949, p. 43). A correlation coefficient is, of course, always relative. It is a property of the population as well as of the two variables. In the case of F as an inbreeding coefficient, relating to all heterallelic neutral loci, its primary function is that of a parameter in the specification of population structure. This is still largely true in other applications in which the peculiarities of a particular locus to which it pertains are important.

There may seem to be a difficulty in the likelihood that the foundation stock may be itself more or less inbred relative to a more remote stock. If, however, there is any heterallelism in the foundation stock in neutral loci, average F of a later period measures the correlation between uniting gametes relative to the array of gene frequencies at such loci, and the decline in heterozygosis relative to an immediate panmictic derivative of the foundation stock. It does not necessarily measure the decline relative to the actual heterozygosis. The foundation stock might conceivably consist of a mixture of homallelic lines ($F = 1$). If the initial matings are made at random, F falls at once to zero and then, on breeding wholly within the stock, gradually rises. It is the decline in heterozygosis that occurs during such a rise in F that is measured.

Malécot (1948) has pointed out that the formula for pedigree F may be interpreted as the probability that the two genes in question are identical by descent from the foundation stock. This holds because the compound path coefficient, $ba' = 0.5$, is interpretable as the probability of identity by descent of a gene with one of those back of it a generation earlier, because the compound path coefficient $b_A{}^2 = 0.5(1 + F_A)$ is interpretable as the probability that the homologous genes of two random gametes of zygote A are identical by descent, and because of the fact that probabilities, like path coefficients, compound along paths by multiplication. Many who use F solely as a measure of inbreeding, relative to the genes of a foundation stock, prefer the simple concept of probability of identity of descent to that of correlation of homologous genes of a certain class. The latter concept, however, is required from the broader standpoint of a group of parameters useful for the description of population structure in general. This is because a correlation coefficient can vary between -1 and $+1$, whereas a probability can vary only between 0 and 1. There will be occasion later to discuss cases of negative F and of values of P in excess of one, implying heterozygosis in excess of that in the panmictic reference population.

Multiple Alleles

In the derivation of the formula for pedigree F by path analysis in the preceding section, there was no reference to specific gene frequencies, to number of alleles, and to values to be assigned to alleles. The only assumptions were those of disomic autosomal heredity and the absence of selective differences. Thus pedigree F, as the correlation between homologous genes of uniting gametes, relative to the gene frequencies of the foundation stock, is wholly a function of the system of mating.

The zygotic frequencies in the case of multiple alleles are easily determined from the principle that under Mendelian heredity any group of alleles may be treated as a single allele. If allele A_i is opposed to all others collectively, it is evident that the frequency of $A_i A_i$ is given by $[(1 - F)q_i{}^2 + Fq_i]$ and that the frequency of its heterozygotes collectively is $2(1 - F) \times q_i(1 - q_i)$. The frequency of the composite allele A_{ij} is $(q_i + q_j)$ and that of its "homozygote" $A_{ij}A_{ij}$ (i.e., A_iA_i, A_iA_j, and A_jA_j collectively) must similarly be $(1 - F)(q_i + q_j)^2 + F(q_i + q_j)$. By subtracting the frequencies of A_iA_i and A_jA_j, the frequency of A_iA_j is found to be $2(1 - F)q_iq_j$. Table 7.4 shows the array of zygotic frequencies implied by the coefficient F.

TABLE 7.4. The frequencies of zygotes with multiple alleles under (1) panmixia; (2) inbreeding measured by F, and (3) complete fixation and the same gene frequencies. Subscripts e and s refer to egg and sperm (Wright 1951).

Zygote	(1) PANMIXIA ($r_{es} = 0$) Frequency	(2) INTERMEDIATE ($r_{es} = F$) Frequency	(3) FIXATION ($r_{es} = 1$) Frequency
A_1A_1	$q_1{}^2$	$(1 - F)q_1{}^2 + Fq_1$	q_1
A_1A_2	$2q_1q_2$	$2(1 - F)q_1q_2$	—
—	—	—	—
A_1A_k	$2q_1q_k$	$2(1 - F)q_1q_k$	—
A_2A_2	$q_2{}^2$	$(1 - F)q_2{}^2 + Fq_2$	q_2
—	—	—	—
A_2A_k	$2q_2q_k$	$2(1 - F)q_2q_k$	—
—	—	—	—
A_kA_k	$q_k{}^2$	$(1 - F)q_k{}^2 + Fq_k$	q_k
Total	1	$(1 - F) + F$	1

Total heterozygosis is given by $2 \sum q_iq_j$, $j > i$, under panmixia, but by $2(1 - F) \sum q_iq_j$ if there is inbreeding measured by F. Thus the formula $F = 1 - (y/y_0)$ still holds.

Since a correlation coefficient that is independent of values arbitrarily assigned to the various alternatives is somewhat unusual, it may be well to give an additional formal demonstration that the correlation in a population with the zygotic distribution of Table 7.4 is in fact F.

Let $V_1, V_2, \ldots, V_k$ be arbitrary values assigned to the alleles. The symbol f, with suitable subscript, is used for proportional frequencies.

(7.11)
$$\bar{G} = \sum_i^k V_if_i = \sum_i^k V_iq_i,$$

(7.12)
$$\sigma_G{}^2 = \sum_i^k V_i{}^2q_i - \left(\sum V_iq_i\right)^2,$$

(7.13)
$$r = \left[\sum_j^k \sum_i^k V_iV_jf_{ij} - \left(\sum V_iq_i\right)^2\right]\Big/\sigma_G{}^2.$$

A frequency, f_{ij}, of an entry in the correlation table has the value $(1 - F)q_iq_j$ if it refers to a heterozygote ($i \neq j$), but $(1 - F)q_i{}^2 + Fq_i$ if it refers to a homozygote ($i = j$). Thus:

(7.14)
$$\sum_j^k \sum_i^k V_iV_jf_{ij} = (1 - F)\left(\sum_i^k V_iq_i\right)^2 + F\left(\sum_i^k V_i{}^2q_i\right),$$

$$(7.15) \qquad r = \left[F\left(\sum_i^k V_i^2 q_i\right) - F\left(\sum_i^k V_i q_i\right)^2 \right] \Big/ \sigma_G^2 = F,$$

from (7.13), (7.14), and (7.12).

F for a Sex-Linked Locus

In complete sex linkage (Fig. 7.3) (males XY, females XX), the constitution of females is equally and completely determined by genes in the X chromosomes of the father and mother, so that $a = \sqrt{\{1/[2(1 + F)]\}}$ as under autosomal heredity. Similarly the constitution of a random gamete produced by a female is correlated with her constitution in the same way as is a random one of the gametes that united to produce her, so that $b = \sqrt{[0.5(1 + F')]}$, again as under autosomal heredity. The constitution of a male, however, is normally completely determined by that of the egg from which he came and completely determines that of any X-bearing sperm which he produces, so that the coefficients b and a' along this path are both one. There can be no inbreeding of the hemizygous males with respect to sex-linked genes and there can be no contribution to the inbreeding coefficient of a female from a common ancestor if there are successive males in the connecting path (Wright 1933a).

The inbreeding coefficient of a female with respect to neutral sex-linked genes is thus:

$$(7.16) \qquad F_f = \sum [0.5^{n(f)}(1 + F_A)]$$

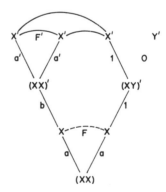

FIG. 7.3. Path diagram for sex-linked heredity (redrawn from Wright 1933a, Fig. 4).

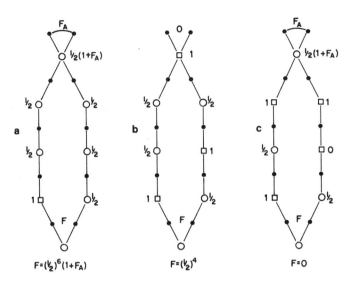

F ɪ ɢ. 7.4. Determination of the inbreeding coefficient for sex-linked genes from an ancestral connection. Three pedigrees. In all of these the autosomal inbreeding coefficient is $(1/2)^7(1 + F_A)$ (Wright 1951, Fig. 13, reprinted by permission, Cambridge University Press).

in which $n(f)$ is the number of females in a path connecting the two gametes under consideration and the summation is restricted to paths which have no males in immediate succession. These points are illustrated in Figure 7.4, which shows three connecting paths, each of which would contribute $0.5^7(1 + F_A)$ to the autosomal inbreeding coefficient but contribute varying amounts to the sex-linked inbreeding coefficient as shown. Drafting errors that escaped attention in Figure 13, Wright 1951, are here corrected.

Genes in the Y chromosome are, of course, transmitted only down the straight male line under complete sex-linkage so that $p_{YY'} = 1$ and all correlations between Y-bearing sperms that trace to a common origin are perfect.

Haldane and Moshinsky (1939) discussed partial sex-linkage by a method that can readily be expressed in terms of path analysis. There is, however, the complication that a specified X- or Y-bearing gamete from a male is not drawn at random, so that the zygote (XY) as the sum of contributions for the X and Y gametes is not transitive. It is simplest to trace the paths from gamete to parental gamete. A path connecting like chromosomes through a male ($p_{XX'}$ or $p_{YY'}$) has the value $1 - c$, and one connecting unlike chromosomes ($p_{XY'}$ or $p_{YX'}$) has the value c where c is the amount of recombination in spermatogenesis. The correlation between sperms from a male ancestor, carrying like chromosomes is

$$(7.17) \qquad r_{XX(m)} = r_{YY(m)} = (1 - c)^2 + c^2 + 2c(1 - c)F_A'.$$

In the case of sperms from a male ancestor carrying unlike chromosomes it is

$$(7.18) \qquad r_{XY(m)} = 2c(1 - c) + [(1 - c)^2 + c^2]F_A'.$$

Since the eggs, all being X-bearing, may be considered to be drawn at random, the contribution of a path through a female has the value 0.5 and the correlation between eggs produced by a female ancestor has the value $0.5(1 + F_A)$ as in the case of autosomal heredity.

The contributions to inbreeding from ancestral connections of the same sorts as in Figure 7.4 are shown in Figure 7.5 except that partial sex-linkage is assumed and the values are given for both daughters and sons (the latter zero under complete sex-linkage).

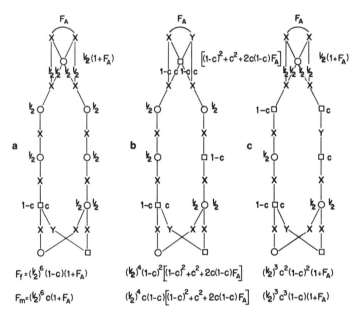

Fig. 7.5. Determination of the inbreeding coefficient for partially sex-linked genes (recombination c) from an ancestral connection. Three pedigrees. In all of these the autosomal inbreeding coefficient is $(1/2)^7(1 + F_A)$.

Polysomic Loci

The method has been extended to the correlation between genes of polysomic loci (Wright 1938c). As brought out in chapter 2, the equilibrium frequency for a pair of alleles in a $2k$-somic is $[(1 - q)a + qA]^{2k}$. Inbreeding brings about deviations in an array of inbred lines. Since there is more than one kind of heterozygote, it is most convenient to measure heterozygosis, y, by the proportion of cases in which pairs of alleles drawn at random from zygotes are different and to define F as the correlation between such random pairs, relative, of course, to the gene frequencies of the total population. The correlation table is then the same as with diploids, and F has the same relation to heterozygosis defined as above.

(7.19) $$F = 1 - y/2q(1 - q) = 1 - y/y_0.$$

It is, however, necessary to distinguish two other correlations between pairs of genes of a zygote: that between genes that entered in the same gamete, F_S, and that between genes brought in by different gametes, F_D. Here F is the weighted average.

(7.20) $$F = [(k - 1)F_S + kF_D]/(2k - 1).$$

Letting a be the coefficient for the path relating zygote to a random one of the genes in the gametes that united to produce it, the equation expressing complete determination of the zygote as the sum of contributions from genes is

$$2ka[a + (2k - 1)aF] = 1,$$

giving

(7.21) $$a = \sqrt{\frac{1}{\{2k[1 + (2k - 1)F]\}}}.$$

Letting b be the coefficient for the path relating a gene of a gamete to the producing zygote, the two expressions for the correlations between component gene and zygote, assuming that no selection intervenes between production by uniting gametes and production of gametes, is

(7.22) $$b = a' + (2k - 1)a'F = \sqrt{\{[1/(2k)][1 + (2k - 1)F']\}}.$$

Thus $ba' = 1/(2k)$ irrespective of inbreeding, as expected from the probability of identity of a gene with one of those a generation earlier.

Correlation F_S would be the same as F' except for the small chance, e, that two genes of the zygote trace to one in the preceding generation. (Cf. chap. 2.)

(7.23) $$F_S = (1 - e)F' + e.$$

Correlation F_D must be found by tracing connecting paths in the ancestry. These connections may be evaluated, as with diploids, by means of the compound path coefficients ba', and $b_A{}^2$ where A is the common ancestor in the path in question. The contribution of a single succession of gene-to-gene paths through n connecting zygotes is $[1/(2k)]^n[1 + (2k - 1)F_A]$.

There are, however, k^2 paths connecting genes in the two gametes of the common ancestor that are involved, and each path splits into k in the next generation except for the two zygotes immediately back of the two genes at the ends of the path in question. Thus each connecting zygotic path in a chain of n zygotes involves k^{n-1} genic paths.

(7.24) $$F_D = \sum \{k^{n-1}[1/(2k)]^n [1 + (2k - 1)F_A]\}$$

$$= (1/k)\left\{\sum 0.5^n[1 + (2k - 1)F_A]\right\}.$$

where summation is by zygotic paths. If $k = 1$, then $F_D = F$ and (7.24) reduces to (7.10).

Correlations between Gametes

Since there was nothing in the demonstrations that required that two genes which are correlated be those in uniting gametes, exactly the same general formulas for F (or F_D for polysomic loci) in terms of ancestral connections can be applied to classes consisting of two genes with any sort of relation to the system of mating. They may be two random gametes from sibs or first cousins or any other designated relatives. Such correlations can be interpreted as the relative decrease in heterallelism (instead of hetero-zygosis) or as the probability of identity by descent from the foundation stock. This principle will be used extensively in later sections. The correlations will be represented by r's with appropriate subscripts, and in some cases it will be convenient to use $P (= 1 - r)$ with the same subscript as r for relative heterallelism.

Sib Mating by Path Analyses

The formulas developed in preceding sections for the values of F and P under autosomal disomic or polysomic loci and for sex-linkage, on the basis of pedigrees tracing back to a foundation, to which they are relative, are completely general but easily applied only where inbreeding is sporadic. In dealing with regular systems of mating it is usually best to trace the paths connecting two gametes back for only one gamete-to-gamete generation in each case and then complete them by the appropriate correlation between the gametes of the preceding generation. Thus if gamete G_1 traces to G_3 and G_4 and gamete G_2 to G_5 and G_6, then $r_{12} = (1/4)(r_{35} + r_{36} + r_{45} + r_{46})$. This may be illustrated by returning to the case of sib mating (Fig. 7.6). There are two kinds of correlations in the preceding generation: between gametes derived at random from the same zygote, $b'^2 = 0.5(1 + F'')$, and between gametes from sibs, with the value F'. There are four connecting paths.

$$
(7.25) \quad \begin{aligned} F &= 0.25[2b'^2 + 2F'] = 0.25[1 + 2F' + F''], \\ P &= 0.5P' + 0.25P''. \end{aligned}
$$

This shows at once that if one starts with heterozygotes, Aa, in which $P'' = 1$, these produce a progeny in which $P' = 0.5$, and the values of P in later generations form a series in which the numerators are Fibonacci numbers if the denominators are doubled in each generation. They are thus in accord with the results of Pearl, Jennings, and Fish referred to earlier, but are derived much more simply (Wright 1921).

With the same mating system, generation after generation, it is to be expected that the ratio of successive terms will approach constancy. Letting $\lambda = P/P' = P'/P''$:

$$
(7.26) \quad \lambda^2 - 0.5\lambda - 0.25 = 0.
$$

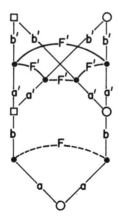

FIG. 7.6. Path diagram for brother-sister mating (redrawn from Wright 1921, II, Fig. 1).

The pertinent (largest) root is $\lambda = 0.25[1 + \sqrt{5}] = 0.80902$ (Wright 1931). The average number of generations for a 50% reduction in heterozygosis is 3.27.

It may be noted that equation (7.26) is an exact divisor of the quartic characteristic equation (7.6) of the matrix of mating types in the case of pairs of alleles, and this must also be true for characteristic equation of the complete 55 × 55 matrix for this case with full allowance for multiple alleles (Haldane 1955). As already brought out, the result for path analysis applies irrespective of the number of alleles.

It is instructive to express the equations from path analysis in matrix form (Wright 1963). Using r_0 here for the correlation between random gametes of the same individual and $r_1 (= F)$ for that between gametes from different individuals (sibs in this case):

$$(7.27) \qquad \begin{aligned} r_0 &= 0.5(1 + r_1'), \\ F = r_1 &= 0.5(r_0' + r_1'). \end{aligned}$$

The corresponding values, $P_0 = 1 - r_0 = 0.5 P_1'$ and $P_1 = 1 - r_1 = 0.5(P_0' + P_1')$ can be arranged in a P-matrix.

$$(7.28) \qquad \begin{array}{c c} & \begin{matrix} P_0' & P_1' \end{matrix} \\ \begin{matrix} P_0 \\ P_1 \end{matrix} & \begin{vmatrix} 0 & 0.5 \\ 0.5 & 0.5 \end{vmatrix} \end{array}$$

The characteristic equation from this matrix is:

$$\begin{pmatrix} -\lambda & 0.5 \\ 0.5 & 0.5 - \lambda \end{pmatrix} = 0,$$

giving

$$(7.29) \qquad \lambda^2 - 0.5\lambda - 0.25 = 0.$$

As before $\lambda = 0.25[1 + \sqrt{5}] = 0.80902$ as the pertinent root.

Thus a 2 × 2 matrix of p's based on gametic unions corresponds to the much more extensive matrix of zygotic unions. The methods are complementary. Path analysis, as a correlation method, deals with only two variables at a time and can give only changes in the frequencies of zygotes. The mating-type method yields explicit expressions for the frequencies of all of the mating types, given the initial frequencies, and thus gives a more complete analysis. The most important result, which can be obtained only by the matrix method, is the proportion of completely fixed matings ($AA \times AA$, $aa \times aa$ etc.). Schäfer (1936) worked this out for sib mating, starting from heterozygotes. It was investigated more generally by Haldane (1937a) in the paper referred to earlier. Haldane showed that after a few generations the proportion of unfixed matings lags about 2.015 generations behind heterozygosis while both decline at the rate $1 - \lambda_1 = 0.19098$ per generation. The mating-type method, however, is practically restricted to very simple cases, whereas path analysis can be applied to any system, regular or irregular, and yields what is much the most important parameter.

Parent-Offspring Mating

Jennings (1916) obtained the rates of decrease of heterozygosis under different types of parent-offspring mating by the mating-type method. These again are more easily derived by path analysis (Wright 1921).

Consider first the mating of offspring with younger parent (Fig. 7.7). It is convenient to use m for the correlation between mated individuals.

$$F = bb'm,$$

$$m = a'b' + a'b''m' = a'b' + a'b''F'/b'b'' = a'b' + a'F''/b',$$

(7.30) $$F = ba'b'^2 + ba'F' = 0.25[1 + F''] + 0.5F'.$$

$$F = 0.25[1 + 2F' + F''],$$

$$P = 0.5P' + 0.25P''.$$

This is the same as for brother-sister mating, irrespective of number, effects, or frequencies of alleles. It agrees with Jennings' result for the case of two alleles.

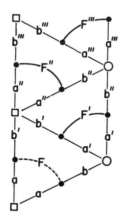

FIG. 7.7. Path diagram for alternating parent-offspring mating (redrawn from Wright 1921, II, Fig. 4).

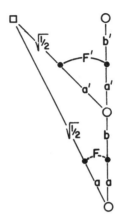

FIG. 7.8. Path diagram for repeated backcrossing to a random male (redrawn from Wright 1921, II, Fig. 2).

Another system of parent-offspring (Fig. 7.8) is that of matings of a single sire with daughters, granddaughters, etc. There is an important complication here in the postulate for path analysis that there be no systematic change in gene frequency in the total array of inbred lines. Assume, however, that lines are started from multiple sires from the same population and hence the same gene frequency at each locus as the females. The coefficient relating gamete to sire has the value $\sqrt{0.5}$.

$$F = bm\sqrt{0.5}, \qquad m = (F/b)\sqrt{2},$$

$$m = a'\sqrt{0.5} + a'b'm' = a'\sqrt{0.5} + a'F'\sqrt{2}$$

(7.31)
$$F = 0.5ba' + ba'F' = 0.25[1 + 2F'],$$

$$P = 0.25[1 + 2P'].$$

In this case there is, of course, no systematic tendency toward fixation of the genotype as a whole. For loci in which the male is known to be homozygous in a particular respect (Fig. 7.9) heterozygosis is halved in each generation of backcrossing. In order to represent this by path analysis, assume that AA and aa males are used in proportion to the frequencies of A and a in the females in order that gene frequency may remain the same.

$$F = bm, \qquad m = F/b,$$

$$m = a' + a'b'm' = a' + a'F'.$$

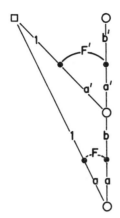

Fᵢɢ. 7.9. Path diagram for repeated backcrossing to a homozygous male (redrawn from Wright 1921, II, Fig. 3).

(7.32)
$$F = ba'[1 + F'] = 0.5(1 + F'),$$
$$P = 0.5P',$$

as expected.

Matings of Half-Sibs and of First and Second Cousins

The systems of half-sib mating that bring about most rapid fixation are those in which one male is mated with two or more females. In Figure 7.10 a male is represented as mated with two females in each generation, one to produce the sire of the next generation and the other to produce two half-sisters of this male, but full sisters of each other. Correlations between gametes that are not shown in Figure 7.10 can easily be deduced.

$$F = (1/4)[b'^2 + 2F' + (1/4)(2b''^2 + 2F'')]$$
$$= (1/16)[(2 + 2F'') + 8F' + (1 + F''') + 2F''].$$

(7.33)
$$F = (1/16)[8F' + 4F'' + F''' + 3] \qquad \text{(Wright 1921),}$$
$$P = (1/16)[8P' + 4P'' + P'''].$$

(7.34) $16\lambda^3 - 8\lambda^2 - 4\lambda - 1 = 0, \qquad \lambda_1 = 0.86995.$

If one male is mated with an indefinitely large number of half-sisters, all assumed to be half-sisters of each other (Fig. 7.11), the correlation between

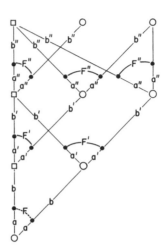

Fɪɢ. 7.10. Path diagram for inbreeding of half-brother to two females, full sisters of each other (redrawn from Wright 1921, II, Fig. 7).

gametes of any two individuals of the same generation is the same as that between uniting gametes.

(7.35)
$$F = (1/4)[b'^2 + 3F'] = (1/8)[6F' + F'' + 1]$$
$$P = (3/4)P' + (1/8)P''. \qquad \text{(Wright 1921)}$$

(7.36)
$$8\lambda^2 - 6\lambda - 1 = 0,$$
$$\lambda_1 = (1/8)(3 + \sqrt{17}) = 0.89039.$$

The formula can easily be found in intermediate cases, but the rate of loss of heterozygotes in all of these lies between 11.0% and 13.0%. A closed herd, headed by one male in each generation, loses about half its heterozygosis every six (5.97) generations. The approach to fixation is thus somewhat more than half that under brother-sister mating. It has the advantage that fixation is being brought about in a much larger population as a unit.

Another system of half-sib mating is that in which each male is mated with two half-sisters but each female is mated with two half-brothers (Fig. 7.12). Such a system may involve an indefinitely large number of both males and females. It may easily be seen, however, that F continually approaches one (Wright 1921). Letting r_0 be the correlation between random gametes from the same zygote, and numbering other correlations according to distance apart, a series of equations may be written from inspection.

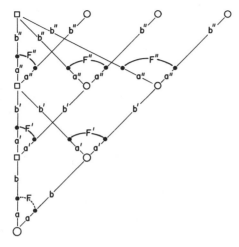

FIG. 7.11. Path diagram for inbreeding in a large herd headed by one male. Females in general half-sisters of each other and of the male (redrawn from Wright 1921, II, Fig. 8).

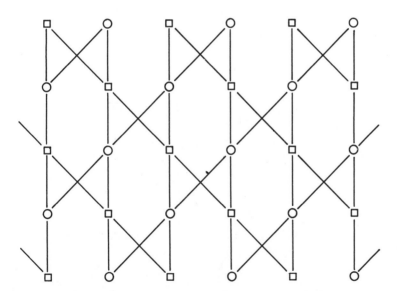

FIG. 7.12. Path diagram for a system in which each individual comes from a mating of half-sibs, otherwise as little related as possible (redrawn from Wright 1921, II, Fig. 9).

(7.37)

$$r_0 = 0.5(1 + r_1'),$$
$$r_1 = F = 0.25(r_0' + 2r_1' + r_2'),$$
$$r_2 = 0.25(r_1' + 2r_2' + r_3'),$$
$$r_x = 0.25[r_{x-1}' + 2r_x' + r_{x+1}'].$$

The number of different ancestors increases by one with each generation that is traced back, and thus without limit if the ends never come together in a single individual. If there were an equilibrium value of F, short of fixation, the primes could be dropped, giving $r_0 = 0.5(1 + r_1)$, $r_1 = 0.5(r_0 + r_2)$, etc. The r's would form an arithmetic series $1:r_0:r_1:r_2$, etc., in the interval 1 to 0, but with introduction of a new r in each generation, and thus increase in all the others, contrary to the hypothesis of equilibrium. The rate of decrease of heterozygosis, P/P', would, however, continually decline instead of approaching a constant value as in the cases with constant N. The increase in F for 50 generations is shown in chapter 12, Figure 12.18.

A similar system is that in which all matings are between first cousins as in Figure 7.13. In this case the number of ancestral matings increases by one with each generation, going backward. Again labeling the correlations between gametes according to distance apart:

(7.38)

$$r_0 = 0.5[1 + r_2'],$$
$$r_1 = 0.5[r_0' + r_2'],$$
$$r_2 = F = 0.25[r_1' + 2r_2' + r_3'],$$
$$r_x = 0.25[r_{x-1}' + 2r_x' + r_{x+1}'].$$

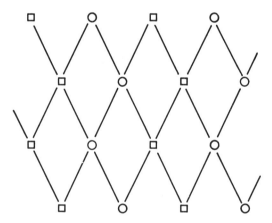

FIG. 7.13. Path diagram for a system in which each individual comes from a mating of first cousins, otherwise as little related as possible (redrawn from Wright 1921, II, Fig. 10).

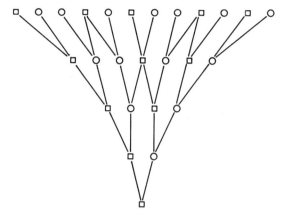

FIG. 7.14. Path diagram for a system in which each individual comes from a mating of half-first cousins, otherwise as little related as possible (redrawn from Wright 1921, II, Fig. 11).

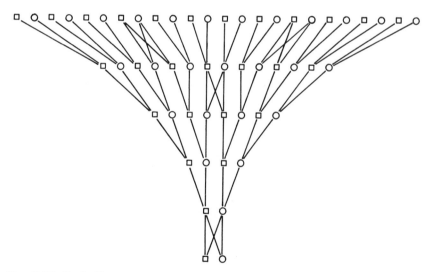

FIG. 7.15. Path diagram for a system in which each individual comes from a mating of second cousins, otherwise as little related as possible (redrawn from Wright 1921, II, Fig. 12).

Again there is no limit to the increase in F short of complete local fixation, but the rate of increase is considerably less than in the preceding case (Wright 1921). The cases of half-sib and first-cousin mating in which the ends are connected to form a circle of constant size will be considered later.

It might be supposed from these cases that there can never be equilibrium short of complete fixation with any consistent system of mating of relatives. This, however, is not the case (Wright 1921). With half-first cousins (Fig. 7.14) there is no necessary connection between uniting gametes except through two of the four grandparents.

$$(7.39) \quad \begin{aligned} F &= (1/16)[b''^2 + 2F''] = (1/32)[1 + 4F'' + F'''], \\ P &= (1/32)[4P'' + P''' + 26]. \end{aligned}$$

An equilibrium is reached when $F = F'' = F'''$ at which $F = 1/27$ and $P = 26/27$.

Similarly with mating of second cousins (Fig. 7.15):

$$(7.40) \quad \begin{aligned} F &= (1/64)[1 + 8F'' + 2F''' + F^{IV}], \\ P &= (1/64)[8P'' + 2P''' + P^{IV} + 52]. \end{aligned}$$

At equilibrium $F = 1/53$, $P = 52/53$.

Mixed Self-fertilization and Random Mating

The present section is concerned with automatic changes in F and P that occur in populations of constant size, N which are not breeding wholly at random.

Consider the case of a population of N monoecious diploids in which fertilization is at random except for a known proportion, h, of self-fertilization. Let E be the correlation between random gametes and F that between uniting gametes, at autosomal loci. Primes indicate preceding generations (Wright 1951).

$$E = (1/N)b^2 + [1 - 1/N]E' \qquad \text{where} \qquad b^2 = 0.5(1 + F'),$$

$$F = hb^2 + (1 - h)E',$$

$$E' = \frac{F - 0.5h(1 + F')}{1 - h},$$

and also

$$E' = \frac{1}{N}\frac{1 + F''}{2} + \left(1 - \frac{1}{N}\right)\left[\frac{2F' - h(1 + F'')}{2(1 - h)}\right].$$

Solving for F:

(7.41)
$$F = [1 + h/2 - 1/N]F' + [1/(2N) - h/2]F'' + 1/(2N),$$
$$P = [1 + h/2 - 1/N]P' + [1/(2N) - h/2]P''.$$

In the improbable case of fertilization wholly at random ($h = 1/N$):

(7.42)
$$P = [1 - 1/(2N)]P',$$
$$\Delta P' = P - P' = -[1/(2N)]P'.$$

Thus in this case, heterozygosis falls off by exactly the proportion $1/(2N)$ of its previous value, per generation. Since the relation to N is simpler in this case than in others it is convenient to take this as the ultimate standard in considering effective size of population, in spite of its improbability.

It might be supposed that the occurrence of self-fertilization plays the most important role in this process, but if self-fertilization is completely excluded ($h = 0$):

(7.43)
$$P = [1 - 1/N]P' + [1/(2N)]P''.$$

If population size remains constant it is to be expected that the ratio of successive values of P will approach a constant value.

Let $P/P' = P'/P'' = \lambda$. This leads to the equation

(7.44)
$$\lambda^2 - [1 - 1/N]\lambda - [1/(2N)] = 0$$

of which the largest root is:

(7.45)
$$\lambda = 0.5[1 - 1/N + \sqrt{(1 + 1/N^2)}],$$

approximately $1 - [1/(2N)][1 - 1/(2N)]$ or even $2N/(2N + 1)$.

Thus $P = [2N/(2N + 1)]P'$ approximately, and the rate of decline of heterozygosis per generation is approximately $\Delta P' = -[1/(2N + 1)]P'$.

Unless N is exceedingly small, this does not differ appreciably from the rate under random fertilization. The effect of exclusion of self-fertilization may be described by stating that in such a population the effective size N_e is slightly larger than in the standard case of random fertilization, as indicated by the approximate formula $N_e = N + 0.5$. The subject of effective size will be discussed in general in the next chapter.

If N is indefinitely great there is no tendency for gene frequency to change and heterozygosis approaches equilibrium rapidly if h is not small (Haldane, 1924b). From (7.41), $F - F' = (h/2)(F' - F'')$.

The increments from initial $F_0 = 0$ (random mating) fall off in geometric progression. Since $F_1 = h/2$, noting that $E_0 = 0$:

(7.46)
$$F_\infty = (h/2)[1 + h/2 + (h/2)^2 + \cdots] = h/(2 - h),$$
$$P_\infty = 2(1 - h)/(2 - h).$$

This value of P_∞ agrees with the ratio of the amount of heterozygosis at equilibrium to that under random mating given by Haldane, who also discussed the effects of selection in this case.

If h is much greater than $1/N$, there is rapid approach to near-equilibrium, as above, before there is much spreading of gene frequencies among the hypothetical multiple populations of size N. We consider here the limiting relation after the rapid effect of selfing has come to an end and F is slowly approaching one. Putting $P/P' = P'/P''$ in 7.41 to find the limiting rate during this phase:

$$(7.47) \quad P = 0.5\{1 + h/2 - 1/N + \sqrt{[(1 - h/2)^2 - (1/N)(h - 1/N)]}\}P',$$

$$(7.48) \quad P \approx \left[1 - \frac{1}{(2 - h)N}\right]P'.$$

The rate of decrease of heterozygosis in this late phase is thus somewhat greater than under random mating $[1/(2N)]P'$: If there is almost 100% self-fertilization, the rate is close to $(1/N)P'$ but the amount of heterozygosis is small. With 100% self-fertilization, no heterozygosis is left in the limiting case considered here $(P = 0)$. The rapid approach to equilibrium $P = 0.5P'$, in each line, is assumed to have reached completion.

One other point that may be noted here is the sampling variance under mixed random mating and selfing. The analysis of zygotic frequencies into random bred and inbred components (Tables 7.3, 7.4) permits a corresponding analysis of the sampling variance for given q (Li, 1955a).

$$(7.49) \quad \sigma^2_{\Delta q} = (1 - F)\frac{q(1 - q)}{2N} + F\frac{q(1 - q)}{N} = \frac{(1 + F)q(1 - q)}{2N}.$$

There have been discussions of mixed random mating and self-fertilization from other standpoints (Bennett and Binet 1956; Workman and Jain 1966).

Sex Ratio and Inbreeding

The most general case for an autosomal disomic locus and separate sexes is that of random mating in a population of N_m males and N_f females. The proportion of matings between full sibs is $1/(N_m N_f)$, between half-sibs $(N_m + N_f - 2)/(N_m N_f)$, and between less closely related individuals $(N_m - 1)(N_f - 1)/(N_m N_f)$ (Wright 1931).

$$(7.50) \quad F = (ba')^2 \left[\frac{1}{N_m N_f}(2b'^2 + 2F') + \frac{N_m + N_f - 2}{N_m N_f}(b'^2 + 3F') \right. $$
$$\left. + \frac{(N_m - 1)(N_f - 1)}{N_m N_f}4F'\right].$$

(7.51)
$$F = F' + \frac{N_m + N_f}{8N_mN_f}(1 - 2F' + F''),$$

$$P = P' - \frac{N_m + N_f}{8N_mN_f}(2P' - P'').$$

The approximate rate of decrease of heterozygosis is $[1/(8N_m) + 1/(8N_f)] \times [1 - 1/(8N_m) - 1/(8N_e)]$.

The expression for P can also be written

$$P = [1 - 1/N_e]P' + (1/2N_e)P'' \quad \text{where} \quad N_e = \frac{4N_mN_f}{(N_m + N_f)}.$$

This is in exactly the same form as in the case of a monoecious population in which self-fertilization is excluded except for replacement of N by $4N_mN_f/(N_m + N_f)$.

If there are equal numbers of males and females ($N_m = N_f = N/2$), then $N_e = N$. It is often convenient to take this as the standard case for comparisons of the inbreeding effect in populations with separate sexes. For comparison with the ultimate standard, a population with completely random union of gametes, 0.5 must be added in both this and the preceding case.

Mixed Sib and Random Mating

Another case of interest is that of separate sexes with $N_P = 0.5N$ permanent pairs and the proportion h of sib matings. The analysis is similar to that for monoecious populations (Wright 1951).

$$E = \frac{1}{N_P}(ba')^2(2F' + 2b'^2) + 4[1 - 1/N_P](ba')^2E'$$

$$= \frac{1}{4N_P}(1 + 2F' + F'') + [1 - 1/N_P]E',$$

$$F = 0.25h(1 + 2F' + F'') + (1 - h)E'.$$

Equating the formulas for E' derivable from the two preceding:

(7.52)
$$F = \left(1 + \frac{h}{2} - \frac{1}{N_P}\right)F' + \left(\frac{1}{2N_P} - \frac{h}{4}\right)F'' + \left(\frac{1}{4N_P} - \frac{h}{4}\right)F''' + \frac{1}{4N_P},$$

$$P = \left(1 + \frac{h}{2} - \frac{1}{N_P}\right)P' + \left(\frac{1}{2N_P} - \frac{h}{4}\right)P'' + \left(\frac{1}{4N_P} - \frac{h}{4}\right)P'''.$$

If there is a random proportion of sib mating ($h = 1/N_P$):

(7.53)
$$P = \left(1 - \frac{1}{2N_P}\right)P' + \frac{1}{4N_P}P''.$$

MATING OF DOUBLE FIRST COUSINS

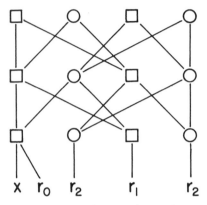

FIG. 7.16. Path diagram for double-first-cousin mating: r_0, r_1, and r_2 designate correlations of indicated gametes with gamete x (Wright 1965c, Fig. 3) (essentially 1921, II, Fig. 5).

This is the same as for random mating with equal numbers of males and females (putting $2N_P = N$).

If sib mating is excluded ($h = 0$):

(7.54)
$$P = \left[1 - \frac{1}{N_P}\right]P' + \frac{1}{2N_P}P'' + \frac{1}{4N_P}P'''.$$

Putting $P/P' = P'/P'' = P''/P''' = \lambda$, and $N_P = N/2$:

(7.55)
$$\lambda^3 - \left[1 - \frac{2}{N}\right]\lambda^2 - \frac{1}{N}\lambda - \frac{1}{2N} = 0.$$

An approximate solution for $x = \lambda - 1$ can easily be found:

$$x^3 + 2\left(\frac{N+1}{N}\right)x^2 + \left(\frac{N+3}{N}\right)x + \frac{1}{2N} = 0.$$

Putting $x^3 = 0$, the approximate value of x ($= \Delta P/P'$) for large N is

(7.56)
$$x \approx -\frac{N}{2(N+1)^2} = -\frac{1}{2[N+2+1/N]}.$$

The effective size of population is approximately $N + 1.5$ in comparison with a population in which sib mating occurs at random, and approximately $N + 2$ in comparison with one in which there is completely random union of gametes.

Maximum Avoidance of Consanguine Mating

The simplest case of N_P pairs with exclusion of sib mating (7.54) is that of double-first-cousin mating ($N_P = 2$) (Wright 1951). It is implied that each pair produces just two offspring to carry on the system.

$$\text{(7.57)} \qquad \begin{aligned} F &= (1/8)(4F' + 2F'' + F''' + 1), \\ P &= (1/8)(4P' + 2P'' + P'''). \end{aligned}$$

$$\text{(7.58)} \qquad P = P' - (1/16)P^{IV}$$

after the first generation in which P is affected.

These formulas can also be derived directly from a diagram for this case alone (Wright 1921). It makes no difference whether each of the pairs produces two offspring of the same sex, as shown, or different sexes (Fig. 7.16). There are three kinds of correlations between gametes of a given generation: between gametes from the same zygote (r_0), between gametes from sibs, (r_1), and between gametes of cousins ($r_2 = F$).

$$\text{(7.59)} \qquad \begin{aligned} r_0 &= b^2 = 0.25[2 + 2r_2'], \\ r_1 &= 0.25[2r_0' + 2r_2'], \\ r_2 &= F = 0.25[2r_1' + 2r_2']. \end{aligned}$$

Substitution in the last gives the same formula (7.57). Putting $P/P' = P'/P'' = P''/P''' = \lambda$ in order to obtain the limiting ratio of successive values of P (Wright 1933a):

$$\text{(7.60)} \qquad 8\lambda^3 - 4\lambda^2 - 2\lambda - 1 = 0 \quad \text{or} \quad \lambda^4 - \lambda^3 - 1/16 = 0,$$
$$\lambda_1 = 0.91964.$$

Fisher (1949) arrived at a 12×12 mating-type matrix in this case and thus a characteristic equation of the twelfth degree. On factoring this, the largest root was contained in a cubic equation, the same as that which had been arrived at by path analysis (7.60).

This sort of analysis can be extended at once to larger populations in which close inbreeding is avoided as much as possible. In the case of quadruple second cousins ($N = 8$) there are four kinds of correlations (Wright 1921) (Fig. 7.17).

$$\text{(7.61)} \qquad \begin{aligned} r_0 &= 0.25[2 + 2r_3'], \\ r_1 &= 0.25[2r_0' + 2r_3'], \\ r_2 &= 0.25[2r_1' + 2r_3'], \\ r_3 &= F = 0.25[2r_2' + 2r_3']. \end{aligned}$$

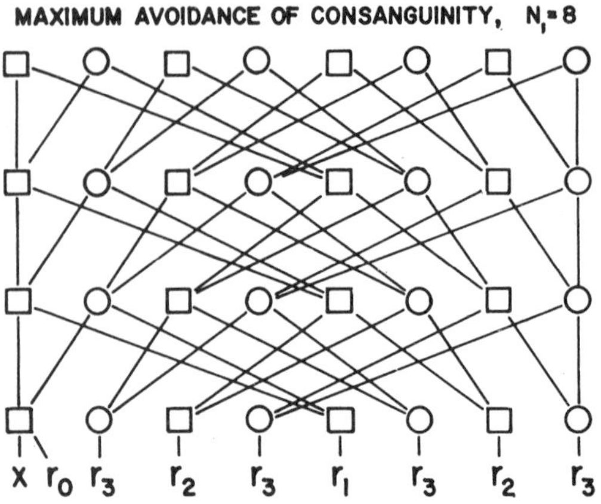

MAXIMUM AVOIDANCE OF CONSANGUINITY, $N_i = 8$

$$X \quad r_0 \ r_3 \quad r_2 \quad r_3 \quad r_1 \quad r_3 \quad r_2 \quad r_3$$

FIG. 7.17. Path diagrams for mating of quadruple second cousins: r_0 to r_3 designate correlations of indicated gametes to gamete x (Wright 1965c, Fig. 1).

$$(7.62) \qquad \begin{aligned} F &= (1/16)[8F' + 4F'' + 2F''' + F^{IV} + 1], \\ P &= (1/16)[8P' + 4P'' + 2P''' + P^{IV}]. \end{aligned}$$

$$(7.63) \qquad P = P' - (1/32)P^{V}$$

after the system has gotten underway.

$$(7.64) \qquad \lambda^5 - \lambda^4 - (1/32) = 0, \qquad \lambda_1 = 0.96378.$$

Similarly in the case of octuple third cousins (Wright 1921), $N = 16$:

$$(7.65) \qquad \begin{aligned} r_0 &= 0.25[2 + 2r_4'], \\ r_1 &= 0.25[2r_0' + 2r_4'], \\ r_2 &= 0.25[2r_1' + 2r_4'], \\ r_3 &= 0.25[2r_2' + 2r_4'], \\ r_4 &= F = 0.25[2r_3' + 2r_4']. \end{aligned}$$

$$(7.66) \qquad \begin{aligned} F &= (1/32)[16F' + 8F'' + 4F''' + 2F^{IV} + F^{V} + 1], \\ P &= (1/32)[16P' + 8P'' + 4P''' + 2P^{IV} + P^{V}]. \end{aligned}$$

$$(7.67) \qquad P = P' - (1/64)P^{VI}$$

after the system has gotten underway.

$$(7.68) \qquad \lambda^6 - \lambda^5 - (1/64) = 0, \qquad \lambda_1 = 0.98298.$$

In general the value of P for populations of size $N = 2^m$ is

$$(7.69) \qquad P = P' - 0.5^{m+2}P^{(m+2)\,\text{primes}}$$

after the system has gotten underway.

(7.70) $$\lambda^{m+1}(1 - \lambda) = 0.5^{m+2}.$$

If $\lambda = 1 - x$,
then

$$2^{m+2}x = \frac{1}{(1 - x)^{m+1}} \approx \frac{1}{1 - (m + 1)x} \approx [1 + (m + 1)x + \cdots]$$

if x is small.

(7.71) $$x \approx 1/[2^{m+2} - (m + 1)] = 1/[4N - (m + 1)].$$

Thus the rate of decrease of heterozygosis ($x = \Delta P/P'$) approaches $1/(4N)$ for large N (Wright 1933a) or more accurately $1/[4N - (m + 1)]$ (A. Robertson 1964). This is only about half the rate given for random mating with $(N/2)$ males, $(N/2)$ females, but the systems differ not only in the avoidance of consanguine mating in the case considered in this section, but in assuming that each parent is represented by exactly two offspring in the next generation, instead of by a random sampling from the whole array of progeny, as assumed under random mating. The consequences of this difference must be considered before a valid comparison can be made.

Circular Mating

It is interesting to compare the effects of a system in which matings are made between individuals that are as closely related as possible without disrupting continuity in a population of given size with those in which consanguinity in mating is avoided as much as possible. Kimura and Crow (1963b) studied the system of mating half sibs around a circle of N ($= 2n$) individuals from this standpoint (Figure 7.18 shows a circle of 8). The correlations to be considered are the same as those presented earlier in discussing such matings in an indefinitely large population, except for the one that closes the circle. It will be convenient to deal with the equations for the P's ($P_x = 1 - r_x$) instead of the correlations themselves, as in (7.37).

(7.72)
$$
\begin{aligned}
P_0 &= 0.5P_1', \\
P_1 &= 0.25[P_0' + 2P_1' + P_2'], \\
P_x &= 0.25[P_{x-1}' + 2P_x' + P_{x+1}'], \\
P_{n-1} &= 0.25[P_{n-2}' + 2P_{n-1}' + P_n'], \\
P_n &= 0.5[P_{n-1}' + P_n'].
\end{aligned}
$$

The values can be calculated generation after generation. Of most interest is the limiting value. This was obtained by Kimura and Crow by arranging

CIRCLE OF HALF-SIB MATINGS, $N_I = 8$

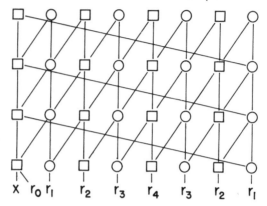

FIG. 7.18. Path diagram for circular half-sib matings: r_0 to r_4 designate correlations of indicated gametes to gamete x (Wright 1965c, Fig. 2).

these P-equations in a matrix. The characteristic equation could then be expressed as a function of a known determinant (Wolstenholme's) on making the substitution $\lambda = 0.5(1 + \cos \theta)$.

It is not necessary, however, to use this determinant, given the above substitution and the definition $\lambda = P/P'$ at the limit (Wright 1965c).

$$P'_{n-1} = P_n'(2\lambda - 1) = P_n' \cos \theta$$

from P_n in (7.72).

$$P'_{n-2} = 2P'_{n-1}(2\lambda - 1) - P_n'$$
$$= P_n'(2 \cos^2 \theta - 1) = P_n' \cos 2\theta$$

from P_{n-1} in (7.72).

$$
\begin{aligned}
P'_{n-3} &= 2P'_{n-2}(2\lambda - 1) - P'_{n-1} \\
(7.73) \qquad &= P_n'[2 \cos 2\theta \cos \theta - \cos (2\theta - \theta)] \\
&= P'[\cos 2\theta \cos \theta - \sin 2\theta \sin \theta] \\
&= P_n' \cos 3\theta.
\end{aligned}
$$

Step by step, and dropping primes:

$$(7.74) \qquad\qquad P_x = P_n \cos (n - x)\theta,$$

including $P_0 = P_n \cos n\theta$.
But

$$P_0 = 0.5P_1' = P_n \cos [(n - 1)\theta/(1 + \cos \theta)].$$

On equating:

(7.75) $$\sin \theta = \cos n\theta / \sin n\theta.$$

With large n, θ becomes small, $\sin \theta$ and $\cos n\theta$ approach θ, and $\sin n\theta$ approaches 1, $\cos \theta$ approaches $\sqrt{(1 - \theta^2)}$ and thus $1 - (\theta^2/2)$, and θ approaches $\pi/[2(n + 1)]$. Finally $1 - \lambda$ approaches $\theta^2/4$.

(7.76) $$1 - \lambda \approx \left[\frac{\pi}{2(N + 2)} \right]^2$$

as given by Kimura and Crow.

In the case of circular mating of first cousins with $N = 2^m$, there are $N/4 + 2$ different kinds of correlations between gametes in a generation. These are the same as those given earlier in the case of an infinite population (7.38) except for termination of the list with $r_{n+1} = 0.5[r_n' + r_{n+1}']$, letting $n = N/4$ in this case. Replacing each r by $1 - P$:

(7.77)
$$P_0 = 0.5P_2'$$
$$P_1 = 0.5[P_0' + P_2']$$
$$\vdots$$
$$P_x = 0.25[P_{x-1}' + 2P_x' + P_{x+1}']$$
$$\vdots$$
$$P_{n+1} = 0.5[P_n' + P_{n+1}']$$

The limiting ratio, $\lambda = P/P'$, was again obtained by Kimura and Crow from the equivalent of the P-matrix, using the same transformation, $\lambda = 0.5(1 + \cos \theta)$, as before. The equations can be solved by the same method as in the preceding case giving:

(7.78) $$P_x = P_{n+1} \cos [(n + 1 - x)\theta]$$

except for P_0, for which there are two equations:

(7.79)
$$P_0 = P_{n+1} \cos [(n - 1)\theta]/(1 + \cos \theta),$$
$$P_0 = 2\lambda P_1 - P_2 = P_{n+1}[(1 + \cos \theta)] \cos n\theta - \cos [(n - 1)\theta].$$

(7.80) $$\sin \theta[2 + \cos \theta] = \cos n\theta / \sin n\theta.$$

This requires that θ be approximately $\pi/2(n + 3)$ leading to $\theta^2/4 = [\pi/4(n + 3)]^2$. Thus

(7.81) $$1 - \lambda \approx \left[\frac{\pi}{N + 12} \right]^2$$

approximately, again as given by Kimura and Crow (1963b).

It may be seen that in both of these cases of mating of close relatives around a circle, the ultimate rate of decrease of heterozygosis is approximately proportional to $1/N^2$ with large N and thus of lower order than in the case of maximum avoidance of consanguine mating or of random mating, under either of which it is approximately proportional to $1/N$. The paradox that avoidance of inbreeding ultimately brings about a more rapid loss of heterozygosis than does its pursuit, to which Kimura and Crow called attention, will be discussed in a later chapter.

Sex-linkage and Inbreeding

The case of sex linkage with N_m males and N_f females is considerably more complicated than the autosomal case. The formula obtained for F (Wright 1933a) has been confirmed by a different method by Kimura (1963).

Two types of mating are to be considered, those in which the mated individuals have the same mother (Fig. 7.19a) and those in which they have different mothers (Fig. 7.19b). The frequency of the former is $1/N_f$ and of the latter, $1 - 1/N_f$.

Case 1, Figure 7.19a:

$$F_{(1)} = 0.25[1 + 2F' + F''].$$

Case 2, Figure 7.19b:

$$F_{(2)} = 0.5[F' + F_f']$$

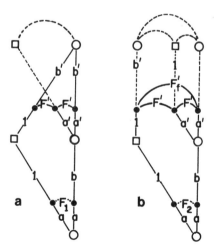

FIG. 7.19. Path diagram for sex-linkage with same (left) or different (right) mother of male and female (redrawn from Wright 1933a, Fig. 3.4).

where F_f' is the correlation between eggs produced by different females of the same generation.

Combining:

(7.82) $$F = 0.5[F' + F_f'] + \frac{1}{4N_f}[1 - 2F_f' + F''].$$

F_f involves the correlation between sperms of different males. Again there are two cases to be considered.

Case 1, Figure 7.20a (mother in common, frequency $1/N_f$):

$$F_{m(1)} = b'^2 = 0.5(1 + F'').$$

Case 2, Figure 7.20b (mother not in common, frequency $1 - 1/N_f$):

$$F_{m(2)} = F_f'.$$

Total

(7.83) $$F_m = F_f' + [1/(2N_f)](1 - 2F_f' + F'') = 2F - F'.$$

There are four cases to be considered in the case of F_f.

Case 1, Figure 7.21a, full sibs, frequency $1/N_mN_f$:

$$F_{f(1)} = (1/4)(1 + b'^2 + 2F') = (1/8)(3 + 4F' + F'').$$

Case 2, Figure 7.21b, mother only in common, frequency $(N_m - 1)/N_mN_f$:

$$F_{f(2)} = (1/4)(b'^2 + 2F' + F_m') = (1/8)(1 + 8F' - F'').$$

Case 3, Figure 7.21c, father only in common, frequency $(N_f - 1)/N_mN_f$:

$$F_{f(3)} = (1/4)(1 + 2F' + F_f').$$

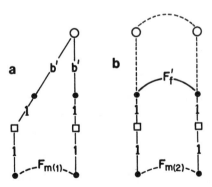

FIG. 7.20. Path diagram for sex-linkage with same (left) or different (right) mother of two males (redrawn from Wright 1933a, Fig. 5.6).

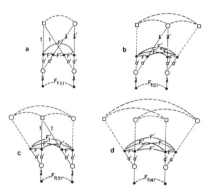

FIG. 7.21. Paths under sex-linkage with same father and mother of two females (top left), different fathers but same mother (top right), different mothers but same father (bottom left), both parents different (bottom right) (redrawn from Wright 1933a, Figs. 7–10).

Case 4, Figure 7.21d, neither parent in common, frequency $(N_m - 1) \times (N_f - 1)/N_m N_f$:

$$F_{f(4)} = (1/4)[F_m' + F_f' + 2F'] = (1/4)[4F' - F'' + F_f'].$$

The following can be derived after considerable reduction:
Total

$$(7.84) \qquad F_f = (1/4)(2F + 3F' - F'') + \frac{1}{4N_m}(1 - 2F' + F'').$$

Substitution in (7.82) yields after some reduction:

$$(7.85) \qquad F = F' + \frac{(N_f + 1)}{8N_f}(1 - 2F' + F'') - \frac{(N_m - 1)(N_f - 1)}{8N_m N_f}(1 - 2F'' + F'''),$$

$$P = P' - \frac{(N_f + 1)}{8N_f}(2P' - P'') + \frac{(N_m - 1)(N_f - 1)}{8N_m N_f}(2P'' - P''').$$

The average rate of decrease of heterozygosis can be obtained as before by putting $P/P' = P'/P'' = P''/P''' = \lambda$ and expressing in terms of $\Delta P/P' = x = \lambda - 1$.

$$(7.86) \quad x^3 + 2(1 + C_1)x^2 + [(1 + C_1) + 2(C_1 - C_2)]x + (C_1 - C_2) = 0$$

where

$$C_1 = \frac{N_f + 1}{8N_f} \quad \text{and} \quad C_2 = \frac{(N_m - 1)(N_f - 1)}{8N_m N_f}.$$

For reasonably large N_m and N_f, x becomes so small that x^3 may be ignored, giving

$$\Delta P = -\frac{C_1 - C_2}{1 + C_1} P' = -\frac{2N_m + N_f - 1}{9N_m N_f + 1} P' \approx -\frac{2N_m + N_f}{9N_m N_f} P'.$$

The effective size of population is thus roughly $N_e = 9N_m N_f/(4N_m + 2N_F)$ which reduces to $(3/4)N$ if $N_m = N_f = N/2$ but is approximately $4.5N_m$ if the number of females is very much greater than the number of males and the latter are heterogametic. In birds in which the females are heterogametic, the roles of N_m and N_f are reversed. In this case, if the number of females is greatly in excess, N_e approaches $2.25N_m$.

Under brother-sister mating $N_m = N_f = 1$ and $P = 0.5P' + 0.25P''$, which is the same as under autosomal heredity.

With one male (XY) and many females, the equation approaches $P = (3/4)P' + (1/8)P''$, which also is the same as under autosomal heredity.

If, however, it is the females that are heterogametic, and there are one male and many females, then $P \approx 0.5P' + 0.25P''$ as under brother-sister mating.

Polysomic Loci and Inbreeding

In the case of a $2k$-somic locus with random union of gametes in a population of N monoecious individuals, the chance of self-fertilization is $1/N$ and of union of gametes from different individuals is $(N - 1)/N$. Giving due weight to these, the equation for F_D (7.24) becomes

$$F_D = (1/N)b^2 + \left(\frac{N - 1}{N}\right)4k^2(ba')^2 F_D',$$

$$F_D = \left(\frac{1}{2Nk}\right)[1 + (2N - 1)(2K - 1)F' - (2N - 2)(k - 1)F''].$$

If e is treated as negligible, $F_S = F'$ by (7.23).

(7.87) $P = \dfrac{1}{2N(2k - 1)} [(6Nk - 4N - 2k + 1)P'$
$$- (2N - 2)(k - 1)P''] \quad \text{(Wright 1938c)}.$$

In the special case of self-fertilization, $N = 1$:

(7.88) $$P = \frac{4k - 3}{4k - 2}P'.$$

This reduces to $0.5P'$ in the case of disomics, as expected, to $(5/6)P'$ in the case of tetrasomics and $(9/10)P'$ in the case of hexasomics, both in agreement with the results of Haldane (1930c) referred to earlier (7.2 and 7.4). For octosomics it reduces to $(13/14)P'$.

(7.89)   If N is large, P approaches $[1 - 1/(2Nk)]P'$.

If self-fertilization is excluded, the frequency of matings between sibs is $2/N(N - 1)$, between half-sibs $4(N - 2)/N(N - 1)$, and between more remote relatives $(N - 2)(N - 3)/N(N - 1)$. Using these weights:

$$F_D = \frac{1}{N(N - 1)}(b^2 + F_D') + \frac{N - 2}{N(N - 1)}(b^2 + 3F_D')$$

$$+ \frac{(N - 2)(N - 3)}{N(N - 1)}F_D'.$$

(7.90)
$$P = \frac{1}{2N(2k - 1)}[(6Nk - 4N - 4k + 2)P'$$
$$- (2Nk - 2N - 4k + 3)P''] \quad \text{(Wright 1938c)}.$$

The simplest special case is that of sib mating $(N = 2)$:

(7.91) $$P = P' - \left(\frac{1}{8k - 4}\right)(2P' - P'').$$

This is the exact equation for given P' and P''. The limiting ratio of P to P', on identifying P/P' and P'/P'', gives the approximate equation

(7.92) $$P = \left[\frac{4k - 3 + \sqrt{[(4k - 2)^2 + 1]}}{8k - 4}\right]P'.$$

Following are special cases (Wright 1938c):

	P (Exact)	P' (Limiting)	
Disomic	$(1/2)P' + (1/4)P''$	$(1/4)(1 + \sqrt{5})P'$	$= 0.80902P'$
Tetrasomic	$(5/6)P' + (1/12)P''$	$(1/12)(5 + \sqrt{37})P'$	$= 0.92356P'$
Hexasomic	$(9/10)P' + (1/20)P''$	$(1/20)(9 + \sqrt{101})P'$	$= 0.95249P'$
Octosomic	$(13/14)P' + (1/28)P''$	$(1/28)(13 + \sqrt{197})P'$	$= 0.96556P'$

In the tetrasomic case, the quadratic equation for the limiting case, given by path analysis, is an exact divisor of the octic characteristic equation that had been obtained by Bartlett and Haldane (1934), and the largest root, 0.92356, is the same. Fisher (1949) arrived at the same octic equation and factored out the same quadratic equation as that from (7.90) for N = 2, k = 2.

The effectiveness of self-fertilization and of sib-mating in reducing heterozygosis may be compared by considering the number of generations required for halving.

Half-period in Generations

	Self-fertilization	Sib-mating
Disomic	1	3.27
Tetrasomic	3.80	8.71
Hexasomic	6.58	14.21
Octosomic	8.58	20.38

Populations of Changing Size

The preceding sections have dealt largely with F and P in arrays of closed populations of constant size N. It is desirable to consider the effect of changing population number.

This is a simple matter in the case of completely random union of gametes, since here the formula for P depends merely on the number in the preceding generation: $P = (1 - 1/2N)P'$ and $\Delta P/P' = -(1/2N)$. If N is any function of time, $N = N_0 f(t)$, and if the numbers are fairly large, the percentage rate may be written:

$$\frac{d \log P}{dt} = -\frac{1}{2N_0 f(t)}.$$

(7.93) $$P = C \exp\left[-\frac{1}{2N_0}\int \frac{dt}{f(t)}\right]$$

where C is a constant such that $P = P_0$ if $t = 0$.

Thus if the population is increasing in geometric series, $f(t) = (1 + r)^t$.

(7.94) $$P = P_0 \exp\left\{-\frac{1}{2N_0}\left[\frac{1 - (1 + r)^{-t}}{\log (1 + r)}\right]\right\} \approx P_0 \exp\left[-\frac{1 - e^{-rt}}{2N_0 r}\right].$$

Populations for which r is negative tend, of course, to extinction, but P decreases at an accelerating rate during the process. If r is zero, $P = P_0 \exp(-t/2N_0)$ as expected. If r is positive, P approaches a limit $P_0 \exp[-1/(2N_0 r)]$ which is close to zero if r is much less than $1/2N_0$ but which declines little if r is much greater.

For populations that are increasing in arithmetic progression,

(7.95) $$f(t) = (1 + rt) \quad \text{and} \quad P = P_0(1 + rt)^{-1/(2N_0 r)}.$$

If r is positive, P approaches zero but with increasing slowness.

The preceding discussion dealt with disomic loci, but in the case of polysomic loci and random union of gametes, the N of the formula is also that of the parental generation. With large N it is merely necessary to substitute kN for N.

The case of a monoecious population with a certain percentage of self-fertilization is more complicated. The values of F and P can be obtained as in equations (7.41) and (7.42), but it is necessary to distinguish between the sizes of successive generations, N' and N. It is also assumed below that h varies.

$$(7.96) \quad P = \frac{1}{2N'(1 - h')} \{[(2 - h - hh')N' - 2(1 - h)]P' $$
$$+ (1 - h)(1 - N'h')P''\}.$$

With random self-fertilization, $h = 1/N$ and $h' = 1/N'$. This reduces to $P = [1 - 1/(2N)]P'$ as expected. With a constant amount of self-fertilization, $h' = h$, it becomes

$$(7.97) \qquad P = 1 + \frac{h}{2} - \frac{1}{N'} \, P' + [1/(2N') - h/2] \, P''.$$

This is the same as (7.41) except that N' is the population number of the grandparental generation.

In many other cases such as that of random mating of N_m males N_f females (7.51), that of N_P permanent pairs and a certain given percentage of sib mating (7.53), and that of polysomic loci, with self-fertilization excluded (7.90), the formula is also unchanged except that N must be interpreted as applying to the grand-parental generation.

In the case of sex-linked heredity, however, N_f applies to the grand-parental generation and N_m to the generation before this.

If there are either irregular or cyclic changes in population size, the value of P after n generations, in the case of random union of gametes, can be written $P_n = P_0 \prod_{i=0}^{n-1} [1 - 1/(2N_i)]$ or if the N's are fairly large, as approximated $P_0[1 - 0.5 \sum_0^{n-1} (1/N_i)]$. The average relation between generations is given by

$$(7.98) \qquad\qquad P = [1 - 1/(2\tilde{N})]P'$$

where $(1/\tilde{N}) = (1/n) \sum_0^{n-1} (1/N_i)$ is the reciprocal of the harmonic mean of the numbers in the generations (Wright 1938a).

CHAPTER 8

Effective Size of Population

In dealing with mating systems in chapter 7, it was pointed out that the concept of "effective population number" is a useful one for comparative purposes. This concept becomes a practical necessity in dealing with natural populations. It is obvious that some sort of abstraction must always be made from crude enumerations to obtain the most significant population number from the standpoint of effects of inbreeding (Wright 1931).

Such effects depend primarily on the number of individuals of reproductive age per generation, not on the total of all ages. There is the further complication that those of reproductive age may differ enormously in productivity. The sex ratio must be taken into account. There is also the difficult problem of overlapping generations in most species. The complications from systematic changes, fluctuations, and cyclic changes have already been touched on. The relations to mode of inheritance and to systems of mating are those to which most attention was given in chapter 7.

Two Kinds of Effective Number

From the standpoint of change in heterozygosis, the effective population number (N_e) may be defined as whatever must be substituted for N in the basic formula in the case of completely random union of gametes in a population of N monoecious individuals:

$$(8.1) \qquad P = [1 - 1/(2N)]P'.$$

Change in heterozygous depends on the cumulative effects of accidents of sampling. The sampling variance, $\sigma^2_{\Delta q}$, of $2N$ gametes drawn at random from the gametic series $(1 - q)a + aA$ is:

$$(8.2) \qquad \sigma^2_{\Delta q} = q(1 - q)/2N.$$

This suggests that effective population number may also be defined by that function of the observed numbers that most accurately replaces N in this formula.

Both formulas have been used extensively for this purpose in dealing with theoretical populations of constant size, in which they agree, but, as brought out by Crow (1954a), changes in heterozygosis and sampling variance have different relations to the generations that make it desirable to distinguish an "inbreeding effective number" based on (8.1) and a "variance effective number" based on (8.2), which he showed may differ enormously in populations that are rapidly changing in size.

Values under Constant Population Size

It is desirable to review briefly the results already obtained with respect to inbreeding effective number in chapter 7, which were almost wholly concerned with populations of constant size. If self-fertilization is excluded in a monoecious population of size N, the formula for P becomes approximately (7.45),

$$(8.3) \qquad P = \left(1 - \frac{1}{2N+1}\right)P', \qquad N_e = N + 0.5.$$

In a random breeding population with equal numbers of the sexes (7.51, $N_m = N_f = N/2$),

$$(8.4) \qquad P = \left(1 - \frac{1}{2N+1}\right)P', \qquad N_e = N + 0.5.$$

If this system is qualified by exclusion of sib mating (7.56),

$$(8.5) \qquad P = \left(1 - \frac{1}{2N+4}\right)P', \qquad N_e = N + 2.$$

This is in relation to the standard case of completely random union of gametes. It becomes approximately $N_e = N + 1.5$ in relation to a random breeding population with equal numbers of males and females.

The deviations of N_e from N in all of those cases are trivial unless N is very small.

Mode of inheritance was found to have more important effects. In the case of a $2k$-somic locus (7.89),

$$(8.6) \qquad P = \left(1 - \frac{1}{2kN}\right)P', \qquad N_e = kN \qquad \text{(if } N \text{ is fairly large).}$$

The frequency of kinds of gametes approaches the binomial $[(1 - q)a + qA]^k$ (chap. 2), and thus the sampling variance for the genes in the $2N$ gametes, necessary to replace the population, approaches the following formula which confirms the figure based on inbreeding effect:

$$(8.7) \qquad \sigma^2_{\Delta q} = q(1 - q)/2kN; \qquad N_e \text{ (Variance)} = kN.$$

In the case of sex-linkage with equal numbers of males and females (7.86, $N_m = N_f = N/2$):

$$(8.8) \qquad P = \left(1 - \frac{1}{1.5N}\right)P', \qquad N_e = 0.75N.$$

The variance of q in a sample of $N/2$ X-chromosomes in fertilized eggs that develop into males (XY) is $2q(1 - q)/N$, and from the N X-chromosomes that develop into females (XX) is $q(1 - q)/N$. On the average, $q = (1/3)q_m + (2/3)q_f$ (chap. 2) giving a result in agreement with the preceding.

$$(8.9) \quad \sigma^2_{\Delta q} = \frac{1}{9}\left[\frac{2q(1 - q)}{N}\right] + \frac{4}{9}\left[\frac{q(1 - q)}{N}\right] = \frac{q(1 - q)}{1.5N}, \; N_e(\text{var}) = 0.75N.$$

Second-order corrections are not included in these formulas.

The Sex-Ratio Effect on N_e

It was shown in chapter 7 that with random mating among N_m males and N_f females the formula (7.51) for change in P indicates the approximate effective population number.

$$(8.10) \qquad N_e = \frac{4N_m N_f}{N_m + N_f}.$$

This reduces to N if $N_m = N_f = N/2$ and thus is the effective population number in terms of separate sexes. It is a close approximation in terms of random union of gametes if 0.5 is added. As noted earlier the extreme case of an indefinitely greater number of females than males indicates $N_e = 4N_m$.

The sampling variance of the $2N_m$ gametes that produce males is $q(1 - q)/2N_m$, and for the $2N_f$ gametes that produce females it is $q(1 - q)/2N_f$. Since the mean gene frequency is $0.5(q_m + q_f)$ the sampling variance is

$$(8.11) \quad \begin{aligned} \sigma^2_{\Delta q} &= 0.25q(1 - q)[1/(2N_m) + 1/(2N_f)] \\ &= q(1 - q)/2\left(\frac{4N_m N_f}{N_m + N_f}\right) \end{aligned} \qquad \text{(Wright 1939b)}.$$

Again there is agreement, ignoring second-order corrections.

Similarly in the case of sex-linked genes (males heterogametic), the approximate formula (7.86) for N_e, derived from that for P, was

$$(8.12) \qquad N_e = \frac{9N_m N_f}{4N_m + 2N_f}.$$

The sampling variance is $q(1 - q)/N_m$ for the N_m X-chromosomes of males (XY) but $q(1 - q)/2N_f$ for the X-chromosomes of females (XX) and thus for the mean $q = [(1/3)q_m + (2/3)q_f]$.

$$(8.13) \quad \sigma^2_{\Delta q} = q(1 - q)\left[\frac{1}{9}\left(\frac{1}{N_m}\right) + \frac{4}{9}\left(\frac{1}{2N_f}\right)\right] = q(1 - q)/2\left(\frac{9N_m N_f}{4N_m + 2N_f}\right)$$

(Wright 1939b).

Again the two methods lead to the same approximate value of N_e.

Formulas (8.8) and (8.9) are for the special case $N_m = N_f = N/2$. If the ratio of N_f to N_m is great, N_e approaches $4.5N_m$, whereas in the opposite case it is $2.25N_f$.

Systematic Change in Population Size

In the case of systematic change of population size, the exact formulas for change in heterozygosis were of the same form as with constant size except that the generations to which the N's pertained had to be designated (chap. 7). In the case of random union of gametes, N_e was the population number of the parental generation, whereas in those in which there was a constant amount of self-fertilization or in which there were separate sexes (and autosomal heredity), N_e referred to the grandparental generation. The concept of a single effective population number broke down in the case of sex-linked heredity since N_f referred to the grandparental generation and N_m referred to a generation earlier.

The sampling variance depends on the gene frequency in the array of gametes produced by the parents and the size of the sample that constitutes the offspring generation. Consideration of the meaning of variance effective number under changing population size will be deferred to a later section. It obviously cannot be expected to be the same as an effective number based on the inbreeding effect in this case.

Fluctuations and Cyclic Changes

The situation is different in the case of fluctuations or cyclic changes about a constant average. As noted in chapter 7 (7.98) the inbreeding effective number may be taken as approximately $\tilde{N}$, the harmonic mean of the numbers over a period, if this is not so long as to bring about appreciable selective changes in gene frequency. The total sampling variance over a cycle of n generations in the standard case is:

$$(8.14) \quad \sigma^2_{\Delta q} = \sum_{1}^{n} [q(1 - q)/2N_i] = q(1 - q)/2\tilde{N} \quad \text{(Wright 1939b).}$$

There is thus agreement with the estimate from change in heterozygosis with some qualification because of the lag of one or two generations in the latter.

If N varies widely, as in the annual cycle in many insects, effective N may be very much smaller than apparent N. To cite an extreme case, if a population increases tenfold in each of five generations, N_o to $10^5 N_o$, before collapsing to its original size, $1/\tilde{N} = (1/6)[1.11111] = 10/54$. $N_e = 5.4 N_o$ by either method over the cycle of six generations in contrast with $\bar{N} = 18,518 N_o$, the arithmetic mean of the numbers.

This bottleneck effect is greatest in cases in which the total population consists of small demes, each likely to become extinct after a few generations but, if so, always replaced sooner or later by a few stray migrants from populations that have persisted. In this way, every deme at any given time has a history of passage through a great many bottlenecks of small numbers on being traced back from place to place, and since a few momentarily flourishing demes may be the source from which many new colonies are founded, large areas or even the whole species may, in the course of time, trace to a single deme that has passed through many bottlenecks (Wright 1938a, 1939b, 1940a).

Differential Productivity

A complication in the estimation of N_e that may be of considerable importance is that of differential productivity of the mature individuals of the ancestral generations. Let N be the number of such individuals in the parental generation and k_i the number of gametes from the ith individual that go into the production of mature individuals of the next generation. In the standard case of N monoecious individuals with random union of gametes, the proportion of self-fertilization is:

$$\sum_{i}^{N} [k_i(k_i - 1)] \bigg/ \left(\sum^{N} k_i\right)\left(\sum k_i - 1\right) = \left[\sum k_i^2 - N\bar{k}\right]\big/ N\bar{k}[N\bar{k} - 1].$$

But $\sum k_i^2 = N[\sigma_k^2 + \bar{k}^2]$, giving the proportion as

(8.15) $\qquad [\sigma_k^2 + \bar{k}(\bar{k} - 1)]/\bar{k}(N\bar{k} - 1)$

instead of $1/N$.

Thus

(8.16) $\qquad N_e = (N\bar{k} - 1)/(\bar{k} - 1 + \sigma_k^2/\bar{k}).$

In the case of a population of constant size, $\bar{k} = 2$:

(8.17) $\qquad N_e = (4N - 2)/(2 + \sigma_k^2)$ $\qquad$ (Wright 1938a, 1939b).

Under random sampling from a total consisting of equal arrays of gametes from all parents, $\sigma_k^2 = N\bar{k}(1/N)(1 - 1/N) = [(N - 1)/N]\bar{k}$. On substituting this in (8.16), $N_e = N$ as expected.

Under experimental conditions, it is possible to take exactly the same number of offspring from every one of the parents for producing the next generation, in which case $\sigma_k^2 = 0$ and $N_e = (N\bar{k} - 1)/(\bar{k} - 1)$ which is greater than N, though not much if $\bar{k}$ is large. If population size is kept constant $(\bar{k} = 2)$, $N_e = 2N - 1$, under which effective population number is practically doubled by selecting exactly two offspring from each parent in each generation.

In nature, however, there are usually much greater differences in productivity than those expected merely from accidents of sampling, and thus an effective population number considerably less than apparent. In the extreme case in which only one member of the parental generation produces all of the parents of the next generation, $\sigma_k^2 = (N - 1)\bar{k}^2$, giving $N_e = 1$ as expected.

Kimura and Crow (1963a) extended the analysis to the case of separate sexes. The case of a monoecious population without self-fertilization is similar. In either of these, it is the number of grandparents (N') instead of parents (N) that must be considered. The proportion of cases in which uniting gametes trace to the same grandparent is $(\sum_i^{N'} [k_i'(k_i' - 1)]/\sum_i^{N'} k')(\sum k' - 1) - 2N$ in this case, listing each pair of grandparental gametes twice as before. The pairs that united to produce parents must be excluded. In this case $\sum_i^{N'} k_i'^2 = N'(\sigma_{k'}^2 + \bar{k}'^2)$ and $N = N'\bar{k}'/2$. Effective population number is

$$(8.18) \qquad N_e = \frac{N'\bar{k}' - 2}{\bar{k}' - 1 + (\sigma_{k'}^2/\bar{k})} = \frac{2N - 2}{\bar{k}' - 1 + (\sigma_{k'}^2/\bar{k})}.$$

If the population is constant in size $(\bar{k} = 2)$: $N_e = (4N - 4)/(2 + \sigma_{k'}^2)$.

In this case, $\sigma_{k'}^2 = [(N' - 2)/N']\bar{k}'$ under random sampling from a total consisting of equal arrays from all grandparents, again giving $N_e = N'$ as expected.

These are the effective population numbers relative to that with equal productivity with equal numbers of males and females (both $N/2$) or in a monoecious population of size N with self-fertilization excluded. As both of these have $N_e = N + 0.5$, approximately, relative to the standard case of random union of gametes, the corrected value of N_e requires addition of about 0.5. Thus for constant population size,

$$(8.19) \qquad N_e = \frac{4N - 3 + 0.5\sigma_{k'}^2}{2 + \sigma_{k'}^2}.$$

If $\sigma_{k'}^2 = 0$, then $N_e = 2N - 1.5$. Again there is practically doubling of effective population number by choosing just two offspring from each parent in each generation.

The Variance Effective Number under Changing Population Size

As noted earlier, it was shown by Crow (1954a) that the variance effective number may differ radically from the estimated inbreeding effective number if population size is changing. The subject was discussed further by Crow and Morton (1955) and, with exhaustive regard to Gaussian corrections, by Kimura and Crow (1963a). For our purpose the somewhat less exact but less tedious approach of the earlier papers seems adequate.

Consider a parental population of size N, with the zygotic array $[xAA + yAA' + zA'A']$ where $x = q^2 + Fq(1 - q)$, $y = 2q(1 - q)(1 - F)$, and $z = (1 - q)^2 + Fq(1 - q)$. The mean variance of the number of A's in individuals about the mean number, $2q$, is given by

$$(8.20) \quad [x(2 - 2q)^2 + y(1 - 2q)^2 + z(0 - 2q)^2] = 2q(1 - q)(1 + F).$$

The variance of the number of A's in a random sample of N individuals is thus $2Nq(1 - q)(1 + F)$ and variance of the proportion of A's in such a sample is $q(1 - q)(1 + F)/2N$.

The variance of the number of A's in the mature individuals of the offspring generation (size $0.5N\bar{k}$) is

$$(8.21) \quad \sum_{}^{N} [x(k - kq)^2 + y[0.5k - kq]^2 + z(0 - kq)^2 + yk/4]$$
$$= 0.5Nq(1 - q)[(\sigma_k{}^2 + \bar{k}^2)(1 + F) + \bar{k}(1 - F)].$$

The variance of the proportion of A's in a sample of $0.5N\bar{k}$ offspring is obtained by dividing by $N^2\bar{k}^2$, the square of the total number of contributing genes:

$$(8.22) \quad \sigma_{q(o)}^2 = q(1 - q)[(\sigma_k{}^2 + \bar{k}^2)(1 + F) + \bar{k}(1 - F)]/2N\bar{k}^2.$$

This variance is compounded of that of the parental generation and the increment $\sigma_{\Delta q}^2$. The latter is thus

$$(8.23) \quad \sigma_{\Delta q}^2 = \frac{q(1 - q)}{2N\bar{k}}[(1 - F) + (1 + F)\sigma_k{}^2/\bar{k}].$$

The estimate of variance effective N for the offspring generation as given by the formula $\sigma^2_{\Delta q} = q(1 - q)/2N_e$ is thus

$$(8.24) \qquad N_e = \frac{2N_o}{(1 - F) + (1 + F)(\sigma_k{}^2/\bar{k})}$$

where $N_o \ (= 0.5N\bar{k})$ is the number of offspring.

The more exhaustive analysis of Kimura and Crow (1963a) arrived at the same formula except that $\sigma_k{}^2$ was multiplied by $N/(N - 1)$.

The F of these formulas is that which measures the deviation of the frequency of heterozygotes from the Hardy-Weinberg expectation within the parental population, $y = 2q(1 - q)(1 - F)$ (referred to as F_{IS} later), not that derived for an array of populations tracing to a foundation stock. It may be negative but is ordinarily very small, and the formula may be taken as practically $N_e = 2N_o/[1 + \sigma_k{}^2/\bar{k}]$.

Crow and Morton (1955) gave the formula for other cases. In that of N_m males and N_f females, let k_{mi} and k_{fi} be the number of gametes contributed by the ith male and ith female, respectively, q_m and q_f the gene frequencies of the sexes, F_m and F_f their inbreeding coefficients relative to the population itself, and q_s and q_e the gene frequencies in sperms and eggs respectively.

$$(8.25) \qquad \sigma^2_{q,e} = \frac{q_f(1 - q_f)}{2N_o}[(1 - F_f) + (1 + F_f)(\sigma^2_{k,f})/\bar{k}_f],$$

$$(8.26) \qquad \sigma^2_{q,s} = \frac{q_m(1 - q_m)}{2N_o}[(1 - F_m) + (1 + F_m)(\sigma^2_{k,m}/\bar{k}_m)],$$

$$(8.27) \qquad \sigma^2_{q,o} = 0.25[\sigma^2_{q,e} + \sigma^2_{q,s}].$$

If there are no differences between q_f and q_m, F_f and F_m, $\sigma^2_{k,f}$ and $\sigma^2_{k,m}$, and $\bar{k}_f$ and $\bar{k}_m$, then

$$(8.28) \qquad \sigma_q{}^2 = \frac{q(1 - q)}{4N_o}[(1 - F_{IS}) + (1 + F_{IS})(\sigma_k{}^2/\bar{k})]$$

as with monoecious diploids.

In the case of sex linkage, the formula for $\sigma^2_{q,e}$ is given above; for sperms (males XY) the formula is

$$(8.29) \qquad \sigma^2_{q,s} = \frac{q_m(1 - q_m)}{N_{o,f}}(\sigma^2_{k,m}/\bar{k}_m).$$

The formula for $\sigma^2_{q_{o,f}}$ (daughters), assuming that $q_f = q_m$, is

$$(8.30) \qquad \sigma^2_{o,f} = \frac{1}{8N_{o,f}}\{q(1 - q)[(1 - F_{1S}) + (1 + F_{1S})(\sigma^2_{k,f}/\bar{k}_f) + 2(\sigma^2_{k,m}/\bar{k}_m)]\}.$$

TABLE 8.1. Comparison of approximate inbreeding effective number in dioecious and monoecious populations and of approximate variance effective number at different values of $\bar{k}$ and $\sigma_k^2/\bar{k}$.

INBREEDING EFFECTIVE NUMBER

Dioecious $N'\bar{k}/[\bar{k} - 1 + \sigma_k^2/\bar{k}]$					Monoecious, Random Unions $N\bar{k}/(\bar{k} - 1 + \sigma_k^2/\bar{k})$				
$\sigma_k^2/\bar{k}'$ \ $\bar{k}$	0	1	2	$N'\bar{k}'$	$\sigma_k^2/\bar{k}$ \ $\bar{k}$	0	1	2	$N\bar{k}$
1	∞	N'	$(1/2)N'$	1	1	∞	N	$(1/2)N$	1
2	$2N'$	N'	$(2/3)N'$	1	2	$2N$	N	$(2/3)N$	1
4	$(4/3)N'$	N'	$(4/5)N'$	1	4	$(4/3)N$	N	$(4/5)N$	1
∞	N'	N'	N'	1	∞	N	N	N	1

VARIANCE EFFECTIVE NUMBER

$2N_0/[1 + \sigma_k^2/\bar{k}]$

$\bar{k}$ \ $\sigma_k^2/\bar{k}$	0	1	2	10
1	$2N_0$	N_0	$(2/3)N_0$	$(2/11)N_0$
2	$2N_0$	N_0	$(2/3)N_0$	$(2/11)N_0$
4	$2N_0$	N_0	$(2/3)N_0$	$(2/11)N_0$
∞	$2N_0$	N_0	$(2/3)N_0$	$(2/11)N_0$

In the case of $2n$-somy,

$$(8.31) \quad \sigma^2_{q,o} = \frac{q(1 - q)}{2nN_o} \{(n - 1)(1 - F_{1S}) + [1 + (n - 1)F_{1S}](\sigma_k^2/\bar{k})\}.$$

It is instructive to compare (see Table 8.1) the inbreeding and variance effective numbers, the former for both the cases dependent on number of grandparents, N', and on number of parents, N, the variance effective number being dependent on number of offspring, N_o. For simplicity, terms of the order of $1/N$ are omitted.

The inbreeding and variance effective numbers all agree if population size is constant ($\bar{k} = 2$), since in this case $N' = N = N_o$. With other values of $\bar{k}$ no real comparison is possible from these tables since the N's refer to different generations. The values are, however, the same (to the approximation used) in the two cases of inbreeding effective number except that those for dioecious populations refer to numbers a generation earlier than those for monoecious populations, with random fertilization. The last column in each of these refers to the maximum possible ratio $\sigma_k^2/\bar{k}$ instead of to a given value and is the case in which all offspring traced to just one individual of the pertinent generation.

The variance effective number for any given ratio $\sigma_k^2/\bar{k}$ is independent of $\bar{k}$, being N_o, the observed number of offspring if there is random sampling ($\sigma_k^2/\bar{k}' = 1$), but is about twice this if all parents have the same number of offspring ($\sigma_k^2 = 0$), and becomes smaller than N_o if there is differential productivity beyond that due to accidents of sampling.

Nei and Murata (1966) have studied the complications that arise where differences in fecundity are hereditary.

CHAPTER 9

Simultaneous Inbreeding and Recombination

It was brought out in chapter 2 that if, for any reason, neutral pairs of alleles are not combined at random in a panmictic population, crossing over, if it occurs at all, will ultimately bring about random combination. Given the gametic array $[wAB + xAb + yaB + zab]$ and thus gene frequencies $q_A = (w + x)$, $q_B = (w + y)$, the deviation from random combination, measured by the correlation $r_{AB} = (w - q_A q_B)/\sqrt{[q_A q_B(1 - q_A)(1 - q_B)]}$ (or merely by the numerator of this expression) which can be written $(wz - xy)$, declines at the average rate of recombination $c = (1/2)(c_f + c_m)$ where c_f and c_m are the rates in oogenesis and spermatogenesis, respectively. It is obvious, however, that if the population is broken up into closed lines in each of which one or the other allele at each locus tends to become homozygous, the lines may all be expected to become fixed before completely random combination has occurred.

Robbins (1918) investigated this matter in the case of self-fertilized lines. He found that on starting from double heterozygotes of the type AB/ab, self-fertilization leads to the proportions $c/(1 + 2c)$ of each of the recombinant types Ab/Ab and aB/aB, with the remainder equally divided between the two original types. If $c = 1/2$, the four types come to be equally numerous.

The corresponding proportions under various systems of mating involving two individuals per generation (sib-mating and parent-offspring mating, both for autosomes and sex chromosomes) were investigated by Haldane and Waddington (1931) who based their calculations on the proportions of all possible types of matings. They noted that "the method of calculation here employed cannot be applied to most other types of inbreeding. It is wholly inapplicable to the important case where a male is bred to a large group of his half-sisters in each generation. The case of double-first-cousin matings with autosomal linkage involves the consideration of 10,000 different pairs of mating types, and other systems are still more complex. It may prove possible to solve such problems by an extension of Wright's (1921) correlation method, but we have been unable to do so."

The method referred to above (path analysis) was applied later to various cases (Wright 1933b).

Kimura (1963) has applied the closely related concept of probability of identity by origin. He confirmed most of the preceding results and made some extensions.

The method of path analysis will be used here. The primary objective is the correlation between two pairs of alleles, referred to above, especially the ultimate value after fixation is complete (r_∞). The amount of recombination in the case in which all gene frequencies are 0.50 (which will be assumed throughout) is given by $(x_\infty + y_\infty) = 2x_\infty = (1/2)(1 - r_\infty)$.

N Monoecious Individuals: Random Fertilization

The simplest case is that of populations of N monoecious individuals with completely random union of gametes, including the proportion $1/N$ of self-fertilization. Figure 9.1 is a diagram which relates the A-locus of a gamete (left) to the B-locus (right): (1) of the same gamete (correlation r), (2) of a different gamete of the same individual (s), and (3) of a *random* gamete from the population (t) (not shown). The latter comes from the same individual (I_i) with frequency $1/N$ and from a different individual (I_j) with frequency $(1 - 1/N)$. The inbreeding coefficients (F') of these individuals are shown but do not enter into the analysis. This depends on the correlation r' between A and B of the same gametes, on the correlation t' between A and B of any other gametes of the preceding generation, on the compound path coefficient relating any gamete of one generation to the one to which it traces in the preceding generation, which as always under diploid autosomal heredity has the value $ba' = 1/2$, and finally on a supplementary path (value g) con-

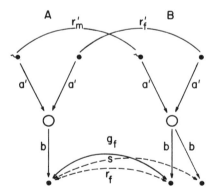

FIG. 9.1. Path diagram for two linked loci in a monoecious population (redrawn from Wright 1933b, Fig. 1).

necting the A and B loci of the same gamete to allow for the additional contribution to r (as compared with s) due to correlated segregation. Chapter 2
dealt with this supplement in the case of indefinitely large panmictic populations. We are concerned here with an indefinitely large population, subdivided into ones of size N, in which therefore there is a correlation (t)
between A and B of random gametes within lines. The correlations after the
system is under way may be written from inspection of the diagram.

(9.1) $$s = (1/4)[2r' + 2t'] = (1/2)(r' + t'),$$

(9.2) $$t = (1/N)s + (1 - 1/N)t' \quad \text{(note that } s \text{ is not primed)},$$

(9.3) $$r = s + g.$$

If there were no crossing over $(c = 0)$, there would be no change in r
which requires (from 9.3 and 9.1) that $g = (1/2)(r' - t')$. If, on the other
hand, there were random recombination $(c = 1/2)$, there would be no
difference between r and s, thus giving $g = 0$. Since recombination at the
frequency c is equivalent to the frequencies $(1 - 2c)$ of complete linkage and
$2c$ of random recombination (chap. 2), the corresponding value of g can be
obtained from the weighted average.

(9.4) $$g = (1/2)(1 - 2c)(r' - t'),$$

(9.5) $$r = s + g = r' - c(r' - t').$$

The rate of change of r can be expressed at once in terms of g, and the
latter can be expressed in terms of its preceding value.

(9.6) $$r - r' = -c(r' - t') = -[2c/(1 - 2c)]g,$$

(9.7) $$\begin{aligned} r - t &= (1 - 1/N)s + g - (1 - 1/N)t' \\ &= [1 - c - 1/(2N)](r' - t'), \end{aligned}$$

(9.8) $$g = (1/2)(1 - 2c)[1 - c - 1/(2N)](r'' - t'')$$
$$= [1 - c - 1/(2N)]g' \quad \text{(after a lag)}.$$

These equations make it possible to calculate the values of the correlations,
generation after generation.

The value of r in the nth generation can readily be obtained from (9.6) and
(9.8). Using subscripts here for generation number, with subscript 1 for the
gametes of the initial random breeding population:

(9.9) $$\sum_{2}^{n} r_i - \sum_{1}^{n-1} r_i = r_n - r_1 = -\left(\frac{2c}{1 - 2c}\right) \sum_{2}^{n} g_i,$$

(9.10)
$$r_n = r_1 - \frac{2c}{1 - 2c} g_2 \left[1 - \left(1 - c - \frac{1}{2N} \right)^{n-1} \right] / \left(c + \frac{1}{2N} \right)$$
$$= r_1 - \frac{4Nc}{(1 - 2c)(2Nc + 1)} g_2 \left[1 - \left(1 - c - \frac{1}{2N} \right)^{n-1} \right].$$

The limiting value, r_∞, is of most interest:

(9.11)
$$r_\infty = r_1 - \frac{4Ncg_2}{(1 - 2c)(2Nc + 1)}.$$

There were typographical errors here in Wright (1933b). The results in cases 1 and 2 were, however, given correctly.

Case 1.—Assume that the population starts from an array of double heterozygotes with the array of gametes

$$\left[\frac{1 - c}{2} AB + \frac{c}{2} Ab + \frac{c}{2} aB + \frac{1 - c}{2} ab \right].$$

The values of r, s, and t in the first generation must be obtained from this array.

$$r_1 = \left[\frac{1 - c}{2} - \frac{1}{4} \right] / \frac{1}{4} = 1 - 2c,$$

$$s_1 = 0, \quad \text{giving} \quad g_1 = 1 - 2c,$$
$$t_1 = 0.$$

The values in later generations may be obtained from (9.5), (9.1), (9.2), and (9.4). After generation 2, g may be obtained from (9.8).

(1)		Later	Generation (2)	(3)
r	$1-2c$	$r'-c(r'-t')$	$(1-2c)(1-c)$	$(1-2c)[(1-c)^2+c/2N]$
s	0	$(1/2)(r'+t')$	$(1/2)(1-2c)$	$(1/2)(1-2c)$
				$\times[1-c+1/(2N)]$
t	0	$t'+[1/(2N)](r'-t')$	$[1/(2N)](1-2c)$	$[1/(2N)](1-2c)$
				$\times[2-c-1/(2N)]$
g	$1-2c$	$(1/2)(1-2c)(r'-t')$	$(1/2)(1-2c)^2$	$(1/2)(1-2c)^2$
				$\times[1-c-1/(2N)]$
				$=g'[1-c-1/(2N)]$

The limiting correlation, r_∞, and proportion of recombinant lines, $2x_\infty$, if $q = 1/2$ are:

(9.12)
$$r_\infty = 1 - 2c \left[\frac{N + 1}{2Nc + 1} \right] = \frac{1 - 2c}{2Nc + 1},$$

(9.13)
$$2x_\infty = \frac{c(N + 1)}{2Nc + 1}.$$

With random recombination ($c = 1/2$), $r_\infty = 0$, and $2x_\infty = 0.50$ as expected.

If Nc is large, the proportion of recombinant lines also approaches 0.50 as expected.

If there is exclusive self-fertilization ($N = 1$):

(9.14)
$$r_\infty = \frac{1 - 2c}{1 + 2c},$$

(9.15)
$$2x_\infty = \frac{2c}{1 + 2c},$$

in agreement with Robbins (1918).

Case 2.—Assume that the population starts from a mixture of homozygotes differing in two loci $[q(AB/AB) + (1 - q)(ab/ab)]$. The initial array of gametes is $[qAB + (1 - q)ab]$ in which $r_1 = 1$, $s_1 = 1$, $t_1 = 0$, and $g_1 = 0$. The array in the next generation is $\{[q - cq(1 - q)]AB + [cq(1 - q)]Ab + [cq(1 - q)]aB + [(1 - q) - cq(1 - q)]ab\}$ in which the correlation between A and B of the same gamete gives $r_2 = 1 - c$, also derivable from (9.5). The values of s_2, t_2, and g_2 can be obtained as before, and again g can be obtained from (9.8) after generation 2.

			Generations	
(1)		Later	(2)	(3)
r	1	$r' - c(r' - t')$	$1 - c$	$(1 - c)^2 + c/2N$
s	1	$(1/2)(r' + t')$	$1/2$	$(1/2)[1 - c + 1/(2N)]$
t	0	$t' + [1/(2N)](r' - t')$	$1/(2N)$	$[1/(2N)][2 - c - 1/(2N)]$
g	0	$(1/2)(1 - 2c)(r' - t')$	$(1/2)(1 - 2c)$	$(1/2)(1 - 2c)[1 - c - 1/(2N)]$
				$= g_2[1 - c - 1/(2N)]$

(9.16)
$$r_\infty = 1 - \frac{2Nc}{2Nc + 1} = \frac{1}{2Nc + 1}.$$

If $q = 1/2$, the proportion of recombinant lines is

(9.17)
$$2x_\infty = \frac{Nc}{2Nc + 1}.$$

Here again the proportion of recombinant lines approaches 50% as expected if Nc is large. The proportion is, however, always slightly less than in the preceding case. Thus with $N = 10$ and $c = 0.1$, the proportion is

36.7% on starting from double heterozygotes but 33.3% on starting from an equal mixture of AB/AB and ab/ab. Even if there is random recombination ($c = 1/2$) the proportion of recombinant lines does not reach 50%, being $N/(2N + 2)$. This is to be expected since the chance of early fixation of $AABB$ or $aabb$ is obviously in excess of that of $AAbb$ or $aaBB$ which is not the case on starting from AB/ab with random combination.

Parent-Offspring Mating

Figure 9.2 illustrates the case of alternating parent-offspring mating. The correlation between two loci in the same gamete is again designated r, in random gametes of the same individual s, and between gametes of mating individuals t. The excess of r over s is again designated g.

(9.18) $s = (1/4)(r' + r'' + 2t')$,

(9.19) $t = (1/2)(s' + t')$,

(9.20) $r = s$ if $c = 1/2$ but $r = (1/2)(r' + r'')$ if $c = 0$.

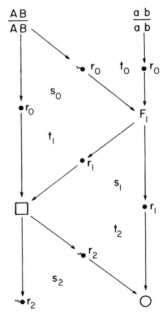

FIG. 9.2. Path diagrams for two linked loci in alternating parent-offspring mating (redrawn from Wright 1933b, Fig. 8).

Assigning these cases the weights $2c$ and $1 - 2c$, respectively, as before:

$$(9.21) \quad r = (1/2)(r' + r'') - (c/2)(r' + r'' - 2t'),$$

$$(9.22) \quad \begin{aligned} g &= (1/4)(1 - 2c)(r' + r'' - 2t') = (1 - 2c)(s - t') \\ &= (1/4)(1 - 2c)(g' + g'' + s' - t'') \end{aligned}$$

$$(9.23) \quad = (1/2)(1 - c)g' + (1/4)(1 - 2c)g'',$$

$$(9.24) \quad \begin{aligned} \sum_3^n g &= \frac{1 - c}{2} \sum_2^{n-1} g + \frac{1 - 2c}{4} \sum_1^{n-2} g \\ &= \frac{1 - c}{2} \left[g_2 + \sum_3^{n-1} g \right] + \frac{1 - 2c}{4} \left[g_1 + g_2 + \sum_3^{n-2} g \right]. \end{aligned}$$

Ultimately g_n, g_{n-1}, and g_{n-2} approach zero.

$$(9.25) \quad \sum_3^\infty g = \frac{1 - 2c}{1 + 4c} g_1 + \frac{3 - 4c}{1 + 4c} g_2,$$

$$(9.26) \quad r = (1/2)(r' + r'') - \frac{2cg}{1 - 2c},$$

$$(9.27) \quad 2\sum_3^n r = \sum_2^{n-1} r + \sum_1^{n-2} r - \frac{4c}{1 - 2c} \sum_3^n g,$$

$$(9.28) \quad 2r_n + r_{n-1} = 2r_2 + r_1 - \frac{4c}{1 - 2c} \sum_3^n g.$$

Ultimately $r_{n-1} = r_n = r_\infty$ and $\sum_3^n g = \sum_3^\infty g$.

$$(9.29) \quad 3r_\infty = 2r_2 + r_1 - \frac{4c}{1 + 4c} \left[g_1 + \frac{3 - 4c}{1 - 2c} g_2 \right].$$

Case 1.—Assume that the initial population consists of double hetero-zygotes, AB/ab, which are mated inter se, and that alternating parent-offspring mating starts from mating them with their offspring. The values $r_1 = 1 - 2c$, $s_1 = t_1 = 0$, and $g_1 = 1 - 2c$ are obvious. The value of s_2 in this case is $(1/2)(r_1 + t_1) = (1/2)(1 - 2c)$.

	(1)	(2)	Generation Later	(3)
r	$1-2c$	$(1-2c)(1-c)$	$(1/2)(1-c)(r'+r'')-ct'$	$(1/2)(1-c)(1-2c)$ $\times (2-c)$
s	0	$(1/2)(1-2c)$	$(1/4)(r'+r''+2t')$	$(1/4)(1-2c)(2-c)$
t	0	0	$(1/2)(s'+t')$	$(1/4)(1-2c)$
g	$1-2c$	$(1/2)(1-2c)^2$	$(1/4)(1-2c)(r'+r''-2t')$	$(1/4)(1-2c)^2(2-c)$ $= \dfrac{1-c}{2} g_2 + \dfrac{1-2c}{4} g_1$

(9.30)
$$r_\infty = \frac{1 - 2c}{1 + 4c}, \qquad 2x_\infty = \frac{3c}{1 + 4c}$$

(Haldane and Waddington 1931; Wright 1933b).

The proportion of recombinants is 50% if $c = 1/2$.

Case 2.—If the population starts from a cross $AB/AB \times ab/ab$ and this is followed by matings of F_1 of each sex to parents and thereafter there is alternating parent-offspring mating along each line, the values of r, s, t, and g in the first three generations are as follows:

	(1)	(2)	Later	(3)
r	1	$1-2c$	$(1/2)(1-c)(r'+r'')-ct'$	$(1-c)^2$
s	1	0	$(1/4)(r'+r''+2t')$	$(1/2)(1-c)$
t	-1	0	$(1/2)(s'+t')$	0
g	0	$1-2c$	$(1/4)(1-2c)(r'+r''-2t')$	$(1/2)(1-2c)(1-c)$

Generation

$$= \left(\frac{1-c}{2}\right)g_2 + \left(\frac{1-2c}{4}\right)g_1$$

(9.31)
$$r_\infty = \frac{3 - 4c}{3(1 + 4c)}, \qquad 2x_\infty = \frac{8c}{3(1 + 4c)} \qquad \text{(Wright 1933b)}.$$

In this case the proportions of recombinant lines reaches only 4/9 even under random assortment.

Sex-linked Inheritance (Male XY)

Under alternating parent-offspring mating, starting from AB/ab females, mated with sons (from any males), heterozygosis is halved in each generation from mother to daughter and the relations of two sex-linked genes are the same as for two linked autosomal genes under self-fertilization (Fig. 9.3).

(9.32)
$$r_\infty = \frac{1 - 2c}{1 + 2c},$$

(9.33)
$$2x_\infty = \frac{2c}{1 + 2c} \qquad \text{(Wright 1933b)}.$$

In the case of brother-sister mating (or one male and many half-sisters in organisms in which the female is heterogametic) the basic formulas become the same as for autosomal genes under alternating parent-offspring mating: The values of r_∞ and $2x_\infty$ are the same as in case 2 of the latter.

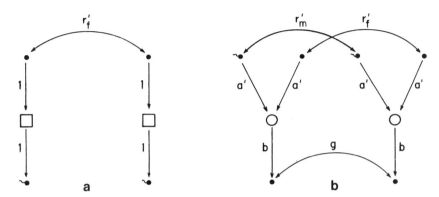

F<small>IG</small>. 9.3. Path diagrams for two sex-linked loci in the same sperm (left) and the same egg (right) (redrawn from Wright 1933*b*, Fig. 2.3).

$$(9.34) \qquad r_\infty = \frac{3 - 4c}{3(1 + 4c)},$$

$$(9.35) \qquad 2x_\infty = \frac{8c}{3(1 + 4c)}$$

(Haldane and Waddington 1931; Wright 1933*b*; Kimura 1963).

It may be added that in the case of N_m males and N_f females, the formulas for the various kinds of correlations in terms of values of the various kinds in preceding generations have been given by Wright (1933*b*) and that Kimura (1963) has obtained the rather complicated formulas for the ultimate values.

Any Number of Males and Females; Autosomal Genes

We consider next the case of autosomal genes and random mating with separate sexes, N_m males and N_f females. The correlations between loci of the same gamete (r) and that between random gametes of the same individual (s) may be expressed in terms of correlations r' and t' of the preceding generation by the same formula as in the case of monoecious populations, t being the correlation between A and B of random gametes of different individuals, irrespective of sex, and hence of uniting gametes. The formula for t is more complicated. The gametes in question may come from full sibs, correlation t_a, with frequency $1/N_m N_f$; from half-sibs, correlation t_b, with frequency $(N_m + N_f - 2)/N_m N_f$; or from non-sibs, correlation t_c, with frequency $(N_m - 1)(N_f - 1)/N_m N_f$. These frequencies, of course, apply only after two generations.

(9.36) $t_a = (1/4)[2s' + 2t']$,

(9.37) $t_b = (1/4)[s' + 3t']$,

(9.38) $t_c = (1/4)[4t']$,

(9.39) $t = \dfrac{1}{N_m N_f}[t_a + (N_m + N_f - 2)t_b + (N_m - 1)(N_f - 1)t_c]$,

(9.40) $= t' + (1/N_e)(s' - t')$ where $N_e = 4N_m N_f/(N_m + N_f)$.

An expression for g in terms of its value in the two preceding generations can be obtained:

(9.41) $$g = r - s = (1/2)(1 - 2c)(r' - t'),$$

as before, and

(9.42) $$r' - t' = 2g/(1 - 2c).$$

Also

(9.43) $$r' - t' = g' + (s' - t').$$

Thus

(9.44) $$s' - t' = \frac{2g}{1 - 2c} - g'.$$

But

(9.45) $s - t = (1/2)(r' + t') - t' - \dfrac{1}{N_e}(s' - t') = (1/2)(r' - t') - \dfrac{1}{N_e}(s' - t')$

(9.46) $s' - t' = \dfrac{g'}{1 - 2c} - \dfrac{1}{N_e}\left[\dfrac{2g'}{1 - 2c} - g''\right]$.

On equating those two expressions for $(s' - t')$:

(9.47) $$g = \left[1 - c - \frac{1}{N_e}\right]g' + \frac{1 - 2c}{2N_e}g'',$$

(9.48) $$r - r' = -c(r' - t'),$$

as before, and

(9.49) $$\sum_2^n r - \sum_1^{n-1} r = -\frac{2c}{1 - 2c}\sum_2^n g,$$

(9.50) $$r_n = r_1 - \frac{2c}{1 - 2c}\left[g_2 + \sum_3^n g\right].$$

But

(9.51)
$$\sum_3^n g = [1 - c - 1/N_e] \sum_2^{n-1} g + \frac{1-2c}{2N_e} \sum_1^{n-2} g_1$$
$$= [1 - c - 1/N_e]\left(g_2 + \sum_3^{n-1} g\right) + \frac{1-2c}{2N_e}\left[g_1 + g_2 + \sum_3^{n-2} g\right].$$

In the limiting case in which g_{n-2}, g_{n-1}, and g_n approach zero:

(9.52) $$\sum_3^\infty g = \{[2N_e(1 - c) - (1 + 2c)]g_2 + (1 - 2c)g_1\}/[2(N_e + 1)c + 1],$$

(9.53) $$r_\infty = r_1 - 2c\left[g_1 + \frac{2N_e}{1 - 2c}g_2\right]\Big/[2(N_e + 1)c + 1].$$

Case 1.—Assume that the population starts from random mating among double heterozygotes, AB/ab.

	(1)	Later	Generation (2)	(3)
r	$1-2c$	$r'-c(r'-t')$	$(1-2c)(1-c)$	$(1-2c)(1-c)^2$
s	0	$(1/2)(r'+t')$	$(1/2)(1-2c)$	$(1/2)[(1-2c)(1-c)]$
t	0	$t'+(1/N_e)(s'-t')$	0	$[1/(2N_e)](1-2c)$
g	$1-2c$	$(1/2)(1-2c)(r'-t')$	$(1/2)(1-2c)^2$	$(1/2)(1-2c)^2(1-c)$

(from (9.47) as well as (9.41))

(9.54) $$r_\infty = 1 - \frac{2(N_e + 2)c}{2(N_e + 1)c + 1} = \frac{1 - 2c}{2(N_e + 1)c + 1},$$

(9.55) $$2x_\infty = \frac{(N_e + 2)c}{2(N_e + 1)c + 1},$$

as given by Wright (1933b) and Kimura (1963).

If N_f is indefinitely large, N_e approaches $4N_m$. Thus in the case of one male and indefinitely many females, $N_e = 4$.

(9.56) $$r_\infty = 1 - \frac{12c}{1 + 10c} = \frac{1 - 2c}{1 + 10c},$$

(9.57) $$2x_\infty = \frac{6c}{1 + 10c}.$$

With equal numbers of males and females, $N_e = N$. The simplest case is that of sib mating, $N = 2$.

$$(9.58) \qquad r_\infty = 1 - \frac{8c}{1 + 6c} = \frac{1 - 2c}{1 + 6c},$$

$$(9.59) \qquad 2x_\infty = \frac{4c}{1 + 6c},$$

as given by Haldane and Waddington (1931).

Case 2.—Assume that the population starts from a mixture $\left[q\!\left(\dfrac{AB}{AB}\right) + (1 - q)\!\left(\dfrac{ab}{ab}\right)\right]$ in both sexes and thereafter splits up into lines of N_m males and N_f females.

Generation

	(1)	(2)	Later	(3)	(4)
r	1	$1-c$	$r'-c(r'-t')$	$(1-c)^2$	$(1-c)(1-c)^2 + c/(2N_e)$
s	1	$1/2$	$(1/2)(r' + t')$	$(1/2)(1-c)$	$(1/2)[(1-c)^2 +1/(2N_e)]$
	0	0	$t'+(1/N_e)(s'-t')$	$1/(2N_e)$	$[1/(2N_e)] \times (2-c-1/N_e)$
g	0	$(1/2)(1-2c)$	$(1/2)(1-2c)(r'-t')$	$(1/2)(1-2c)(1-c)$	$\dfrac{(1-2c)}{2}[(1-c)^2 -1/(2N_e)]$

$$(9.60) \qquad r_\infty = 1 - \frac{2N_e c}{2(N_e + 1)c + 1} = \frac{1 + 2c}{2(N_e + 1)c + 1}$$
(incorrect in Wright 1933b).

If $q = 1/2$:

$$(9.60a) \qquad 2x_\infty = \frac{N_e c}{2(N_e + 1)c + 1}.$$

Again there is approach to 50% recombinant lines if $N_e c$ is large but always somewhat less than 50% even under random combination. In the simplest case, $N_m = N_f = 2$, $2x_\infty = 4c/(10c + 1)$ in contrast with $6c/(10c + 1)$ if the population starts from AB/ab.

Monoecious Populations, No Self-fertilization

The basic equations are the same as in populations with equal numbers of males and females. The history either on starting from double heterozygotes or from a mixture of homozygotes differing at two loci is, in consequence, the same as in the preceding section.

Maximum Avoidance of Consanguine Mating

In the case of matings of double first cousins, there are four types of correlations between two loci to consider: (1) that between loci of the same gamete (r); that between loci of gametes of the same individual (s); that between loci of gametes of sibs (t); and that between loci of gametes of cousins, including the uniting gametes (u).

$$(9.61) \qquad r = r' - c(r' - u'),$$

$$(9.62) \qquad s = (1/2)(r' + u'),$$

$$(9.63) \qquad t = (1/2)(s' + u'),$$

$$(9.64) \qquad u = (1/2)(t' + u'),$$

$$(9.65) \qquad g = r - s = (1/2)(1 - 2c)(r' - u').$$

The relation of g to its value in preceding generations can be found as follows:

$$(9.66) \quad r' - u' = 2g/(1 - 2c) \qquad \text{from (9.65)}$$

$$(9.67) \quad r' - u' = -\frac{(r - r')}{c} = -\frac{(s - s') + (g - g')}{c} \qquad \text{since } r = s + g,$$

$$(9.68) \quad s - s' = g' - g - \frac{2cg}{1 - 2c} \qquad \text{from (9.66), (9.67),}$$

$$(9.69) \quad s' - u' = \frac{2g}{1 - 2c} - g' \qquad \text{from (9.65), (9.66),}$$

$$(9.70) \quad \begin{aligned} s' - u' &= (1/2)(r'' - t'') \\ &= (1/2)[g'' + (s'' - s''') + (1/2)(s''' - u''')] \\ &= (1/2)g'' + (1/4)g''', \end{aligned}$$

$$(9.71) \quad \begin{aligned} g &= \frac{1 - 2c}{2}(r' - u') \\ &= \frac{1 - 2c}{2}[(r' - s') + (s' - u')] \qquad \text{from (9.66),} \end{aligned}$$

$$g = \frac{1 - 2c}{2}(g' + g''/2 + g'''/4) \qquad \text{after a lag,}$$

$$(9.72) \quad \begin{aligned} \sum_{4}^{\infty} g &= \frac{1 - 2c}{2}\left[\sum_{3}^{\infty} g + (1/2)\sum_{2}^{\infty} g + (1/4)\sum_{1}^{\infty} g\right] \\ &= \frac{1 - 2c}{2}\left[g_3 + \sum_{4}^{\infty} g + (1/2)g_2 + (1/2)g_3 + (1/2)\sum_{4}^{\infty} g \right. \\ &\qquad \left. + (1/4)g_1 + (1/4)g_2 + (1/4)g_3 + (1/4)\sum_{4}^{\infty} g\right] \end{aligned}$$

(9.73) $$= \frac{1 - 2c}{1 + 14c}\,[g_1 + 3g_2 + 7g_3],$$

(9.74) $$r_2 - r_1 = -\frac{2c}{1 - 2c}\,g_2 \qquad \text{from (9.61), (9.66)},$$

(9.75) $$\sum_2^\infty r - \sum_1^\infty r = -\frac{2c}{1 - 2c}\left[g_2 + g_3 + \frac{1 - 2c}{1 + 14c}\,(g_1 + 3g_2 + 7g_3)\right]$$
$$\text{from (9.73), (9.71)},$$

(9.76) $$r_\infty = r_1 - \frac{2c}{(1 - 2c)(1 + 14c)}\,[(1 - 2c)g_1 + (4 + 8c)g_2 + 8g_3].$$

Assume that the initial population consists of double heterozygotes, AB/ab. The correlations in the first four generations are as follows:

Generation

	(1)	Later	(2)	(3)	(4)
r	$1-2c$	$r'-c(r'-u')$	$(1-2c)(1-c)$	$(1-2c)(1-c)^2$	$(1-2c)(1-c)^3$
s	0	$(1/2)(r'+u')$	$(1/2)(1-2c)$	$(1/2)(1-2c)(1-c)$	$(1/2)(1-2c)$ $\times(1-c)^2$
t	0	$(1/2)(s'+u')$	0	$(1/4)(1-2c)$	$(1/4)(1-2c)$ $\times(1-c)$
u	0	$(1/2)(t'+u')$	0	0	$(1/8)(1-2c)$
g	$1-2c$	$\dfrac{1-2c}{2}(r'-u')$	$\dfrac{(1-2c)^2}{2}$	$\dfrac{(1-2c)^2(1-c)}{2}$	$\dfrac{(1-2c)^2(1-c)^2}{2}$

(9.77) $$r_\infty = 1 - \frac{16c}{1 + 14c} = \frac{1 - 2c}{1 + 14c},$$

as given by Wright (1933b).

(9.78) $$2x_\infty = \frac{8c}{1 + 14c}.$$

An obvious slip ($16c$ for $8c$) is corrected here.

In the case of quadruple second cousins, the iteration formula for g is extension of that for double first cousins (and sibs):

(9.79) $$g = \frac{1 - 2c}{2}\,[g' + (1/2)g'' + (1/4)g''' + (1/8)g^{\mathrm{IV}}],$$

(9.80) $$r_\infty = 1 - \frac{32c}{1 + 30c} = \frac{1 - 2c}{1 + 30c},$$

(9.81) $$2x_\infty = \frac{16c}{1 + 30c}.$$

The general formula under maximum avoidance and starting from AB/ab is as follows:

$$(9.82) \qquad r_\infty = 1 - \frac{4Nc}{2(2N-1)c+1} = \frac{1-2c}{2(2N-1)c+1},$$

$$(9.83) \qquad 2x_\infty = \frac{2Nc}{2(2N-1)c+1}$$

as given by Wright (1933b).

The ultimate correlation is zero if $c = 0.50$ as in the other cases starting from double heterozygotes.

In a large population the ultimate correlation is only half as great as that given for random mating in a population of the same size, but in the latter case it was assumed that the parents of any generation are drawn at random from offspring of the preceding generation instead of just two per individual. Using the formula of Crow and Kimura, N in the case of random mating and separate sexes (9.54) must be replaced by $2N - 2$ to reduce to the latter basis. This changes $(1 - 2c)/[2(N + 1)c + 1]$ to $(1 - 2c)/[2(2N - 1)c + 1]$ which is identical with r_∞ under maximum avoidance.

Circular Half-sib mating

At the opposite extreme from the maximum avoidance of consanguine mating is the circular system of mating half-sibs (also with just two offspring per parent). The simplest case is that of a circle of two males and two females. Using r for the correlation between two loci in the same gamete, s for that in random gametes of the same individual, t for that in random gametes of half-sibs (and thus of uniting gametes), and u for that in random gametes of cousins, the basic equations are as follows:

$$(9.84) \qquad r = r' - c(r' - t'), \qquad\qquad (9.84a) \quad r - r' = -c(r' - t');$$

$$(9.85) \qquad s = (1/2)(r' + t'), \qquad\qquad (9.85a) \quad r' + t' = 2s;$$

$$(9.86) \qquad t = (1/4)(s' + 2t' + u'), \qquad (9.86a) \quad u' = 4t - s' - 2t';$$

$$(9.87) \qquad u = (1/2)(t' + u'),$$
$$(9.87a) \quad 2u = t' + u' = 4t - s' - t';$$

$$(9.88) \qquad g = r - s = (1/2)(1 - 2c)(r' - t'),$$
$$(9.88a) \quad r' - t' = 2g/(1 - 2c);$$

$$(9.89) \qquad r' = s' + g' = s + g/(1 - 2c) \qquad \text{from (9.85a), (9.88a)},$$
$$(9.89a) \quad s - s' = g' - [g/(1 - 2c)];$$

(9.90) $t' = s - [g/(1 - 2c)]$ from (9.85a), (9.88a),

(9.90a) $s - t' = g/(1 - 2c)$;

(9.91) $8(t - t') = (s' - t'') + (s' - s'')$ from (9.86a), (9.87a);

(9.92) $8(t - t') = g''$ from (9.91), (9.90a), (9.89a);

(9.93) $4(t - t') = (s' - s'') + 2(t' - t'') + (u' - u'')$ from (9.86);

(9.94) $(u - u') = g/(1 - 2c) - (1/2)g' - (1/4)g''$

from (9.84a), (9.89a), (9.92);

(9.95) $g - g' = \dfrac{1 - 2c}{2}[(r' - r'') - (t' - t'')]$ from (9.88);

(9.96) $g = g'(1 - c) - \dfrac{1 - 2c}{16}g'''$

from (9.95), (9.84a), (9.88a), (9.92) after a lag;

(9.97) $\displaystyle\sum_{2}^{n} r - \sum_{1}^{n-1} r = r_n - r_1 = -\frac{2c}{1 - 2c}\sum_{2}^{n} g$ from (9.84a), (9.85a).

The values of r, s, t, u, and g for four generations are as follows, noting that g_4 is the first that can be derived from (9.96) as well as (9.88):

	(1)	Later	Generation (2)	(3)	(4)
r	$1 - 2c$	$r' - c(r' - t')$	$(1-2c)(1-c)$	$(1-2c)(1-c)^2$	$(1-2c)[(1-c)^3 + c/8]$
s	0	$(1/2)(r' + t')$	$(1/2)(1-2c)$	$(1/2)(1-2c) \times (1-c)$	$(1/2)(1-2c) \times [(1-c)^2 + 1/8]$
t	0	$(1/4)(s' + 2t' + u')$	0	$(1/8)(1-2c)$	$(1/8)(1-2c) \times (3/2 - c)$
u	0	$(1/2)(t' + u')$	0	0	$(1/16)(1-2c)$
g	$1 - 2c$	$\left(\dfrac{1-2c}{2}\right)(r' - t')$	$(1/2)(1-2c)^2$	$(1/2)(1-2c)^2 \times (1-c)$	$(1/2)(1-2c)^2 \times [(1-c)^2 - 1/8]$

(9.98) $\displaystyle\sum_{4}^{n} g = (1 - c)\left[g_3 + \sum_{4}^{n-1} g\right] - \frac{1 - 2c}{16}\left[g_1 + g_2 + g_3 + \sum_{4}^{n-3} g\right]$

from (9.96).

The limiting value when g_{n-3}, etc., approach zero is

(9.99) $\displaystyle\sum_{4}^{\infty} g = [16(1 - c)g_3 - (1 - 2c)(g_1 + g_2 + g_3)]/[1 + 14c].$

$$(9.100) \qquad r_\infty = r_1 - \frac{2c}{1 - 2c} \left[g_2 + g_3 + \sum_4^\infty g \right],$$

$$(9.101) \qquad r_\infty = 1 - \frac{16c}{1 + 14c} = \frac{1 - 2c}{1 + 14c},$$

$$(9.102) \qquad 2x_\infty = \frac{8c}{1 + 14c}.$$

Kimura (1963) gives the proportion of recombinant lines in the general case of circular half-sib mating as $2Nc/[2(2N - 1)c + 1]$ as derived by his probability method. Formula (9.102) for the case $N = 4$ is in agreement.

These results are exactly the same as under maximum avoidance and for random mating with separate sexes and effective number N if there are exactly two offspring per individual in all of them. This is somewhat surprising since it was shown earlier that the fixation processes follow different courses.

It appears that the absence of lag and the initial relatively rapid rate of loss of heterozygosis under circular half-sib mating, as compared with the considerable lag and slower rate of loss under maximum avoidance of consanguinity, are exactly compensated for, with respect to the ultimate correlation between loci and the ultimate amount of recombination at fixation, by the greater persistence of heterozygosis under the former system, due to its continually declining rate of loss, in contrast with the steady rate of loss in the latter. Random mating with no such lag as that under maximum avoidance, but a slightly slower rate of loss, also shows exact compensation at fixation.

Comparisons among Systems of Inbreeding

A number of ways have been presented above for describing the extent to which recombination occurs among inbred lines derived from a parent population in which there is not random combination, whether because this population is the result of a cross or of a mixture. One of these is to find the correlation r between two loci within the same gamete. Because of the derivation by path analysis, this is independent of the number, effects, or frequencies of the alleles at these loci. This correlation decreases in the array of inbred lines until the situation is frozen by complete fixation. The value r_∞ at this point has been given in all cases. It would be possible to calculate r at any preceding stage by the same method.

The situation can be described equally well by means of the excess correlation $g = r - s$, between loci of the same gamete as compared with the

TABLE 9.1. Population of N monoecious individuals with random fertilization including self-fertilization. Proportion of recombinant lines when $F = 1$.

	FROM $\frac{AB}{ab}$, $2x_\infty = \frac{(N+1)c}{1+2Nc}$				FROM $\left(0.50\frac{AB}{AB} + 0.50\frac{ab}{ab}\right)$, $2x_\infty = \frac{Nc}{1+2Nc}$			
	c							
N	0.01	0.05	0.20	0.50	0.01	0.05	0.20	0.50
1	0.0196	0.0909	0.2857	0.5000	—	—	—	—
2	.0288	.1250	.3333	.5000	0.0192	0.0833	0.2222	0.3333
4	.0463	.1786	.3846	.5000	.0370	.1429	.3077	.4000
8	.0776	.2500	.4286	.5000	.0690	.2222	.3810	.4444
100	0.3367	0.4591	0.4927	0.5000	0.3333	0.4545	0.4878	0.4950

correlation in different gametes of the same individual. This is a somewhat more complicated concept than r, but has the advantage that recurrence formulas in terms of the values of g of preceding generations were obtained in all cases.

The simplest concept is the actual proportion of recombinant lines at fixation in the case of two pairs of alleles with gene frequencies all 0.50. This is used in Tables 9.1 to 9.4 as the basis for comparison of the effects of the various inbreeding systems. In Table 9.1 (lines of N monoecious individuals with random self-fertilization) and Table 9.2 (lines of N_m males, N_f females, $N_e = 4N_mN_f/(N_m + N_f)$ or of N_e self-incompatible monoecious individuals), the results are given for an initial cross (AB/ab) and for an initial equal mixture $[(1/2)(AB/AB) + (1/2)(ab/ab)]$. In both cases the offspring are

TABLE 9.2. Populations of dioecious individuals of effective size N_e (N_m = males, N_f = females). $N_e = 4N_mN_f/(N_m + N_f)$ or else of N_e self-incompatible monoecious individuals. Proportion of recombinant lines when $F = 1$.

	FROM $\frac{AB}{ab}$, $2x_\infty = \frac{(N_e+2)c}{1+2(N_e+1)c}$				FROM $\left(0.50\frac{AB}{AB} + 0.50\frac{ab}{ab}\right)$, $2x_\infty = \frac{N_ec}{1+2(N_e+1)c}$			
	c							
N_e	0.01	0.05	0.20	0.50	0.01	0.05	0.20	0.50
2	0.0377	0.1538	0.3636	0.5000	—	—	—	—
4	.0545	.2000	.4000	.5000	0.0364	0.1333	0.2667	0.3333
8	.0847	.2632	.4348	.5000	.0678	.2105	.3478	.4000
100	0.3377	0.4595	0.4928	0.5000	0.3311	0.4505	0.4831	0.4902

TABLE 9.3. Populations of $N/2$ males, $N/2$ females, in which each individual is the parent of just two of the next generation whether there is (1) maximum avoidance of consanguineous mating, (2) random mating, or (3) circular half-sib mating. Proportion of recombinant lines when $F = 1$. Starting from AB/ab. In all three cases $2x_\infty = 2Nc/[2(2N - 1)c + 1]$.

c N	0.01	0.05	0.20	0.50
4	0.0702	0.2353	0.4211	0.5000
8	.1231	.3200	.4571	.5000
16	0.1975	0.3902	0.4776	0.5000

assumed to be random samples. In Table 9.3 it is assumed that each parent provides just two mating individuals to the next generation whatever the system of mating. Table 9.4 deals with alternate parent-offspring mate (for autosomal and sex-linked loci) and with sib mating under sex-linkage.

While there is random combination of the loci among the fixed lines that trace to a cross, random combination is not fully attained among loci that trace to a mixture of lines, although the deviation is slight if the lines are large. It is hampered more by strong than by weak linkage. With a given strength of linkage and a given number in the inbred lines, it is hampered more by completely random union of gametes (Table 9.1) than if there is

TABLE 9.4. Proportion of recombinant lines when $F = 1$, under alternate parent-offspring mating for two autosomal loci (2 cases), sex-linked loci under sib mating, or (in fowls) one male (XX) and many females (XY).

Alternate Parent-Offspring	0.01	0.05	0.20	0.50
From $\dfrac{AB}{AB} \times \dfrac{ab}{ab}$, $F_1 \times F_1, F_2 \times F_1$, etc., $\dfrac{3c}{1 + 4c}$	0.0288	0.1250	0.3333	0.5000
From $\dfrac{AB}{AB} \times \dfrac{ab}{ab}$, $F_1 \times$ parents, etc., $\dfrac{8c}{3(1 + 4c)}$	.0256	.1111	.2962	.4444
Sex-linkage $\dfrac{AB}{ab} \times \dfrac{AB}{Y} + \dfrac{ab}{Y}$, etc., $\dfrac{2c}{1 + 2c}$	.0196	.0909	.2857	.5000
Sib mating under sex-linkage or $1\circlearrowleft XX$, many $\circleplus$'s XY (fowls), $\dfrac{8c}{3(1 + 4c)}$	0.0256	0.1111	0.2962	0.4444

self-incompatibility or separate sexes (Table 9.2). It is hampered less if exactly two offspring are taken from each parent, whatever the system of mating (Table 9.3), than if the offspring are a random sample from those produced by the parental generation.

Inbreeding Coefficients for Multiple Loci

A wholly different aspect of the joint effects of inbreeding and recombination has been investigated by Schnell (1961) by a generalization of the inbreeding coefficient to describe the effects of inbreeding at multiple loci.

He proposed a set of 2^k coefficients (sum 1) for the set of k loci under consideration, each the probability that an individual is homozygous by known descent with respect to certain of the loci and heterozygous by descent in the remaining ones. Thus there are two coefficients with respect to a single locus (the inbreeding coefficient F and the panmictic index $P = 1 - F$), four for two loci, eight for three loci, and so on.

While F does not depend on the number, effects, or frequencies of alleles, and thus depends only on the system of inbreeding, the others depend not only on the system of inbreeding but on specification of the linkage relations.

The values are simple if there is no linkage and no self-fertilization, since in this case fixation of each locus is independent of that at the others. The array of coefficients, if loci are distinguished by numerical subscripts, is given by the terms of $(F_1 + P_1)(F_2 + P_2) \cdots (F_k + P_k)$ where all F's have the same value, and the same is true of the P's. If specific loci are not distinguished, the $(k + 1)$ kinds of coefficients and the number of each kind are given by the expansion of $(F + P)^k$.

The reduction to $(k + 1)$ kinds of coefficients by value (k independent) is possible if $k = 2$ for a specified amount of recombination, but if k is greater than 2, the amounts of recombination between pairs are not all the same (unless $c = 0.50$ for all) and loci must be distinguished.

The recombination values for all pairs of loci are not enough to specify the gametic frequencies. An individual produces 2^k kinds of gametes if heterozygous for k loci. Since these come in pairs of complementaries of equal frequency, and since the sum of the frequencies is one, the number of parameters required for specification is $2^{k-1} - 1$. There are $(1/2)k(k - 1)$ recombination values for k pairs of alleles. This is enough up to three loci but one more datum must be drawn on in the case of four loci, five more in the case of five loci, and so on.

Schnell supplemented the ordinary recombination values with values that refer to noncontiguous pairs. Using c with appropriate subscripts for recombination values, c_{AB}, c_{BC}, and c_{CD} refer to successive regions in the set

$ABCD$, c_{AC} refers to region $(AB) + (BC)$, c_{BD} refers to $(BC) + (CD)$, and c_{AD} refers to $(AB) + (BC) + (CD)$. His supplementary recombination value c_{ABCD} refers to noncontiguous regions, (AB) and (CD), being defined as the frequency of recombination in (AB) associated with absence of recombination in (CD), plus the reverse. The value does not depend on knowledge of the correct order of the loci.

This permits specification of the eight complementary pairs of gamete frequencies, γ's, in terms of recombination values in a symmetrical way. Using subscripts 0 and 1 for maternal and paternal alleles, respectively, the set of linear orthogonal equations may be written as in (9.103) ($\gamma_{1111} = \gamma_{0000}$).

(9.103)

$$\gamma_{0000} = (1/2) \quad -(1/8)c_{AB} - (1/8)c_{AC} - (1/8)c_{AD} - (1/8)c_{BC} - (1/8)c_{BD} - (1/8)c_{CD} - (1/8)c_{ABCD}$$

$$\gamma_{1000} = \gamma_{0111} = +(1/8)c_{AB} + (1/8)c_{AC} + (1/8)c_{AD} - (1/8)c_{BC} - (1/8)c_{BD} - (1/8)c_{CD} + (1/8)c_{ABCD}$$

$$\gamma_{0100} = \gamma_{1011} = +(1/8)c_{AB} - (1/8)c_{AC} - (1/8)c_{AD} + (1/8)c_{BC} + (1/8)c_{BD} - (1/8)c_{CD} + (1/8)c_{ABCD}$$

$$\gamma_{0010} = \gamma_{1101} = -(1/8)c_{AB} + (1/8)c_{AC} - (1/8)c_{AD} + (1/8)c_{BC} - (1/8)c_{BD} + (1/8)c_{CD} + (1/8)c_{ABCD}$$

$$\gamma_{0001} = \gamma_{1110} = -(1/8)c_{AB} - (1/8)c_{AC} + (1/8)c_{AD} - (1/8)c_{BC} + (1/8)c_{BD} + (1/8)c_{CD} + (1/8)c_{ABCD}$$

$$\gamma_{1100} = \gamma_{0011} = -(1/8)c_{AB} + (1/8)c_{AC} + (1/8)c_{AD} + (1/8)c_{BC} + (1/8)c_{BD} - (1/8)c_{CD} - (1/8)c_{ABCD}$$

$$\gamma_{1010} = \gamma_{0101} = +(1/8)c_{AB} - (1/8)c_{AC} + (1/8)c_{AD} + (1/8)c_{BC} - (1/8)c_{BD} + (1/8)c_{CD} - (1/8)c_{ABCD}$$

$$\gamma_{1001} = \gamma_{0110} = +(1/8)c_{AB} + (1/8)c_{AC} - (1/8)c_{AD} - (1/8)c_{BC} + (1/8)c_{BD} + (1/8)c_{CD} - (1/8)c_{ABCD}$$

The recombination values, ranging from 0 to 0.5, are conveniently replaced by linkage values $\lambda = 1 - 2c$ ranging from 1 to 0. For two loci:

$$(9.104) \qquad \begin{aligned} \gamma_{00} &= \gamma_{11} = (1/4)[1 + \lambda_{AB}], \\ \gamma_{10} &= \gamma_{01} = (1/4)[1 - \lambda_{AB}]. \end{aligned}$$

Schnell's inbreeding function for a single locus, φ_A or φ_B, is, as noted, the same as the inbreeding coefficient F. That for a set, R, is designated φ_R. In the case of an individual derived by one generation of self-fertilization, sets of genes of the uniting gamete are identical by descent if, and only if, the genes at each locus trace to the same gene in one of the gametes that united to produce the parent.

$$(9.105) \qquad \varphi_A = \gamma_0^2 + \gamma_1^2 = 1/2,$$

$$(9.106) \qquad \varphi_{AB} = \gamma_{11}^2 + \gamma_{10}^2 + \gamma_{01}^2 + \gamma_{00}^2 = (1/4)(1 + \lambda_{AB}^2),$$

$$(9.107) \qquad \varphi_{ABC} = (1/8)(1 + \lambda_{AB}^2 + \lambda_{AC}^2 + \lambda_{BC}^2),$$

$$(9.108) \qquad \varphi_{ABCD} = (1/16)(1 + \lambda_{AB}^2 + \lambda_{AC}^2 + \lambda_{AD}^2 + \lambda_{BC}^2 + \lambda_{BD}^2 + \lambda_{CD}^2 + \lambda_{ABCD}^2).$$

Schnell uses $\xi_{R(Q)}$ generally for the probability of homozygosis by descent at the subset Q and heterozygous by descent at the remaining loci in the total set R. φ_R is the special case of homozygosis by descent at all loci. He uses π_R for the opposite extreme case.

The relations among these coefficients in the cases of two and three loci are shown in (9.109) and (9.110) in terms of the π's, for which recurrence formulas, discussed later, are in general simpler than for the others.

$$
\begin{aligned}
\xi_{AB()} &= & \pi_{AB} \\
\xi_{AB(A)} &= & \pi_B - \pi_{AB} \\
(9.109) \qquad \xi_{AB(B)} &= \pi_A & - \pi_{AB} \\
\xi_{AB(AB)} &= 1 - \pi_A - \pi_B + \pi_{AB} = \varphi_{AB}
\end{aligned}
$$

$$\text{Total} = 1$$

$$
\begin{aligned}
\xi_{ABC()} &= & & & \pi_{ABC} \\
\xi_{ABC(A)} &= & & \pi_{BC} & - \pi_{ABC} \\
\xi_{ABC(B)} &= & & \pi_{AC} & - \pi_{ABC} \\
\xi_{ABC(C)} &= & & \pi_{AB} & - \pi_{ABC} \\
(9.110) \qquad \xi_{ABC(AB)} &= & \pi_C & - \pi_{AC} - \pi_{BC} & + \pi_{ABC} \\
\xi_{ABC(AC)} &= & \pi_B & - \pi_{AB} & - \pi_{BC} + \pi_{ABC} \\
\xi_{ABC(BC)} &= \pi_A & & - \pi_{AB} - \pi_{AC} & + \pi_{ABC} \\
\xi_{ABC(ABC)} &= 1 - \pi_A - \pi_B - \pi_C & + \pi_{AB} + \pi_{AC} + \pi_{BC} & - \pi_{ABC} = \varphi_{ABC}
\end{aligned}
$$

$$\text{Total} = 1$$

The sets for larger numbers of loci are analogous.

Narain (1965) gave the recurrence formulas for self-fertilization. Indicating the preceding generation by a prime:

(9.111) $\pi_A = (1/2)\pi_A'$ (same as $P = (1/2)P'$),

(9.112) $\pi_{AB} = (1/4)(1 + \lambda_{AB}^2)\pi_{AB}'$,

(9.113) $\pi_{ABC} = (1/8)(1 + \lambda_{AB}^2 + \lambda_{AC}^2 + \lambda_{BC}^2)\pi_{ABC}'$,

(9.114) $\pi_{ABCD} = (1/16)(1 + \lambda_{AB}^2 + \lambda_{AC}^2 + \lambda_{AD}^2 + \lambda_{BC}^2 + \lambda_{BD}^2 + \lambda_{CD}^2 + \lambda_{ABCD}^2)\pi_{ABCD}'$.

For an individual that is heterozygous in all of the given loci, $\pi_R = 1$. The value of π_R in the nth generation, $\pi_R^{(n)}$, is obviously merely the appropriate coefficient above, raised to the nth power. The coefficients for homozygosis at one or more loci can readily be derived from the equations. It may readily be verified that φ_R after one generation is the same as π_R. Values for two loci are given in (9.115).

$$
\begin{aligned}
\pi_{AB}^{(n)} &= & (1/4)(1 + \lambda_{AB}^2)^n \\
\xi_{AB(A)}^{(n)} &= (1/2)^n & -(1/4)(1 + \lambda_{AB}^2)^n \\
(9.115) \qquad \xi_{AB(B)}^{(n)} &= (1/2)^n & -(1/4)(1 + \lambda_{AB}^2)^n \\
\varphi_{AB}^{(n)} &= 1 - 2(1/2)^n & +(1/4)(1 + \lambda_{AB}^2)^n
\end{aligned}
$$

The mean and variance of the number of loci homozygous by descent in any population were given by Schnell (1961) as follows, where k is the number of loci involved:

$$(9.116) \qquad M = kF,$$

$$(9.117) \qquad \sigma_M{}^2 = k(1 - kF)F + 2\sum \varphi_{ij},$$

where the summation refers to all distinct pairs of loci and thus has $(1/2)k(k - 1)$ terms.

The proportion of the residual lines that become completely homozygous by descent in each generation is given by $(\varphi - \varphi')/(1 - \varphi')$ (Narain 1965).

The properties of populations with respect to two or three loci during five generations of self-fertilization (from tables given by Narain, 1965) $c_{AB} = 0.30$, $c_{BC} = 0.20$, no interference, are given in Table 9.5 for comparison with the obvious values for a single loci.

The application of these principles to other systems of inbreeding than self-fertilization is much more complicated. A few examples were given by Schnell.

TABLE 9.5. The inbreeding functions under five generations of self-fertilization for one, two, or three loci, the mean (M) and variance $(\sigma_M{}^2)$ of the number of loci homozygous by descent, and the proportion $\delta\varphi_s/(1 - \varphi_s')$ of the residual lines that become completely homozygous by descent in each generation.

	GENERATIONS					
	0	1	2	3	4	5
$\pi_A = P$	1	0.5000	0.2500	0.1250	0.0625	0.0313
$\varphi_A = F$	0	0.5000	0.7500	0.8750	0.9375	0.9687
M	0	0.5000	0.7500	0.8750	0.9375	0.9687
$\sigma_M{}^2$	0	0.2500	0.1875	0.1094	0.0586	0.0303
$\delta\varphi_A/(1 - \varphi_A')$	—	0.5000	0.5000	0.5000	0.5000	0.5000
π_{AB}	1	0.2900	0.0841	0.0244	0.0071	0.0020
$\xi_{AB(A)}$	0	0.2100	0.1659	0.1006	0.0554	0.0292
$\xi_{AB(B)}$	0	0.2100	0.1659	0.1006	0.0554	0.0292
φ_{AB}	0	0.2900	0.5841	0.7744	0.8821	0.9396
M	0	1.0000	1.5000	1.7500	1.8750	1.9375
$\sigma_M{}^2$	0	0.5800	0.4182	0.2363	0.1236	0.0628
$\delta\varphi_{AB}/(1 - \varphi_{AB}')$	—	0.2900	0.4142	0.4576	0.4774	0.4877
π_{ABC}	1	0.1972	0.0389	0.0077	0.0015	0.0003
M	0	1.5000	2.2500	2.6250	2.8125	2.9062
$\sigma_M{}^2$	0	1.0300	0.7221	0.3970	0.2025	0.1004
$\delta\varphi_{ABC}/(1 - \varphi_{ABC}')$	—	0.1928	0.3538	0.4222	0.4562	0.4747

CHAPTER 10

Inbreeding and Selection

Chapters 8 and 9 have dealt with the effects of inbreeding on a single completely neutral locus and on two or more such loci, respectively. It is safe to assume, however, that there is usually more or less selection at any locus, or if not, at a linked locus.

Weak Selection

The situation is simple enough if the population is close to equilibrium because of balancing of opposed pressures and a constant amount of inbreeding measured by F (Wright 1942).

Genotype	Frequency	w_R	w_I	
AA	$(1-q)^2(1-F)+(1-q)F$	1	1	$\bar{w}_R = 1 - 2sq(1-q) - tq^2$
(10.1) Aa	$2q(1-q)(1-F)$	$1-s$		$\bar{w}_I = 1 - tq$
aa	$q^2(1-F)+qF$	$1-t$	$1-t$	

Gene frequency is here treated as if composed of a diploid randombred component with selective values w_R for which by itself

$$\Delta q_R = q(1-q) \sum \left(w_R \frac{\partial f_R}{\partial q} \right) \Big/ 2\bar{w}_R$$

and a haploid component with selective values w_I for which by itself,

$$\Delta q_I = q(1-q) \sum \left(w_I \frac{\partial f_I}{\partial q} \right) \Big/ \bar{w}_I.$$

There may be multiple alleles. The actual component of rate of change of gene frequency due to selection is given by the weighted average (weights $(\bar{w}_R/\bar{w})(1-F)$ and $(\bar{w}_I/\bar{w})F$):

$$(10.2) \quad \Delta q = \frac{q(1-q)}{\bar{w}} \left[\frac{1-F}{2} \sum \left(w_R \frac{\partial f_R}{\partial q} \right) + F \sum \left(w_I \frac{\partial f_I}{\partial q} \right) \right].$$

The difference from the formula in the absence of inbreeding is brought out best by putting this in the form

$$\Delta q = \frac{q\,(1-q)}{2\bar{w}}\left[\sum\left(w\,\frac{\partial f}{\partial q}\right) + F\sum\left(w_I\,\frac{\partial f_I}{\partial q}\right)\right],$$

which differs only in the last term (0 if no inbreeding).

In the case above with constant w's:

$$\sum\left(w_R\,\frac{\partial f}{\partial q}\right) = \frac{\partial \bar{w}_R}{\partial q} = -2s(1-2q) - 2tq \quad \text{and} \quad \sum\left(w_I\,\frac{\partial f_I}{\partial q_I}\right) = \frac{\partial w_I}{\partial q} = -t.$$

(10.3) $$\Delta q = -\frac{q(1-q)}{\bar{w}}[(1-F)[s-(2s-t)q] + Ft].$$

This was applied by Dobzhansky and Wright (1941) to the case of lethals held in equilibrium in wild populations of Drosophila pseudoobscura. The loci in this case were far from neutrality, but s was assumed to be very small and the production of homozygous lethals exceedingly rare.

In the case of semidominance this reduces to

(10.4) $$\Delta q = -sq\,\frac{(1-q)}{\bar{w}}[1+F].$$

In all of the above cases it must be supposed that these components due to selection are balanced by components due to mutation or immigration.

In the case of overdominance, however, this need not be the case. Letting s be the selective disadvantage of AA, and t of aa.

(10.5) $$\Delta q = q(1-q)[(s-Ft) - (s+t)(1-F)q]/\bar{w}.$$

If the selection pressure is not balanced, one allele tends toward fixation. If the pressure is slight, the selective difference being, for example, less than the reciprocal of ten times the effective population size, the relative decrease in heterozygosis is not affected to an extent that is ordinarily important, but the effect of strong selection at the same or a closely linked locus is, of course, very important. The extreme case is that of balanced lethals in which there can be no change from 100% heterozygosis by any sort of consanguine mating.

Inbreeding and Diverse Patterns of Selection

As in the preceding chapters, it will be assumed that an array of many separate lines traces to the foundation stock and that all are subject to the same conditions. For simplicity only pairs of alleles will be considered for the most part, noting that a group of alleles with the same selective values may be treated as if one. If there are more than two such groups, the number is usually reduced rather rapidly to one or two within each line under close inbreeding. The frequency array for the population will be represented as $x(a_1a_1){:}y(a_1a_2){:}z(a_2a_2)$. Selective value relative to a standard has been represented by w. This symbol will be used here for relative selective values in general, but it will be desirable in some cases to distinguish between values based on viability of offspring before mating (v) and on fecundity (u). This use of u and v must not be confused with the use elsewhere of these symbols for mutation rates. The symbol t will be used here for the product, uv.

The first attack on this problem was by Hayman and Mather (1953). They considered the case in which all homozygotes have the same selective value (v) relative to all heterozygotes, whether within the same progeny or not. The simplest case is that of self-fertilization. Starting from the array $(1 - y_0)(a_1a_1, a_2a_2) + y_0(a_1a_2)$, the array of lines in the next generation is as follows. The subscripts of y refer to generation.

	Offspring	Contributions by Parents	
		(a_1a_1, a_2a_2)	(a_1a_2)
(10.6)	$(a_1a_1, a_2a_2)(1 - y_1)$	$(v/s_1)(1 - y_0) + [v/(2s_1)]y_0$	
	$(a_1a_2) \qquad y_1$	$[1/(2s_1)]y_0$	
	Total 1	$= (v/s_1)(1 - y_0) + [(1 + v)/(2s_1)]y_0$	
	where s_1	$= v + (1/2)(1 - v)y_0$	

The generation matrix that yields the offspring frequencies in a total population of constant size, on multiplication into the column factor of parental frequencies is thus:

$$(10.7) \qquad \begin{vmatrix} v/s_1 & v/(2s_1) \\ 0 & 1/(2s_1) \end{vmatrix}.$$

The authors, however, used what may be called for convenience the numerator matrix by multiplying throughout by the sum s_1.

$$(10.8) \qquad \begin{vmatrix} v & v/2 \\ 0 & 1/2 \end{vmatrix}.$$

Multiplication into the column vector of parental frequencies here yields offspring frequencies that are in the proper ratio to each other but continually declining in total number. The characteristic equation derived from this matrix has the roots v and $1/2$. As the inbreeding proceeds, the larger root dominates the relative frequencies more and more. Thus there is a qualitative difference in the ultimate result depending on whether v is less than $1/2$ or not. With $v \gtrless 1/2$, the lines move toward complete fixation. With $v < 1/2$ the tendency toward fixation comes to be balanced by the loss of homallelic lines. The extreme case is that of balanced lethals, $v = 0$, in which homallelic lines cannot be formed at all.

The authors also gave formulas for the relative frequencies of homozygotes after n generations and for the equilibrium, $y_\infty = (1 - 2v)/(1 - v)$, if $v < 1/2$ in this case.

They went on to determine the condition for persistence of heterozygosis under sib mating, assuming the occurrence of selection against homozygotes of the same sort as above. The numerator matrix from the recurrence equations (4×4 matrix) yielded the following characteristic equation:

(10.9) $\quad (\lambda - v)\{4(1 + v)^2\lambda^3 - 2(1 + v)(1 + 2v)\lambda^2 - v^2(1 + v)\lambda + v^3\} = 0.$

This is for a pair of alleles. The full 7×7 matrix allowing for four possible alleles, which they gave, includes two additional submatrices and thus yields three more factors, but the latent roots from these are never the largest, reflecting the inevitable reduction to two alleles.

The largest root of the second factor above is $\lambda_2 = (1/4)[1 + \sqrt{5}] = 0.8090$ if $v = 1$ (as given in chapter 7 for pure sib mating). It is 0.5 if $v = 0$ and intermediate for other values of v. The value at which it is the same as the root $\lambda_1 = v$ from the first factor is found by putting $\lambda = v$ in the cubic which becomes $4v^5 + 3v^4 - 2v^3 - 2v^2 = 0$, the largest root of which is 0.7633. This is Hayman and Mather's critical value of v. With this or larger values there is approach to complete fixation (as with $v = 1$) while with smaller values there is an equilibrium at which heterozygosis is permanently maintained.

This method was used to find the critical value under a number of other systems of inbreeding. Two cases were considered under each: (1) equally low relative selective values of both homozygotes, $v_2 = v_1$, and (2) complete lethality of one homozygote ($v_2 = 0$). In the following table parent-offspring mating refers to alternate mating of individuals with parent and offspring, assuming that all selective loss of homozygotes precedes the first mating. Half-sib mating refers to groups composed of one male and half-sisters which are half-sisters of each other.

	Critical Value	
	$v_1 = v_2$	$v_1, (v_2 = 0)$
Selfing	0.500	0.500
Sib mating	.763	.660
Parent-offspring	.750	.654
Half-sib	.812	.691
Double first cousin	0.855	0.768

248   INBREEDING AND SELECTION

It was pointed out that in the cases of equally low viability of both homo-zygotes, there must be a value of v at which there would be the same pro-portions of the three genotypes in the whole population, as under random mating, $1a_1a_1 : 2a_1a_2 : 1a_2a_2$, in spite of the subdivision into inbreeding lines. They gave this value of v as $1/3$ in the case of self-fertilization (from $\hat{y} = (1 - 2v)/(1 - v) = 1/2$); as 0.554 in the case of sib mating and as 0.528 in parent-offspring mating.

Haldane (1956) criticized the use of the characteristic equation of the numerator matrix by Hayman and Mather. He held that the characteristic equation should be used only if based on the full recurrence equations of a population of constant size and then only if these are linear, which they are not in the above case. Starting from the full recurrence equations under various hypotheses with respect to the operation of selection under selfing, he derived, by algebraic manipulation, the formula for the amount of heterozygosis, y_n, in any generation and the limiting amount, $\hat{y}$, if $v < 1/2$ in the case considered by Hayman and Mather.

Hayman and Mather in a reply (1956) maintained the legitimacy of their procedure. They were clearly correct insofar as derivation of the critical value is concerned. They did not, however, bring out in this or their earlier paper how they derived y_n or its limiting value. These quantities are not in general derivable at all from their characteristic equation by itself. This does not for example involve the second element of the first row in the 2×2 matrix discussed first. This element (involved in s) undoubtedly affects y_n.

The simplest method of making these calculations seems in general to be that of Reeve (1957). He used the numerator matrix but not its charac-teristic equation. He started from the following table for analysis of the general case of self-fertilization. The mode of selection is described by four parameters: v_1 and v_2 for the viabilities of a_1a_1 and a_2a_2, respectively, relative to that of a_1a_2, and the overall productivities, t_1 and t_2 of a_1a_1 and a_2a_2 as parents, taking account of both their fecundities u_1, u_2 relative to that of a_1a_2, and the viabilities of their offspring ($t_1 = u_1v_1$, $t_2 = u_2v_2$). The overall productivity of a_1a_2 is not 1 but $0.5(1 + \bar{v})$.

	Offspring genotypes	Contributions by Parental Lines		
		a_1a_1	a_1a_2	a_2a_2
	a_1a_1	t_1	$(1/4)v_1$	0
(10.10)	a_1a_2	0	$1/2$	0
	a_2a_2	0	$(1/4)v_2$	t_2
	Lost	$1 - t_1$	$(1/2)(1 - \bar{v})$	$1 - t_2$
	Total	1	1	1

The product of the matrix of survivors (numerator matrix) into the column vector of initial frequencies gives the relative frequencies after a generation of selfing, from which the absolute frequencies can be derived by dividing by the sum. Since the relative frequency of a_1a_2 is $1/2$, it is convenient to multiply throughout by two which of course does not affect the proportions but makes them relative to one for a_1a_2.

$$(10.11) \quad \begin{vmatrix} 2t_1 & (1/2)v_1 & 0 \\ 0 & 1 & 0 \\ 0 & (1/2)v_2 & 2t_2 \end{vmatrix} \begin{vmatrix} x_0 \\ y_0 \\ z_0 \end{vmatrix} = \begin{vmatrix} 2t_1x_0 + (1/2)v_1y_0 \\ y_0 \\ 2t_2z_0 + (1/2)v_2y_0 \end{vmatrix} = \begin{vmatrix} S_1x_1 \\ S_1y_1 \\ S_1z_1 \end{vmatrix}.$$

The relative frequencies in the nth generation can be obtained by carrying through this process n times or, what is the same thing, because of the associative property of matrix multiplication, multiplying the nth power of the numerator matrix into the initial frequency vector. This nth power is easily expressed in this case.

$$(10.12) \quad \begin{vmatrix} 2t_1 & (1/2)v_1 & 0 \\ 0 & 1 & 0 \\ 0 & (1/2)v_2 & 2t_2 \end{vmatrix}^n \begin{vmatrix} x_0 \\ y_0 \\ z_0 \end{vmatrix} = \begin{vmatrix} (2t_1)^n x_0 + \dfrac{v_1}{2}\dfrac{(2t_1)^n - 1}{2t_1 - 1} y_0 \\ y_0 \\ (2t_2)^n z_0 + \dfrac{v_2}{2}\dfrac{(2t_2)^n - 1}{2t_2 - 1} y_0 \end{vmatrix} = \begin{vmatrix} S_nx_n \\ S_ny_n \\ S_nz_n \end{vmatrix}.$$

Thus $y_n = y_0/S_n$

$$y_n = y_0 \bigg/ \bigg\{ (2t_1)^n x_0 + (2t_2)^n z_0 + \bigg[\frac{v_1}{2}\frac{(2t_1)^n - 1}{2t_1 - 1} + 1 + \frac{v_2}{2}\frac{(2t_2)^n - 1}{2t_2 - 1} \bigg] y_0 \bigg\}.$$
(10.13)

All of the cases considered by Haldane are included in this formula.

Returning to Hayman and Mather's approach, the characteristic equation of the original numerator matrix (in which the sums of the columns, including the row of losses, are all 1) is $(\lambda - 1/2)(\lambda - t_1)(\lambda - t_2) = 0$. This indicates a critical value of the larger t at $1/2$.

If both t_1 and t_2 are less than $1/2$, there is approach to the limiting ratio:

$$(10.14) \quad \frac{v_1}{2(1 - 2t_1)}\, a_1a_1 : 1a_1a_2 : \frac{v_2}{2(1 - 2t_2)}\, a_2a_2.$$

All three types continue if neither v_1 nor v_2 is zero. Otherwise one or both of the homozygotes does not exist. If t_1 is greater than t_2 and not less than $1/2$, then a_1a_1 tends toward fixation, and correspondingly with a_2a_2 if t_2 is greater than t_1. If $t_1 = t_2 \geqslant 1/2$ and the population starts from a_1a_2, there are eventually only lines of a_1a_1 and of a_2a_2 in the ratio $v_1:v_2$, but the slightest difference between t_1 and t_2 leads ultimately to elimination of the allele that is less favorable in this respect.

It is instructive to compare the effects of different kinds of selection under the assumption that the homozygotes are equivalent with respect to both aspects of selection, $t_1 = t_2$ and $v_1 = v_2$.

Following are four matrices, the first from complete recurrence equations, the others merely from the numerators.

$$(10.15) \quad \begin{array}{c}(1)\\ \begin{vmatrix} 1 & v(1+v) \\ 0 & 1/(1+v) \end{vmatrix}\end{array} \quad \begin{array}{c}(2)\\ \begin{vmatrix} u & 1/2 \\ 0 & 1/2 \end{vmatrix}\end{array} \quad \begin{array}{c}(3)\\ \begin{vmatrix} v & v/2 \\ 0 & 1/2 \end{vmatrix}\end{array} \quad \begin{array}{c}(4)\\ \begin{vmatrix} uv & v/2 \\ 0 & 1/2 \end{vmatrix}\end{array}$$

Case 1 is that of selection exclusively *within* the self-fertilized lines. All lines are carried along equally whether by deliberate plan or because selection is due wholly to competition within progenies without effect on the total number of survivors. Heterozygosis falls off in geometric progression toward complete loss, unless $v = 0$, the case of balanced lethals.

$$(10.16) \qquad y_n = \left(\frac{1}{1+v}\right)^n y_0.$$

Case 2 is that of selection exclusively *among* lines, whether deliberately, or because of inherent differences in fecundity but not in viability, $t_1 = t_2 = u$ and $v_1 = v_2 = 1$. If $u < 1/2$, $\hat{y}_n = (1 - 2u)/(2 - 2u)$.

Case 3 is that of differential viability of homozygotes and heterozygotes but equal fecundity ($t_1 = t_2 = v_1 = v_2$), the case already considered. If $v < 1/2$, then $\hat{y}_n = (1 - 2v)/(1 - v)$.

Case 4 is that in which homozygotes differ from heterozygotes equally in both viability and fecundity, $u_1 = u_2 = v_1 = v_2$. If $t = uv < 1/2$, then $\hat{y}_n = (1 - 2t)/(1 + v - 2t)$.

Values of $\hat{y}_n$ corresponding to different selective values, $w \; (= u, v, \text{ or } t)$ are shown in Table 10.1. Cases 4 and 5 are both examples of case 4 above but in case 4, t is assigned the same values as u or v in cases 1 to 3, while in case 5, u and v are assigned these values and $t = w^2$.

The decreases in heterozygosis, y_n for twenty generations, under patterns 1 to 5, each with selective values $w \; (= 0.75, 0.50, \text{ and } 0.25)$ are illustrated in Figures 10.1, 10.2, and 10.3, respectively. In each figure the decrease under self-fertilization in the absence of selection ($w = 1$) is also shown.

A disadvantage of 25% ($w = 0.75$) must be considered strong selection in all the patterns of selection, though in all of those represented heterozygosis tends toward eventual extinction, and in all but case 5 (in which t is 0.5625), more than 95% of the heterozygosis is lost in seven generations of selfing, only two more generations than in the absence of selection. It is evident that if either viability or fecundity, or even both, is depressed in homozygotes at

TABLE 10.1. The limiting frequency of heterozygotes in various patterns of selective value, w ($= u$, v, or t) in five cases indicated by the matrices at the top and discussed in the text. The homozygotes in each case are equivalent.

w (u, v, or t)	Case 1 $\begin{vmatrix} 1 & v/(1+v) \\ 0 & 1/(1+v) \end{vmatrix}$ $\hat{y}$	Case 2 $\begin{vmatrix} u & 1/2 \\ 0 & 1/2 \end{vmatrix}$ $\dfrac{1-2u}{2-2u}$	Case 3 $\begin{vmatrix} v & v/2 \\ 0 & 1/2 \end{vmatrix}$ $\dfrac{1-2v}{1-v}$	Case 4 $\begin{vmatrix} t & (1/2)\sqrt{t} \\ 0 & 1/2 \end{vmatrix}$ $\dfrac{1-2t}{1-2t+\sqrt{t}}$	Case 5 $\begin{vmatrix} uv & v/2 \\ 0 & 1/2 \end{vmatrix}$ $\dfrac{1-2uv}{1+v-2uv}$
1.00	0	0	0	0	0
0.90	0	0	0	0	0
0.80	0	0	0	0	0
0.70	0	0	0	0	0.0278
0.60	0	0	0	0	0.3182
0.50	0	0	0	0	0.5000
0.40	0	0.1667	0.3333	0.2402	0.6539
0.30	0	.2857	0.5714	0.4221	0.7321
0.20	0	.3750	0.7500	0.5730	0.8214
0.10	0	.4444	0.8889	0.7167	0.9074
0	1.000	0.5000	1.0000	1.0000	1.0000

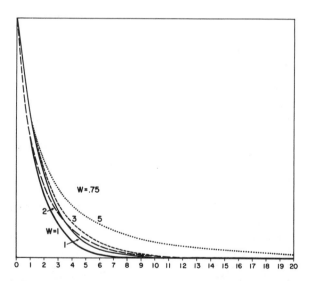

FIG. 10.1. Comparison of patterns of selection as described in the text. For homozygotes: $W = (u$, v, or $t) = 0.75$. Case 4, between cases 2 and 3 in effect, is not shown. The case of no selection, $W = 1$, is shown.

252

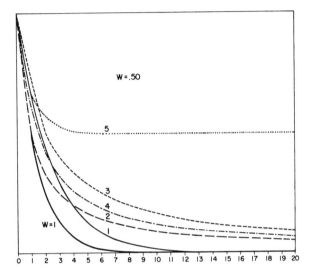

FIG. 10.2. Same as Figure 10.1 except for stronger selection, $W = 0.50$

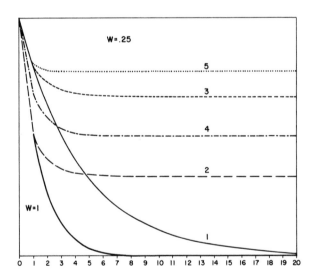

FIG. 10.3. Same as Figure 10.1 except for very strong selection, $W = 0.25$

each of any number of independent loci by amounts up to perhaps 10%, the departure from the theory of self-fertilization without selection is not important for most purposes. Selective disadvantages of 25% in both aspects, however, produce great delay in reaching a loss of 95% of the heterozygosis, about twelve generations being required in case 5 and very great delay in going much beyond this. Selection of a given degree exclusively within lines (case 1) permits more rapid fixation than selection among lines (case 2) after the first few generations, the eventual ratio of successive amounts of heterozygosis being $1/(1 + w) = 0.571$ in the former but $1/(2w) = 0.667$ in the latter, both in contrast with 0.500 in the absence of selection.

The case of $w = 0.50$ in Figure 10.2 is the largest value of w at which there is eventual loss of heterozygosis in cases 2, 3, and 4. The delay in the fixation process is not especially serious if there is no selection among lines (case 1) although, somewhat surprisingly, there is more delay for three generations than in case 2, in which the selection is exclusively among lines. Some heterozygosis persists, however, almost indefinitely in cases 2, 3, and 4 with 50% loss in overall productivity of matings. In case 5 in which there is 50% depression in both viability and fecundity and thus 75% in overall productivity per mating, 50% of the heterozygosis is retained indefinitely.

In the case of $w = 0.25$ in Figure 10.3, case 1 is the only one of those considered in which fixation is ultimately complete, and it is here greatly delayed in comparison with the process in the absence of selection. The greater delay in loss of heterozygosis and higher frequency of heterozygotes where an equilibrium is attained in case 4 than in case 2, and the still greater delay in case 3, are of course as expected.

Reeve (1955) has compared the effects of selection exclusively within lines in various systems of close inbreeding: self-fertilization, sib mating, half-sib mating, and double-first-cousin mating. Since the matrix based on the full recurrence equations is linear in this case, the limiting rate of reduction of heterozygosis, after a few generations, is the largest root of the characteristic equation (excluding the class of homallelic lines) according to the method of Bartlett and Haldane (1934). Viabilities within lines are assumed to be in the ratio $v_1(a_1a_1):1(a_1a_2):v_2(a_2a_2)$.

In the case of self-fertilization $\lambda = 1/[1 + (1/2)v_1 + (1/2)v_2]$ as expected from the preceding section.

In the case of sib mating, Reeve obtained the following characteristic equation from the 4×4 matrix, excluding homallelic lines:

$$(10.17) \quad \lambda^4 - (2Av_1 + 2Bv_2 + 4C)\lambda^3 + \{(4AB - 2C)v_1v_2 + 4ACv_1 + 4BCv_2\}\lambda^2 + (4ACv_1{}^2v_2 + 4BCv_1v_2{}^2)\lambda - 8ABCv_1{}^2v_2{}^2 = 0$$

where $A = 1/(1 + v_1)^2$, $B = 1/(1 + v_2)^2$, $C = 1/(2 + v_1 + v_2)^2$.

If $v_1 = v_2 = v$:

$$(10.18) \quad \left[\lambda - \frac{2v}{(1+v)^2} \right] \left[\lambda^3 - \frac{1+2v}{(1+v)^2} \lambda^2 - \frac{v^2}{2(1+v)^2} \lambda + \frac{v^3}{(1+v)^4} \right] = 0.$$

If $v_2 = 0$:

$$(10.19) \quad (1+v)^2(2+v)^2\lambda^2 - [2v(2+v)^2 + 4(1+v)^2]\lambda + 4v = 0.$$

The pattern of half-sib mating considered was that in which a male is mated with two half-sisters, full sisters of each other (instead of half-sisters of each other as considered by Hayman and Mather). The limiting values of λ were shown in chapter 7 to be 0.8700 in the former, 0.8904 in the latter. These compare with 0.5000 for self-fertilization, 0.8090 for sib mating, and 0.9196 for double-first-cousin mating in the absence of selection. This sort of half-sib mating yields an 8×8 matrix in the case $v_1 = v_2$ and a 4×4 matrix in that in which $v_2 = 0$, both after exclusion of the homallelic lines.

Double-first-cousin (DFC) mating yields a 12×12 matrix if $v_1 = v_2$ and a 5×5 matrix if $v_2 = 0$, both excluding homallelic lines. The matrices were given by Reeve in the preceding four cases. The largest roots were obtained by repeated matrix multiplication in these cases instead of by writing and solving the characteristic equations.

Table 10.2 shows the limiting ratios, λ, of heterozygosis in successive generations (largest root) in these cases with $v_1 = v_2$ or with $v_2 = 0$.

TABLE 10.2. Limiting ratios of heterozygosis in successive generations

SURVIVAL OF HOMOZYGOTES	λ			
	Selfing	Sib	Half-sib	DFC
$v_1 = v_2$ 1.	0.5000	0.8090	0.8700	0.9196
0.8	.5556	.8512	.9068	.9503
0.6	.6250	.8968	.9433	.9761
0.4	.7143	.9429	.9751	.9930
0.2	.8333	.9824	.9954	.9994
$v_2 = 0$ 1.	.6667	.8067	.8367	.8706
0.8	.7143	.8566	.8878	—
0.6	.7692	.9075	.9363	.9632
0.4	.8333	.9541	.9752	—
0.2	0.9091	0.9880	0.9964	0.9994

The number of generations required to halve the amount of heterozygosis is given by $n = \log_{10} 0.5 / \log_{10} \lambda$. These are given in Table 10.3.

The half-period for loss of heterozygosis is considerably greater under selfing if one homozygote is lethal, the other with selective value v_1, than if $v_2 = v_1$. There is little difference under sib mating or half-sib mating unless v is rather small. The half-period is in fact a little less if $v_2 = 0$ and v is not

TABLE 10.3. Half-periods for heterozygosis under the indicated conditions

		Selfing	Sib	Half-sib	DFC
$v_1 = v_2$	1.	1.00	3.27	4.97	8.27
	0.8	1.18	4.30	7.08	13.60
	0.6	1.47	6.36	11.88	28.67
	0.4	2.88	11.79	27.49	98.4
	0.2	3.80	38.94	149.77	1158.
$v_2 = 0$	1.	1.71	3.22	3.89	5.00
	0.8	2.06	4.48	5.83	—
	0.6	2.64	7.14	10.53	18.49
	0.4	3.80	14.74	27.04	—
	0.2	7.27	57.56	190.53	1158.

small. This tendency increased under double-first-mating. It requires about the same enormous number of generations, over 1,150, to halve heterosis if $v_1 = v_2 = 0.2$ or $v_1 = 0.2$, $v_2 = 0$, while with less severe selection the half-period is considerably less if a_2a_2 is lethal.

With 20% disadvantage of both homozygotes in viability, which is fairly strong selection, the half-period is increased by 17.9% under selfing, 31.5% under sib mating, 42.4% under half-sib mating, and 64.4% under double-first-cousin mating. We may again conclude that weak selection causes relatively little delay in fixation by self-fertilization. The amount of delay increases considerably, however, with decrease in the closeness of the inbreeding.

Reeve (1955) also worked out a number of cases under sib mating in which v_1 and v_2 are different but neither is zero. Among other things, he worked out the limiting relative frequencies of mating types under sib, half-sib, and double-first-cousin mating where $v_1 = v_2$.

He noted the likelihood, on the basis of experimental results, that the viabilities of homozygotes would decrease as the amount of fixation rises, so that heterozygosis may be lost almost as rapidly as under the uncomplicated theory of inbreeding in the early stages but with increasing slowness as the process goes on.

The Effect of Linkage with a Lethal on the Course of Inbreeding

It will be assumed here that there are no selective differences among the alleles at the locus under consideration. As noted earlier, heterozygosis at such a locus may be influenced by selection at a linked locus. The extreme case for a given amount of recombination is that of linkage with balanced lethals. There is the same situation, mathematically, if the neutral pair of alleles is linked with a pair of alleles with conspicuous effects that are deliberately kept heterozygous, for the purpose of introducing the segregating pair into an otherwise homallelic strain.

The effect under self-fertilization is easily obtained. Letting a_1, a_2 be the neutral locus and l_1, l_2 balanced lethals (or nonlethals deliberately kept heterozygous in making matings) and letting c be the amount of recombination, it is merely necessary to make a table of uniting gametes to find that:

$$(10.20) \quad \frac{a_1 l_1}{a_2 l_2} \times \frac{a_1 l_1}{a_2 l_2} \Rightarrow c(1-c)\frac{a_1 l_1}{a_1 l_2} + (1-c)^2 \frac{a_1 l_1}{a_2 l_2}$$
$$+ c(1-c)\frac{a_2 l_1}{a_2 l_2} + c^2 \frac{a_1 l_2}{a_2 l_1}.$$

Thus heterozygosis decreases by $2c(1-c)$ per generation.

$$(10.21) \quad y_n = [1 - 2c(1-c)]^n y_0.$$

The case of balanced lethals, k_1/k_2, l_1/l_2 on each side of genes a_1, a_2 can be worked out similarly, letting c_1 and c_2 be the amounts of recombination in the regions k to a and a to l, respectively, and d the amount of double crossing over. A triple heterozygote, $k_1 a_1 l_1/k_2 a_2 l_2$ produces $1 - c_1 - c_2 + d$ noncrossovers, $c_1 - d$ crossovers in region 1 and $c_2 - d$ in region 2. Of the 64 combinations of gametes, sixteen are viable. Assembling these, the proportion of triple heterozygotes among the offspring is:

$$(10.22) \quad y_n = \left[\frac{(1 - c_1 - c_2 + d)^2 + (c_1 - d)^2 + (c_2 - d)^2 + d^2}{(1 - c_1 - c_2 + 2d)^2 + (c_1 + c_2 - 2d)^2}\right] y_{n-1}.$$

Noting that the amount of recombination, c_3, between k and l is $(c_1 + c_2 - 2d)$,

$$(10.23) \quad y_n = \left[1 - \frac{2c_1 c_2 + 2d(1 - 2c_1 - 2c_2 + 2d)}{(1 - c_3)^2 + c_3^2}\right] y_{n-1}.$$

If there is no interference, as expected if c_3 is large, then $d = c_1 c_2$ and

$$(10.24) \quad y_n = \frac{[1 - 2c_1(1 - c_1)][1 - 2c_2(1 - c_2)]}{(1 - c_3)^2 + c_3^2} y_{n-1}.$$

If $c_1 = c_2$, this becomes:

$$(10.25) \quad y_n = \left[1 - \frac{C^2}{(1 - C)^2 + C^2}\right] y_{n-1} \quad \text{where} \quad C = 2c(1-c).$$

If there is complete interference, as expected if c_3 is small, then $d = 0$ and

$$(10.26) \quad y_n = \left[1 - \frac{2c_1 c_2}{(1 - c_1 - c_2)^2 + (c_1 + c_2)^2}\right] y_{n-1}.$$

If $c_1 = c_2$ this becomes

$$(10.27) \quad y_n = \left[1 - \frac{2c^2}{(1 - 2c)^2 + 4c^2}\right] y_{n-1} = \left[1 - \frac{2c^2}{1 - 4c + 8c^2}\right] y_{n-1}.$$

These all agree with formulas given by Reeve (1957).

The effects under sib mating of enforced heterozygosis $Dd \times Dd$ (or balanced lethals) at a linked locus were analyzed by Bartlett and Haldane (1935) on the basis of the matrix of types of mating. They also dealt with enforced heterozygosis in only one parent (all matings of the type $Dd \times dd$), which is very important in introducing a segregating pair into a homallelic line but corresponds to the unusual natural case of balanced lethals in one sex, fully viable homozygotes in the other. They also considered sex linkage and some other cases. Some extensions, especially with respect to patterns involving backcrossing, of great practical value, have been made by Green and Doolittle (1963).

Inbreeding with Forced Heterozygosis of a Linked Locus

The principal parameter, F, can, however, be obtained more simply by focusing on gametic instead of zygotic unions and can be readily extended to populations of any size by using path analysis. Consider the case of a population of N_m males and N_f females in which every mating is of the type $Dd \times Dd$ with respect to the marker (Wright 1963). The objective is the ratio $\lambda = P/P'$ for linked genes A, a. It will be assumed that these are related symmetrically to D and d in the total population. Let c_o and c_s be the amounts of recombination in oogenesis and spermatogenesis, respectively. Figure 10.4 shows first the relation between a sperm carrying D, (D_s) and an ovum carrying d, (d_o). Gamete D_s may derive its A allele from either of the uniting gametes of the preceding generation but with probability $(1 - c_s)$ from the D gamete and probability c_s from the d gamete. These are the path coefficients in these cases. Similarly the A allele of gamete d_o is related to the d gamete of the preceding generation by a path coefficient with the value $(1 - c_o)$ and to the D gamete by one with value c_o. The correlation between the A alleles of D_s and of d_o is designated $r_{so(N)}$ in which the subscript N indicates nonidentical D alleles. The correlation between uniting gametes (F) is of this sort. The correlation between A alleles of sperm and egg that carry identical D alleles $(r_{so(I)})$ and the corresponding correlations between two sperms $(r_{ss(N)}, r_{ss(I)})$ and between two eggs $(r_{oo(N)}, r_{oo(I)})$ are also of concern. Because of the postulated symmetry of the system of mating, it makes no difference whether a parent came from the union of D sperm with d ovum or the reverse. Thus the correlation between A alleles both associated with

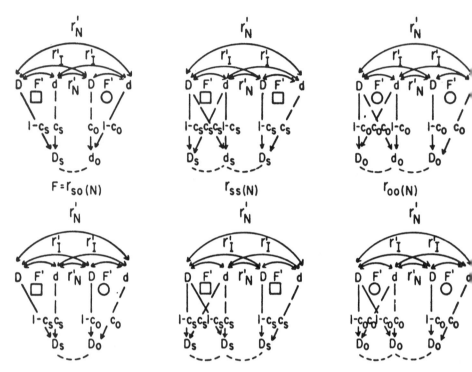

FIG. 10.4. Path diagrams for analysis of six types of gametic loci with respect to a linked marker locus D, in a population of Dd males and Dd females (Wright 1963, Fig. 15, reprinted by permission, Holden-Day).

D or both with d is the average of $r_{ss(I)}$, $r_{so(I)}$, and $r_{oo(I)}$ with weights of $1/4$, $2/4$, and $1/4$, respectively.

$$(10.28) \qquad r_I = (1/4)[r_{ss(I)} + 2r_{so(I)} + r_{oo(I)}].$$

Similarly:

$$(10.29) \qquad r_N = (1/4)[r_{ss(N)} + 2r_{so(N)} + r_{oo(N)}].$$

On tracing the connecting paths in Figure 10.4 it is found that

$$(10.30) \qquad r_{so(N)} = F = [(1 - c_s)(1 - c_o) + c_s c_o]r_N' \\ + [c_s(1 - c_o) + (1 - c_s)c_o]r_I'.$$

If d_o is replaced by D_o, coefficients c_o and $(1 - c_o)$ must be exchanged; and, if D_s is replaced by d_s, c_s and $(1 - c_s)$ must be exchanged. Union of d_s with D_o gives the same result as above.

(10.31) $r_{so(I)} = [(1 - c_s)(1 - c_o) + c_s c_o]r_I' + [c_s(1 - c_o) + (1 - c_s)c_o]r_N'.$

In the case of correlations between two sperms or between two eggs, the probabilities that they are produced by the same individual $1/N_m$ and $1/N_f$, respectively, and the probabilities that they are produced by different individuals, must be taken into account.

(10.32) $r_{ss(I)} = (1/N_m)\{[(1 - c_s)^2 + c_s^2] + 2c_s(1 - c_s)F'\}$
$+ [(N_m - 1)/N_m]\{[(1 - c_s)^2 + c_s^2]r_I' + 2c_s(1 - c_s)r_N'\}.$

(10.33) $r_{ss(N)} = (1/N_m)\{[(1 - c_s)^2 + c_s^2]F' + 2c_s(1 - c_s)\}$
$+ [(N_{m-1})/N_m]\{[(1 - c_s)^2 + c_s^2]r_N' + 2c_s(1 - c_s)r_I'\}.$

The formulas for $r_{oo(I)}$ and $r_{oo(N)}$ are analogous, merely replacing subscripts m by f and s by o.

It is convenient to let $l_s = 2c_s(1 - c_s)$, $l_o = 2c_o(1 - c_o)$, and $l_m = c_s(1 - c_o) + (1 - c_s)c_o$ and $a = (N_{m-1})/N_m$, $b = (N_f - 1)/N_f$. The equations for r_N and r_I can be written from the appropriate averages. A further condensation of symbolism is desirable.

$$u = (1 - l_m), \qquad v = l_m,$$
$$w = (1/4)[(1 - l_s)(1 - a) + (1 - l_o)(1 - b)],$$
(10.34) $$x = (1/4)[l_s(1 - a) + l_o(1 - b)],$$
$$y = (1/4)[2(1 - l_m) + (1 - l_s)a + (1 - l_o)b],$$
$$z = (1/4)[2l_m + l_s a + l_o b].$$

The correlations F, r_N, and r_I can then be written as follows:

$$F = ur_N' + vr_I',$$
(10.35) $$r_N = wF' + yr_n' + zr_I' + x,$$
$$r_I = xF' + zr_N' + yr_I' + w.$$

Since the sums of the coefficients are equal to 1 in all cases, the constant terms disappear on substituting $r = 1 - P$ in each case. This leads to the P-matrix, the characteristic equation of which is as follows:

(10.36) $$\begin{vmatrix} -\lambda & u & v \\ w & y - \lambda & z \\ x & z & y - \lambda \end{vmatrix} = 0.$$

$\lambda^3 - \lambda^2(2y) + \lambda[y^2 - z^2 - uw - vx] + [uwy + vxy - uxz - vwz] = 0.$

The largest root gives the ratio of heterozygosis in successive generations.

In the case of sib mating ($N_m = N_f = 1$ and $a = b = 0$) this reduces to the following, which could have been derived much more simply if these assumptions had been made in the first place:

$$(10.37) \quad \begin{aligned} \lambda^3 - \lambda^2(1 - l_m) - (\lambda/4)[1 - (l_s + l_o)(1 - 2l_m) \\ + (1/8)(2 - l_s - l_o)(1 - 2l_m)] = 0. \end{aligned}$$

It is interesting to note that if there is random assortment in one sex ($l_m = 1/2$) the equation reduces to that for sib mating with random assortment in both sexes.

If there is equal crossing over in both sexes, $c_s = c_o = c$, and $l_s = l_o = l_m = l = 2c(1 - c)$:

$$(10.38) \quad \lambda^3 - \lambda^2(1 - l) - (\lambda/4)[1 - 2l(1 - 2l)] + (1/4)(1 - l)(1 - 2l) = 0.$$

Bartlett and Haldane (1935) and Green and Doolittle (1963) arrived at a quartic equation in terms of $\mu = 2\lambda$ from the matrix of mating types in this case. The above cubic is an exact divisor and yields the same value of λ.

If there is no crossing over in one sex as in Drosophila ($c_s = 0$, and $l_s = 0$, $l_m = c_o$) then:

$$(10.39) \quad \begin{aligned} \lambda^3 - \lambda^2(1 - c_o) - (\lambda/4)[1 - l_o(1 - 2c_o)] \\ + (1/8)(2 - l_o)(1 - 2c_o) = 0. \end{aligned}$$

On substituting $\lambda = \mu/2$, this is an exact divisor of the quartic equation of Bartlett and Haldane for this case. The conclusions on the rate of decrease of heterozygosis are again in exact agreement.

To hold together a line considerably larger than under sib mating, attention is directed to the limiting case of one male ($a = 0$) and exclusive mating with half sisters ($b = 1$). With equal crossing over in both sexes the characteristic equation is

$$(10.40) \quad \begin{aligned} \lambda^3 - (3\lambda^2/2)(1 - l) + (\lambda/16)[5(1 - l)^2 - 13l^2] \\ + (3/16)(1 - l)(1 - 2l) = 0. \end{aligned}$$

The case in which the marker gene is maintained by matings of type ($Dd \times dd$) can be analyzed similarly (Wright 1963). It was assumed that all males are Dd and that all females are dd so that only recombination in spermatogenesis (here c) is involved. Letting S and s in subscript represent sperms carrying D and d, respectively, there are six kinds of correlations to consider (r_{So}, r_{so}, r_{SS}, r_{Ss}, r_{ss}, and r_{oo}) (Fig. 10.5). There is no difficulty in constructing gametic diagrams in each case from which the formulas for the correlations can be written by inspection. Note that both r_{So} and r_{so} are correlations between uniting gametes.

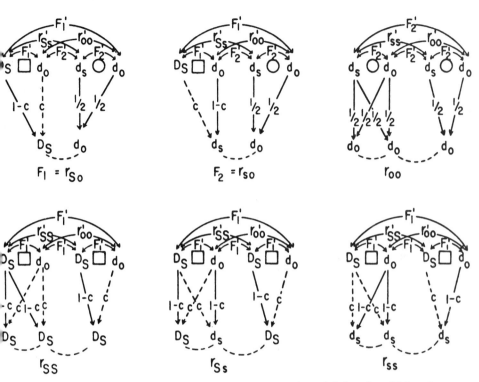

FIG. 10.5. Same as Figure 10.4 except in a population of Dd males, dd females (Wright 1963, Fig. 16, reprinted by permission, Holden-Day).

	r'_{So}	r'_{so}	r'_{SS}	r'_{Ss}	r'_{ss}	r'_{oo}	1
$r_{So} = F_m$	$(1/2)(1-c)$	$(1/2)c$	0	$(1/2)(1-c)$	0	$(1/2)c$	0
$r_{so} = F_f$	$(1/2)c$	$(1/2)(1-c)$	0	$(1/2)c$	0	$(1/2)(1-c)$	0
r_{SS}	l	0	$(1-c)^2a$	0	0	c^2a	$(1-l)(1-a)$
r_{Ss}	$1-l$	0	$(1/2)la$	0	0	$(1/2)la$	$l(1-a)$
r_{ss}	l	0	c^2a	0	0	$(1-c)^2a$	$(1-l)(1-a)$
r_{oo}	0	$1/2$	0	0	$(1/4)b$	$(1/4)b$	$(1/2)(1-b)$

(0.41)

The P matrix is the same except for elimination of the constant terms in the last column. The characteristic equation is thus a rather complicated sextic for which the original paper may be consulted (Wright 1963).

There is considerable simplification in the case of one male ($a = 0$). The limiting case of an indefinitely large number of females ($b = 1$) yields:

(10.42)
$$\lambda^4 - (\lambda^3/4)(5 - 4c) - (\lambda^2/4)[1 - 2(1 - c)l] \\ + (\lambda/16)(1 - 2c)(7 - 10c + 8c^2) + (1/16)(1 - 2c)(1 - l) = 0.$$

The case of one *dd* male but many *Dd* females is more complicated.

(10.43) $\lambda^5 - \lambda^4(1 - c)(2 - c) - (\lambda^3/4)[c + 2(1 - c)(1 - l) - 4(1 - c)^3]$
$+ (\lambda^2/16)(1 - 2c)[2(3 - 2l) + 4(1 - c)][c + 2(1 - c)^2]$
$+ (\lambda/16)(1 - 2c)[2(1 - l) - 2(1 - c)^2(3 - 4c) + 2cl]$
$- (1/8)(1 - 2l)(1 - c)^2 = 0.$

In the case of sib mating ($a = 0$, $b = 0$):

(10.44) $\lambda^4 - \lambda^3(1 - c) - (\lambda^2/4)[c + 2(1 - c)(1 - l)]$
$+ (\lambda/8)(1 - 2c)(3 - 2l) + (1/8)(1 - 2c)(1 - l) = 0.$

The equation obtained by substituting $\lambda = \mu/2$ is an exact divisor of the quintic equation derived by Bartlett and Haldane and by Green and Doolittle from the matrix of mating types in this case and maximum λ is in agreement.

Next we will consider the case in which the marker gene is sex-linked with males dY and females Dd (Fig. 10.6). There are six types of correlations to

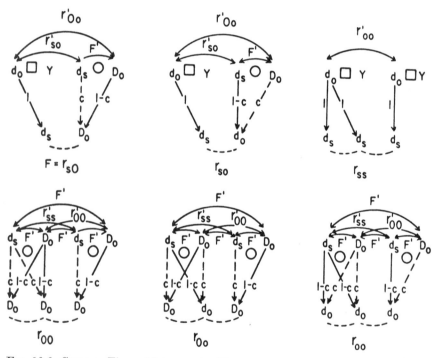

FIG. 10.6. Same as Figure 10.4 except with respect to a sex-linked marker locus D in a population of dY males, Dd females (Wright 1963, Fig. 17, reprinted by permission, Holden-Day).

consider $(r_{sO} = F, r_{so}, r_{OO}, r_{Oo}, r_{oo}, r_{ss})$ in which capital subscripts indicate that D is carried, small subscripts that d is carried. The gametic diagrams are easily constructed.

$$
\begin{array}{ccccccccc}
 & & r'_{sO} & r'_{so} & r'_{OO} & r'_{Oo} & r'_{oo} & r'_{ss} & 1 \\
 & r_{sO} = F & 0 & c & 0 & 1-c & 0 & 0 & 0 \\
 & r_{so} & 0 & 1-c & 0 & c & 0 & 0 & 0 \\
(10.45) & r_{OO} & l & 0 & (1-c)^2 b & 0 & 0 & c^2 b & (1-l)(1-b) \\
 & r_{Oo} & 1-l & 0 & c(1-c)b & 0 & 0 & c(1-c)b & l(1-b) \\
 & r_{oo} & l & 0 & c^2 b & 0 & 0 & (1-c)^2 b & (1-l)(1-b) \\
 & r_{ss} & 0 & 0 & 0 & 0 & a & 0 & 1-a
\end{array}
$$

Again the P matrix is the same except for omission of the last column and again the characteristic equation is sextic.

In the case of a single male $(a = 0, r_{ss} = 1)$ the last two rows and columns in the P matrix drop out and the characteristic equation becomes:

$$
\begin{aligned}
(10.46) \quad & \lambda^4 - \lambda^3(1 - c)[1 + (1 - c)b] - \lambda^2(1 - c)[(1 - l) - (1 - c)^2 b] \\
& + \lambda(1 - 2c)[(1 - l) + (1 - c)^3 b] - (1 - 2c)^2(1 - c)^2 b = 0.
\end{aligned}
$$

Under sib mating (both $a = 0$ and $b = 0$) the characteristic equation reduces to the form derived by Bartlett and Haldane from the mating type matrix.

$$
(10.47) \quad \lambda^3 - \lambda^2(1 - c) - \lambda(1 - c)(1 - l) + (1 - 2c)(1 - l) = 0.
$$

If there is random assortment in any of these cases, the characteristic equation reduces to forms given earlier.

Table 10.4 shows the limiting rate of decrease of heterozygosis per generation $(1 - \lambda)$ under systems with one male and either one or indefinitely many females and various amounts of recombination, here assumed equal in males and females.

TABLE 10.4. Limiting rates of decrease of heterozygosis under various systems of mating and various rates of crossing over between a neutral gene and the marker.

♂ ♀	0.02	0.05	0.10	0.20	0.30	0.40	0.50
$1Dd \times 1Dd$	0.0371	0.0821	0.1326	0.1766	0.1886	0.1908	0.1910
$1Dd \times 1dd$	.0257	.0593	.1016	.1486	.1730	.1865	.1910
$1dY \times 1Dd$	.0100	.0251	.0501	.0987	.1419	.1746	.1910
$1Dd \times \infty Dd$	.0343	.0666	.0916	.1060	.1090	.1096	.1096
$1Dd \times \infty dd$	.0246	.0505	.0727	.0914	.1016	.1076	.1096
$1dd \times \infty Dd$	.0149	.0343	.0587	.0854	.0983	.1028	.1096
$1dY \times \infty Dd$	0.0051	0.0128	0.0255	0.0503	0.0736	0.0940	0.1096

With loose linkage with the marker ($c = 0.40$), the rate of loss of hetero-zygosis is not much less than under random assortment (19.10% for sib mating, 10.96% for one male and many half sisters) but is distinctly less for sex-linked genes than for autosomal ones. With tight linkage ($c = 0.02$) fixation occurs more rapidly if both parents are heterozygous in the marker than if only one is, and it makes little difference whether there is only one female or many. In matings of type $Dd \times dd$ and many females, fixation occurs more rapidly if it is the male that is heterozygous. Loss of heterozygosis is very slow for sex-linked genes that are tightly linked and, whatever the amount of recombination, is only about half as great with many females as with one.

Retention of Linked Genes during Backcrossing

The problem of introducing a gene into an established isogenic line is as important, practically, as that of maintaining one in heterozygous state in such a line. In the case of a recognizable dominant or semidominant gene the obvious method is repeated backcrossing. The question here is the number of backcross generations required to remove genes that are intro-duced along with the desired gene in the first cross.

Of those that are in other chromosomes 50% tend to be eliminated in each backcross generation. Those that are linked can be eliminated only by re-combination. The proportion of heterozygosis with respect to loci with the proportion c of recombination is obviously given by $P = (1 - c)P'$. A considerable portion of the chromosome on each side of the gene that is being introduced may be expected to remain intact through a great many backcrosses. Assuming a uniform distribution of c, the average length after n generations is given by the following:

$$(10.48) \qquad L = \int_c^{1/2} (1 - c)^{n-1} \, dc = \frac{1}{n} [1 - (1/2)^n] \approx 1/n.$$

Bartlett and Haldane (1935) gave the following approximate results for large n in various cases that they considered:

Mean length of chromosome heterozygous on each side of the introduced locus after n generations (n large):

Introduction of dominant	$1/n$
Introduction of autosomal recessive ($c_s = c_o$)	$2/n$
Same except $c_s = 0$ as in Drosophila	$4/n$
Introduction of sex-linked recessive	$4/n$
Self-fertilization	$1/(2n)$

Sib mating, autosomal lethal selected ($c_s = c_o$) $1/(3n)$
Same except $c_s = 0$ $2/(3n)$
Sib mating, sex-linked lethal selected $(1/n)[1 - (1/3)(-1)^n]$
Sib mating, partial sex linkage or heterostylism $1/(2n)$
Sib mating, self-incompatibility $2/(3n)$

Introduction of a Gene into an Isogenic Line

Green and Doolittle (1963) have given a detailed analysis by means of Bartlett and Haldane's matrix method of the methods found useful by the Jackson Memorial Laboratory for introducing genes into inbred strains of mice. The simplest is, of course, that of introducing a dominant or partially dominant gene as discussed above. A recessive mutant can be introduced by what they call the cross-intercross method (Fig. 10.7). A cross is made to the inbred strain. The crossbreds are intercrossed to produce recessive segregants with which the process is repeated until the chance that linked genes are being carried along is considered to be sufficiently small.

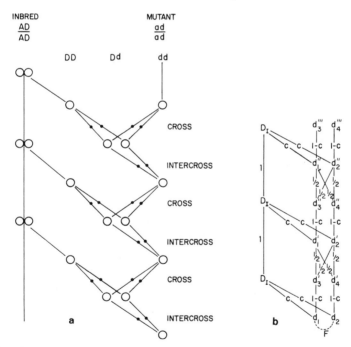

FIG. 10.7. Path diagrams for cross-intercross system of introducing a recessive gene into an inbred strain (Fig. 10.7a redrawn from Green and Doolittle 1963, Fig. 5, by permission, Holden-Day).

In order to analyze by path analysis, constancy of gene frequencies must be maintained by postulating equal use of inbred strains $AD \times AD$ and aD/aD in crossing with mutant strains ad/ad and Ad/Ad respectively as in the discussion of backcrossing in chapter 7. Figure 10.7b shows only gamete-to-gamete paths. All gametes from a given inbred strain are supposed to be alike (D_I). The coefficients relate to a locus linked with D, d. The values of the path coefficients are obvious from the earlier discussion.

$$F = c^2 + 2c(1 - c)r_{13} + (1 - c)^2 r_{34},$$
$$r_{24} = (1/2)(1 + F'),$$
$$r_{13} = [F - c^2 - (1/2)(1 - c^2) - (1/2)(1 - c^2)F']/2c(1 - c).$$

Also

$$r_{13} = c + (1 - c)r'_{13}.$$

These can be solved for F and hence for $P = 1 - F$. After some reduction:

$$P = (1/2)(1 - c)[(3 - c)P' + (1 - c)^2 P''].$$

Letting $P/P' = P'/P'' = \lambda$ to find the limiting ratio:

(10.49) $\lambda^2 - (1/2)(1 - c)(3 - c)\lambda + (1/2)(1 - c)^3 = 0.$

The larger root is $\lambda_1 = 1 - c$, the other being $\lambda_2 = (1/2)(1 - c)^2$.

Thus the relation $P = (1 - c)P'$ is approached except that a cycle of two generations is implied.

A recessive that can be carried only in the heterozygous condition because of lethality or low viability or low fertility requires test intercrosses to select heterozygotes for each backcross.

A method that saves some time is what is called the cross-backcross-intercross system (Fig. 10.8). It is desired to introduce the viable recessive d while eliminating linked genes as far as practicable. The progeny of the first cross are backcrossed to the inbred strain, producing 50% DD and 50% Dd, the latter composed of $[(1 - c)(AD/ad) + c(AD/Ad)]$. A sufficient number of intercrosses are made to produce recessive dd with gene frequency $\{(1 - c)^2 a + [1 - (1 - c)^2]A\}$. These are crossed to the inbreds AD/AD. In the following backcross the 50% that are Dd form the array $[(1 - c)^3(AD/ad) + [1 - (1 - c)^3](AD/Ad)]$ and in the recessives extracted from intercrosses, the gene frequency at the A locus becomes $\{(1 - c)^4 a + [1 - (1 - c)^4]A\}$ and so on. Thus $P = (1 - c)^2 P'$ in a cycle of three generations in this system. This result can readily be derived from path analysis in the gamete to gamete system of Figure 10.8b.

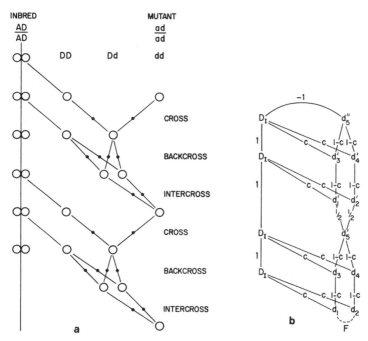

FIG. 10.8. Path diagrams for cross-backcross-intercross system of introducing a recessive gene into an inbred strain (Fig. 10.8a redrawn from Green and Doolittle 1963, Fig. 7, by permission, Holden-Day).

The rate in generations can be further reduced at the expense of carrying a considerable number of backcross lines in each cycle by making repeated backcrosses before making test crosses to discover animals that are still heterozygous. Thus an inbred strain of spotted guinea pigs (ss) was crossed with an inbred self-colored strain (SS) with the production of self-colored or nearly self-colored offspring (Ss). These were backcrossed to the self-colored strain for two generations along many independent lines producing young 7/8 blood of the self-colored strain and expected to consist of about 75% SS, 25% Ss. There was no difficulty in finding heterozygotes by means of test crosses to ss and extracting recessives by intercrossing of those proved to be Ss, in which the effect of ss on a gametic background was largely that of the other inbred strain (Wright and Chase 1936) (data volume 1, Table 15.10). Such a system of backcrosses could be carried considerably farther before test crossing if the cutting down of the number of generations before achieving a high degree coisogenicity were more important than the additional space required to insure the presence of heterozygotes at the end of the series of backcrosses and to make the necessary test crosses.

Linkage and Selection under Self-fertilization

The effect of selection other than enforced heterozygosis at a linked locus cannot be dealt with by path analysis because of its nonlinear effects. Reeve (1957) made a thorough analysis in the case of self-fertilization. It required a 6 × 6 matrix. Representing the relative selective values of d_1d_1 and d_2d_2 at the linked locus by v_1 and v_2 within matings, t_1 and t_2 among matings as before, using c for amount of recombination and $C = 2c(1 - c)$ also as before, and using a_xa_x for $(a_1a_1 + a_2a_2)$ at the neutral locus under consideration, the generation matrix, multiplied throughout by two, was as follows:

Parent Lines

Progeny Lines	$\dfrac{a_xd_1}{a_xd_1}$	$\dfrac{a_xd_1}{a_xd_2}$	$\dfrac{a_xd_2}{a_xd_2}$	$\dfrac{a_1d_1}{a_2d_1}$	$\dfrac{a_1d_1}{a_2d_2}$	$\dfrac{a_1d_2}{a_2d_2}$
$\dfrac{a_xd_1}{a_xd_1}$	$2t_1$	$(1/2)v_1$	0	t_1	$(1/2)v_1(1 - C)$	0
$\dfrac{a_xd_1}{a_xd_2}$	0	1	0	0	C	0
$\dfrac{a_xd_2}{a_xd_2}$	0	$(1/2)v_2$	$2t_2$	0	$(1/2)v_2(1 - C)$	t_2
$\dfrac{a_1d_1}{a_2d_1}$	0	0	0	t_1	$(1/2)v_1C$	0
$\dfrac{a_1d_1}{a_2d_2}$	0	0	0	0	$1 - C$	0
$\dfrac{a_1d_2}{a_2d_2}$	0	0	0	0	$(1/2)v_2C$	t_2

(10.50)

The nth power of this matrix is not excessively complicated but will not be given here. On starting from double heterozygotes a_1d_1/a_2d_2 and thus from $y_0 = 1$, the amount of heterozygosis in the nth generation came out as follows:

$$(10.51)\quad y_n = \frac{\dfrac{v_1C}{2}\left[\dfrac{(t_1)^n - (1 - C)^n}{t_1 - (1 - C)}\right] + (1 - C)^n + \dfrac{v_2C}{2}\left[\dfrac{(t_2)^n - (1 - C)^n}{t_2 - (1 - C)}\right]}{\dfrac{v_1}{2}\left[\dfrac{(2t_1)^n - 1}{2t_1 - 1}\right] + 1 + \dfrac{v_2}{2}\left[\dfrac{(2t_2)^n - 1}{2t_2 - 1}\right]}.$$

This reduces to equation (10.13) (with $x_0 = z_0 = 0$) if linkage is complete ($C = 0$) and to $(1 - C)^n$ in the case of balanced lethals (10.21) (with $v_1 = v_2 = 0$) as expected.

With very strong selection (t_1, t_2, v_1, v_2 all small) at the linked locus a high level of heterozygosis is maintained at the neutral locus and $t_1{}^n$ and $t_2{}^n$ may be ignored after a few generations.

$$(10.52) \quad y_n = (1 - C)^n \left[\frac{v_1 C}{2(1 - C - t_1)} + 1 + \frac{v_2 C}{2(1 - C - t_2)} \right] \Big/ \left[\frac{v_1}{2(1 - 2t_1)} + 1 + \frac{v_2}{2(1 - 2t_2)} \right]$$

$$= k(1 - C)^n$$

where k is a constant.

In Table 10.5 are some of the examples given by Reeve (with a few extensions) with $v_1 = v_2 = v$ and $t_1 = t_2 = t$. Case 1 refers to selection (at the linked locus) exclusively within lines; case 2 to selection exclusively among lines; case 3 to equal selection within and among lines, and case 4 to balanced lethals. These are given for both $c = 0.20$ and $c = 0.05$. The case of no selection ($c = 0.50$ or $v = t = 1$) is given first for comparison.

TABLE 10.5. Amounts of heterozygosis at a neutral locus after the indicated numbers of generations under self-fertilization and various conditions of selection (v, t) at a linked locus with 20% or 5% crossing over, in comparison with the amounts in the absence of linkage, $c = 0.50$.

Genera- tion	$c = 0.50$ or $v = 1$ $t = 1$	$c = 0.20$			
		Case 1 $v = 0.50$ $t = 0.75$	Case 2 $v = 1.0$ $t = 0.50$	Case 3 $v = 0.50$ $t = 0.50$	Case 4 $v = 0$ $t = 0$
1	0.500	0.560	0.500	0.560	0.680
2	.250	.307	.280	.326	.462
4	.063	.089	.097	.116	.214
8	.004	.007	.013	.017	.046
12	0.000	0.000	0.002	0.003	0.010
		$c = 0.05$			
1		0.635	0.500	0.635	0.909
2		.399	.317	.443	.819
4		.154	.163	.247	.671
8		.022	.062	.101	.450
12		0.003	0.029	0.048	0.302

Where selection is exclusively within lines (as in case 1), the linked locus tends toward fixation and after a few generations heterozygosis declines rapidly in the neutral locus a_1, a_2 even with close linkage ($c = 0.05$). In cases 2 and 3 above, t is at the critical value, 1/2, that just allows fixation at the linked locus. The decline in heterozygosis at locus a_1, a_2, though considerably less than in case 1, is very much more rapid with $c = 0.05$ than with balanced lethals. Somewhat loose linkage ($c = 0.20$) permits a fairly rapid decline in all cases.

Linkage and Selection under Sib Mating

Reeve and Gower (1958) worked out the effects under sib mating of equal selection against both homozygotes at a linked locus. They considered both selection exclusively within lines and equal selection within and among lines. These required 19 × 19 matrices. The calculation of the nth powers was made by an electronic digital computer. Tables 10.6 and 10.7 give the limiting ratios of heterozygosis at the neutral locus in successive generations for various selective values, v, at the linked locus and amount of recombination c.

TABLE 10.6. Limiting ratios (λ_∞) of heterozygosis at a given neutral locus in successive generations with given selection (v) at a linked locus exclusively within lines (case 1) or with equal selection (v_0) within and among lines (case 2), and given amounts of crossing over under sib mating.

CASE 1

c	$v = 0.8$	$v = 0.6$	$v = 0.4$	$v = 0.2$	$v = 0.1$
0.25	0.8090	0.8090	0.8090	0.8090	—
.20	.8090	.8090	.8090	.8139	0.8221
.15	.8090	.8090	.8090	.8314	.8390
.10	.8090	.8090	.8319	.8614	.8687
0.05	.8090	.8369	.8774	.9100	.9185
0	0.8512	0.8968	0.9429	0.9824	0.9952

	CASE 2				Case 1 / Case 2
c	$v = 0.8$	$v = 0.6$	$v = 0.4$	$v = 0.2$	$v = 0$
0.25	0.8090	0.8238	0.8216	0.8187	0.8154
.20	.810	0.8357	0.8329	0.8289	0.8234
.15	.8265	0.8552	0.8519	0.8469	0.8389
.10	.8565	0.8863	0.8829	0.8774	0.8674
0.05	.9014	0.9335	0.9310	0.9266	0.9179
0	0.9638	1.0	1.0	1.0	1.0

The rate $\lambda = 0.8090$ that appears in many cases (see Table 10.6), especially under case 1, is the same as for pure sib mating $v = 1$ (or $c = 0.50$). It requires, however, many more generations to reach this with $v < 1$ and $c < 0.50$. The bottom row ($c = 0$) in both cases is that for selection of the sort indicated at the locus itself. The last column in the lower part of the table is that for linkage with balanced lethals. One apparently surprising point, noted by Reeve, is that in case 2 the limiting value of λ is maximum at about $v = 0.6$ instead of $v = 0$. Where selection is exclusively within lines, limiting λ rises consistently with reduction in selective value as expected. The joint effects of selection within and among lines at the linked locus in maintaining heterozygosis are more complicated.

The speed of inbreeding in any generation, relative to that under uncomplicated sib mating, is given by the ratio $\log \lambda_{n(v,c)}/\log \lambda_{n(1)}$ where $\lambda_{n(1)}$ is that in the absence of selection. Some of the figures given by Reeve for the two cases are shown in Table 10.7.

TABLE 10.7. Relative speed of inbreeding in cases 1 and 2 at generations 10 and after constancy is reached, as percentages of that under uncomplicated sib mating.

c	n	v Case 1				v Case 2				Case 1 Case 2
		0.8	0.6	0.4	0.2	0.8	0.6	0.4	0.2	0
0.25	10	99.6	98.9	97.6	96.2	96.5	92.8	92.8	94.4	96.3
	∞	100	100	100	100	100	91.5	92.7	94.4	96.3
.15	10	98.2	94.7	89.1	83.2	89.2	77.5	75.9	78.4	83.0
	∞	100	100	100	87.1	90.0	73.8	75.6	78.4	82.9
.05	10	91.2	77.2	59.7	44.3	67.8	40.4	34.5	36.0	40.5
	∞	100	84.0	61.7	44.5	49.0	32.5	33.7	36.0	40.4
.01	10	83.3	61.0	36.9	28.7	51.3	16.4	8.4	8.1	9.4
	∞	82.1	58.0	35.2	16.4	24.2	7.1	7.4	8.0	9.2
0.0	10	76.0	51.4	27.7	8.4	39.7	0.0	0.0	0.0	0.0
	∞	76.0	51.4	27.8	8.4	17.4	0.0	0.0	0.0	0.0

If selection is exclusively within lines (case 1) it makes little difference how strong the selection against homozygotes is, if c is as great as 0.25 and such selection must be very severe to interfere much with inbreeding if c is 0.15. Even 20% selective elimination ($v = 0.8$) is moderately severe but causes little interference with c as small as 0.05. Such selection at the locus itself ($c = 0$) reduces the rate of inbreeding by about 24%.

There is more interference if there is also selection among lines (case 2), this being ultimately greatest, as noted above, at about $v = 0.6$, but at a lower value of v in the early generations, as shown for generation 10. There is no very serious effect if c is as great as 0.25, about a 26% reduction in speed ultimately if $c = 0.15$, $v = 0.6$ and much more serious slowing down at $c = 0.05$. The speed is reduced to zero at generation 10 as well as later by selective values at the locus itself ($c = 0$) that are less than Hayman and Mather's critical value 0.7633.

A different approach to joint effects of inbreeding and selection based on incorporation of selection effects into a generalized "fixation" index, F, will be taken up in chapter 12.

CHAPTER 11

Assortative Mating

This chapter is concerned with pure assortative mating (no selection) in populations so large that there are no random changes in gene frequency that need to be considered.

Assortative Mating at a Single Locus

In the one-factor case with recognizable heterozygotes and perfect assortative mating of all three genotypes, the percentage of heterozygotes is obviously halved in each generation with equal contributions to each homozygous class, leading to complete fixation in the proportions in which the genes were present in the original population.

With complete dominance, the end result is the same but heterozygosis is reduced more slowly. Starting from $(q - y_0/2)AA + y_0Aa + (1 - q - y_0/2)aa$, the proportion of matings of dominant with dominant is $q + y_0/2$. Taking due account of the relative frequencies of the three possible types of mating, the proportion of homozygous dominants becomes $2q^2/(2q + y_0)$, of heterozygotes $2y_0q/(2q + y_0)$, and of recessive $(2q + y_0 - 2y_0q - 2q^2)/(2q + y_0)$. Jennings (1916) gave the case of $q = 1/2$, starting from panmixia, in which the proportion of heterozygotes falls off in the series $1/2, 1/3, 1/4, 1/5, \ldots, 0$. Wentworth and Remick (1916) dealt with the general case.

There have been later studies of simple patterns by Haldane (1924b), Breese (1956), Workman (1964), and O'Donald (1960).

Multifactorial Assortative Mating

The situation becomes more complicated in multifactorial cases. Fisher (1918) investigated the effects on the correlations between relatives where there is equilibrium under partial assortative mating with respect to a character affected by many dominant genes and by environmental factors. The progressive effects were investigated from a different viewpoint by Wright

(1921) under the simplifying assumptions that all pairs of alleles are equivalent, all are semidominant and additive, and all have gene frequency 0.50.

The nature of the problem may be illustrated by carrying through the operations directly in a very simple case: two equivalent completely additive pairs of alleles, both gene frequencies 0.50 and no environmental effects, under perfect assortative mating. Table 11.1a shows the relative frequencies

TABLE 11.1. Perfect assortative mating with two equivalent loci. (a) Genotypes of random breeding population, (b) Gametes produced by five phenotypes, (c) Correlation array of uniting gametes, (d) Genotypes after one generation.

PARENTAL GENOTYPES					PHENOTYPES	GAMETES				
	BB	Bb	bb	Total	+ genes	AB	Ab	aB	ab	Total
AA	1	2	1	4	(4)	1				1
Aa	2	4	2	8	(3)	2	1	1		4
aa	1	2	1	4	(2)	1	2	2	1	6
Total	4	8	4	16	(1)		1	1	2	4
					(0)				1	1
		(a)			Total	4	4	4	4	16
							(b)			

UNITING GAMETES						OFFSPRING GENOTYPES			
	AB	Ab	aB	ab	Total		BB	Bb	bb	Total
AB	13	5	5	1	24	AA	13	10	7	30
Ab	5	7	7	5	24	Aa	10	16	10	36
aB	5	7	7	5	24	aa	7	10	13	30
ab	1	5	5	13	24	Total	30	36	30	96
Total	24	24	24	24	96			(d)		
		(c)								

of the nine genotypes under random mating. Table 11.1b gives the gametic arrays for each of the five phenotypes. In calculating frequencies of unions among the various types of gametes, it must be borne in mind that 6/16 of the matings are within the middle phenotype, 4/16 within those with one plus factor and also with three plus factors, and 1/16 within each of the extreme classes. The relative frequencies are given in Table 11.1c and the composition of the resulting population in Table 11.1d. The correlation between gametes with respect to a single locus (F) has changed from 0 to 1/4, with respect to the total for both gametes (F_T) from 0 to 1/2. The proportion of heterozygosis has changed from 1/2 to 3/8. The genetic and phenotypic variances, here the same, have risen from 1 to 3/2.

By repeating this process, the compositions of any number of generations may be found. The values of F form the series 0, 1/4, 3/8, 15/32, 35/64; those of F_T: 0, 1/2, 2/3, 3/4, 70/87; those for heterozygosis: 1/2, 3/8, 10/32, 17/64, 29/128; and those for the variance: 1, 3/2, 15/8, 35/16, 157/64 if each plus gene makes a unit contribution to the phenotype.

The work is rather tedious even in this very simple case. It is not difficult, however, to obtain general formulas by path analysis as long as the gene effects are additive. Dominance and factor interaction present serious complications that will not be considered here. It will also be assumed that there are no genetic-environmental interactions.

General Formulas

Relations between phenotypic assortative mating and heritability may be considered first. Such assortative mating between prospective parents, P_1 and P_2 (Fig. 11.1), creates correlations between the factors back of P_1 and those back of P_2. (In what follows, second-order subscripts will be replaced by first-order subscripts in parentheses.) Assume that $r_{P(1)H(1)} = r_{P(2)H(2)} = h$ and that $r_{P(1)E(1)} = r_{P(2)E(2)} = e$, so that $h^2 + e^2 = 1$. Because of symmetry, $r_{E(1)H(2)} = r_{H(1)E(2)}$.

(11.1) $\qquad r_{P(1)P(2)} = h^2 r_{H(1)H(2)} + 2her_{H(1)E(2)} + e^2 r_{E(1)E(2)}.$

The directions of arrows relating to P_1 and P_2 may be reversed to indicate determination of the correlations by assortative mating $r_{P(1)P(2)}$. This is done in Figure 11.2.

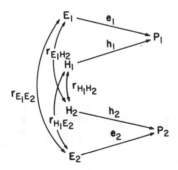

FIG. 11.1. Path diagram relating the phenotypes of the parents (P_1, P_2) to each other through their heredities (H_1, H_2) and their environments (E_1, E_2) under assortative mating.

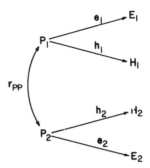

FIG. 11.2. Path diagram relating the parental heredities (H_1, H_2) and environments (E_1, E_2) to each other through the phenotypes (P_1, P_2) under assortative mating.

The correlations $r_{P(1)E(1)} = r_{P(2)E(2)}$ and $r_{P(1)H(1)} = r_{P(2)H(2)}$ are unaffected, so that the reversed path coefficients are also e and h, respectively. The correlation between parental genotypes is $r_{H(1)H(2)} = h^2 r_{P(1)P(2)}$, between parental environments is $r_{E(1)E(2)} = e^2 r_{P(1)P(2)}$, and between genotype of one and environment of the other is $r_{H(1)E(2)} = r_{E(1)H(2)} = her_{P(1)P(2)}$. Thus equation (11.1) can be written:

$$(11.2) \quad r_{P(1)P(2)} = (h^4 + 2h^2e^2 + e^4)r_{P(1)P(2)} = (h^2 + e^2)^2 r_{P(1)P(2)} = r_{P(1)P(2)}.$$

In what follows, only the genetic assortative mating $m = r_{H'(1)H'(2)} = h'^2 r_{P(1)P(2)}$ will be considered at first in the analysis, but it must be remembered that the phenotypic correlation is actually primary.

It is convenient to consider the case of two loci with effects additive within and between loci but with no restrictions on gene frequencies or magnitudes of effects or on the recombination rate c. In Figure 11.3 the genotypic effect H is represented as composed of contributions L_A and L_B from loci A and B, respectively (path coefficients l_A and l_B, respectively). These are analyzed into gene effects assuming that the uniting gametes were A_1B_1 and A_2B_2. The path coefficient relating locus effect to gene effect is represented as $a_A \, (= \sqrt{\{1/[2(1 + F_A)]\}})$ at the A locus and as $a_B \, (= \sqrt{\{1/[2(1 + F_B)]\}})$ at the B locus. The correlation between linked genes is represented by s and that between the A allele in one gamete and the B allele in the other by d.

$$(11.3) \quad r_{L(A)A} = a_A(1 + F_A); \quad r_{L(B)B} = a_B(1 + F_B);$$

$$(11.4) \quad r_{L(A)B} = a_A(s + d); \quad r_{L(B)A} = a_B(s + d);$$

$$(11.5) \quad r_{L(A)L(B)} = a_A a_B(2s + 2d) = (s + d)/\sqrt{[(1 + F_A)(1 + F_B)]}.$$

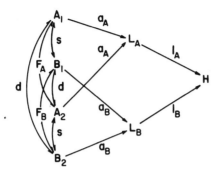

FIG. 11.3. Path diagram analyzing heredity (H) into contributions (L_A, L_B) from two loci and relating these to each other through their component genes, under assortative mating.

The variances at the two loci in the absence of assortative mating (subscript 0) will be taken as basic data.

(11.6) $$\sigma^2_{L(A)(0)} = 2q_A(1 - q_A)\alpha^2$$

where α is the excess contribution of A over a;

(11.7) $$\sigma^2_{L(B)(0)} = 2q_B(1 - q_B)\beta^2$$

where β is the excess contribution of B over b.

If there is assortative mating that gives fixation indices of F_A and F_B at the two loci:

(11.8) $$\sigma^2_{L(A)} = \sigma^2_{L(A)(0)}(1 + F_A); \qquad \sigma^2_{L(B)} = \sigma^2_{L(B)(0)}(1 + F_B);$$
$$\sigma_H^2 = \sigma^2_{L(A)} + \sigma^2_{L(B)} + 2\sigma_{L(A)}\sigma_{L(B)}r_{L(A)L(B)};$$

(11.9) $$\sigma_H^2 = \sigma^2_{L(A)(0)}(1 + F_A) + \sigma^2_{L(B)(0)}(1 + F_B) + 2\sigma_{L(A)(0)}\sigma_{L(B)(0)}(s + d).$$
$$l_A = \sigma_{L(A)}/\sigma_H; \qquad l_B = \sigma_{L(B)}/\sigma_H;$$
$$l_A a_A = \sigma_{L(A)(0)}/\sigma_H\sqrt{2}; \qquad l_B a_B = \sigma_{L(B)(0)}/\sigma_H\sqrt{2};$$
$$r_{AH} = l_A a_A(1 + F_A) + l_B a_B(s + d);$$

(11.10) $$r_{AH} = [\sigma_{L(A)(0)}(1 + F_A) + \sigma_{L(B)(0)}(s + d)]/\sigma_H\sqrt{2}.$$

Equations (11.9) and (11.10) permit σ_H^2 and r_{AH} (r_{BH} by symmetry) to be expressed in terms of F_A, F_B, s, and d of the same generation and the basic data.

In Figure 11.4,

(11.11) $$b_A = r_{L'(A1)A(1)} = r_{L'(A1)A'(1)} = a_A'(1 + F_A') = \sqrt{[(1 + F_A')/2]};$$
$$b_B = \sqrt{[(1 + F_B')/2]},$$

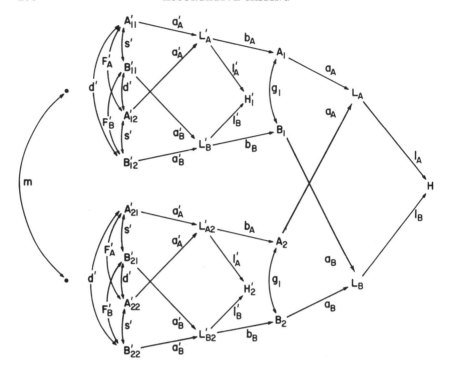

Fig. 11.4. Path diagram analyzing heredity (H) into contributions (L_A, L_B) from two loci (as in 11.3) but carrying the analysis back to genes of the parental generation (here primed), under assortative mating: $r_{H_1'H_2'} = m$.

$$(11.12) \quad F_A = r_{A1 \cdot A2} = b_A{}^2 r_{L'(A1)L'(A2)}; \quad \text{thus} \quad r_{L'(A1)L'(A2)} = 2F_A/(1 + F_A').$$

Also

$$(11.13) \quad r_{L'(A1)L'(A2)} = 4a'_A{}^2 r_{A'(11)A'(21)} = 2r_{A'(11)A'(21)}/(1 + F_A');$$

thus

$$(11.14) \quad r_{A'(11)A'(21)} = F_A$$

as expected, and

$$(11.15) \quad r_{A(1)B(1)} = s = b_A b_B r_{L'(A1)L'(B1)} + g = \frac{s' + d'}{2} + g,$$

from (11.11), (11.5), where g is the contribution of linkage to the correlation of linked genes. But also:

(11.16) $$s = (1 - c)s' + cd'.$$

If $c = 0$, then $s = s'$; if $c = 1/2$, then $s = (1/2)(s' + d')$.

(11.17) $$g = s - \frac{s' + d'}{2} = (1/2 - c)(s' - d'),$$

$$d = r_{A(1)B(2)} = r_{B(1)A(2)} = b_A b_B r_{L'(A1)L'(B2)} = 4(b_A a_A')(b_B a_B')r_{A'(11)B'(21)}$$

(11.18) $$d = r_{A'(11)B'(21)}.$$

From Figure 11.5, with arrows reversed:

(11.19) $$F_A \doteq (r_{A'H'})^2 m, \qquad F_B = (r_{B'H'})^2 m;$$

(11.20) $$d = r_{A'H'} r_{B'H'} m = \sqrt{(F_A F_B)}.$$

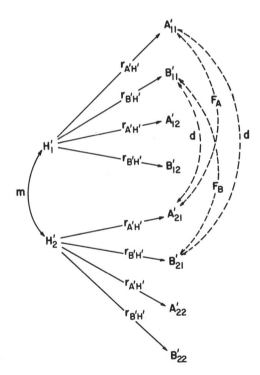

FIG. 11.5. Path diagram relating parental genes (primed) to each other, through the parental heredities, with correlation m.

Returning to Figure 11.4:

$$m = r_{H'(1)H'(2)} = 4(l_A'a_A')^2 r_{A'(11)A'(21)} + 8(l_A'a_A')(l_B'a_B')r_{A'(11)B'(21)}$$
$$+ 4(l_B'a_B')^2 r_{B'(11)B'(21)}$$

(11.21) $m = 2[\sigma^2_{L'(A)(0)}F_A' + 2\sigma_{L'(A)(0)}\sigma_{L'(B)(0)}\sqrt{(F_A'F_B')} + \sigma^2_{L'(B)(0)}F_B']/\sigma^2_{H'}.$

Equations (11.16) and (11.19) permit s, F_A, and F_B to be expressed in terms of parameters of the parental generation, and (11.20) and (11.21) permit d and m to be derived from parameters of the parental generation. This gives all coefficients in terms of the basic data from an initial panmictic population.

$$F_{A(0)} = F_{B(0)} = s_0 = d_0 = 0;$$
$$\sigma^2_{L(A)(0)} = 2q_A(1 - q_A)\alpha^2; \qquad \sigma^2_{L(B)(0)} = 2q_B(1 - q_B)\beta^2;$$

(11.22) $\sigma^2_{H(0)} = \sigma^2_{L(A)(0)} + \sigma^2_{L(B)(0)}; \qquad r_{HA(0)} = \sigma_{L(A)(0)}/\sigma_{H(0)}\sqrt{2};$

$$\sigma^2_{P(0)} = \sigma^2_{H(0)} + \sigma_E^2; \qquad h_0{}^2 = \sigma^2_{H(0)}/\sigma^2_{P(0)}.$$

The parameters for later generations can be derived step by step for any succession of values of the assortative mating $r_{P(1)P(2)}$ or of $m = r_{P(1)P(2)}h^2$. It is simplest to assume that $r_{P(1)P(2)}$ is constant, but actually it would be likely to rise as σ_P^2 rises. The results can easily be generalized for any number of loci. It will, however, be assumed here that $c = 1/2$ for all pairs.

(11.23) $F_A = mr^2_{H'A'}$

and similarly for other loci;

(11.24) $d_{AB} = \sqrt{(F_A F_B)}$

and similarly for other pairs;

(11.25) $s_{AB} = (1/2)(s'_{AB} + d'_{AB})$

and similarly for other pairs.

(11.26) $\sigma_H^2 = \sum_i [\sigma^2_{L(i)(0)}(1 + F_i)] + 2 \sum_{ij} [\sigma_{L(i)(0)}\sigma_{L(j)(0)}(s_{ij} + d_{ij})], \qquad j > i$

(11.27) $r_{HA} = [\sigma_{L(A)(0)}(1 + F_A) + \sum_i \sigma_{L(i)(0)}(s_{Ai} + d_{Ai})]/\sigma_H\sqrt{2}, \qquad i \neq A$

similarly for other loci with terms in sum involving all other loci in each case.

(11.28) $\sigma_P = \sigma_E^2 + \sigma_H^2;$

(11.29) $h^2 = \sigma_H^2/\sigma_P^2, \qquad e^2 = \sigma_E^2/\sigma_P^2;$

(11.30) $m = r_{P(1)P(2)}h^2.$

A simple special case is that in which there are n equivalent factors all with gene frequency $1/2$. In this case:

(11.31) $\quad s = (1/2)[F' + s']$,

(11.32) $\quad F = \dfrac{m}{2n}[1 + nF' + (n - 1)s'] = \dfrac{m}{2n}[1 + F' + 2(n - 1)s]$

from (11.23) to (11.27)

(11.33) $\quad \sigma_H^2 = n\sigma_{L(0)}^2[1 + nF + (n - 1)s], \qquad \sigma_{H'}^2 = \dfrac{2n^2}{m}\sigma_{L(0)}^2 F$

after the first generation.

So far we have considered coefficients relating to single genes. Those relating to whole gametes are also of interest. Figure 11.6 is like Figure 11.3 except that the genotype is analyzed into contributions from two gametes instead of into two (or more) loci. The coefficient, relating gamete to contributing gene, is represented by z_A or z_B.

(11.34) $\quad z_A^2 = \sigma_A^2/\sigma_G^2 = q_A(1 - q_A)\alpha^2/\sigma_G^2, \quad$ etc.;

(11.35) $\quad \sigma_G^2 = \sigma_A^2 + \sigma_B^2 + \cdots + 2\sigma_A\sigma_B s + \cdots$.

The correlation (F_T) between uniting gametes is

(11.36)
$$F_T = z_A^2 F_A + z_B^2 F_B + \cdots + 2z_A z_B d + \cdots;$$
$$F_T = \dfrac{\sigma_A^2 F_A + \sigma_B^2 F_B + \cdots + 2\sigma_A\sigma_B\sqrt{(F_A F_B)} + \cdots}{\sigma_A^2 + \sigma_B^2 + \cdots + 2\sigma_A\sigma_B s + \cdots} .$$

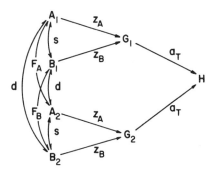

FIG. 11.6. Path diagram analyzing heredity (H) into contributions (G_1, G_2) from the uniting gametes and these into contributions of the genes of the two loci under assortative mating.

If there are n equivalent loci:

(11.37) $$F_T = \frac{n\sigma_A{}^2[F_A + (n-1)F_A]}{n\sigma_A{}^2[1 + (n-1)s]} = \frac{nF_A}{1 + (n-1)s}.$$

Figure 11.7 traces a genotype H to the two parental genotypes (correlation m) through the uniting gametes.

(11.38) $$2a_T{}^2(1 + F_T) = 1, \qquad a_T{}^2 = 1/[2(1 + F_T)];$$

(11.39) $$F_T = b_T{}^2 m, \qquad b_T{}^2 = F_T/m.$$

Coefficients a_T and b_T will be used in chapter 15 in determining the correlations between relatives.

In the simple case discussed near the beginning of this chapter, there were two equivalent additive loci ($n = 2$), $q_{A(0)} = q_{B(0)} = 0.5$ perfect assortative mating ($m = 1$), and $F_{A(0)} = s_0 = 0$, $\sigma^2_{L(0)} = 0.5\alpha^2$. The pertinent formulas are:

(11.40) $$s = (1/2)(F' + s'),$$

(11.41) $$F_A = (1/4)(1 + 2F' + s'),$$

(11.42) $$y = (1 - F_A)y_0,$$

(11.43) $$F_T = 2F_A/(1 + s),$$

(11.44) $$\sigma_H{}^2 = (1 + 2F_A + s)\alpha^2, \qquad \sigma^2_{H'} = 4F_A\alpha^2$$

after a generation.

These agree with the results of direct calculation. Fixation index F and $\sigma_H{}^2/\sigma^2_{H(0)}$ appear under $r_{PP} = 1$, $h_0{}^2 = 1$, and $n = 2$ in Tables 11.2 and 11.3.

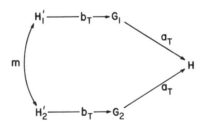

FIG. 11.7. Path diagram analyzing heredity (H) into contributions (G_1, G_2) from the uniting gametes (as in 11.6) but relating these through the parental heredities, under assortative mating.

TABLE 11.2. Fixation indexes (F) for various numbers of equivalent loci (n) in successive generations of assortative mating $r_{P(1)P(2)}$, with initial heritability h_0^2.

Generation	$r_{P(1)P(2)} = 1$ $h_0^2 = 1$				$r_{P(1)P(2)} = 1$ $h_0^2 = 0.5$		$r_{P(1)P(2)} = 0.5$ $h_0^2 = 1$		$r_{P(1)P(2)} = -1$ $h_0^2 = 1$	
	$n = 1$	2	4	10	1	4	1	4	1	4
0	0	0	0	0	0	0	0	0	0	0
1	0.500	0.250	0.125	0.050	0.250	0.063	0.250	0.063	−0.500	−0.125
2	0.750	0.375	0.188	0.075	.347	.087	.313	.078	−.250	−.063
3	0.875	0.469	0.242	0.099	.387	.106	.328	.088	−.375	−.070
4	0.938	0.547	0.293	0.122	.403	.123	.332	.095	−.313	−.066
5	0.969	0.613	0.340	0.144	.409	.138	.333	.100	−.344	−.067
10	0.999	0.825	0.534	0.249	.414	.191	.333	.109	−.333	−.067
15	1.000	0.921	0.670	0.340	.414	.220	.333	.111	−.333	−.067
∞	1.000	1.000	1.000	1.000	0.414	0.261	0.333	0.111	−0.333	−0.067

TABLE 11.3. Ratio of genotypic variance (σ_H^2) under assortative mating to the initial value ($\sigma_{H(0)}^2$). Heritability is complete in all cases except in two columns. In column 6 it rises in seven generations from 0.500 to 0.586. In column 7 it rises from 0.500 to 0.651 in five generations, to 0.695 in 10 generations and ultimately to 0.739.

Generation	$r_{P(1)P(2)} = 1$ $h_0^2 = 1$				$r_{P(1)P(2)} = 1$ $h_0^2 = 0.5$		$r_{P(1)P(2)} = 0.5$ $h_0 = 1$		$r_{P(1)P(2)} = -1$ $h_0^2 = 1$	
	$n = 1$	2	4	10	1	4	1	4	1	4
0	1.000	1.000	1.000	1.000	1.000	1.000	1.000	1.000	1.000	1.000
1	1.500	1.500	1.500	1.500	1.250	1.250	1.250	1.250	0.500	0.500
2	1.750	1.875	1.938	1.975	1.347	1.441	1.313	1.407	0.750	0.563
3	1.875	2.188	2.344	2.438	1.387	1.602	1.328	1.516	0.626	0.531
4	1.938	2.451	2.723	2.888	1.402	1.741	1.332	1.593	0.688	0.535
5	1.968	2.679	3.076	3.327	1.409	1.862	1.333	1.647	0.656	0.533
10	2.000	3.401	4.518	5.359	1.414	2.279	1.333	1.755	0.667	0.533
15	2.000	3.729	5.538	7.144	1.414	2.509	1.333	1.774	0.667	0.533
∞	2.000	4.000	8.000	20.000	1.414	2.828	1.333	1.778	0.667	0.533

Progressive Effects with Equivalent Loci

Equations (11.31), (11.32), and (11.33) are all that are needed for obtaining the fixation index F and the ratio of the phenotypic variance to its original value, $\sigma_H^2/\sigma_{H(0)}^2$, generation after generation, where there is complete determination by heredity ($h_0^2 = 1$, $m = r_{P(1)P(2)}$), assuming that $r_{P(1)P(2)}$ is constant. This applies to all columns in Tables 11.2 and 11.3 except 6 and 7. Where there are environmental contributions, here assumed constant with the value $\sigma_E^2 = \sigma_{H(0)}^2(1 - h_0^2)/h_0^2$ (from $h_0^2 = \sigma_{H(0)}^2/(\sigma_{H(0)}^2 + \sigma_E^2)$), it is necessary to calculate h^2 for each generation:

$$(11.45) \qquad h^2 = \sigma_H^2/[\sigma_H^2 + \sigma_{H(0)}^2(1 - h_0^2)/h_0^2].$$

This formula as well as (11.31)–(11.33) was used in calculating the entries in columns 6 and 7 in Tables 11.2 and 11.3.

Under perfect assortative mating and complete determination by heredity (columns 2–5) there is no limit short of complete fixation. The rate of fixation is very rapid if the character depends on only one pair of alleles (as already noted), is fairly rapid with two equivalent loci, but is slow with as many as ten. The variance, however, increases more rapidly the greater the number of loci (after the first generation) and reaches $2n$ times its initial value.

With perfect assortative mating but only 50% determination by heredity the F rapidly approaches a limit (0.414) if there is only one pair of loci but rather slowly approaches a lower limit (0.261) if there are four equivalent loci. The increases in variance are relatively small, but again larger the greater the number of loci.

With the same initial genotypic assortative mating, $m = 0.5$, but because of imperfect assortative mating ($r_{PP} = 0.5$), complete determination by heredity, F rises more slowly and approaches a lower limit ($F = 0.333$ if $n = 1$, $F = 0.111$ if $n = 4$) than in the preceding cases. The increases in variance are also less. The reason is that m remains constant in this case (0.5) while in the preceding cases it rose rapidly toward 0.586 with one locus from 0.500 somewhat slowly toward 0.739 with four loci.

Finally, with perfect disassortative mating and complete determination by heredity, F reaches a maximum negative value at once (-0.500 if $n = 1$, -0.125 if $n = 4$) and thereafter oscillates toward limiting values of -0.333 and -0.067, respectively. The variance ratio ($\sigma_H^2/\sigma_{H(0)}^2$) reaches its minimum value (0.500) at once and oscillates toward limiting value of 0.667 with $n = 1$ and 0.533 with $n = 4$.

Equilibrium

The situation at equilibrium may be found by dropping primes in all equations. It will be assumed that recombination is at random.

$$(11.46) \qquad s_{ij} = d_{ij} = \sqrt{(F_i F_j)},$$

$$(11.47) \quad \sigma_H^2 = \sum_i [\sigma_{L(i)(0)}^2(1 + F_i)] + 4 \sum_{ij} [\sigma_{L(i)(0)}\sqrt{F_i}\, \sigma_{L(j)(0)}\sqrt{F_j}], \qquad j > i$$

$$(11.48) \quad \sigma_H^2 = \sum_i [\sigma_{L(i)(0)}^2(1 - F_i)] + 2\left[\sum_i \sigma_{L(i)(0)}\sqrt{F_i}\right]^2, \quad i \text{ includes all loci}$$

$$(11.49) \quad r_{AH} = \left[\sigma_{L(A)(0)}(1 - F_A) + 2\sqrt{F_A} \sum_i (\sigma_{L(i)(0)}\sqrt{F_i}) \right] \sigma_H \sqrt{2}.$$

i includes all loci

Let

$$X_i = \sigma^2_{L(i)(0)}(1 - F_i) + 2(\sigma_{L(i)(0)}\sqrt{F_i}) \sum_j (\sigma_{L(j)(0)}\sqrt{F_j}).$$

Then

$$(11.50) \qquad\qquad \sigma_H{}^2 = \sum X_i,$$

$$(11.51) \qquad\qquad r_{AH} = X_A / \sigma_{L(A)(0)} \Big/ \left(2 \sum X_i \right)$$

$$(11.52) \qquad \sigma^2_{L(A)(0)} F_A = \sigma^2_{L(A)(0)} m r^2_{AH} = m X_A{}^2 / 2 \sum X_i,$$

$$(11.53) \quad 2\sigma_{L(A)(0)}\sqrt{F_A} \sum [\sigma_{L(i)(0)}\sqrt{F_i}] = 2X_A \Big/ \left(\sqrt{\frac{m}{2 \sum X_i}} \right) \sum \left(X_i \Big/ \left(\sqrt{\frac{m}{2 \sum X_i}} \right) \right)$$

$$= m X_A,$$

$$(11.54) \qquad\qquad X_i = \sigma^2_{L(i)(0)} - \frac{m X_i{}^2}{2 \sum X_i} + m X_i,$$

$$(11.55) \qquad\qquad \frac{m X_i{}^2}{2 \sum X_i} + X_i(1 - m) - \sigma^2_{L(i)(0)} = 0.$$

The set of equations of this type (11.55) for all loci (all i's) permit solution of the X_i's for given m, given $\sigma^2_{L(i)(0)}$ and trial values of $\sum X_i$, since by repeated trial the sum of the X_i's may be made to equal the final trial value of $\sum X_i$.

The values of the fixation indices are readily found:

$$(11.56) \qquad F_i = 1 - (1 - m)X_i / \sigma^2_{L(i)(0)} = m X_i{}^2 / 2\sigma^2_{L(i)(0)} \sum X_i.$$

The simplest multifactorial case is that in which all of the loci are equivalent in effect and gene frequency:

$$(11.57) \qquad\qquad \frac{mX}{2n} + X(1 - m) - \sigma^2_{L(0)} = 0,$$

$$(11.58) \qquad\qquad X = \frac{2n\sigma^2_{L(0)}}{2n(1 - m) + m},$$

$$(11.59) \qquad\qquad F = \frac{m}{2n(1 - m) + m} \qquad\qquad \text{(Wright 1921).}$$

The effects on the genetic variance of characters are also of interest:

(11.60) $\sigma_H{}^2/\sigma_{L(0)}^2 = 2n^2/[2n(1 - m) + m]$,

(11.61) $\sigma_H{}^2/\sigma_{H(0)}^2 = 2n/[2n(1 - m) + m]$ since $\sigma_{H(0)}^2 = n\sigma_{L(0)}^2$.

Limiting values of F and $\sigma_H{}^3/\sigma_{H(0)}^2$ under various conditions are shown in Figure 11.4.

The case with two nonequivalent loci is readily solved:

(11.62)
$$\frac{mX_A{}^2}{2(X_A + X_B)} + X_A(1 - m) - \sigma_{L(A)(0)}^2 = 0;$$

$$\frac{mX_B{}^2}{2(X_A + X_B)} + X_B(1 - m) - \sigma_{L(B)(0)}^2,$$

(11.63) $\dfrac{m}{2}(X_A - X_B) + (X_A - X_B)(1 - m) - (\sigma_{L(A)(0)}^2 - \sigma_{L(B)(0)}^2) = 0.$

Thus

(11.64) $(X_A - X_B) = 2[\sigma_{L(A)(0)}^2 - \sigma_{L(B)(0)}^2]/(2 - m) = K,$

(11.65) $X_B = X_A - K,$

(11.66) $X_A{}^2[4 - 3m] - X_A[2K(1 - m) + 4\sigma_{L(A)(0)}^2] + 2K\sigma_{L(A)(0)}^2 = 0.$

The limiting values of F and of the $\sigma_H{}^2/\sigma_{H(0)}^2$ are given over a much wider range of conditions in Table 11.4 than in Tables 11.2 and 11.3. High values of F are reached with perfect assortative mating and high heritability even with as many as ten equivalent pairs of alleles, in which case the increase in the variance ratio is great. With high but not perfect assortative mating, F reaches high values only if heritability is perfect or nearly so and there are only one or two loci. The maximum limiting negative value of F (-0.333) requires perfect disassortative mating and complete determination by heredity.

In general, the limiting values of F, whether positive or negative, are small. The variance ratio $(\sigma_H{}^2/\sigma_{H(0)}^2)$ may show considerable increase with moderately strong assortative mating and fairly high heritability, especially if many loci are involved. Similarly, moderately strong disassortative mating and fairly high heritability reduce the variance ratio considerably, the lowest value shown being 0.513 with $r_{P(1)P(2)} = -1$, $h_0{}^2 = 1$, and $n = 10$.

Dominance has not been considered. The variance of dominance deviations at equilibrium may be treated approximately as if a constant, and added to the nongenetic variance, as assumed by Fisher (1918), if the limiting value of F is small.

TABLE 11.4. Limiting values of F and $\sigma_{H}^{2}/\sigma_{H(0)}$ under assortative mating as described in the first two columns. If $h_0^2 < 1$, heritability, h^2, rises under positive assortative and declines under disassortative mating according to the formula $R/[(1 - h_0^2)/h_0^2 + R]$.

$r_{P(1)P(2)}$	h_0^2	m_0	F_∞ No. of Equal Pairs of Alleles				$R = \sigma_{H\infty}^2/\sigma_{H(0)}^2$ No. of Equal Pairs of Alleles			
			1	2	4	10	1	2	4	10
1.00	1.00	1.00	1.0000	1.0000	1.0000	1.0000	2.000	4.000	8.000	20.000
	0.75	0.75	.7208	.6991	.6848	.6745	1.721	2.097	5.794	13.816
	0.50	0.50	.4142	.3333	.2612	.1827	1.414	2.000	2.838	4.472
	0.25	0.25	.1623	.0972	.0544	.0236	1.162	1.292	1.381	1.448
0.75	1	0.7500	.6000	.4286	.2727	.1304	1.600	2.286	2.909	3.478
	0.75	0.5625	.4376	.3068	.1946	.0917	1.438	1.921	2.362	2.742
	0.50	0.3750	.2649	.1706	.1029	.0455	1.265	1.512	1.720	1.865
	0.25	0.1875	.1129	.0634	.0339	.0141	1.113	1.190	1.236	1.269
0.50	1	0.500	.3333	.2000	.1111	.0476	1.333	1.600	1.778	1.905
	0.75	0.375	.2457	.1459	.0806	.0344	1.246	1.438	1.564	1.654
	0.50	0.250	.1547	.0883	.0476	.0200	1.155	1.265	1.333	1.380
	0.25	0.125	.0704	.0376	.0195	.0080	1.070	1.113	1.137	1.152
0.25	1	0.2500	.1429	.0769	.0400	.0164	1.143	1.231	1.280	1.311
	0.75	0.1855	.1063	.0570	.0296	.0121	1.106	1.171	1.207	1.230
	0.50	0.1250	.0690	.0365	.0188	.0076	1.069	1.109	1.131	1.145
	0.25	0.0625	.0331	.0170	.0087	.0035	1.033	1.051	1.061	1.066
−0.50	1	−0.500	−.2000	−.0909	−.0435	−.0169	0.800	0.727	0.696	0.678
	0.75	−0.375	−.1521	−.0696	−.0334	−.0130	0.848	0.791	0.767	0.752
	0.50	−0.250	−.1056	−.0491	−.0237	−.0093	0.894	0.853	0.834	0.823
	0.25	−0.125	−.0364	−.0269	−.0132	−.0052	0.964	0.919	0.908	0.901
−1.00	1	−1.00	−.3333	−.1429	−.0667	−.0256	0.667	0.571	0.533	0.513
	0.75	−0.75	−.2566	−.1111	−.0521	−.0202	0.743	0.667	0.635	0.616
	0.50	−0.50	−.1835	−.0814	−.0385	−.0149	0.816	0.756	0.730	0.716
	0.25	−0.25	−.1032	−.0476	−.0234	−.0090	0.897	0.857	0.836	0.829

Tables 11.5 and 11.6 are intended to illustrate the consequences of unequal contributions in the case of a pair of alleles. Various degrees of assortative and disassortative mating are assumed, but with complete determination by heredity in all cases. The limiting values of F, for the more important locus, range from close to the value for a single locus if the second locus has little effect to an approach to that of either of two equivalent loci. Limiting F for the less important locus ranges from 0 toward equality with the more important one, as its contribution approaches equality.

TABLE 11.5. Limiting values of F for given r_{PP}, $h^2 = 1$, with one locus, or with two loci and gene contributions as indicated, assuming complete determination by heredity but various degrees of assortative mating.

n	α	$r_{PP} = 1$	$+0.75$	$+0.50$	$+0.25$	0	-0.50	-1.00
1	1.000	1	$+0.600$	$+0.333$	$+0.143$	0	-0.200	-0.333
2	1.000	1	$+.552$	$+.300$	$+.128$	0	$-.177$	$-.295$
	0.125	1	$+.213$	$+.067$	$+.020$	0	$-.017$	$-.023$
2	1.000	1	$+.522$	$+.276$	$+.116$	0	$-.158$	$-.261$
	0.250	1	$+.289$	$+.056$	$+.033$	0	$-.031$	$-.045$
2	1.000	1	$+.482$	$+.243$	$+.099$	0	$-.135$	$-.206$
	0.500	1	$+.363$	$+.152$	$+.054$	0	$-.070$	$-.084$
2	1.000	1	$+.429$	$+.200$	$+.077$	0	$-.091$	$-.143$
	1.000	1	$+0.429$	$+0.200$	$+0.077$	0	-0.091	-0.143

TABLE 11.6. Limiting values of the ratio R of the genotypic variance (σ_H^2) to its initial value ($\sigma_{H(0)}^2$) under the same conditions as in Table 11.5.

n	α	$r_{PP} = 1$	$+0.75$	$+0.50$	$+0.25$	0	-0.50	-1.00
1	1.000	2.000	1.600	1.333	1.143	1	0.800	0.667
2	1.000 0.125	3.257	1.944	1.452	1.179	1	.773	.632
2	1.000 0.250	3.600	2.097	1.516	1.201	1	.755	.609
2	1.000 0.500	3.886	2.231	1.575	1.222	1	.742	.584
2	1.000 1.000	4.000	2.286	1.600	1.231	1	0.727	0.571

It should be added finally that assortative mating is especially likely to occur in situations which also bring about a correlation between the heredities and environments of individuals. This is obviously the case in man and domestic animals. Going back to Figure 11.1,

$$r_{P(1)H(1)} = h_1 + e_1 r_{H(1)E(1)},$$
$$r_{P(1)E(1)} = h_1 r_{H(1)E(1)} + e_1,$$

(11.67) $$h_1 = (r_{P(1)H(1)} - r_{P(1)E(1)} r_{H(1)E(1)})/(1 - r^2_{H(1)E(1)}),$$

(11.68) $$e_1 = (r_{P(1)E(1)} - r_{P(1)H(1)} r_{H(1)E(1)})/(1 - r^2_{H(1)E(1)}).$$

In Figure 11.2, h_1 must be replaced by $r_{P(1)H(1)}$, e_1 by $r_{P(1)E(1)}$, and similarly with h_2 and e_2.

$$r_{H(1)H(2)} = r_{P(1)H(1)} r_{P(2)H(2)} r_{P(1)P(2)},$$
$$r_{H(1)E(2)} = r_{P(1)H(1)} r_{P(2)E(2)} r_{P(1)P(2)},$$
$$r_{E(1)H(2)} = r_{P(1)E(1)} r_{P(2)H(2)} r_{P(1)P(2)},$$
$$r_{E(1)E(2)} = r_{P(1)E(1)} r_{P(2)E(2)} r_{P(1)P(2)}.$$

Returning to Figure 11.1,

$$r_{P(1)P(2)} = h_1 h_2 r_{H(1)H(2)} + h_1 e_2 r_{H(1)E(2)} + e_1 h_2 r_{H(2)E(1)} + e_1 e_2 r_{E(1)E(2)},$$

which reduces to $r_{P(1)P(2)}$, demonstrating the consistency of the values of h_1, e_1, h_2, and e_2 in this figure where there are correlations between heredity and environment.

CHAPTER 12

Population Structure

Introduction

There are species which breed so nearly at random throughout their whole range that zygotic frequencies may be assumed to be very nearly of the Hardy–Weinberg type and evolutionary change may be treated accordingly. This is probably unusual. We have already considered deviations from randomness due to mating according to relationship, and mating according to phenotypic similarity. We will consider here deviations due to more-or-less complete spatial isolation of local populations within the species.

The simplest pattern of subdivision to deal with mathematically is the "island model." In this, in pure form, the population is divided into groups that are panmictic within themselves, except for reception of small proportions of immigrants, representative of the population as a whole.

In most actual cases, immigrants come largely from neighboring groups and there is more or less "isolation by distance." Such patterns may be classified by the degree of continuity of the population. The island model passes into the "stepping stone" model, this into the model of a continuum with scattered clusters of high density, and this into the model of a uniform continuum.

Each of these may be classified according to the number of dimensions of continuity. There may be significant differentiation only along a single line, as in a chain of islands, a long narrow mountain valley, or the shore line of a lake or sea. There may be branching as in a river system, or differentiation in all directions as in an archipelago, a forest, a prairie, or a large body of water.

If sufficiently extensive, any of the above patterns may be treated as hierarchic by subdivision of the whole into a number of primary subdivisions, these into a number of secondary ones, and so on down to groups that may be treated as homogeneous within themselves. The convenient term "deme" of Gilmour and Gregor (1939) has come to be used for this ultimate unit of population, though in a narrower sense (gamodeme) than they proposed. In the case of a continuum, it is sometimes more convenient to refer to the "neighborhood," defined as the population of a region in a continuum from which the parents of individuals born near the center may be treated as if drawn at random (Wright 1946).

Populations have structure in time as well as in space. There may be systematic changes in population number or wide fluctuations or cyclic changes. There may be changes in state of subdivision, including both branching and anastomosing of branches that produce a reticular structure in time. A single existent population may sometimes be thought of to advantage as one of an infinite number of possible populations that might have been derived from a specified ancestral population, a device used in chapter 7 in dealing with systems of mating in laboratory experiments. This is especially useful in dealing with breeds of livestock for which pedigrees are available.

The Island Model

The model of population structure to be considered here is of that of a population subdivided into random breeding islands with populations of size N of which the proportion m consists of immigrants that may be considered a random sample of the total species.

Since the islands may be expected to become differentiated from each other, a correlation between uniting gametes is implied, based on the proportion of cases $(1 - m)^2$, in which both are of local origin. The standard case of completely random union of gametes is assumed (Wright 1931, 1943a, 1951).

$$(12.1) \quad F = (1 - m)^2 \left[\frac{1}{N} b^2 + \frac{N - 1}{N} F' \right] = (1 - m)^2 \left[\frac{1}{2N} + \frac{2N - 1}{2N} F' \right].$$

On attainment of a steady state, $F = F'$:

$$(12.2) \quad F = (1 - m)^2 / [2N - (2N - 1)(1 - m)^2].$$

If m is small this approaches the formula

$$(12.3) \quad F = 1/(4Nm + 1).$$

Migration may, as before, be supplemented by reversible mutation (rates u, v) replacing m by $(m + u + v)$.

Before discussing this formula, it is desirable to consider how much differentiation among the islands is expected from given values of N and m. A deme with gene frequency q_D tends to return toward the population average q_T by the amount $\Delta q = -m(q_D - q_T)$. Thus a deviation from the average $(q_D - q_T)$, tends to be reduced to $(1 - m)(q_D - q_T)$ in the next generation. The mean sampling variance of $q_D + \Delta q_D$ among n islands is

$$(12.4) \quad \frac{1}{2Nn} \sum_i^n [q_D - m(q_D - q_T)][(1 - q_D + m)(q_D - q_T)]$$

$$= \frac{1}{2N} [q_T(1 - q_T) - (1 - m)^2 \sigma^2_{q(D)}].$$

where $\sigma^2_{q(D)}$ is the variance of values of q in demes within the total array, T. On attainment of a steady state:

$$(12.5) \quad \sigma^2_{q(D)} = (1 - m)^2 \sigma^2_{q(D)} + \frac{1}{2N} [q_T(1 - q_T) - (1 - m)^2 \sigma^2_{q(D)}],$$

$$(12.6) \quad \sigma^2_{q(D)} = q_T(1 - q_T)/[2N - (2N - 1)(1 - m)^2],$$

$$(12.7) \quad \sigma^2_{q(D)} = \frac{q_T(1 - q_T)}{4Nm + 1},$$

approximately, if m is small.

These formulas all involve the assumption that the genes in question are completely neutral and that nothing is involved in changes in gene frequency but accidents of sampling and dispersion. Since Nm is the number of immigrants per generation, the quantity $4Nm + 1$ would ordinarily be rather large and thus F (from (12.3)) and $\sigma^2_{q(D)}$ (from (12.7)) would ordinarily be very small. However, N is the *effective* population number which may be much less than the apparent number of mature individuals for the reasons discussed in chapter 8. Moreover, the island model is one that would rarely be realized in nature in pure form. Ordinarily immigrants would come largely from neighboring demes and would be expected to differ little in gene frequency. Letting m_e be the effective proportion of immigration and q_I the gene frequency in the immigrants, $m_e = m[(q_D - q_I)/(q_D - q_T)]$. Thus effective $N_e m_e$ may be much smaller than its apparent value because of smallness of both N_e and m_e. This is a sort of stepping-stone model.

If N is eliminated from (12.2) and (12.6):

$$(12.8) \quad F = \frac{(1 - m)^2 \sigma^2_{q(D)}}{q_T(1 - q_T)}.$$

This is the ratio of the variance of mean gene frequencies of subdivisions, excluding sampling variance in the last generation, to the limiting value, $q_T(1 - q_T)$, that would be found if there were fixation in all subdivisions without change in total gene frequency. It is apparent that a rather small value of F may be associated with a very considerable amount of differentiation among the subdivisions. Thus if the values of q for subdivisions range from about 0.25 to 0.75 about $q = 0.50$ with a standard deviation of 0.10, the value of F would be only 0.04. Even a standard deviation of mean gene frequencies of 0.05 and range from about 0.38 to 0.62 is hardly negligible, although the corresponding value of F ($= 0.01$) may seem so.

This equation (12.8) adds another interpretation of F to those already given, and a possible way of estimating it as an inbreeding coefficient in subdivided populations, provided it is known that the loci in question are neutral and the subdivisions panmictic.

If there is no assurance on these points, a statistic pertaining to the population and locus can be calculated from formula (12.7), but its meaning is obscure unless it can be derived in a way that does not involve N. This can be done from consideration of heterozygosis in the total population and its subdivisions. That in the total population was shown (chap. 7) to be

$$(12.9) \qquad y_T = 2q_T(1 - q_T)(1 - F).$$

Here, F is the fixation index in the broad sense. Let $2q_D(1 - q_D)$ be the amount of heterozygosis with respect to the gene in question in a typical subdivision. This implies that there is no deviation from the Hardy–Weinberg expectation from any cause locally. The average for all subdivisions is

$$(12.10) \qquad y_T = \frac{2}{n} \sum_{}^{n} q_D(1 - q_D) = 2\left[q_T - \frac{1}{n} \sum q_D^2\right].$$

The quantity $(1/n) \sum q_D^2 = \sigma_{q'(D)}^{2} + q_T^2$ where $\sigma_{q'(D)}^2$ applies to the parental generation and thus equals $(1 - m)^2 \sigma_{q'(D)}^2$

$$(12.11) \qquad y_T = 2q_T(1 - q_T) - 2\sigma_{q'(D)}^{2}.$$

This important formula is due to Wahlund (1928).

$$(12.12) \qquad \sigma_{q'(D)}^{2} = (1 - m)^2 \sigma_{q(D)}^2 = q_T(1 - q_T)F.$$

This is the same as (12.8). Thus the ratio of the variance of gene frequencies (excluding the immediate sampling variance) to its limiting value can be interpreted as the correlation between uniting gametes only if $F = 0$ within the subdivisions.

The F-Statistics of Hierarchic Populations

This consideration of the island model leads to a more general treatment of population structure (Wright 1943a, 1946, 1951, 1965c). Nothing will be assumed here with respect to the degree of isolation of the subdivisions (S) of a total population (T) or of their arrangement in space. They may be completely isolated at one extreme, or merely arbitrarily bounded portions of a continuum, at the other. Their gene frequencies may be distributed at random in the total population or in an orderly cline.

The correlation between gametes that unite to produce the individuals (I) relative to the gametes of the total population will be represented by F_{IT} which is the same as the F of preceding sections. The average over all subdivisions of the correlation between uniting gametes relative to those of their own subdivision is F_{IS}. The correlation between random gametes within subdivisions, relative to gametes of the total population, is F_{ST}. The list can be extended if there is further subdivision.

The amount of heterozygosis in the total population in general is given in (12.9), on substituting F_{IT} for F.

Wahlund's formula (12.11) still holds. Equation (12.12) applies to the variance of gene frequencies of demes within the total $\sigma^2_{q(DT)}$, which is the terminology to be used from this point instead of $\sigma^2_{q(D)}$.

$$\sigma^2_{q(DT)} = q_T(1 - q_T)F_{IT},$$

where $\sigma^2_{q(DT)}$ here for simplicity excludes the immediate sampling variance.

It should be noted that the correlation between random gametes drawn from demes (F_{DT}) is the same as F_{IT} under the assumption of random mating within demes.

Consider next division of the total into subdivisions (S) that are themselves inbred. As before, $y_T = 2q_T(1 - q_T)(1 - F_{IT})$, but as an average:

$$y_T = \frac{2}{n} \sum^n [q_{ST}(1 - q_{ST})(1 - F_{IS})],$$

(12.13) $$y_T = 2(1 - \bar{F}_{IS})\left[q_T - (1/n) \sum q^2_{ST}\right]$$

assuming that F_{IS} and q_S are independent,

$$\sigma^2_{q(ST)} = (1/n) \sum (q_{ST} - q_T)^2 = (1/n) \sum^n q^2_{ST} - q_T{}^2.$$

Dropping the bar over F_{IS} for simplicity:

(12.14) $$y_T = 2[(1 - F_{IS})q_T(1 - q_T) - \sigma^2_{q(ST)}].$$

Thus

(12.15) $\sigma^2_{q(ST)} = q_T(1 - q_T)(F_{IT} - F_{IS})/(1 - F_{IS}).$

If, now, random mating is instituted in the subdivision there would be no change in their gene frequencies and hence none in $\sigma^2_{q(ST)}$, but now

(12.16) $\sigma^2_{q(ST)} = q_T(1 - q_T)F_{ST}.$

Thus

(12.17) $F_{ST} = (F_{IT} - F_{IS})/(1 - F_{IS}).$

This is simplified, if expressed in terms of panmictic indices $(P = 1 - F)$, to

(12.18) $P_{IT} = P_{IS}P_{ST}.$

If there are secondary subdivisions into local races (R) which may themselves be inbred $(F_{IR} \neq 0)$, then $P_{IS} = P_{IR}P_{RS}$ and $P_{IT} = P_{IR}P_{RS}P_{ST}$. Such analysis may be continued as far as there is hierarchic subdivision.

The quantity $F_{ST} = (\sigma^2_{q(ST)}/[q_T(1 - q_T)])$, is the ratio of the actual variance of the subdivisions to its maximum possible value $q_T(1 - q_T)$ that is expected if the subdivisions are completely isolated and each completely fixed, thus forming the array $[q_T AA + (1 - q_T)aa]$. It is thus necessarily positive. While usually positive, F_{IS} is negative if there is systematic avoidance of consanguine mating within subdivisions. If there is systematic subdivision, whether into demes $(F_{IS} = 0$ and $F_{IT} = F_{ST})$ or into inbred groups, F_{IT} is positive but it can be negative if there is little or no systematic subdivision and there is prevailing avoidance of consanguine mating.

Isolation by Distance

A group of "islands" in which each one exchanges population only with those that surround it passes into a continuum with clusters of high density, and this into one that is of uniform density in which any local differentiation from sampling depends merely on limitation of the range of dispersion.

In this last case, the properties turn out to depend largely on the population number of the "neighborhood," defined as that of an area from which the parents of central individuals may be treated as if drawn at random. Let N_1, N_1', N_1'', etc., be the population numbers of neighborhoods in the current and preceding generations; N_2', N_2'', N_2''', etc., those of the grandparental generations; and in general N_x, with the appropriate number of primes, those from which the ancestors of generation X may be considered to have been drawn at random. Let F_{1S}, F_{2S}, ..., F_{XS}, with primes to indicate generation (Fig. 12.1), be the correlations between random gametes of the

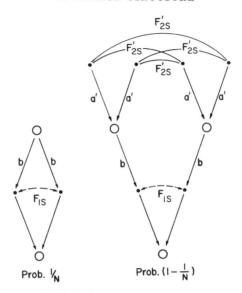

F$_{\mathrm{IG}}$. 12.1. Path diagram for isolation by distance (redrawn from Wright 1943a, text figure).

area indicated by the first subscript, relative to the area of population number N_S (Wright 1943a, 1951):

$$F_{1S} = \frac{1}{N_1} b^2 + 4\left[1 - \frac{1}{N_1}\right](ba')^2 F'_{2S}$$

$$= \frac{1}{2N_1}(1 + F'_{1S}) + \left[1 - \frac{1}{N_1}\right]F'_{2S},$$

(12.19)

$$F'_{2S} = \frac{1}{2N_2}(1 + F''_{1S}) + \left[1 - \frac{1}{N_2}\right]F''_{3S},$$

$$F''_{3S} = \frac{1}{2N_3}(1 + F'''_{1S}) + \left[1 - \frac{1}{N_3}\right]F'''_{4S}, \text{ etc.}$$

If the first subscript equals or exceeds S, then F is assumed to be zero. These are the basic formulas.

Assume now that conditions are static and that a steady state has been reached so that primes may be dropped. These F's are of the nature of F_{IS}.

$$F_{1S} = \left(\frac{1 + F_{1S}}{2}\right)\left[\frac{1}{N_1} + \frac{1}{N_2}\left(1 - \frac{1}{N_1}\right)\right.$$

(12.20)

$$\left. + \frac{1}{N_3}\left(1 - \frac{1}{N_1}\right)\left(1 - \frac{1}{N_2}\right) + \cdots + \frac{1}{N_S}\prod_{X=1}^{S-1}\left(1 - \frac{1}{N_X}\right)\right].$$

The series in brackets, with terms

$$t_1 = \frac{1}{N_1}, \qquad t_x = \left[\frac{N_{x-1} - 1}{N_x}\right]t_{x-1}$$

up to t_S, will be referred to as $\sum t$. Various assumptions will be made with respect to the N's.

(12.21)
$$F_{1S} = \left(\frac{1}{2}\right)(1 + F_{1S})\sum t,$$

$$F_{1S} = \sum t / (2 - \sum t).$$

This permits calculation, step by step, of the inbreeding coefficients of neighborhoods relative to populations of any size for which N_S/N_1 is not so great as to make this impracticable.

A simple formula for $\sum t$ has been pointed out by D. J. Hooton (Wright 1951):

$$N_S t_S = N_{S-1} t_{S-1} - t_{S-1}$$
$$N_{S-1} t_{S-1} = N_{S-2} t_{S-2} - t_{S-2}$$

(12.22)
$$\vdots \qquad \qquad \vdots \qquad \qquad \vdots$$

$$N_3 t_3 = N_2 t_2 \qquad - t_2$$
$$N_2 t_2 = N_1 t_1 \qquad - t_1$$
$$\overline{N_S t_S = N_1 t_1 \qquad - \sum_{x=1}^{S-1} t_x}$$

by addition.

(12.23)
$$\sum_{x=1}^{S-1} t_x = 1 - N_S t_S,$$

(12.24)
$$F_{1S} = \frac{1 - N_S t_S}{1 + N_S t_S}, \qquad N_S t_S = \prod_{x=1}^{S-1}\left(1 - \frac{1}{N_x}\right)$$

from (12.20).

Since t_S depends on all of the preceding t's, direct use of this formula depends on knowledge of these. Even in connection with step-by-step calculation, it is, however, of great value as a final check on the estimate of F_{1S}.

Local Inbreeding along a Linear Range

The simplest pattern involving isolation by distance is that of a population with a uniform, essentially one-dimensional range (parents drawn from the whole width), along which the distances between birthplaces of parents and offspring have the same normal distribution in all generations. The distribution of ancestors of generation X would be compounded of X parent-offspring distributions and would thus be normal with variance X times that of the latter, assuming random dispersion. The effective population number of the ancestral population would be proportional to the standard deviation and thus is $X^{1/2}N$.

$$N_X = X^{1/2}N_1, \qquad N_S = S^{1/2}N_1, \qquad t_1 = \frac{1}{N_1},$$

(12.25) $\qquad t_X = \dfrac{(X-1)^{1/2}N_1 - 1}{X^{1/2}N_1} t_{X-1} \qquad \text{for } 1 < X \leq S,$

(12.26) $\qquad \dfrac{\Delta t_{X-0.5}}{t_{X-0.5}} \approx \dfrac{2(t_X - t_{X-1})}{t_X + t_{X-1}} = \dfrac{2N_1[(X-1)^{1/2} - X^{1/2}] - 2}{N_1[(X-1)^{1/2} + X^{1/2}] - 1}.$

On treating this as the slope and replacing $X - 0.5$ by X:

(12.27) $\qquad \dfrac{dt}{t\,dX} = \dfrac{2N_1[(X-0.5)^{1/2} - (X+0.5)^{1/2}] - 2}{N_1[(X-0.5)^{1/2} + (X+0.5)^{1/2}] - 1}.$

On expanding the radicals and integrating:

(12.28) $\qquad N_1 t_X \approx C\,[X^{1/2} - 1/(2N_1)]^{-[1 + (1/N_1)^2]} \exp\left(-2X^{1/2}/N_1\right),$

ignoring small terms, $1/(32X^2)$ and less.

Comparisons of actual and calculated values of t indicate that estimates of C approach stability after a few terms. The sum $\sum t$ may be calculated by steps (12.25) for a considerable number (S_1) of terms and then supplemented by the approximate formula,

(12.29) $\qquad \displaystyle\sum_{S_1}^{S_2-1} t_X \approx C\,[\exp\left(-2S_1^{1/2}/N_1\right) - \exp\left(-2S_2^{1/2}/N_1\right)],$

in which C is to be taken so that $\sum^\infty t = 1$.

$$C = \left(1 - \sum t_{S(1)}\right)\Big/ \exp\left(-2S_1^{1/2}/N_1\right).$$

Figure 12.2 shows how F_{IS} (here same as F_{1S}) rises with increase in S. There is almost complete local fixation in populations consisting of thousands of neighborhoods if the effective size of the neighborhoods is less than the corresponding number of individuals. The expression $F_{IS} = \sigma^2_{q(IS)}/q_S(1 - q_S)$ suffers, however, from the disadvantage that the denominator as well as the numerator changes.

Of greater interest is the amount of differentiation among areas of any given effective population number within some constant large total, measured

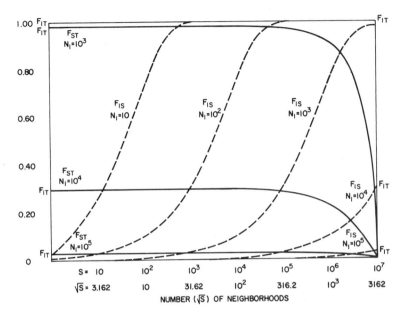

FIG. 12.2. F_{IS} and F_{ST} in relation to length of region (number of neighborhoods in a linear continuum) within a total of 10^7 neighborhoods (redrawn from Wright 1943a, Figs. 4, 6, except ordinates F instead of $\sqrt{F}$).

by $F_{ST} = (F_{IT} - F_{IS})/(1 - F_{IS}) = \sigma^2_{q(ST)}/[q_T(1 - q_T)]$. The first ordinate ($F_{IT}$) in the curve for F_{ST} for a given value of N_1 (Fig. 12.2) is the same as the last in that for F_{IT}. It may be seen that differentiation among neighborhoods of considerable size extends to populations composed of numerous neighborhoods.

Isolation by Distance over a Uniform Area

In the case of an area continuum in which the parent-offspring distances are distributed normally, the effective number in ancestral generation, X, is X times that in a neighborhood.

$$N_X = XN_1, \qquad N_S = SN_1, \qquad t_1 = 1/N_1,$$

(12.30) $$t_X = \frac{(X - 1)N_1 - 1}{XN_1} t_{X-1}.$$

In this case, also, a formula for t can be obtained from the approximate relative slope, and $\sum t$ by integration.

$$(12.31) \qquad \frac{\Delta t_{(X-0.5)}}{t_{(X-0.5)}} = -\frac{2(N_1 + 1)}{N_1(2X - 1) - 1},$$

$$(12.32) \qquad \frac{dt}{t\,dX} = -\frac{2(N_1 + 1)}{2N_1 X - 1}, \qquad t = \frac{C}{N_1}\left(X - \frac{1}{2N_1}\right)^{-(N_1+1)/N_1},$$

$$(12.33) \qquad \sum_{S_1}^{S_2-1} t_X = C\left\{ \left[S_1 - \frac{1}{2} - \frac{1}{2N_1}\right]^{-1/N_1} - \left[S_2 - \frac{1}{2} - \frac{1}{2N_1}\right]^{-1/N_1} \right\}.$$

The first 40 or 50 terms had best be obtained step by step from (12.30). This permits C to reach stability.

In this case, also, the value of $\sum t$ can be obtained from equations (12.20) and (12.24).

$$(12.34) \quad \log\,(N_S t_S) = \log \sum_{X=1}^{S-1}\left[1 - \frac{1}{XN_1}\right]$$

$$= -\left[\frac{1}{N_1}\sum\frac{1}{X} + \frac{1}{2N_1^2}\sum\frac{1}{X^2} + \frac{1}{3N_1^3}\sum\frac{1}{X^3} + \cdots\right]$$

$$= -\left\{\frac{1}{N_1}[\log\,(S - 0.5) + 0.5772]\right.$$

$$+ \frac{1}{2N_1^2}\left[1.6449 - \frac{2}{2S - 1}\right]$$

$$\left. + \frac{1}{3N_1^3}\left[1.202 - \frac{2}{(2S - 1)^2}\right] + \cdots\right\}.$$

Again $N_S t_S$ approaches zero as S is increased and $F_{IS} = (1 - N_S t_S)/(1 + N_S t_S)$ approaches one.

The rate of increase of F for given N_1 is very much less than in the case of a linear range. Figure 12.3 shows the values of F_{IS} (here same as F_{1S}) for neighborhoods of various sizes relative to larger populations, N_S, up to $N_T = 10^7 N_1$.

The coefficients F_{ST}, measuring the relative variabilities of larger populations within the total are again of more interest because they are not dependent on knowledge of the neighborhoods and because the variances are relative to a constant limiting value.

From this figure it is apparent that the amount of random differentiation of even rather small populations is slight in an area continuum unless the effective population of neighborhoods is very small. There is much differentiation if N_1 is of the order of 20 or less, differentiation is not negligible up to $N_1 = 200$, but there is almost the equivalent of universal panmixia (with respect to sampling effects) if N_1 is larger than 1,000.

It is also important, however, that if there is considerable differentiation

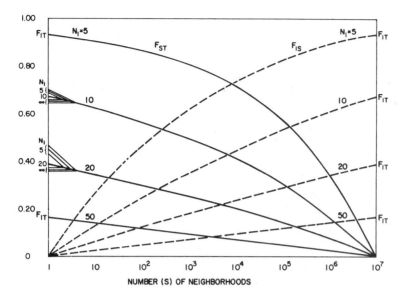

FIG. 12.3. F_{IS} and F_{ST} in relation to size of region (number of neighborhoods in an area continuum) within a total of 10^7 neighborhoods. The effects on F_{ST} of increasing N_1 greatly (∞) or of reducing it to five from $N_1 = 10$ or 20 are shown for three generations (redrawn from Wright 1943a, Figs. 1, 3, except ordinates F instead of $\sqrt{F}$).

of neighborhoods, from accidents of sampling, this builds up differentiation of much larger areas. There is some differentiation even of large fractions of the total under the postulates considered so far. Important qualifications will be considered later.

The process by which a pattern of differentiation of large areas is built up from random differentiation of small neighborhoods is necessarily exceedingly slow as may be realized from the smallness of the terms after the first few in the series $\sum t$ for areas. This can be brought out well by considering the effect of an abrupt change in effective size of neighborhood on the F_{ST} curve. Figure 12.3 shows the effect of a reduction of N_1 from 10 or 20 to 5 for three successive generations, using the basic formulas. Such a reduction causes an abrupt rise at the extreme left side of the curve which continues and spreads slowly to the right until in the course of an enormous number of generations the whole curve is raised to the new equilibrium. It requires as many generations of persistence of the new value of N as the number of neighborhoods (S) included in the area under consideration before the rise begins to affect the variance of such areas within the total.

Conversely, an increase in the size of neighborhood produces a flattening of the curve that spreads in similarly slow fashion to ever larger areas until the whole curve comes to equilibrium for the new N_1. Figure 12.3 shows the effect for three successive generations of such a great increase in N_1 that the curve is ultimately flattened completely.

The effect of increased dispersion is similar to that of increased density of population in increasing N_1 and conversely, except that with changes in dispersion, the area of neighborhoods and hence the number included in a given total area is changed which is not the case with changes in density.

Size of Neighborhood

So far it has merely been assumed that there is a certain effective size of neighborhood in relation to a given normal distribution of parent-offspring distances without specifying what the relation is.

Consider first the situation in a population of uniform density along a linear range. Assume that the distance X of a parent relative to offspring may be represented by the normal distribution (Wright 1946).

$$(12.35) \qquad y = \frac{1}{\sigma\sqrt{(2\pi)}} \exp\left(\frac{-X^2}{2\sigma^2}\right).$$

Let n be the number of potential parents in a strip of length 2σ. The density per unit distance is $d = n/(2\sigma)$. The average length of the territory occupied by an individual is

$$(12.36) \qquad \frac{1}{d} = \frac{2\sigma}{n} = \int_{X_1-\sigma/n}^{X_1+\sigma/n} dX.$$

The chance that a particular gamete comes from a particular member of the parental generation, X_i, is y_i/d. The chance that two uniting gametes come from the same individual (still assuming the standard case of a monoecious population with random self-fertilization) is thus $\sum (y_i/d)^2$ where the summation applies to all individuals in the parental generation. This is the expression to be equated to $1/N_1$.

$$(12.37) \quad \frac{1}{N_1} = \sum_{-\infty}^{+\infty} \left[\frac{2\sigma}{n} y_i^2 \int_{X_i-\sigma/n}^{X_i+\sigma/n} dX\right] = \frac{2\sigma}{n} \int_{-\infty}^{+\infty} y^2 \, dX$$

$$= \frac{2\sigma}{n} \int_{-\infty}^{+\infty} \left[\frac{\exp(-X^2/\sigma^2)}{2\pi\sigma^2}\right] dX$$

$$= \frac{1}{n\sqrt{\pi}} \int_{-\infty}^{+\infty} \left\{\frac{\exp[-X^2/2(\sigma/\sqrt{2})^2]}{(\sigma/\sqrt{2})\sqrt{(2\pi)}}\right\} dX = 1/n\sqrt{\pi},$$

$$(12.38) \quad N_1 = n\sqrt{\pi} = 2\sigma \, d\sqrt{\pi} = 3.545\sigma \, d.$$

Effective N_1 is thus equivalent to the otherwise effective number along a strip 3.545σ long. About 92.4% of the actual parents of central individuals would fall within $\pm\sigma d\sqrt{\pi}$.

This method of relating N to σ and d can be extended to populations that are continuous over an area. Let

$$(12.39) \qquad y = \left[\frac{1}{2\pi\sigma^2}\right] \exp\left[-(X_1{}^2 + X_2{}^2)/(2\sigma^2)\right]$$

be the distribution of birthplaces of parents relative to those of offspring. Let n be the number of potential parents in a square 2σ on a side. The density per unit area is $d = n/(4\sigma^2)$. The average area occupied by an individual may be written

$$(12.40) \qquad \frac{1}{d} = \frac{4\sigma^2}{n} = \int_{X_1-\sigma/n}^{X_1+\sigma/n} \int_{X_2-\sigma/n}^{X_2+\sigma/n} dX_1\, dX_2.$$

The probability that two uniting gametes come from the same individual may be written

$$(12.41) \qquad \frac{1}{N_1} = \frac{4\sigma^2}{n} \int_{-\infty}^{+\infty} \int_{-\infty}^{+\infty} y^2\, dX_1\, dX_2 = \frac{1}{n\pi},$$

$$(12.42) \qquad N_1 = n\pi = 4\pi\sigma^2 d = 12.566\sigma^2 d.$$

Effective N_1 is equivalent to the otherwise effective population number in a circle of radius 2σ. Such circles would include 86.5% of the parents of central individuals.

Nonnormal Dispersion

Normal distributions of parents relative to offspring are to be expected if dispersion occurs by a long succession of random movements, irrespective of the nature of the distribution of the single steps. In many cases, however, the distribution after a few steps may be far from normal. The dispersion of marked Drosophilas, described in volume I, chapters 6, 10, and 11, was found to be highly leptokurtic after one day (γ_2 about 5.9), but substantially normal in a week. Bateman (1947) has found that the flights of bees, carrying pollen from flower to flower, were highly leptokurtic. This was also found by J. W. Wright (1952) to be true of wind-borne pollen from a variety of trees.

Bateman found that the formula $y = y_0 \exp(-bX^n)$ is useful in describing such distributions. This is normal if the exponent n (unrelated to n in the previous section) is 2, but leptokurtic if less. He found values of $1/2$ to 1 to be characteristic. The writing of the formulas is somewhat simplified by using $1/a$ for n.

(12.43) $$y = y_0 \exp\left(-bX^{(1/a)}\right),$$

(12.44) $$y_0 = b^a/[2\Gamma(a + 1)],$$

(12.45) $$\sigma^2 = b^{-2a}\Gamma(3a)/\Gamma(a),$$

(12.46) $$\gamma_2 + 3 = \Gamma(a)\Gamma(5a)/[\Gamma(3a)]^2.$$

On using this distribution in place of the normal curve in the preceding discussion, the effective values of N_1 can readily be found for both linear and area continua.

(12.47) $$N_1 \text{ (line)} = 2^{a+1}\Gamma(a + 1)\left[\frac{\Gamma(a)}{\Gamma(3a)}\right]^{1/2}\sigma d$$

(12.48) $$N_1 \text{ (area)} = 2^{2a}[\Gamma(3a + 1)\Gamma(a)/\Gamma(3a)]\pi\sigma^2 d$$

Table 12.1 shows some special cases, including the limiting cases of an island distribution, $a = 0$, and the normal distribution $a = 0.5$.

Population number of neighborhood in each case is plotted (in terms of σd, for linear, $\pi\sigma^2 d$ for area distributions) against kurtosis (γ_2) in Figure 12.4. In that of a linear continuum, N_1 rises from $3.464\sigma d$ in the limiting case of no dispersion to a high value of about $3.7\sigma d$ in a platykurtic distribution, γ_2 about 0.25; falls slightly for a normal distribution ($3.545\sigma d$), and continues to decline, reaching about $1.35\sigma d$ at $\gamma_2 = 30$, the highest leptokurtosis in the figure. Since the standard deviation of ancestral distances tends to be $\sigma\sqrt{X}$ in the Xth ancestral generation, the corresponding popu-

TABLE 12.1. Midordinate (y_0), variance (σ^2), γ_2, size of neighborhood, N_1, in a linear continuum or in an area continuum, for different values of a in the distribution $y = y_0 \exp\left(-bx^{1/a}\right)$.

a	y_0	σ^2	γ_2	N_1 (Line) $\times \sigma d$	N_1 (Area) $\times \pi\sigma^2 d$
0	$0.5000/L$	$0.3333L^2$	-1.20	3.464	3
0.25	$.5516b^{0.25}$	$0.3380b^{-0.5}$	-0.8116	3.708	3.708
0.50	$.5642b^{0.50}$	$0.5000b^{-1}$	0	3.545	4
0.75	$.5541b^{0.75}$	$0.9246b^{-1.5}$	$+1.222$	3.215	4.067
1.00	$.5000b$	$2.0000b^{-2}$	$+3$	2.828	4
1.50	$.3761b^{1.5}$	$13.125\ b^{-3}$	$+9.257$	2.076	3.657
2.00	$.2500b^2$	$120\quad b^{-4}$	$+22.20$	1.461	3.20
2.50	$.1505b^{2.5}$	$1,407.6\quad b^{-5}$	$+48.95$	1.002	2.728
3.00	$0.0833b^3$	$20,160\quad b^{-6}$	$+104.25$	0.676	2.286

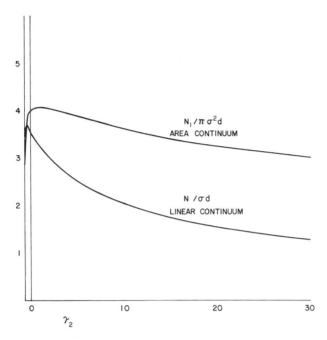

Fig. 12.4. The multiple of σd (d = density) in a linear continuum and the multiple of $\pi\sigma^2 d$ in an area continuum which define size of neighborhood, in relation to the kurtosis (γ_2) of the distribution of unidirectional parent-offspring distances (standard deviation = σ).

lation number N_X is smaller if the parent-offspring distribution is leptokurtic than if normal, but approaches that for a normal distribution as X increases, recalling (vol. 1, eq. 8.25) that γ_2 of the compound of K similar equivalent independent variables is only $1/K$ times that of each component. The curve F_{1S} with leptokurtic parent-offspring distribution thus starts like that for a normal distribution with the same small N_1 but flattens out because N_X becomes increasingly greater as the kurtosis of the ancestral populations decreases. Ultimately it becomes approximately parallel to the curve for F_{1S} of a population with normal parent-offspring distribution and thus N_1 with the relatively high value $3.545\sigma d$. An extreme case is shown in Figure 12.5 in which the F_{1S} for initial $\gamma_2 = 20$, $N_1 = 4.32$ ($= 1.53\sigma d$) is compared with that for $\gamma_2 = 0$, $N_1 = 4.32$ and that for $\gamma_2 = 0$, $N_1 = 10$ ($= 4.32 \times 3.545/1.53$) which it comes to resemble, allowing for a lag in the latter, as the ancestral distances approach normality.

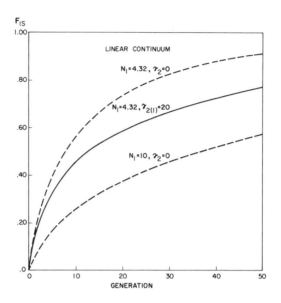

FIG. 12.5. F_{IS} for ancestral populations up to 50 generations in a linear continuum with neighborhood size $N_1 = 4.32$ and parent-offspring distributions that are normal ($\gamma_2 = 0$) or very leptokurtic ($\gamma_2 = 20$). F_{IS} in the latter case comes to resemble (with a lag) the values with $N_1 = 10$, $\gamma_2 = 0$, also shown.

It might be supposed that the standard deviation of a leptokurtic distribution extends out so far in relation to the main body of the frequencies that a leptokurtic parent-offspring distribution would imply a large population number for a given parental variance. Figure 12.6 shows linear half distributions in the cases $a = 2, 1, 0.5$ (normal) and 0, taking the half-length (R) of the neighborhood as the unit. It may be seen that the above supposition is not correct. This can be brought out numerically by calculating what fraction the quartile distance, including half the parents, forms of the total length of the neighborhood ($2R$). It comes out 0.354 in the case of the very leptokurtic distribution with $a = 2$, $\gamma_2 = 22.2$; slightly less (0.347) if $a = 1$, $\gamma_2 = 2.828$; and somewhat greater (0.380) for the normal distribution $a = 0.5$, $\gamma_2 = 0$. The length of the neighborhood can be taken as about 2.8 times the range that includes half the parents without much error, irrespective of the kurtosis.

The relation of N_1 in terms of $\pi\sigma^2 d$ to γ_2 in the case of an *area* continuum changes relatively little with increasing kurtosis, and the maximum is at about $\gamma_2 = 1$ (Fig. 12.4). In the same extreme case above ($\gamma_2 = 20$, $N_1 = 3.25\pi\sigma^2 d$ for the parent-offspring distribution), N_1 is taken as 8.13, which

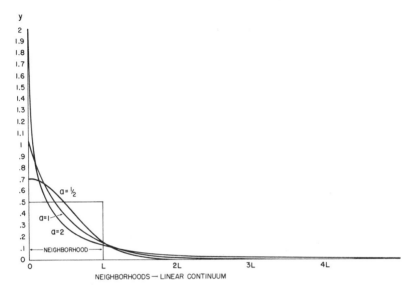

FIG. 12.6. Parent-offspring half distributions in a linear continuum, if rectangular ($a = 0$, $\gamma_2 = -1.2$), normal ($a = 0.5$, $\gamma_2 = 0$), moderately leptokurtic ($a = 1$, $\gamma_2 = 3$), or very strongly leptokurtic ($a = 2$, $\gamma_2 = 22.2$) on a scale of number of neighborhoods.

corresponds to 10 ($= 8.13 \times 4/3.25$) for $\gamma_2 = 0$. The curve for F_{1S} again lies between those with normal parent-offspring distributions with $N_1 = 8.13$ and $N_1 = 10$ respectively (Fig. 12.7). The distributions of frequencies of parents in concentric rings about offspring are shown in Figure 12.8 for the same values of a as in the linear case (2, 1, 0.5, and 0) in terms of the radius (R) of the neighborhood as the unit. The quartile deviation is $0.689R$ if $a = 2$; $0.589R$ if $a = 1$; $0.594R$ if $a = 0.5$; and $0.707R$ in the island model ($a = 0$). These are not as close as in the linear case but if kurtosis is between 0 and 3 the radius of the neighborhood may be taken as $1.7QD$ with little error. There is closer agreement on the basis of the distance that includes 40% of the parents. The radius of the neighborhood is about 2.0 times this distance for $\gamma_2 = 0$ to 22.

Effect of Universal Dispersion or of Reversible Mutation

It will be assumed here that the distribution of parents relative to offspring is bivariate normal, but that local fixation is prevented either by a small amount (m) of dispersion over the entire range or by the mathematically

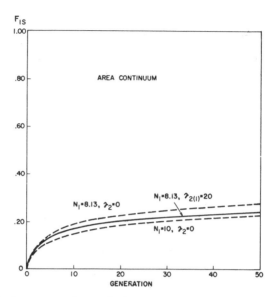

FIG. 12.7. F_{IS} for ancestral populations up to 50 generations for an area continuum, $N_1 = 8.13$, and unidirectional parent-offspring distributions that are normal ($\gamma_2 = 0$) or very leptokurtic ($\gamma_2 = 20$). F_{IS} in the latter case comes to resemble (with a lag) the values for $N_1 = 10$, $\gamma_2 = 0$.

equivalent process of reversible mutation at rates u and v. For simplicity, $(m + u + v)$ will be represented by m. The formula for $N_1 \sum t$ in the case of an area continuum is as follows (Wright 1943a):

$$(12.49) \quad N_1 \sum_{X=1}^{S-1} t_X = (1 - m)^2 + \frac{1}{2}(1 - m)^4\left(1 - \frac{1}{N_1}\right)$$

$$+ \frac{1}{3}(1 - m)^6\left(1 - \frac{1}{N_1}\right)\left(1 - \frac{1}{2N_1}\right) + \cdots + \left(\frac{1}{S}\right)(1 - m)^{2S} \prod_{X=1}^{S-1}\left(1 - \frac{1}{SN_1}\right).$$

The factor $(1 - m)^{2X}$ is approximately $1 - 2mX$ if $2mX$ is small. The effect on $\sum t$ and hence on F_{1S} is negligible for most purposes if X is less than $1/(10m)$. If X is greater than $3/m$, then $(1 - m)^{2X}$ becomes less than 0.0025 and the contributions of such terms to $\sum t$ become negligible for most purposes. The curve representing F_{1S} in relation to $\log S$ follows closely that with $m = 0$ up to about $S = 1/(10m)$ and then rapidly levels off toward an asymptote that is less than one. This asymptote can be estimated (Wright 1943a) by an integration formula that was accurate but rather

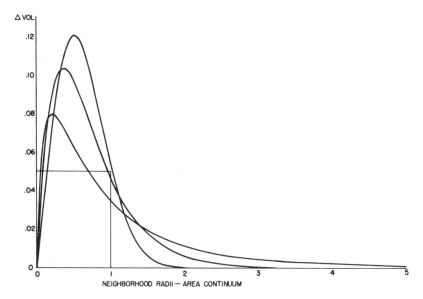

Fɪɢ. 12.8. The distribution of parents in concentric rings in an area continuum about offspring if the unidirectional distribution is rectangular ($a = 0$, $\gamma_2 = -1.2$), normal ($a = 0.5$, $\gamma_2 = 0$), moderately leptokurtic ($a = 1$, $\gamma_2 = 3$), or very strongly leptokurtic ($a = 2$, $\gamma_2 = 22.2$) on a scale of neighborhood radii.

cumbersome. The same values have been obtained by a simple formula suggested by A. Robertson (Wright 1951).

This depends on writing

$$(12.50) \qquad \sum_{y=1}^{\infty} t_X = \left[(1 - m)^2 \frac{1}{N_1} - \frac{(1 - m)^4}{2!} \frac{1}{N_1} \left(\frac{1}{N_1} - 1 \right) \right.$$

$$\left. + \frac{(1 - m)^6}{3!} \frac{1}{N_1} \left(\frac{1}{N_1} - 1 \right) \left(\frac{1}{N_1} - 2 \right) - \cdots \right]$$

$$= 1 - [1 - (1 - m)^2]^{1/N_1}.$$

Figure 12.9 shows the relation of F_{ST} to S up to $S = T = 10^8$ for values of m from 10^{-1} to 10^{-8} and $N_1 = 20$. The curve F_{ST} starts at the asymptotic value of F_{1S} and declines to zero at a value of S less than 10^8. Thus differentiation of large areas is built up only to a certain population size, N_S, of about $(3/m)N_1$.

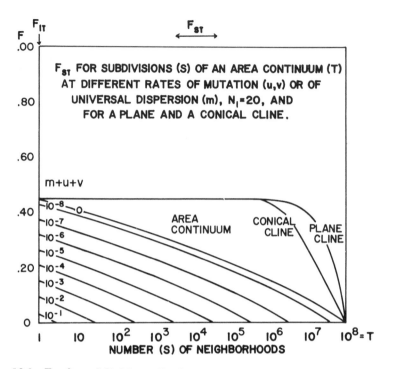

FIG. 12.9. F_{ST} for subdivisions (S) of an area continuum $(T$ neighborhoods) at different rates of mutation (u, v) or of universal dispersion (m) with $N_1 = 20$, and for a plane and a conical cline (Wright 1965c, Fig. 5).

Systematic pressures (Δq) involving the same selection over the entire range have roughly similar effects to those due to dispersion or mutation except that they are not linear. They may be treated similarly in cases in which there is only moderate deviation from equilibrium (F small) by using the best linear expression for Δq near the equilibrium point, $\hat{q}$ (Wright 1943a). It follows that random differentiation can extend to large areas only if the alleles in question are almost neutral.

Diversity in degree and direction of selection among localities is, of course, a wholly different matter and may bring about great differentiation among large areas if not overbalanced by immigration.

Vegetative Reproduction

A mixture of clones may be expected to vary in their relative frequencies over a continuous range because of accidents of sampling to an even greater extent than if there were local inbreeding. The correlation to be considered obviously cannot be that between uniting gametes. That between random individuals of a neighborhood (E_{1S}) relative to a given population (S) may, however, be considered. The neighborhood, size N_1, may be defined as that from which the parent of central individuals may be considered to have been drawn at random (Wright 1946).

$$E_{1S} = \frac{1}{N_1} + \left(1 - \frac{1}{N_1}\right)E'_{2S},$$

(12.51)
$$E'_{2S} = \frac{1}{N_2} + \left(1 - \frac{1}{N_2}\right)E''_{3S},$$

$$E''_{3S} = \frac{1}{N_3} + \left(1 - \frac{1}{N_3}\right)E'''_{4S}.$$

Again primes may be dropped if the same population structure has continued for a great many generations:

(12.52) $\quad E_{1S} = \dfrac{1}{N_1} + \dfrac{1}{N_2}\left(1 - \dfrac{1}{N_1}\right)$

$$+ \frac{1}{N_3}\left(1 - \frac{1}{N_1}\right)\left(1 - \frac{1}{N_2}\right) + \cdots + \frac{1}{N_S}\overset{S-1}{\prod}\left(1 - \frac{1}{N_X}\right).$$

In this case

(12.53) $\qquad E_{1S} = \sum t = N_1 t_1 - N_S t_S = 1 - N_S t_S.$

In both linear ranges and areas, E_{1S} approaches one as S is increased without limit. For given N_1 and N_S, E_{1S} is about twice as great for small values as F_{1S} under random union of gametes. The population number of neighborhoods is the same as before for both linear ranges and areas.

Monoecious Populations with More or Less Self-fertilization

The slightness of the effects of minor divergences from completely random union of gametes on inbreeding within closed systems indicates that the effects of F under isolation by distance may be expected to be rather small. A number of cases have been studied.

Let E_{1S} and F_{1S} be the correlations between random gametes from neighborhoods and between uniting ones, respectively, relative to an array of S neighborhoods, each of effective size N_1. Consider first the case of equal

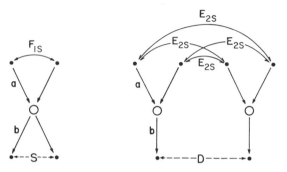

FIG. 12.10. Path diagrams for a monoecious population with a mixture of self-fertilization (left) and crossing (right) (redrawn from Wright 1946, Fig. 1).

dispersion from both parents (e.g., by seed) and the proportion h of self-fertilization (Fig. 12.10):

(12.54)
$$E_{1S} = \frac{1}{N_1} b^2 + \left(1 - \frac{1}{N_1}\right) E'_{2S},$$

(12.55)
$$F_{1S} = hb^2 + (1 - h)E'_{2S}.$$

In the case of an area continuum these lead to the equations

(12.56)
$$E_{1S} = \frac{(N_1 - 1)\sum t}{(N_1 - 1) + N_1(1 - h)(1 - \sum t)},$$

$$t_1 = \frac{1}{N_1}, \qquad t_X = \left[\frac{(X - 1)N_1 - 1}{XN_1}\right] t_{X-1},$$

It may be well to note that in the discussion of this and of the following special cases in Wright 1946, "$\sum t$" referred to $N_1 \sum t$ here.

(12.57)
$$E_{1S} = \frac{(N_1 - 1)(1 - N_S t_S)}{N_1[1 + (1 - h)N_S t_S] - 1},$$

(12.58)
$$F_{1S} = \frac{N_1[1 - (1 - h)N_S t_S] - 1}{N_1[1 + (1 - h)N_S t_S] - 1}.$$

In the case of random self-fertilization ($h = 1/N_1$), both of these reduce to $(1 - N_S t_S)/(1 + N_S t_S)$ as obtained before. Exclusion of self-fertilization ($h = 0$) makes little difference in either case unless N_1 is very small.

If there is exclusive self-fertilization ($h = 1$), then F_{1S} approaches one relative to any population containing more than one clone. The correlation between gametes approaches $E_{1S} = 1 - N_S t_S$ as in vegetatively produced clones.

The variance of the frequency of a given gene among neighborhoods within a more comprehensive population is

$$(12.59) \qquad \sigma^2_{q(IS)} = q_S(1 - q_S)E_{1S}.$$

N_P Permanent Pairs

Assume separate sexes with equal dispersion, N_P permanent pairs in neighborhoods, and the proportion h of sib mating (Fig. 12.11).

In this case the number of pairs in a neighborhood, $N_P = (1/2)N_1$, takes the place of N_1 in the analysis and similarly with N_{PX} (the number of pairs in the Xth ancestral generation). The distances between pairs in the parent and offspring generation refer to the locations at which pairing is established instead of to birthplaces. The standard deviation σ_P of such distances is, however, the same on the average as that for birthplaces. The densities of pairs d_P is half that of individuals. Thus the formulas are the same for pairs or individuals.

For linear ranges,

$$(12.60) \qquad N_P = 2\pi^{1/2}\sigma_P\, d_P \qquad \text{or} \qquad N_1 = 2\pi^{1/2}\sigma\, d.$$

For area ranges,

$$(12.61) \qquad N_P = 4\pi\sigma_P{}^2\, d_P \qquad \text{or} \qquad N_1 = 4\pi\sigma^2\, d.$$

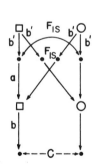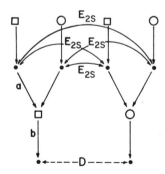

FIG. 12.11. Path diagrams for populations of N_P permanent pairs with mixture of sib mating (left) and more remote matings (right) (redrawn from Wright 1946, Fig. 2).

Let C_{1S} be the correlation between gametes produced by siblings, D_{1S} that between gametes of nonsiblings from the same neighborhood, D_{XS} that for the Xth ancestral generation, E_{1S} that between gametes from the same neighborhood, E_{XS} that between gametes of the Xth ancestral generation, and F_{1S} that between uniting gametes. In the steady state for area continuum:

$$C_{1S} = \frac{1}{4}(1 + 3F_{1S}),$$

$$D_{1S} = \frac{1}{4}(4E_{2S}), \qquad D_{XS} = E_{(X+1)S},$$

$$E_{1S} = \frac{1}{N_P}C_{1S} + \left(1 - \frac{1}{N_P}\right)E_{2S},$$

$$E_{XS} = \frac{1}{XN_P}C_{1S} + \left(1 - \frac{1}{XN_P}\right)E_{(X+1)S},$$

$$F_{1S} = hC_{1S} + (1 - h)E_{2S}.$$

These lead to the equations

$$
\text{(12.62)} \qquad
\begin{aligned}
E_{1S} &= \frac{(N_P - 1)\sum t_P}{[(N_P - 1) + 3N_P(1 - h)(1 - \sum t_P)]} \\
&= \frac{(N_P - 1)(1 - N_P t_{PS})}{[(N_P - 1) + 3N_P(1 - h)N_{PS}t_{PS}]},
\end{aligned}
$$

$$
\text{(12.63)} \qquad
\begin{aligned}
F_{1S} &= \frac{h(N_P - 1) + (1 - h)(N_P \sum t_P - 1)}{[(N_P - 1) + 3N_P(1 - h)(1 - \sum t_P)]} \\
&= \frac{(N_P - 1) - N_P(1 - h)N_{PS}t_{PS}}{[(N_P - 1) + 3N_P(1 - h)N_{PS}t_{PS}]}.
\end{aligned}
$$

There is little difference whether sib mating is at random ($h = 1/N_P$) so that $E_{1S} = F_{1S} = (1 - N_{PS}t_{PS})/(1 + 3N_{PS}t_{PS})$ or is excluded ($h = 0$). If there is exclusive sib mating ($h = 1$), there is again approach to complete fixation ($F_{1S} = 1$) and to $E_{1S} = 1 - N_{PS}t_{PS}$.

These formulas can be compared most easily with those for the standard case, but with only half as many individuals in a neighborhood. The correlations are considerably higher than in monoecious populations of the same population number.

Separate Sexes with Random Mating

Assume N_m males and N_f females per neighborhood, random mating, and equal dispersion of sons and daughters (Fig. 12.12). There are four types of

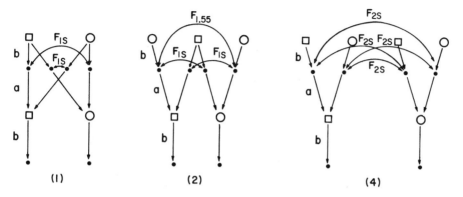

FIG. 12.12. Path diagrams for random mating population of N_m males, N_f females. (1) is for sib mating, (2) is for paternal half-sib mating (maternal half-sib mating analogous), and (4) is for more remote matings (redrawn from Wright 1946, Fig. 3).

mating to consider: (1) full-sib, with probability $1/(4N_mN_f)$, there being $2N_m$ males and $2N_f$ females in the preceding generation; (2) paternal half-sib, with probability

$$\frac{1}{2N_m}\left(1 - \frac{1}{2N_f}\right);$$

(3) maternal half-sib, with probability

$$\frac{1}{2N_f}\left(1 - \frac{1}{2N_m}\right)$$

and those (4) not immediately related with probability

$$\left(1 - \frac{1}{2N_m}\right)\left(1 - \frac{1}{2N_f}\right).$$

The condition $F_{1.5S}$ between gametes of mates of the same individual is slightly less than F_{1S}, but greater than F_{2S}, that between gametes of random individuals of a double neighborhood.

$$(12.64) \quad F_{1S} = \frac{1}{4N_mN_f}\left[\frac{1 + 3F_{1S}}{4} + (2N_m + 2N_f - 2)\left(\frac{1 + 5F_{1S} + 2F_{1.5S}}{8}\right)\right.$$
$$\left. + (2N_m - 1)(2N_f - 1)F_{2S}\right].$$

Collecting terms, multiplying N_m and N_f by X, and replacing F_{2S} by $F_{(X+1)S}$:

$$(12.65) \quad F_{XS} = \frac{(N_m + N_f)}{2XN_mN_f} \left[\frac{1 + 5F_{1S} + 2F_{1.5S}}{8} \right]$$

$$+ \left[1 - \frac{N_m + N_f}{2XN_mN_f} \right] F_{(X+1)S} - \left[\frac{F_{1S} + F_{1.5S} - 2F_{(X+1)S}}{8X^2N_mN_f} \right].$$

The last term is very small. An approximate solution may be obtained by ignoring it and ignoring the slight difference between F_{1S} and $F_{1.5S}$. It is convenient to write $N' = 2N_fN_m/(N_m + N_f)$ (which is $0.5N_e$). Note that if $N_m = N_f$, N' is the number of males (or females), while if females greatly outnumber males, N' approaches $2N_m$.

$$(12.66) \quad F_{XS} \approx \frac{1}{XN'} \left[\frac{1 + 7F_{1S}}{8} \right] + \left[1 - \frac{1}{XN'} \right] F_{(X+1)S},$$

$$(12.67) \quad F_{1S} \approx \frac{\sum t}{8 - 7\sum t},$$

where $\sum t$ depends as usual on whether an areal or linear continuum is in question. In either case it approaches one as the number of terms is increased indefinitely, so that as in the other cases there is an approach to local fixation.

Dispersion of Male Gametes Only

The assumption that the distribution of parent-offspring distances is the same for parents of both sexes often does not apply. Thus among plants dispersal of seeds may be negligible in comparison with that of pollen. We will consider here the limiting case in which all dispersal is by pollen (Fig. 12.13). It is further assumed that all individuals are hermaphoditic, with self-fertilization occurring to any specified extent, h. In the case of a linear distribution, the distribution of pollen parent about progeny (and ovule parent) will be assumed to be univariate normal with standard deviation σ, apart from excess (or defect) of the midclass due to excess (or defect) in amount of self-fertilization relative to that under random fertilization. Letting n be the number of individuals in a strip 2σ long, the average density is $d = n/2\sigma$. Let N_1 be the effective number of individuals in the neighborhood that function as pollen parents without taking cognizance of excess self-fertilization. Then the chance of self-fertilization under random union is $1/N_1 = (2\sigma/n)y_0$ where y_0 is the midordinate of the normal distribution. It is

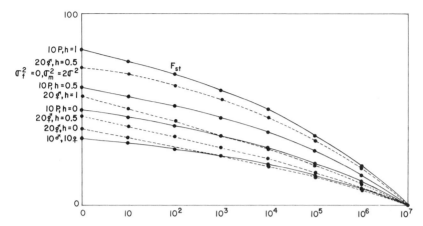

FIG. 12.13. Path diagrams for case of dispersion of pollen only (redrawn from Wright 1946, Fig. 4).

assumed that N_1 is sufficiently large that the midclass can be represented reasonably well by the product of midordinate into class range. Thus

(12.68)
$$1/N_1 = 2\sigma/(n\sigma\sqrt{(2\pi)}) = (1/n)\sqrt{(2/\pi)},$$
$$N_1 = n\sqrt{(\pi/2)} = \sigma\,d\sqrt{(2\pi)} = 2.50\sigma\,d.$$

In the case of area continuity, it is assumed that the distribution of pollen parents is bivariate normal relative to ovule parents and progeny. Letting n be the number of individuals in a square 2σ on a side, the average density is $n/(4\sigma^2)$. Defining N_1 as above, the chance of self-fertilization under random union of gametes in the neighborhood is $4\sigma^2 y_0/n$.

(12.69)
$$1/N_1 = 4\sigma^2/[n(2\pi\sigma^2)] = 2/(\pi n),$$
$$N_1 = \pi n/2 = 2\pi\sigma^2\,d = 6.28\sigma^2\,d.$$

Thus N_1 is equivalent to the number of individuals in a circle of radius $\sigma\sqrt{2}$. It is half as great as in the case of an equally dense monoecious population with the same amount of dispersion of both male and female gametes as of male gametes in this case. If the variance of pollen dispersal is twice that of the preceding cases, but d is the same, the formulas for N_1 become the same as in those in both linear ranges and areas.

Let r be the proportion of the pollinations that may be considered as at random from the neighborhood, and thus $(1 - r)$ the excess self-fertilization. Assuming that N_1 is at least two, the variance of pollen parents is $r\sigma^2$ (area continuity). The total proportion of self-fertilization is $h = r/N_1 + (1 - r)$.

The correlation, E, between ovules and pollen grains that contribute to adjacent zygotes and that, F, between those that unite may be analyzed as indicated in Figure 12.14.

$$(12.70) \qquad E_{1S} = \frac{C_{1S}}{N_1} + \frac{N_1 - 1}{N_1} D_{1S},$$

$$(12.71) \qquad F_{1S} = hC_{1S} + (1 - h)D_{1S}.$$

In cases of cross-pollination, the variance of father's mother, relative to mother's mother, is the same as that of father relative to mother (σ^2) because of the postulated absence of dispersion in the female line. The correlation between ovules from which fathers and mothers (where different) were derived is thus E_{1S}. The variance of father's father about mother's mother (father and mother different) is $(1 + r)\sigma^2$, corresponding to an effective population of $(1 + r)N_1$ if area continuity or $N_1\sqrt{(1 + r)}$ if linear continuity. The same is true for father's mother relative to mother's father. The correlation between these grandparents may be called E_{2S}. The variance of father's father relative to mother's father (father and mother different) is $(1 + 2r)\sigma^2$ corresponding to an effective population of $(1 + 2r)N_1$ if area continuity and $N_1\sqrt{(1 + 2r)}$ if linear continuity. The correlation between these grandparents will be called E_{3S}.

The spores produced by the Xth ancestral generation where the parents are different are drawn from populations with variances $[1 + (X - 2)r]\sigma^2$,

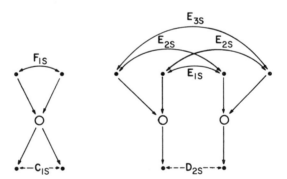

Fig. 12.14. F_{IS} and F_{ST}, all with $N_1 = 20$. Various systems of mating are compared (10 ♂, 10 ♀ at random; 20 ⚥ with various amounts of self-fertilization $h = 0$, 0.5, or 1; 10P permanent pairs, with sib mating $h = 0$, 0.5, or 1; and 20 ⚥ with no dispersal of ovules, double dispersion variance of pollen either with random self-fertilization, broken line close to 20 ♂, $h = 0$, or with about 50% self-fertilization) (redrawn from Wright 1951, Fig. 9, by permission, Cambridge University Press).

$[1 + (X - 1)r]\sigma^2$, and $[1 + Xr]\sigma^2$ according as ovule-ovule, ovule-pollen, or pollen-pollen. The effective population numbers are proportional, $[1 + (X - 2)r]N_1$, etc., if area continuity, and proportional to the square roots, $N_1\sqrt{[1 + (X - 2)r]}$, etc., if linear continuity. Thus if D_{XS} is the correlation between spores from different individuals of this generation:

$$D_{XS} = (E_{XS} + 2E_{(X+1)S} + E_{(X+2)S})/4,$$
$$C = b^2 = (1 + F_{1S})/2.$$

With area continuity

$$E_{1S} = \frac{C}{N_1} + \frac{N_1 - 1}{4N_1}(E_{1S} + 2E_{2S} + E_{3S})$$

$$E_{2S} = \frac{C}{(1 + r)N_1} + \frac{(1 + r)N_1 - 1}{4(1 + r)N_1}(E_{2S} + 2E_{3S} + E_{4S})$$

(12.72) :

$$E_{XS} = \frac{C}{[1 + (X - 1)r]N_1} + \frac{[1 + (X - 1)r]N_1 - 1}{4[1 + (X - 1)r]N_1}$$
$$\times (E_{XS} + 2E_{(X+1)S} + E_{(X+2)S}).$$

The equations above are obviously satisfied if all E's are equal to one, which, as in the preceding cases, is the limiting value approached as S is made indefinitely large. The attempt to solve for E_{1S} with finite N_S leads (as in case 3) to an unmanageable series. An approximate solution may be obtained by writing:

$$[E_{XS} + 2E_{(X+1)S} + E_{(X+2)S}]/4 = E_{(X+1)S} + \Delta_{(X+1)S}.$$

Since $\Delta_{(X+1)S} = (1/4)[(E_{XS} - E_{(X+1)S})] - [(E_{(X+1)S} - E_{(X+2)S})]$ is one fourth of the second differences of the E's which must be very nearly in arithmetic progression, the Δ's must be very small and a close approximation should be obtained by ignoring them.

(12.73)
$$E_{1S} = C_{1S}\left[\frac{1}{N_1} + \left(\frac{1}{N_2}\right)\left(1 - \frac{1}{N_1}\right) + \left(\frac{1}{N_3}\right)\left(1 - \frac{1}{N_1}\right)\left(1 - \frac{1}{N_2}\right)\cdots\right]$$
$$= C_{1S}\sum t$$

where $N_X = [1 + (X - 1)r]N_1$. The sum of the series can be evaluated as before:

$$\sum t = 1 - N_S t_S = 1 - [1 + (S - 1)r]N_1 t_S.$$

From equations above,

$$D_{1S} = E_{2S} = (N_1 E_{1S} - C_{1S})/(N_1 - 1),$$
$$F_{1S} = C_{1S}(1 - r) + rE_{1S},$$
$$C_{1S} = (1 + rE_{1S})/(1 + r),$$

(12.74) $E_{1S} = \left(\dfrac{1 + rE_{1S}}{1 + r}\right) \sum t = \sum t \,/ [1 + r(1 - \sum t)]$,

(12.75) $F_{1S} = [1 + r(2E_{1S} - 1)]/(1 + r)$.

If self-fertilization is at random ($r = 1$), this reduces to

(12.76) $E_{1S} = \dfrac{1 - SN_1 t_S}{1 + SN_1 t_S}$.

This is the same formula as that obtained for a monoecious population with equal dispersion of both parents to offspring and random self-fertilization, but there is greater differentiation for a given density of population and given dispersion of pollen than in the latter since effective N_1 is only half as great.

If there is exclusive self-fertilization ($r = 0$), then $F = 1$ as expected.

The relative amounts of differentiation, measured by F_{ST}, of populations ranging from single neighborhoods ($N_1 = 20$ in all cases) up to a total of 10^8 neighborhoods in an area continuum, assuming no mutation or long-range dispersal, are compared in Figure 12.14 according to mating system. Among the systems shown, there is least differentiation (except among very small populations), with monoecious individuals and either equal dispersion of male and female heredities ($\sigma_m = \sigma_f = \sigma$, as with exclusive dispersal by seed) or twice as much dispersion of pollen ($\sigma_m = 2\sigma$) associated with no seed dispersal ($\sigma_f = 0$). In neither case does it make any appreciable difference whether self-fertilization occurs at random ($h = 0.05$) or is excluded ($h = 0$). Random mating of equally dispersing males and females (both σ) gives about the same differentiation of neighborhoods but appreciably more of larger areas. Permanent pairing with random or no sib mating and equal dispersal, σ, of the sexes gives considerably more differentiation, and more than with monoecious individuals with 50% self-fertilization or even 100% for areas of more than $50N$ associated with equal dispersal, σ, of male and female heredities. The case of permanent pairs, with 50% sib mating and equal dispersion, σ, of the sexes shows consistently more differentiation than any of the preceding. Still more is shown by monoecious individuals, 50% self-fertilization and no dispersal of seeds ($\sigma_k = 0$) but doubled dispersion of pollen ($\sigma_m = 2\sigma$). The greatest amount of differentiation of populations of all sizes is found where there are permanent pairs with 100% self-fertilization.

Randomly Distributed Clusters

It is next of interest to consider how the theory of isolation by distance must be modified if, instead of uniform density, there is a pattern of randomly distributed clusters each with a small amount of exchange with those that are closest. Assume that the parents of any individual are largely drawn from a cluster with effective population number, M. Assume that the effective number from which ancestors are drawn increases linearly with the number of generations, the increment N being smaller than M because of the low density between clusters. Let $M = kN$. Then $N_X = (k + X - 1)N$ for the xth ancestral generation.

$$F_{1S} = \frac{1}{kN}\left(\frac{1 + F'_{1S}}{2}\right) + \left(1 - \frac{1}{kN}\right)F'_{2S},$$

(12.77)

$$F'_{2S} = \frac{1}{(k+1)N}\left(\frac{1 + F'_{1S}}{2}\right) + \left(1 - \frac{1}{(k+1)N}\right)F''_{3S}, \text{ etc.}$$

When a steady state is reached and primes are dropped:

$$F_{1S} = \frac{1 + F_{1S}}{2}\left[\frac{1}{kN} + \frac{1}{(k+1)N}\left(1 - \frac{1}{kN}\right) + \cdots\right.$$

$$\left. + \frac{1}{(k+S-1)N}\prod_{X=2}^{S}\left(1 - \frac{1}{(k+X-2)N}\right)\right]$$

(12.78) $\quad F_{1S} = \sum t_S' / [2 - \sum t_S'], \qquad$ where $\qquad \sum t_S' = \sum_{X=1}^{S-1} t_X'$

and

$$t_X' = \frac{(k+X-2)N - 1}{(k+X-1)N}t_{X-1}', \qquad X > 1, \qquad t_1' = 1/(kN)$$

(12.79) $\quad \sum t_S' = kNt_1' - (k+S-1)Nt_S' = 1 - (k+S-1)Nt_S',$

$$F_{1S} = \frac{1 - (k+S-1)Nt_S'}{1 + (k+S-1)Nt_S'}.$$

Note that t_X' can be expressed in terms of t_X (12.20) by the formula

(12.80) $\qquad t_X' = t_{k+X-1} \Big/ \prod_1^{k-1}\left(1 - \frac{1}{XN}\right) = t_{k+X-1}/kNt_k$

The values of F_{IS} (same as F_{1S}) and F_{ST} can be found for any given set of values of N and S. Figure 12.15 shows those for $N = 20$ and various values of k from 1 to 10^4 and values of S up to 10^8. The size of the total populations under consideration is thus $20 \times (10^8 + k - 1)$.

The values of F_{IS} for clusters of size kN are parallel to those for neighborhoods of size 20 ($k = 1$) but hardly begin to rise until S is equal to k. The differentiation of clusters of size 200,000 within this total is about half that

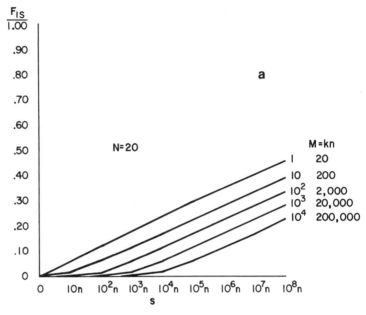

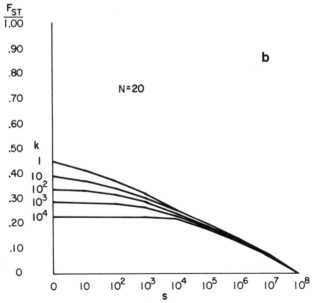

FIG. 12.15. F_{IS} (above) F_{ST} (below) where $N = 20$ is the increment to ancestral population size per generation and $M = kN$ is the neighborhood size (redrawn from Wright 1951, Fig. 11, by permission, Cambridge University Press).

of neighborhoods of size 20. The differentiation of large populations ($S > 10^4$) does not differ much for values of k from 1 to 10^4. These conclusions are, however, subject to the assumption that there is no long-range dispersion or mutation ($m + u + v < 10^{-8}$).

Correlation in Relation to a Distance in a Continuum

An important property of continuous populations is the falling off of the correlation between the gene frequencies of local populations according to their distance apart. Malécot (1948) focused on this in a study of isolation by distance by a wholly different mathematical method from that used here. Kimura (1953) and Kimura and Weiss (1964) have studied clusters (the "stepping-stone model") from this standpoint but by still another mathematical method. This correlation can be estimated roughly by the present method (Wright 1951).

The average distance apart of two neighborhoods drawn at random from an area with a population of size SN_1 is of the order of $\sigma\sqrt{S}$ where σ is the standard deviation of dispersion along one coordinate. The variance of the difference in gene frequency between two such neighborhoods is $2\sigma^2_{q(IS)}$. If, however, differences among subpopulations of this size are considered over a more comprehensive population of size TN_1, the correlation $r_{q(1)q(2)(ST)}$ between the pairs from the same subpopulation relative to all pairs within the total must be taken into account in the variance of difference.

(12.81) $$2\sigma^2_{q(IS)} = 2\sigma^2_{q(IT)}(1 - r_{q(1)q(2)(ST)}),$$

(12.82) $$r_{q(1)q(2)(ST)} = 1 - \frac{\sigma^2_{q(IS)}}{\sigma^2_{q(IT)}} = \frac{\sigma^2_{q(ST)}}{\sigma^2_{q(IT)}} = \frac{q_T(1 - q_T)F_{ST}}{q_T(1 - q_T)F_{IT}} = \frac{F_{ST}}{F_{IT}}.$$

Thus the correlation between the gene frequencies of neighborhoods at an average distance of about $\sigma\sqrt{S}$ apart relative to the total population N_T is given approximately by the ratio of F_{ST}/F_{1T}.

Both Malécot (1948) and Kimura and Weiss (1964) found that the correlation coefficient between gene frequencies decreases approximately exponentially. Using d as distance, m_1 as the amount of immigration from neighboring clusters, and m_∞ as that from a random sample of the species as whole, the latter authors obtained the relations:

$$r_{q(1)q(2)} \propto e^{-Ad}, \qquad A = \sqrt{(2m_\infty/m_1)}$$

in one dimension,

(12.83) $$r_{q(1)q(2)} \propto e^{-Bd}/\sqrt{d}, \qquad B = \sqrt{(4m_\infty/m_1)}$$

in two dimensions,

$$r_{q(1)q(2)} \propto e^{-Cd}/d, \qquad C = \sqrt{(6m_\infty/m_1)}$$

in three dimensions.

A wholly different aspect of dispersion was involved in Fisher's (1937) attempt to describe the wave of advance of an advantageous gene.

Application of F-Statistics to Breeding Systems

It is instructive to apply the F-statistics to the systems of mating discussed in chapter 7 (Wright 1965c). In these systems, the closed lines are to be considered as subdivisions (S) of an indefinitely large array of such lines (T), derived from the same foundation stock. The inbreeding coefficients are thus of the type F_{IT}. The average of the correlations among all gametes of a line, relative to this total, is F_{ST}; the average between uniting gametes relative to the gametes of their own lines is F_{IS}, and must be calculated from F_{IT} and F_{ST} (formula 12.17).

In connection with the interpretation of F_{IS}, it is interesting to begin with the extreme case of sib mating. There are two kinds of correlations in a generation: between gametes of the same individual (r_0) and between gametes of different individuals ($r_1 = F_{IT}$).

$$(12.84) \quad r_0 = (1/2)(1 + r_1'),$$

$$(12.85) \quad \begin{aligned} r_1 &= F_{IT} = (1/2)(r_0' + r_1') = (1/4)[2F' + F'' + 1], \\ P_{IT} &= (1/2)P_{IT}' + (1/4)P_{IT}''. \end{aligned}$$

Since these types are equally numerous,

$$(12.86) \quad \begin{aligned} F_{ST} &= (1/2)(r_0 + r_1) = (1/4)(2F + F' + 1), \\ P_{ST} &= (1/2)P_{IT} + (1/4)P_{IT}'. \end{aligned}$$

Thus F_{IT} is identical with F_{ST} of the preceding generation and the ratio P_{ST}/P_{IT} rapidly approaches λ ($= 0.80902$).

$$(12.87) \quad F_{IS} = (F_{IT} - F_{ST})/(1 - F_{ST}), \quad P_{IS} = P_{IT}/P_{ST} = P_{ST}'/P_{ST}.$$

The values of F_{IT}, F_{ST}, and F_{IS} for seven generations of sib mating are shown in Table 12.2.

TABLE 12.2. The values of F_{IT}, F_{ST}, and F_{IS} for seven generations under sib mating.

	0	1	2	3	4	5	6	7
F_{IT}	0	0.2500	0.3750	0.5000	0.5937	0.6719	0.7344	0.7852
F_{ST}	0.2500	0.3750	0.5000	0.5937	0.6719	0.7344	0.7852	0.8262
F_{IS}	-0.3333	-0.2000	-0.2500	-0.2308	-0.2381	-0.2353	-0.2364	-0.2360

Thus F_{IS} is always negative. It rapidly approaches $(\lambda - 1)/\lambda$ ($= -0.23607$) in oscillatory fashion.

The question may arise whether F_{IS} has any meaning in a population of two individuals. The correlation between egg and sperm is indeterminate (0/0) unless both parents are heterozygous, in which case it is zero. Even if the correlation arrays are made diagonally symmetrical by tabulating gamete against gamete, irrespective of kind, the coefficient is indeterminate if both parents are homozygous in the same allele, a class of mating that approaches 100% in frequency as the inbreeding proceeds.

This difficulty disappears, however, if the various types of mating are weighted by their variances in the direct calculation of F_{IS}. The essentially different kinds of matings, with their correlation arrays and their variances, and the correlation coefficients are given in Table 12.3, noting that A and a may be exchanged with no essential change in kind.

TABLE 12.3. Values of gene frequencies (q), variance (σ^2), and correlation between uniting gametes (r) in four types of sib matings.

	$AA \times AA$		$AA \times aa$		$AA \times Aa$		$Aa \times Aa$	
	0	1	0.50	0	0.25	0.50	0.25	0.25
	0	0	0	0.50	0	0.25	0.25	0.25
q	0	1	0.50	0.50	0.25	0.75	0.50	0.50
	$\sigma^2 = 0$		$\sigma^2 = 0.25$		$\sigma^2 = 0.1875$		$\sigma^2 = 0.25$	
	$r = 0/0$		$r = -1$		$r = -0.3333$		$r = 0$	

The frequencies of these types in seven successive generations of sib mating and the weighted average of the correlations (F_{IS}) are shown in Table 12.4.

It may be seen that the actual weighted averages, $\overline{F}_{IS}$, agree exactly with values calculated from F_{IT} and F_{ST}. $\overline{F}_{IS}$ can thus be given a concrete meaning even in this very extreme case. It cannot of course be interpreted as a probability because of its negative value.

Turning now to the maximum avoidance system with population number $N = 2^m$, the $m + 1$ kinds of correlations have been given earlier (chapter 7):

(12.88) $\quad F_{IT} = (1/2)F'_{IT} + (1/4)F''_{IT}$

$$+ (1/8)F'''_{IT} + \cdots + \frac{1}{2^{m+1}} (F_{IT})^{(m+1)\,\text{primes}}.$$

The average correlation between gametes is given by

(12.89) $\qquad F_{ST} = \frac{1}{N}[r_0 + r_1 + 2r_2 + 4r_3 + \cdots + 2^{m-1}r_m].$

TABLE 12.4. Types of sib matings, the values of r and σ^2 for each (from Table 12.3), and the frequencies of these types for seven successive generations. The weighted average for $\bar{F}_{IS}$ is the same as that calculated from F_{IT} and F_{ST}, Table 12.2.

FREQUENCIES OF MATINGS BY GENERATIONS

Mating	$r\ (=F_{IS})$	σ^2	0	1	2	3	4	5	6	7
$AA \times AA$ $aa \times aa$	0/0	0	0.1250	0.2812	0.4141	0.5254	0.6157	0.6891	0.7484	0.7965
$AA \times aa$	-1	.2500	.1250	.0313	.0391	.0254	.0220	.0172	.0141	.0113
$AA \times Aa$ $aa \times Aa$	-0.3333	.1875	.5000	.3750	.3437	.2734	.2246	.1812	.1469	.1187
$Aa \times Aa$	0	0.2500	0.2500	0.3125	0.2031	0.1758	0.1377	0.1125	0.0906	0.0734
Total			1.0000	1.0000	1.0000	1.0000	1.0000	1.0000	1.0000	1.0000
$\bar{F}_{IS} = \dfrac{\sum (r\sigma^2 f)}{\sum (\sigma^2 f)}$			-0.3333	-0.2000	-0.2500	-0.2308	-0.2381	-0.2353	-0.2364	-0.2360

All of the r's or P's can readily be expressed in terms of F_{IT}'s or P_{IT}'s. Thus in the case of 16-fold fourth cousins ($N = 32$):

$$(12.90) \quad P_{ST} = \frac{1}{128}[64P_{IT} + 32P'_{IT} + 15P''_{IT} + 7P'''_{IT} + 3P^{iv}_{IT} + P^{v}_{IT}],$$

$$(12.91) \quad P_{IS} = P_{IT}/P_{ST},$$

limiting value: $128\lambda^5/[64\lambda^5 + 32\lambda^4 + 15\lambda^3 + 7\lambda^2 + 3\lambda + 1] = 1.04207,$

$$(12.92) \quad F_{IS} = 1 - P_{IS},$$

limiting value: -0.04207.

Values of $1 - \lambda$ are given in Table 12.5 and of F_{IS} in Table 12.6.

In the case of circular mating of half-sibs, population number $N = 2^m$, the limiting value of $1 - \lambda$ has been given (chapter 7) as $[\pi/(2N + 4)]^2$. All of the gametic correlations appear twice around the circle except r_0 and r_n since $r_{N-X} = r_X$. Thus

$$F_{ST} = (1/N)\left[r_0 + \sum_{1}^{n-1} 2\,r_X + r_n\right]$$

and P_{IS} approaches a limiting value that can be obtained as the limiting value of

$$NP_1\bigg/\left[P_0 + 2\sum_{1}^{n-1} P_X + P_0\right]$$

in terms of the cosine formulas given for the various r's, after calculating θ.

In the case of circular mating of first cousins, $N = 2^m$, the values of the various gametic correlations and their limiting values have been given in chapter 7. The limiting value of $1 - \lambda$ was given as $[\pi/(N + 12)]^2$.

The correlations r_0 and r_1 appear only once around the circle, r_{n+1} appears twice, and all the others four times.

$$(12.93) \qquad F_{ST} = \frac{1}{N}\left[r_0 + r_1 + 4\sum_{1}^{n} r_X + 2r_{n+1}\right].$$

The limiting values of P_{IS} can readily be found.

Figure 12.16 compares the modes of approach toward fixation, F_{IT}, under various systems of mating, including the preceding three, in populations of size eight, starting in all cases from the first generation that shows an increase and thus not allowing for the lags in starting from random breeding stocks. The most rapid of these is that with one male and seven females with replacement by one random male and seven random females ($1 - \lambda = 0.1228$). The next is similar except that there are four males and four females

PROGRESS OF FIXATION IN POPULATIONS OF EIGHT

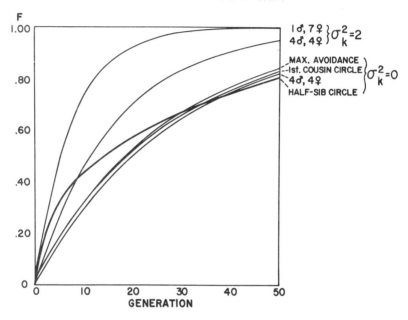

FIG. 12.16. Progress of fixation in populations of eight (Wright 1965c, Fig. 7)

$(1 - \lambda = 0.0586)$. The maximum avoidance system (quadruple second cousins) comes next $(1 - \lambda = 0.0362)$ but differs little from circular mating of first cousins $(1 - \lambda = 0.0347)$ and mating of four males and four females with selection of just two offspring from each parent $(1 - \lambda = 0.0344)$ as in the preceding two. The progress under circular mating of half-sibs follows a very different course from any of the others. There is almost as rapid an early rise as with one male and seven females, but this is followed by crossing of all of the other lines and much the lowest ultimate rate (0.0249).

Table 12.5 compares the limiting rates of decrease of heterozygosis, $1 - \lambda$, in various sizes of population. This is always slightly greater under maximum avoidance $(N > 2)$ than under random mating with equal number of males and females and just two offspring per parent in both. Circular mating of first cousins is the same system as maximum avoidance if $N = 4$ but has a slightly lower rate if $N = 8$ and a slightly higher one than under the random system. With $N = 16$ or more, the rate becomes less than in either of the others. The limiting rate under circular half-sib mating is

329

TABLE 12.5. The limiting rates of decrease of heterozygosis $(1 - \lambda)$ under six closed systems of mating with different size of population (N). In the first two systems, the parents are drawn at random $(\sigma_K^2 = 2)$; in the others just two are used from each parent of the preceding generation $(\sigma_K^2 = 0)$.

	$\sigma_K^2 = 2$		$\sigma_K^2 = 0$			
N	$1\male$ $(N-1)\female$'s	$(N/2)\male$'s $(N/2)\female$'s	Maximum Avoidance	$(N/2)\male$'s $(N/2)\female$'s	Circle of First Cousins	Circle of Half-sibs
2	0.1910	0.1910	0.1910	0.1910	—	—
4	.1396	.1096	.0804	.0764	0.0804	0.0727
8	.1228	.0586	.0362	.0344	.0347	.0249
16	.1159	.0303	.0170	.0164	.0142	.0076
32	.1120	0.0154	0.0082	0.0080	0.0053	0.0021
Large	0.1096	$1/[2N + 1]$	$1/[4N - (m + 1)]$	$1/[4N - 3]$	$[\pi/(N + 12)]^2$	$[\pi/(2N + 4)]^2$

always the lowest of those considered here and becomes very much so as N is increased. The greater tendency, under this system, to maintain hetero-zygosis than under maximum avoidance was the paradox (chap. 7) discussed by Kimura and Crow (1963b). A. Robertson (1964) has discussed this from a somewhat different viewpoint.

Table 12.6 gives the correlations, F_{IS}, between uniting gametes relative to their own lines in the three systems in which there is not random mating. It is, of course, always negative under maximum avoidance, but approaches zero as N is increased.

TABLE 12.6. The limiting correlation between uniting gametes relative to the array of the same line (F_{IS}) in systems in which there is not random mating.

N	Maximum Avoidance	Circle of First Cousins	Circle of Half-Sibs
2	− 0.2361	—	—
4	− .1824	− 0.1824	− 0.0784
8	− .1170	− .0733	+ .2221
16	− .0711	+ .1011	+ .5160
32	− 0.0421	+ 0.3293	+ 0.7274

Circular first-cousin mating passes from negative F_{IS} if $N = 4$ (same as maximum avoidance) to positive at some population size between 8 and 16. Even with circular half-sib mating, F_{IS} is negative if $N = 4$, but becomes positive between this and $N = 8$ and reaches the high value $+0.73$ if $N = 32$.

Figure 12.17 compares the ways in which F_{IT}, F_{IS}, and F_{ST} change in the course of 50 generations, after starting lines of 8 or 32 from random breeding stock under the two extreme systems. Under maximum avoidance, F_{ST} (measuring the permanent inbreeding effect) is always higher than F_{IT} (measuring the momentary total effect) because of negative F_{IS}. It was brought out in Figure 12.16 that even in populations of eight, F_{IT} is very slightly higher (after the initial lag) under maximum avoidance than under random mating. Thus F_{ST} is still more in excess under the former, since $F_{ST} = F_{IT}$ under random mating. These differences are, however, slight even in populations of eight and become less in larger populations, as shown for $N = 32$.

The very different character of the progress of F_{IT} under circular half-sib mating as compared with random mating in populations was brought out in Figure 12.16. It is evident from Figure 12.17 that this is due to the rapid rise

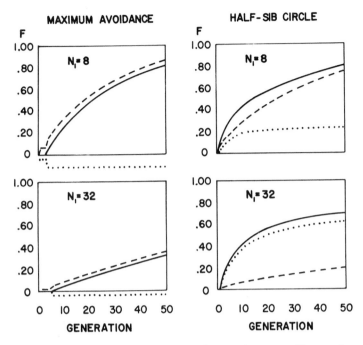

Fɪɢ. 12.17. Rise of F_{IT} in 50 generations under maximum avoidance of consanguine mating in populations of 8 and 32 and in half-sib circles, also in populations of 8 and 32. Solid lines = F_{IT}; broken lines = F_{ST}; dotted lines = F_{IS} (Wright 1965c, Fig. 8).

and approach to constancy of positive F_{IS}. Because of positive F_{IS}, F_{ST} is always lower than F_{IT}. With larger N, illustrated by the case of $N = 32$, there is an almost qualitative difference. At first F_{IT} is almost wholly dominated by the large amount of current inbreeding measured by F_{IS}, while the more permanent differentiation of lines as wholes, measured by F_{ST}, builds up very slowly. The excess correlation between adjacent individuals tends to maintain different alleles in different regions around the circle. There is an approach to the situation found in a population that is broken up into permanently distinct isogenic lines, which has been recognized as the best way to maintain the potentiality for maximum heterozygosis (realizable by crossing) since Shull (1908) and Jones (1918) developed the theoretical basis for the enormously successful hybrid corn program. The basis for the exceedingly low rates of decrease of heterozygosis in large populations under circular systems of mating, demonstrated by Kimura and Crow (1963b), is obvious from Figure 12.17.

The open systems of half-sib and first-cousin mating in infinite populations were studied as first approaches to the problem of isolation by distance. They were not very satisfactory models, however, and at the time the results were merely presented without discussion (Wright 1921). When more satisfactory models were studied later (Wright 1940a, 1943a, 1946, 1951), it did not seem worthwhile to go back to these very artificial systems. It is instructive, however, in the present context to do so; first for the open system of half-sib mating and then for the corresponding closed circle of 32 individuals.

Figure 12.18 shows the values of F under half-sib mating in an infinite population, carried to generation 50 instead of merely 15 as in 1921. This is compared with the progress of F_{IT} under linear isolation by distance with neighborhoods of various sizes. Parent-offspring distances are assumed to be distributed normally, and hence variances of ancestral populations rise linearly with number of generations, but sizes of these populations rise only as the square roots of the latter. In the case of the half-sib system, the parent-offspring distance is constant and equals 0.50 in terms of the distance

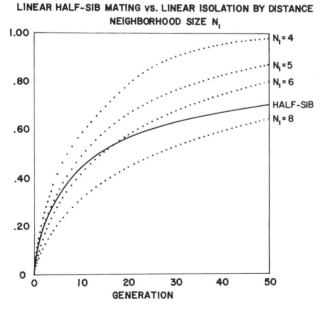

FIG. 12.18. Rise of F in 50 generations in indefinitely large half-sib circle and under linear isolation by distance with neighborhood sizes of 4, 5, 6, or 8 (Wright 1965c, Fig. 9).

between adjacent individuals. The grandparental distances have a 1:2:1 distribution about zero, the great-grandparental a 1:3:3:1 distribution, and the great-great-grandparental a 1:4:6:4:1 distribution. The variances rise linearly (0.25, 0.50, 0.75, 1.00, etc.) as in the model for linear isolation by distance. On the other hand, the range also rises linearly (1, 2, 3, 4, etc.), as does the number of different ancestors (2, 3, 4, 5, etc.) in contrast with the sizes of ancestral populations in the model of linear isolation by distances which rise only as the square root of the number of ancestral generations. This difference is due to the fact that in the half-sib model the parental distribution is as platykurtic as possible and the ancestral distributions only gradually approach normality instead of all being normal.

At first sight, it would appear that the size of "neighborhood" to be used in making a comparison should be two, since each individual is produced by two adjacent individuals. This, however, does not allow for the differences between drawing at random from normally distributed parents and taking exactly two offspring from each parent. The most nearly corresponding effective number under linear isolation by distance is thus expected to be considerably larger than two.

On calculating the values of F by generations with $N = 4$ by the formula (12.19 with $N_X = N_1\sqrt{X}$) for the linear model, it turns out that these rise much too rapidly. With $N = 5$ the values start out rather similarly (actually very slightly too small) but soon are considerably in excess. With $N = 6$, the values are too small for 16 generations but are considerably too large at 50 generations. Even with $N = 8$, the course of F under the linear model is clearly rising toward that under the half-sib model, though still below at 50 generations.

The difference in form of the course of F under the two systems can be accounted for by the differences discussed above. In the half-sib system the effective number of ancestors in ancestral generation X is somewhat between $\sqrt{X}$, expected if parental and all ancestral distributions were normal, and X. There is in consequence greater damping of progress than under the linear model in which this number varies with $\sqrt{X}$.

The increase in F_{IT} in the circular half-sib system, $N = 32$, does not differ appreciably from that in the infinite population (Fig. 12.18) up to 50 generations. It is of interest to make an analysis in terms of subdivisions of the total circle, similar to that discussed earlier for the models of isolation by distance. Since S has been used for the whole circle in relation to an infinite array of such groups, it will be convenient to use X for portions of the circle, of length X in the sense used earlier, but giving only half-weight to the terminal individuals. The smallest such portion ($X = 1$) includes two individuals with correlations between gametes of r_0 and r_1 in equal frequencies.

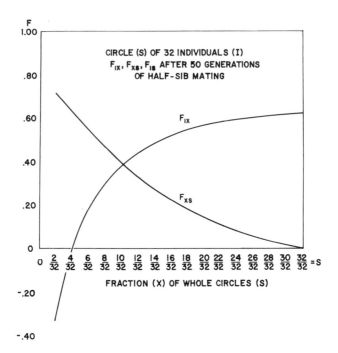

FIG. 12.19. Circle (S) of 32 individuals (I): F_{IX}, F_{XS}, F_{IS} after 50 generations of half-sib mating (Wright 1965c, Fig. 10).

The next to be considered $(X = 2)$ includes four individuals with gametic correlations of r_0, r_1, and r_2 in frequencies 0.25, 0.50, and 0.25, respectively. The distance, $X = 16$, includes all 32 individuals.

Since the total of all groups (T) is subdivided into groups (S) of size 32 and these into portions (X), the panmictic index for individuals relative to the total can be analyzed into three factors, $P_{IT} = P_{IX}P_{XS}P_{ST}$. Table 12.7 shows the values of r_X for all values of X from 0 to 31 for the 50th generation based on calculations for all previous generations. Correlation F_{IT} is 0.69822 and thus $P_{IT} = 0.30178$; P_{ST} is 0.80187 and P_{IS} is thus 0.37635. Thus F_{ST} $(= 0.19813)$ is far below its limiting value while F_{IS} $(= 0.62365)$ is not very far below its limiting value 0.72736 (cf. Table 12.6). The coefficients involving X were found as follows for each X:

$$(12.94) \quad P_X = 1 - r_X,$$

$$(12.95) \quad P_{XT} = (1/X)\left[(1/2)P_0 + \sum_1^{X-1} P_i + (1/2)P_X\right], \qquad F_{XT} = 1 - P_{XT},$$

(12.96) $P_{IX} = P_{IT}/P_{XT} = 0.30178/P_{XT}$, $F_{IX} = 1 - P_{IX}$,

(12.97) $P_{XS} = P_{IS}/P_{IX} = 0.37635/P_{IX}$, $F_{XS} = 1 - P_{XS}$.

The values of F_{XT} (Table 12.7) are of little interest in themselves. The correlations F_{IX} (also Table 12.7) between uniting gametes relative to the array of their own fractional group are, however, of interest (Fig. 12.19). The correlation between uniting gametes relative to the array of gametes from two neighboring individuals is $F_{I1} = -0.329$. Correlation $F_{I2} = -0.009$ is virtually zero indicating that such groups of four individuals (effective number about 6 by Kimura and Crow's formula) are roughly equivalent to neighborhoods. Beyond this, F_{IX} rises gradually as X increases toward the value $F_{IS} = 0.624$. In the last column of Table 12.7, F_{XS} measures the amount of differentiation of the fractional groups relative to that of complete local fixation ($q_S(1 - q_S)$). It falls from 0.717 for random groups of 2 to 0.222 for random groups of 16 (half of the circle) and to 0.016 for random groups of 30. That for "neighborhoods" (groups of 4) is approximately 0.627. This brings out in another way the strong local differentiation within the circles that interferes with the progress of fixation of circles as wholes as measured by F_{ST}.

TABLE 12.7. Analysis of system of circular half-sib mating, $N = 32$ with S pertaining to a single group of the 50th generation, T to the totality of all such groups, and X (in F_{XT}, F_{IX}, and F_{XS}) to portions of groups terminating at distance X (in r_X, the correlation between gametes of individuals at this distance). Terminal distances have half-weight.

Distance	r_X	F_{XT}	F_{IX}	F_{XS}
0	0.8477	0.8477	—	—
1 = 31	.6982	.7730	− 0.3293	0.7169
2 = 30	.5594	.7009	− .0090	.6270
3 = 29	.4354	.6331	+ .1776	.5424
4 = 28	.3288	.5703	+ .2977	.4641
5 = 27	.2406	.5132	+ .3801	.3929
6 = 26	.1704	.4619	+ .4392	.3289
7 = 25	.1167	.4164	+ .4829	.2722
8 = 24	.0772	.3765	+ .5160	.2224
9 = 23	.0493	.3417	+ .5416	.1790
10 = 22	.0304	.3115	+ .5617	.1414
11 = 21	.0181	.2854	+ .5777	.1088
12 = 20	.0104	.2628	+ .5906	.0806
13 = 19	.0057	.2432	+ .6012	.0562
14 = 18	.0032	.2261	+ .6100	.0349
15 = 17	.0019	.2113	+ .6174	0.0163
16	0.0015	0.1981	+ 0.6237	0

Crossbreeding and Inbreeding

This section will be concerned with populations derived from crosses among inbred strains. No selection among genotypes will be assumed, so that path analysis is possible.

Consider first an array of more or less completely fixed inbred strains among which all possible crosses are made in equal numbers. Assume that there are n such strains with correlation F_{ST} between representatives of a locus within strains, relative to the total array of such genes in the foundation strains, and with an average correlation F_{CT} between the representative of the locus in different strains. Assume that random matings are made among the crossbreds. The question to be considered is the correlation between random representatives of the locus in the second and later randombred generations, again relative to the gene frequencies in the foundation lines.

The parents of the first randombred generation (Fig. 12.20) may both come from the same cross between inbred strains in which case they may have (1a) no actual parent in common, or (1b) one parent in common, or (1c) both parents in common. The value of correlation between random gametes from each may be read off from Figure 12.20.

(12.98a) $$F = (1/2)F_{ST} + (1/2)F_{CT},$$

(12.98b) $$F = (1/8)(1 + 3F_{ST}) + (1/2)F_{CT},$$

(12.98c) $$F = (1/4)(1 + F_{ST}) + (1/2)F_{CT}.$$

If the inbred strains are all completely fixed ($F_{ST} = 1$), these all become $F = (1/2)(1 + F_{CT})$.

The parents may come from crosses that have one inbred strain in common. They may (2a) have no actual parent in common or (2b) have one parent in common.

(12.99a) $$F = (1/4)F_{ST} + (3/4)F_{CT},$$

(12.99b) $$F = (1/8)[1 + F_{ST}] + (3/4)F_{CT}.$$

These again become the same if $F_{ST} = 1$, giving $F = (1/4)(1 + 3F_{CT})$.

Finally the parent may come (2c) from crosses that have no inbred strain in common.

(12.100) $$F = F_{CT}.$$

Under the assumption of completely random mating among the progeny of the $(1/2)n(n - 1)$ different crosses, the proportion of the first case would be $2/[n(n - 1)]$, of the second case $4(n - 2)/n(n - 1)$ and of the third case $(n - 2)(n - 3)/n(n - 1)$. Assume for simplicity that no actual parents are in common.

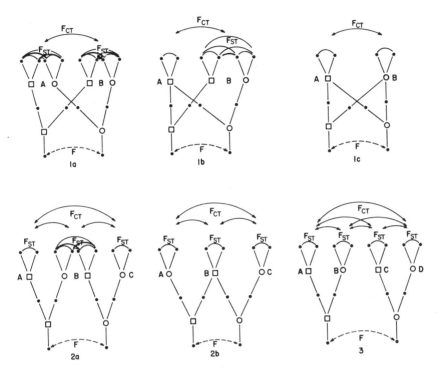

FIG. 12.20. Path diagrams for analysis of crossing of inbred lines: (1a), (1b), and (1c) relate to equations (12.98), (2a) and (2b) relate to equations (12.99), and (3) relates to equation (12.100).

$$(12.101) \quad F = \frac{2}{n(n-1)} [(1/2)F_{ST} + (1/2)F_{CT}]$$

$$+ \frac{4(n-2)}{n(n-1)} [(1/4)F_{ST} + (3/4)F_{CT}] + \frac{(n-2)(n-3)}{n(n-1)} F_{CT}$$

$$= \left(\frac{1}{n}\right) F_{ST} + \left(\frac{n-1}{n}\right) F_{CT}.$$

The value of F_{CT} can easily be found if every strain is completely fixed with respect to one allele or other at the locus in question ($F_{ST} = 1$) assuming of course that more than one allele is present. Let V_i be any arbitrary value assigned to allele A_i.

$$(12.102) \quad F_{CT} = \left[\frac{\sum V_i V_j}{n(n-1)} - \frac{(\sum V_i)^2}{n^2}\right] \bigg/ \left[\frac{\sum V_i^2}{n} - \frac{(\sum V_i)^2}{n^2}\right], \qquad i \neq j.$$

But

(12.103) $\quad \sum_{i \neq j}^{n(n-1)} V_i V_j = \sum_{j=1}^{n} \sum_{i=1}^{n} V_i V_j - \sum^{n} V_i^2 = \left(\sum^{n} V_i \right)^2 - \sum^{n} V_i^2,$

(12.104) $\quad F_{CT} = \dfrac{n[(\sum^{n} V_i)^2 - \sum^{n} V_i^2] - (n-1)(\sum^{n} V_i)^2}{n(n-1) \sum^{n} V_i^2 - (n-1)(\sum^{n} V_i)^2} = -\dfrac{1}{n-1}.$

Substituting the values $F_{ST} = 1$ and $F_{CT} = -1/(n-1)$:

(12.105) $\qquad\qquad\qquad\qquad F = 0.$

With continued random mating in an indefinitely large population derived from the crosses, F continues to be zero. These results are, of course, expected, since there has been no change in gene frequency from that present in the array of inbred lines. The value $F_{CT} = -1/(n-1)$ could have been deduced from this consideration. The point of interest here is in the comparison of the phenotypic averages of the inbreds ($F = 1$), the crosses among them ($F = F_{CT} = -1/(n-1)$) and the randombred derivatives ($F = 0$). If the effects of loci are additive but there is dominance to any extent, the mean $M(F)$ of a population with coefficient F is related to the means of randombred population ($M(0)$) and completely fixed populations ($M(1)$), all with the same gene frequencies, by the formula

(12.106) $\qquad M(F) = M(0) - F[M(0) - M(1)] \qquad$ (Wright 1922b).

In the present case, the mean of the crossbreds should exceed that of the randombreds by $1/(n-1)$ times the excess of the randombreds over the inbreds.

If the n inbred strains are assumed to be a random sample from an indefinitely large number that might have been produced from an original randombred stock, F_{CT} must be assumed to be zero relative to the array of gene frequencies in the latter. In this case $F = (1/n)F_{ST}$ for the derived randombreds or $F = (1/n)$ if $F_{ST} = 1$. In the terminology above $M(0)$ here refers to the crossbreds ($F_{CT} = 0$), $M(1)$ still refers to the inbreds ($F_{ST} = 1$), and $M(F)$ refers to the derived randombreds ($F = 1/n$). Thus random mating should result in a loss of the proportion $1/n$ of the excess of the crossbreds over the inbreds (Wright 1922b). This is, of course, equivalent to the previous expression. In the case of hybrid corn ($n = 4$), random mating of the fourway hybrid seed should result in a loss of 25% of the excess vigor.

In this connection it is of interest to consider the descendants of a three-way cross of the type $A(BC)$. Assuming that there are no parents in common at any point:

(12.107) $\qquad\qquad F = (3/8)F_{ST} + (5/8)F_{CT}.$

If it is assumed as the other extreme that the final cross is between a single A individual and a single (BC) hybrid in each case:

(12.108) $F = 1/4 + (1/8)F_{ST} + (5/8)F_{CT}.$

In either case, $F = 3/8$ if $F_{ST} = 1$ and $F_{CT} = 0$ (inbreds of a random sample) instead of $F = 1/3$ for the case in which the ancestry traces equally to three inbred strains.

A system, used for maintaining hybrid vigor in swine (Winters 1952), is to mate the females of a herd with a male from a different pure breed in each generation around a cycle of several generations. Preferably more-or-less inbred strains are used. Figure 12.21 gives a diagram of a case in which four strains are used in rotation, starting from a herd that is unrelated to any of them. A correlation of F_{ST} is assumed between random gametes within any strain and one of F_{CT} between random gametes of different strains. The

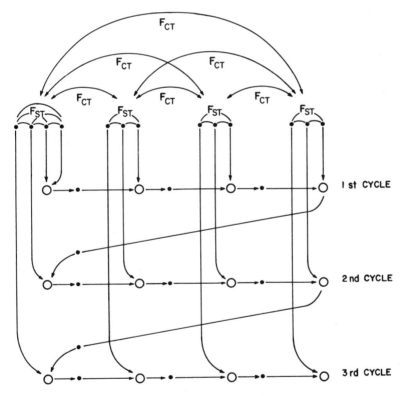

Fig. 12.21. Path diagram for cyclic mating of four breeds

values of F are thus relative to a randombred stock with the gene frequencies of the given set of strains. It is assumed that no male is used in successive cycles. The correlations for the offspring of males of each of four, A, B, C, and D, used in rotation, can be found from inspection. The contributions of each are listed separately in Table 12.8.

In a cycle of n breeds, the coefficient of F_{ST} is zero in the first cycle, $(1/2)^n$ in the second, $[(1/2)^n + (1/2)^{2n}]$ in the third, $[(1/2)^n + (1/2)^{2n} + (1/2)^{3n}]$ in the fourth, which rapidly approach $1/(2^n - 1)$. The sum of the coefficients of F_{CT} and F_{ST} is $1 - (1/2)^{k-1}$ where k is number of males that have been used in succession. The coefficient of F_{CT} rapidly approaches $(2^n - 2)/(2^n - 1)$ or practically one. Thus the system maintains a negative inbreeding coefficient (measuring amount of heterosis) which is less than that of first crosses between the strains F_{CT} by only about $[1/(2^n - 1)]F_{CT}$.

If the strains are treated as a random sample of a more comprehensive population so that $F_{CT} = 0$ and are assumed to be completely fixed so that $F_{ST} = 1$, the system soon leads to an inbreeding coefficient of $1/(2^n - 1)$ in agreement with Carmon, Stewart, Cockerham, and Comstock (1956).

Selection in Relation to Population Structure

The most important aspect of population structure is no doubt that due to differences in the conditions of selection in different parts of the range of the species. Unfortunately it is difficult to get much beyond qualitative description. F-statistics may be obtained but are necessarily specific for each pair of alleles. The most generally useful parameter is F_{ST}, defined as the ratio of the variance of the mean gene frequency for areas of a given size, relative to the limiting value for complete fixation of such areas according to the observed overall frequency, which may in principle be obtained for all pairs of alleles.

$$(12.109) \qquad F_{ST} = \sigma^2_{q(ST)}/q_T(1 - q_T).$$

As a simple example consider the case of local selection, s, balanced by immigration, assuming semidominance (Wright 1965c):

$$(12.110) \qquad \Delta q_S = sq_S(1 - q_S) - m(q_S - q_T),$$

$$(12.111) \qquad \dot{q}_S = q_T[1 + (s/m)(1 - q_T)]$$

$$\text{(approximately, if } s \ll m),$$

$$(12.112) \qquad \dot{\sigma}^2_{q(S)} = \sigma^2_{q(ST)} = \sigma^2_{(s/m)}q_T^2(1 - q_T)^2,$$

$$(12.113) \qquad F_{ST} = \sigma^2_{(s/m)}q_T(1 - q_T).$$

TABLE 12.8. Contributions of four inbred strains to inbreeding under cyclic mating.

CYCLE	♂	A	B	C	D	COEFFICIENTS OF F_{ST}	F_{CT}
1	A	0	—	—	—	0	0
	B	$\left(\frac{1}{2}\right)F_{CT}$	—	—	—	0	$\frac{1}{2}$
	C	$\left(\frac{1}{4}\right)F_{CT}$	$\left(\frac{1}{2}\right)F_{CT}$	—	—	0	$\frac{3}{4}$
	D	$\left(\frac{1}{8}\right)F_{CT}$	$\left(\frac{1}{4}\right)F_{CT}$	$\left(\frac{1}{2}\right)F_{CT}$	—	0	$\frac{7}{8}$
2	A	$\left(\frac{1}{16}\right)F_{ST}$	$\left(\frac{1}{8}\right)F_{CT}$	$\left(\frac{1}{4}\right)F_{CT}$	$\left(\frac{1}{2}\right)F_{CT}$	$\frac{1}{16}$	$\frac{7}{8}$
	B	$\left(\frac{1}{2}+\frac{1}{32}\right)F_{CT}$	$\left(\frac{1}{16}\right)F_{ST}$	$\left(\frac{1}{8}\right)F_{CT}$	$\left(\frac{1}{4}\right)F_{CT}$	$\frac{1}{16}$	$\frac{7}{8}+\frac{1}{32}$
	C	$\left(\frac{1}{4}+\frac{1}{64}\right)F_{CT}$	$\left(\frac{1}{2}+\frac{1}{32}\right)F_{CT}$	$\left(\frac{1}{16}\right)F_{ST}$	$\left(\frac{1}{8}\right)F_{ST}$	$\frac{1}{16}$	$\frac{7}{8}+\frac{3}{64}$
	D	$\left(\frac{1}{8}+\frac{1}{128}\right)F_{CT}$	$\left(\frac{1}{4}+\frac{1}{64}\right)F_{CT}$	$\left(\frac{1}{2}+\frac{1}{32}\right)F_{CT}$	$\left(\frac{1}{16}\right)F_{ST}$	$\frac{1}{16}$	$\frac{7}{8}+\frac{7}{128}$
3	A	$\left(\frac{1}{16}+\frac{1}{256}\right)F_{ST}$	$\left(\frac{1}{8}+\frac{1}{128}\right)F_{ST}$	$\left(\frac{1}{4}+\frac{1}{64}\right)F_{CT}$	$\left(\frac{1}{2}+\frac{1}{32}\right)F_{CT}$	$\left(\frac{1}{16}+\frac{1}{256}\right)$	$\frac{7}{8}+\frac{7}{128}$

Here, F_{ST} is not only specific for the particular pair of alleles in question but also varies with gene frequency, both in contrast with F_{ST} resulting from the balancing of accidents of sampling by immigration in the case of neutral alleles.

The way in which F_{ST} falls off with increasing size of area depends on how the selective differences among neighborhoods and larger areas are distributed. An especially important case is that of a cline (Wright 1965c).

As the simplest case, consider a cline along a single line of length L, along which gene frequency, q, rises linearly from one end to the other because of changes in the balance between selection and immigration. The variance of q for neighborhoods over the total length is:

$$(12.114) \quad \sigma^2_{q(IT)} = \frac{1}{q_L - q_0} \int_{q_0}^{q_L} (q - \bar{q})^2 dq = (1/12)(q_L - q_0)^2 \quad \text{if}$$

$$\bar{q} = (1/2)(q_L + q_0).$$

The variance of q within subdivisions of length L/n is $1/n^2$ times this.

$$(12.115) \qquad \sigma^2_{q(IS)} = \frac{1}{12n^2} (q_L - q_0)^2.$$

Thus

$$(12.116) \qquad \sigma^2_{q(ST)} = \sigma^2_{q(IT)} - \sigma^2_{q(IS)} = \frac{(q_L - q_0)^2}{12} (1 - 1/n^2).$$

There is no appreciable reduction of $\sigma^2_{q(ST)}$ and hence of F_{ST} for subdivisions constituting one-hundredth of the total and very little (1%) for those constituting one-tenth of it as compared with the values for neighborhoods.

Of more interest is the case of a large square area in which a gene frequency changes uniformly for strips parallel to one edge. The value of $\sigma^2_{q(ST)}$ for such strips is as above, but if each of these is divided into n squares and thus the total into n^2 areas, $\sigma^2_{q(ST)}$ or F_{ST} declines according to the fraction that the subdivisions under consideration form of the total: 10% for areas that are one-tenth of the total, 1% for areas that are one-hundredth of the total, etc. If the total consists of millions of neighborhoods, and F_{ST} is plotted against the logarithm of the size of subdivision in terms of neighborhoods, it remains substantially constant up to areas consisting of many thousands of neighborhoods but drops off precipitously for those larger than 1% of the total. This contrasts with the nearly linear decline of F_{ST} that depends on the amount of long-range dispersion or mutation in the case of neutral alleles subject to isolation by distance (Fig. 12.9).

If instead of a single cline there is an alternation of rising and falling clines, gene frequency will vary little for subdivisions corresponding to whole clines or more ($F_{ST} = 0$) but F_{ST} will remain high for areas up to about 1% of those that encompass whole clines. Thus if there are ten alternating clines in the total, the precipitous decline in the curve for F_{ST} will be shoved back to subdivision 10% of the size of those shown in Figure 12.5.

Instead of a plane cline, there may be uniform change of gene frequency in all directions from a high (or low) center, constituting a conical cline. With seven equal areas (a central one surrounded by six others) the variance of area averages is 51.6% of that of small neighborhoods. With 19 such areas in two concentric zones about a central one, the corresponding figure is 78.9%. With 37 equal areas in three concentric zones about a central one it is 88.7%, and in the case of 61 it is 93%. In a total consisting of millions of neighborhoods, the curve for F_{ST} is still virtually level over most of the range of areas on a logarithmic scale, but conspicuous decline begins with smaller fractions of the total than in the case of a plane cline (Fig. 12.9). Thus there is in general much less falling off of differentiation in relation to increasing size of area in any pattern of clines than in the typical pattern from balancing of the inbreeding effect by dispersion.

Selection tends to bring about deviations from the Hardy–Weinberg distribution. The relation between F as the correlation between the alleles of individuals in a population and the amount of heterozygosis under the Hardy–Weinberg distribution is the same as that due to inbreeding, assuming as before that no distinction is made between alleles that enter from males or females. Where selection is different in the sexes, the correlation array must be made symmetrical by combining tabulations of egg against sperm and of sperm against egg.

As a simple example, consider the case of a locus in which there is a steady state because of selection against both homozygotes in favor of the heterozygotes.

$$\text{Frequency} \quad W \qquad \overline{W} = 1 - sq^2 - t(1-q)^2$$

$$AA \quad q^2 \qquad 1-s \qquad \Delta q = -(s+t)q(1-q)(q-\hat{q}), \quad \hat{q} = \frac{t}{s+t}$$

(12.117) $\quad Aa \quad 2q(1-q) \quad 1 \qquad \hat{W} = 1 - st/(s+t)$

$$aa \quad (1-q)^2 \quad 1-t$$

Calculation of the correlation between the alleles gives the negative fixation index after selection:

(12.118) $$F = -st/(s + t - st).$$

The panmictic index, $P = (s + t)/(s + t - st)$, is greater than one.

If, however, there is not equilibrium, so that gene frequencies are not the same after selection as before, the formulas for F and for ΔF are rather complicated, whether in terms of gene frequencies before or after selection.

This sort of use of the fixation index has been extended by Jain and Workman (1967).

`CHAPTER 13

Stochastic Distributions of Gene Frequencies: Single Genes

The Variance of Gene Frequencies under Inbreeding

It was shown in chapter 7 that random sampling tends to bring about a decrease in heterozygosis in populations of finite size with respect to loci that are not subject to systematic pressures. Assuming that all populations are of the same size, N, and that all start from the same gene frequency, q_0, the above result implies that a spreading of the values of q occurs among the populations in both directions from q_0, leading eventually to loss or fixation ($q = 0$ or $q = 1$) in increasing numbers of them. The first problem is to find the rule according to which the variance, σ_q^2, increases in this process (Wright 1942).

A random sample of $2N$ gametes from the gene array, $(1 - q)a + aA$, will be distributed in the next generation according to the expansion of $[(1 - q)a + qA]^{2N}$ with variance $\sigma_{q(1)}^2 = q_0(1 - q_0)/2N$.

The increment of variance in the second generation will be slightly less.

$$(13.1) \qquad \sigma_{\delta q(2)}^2 = \frac{1}{2N} \int_0^1 q(1 - q)f_1 dq$$

in which the f_1's are the frequencies of the values of q in the first generation.

$$\sigma_{\delta q(2)}^2 = \frac{1}{2N} [\bar{q}(1 - \bar{q}) - \sigma_{q(1)}^2]$$

in which $\bar{q} = q_0$. Thus:

$$\sigma_{q(2)}^2 = \sigma_{q(1)}^2 + \sigma_{\delta q(2)}^2 = \sigma_{q(1)}^2 \left(1 - \frac{1}{2N}\right) + \frac{\bar{q}(1 - \bar{q})}{2N}$$

$$(13.2)$$

$$= \frac{\bar{q}(1 - \bar{q})}{2N} \left[1 + \left(1 - \frac{1}{2N}\right)\right].$$

Similarly in any later generation:

(13.3)
$$\sigma^2_{q(n)} = \sigma^2_{q(n-1)} + \frac{1}{2N} \int_0^1 q(1-q)f_{n-1}dq$$
$$= \sigma^2_{q(n-1)}\left(1 - \frac{1}{2N}\right) + \frac{\bar{q}(1-\bar{q})}{2N},$$

(13.4)
$$\sigma^2_{q(n)} = \frac{\bar{q}(1-\bar{q})}{2N}\left[1 + \left(1 - \frac{1}{2N}\right) + \left(1 - \frac{1}{2N}\right)^2 + \cdots \right.$$
$$\left. + \left(1 - \frac{1}{2N}\right)^{n-1}\right],$$

(13.5) $$\qquad \sigma^2_{q(n)} = \bar{q}(1-\bar{q})\left[1 - \left(1 - \frac{1}{2N}\right)^n\right] \approx \bar{q}(1-\bar{q})[1 - e^{-n/2N}].$$

This is the required rule. In early generations, the variance rises approximately with the number of generations, but as n becomes large it approaches $\bar{q}(1-\bar{q})$ which is the variance of the array of fixed populations, $(1-\bar{q})aa + \bar{q}AA$, with same mean gene frequency as at first. The variance is only 63% of the final value in $2N$ generations, 86% in $4N$ generations, and 95% in $6N$ generations.

On starting from an intermediate value of q_0, the distribution spreads and flattens. On starting from one of the subterminal classes $q = 1/(2N)$ or $1 - 1/(2N)$, there would be much immediate loss or fixation, but excluding these, the distribution of the rest will spread toward intermediate frequencies and thus also flatten. It may be expected that the intermediate portion of the distribution will approach a certain constant form although all classes will decline as loss and fixation proceed.

Distributions under Pure Inbreeding

The first attempt to determine this form was made by Fisher (1922), who represented the process by a differential equation of the type of the heat diffusion equation. He used a transformation $\theta = \cos^{-1}(1 - 2q)$, instead of q, in order to make the sampling variance uniform throughout the range between $q = 0$ and $q = 1$. He came out with a uniform rate of fixation, $1/(4N)$.

This, however, disagreed with the rate $1/(2N)$ which had been obtained by path analysis. Since the cause of the discrepancy was not wholly clear, I tried to obtain the distribution by another method, without the above transformation (Wright 1929a). This was based on the concept that a class of populations, characterized by any given gene frequency q, makes a contribution in the next generation to the class characterized by gene frequency q_1 according to the appropriate term in the expansion of $[(1 - q)a + aA]^{2N}$, i.e.,

$$\binom{2N}{2Nq_1}[q^{2Nq_1}(1 - q)^{2N(1-q_1)}]f(q),$$

where $f(q)$ is the frequency of gene frequency q (Wright 1931).

If there is to be constancy of the form of the distribution, but decay of all class frequencies at the rate $1/(2N)$, the sum of the contributions from all classes to any given class must be the same as the preceding frequency in the latter class except for reduction by $1/(2N)$.

$$(13.6) \quad \frac{(2N)!}{(2Nq_1)!\,[2N(1 - q_1)]!} \sum_0^1 [q^{2Nq_1}(1 - q)^{2N(1-q_1)}]f(q) = \left[1 - \frac{1}{2N}\right]f(q_1).$$

Since q varies by very small steps if N is large, an approximation should be obtainable by dealing with q as if varying continuously between 0 and 1, thus replacing summation by integration, $f(q)$ by $\varphi(q)dq$ and $f(q_1)$ by $\varphi(q_1)/(2N)$, except very near the boundaries 0 and 1.

$$(13.7) \quad \frac{\Gamma(2N)}{q_1(1 - q_1)\Gamma(2nq_1)\Gamma[2N(1 - q_1)]} \int_0^1 q^{2Nq_1}(1 - q)^{2N(1-q_1)}\varphi(q)dq$$
$$= \left(1 - \frac{1}{2N}\right)\varphi(q_1).$$

If $\varphi(q) = 1$, the left-hand member becomes $2N/(2N + 1)$ which is very nearly the same as the right-hand member which is $(2N - 1)/2N$. The rectangular distribution,

$$(13.8) \quad \varphi(q) = 1,$$

is thus indicated to be a close approximation (Fig. 13.1).

Kimura (1955b, 1956a) has gone into the distribution of three or more alleles where there is equilibrium of form but steady decay, in the absence of all evolutionary pressures. The distribution ultimately becomes flat and falls off at the rate of $3/2N$ per generation. The total distribution of each as opposed to all others is, of course, of the near-rectangular type falling off $1/(2N)$ per generation.

Returning to the discrete distribution, this would indicate the frequency $f = 1/(2N)$ (or strictly $1/(2N - 1)$, there being $2N - 1$ classes between 0 and 1). The amounts of loss and fixation are each $1/(4N)$ (to give a total rate of $1/(2N)$). Thus it appears that the amounts of loss and fixation are almost exactly half the frequency of the corresponding subterminal class. The actual expected amount of fixation can, however, be estimated from the binomial

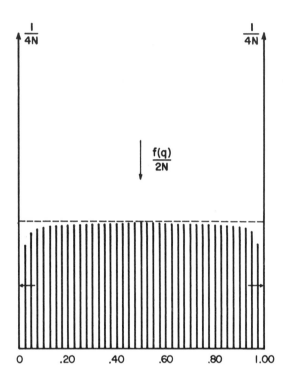

FIG. 13.1. Declining distribution of gene frequencies at a steady state with respect to form in a population of size N, in the absence of any systematic pressure. There is fixation of each homozygote at the rate $1/(4N)$ per generation (modified from Wright 1931, Fig. 3).

distributions from classes near the ends, which are approximately Poisson distributions if N is large. The contribution to loss from the class with gene frequency $m/2N$ is thus e^{-m}. The total contribution to loss is thus

$$(13.9) \quad (e^{-1} + e^{-2} + e^{-3} + \cdots)f\left(\frac{1}{2N}\right) = \frac{e^{-1}}{1 - e^{-1}}f\left(\frac{1}{2N}\right) = 0.582 f\left(\frac{1}{2N}\right),$$

instead of $0.5f(1/(2N))$ as implied above.

The situation is the same at the other end of the distribution. This shows that the distribution must dip somewhat from the rectangular form $\varphi(q) = 1$ near the boundaries. The subterminal class would have to be $0.777/(2N)$ if it were the only one with frequency less than $1/(2N)$ but will actually be larger than this because of spreading of the dip to higher classes.

The equilibrium distribution can readily be found exactly in the extreme case of populations of two monoecious individuals with random union of gametes (Wright 1931). The following equations can be set up for the progeny of populations with one to three representatives of the gene (A) in question, letting x be the frequency of those with the $2A:2a$, and y with $3A$ to $1a$ or $1a:3A$, including the fixed classes, so that $x + 2y = 1$.

	Parent population	$4A$	$3A:1a$	$2A:2a$	$1A:3a$	$4a$
	$3A:1a$ $256y \rightarrow$	$81y$	$+$ $108y$	$+$ $54y$	$+$ $12y$	$+$ $1y$
(13.10)	$2A:2a$ $256x \rightarrow$	$16x$	$+$ $64x$	$+$ $96x$	$+$ $64x$	$+$ $16x$
	$1A:3a$ $256y \rightarrow$	$1y$	$+$ $12y$	$+$ $54y$	$+$ $108y$	$+$ $81y$

The proportion that becomes homallelic, $4A + 4a$, is $(164y + 32x)/256$.

If there is equilibrium, $y = (120y + 64x)/(256 - 164y - 32x)$ yielding

$$(13.11) \qquad y = 8/25 = 0.32, \qquad x = 9/25 = 0.36.$$

The rate of decay is $1/4$, or exactly $1/(2N)$, as expected in this case.

Thus even in this extreme case the proportion in the subterminal classes $(y = 0.32)$ is not very much less than that in the middle class $(x = 0.36)$.

There is a greater dip in the subterminal classes in the case of a monoecious population of two with self-fertilization excluded or the equivalent case of brother-sister mating. As noted in chapter 7, the proportion of fixation is less than $1/(2N)$, being $(1/4)(3 - \sqrt{5}) = 0.191$. On solving the equations of equilibrium, we obtain the following:

	Mating	Frequency
	$AA \times Aa$	$7 - 3\sqrt{5} = 0.2918$
(13.12)	$Aa \times Aa$	$-22 + 10\sqrt{5} = 0.3607$
	$AA \times aa$	$9 - 4\sqrt{5} = 0.0557$
	$Aa \times aa$	$7 - 3\sqrt{5} = 0.2918$
	1	1.0000

The case of random union of gametes in populations of three monoecious individuals can also readily be solved from the equations of equilibrium. The rate of fixation comes out $1/6$, or exactly $1/(2N)$, as expected.

	Population	Frequency
	$5A:1a$	0.1830
	$4A:2a$	.2098
(13.13)	$3A:3a$	.2144
	$2A:4a$	.2098
	$1A:5a$	0.1830
		1.0000

Fisher, on inspection of the preceding results in manuscript, corrected his equation (Fisher 1930a,b) by adding a term made necessary by the transformation of scale (the second on the right side below).

$$(13.14) \qquad \frac{\partial y}{\partial t} = \frac{1}{4N} \frac{\partial^2 y}{\partial \theta^2} + \frac{1}{4N} \frac{\partial}{\partial \theta} (y \cot \theta),$$

from which $y = A_0 e^{-t/2N} \sin \theta$, $t =$ number of generations. This confirms $1/(2N)$ as the rate of decay.

Applying the transformation $\theta = \cos^{-1} (1 - 2q)$, $\sin \theta = 2\sqrt{[q(1 - q)]}$, and

$$\frac{\partial \theta}{\partial q} = \frac{1}{2\sqrt{[q(1 - q)]}},$$

it may be seen that the sine curve, on Fisher's scale, transforms into a rectangular distribution relative to gene frequencies.

A similar problem, the extinction of surnames in human populations, had been raised by Galton and solved by Watson in a different way (Watson and Galton 1874) (cf. Harris 1963). Fisher (1930a,b) used this method of branching processes to obtain an expression for the departure from the rectangular distribution on the scale of gene frequencies in the case of large populations. It came out approximately $[1 - 1/(6m)]$ where m is the number of representatives of one of the alleles. The exact ratio to the subterminal frequency as given by the formula is given below where f_m is the frequency in the class with m representatives of the gene.

	m	$1 - 1/(6m)$	f_m
	1	0.833333	0.818203
	2	.913333	.916762
	3	.944444	.944923
(13.16)	4	.958333	.958266
	5	.966667	.966634
	6	0.972222	0.972225
	—	—	—
	—	—	—
	$\sum e^{-m} f_m$	0.505080	0.500000

With these class frequencies, $\sum e^{-m} f_m = 0.500,000$. The amount of fixation is thus just half the frequency of the subterminal class in the formula before correction as shown for populations of two or three. (See Fig. 13.1.)

The problem of determining the form of the distribution at any stage between an initial single value of q and this limiting form for unfixed genes has been solved by Kimura (1955a). Figures 13.2a and 13.2b illustrate results in the cases in which $q_0 = 0.50$ and $q_0 = 0.10$, respectively. It requires some $2N$ generation to arrive at an almost flat distribution in the former case with

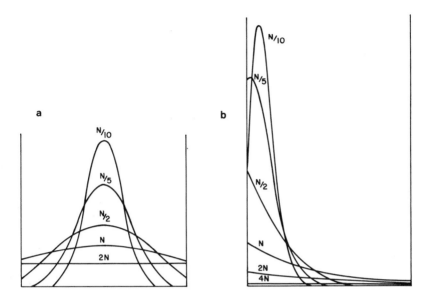

FIG. 13.2. Changing distribution of gene frequencies in a population of size N, in the absence of any systematic pressures: (a) on starting from $q = 0.50$; (b) on starting from $q = 0.10$ (redrawn from Kimura 1955a, Fig. 2).

about 50% of the genes still unfixed, while it requires over $4N$ generations in the latter, by which time more than 90% have been fixed.

Multiple Cytoplasmic Particles

A somewhat similar distribution arises where cells contain a certain number of entities, each of which duplicates, and just half are apportioned to each daughter at random with respect to alternative forms. As noted in chapter 6 and volume 1 chapter 4, this process has been postulated for various cytoplasmic entities involved in nongenic inheritance, especially of chlorophyl variegation (Gregory 1915; Michaelis 1959; Rhoades 1943, 1946). It has also been postulated for macronuclear constituents in ciliates (Sonneborn 1943; Nanney and Allen 1959).

The simplest case is that of two plastids, one green (G) and one colorless (W), in the initial cell. Duplication and random segregation of kinds would yield GG-WW or GW-GW with relative frequencies 1:2. Thus two-thirds of the daughter cells from such segregations retain the mixed condition, while one-sixth are true breeding green and one-sixth true breeding white. Only $(2/3)^n$ are mixed after n divisions.

With a larger number of plastids, homogeneous sets arise less frequently. Assume np of one type and nq of the other, where $p + q = 1$. Duplication and random segregation except for maintenance of the number, n, gives the ratio np_1 to nq_1 with the following frequency, as may be seen from the numbers of combinations in sets of np_1 and nq_1 and in the total (Correns and Wettstein 1937; Michaelis 1955):

$$(13.17) \qquad f_{q(1)} = \frac{(n!)^2(2np)!\,(2nq)!}{(2n)!\,(np_1)!\,(2np - np_1)!\,(nq_1)!\,(2nq_1 - nq_1)!},$$

This implies symmetrical spreading from the initial composition, best seen by writing $x = n(q_1 - q)$ for the deviation from initial nq.

$$(13.18) \quad f_{q(1)} = \frac{(n!)^2(2np)!\,(2nq)!}{(2n)!}\left[\frac{1}{(np + x)!\,(np - x)!\,(nq + x)!\,(nq - x)!}\right].$$

The variance from a single element taken at random from the duplicated array, $[2npa + 2nqA]$, is pq. If $2n$ were taken, each wholly at random, the variance of the total would be $2npq$. The total, however, has by hypothesis zero variance, which implies a negative correlation, r, among the elements in their contributions to it.

$$2npq + 2n(2n - 1)rpq = 0,$$

$$r = -\frac{1}{2n - 1}.$$

If n elements are taken from the total array, the variance of their total is as follows, using the above value of r:

$$(13.19) \qquad \begin{aligned} \sigma^2_{\Delta nq} &= npq + n(n - 1)rpq = npq[1 + (n - 1)r] = \frac{n^2pq}{2n - 1}, \\ \sigma^2_{\Delta q} &= pq/(2n - 1). \end{aligned}$$

The limiting form of the distribution may be obtained from the slope at $x + 1/2$ and $x - 1/2$. Ignoring second-order terms:

$$(13.20) \qquad \begin{aligned} \Delta f &= -f\left[\frac{2(n + 1)x}{n^2pq + x^2}\right] \approx \frac{df}{dx}, \\ f &\approx y_0\left(1 + \frac{x^2}{n^2pq}\right)^{-(n + 1)}, \end{aligned}$$

where $y_0 \approx 1/\sqrt{(\pi npq)}$ by Stirling's theorem.

$$(13.21) \qquad \begin{aligned} \mu_2 &= \frac{n^2pq}{2n - 1} \qquad \text{as above,} \\ \mu_3 &= 0 \\ \mu_4 &= \frac{3(2n - 1)}{2n - 3}\mu_2{}^2, \qquad \gamma_2 = 6/(2n - 3) \end{aligned}$$

This curve is only slightly leptokurtic, with large n, and approaches normality as n increases. The variance is correct for even the smallest values of n. The kurtosis of actual distributions is, however, not at all closely approximated unless n is large.

The distribution may be expected to spread generation after generation until fixation of the two types of element approaches a constant rate (some $2n$ generations on starting from equal number) after which the unfixed distribution should be nearly constant in form and symmetrical but falling off at a constant rate, k per generation. The contribution of newly fixed sets to the variance is thus $k/4$, and that of the unfixed sets is $(1 - k)$ times that in the preceding generation (σ_q^2). The increment of variance over that of unfixed sets of the preceding generation being $pq/(2n - 1)$ where $pq = 1/4$ when symmetry is attained, we have

$$\sigma_q^2 + 1/[4(2n - 1)] = (1 - k)\sigma_q^2 + k/4,$$

(13.22) $$k = 1/(2n - 1).$$

The rate of decay is thus $1/(2n - 1)$ and the rate of fixation of homogeneous sets of either sort is $1/(4n - 2)$.

The Fokker–Planck equation, given later (13.119), is satisfied by a rectangular distribution $\varphi(q) = 1$, as in the Mendelian case, although the rate of decay is only about half as great. There is, however, more dip near the extremes. The steady form distribution for $n = 16$ is shown in Figure 13.3.

There are likely to be complications. There may be an approach to equational apportionment of duplicants with consequent delay in segregation. On the other hand, duplicants may tend to remain together, giving more rapid segregation. Moreover, the number of elements apportioned to daughter cells is likely to be unequal.

The case of n similar entities, which duplicate with random apportionment of the numbers, is important. This may apply to B chromosomes of maize, kappa particles in Paramecium (Sonneborn 1943), and particles that carry respiratory enzymes in yeast (Ephrussi 1953). There may be the qualification, demonstrated in the case of the kappa particles (Preer 1950), that duplication of the particles may not keep in step with cell division. We will consider here, however, only the case in which duplication is synchronous with cell division so that the mean number is conserved.

With a given initial number, n, the distribution in the next generation is $[(1/2)(0) + (1/2)(1)]^{2n}$. The total frequency array spreads rapidly. The spread is asymmetrical because the immediate variance from cells $(n/2)$ is proportional to the number of particles. Table 13.1 shows the distribution for eight generations on starting from a single particle. In the eighth generation the particle is absent in about 70% of the cell descendants, but more than

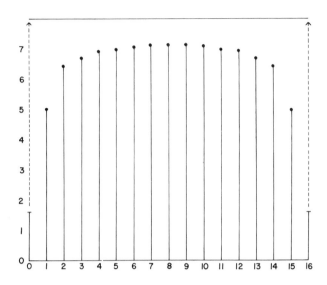

FIG. 13.3. Declining distribution of number of green plastids among cells with 16 mixed kinds, at a steady state with respect to form, assuming that duplication at cell division is followed by random segregation of 16 to each daughter cell. Each kind of homogeneous set is fixed at the rate $1/(4n - 2) = 1/62$.

10% have four or more, more than 1% nine or more, and about 0.1% thirteen or more.

Where the products of cell division are different organisms, there is likely to be selection. Moreover, there may be recurrent mutation. Thus Ephrussi accounted for the regular occurrence of about 1% yeast cells lacking respiratory enzymes because of absence of the pertinent cytoplasmic particles as the consequence of a balance between mutation rate, segregation of particles, and selection against total absence.

The Steady State Distributions under Mutation and Immigration

The changing distributions of gene frequencies under inbreeding, uncomplicated by systematic pressures, are of interest for laboratory experiments but of little importance in the theory of evolution. In nature, in the absence of any secular trend in conditions, each gene frequency may be expected to approach a certain equilibrium value under the pressures of recurrent mutation, selection, and immigration (as brought out in preceding chapters), but

TABLE 13.1. Distribution through eight cell divisions of entities, starting from one, if these duplicate with each cell division and are apportioned to daughter cells at random.

GENERATION	0	1	2	3	4	5	6	7	8	9	10	11	12	13	14	15	16	17	18	Percentage Fixed
0	0	1	0																	
1	0.2500	0.5000	0.2500																	25.000
2	.3906	.3125	.2188	0.0625	0.0156															18.750
3	.4834	.2173	.1765	.0776	.0326	0.0093	0.0027	0.0005	0.0001											15.234
4	.5502	.1612	.1427	.0767	.0404	.0173	.0074	.0027	.0010	0.0003	0.0001									12.913
5	.6008	.1249	.1171	.0710	.0426	.0221	.0115	.0055	.0026	.0011	.0005	0.0002	0.0001							11.246
6	.6406	.1000	.0976	.0641	.0420	0245	.0143	.0079	.0043	.0023	.0012	.0006	.0003	0.0001	0.0001	0.0001				9.981
7	.6729	.0820	.0826	.0575	.0400	.0253	.0160	.0098	.0059	.0034	.0020	.0011	.0006	.0004	.0002	.0001	0.0001	0.0001		8.984
8	0.6996	0.0686	0.0708	0.0515	0.0375	0.0252	0.0169	0.0110	0.0071	0.0045	0.0028	0.0018	0.0011	0.0007	0.0004	0.0002	0.0001	0.0001	0.0001	8.178

this equilibrium may be expected to be disturbed continually by random processes, always including the effects of accidents of sampling but also in general those of fluctuations in the systematic pressures. The opposition between the effects of the systematic pressures directed toward the equilibrium value, $\hat{q}$, and the cumulative effects of random processes should result in a probability distribution that describes the frequency of occurrence of each value of the gene frequency, in the long run. This distribution is also that manifested at any given moment by this gene in an array of populations of the same size, all subject to the same conditions. A third interpretation is the distribution, in a single population, at any given moment, of the frequencies of all genes that are subject to exactly the same pressures and random processes.

These are, of course, all highly idealized situations, never fully realized in nature. Size of population, for example, is continually changing. It is indeed the essence of interdemic selection that some local populations are increasing systematically and others decreasing. As a population increases, sampling variance decreases and the probability distribution contracts, and vice versa. A formula that attempted to express this process in full would be so complicated as to be of little use for our purpose. Thus population size, N, will be treated in the formulas as if constant. The effect of fluctuations or of cyclic changes will be taken care of by use of the concept of effective population size, as discussed in chapter 7. The effect of systematic change will be indicated only by comparison of the steady state distributions at different values of N. Similar considerations apply to changes in the systematic pressures. For mathematical treatment of systematic changes in N, the reader may consult Feller (1955, 1966).

Since a particular gene in a particular population has only one gene frequency at a given time, the steady state distribution derived from the momentary pressures and random processes is to be looked upon as an index of momentary potentialities rather than as something that can be expected to be actually realized, except very roughly, as indicated above.

The distribution for a single gene is indeed not in itself of much importance, but the multifactorial distribution for all loci involved in an interaction system is of primary importance in the aspect of evolutionary theory in which the steps consist of transitions from control by one interaction system to control by a superior one. This can occur only if such transitions are made possible by joint action of random processes and selection. The distributions for single genes are mainly important as cross sections of the unwieldy multifactorial distributions considered in the next chapter.

This steady state distribution can be arrived at in various ways. It is desirable to derive it first for the limiting case in which mutation is occurring in both directions but at so low a rate that its effect is negligible except in preventing permanent fixation of either allele. The appropriate integral equation is identical with (13.7) except that there is no decay of frequencies (right-hand member merely $\varphi(q_1)$).

It may be found by trial that the equation is now satisfied if $\varphi(q) = C_1/q$ or $C_2/(1 - q)$ or a combination:

$$(13.23) \qquad \varphi(q) = \frac{C_1}{q} + \frac{C_2}{1 - q}.$$

This equation takes no account, however, of the exchanges between the terminal classes, $f(0)$, $f(1)$, and the neighboring classes. Assuming that the amount of loss or fixation from these per generation is equal to about half the *theoretical* frequency of the adjacent subterminal classes $f[1/(2N)]$ and $f[1 - 1/(2N)]$, respectively, as found exactly in the case of the pure inbreeding effect, and that the rates of mutation from and to the gene in question are u and v respectively, the balance of exchanges may be written:

$$(13.24) \quad \begin{aligned} 2Nvf(0) &= (1/2)f[1/(2N)], \\ 2Nuf(1) &= (1/2)f[1 - 1/(2N)]. \end{aligned}$$

Under the assumption that mutation pressures are negligible except for these terminal exchanges, nearly all populations may be expected to accumulate in the terminal classes with unchanged mean gene frequencies.

$$(13.25) \quad \begin{aligned} f(0) &\approx 1 - \bar{q} = u/(u + v), \\ f(1) &\approx \quad\;\; \bar{q} = v/(u + v). \end{aligned}$$

In a steady state, the amounts of mutation at both boundaries must be the same, approximately $2Nuv/(u + v)$. This implies that $f[1/(2N)] = f[1 - 1/(2N)]$ and that the steady state distribution is symmetrical in the heterallelic portion (Fig. 13.4).

$$(13.26) \quad \varphi(q) = C/q(1 - q), \qquad C = 1/\{2[\log (2N - 1) + 0.577]\}$$

(Wright 1931).

If C_1 and C_2 are not the same there is a net flux from one terminal class to the other, without appreciable effect on the intermediate classes in the limiting case of extremely low mutation rates.

On calculation, the amount of loss or fixation from the classes near the boundary is only 0.4587 times the theoretical subterminal frequency. For the amount of fixation to be exactly 0.5 times this frequency, the actual frequency must be somewhat greater than given by the formula, contrary to the situation in a rectangular distribution. Most of the contribution to loss or fixation is due to the subterminal class. It would have to be 1.112 times its value, calculated by the above formula for loss or fixation, to be brought up to 0.5 times the uncorrected value.

The exact distribution can readily be calculated in the case of populations of three monoecious individuals (Wright 1931):

	Population	Exact	Frequency $Cq^{-1}(1 - q)^{-1}$
	$5A{:}1a$	0.275	0.263
	$4A{:}2a$	.154	.164
(13.27)	$3A{:}3a$	.141	.146
	$2A{:}4a$	.154	.164
	$1A{:}5a$	0.275	0.263
		0.999	1.000
	Terminal exchange	0.108	0.110

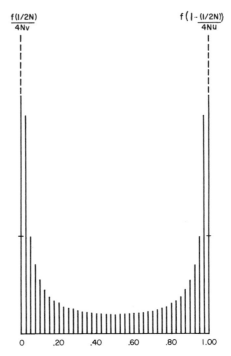

Fig. 13.4. Steady state distribution of gene frequencies with very low mutation rates, u and v (redrawn from Wright 1931, Fig. 5).

The terminal exchange is here $5/12$ ($= (2N - 1)/4N$) times the estimated subterminal class from the formula $Cq^{-1}(1 - q)^{-1}$.

Fisher (1930a) calculated the actual values for the distribution of neutral mutations corresponding to the approximate distribution C/q, discussed later. This does not differ appreciably from $Cq^{-1}(1 - q)^{-1}$ in the subterminal region.

	m	Exact	Cq^{-1}
	1	1.120458	1.000000
	2	0.476886	0.500000
(13.28)	3	0.335932	0.333333
	4	0.250548	0.250000
	5	0.199881	0.200000
	—	—	—
	$\sum e^{-m}f_m$	0.500000	0.458675

If there are systematic pressures (Δq) on gene frequency that must be taken into account, and random processes are represented only by those from accidents of sampling, the equilibrium condition is represented by the following, using p for $1 - q$:

$$(13.29) \quad \frac{\Gamma(2N)}{p_1 q_1 \Gamma(2Np_1)\Gamma(2Nq_1)} \int_0^1 (q + \Delta q)^{2Nq_1}(p - \Delta q)^{2Np_1}\varphi(q)dq = \varphi(q_1).$$

Approximate solutions were obtained (Wright 1931) in the case of reversible recurrent mutation by assuming that $\varphi(q)$ is of the type $q^x(1 - q)^y$. In the case of selection in favor of a semidominant gene, the form $e^{2Nsq}(C_0 + C_1 q + C_2 q^2 + \cdots)/q(1 - q)$ was assumed and (Wright 1938b, 1942) in the case of selection with any degree of dominance ($\Delta q = (s + tq)q(1 - q)$), the same form was assumed except for addition of the term Ntq^2 to the exponent of e.

We will return to this method in connection with the case of steady flux. The most general solution for a steady state by this method was for the case $\Delta q = v(1 - q) - uq - m(q - Q) + (s + tq)q(1 - q)$, and $\sigma_{\Delta q}^2 = q(1 - q)/2N$:

$$(13.30) \quad \varphi(q) = Ce^{4Nsq + 2Ntq^2}q^{4N(mQ + v) - 1}(1 - q)^{4N[m(1 - Q) + u] - 1}.$$

The method depends on evaluation of infinite series, and the variability is restricted to that due to sampling. We will take up next a more general method of obtaining steady state distributions.

Steady State with Respect to all Moments

The formula was obtained (Wright 1937, 1938b) by equating the mean and variance of the distribution before and after the occurrence of any systematic change (Δq) and any random change (δq). This mode of demonstration was later extended to include identity of all moments before and after (Wright 1952b). The basic equation is as follows:

$$(13.31) \quad \sum_{q=0}^{1} \sum_{\delta q = -q}^{1-q} \left\{ [q - \bar{q} + \Delta q + \delta q]^n f(\delta q)f(q) = \sum_{q=0}^{1} (q - \bar{q})^n f(q) \right\}.$$

On expanding the left-hand member in powers of $(q - \bar{q})$ and of $(\Delta q + \delta q)$, the first term cancels the right-hand member. It is to be noted that the following hold for *random* deviations which are *uncorrelated* with deviations of q from $\bar{q}$, and with δq:

$$\sum [\delta q f(\delta q)] = 0,$$
$$\sum [(\delta q)^2 f(\delta q)] = \sigma_{\delta q}^2 = \sigma_{\Delta q}^2,$$
$$\sum \sum \{[\delta q (q - \bar{q})] f(\delta q) f(q)\} = 0,$$
$$\sum \sum \{[\delta q \Delta q] f(\delta q) f(q)\} = 0.$$

It may be well to note that while "Δq" should logically refer to the total change and thus $\overline{\Delta q}$ to the systematic component, it has seemed best to use the simpler form, Δq, throughout for the latter, and to use ($\Delta q + \delta q$), as above for the total change.

Unless $\sigma^2_{\Delta q}$ is of the order Δq or greater, the latter dominates so much that the distribution spreads very little from the equilibrium value, $\hat{q}$. The case of most interest is that in which $(\Delta q)^2$, $(\delta q)^3$, $\Delta q (\delta q)^2$, and higher powers may be treated as negligible. With these assumptions (13.31) reduces to the following:

$$(13.32) \quad \sum_{q=0}^{1} (q - \bar{q})^{n-1} \Delta q f(q) + \left(\frac{n-1}{2}\right) \sum_{q=0}^{1} [(q - \bar{q})^{n-2}\sigma^2_{\Delta q} f(q)] = 0.$$

It is convenient to substitute integration for summation, $\varphi(q)\ dq$ for $f(q)$, and represent $\Delta q \varphi(q)\ dq$ as the differential, $d\chi(q)$, of a new function

$$(13.33) \quad \int_0^1 (q - \bar{q})^{n-1} d\chi(q) + \frac{n-1}{2} \int_0^1 (q - \bar{q})^{n-2}\sigma^2_{\Delta q}\varphi(q)\ dq = 0.$$

On integrating the first term by parts, it becomes

$$(13.34) \quad [\chi(q)(q - \bar{q})^{n-1}]_0^1 - (n-1) \int_0^1 \chi(q)(q - \bar{q})^{n-2}\ dq.$$

If $n = 1$, then $[\chi(q)]_0^1 = 0$, from (13.33) and (13.34). Thus

$$(13.35) \quad \chi(1) = \chi(0)$$

and

$$(13.36) \quad \begin{aligned} [\chi(q)(q - \bar{q})^{n-1}]_0^1 &= \chi(1)[(1 - \bar{q})^{n-1} - (-\bar{q})^{n-1}] \\ &= (n-1)\chi(1) \int_0^1 (q - \bar{q})^{n-2}\ dq. \end{aligned}$$

Equation (13.33) now becomes

$$(13.37) \quad \int_0^1 (q - \bar{q})^{n-2}[\chi(1) - \chi(q) + (1/2)\sigma^2_{\Delta q}\varphi(q)]\ dq = 0.$$

Thus *all* moments are the same before and after occurrence of change of gene frequency, if the following holds:

$$(13.38) \quad \chi(q) - \chi(1) = (1/2)\sigma^2_{\Delta q}\varphi(q).$$

From this and the definition of $d\chi(q)/dq$:

$$(13.39) \quad \begin{aligned} \frac{d}{dq} \log [\chi(q) - \chi(1)] &= \frac{d\chi(q)}{dq} \Big/ [\chi(q) - \chi(1)] \\ &= 2\ \Delta q \varphi(q)/\sigma^2_{\Delta q}\varphi(q), \end{aligned}$$

(13.40) $\log [\chi(q) - \chi(1)] = \log (C/2) + 2 \int (\Delta q/\sigma_{\Delta q}^2)\, dq$,

(13.41) $\chi(q) - \chi(1) = (C/2) \exp \left[2 \int \Delta q/\sigma_{\Delta q}^2 \right] dq$.

Equating the two expressions for $\chi(q) - \chi(1)$ of (13.38) and (13.41):

(13.42) $\varphi(q) = (C/\sigma_{\Delta q}^2) \exp \left[2 \int (\Delta q/\sigma_{\Delta q}^2) \right] dq$, $\quad C \int_0^1 \varphi(q)\, dq = 1$.

This is the desired formula. The most general steady state solution yielded by the integral equation (13.30) is given at once by substitution of Δq and $\sigma_{\Delta q}^2$ in (13.42).

The Fokker–Planck Equation

Formula (13.42) can also be derived as the steady state solution of the Fokker–Planck partial differential equation of physics, also known as the Kolmogorov forward equation (Wright 1945b).

Equation (13.38) was arrived at as the condition that all moments remain unchanged. Recalling that $d\chi(q)/dq$ was defined as $\Delta q\varphi(q)$, it may be seen that differentiation with respect to q leads to the following ordinary differential equation, of which (13.42) is the solution:

(13.43) $\Delta q\varphi(q) - (1/2) \dfrac{d}{dq} [\sigma_{\Delta q}^2 \varphi(q)] = 0$.

In this, $\Delta q\varphi(q)$ is obviously the proportion of the frequencies that tends to be carried past the specified value of q in a generation by the systematic pressure, while the other term, recalling that $\sigma_{\Delta q}^2 = \sum (\delta q)^2 f(\delta q)$, represents, somewhat less obviously, the net proportion that tends to be carried past q in the opposite direction in a generation by random processes.

If we consider a case in which these terms do not balance, the difference, at a specified value of q and a specified time (t), between the amounts of change in the above two proportions over a class range should give the change in the frequency of this class in a generation.

(13.44) $\dfrac{\partial \varphi(q, t)}{\partial t} = (1/2) \dfrac{\partial^2}{\partial q^2} [\sigma_{\Delta q}^2 \varphi(q, t)] - \dfrac{\partial}{\partial q} [\Delta q\varphi(q, t)]$.

This is the Fokker–Planck equation, which reduces to (13.43) if the left-hand member is zero, and hence gives (13.42) as its solution for the steady state.

Special Cases

We will come back to this equation later. It is desirable now to take up various special steady states.

The simplest cases are those in which the gene frequencies are affected only by the linear pressures from recurrent mutation or immigration, apart from accidents of sampling. In most cases, substitution of the formulas for Δq and $\sigma^2_{\Delta q}$ in (13.42) leads to expressions that require numerical integration for determination of the coefficient C, and such properties as mean and variance. In these cases, however, there is no difficulty.

Recurrent Mutation

$$\Delta q = v(1 - q) - uq, \qquad \sigma^2_{\Delta q} = q(1 - q)/2N,$$

(13.45) $$\varphi(q) = \frac{\Gamma(4Nu + 4Nv)}{\Gamma(4Nu)\Gamma(4Nv)} q^{4Nv-1}(1 - q)^{4Nu-1},$$

(13.46) $$\bar{q} = \int_0^1 q\varphi(q)\, dq = \frac{v}{u + v} = \hat{q},$$

(13.47) $$\sigma_q{}^2 = \int_0^1 (q - \bar{q})^2\varphi(q)\, dq = \frac{\bar{q}(1 - \bar{q})}{4N(u + v) + 1}.$$

Immigration

$$\Delta q = -m(q - Q) = mQ(1 - q) - m(1 - Q)q, \qquad \sigma^2_{\Delta q} = q(1 - q)/2N,$$

(13.48) $$\varphi(q) = \frac{\Gamma(4Nm)}{\Gamma(4NmQ)\Gamma[4Nm(1 - Q)]} q^{4NmQ-1}(1 - q)^{4Nm(1-Q)-1},$$

(13.49) $$\bar{q} = Q.$$

The Fokker–Planck equation was applied to this case by Kolmogorov (1935) who noted the agreement with the result from the integral equation (Wright 1931).

(13.50) $$\sigma_q{}^2 = \frac{Q(1 - Q)}{4Nm + 1}.$$

The formulas are essentially the same, mQ and $m(1 - Q)$ in the case of immigration taking the place of v and u, respectively, and m that of $(u + v)$.

The formula for the variance, derived here from the distribution, agrees with the formula $\sigma_q{}^2 = Q(1 - Q)/[2N - (2N - 1)(1 - m)^2]$ derived from other considerations in chapter 12 (12.6) if the term $(-2Nm^2 - 2m + m^2)$ is negligible.

Figure 13.5 shows forms taken by the distribution with $Q = 0.5$ and various values of Nm and the corresponding values of $F = 1/(4Nm + 1)$.

If N and m are taken literally, the product Nm is the actual number of

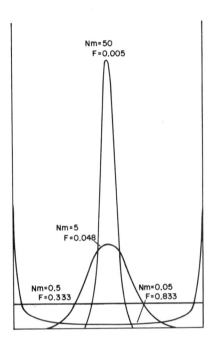

FIG. 13.5. Steady state distributions of gene frequencies under immigration at the rate m in populations of size N for various values of Nm. The corresponding values of F are shown (essentially from Wright 1931, Fig. 6).

immigrants per generation and it may be seen from the formula that the variance would ordinarily be exceedingly small. However, as brought out in chapter 12, effective N may usually be expected to be much smaller than the number of mature individuals, and effective m may be expected to be much smaller than the actual proportion of immigrants because of the usual strong correlation between the gene frequency of the latter and that of the deme that receives them. As may be seen from Figure 13.5, random drift with $Q = 0.5$ extends to occasional fixation if effective Nm is 0.5; is fairly extensive if effective Nm is 5, and is not negligible if $Nm = 50$.

Selection Balanced by Mutation

The simplest case under this head is that in which there is semidominance. In reference to the favorable allele:

(13.51)
$$\Delta q = v(1 - q) - uq + sq(1 - q),$$
$$\sigma_{\Delta q}^2 = q(1 - q)/2N,$$
$$\varphi(q) = Ce^{4Nsq}q^{4Nv-1}(1 - q)^{4Nu-1}.$$

This may be compared with the case of complete dominance of the favorable allele.

(13.52)
$$\Delta q = v(1 - q) - uq + tq(1 - q)^2,$$
$$\sigma^2_{\Delta q} = q(1 - q)/2N,$$
$$\varphi(q) = Ce^{-2Nt(1-q)^2}q^{4Nv-1}(1 - q)^{4Nu-1}.$$

Figure 13.6 compares these distributions in cases in which $u = v$, with semidominance in a, b, and c and recessiveness in d, e, and f. Effective population size ranges from $1/(40u)$ in a and d, $10/(40u)$ in b and e, and $100/(40u)$ in c and f; and selection is practically negligible (solid line $s = u/10$ and $t = u/5$), or of the order of the mutant rate (not distinguishable from preceding in a and d, broken line in b and e, with $s = u$ and $t = 2u$), or of higher order (dotted line, $s = 10u$ and $t = 20u$). In the more usual cases in which the selection coefficient is 100-fold or more greater than the mutation rate, the distributions would be crowded toward the right side with mean of $1 - u/s$ in the case of semidominance, and $1 - \sqrt{(u/t)}$ is that of complete dominance, assuming a large enough effective N to give an i-shaped distribution ($4Nv$, $4Nu$ greater than 1). The value of v, if small, is unimportant in these cases.

A great many deleterious genes are undoubtedly carried in all natural populations at low frequencies by this mechanism. This includes recessive lethals. The distribution of these is thus of considerable interest (Wright 1937). The term $\bar{w} = 1 - tq^2$ in the denominator of the formula for selection pressure is not here treated as if one.

(13.53)
$$\Delta q = v(1 - q) - q^2(1 - q)/(1 - q^2) = v(1 - q) - q^2/(1 + q),$$
$$\varphi(q) = C(1 - q^2)^{2N}q^{4Nv-1}(1 - q)^{-1}.$$

The mean can be expressed in gamma functions by substitution of x for q^2 and ignoring $(1 - q)^{-1}$, which is very nearly one throughout the distribution.

(13.54)
$$C = \frac{2(1 + v)\Gamma[2N(1 + v)]}{\Gamma(2N)\Gamma(2Nv)},$$

(13.55)
$$\bar{q} \approx \frac{\Gamma(2Nv + 0.5)\Gamma(2N + 2Nv)}{\Gamma(2Nv)\Gamma(2N + 2Nv + 0.5)} \approx \frac{\Gamma(2Nv + 0.5)}{\Gamma(2Nv)\sqrt{(2N)}}.$$

For values of $2Nv$ that are considerably larger than one, this approaches $\sqrt{v}$, the equilibrium point, as expected. If, on the other hand, $2Nv$ is a small fraction, q approaches $v\sqrt{(2\pi N)}$.

Figure 13.7 shows some of the forms taken by the distribution of a recessive lethal maintained by a mutation rate of 10^{-5} in populations of various sizes. The mean gene frequency is $v = 0.0032$ in very large populations.

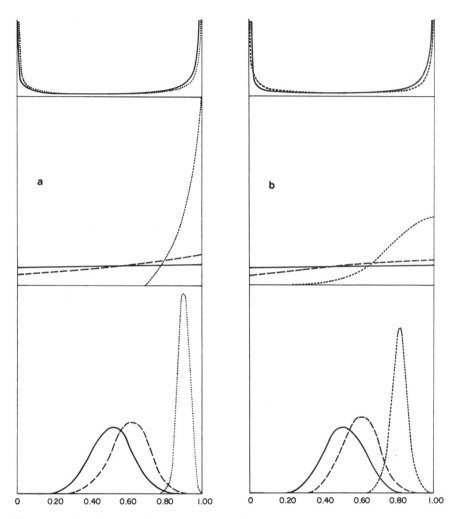

FIG. 13.6. Steady state distributions of gene frequencies where weak selection is balanced by recurrent mutation. Semidominant selection at the left (a, b, c), dominant at the right (d, e, f), with values given in the text (essentially from Wright 1937, Figs. 1–6).

This is approximately realized in the case of $N = 10^6$. With $N = 10^5$, the gene is always present but $\bar{q}$ is slightly reduced (0.0030). With $N = 10^4$, the gene is absent about 15% of the time and $\bar{q} = 0.0020$. With $N = 10^3$, it is

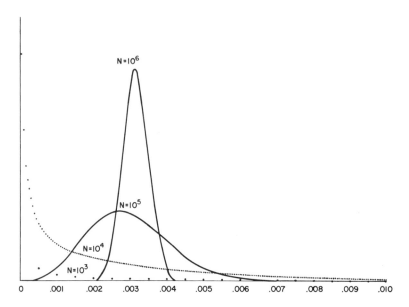

FIG. 13.7. Steady state distributions of lethal recessive genes which recur at the rate 10^{-5} per generation in populations of various sizes (Wright 1937, Fig. 9).

absent about 87% and $\bar{q} = 0.0008$. The case of 10^2 is not shown because the gene is absent about 99% of the time and $\bar{q}$ is only 0.00026. In selfed lines ($N = 1$) the gene is absent 99.996% of the time giving $\bar{q} = 0.00002$ ($= 2v$).

Nei (1968) has derived an approximate distribution for completely recessive *individuals* ($t = q^2$) with selective disadvantage s, by ignoring the usually negligible term $(1 - q)^{-1}$ in the full formula.

$$\varphi(t) \approx [(2Ns)^{2Nv} e^{-2Nst} t^{2Nv-1}]/\Gamma(2Nv).$$

He gives the mean gene frequency as approximately

$$\bar{q} = \Gamma(2Nv + 0.5)/[\Gamma(2Nv)/\sqrt{(2Ns)}]$$

in agreement with (13.55) for $s = 1$.

Similarly, he has derived an approximate distribution for incompletely recessive lethals, with selective disadvantage, s, of heterozygotes:

$$\varphi(q) \approx [(4Ns)^{4Nv} e^{-4Nsq} q^{4Nv-1}]/\Gamma(4Nv)$$

with mean v/s and variance $\bar{q}/(4Ns)$.

Heterotic Alleles and Mutation

Heterotic alleles were described in chapter 3 as giving stable equilibrium at $\hat{q} = t/(s + t)$ where s is the selective disadvantage of the gene in question and t that of its allele relative to the heterozygote. This, however, refers to populations so large that the effects of accidents of sampling are negligible. Otherwise there is an appreciable chance that all gametes may happen to carry the same allele in some generation, a situation from which the other can only be restored by mutation or immigration. Reversible mutation will be assumed.

$$\Delta q = v(1 - q) - uq - (s + t)q(1 - q)(q - \hat{q}), \qquad \hat{q} = t/(s + t),$$

$$(13.56) \qquad \varphi(q) = Ce^{-2N(s + t)(q - \hat{q})^2}q^{4Nv - 1}(1 - q)^{4Nu - 1}.$$

Figures 13.8a and 13.8b illustrate symmetrical ($\hat{q} = 0.50$) and asymmetrical ($\hat{q} = 0.667$) cases.

In the absence of mutation (or immigration), the probability of complete fixation of one or the other allele is of course greater the smaller the value of $N(s + t)$ and, especially as brought out by A. Robertson (1962), the greater the deviation of q from 0.50. Robertson found that if the equilibrium frequency lies outside the range 0.2 and 0.8, selection for the heterozygote may, over a large range of population sizes, in fact magnify the effect of reduced size in leading to fixation. This was based on consideration of the ratio of fixation under heterotic selection in the absence of mutation to that due to the inbreeding effect by itself, $1/(2N)$. Similarly, he showed that the amount of heterozygosis at equilibrium in the presence of both reversible recurrent mutation and heterozygous advantage may be less than that under the same mutation rates alone if the equilibrium value due to the selection is far from 0.50. He found that the range of equilibrium gene frequencies over which heterozygote advantage always conserves variability is slightly greater than that invariably leading to retardation of fixation in the absence of mutation. It covers the values 0.15 to 0.85 and is at its narrowest when $N(s + t) = 8$. He found that as the equilibrium values become more extreme, it becomes necessary to go to higher values of $N(s + t)$ before the selection increases the genetic variability above that found in its absence, the critical value being 50 if $\hat{q} = 0.1$ or 0.9 and 420 if $\hat{q} = 0.05$ or 0.95.

Some of the properties of the distribution are shown in Table 13.2 for populations of 100, 1000, and 10000 ($u = v = 10^{-6}$) and with various values of the larger selection coefficient ($s = 1$, 0.1, and 0.01) and various values of the equilibrium value for selection ($\hat{q} = 0.50$ from $t = s$, $\hat{q} = 0.30$ from $t = (3/7)s$, and $\hat{q} = 0.10$ from $t = (1/9)s$). The proportions in the heterallelic classes and in the two homallelic classes, f_0 and f_1, are shown, and

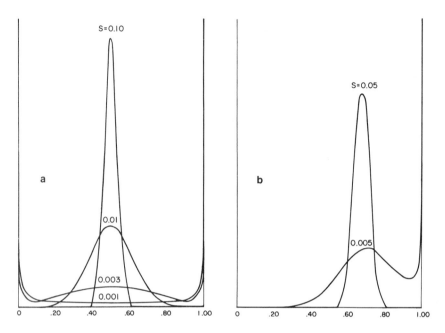

FIG. 13.8. Steady state distributions of heterotic genes in populations of 1,000: (a) with equal selection against both homozygotes (s = 0.001, 0.003, 0.01, or 0.1); (b) with twice as much selection against one (t = 0.01 or 0.10) as against the other (s = 0.005 or 0.05), $\hat{q}$ = $t/(s + t)$ = 2/3. There must be mutation at an appreciable rate to balance fixation in the asymmetrical case, the ordinates in which are much exaggerated (Wright 1948, Fig. 6; 1964, Fig. 3, by permission, Univ. of Wisconsin Press, © 1964 by The Regents of Univ. of Wisconsin).

also the mean and standard deviation of the distribution, both including and excluding the homallelic classes. These means and standard deviations have been calculated by numerical integration from ordinates at frequent values of q, especially near the extremes.

In the case of populations of 10,000 the distributions are all compact i-shaped ones, with no appreciable fixation, except in that with weakest selection and lowest $\hat{q}$ from selection (s = 0.01, $\hat{q}$ = 0.10) in which case the more favorable allele is fixed nearly half the time, and the mean, $\bar{q}$, is much less than 0.10, not only in the total distribution but even in the unfixed portion ($\bar{q}$ = 0.0612). Some explanation may seem required for the existence of any variability in the case of balanced lethals (s = 1, t = 1) since only heterozygotes, $\hat{q}$ = 0.50, can be present. The formula for the distribution was derived, however, on the assumption that in the preceding generation it

TABLE 13.2. Properties of the distribution of gene frequencies where there is selection against both homozygotes and recurrent mutation in both directions, $u = v = 10^{-6}$ and $N = 10^2, 10^3$, or 10^4. Selective disadvantage of less favorable homozygotes (if different): $s = 1$ (lethal), 0.1, or 0.01. Equilibrium value relative to selection $\hat{q} = t/(s + t) = 0.50, 0.30$, or 0.10. The frequencies of fixation, $f(0)$ and $f(1)$, and $\bar{q}$ and σ_q, are shown for both the total distribution and the heterallelic portion.

N	s	$\hat{q}$	f_0	$1-f_0-f_1$	f_1	$\bar{q}$	σ_q	$\bar{q}$	σ_q
				Amounts of Fixation		Total Distribution		Exclusive of $f(0)$ and $f(1)$	
10^2	0.01	0.50	0.4983	0.0034	0.4983	0.5000	0.4996	0.5000	0.3653
		.30	.7540	0.0028	.2432	.2442	.4293	.3462	.3495
		.10	.8524	0.0021	.1452	.1459	.3526	.2686	.3207
	0.1	.50	.0947	0.8106	.0947	.5000	.2456	.5000	.1196
		.30	.9901	0.0098	0	.0023	.0276	.2368	.1424
		.10	.9979	0.0021	0	.0002	.0055	.0791	.0904
	1	.50	0	1	0	.5000	.0351	—	—
		.30	0	1	0	.2965	.0391	—	—
		.10	.9947	0.0053	0	.0004	0063	0727	.0481
10^3	0.01	.50	.0009	0.9982	0.0009	.5000	.1382	.5000	.1199
		.30	.8941	0.1059	0	.0232	.0844	.2196	.1558
		.10	.9703	0.0297	0	.0017	.0175	.0572	.0837
	0.1	.50	0	1	0	.5000	.0351	—	—
		.30	0	1	0	.2965	.0408	—	—
		.10	.9305	0.0695	0	.0045	.0212	.0644	.0456
	1	.50	0	1	0	.5000	.0108	—	—
		.30	0	1	0	.2997	.0129	—	—
		.10	0	1	0	.0979	.0141	—	—
10^4	0.01	.50	0	1	0	.5000	.0245	—	—
		.30	0	1	0	.2966	.0407	—	—
		.10	0.4864	0.5136	0	.0315	.0482	0.0612	0.0519
	0.1	.50	0	1	0	.5000	.0078	—	—
		.30	0	1	0	.2997	.0129	—	—
		.10	0	1	0	.0980	.0149	—	—
	1	.50	0	1	0	.5000	.0035	—	—
		.30	0	1	0	.3000	.0041	—	—
		0.10	0	1	0	0.0998	0.0047	—	—

has been modified by accidents of sampling (δq) as well as by systematic pressures (Δq). It thus applies to distribution of gametes, instead of zygotes. The selection in the case of balanced lethals brings all gene frequencies to the value 0.50, but sampling gives a standard deviation of $\sqrt{[\bar{q}(1 - \bar{q})/2N]}$ which in this case is 0.0035.

In the case of $N = 1,000$, there is no appreciable fixation if one of the alleles is lethal ($s = 1$) even if $\hat{q}$ is as low as 0.10. There is also no appreciable fixation and little depression of the mean if $s = 0.1$ and $\hat{q}$ is 0.50 or 0.30, but if $\hat{q}$ is 0.10, the favorable gene is fixed 93% of the time and the mean is much reduced (from 0.10 to 0.0644) when both alleles are present. If $s = 0.01$ there is a little fixation even in the symmetrical case ($\hat{q} = 0.50$ and $f_0 = f_1 = 0.0009$). In this case the standard deviation in the unfixed portion is very large even though still i-shaped ($\sigma = 0.1199$). With $s = 0.01$ and $\hat{q} = 0.30$, the favorable allele is fixed most of the time ($f_0 = 0.8941$) and the distribution spreads over most of the range. With $s = 0.01$, $\hat{q} = 0.10$, the favorable allele is fixed 97.03% of the time, the mean frequency when present at all has fallen to 0.0572. There is still, however, rather wide variation ($\sigma = 0.0837$ in the unfixed portion).

In the case of $N = 100$, appreciable fixation is avoided only if selection against both homozygotes is strong ($s = 1$, $\hat{q} = 0.50$ or 0.30 among cases in the table). If the unfavorable allele is lethal ($s = 1$) and $\hat{q} = 0.10$, the favorable allele is nearly always fixed ($f_0 = 0.9947$) and the mean frequency of the lethal when present at all is only 0.0727. In the symmetrical case with $s = t = 0.1$ and $\hat{q} = 0.50$, there is considerable fixation ($f_0 = f_1 = 0.0947$). With $s = 0.1$ and $\hat{q} = 0.30$, the favorable allele is fixed nearly all of the time ($f_0 = 0.9901$), but there is so much variability when both are present that the chance of fixation of the unfavorable allele is not wholly inappreciable (0.00001). It becomes so if $q = 0.10$, in which case the favorable allele is fixed 99.79% of the time. With selection against both homozygotes only 0.01 or less there is fixation of one or the other nearly all of the time. If $\hat{q} = 0.50$, then $f_0 = f_1 = 49.83\%$. If $s = 0.01$ and $\hat{q} = 0.30$, the favorable allele is fixed 75.40% of the time but the unfavorable one is fixed 24.32% of the time. Even if $s = 0.01$ and $\hat{q} = 0.10$, the unfavorable allele is fixed 14.52% of the time, the favorable one of course being fixed nearly all of the rest of the time (85.24%).

Selection a Function of Gene Frequency

As brought out in chapter 5, it becomes necessary to use the formula

$$(13.57) \qquad \Delta q = q(1 - q) \sum \left(W \frac{\partial f}{\partial q} \right) \bigg/ 2\overline{W}$$

for selection pressure in cases in which selection is a function of gene frequencies, this, however, can always be put in the more convenient form

$$(1/2)q(1 - q) \frac{dF(W/\overline{W})}{dq}$$

in the case of single genes. In conjunction with the sampling variance, this leads to the following for the distribution of gene frequencies:

$$(13.58) \qquad \varphi(q) = Ce^{2NF(W/\overline{W})}q^{4NmQ-1}(1 - q)^{4Nm(1-Q)-1},$$

in which mQ may be supplemented or replaced by v, and $m(1 - Q)$ by u where required.

We will consider only the simple case in which each allele has a selective advantage when rare, but a disadvantage above a critical frequency, and heterozygotes are always exactly intermediate so that there is no complication from the effects of heterotic advantage. A small amount of recurrent mutation in each direction is assumed to prevent possible irreversible fixation.

	f	W	
A_1A_1	q^2	$1 + a - bq$	$\overline{W} = 1 - (a - bq)(1 - 2q)$
A_1A_2	$2q(1 - q)$	1	$\Delta q = v(1 - q) - uq + q(1 - q)(a - bq)$
A_2A_2	$(1 - q)^2$	$1 - a + bq$	$\hat{q} = a/b, \qquad a < b$

$$(13.59) \qquad \varphi(q) = Ce^{-2Nb(q-\hat{q})^2}q^{4Nv-1}(1 - q)^{4Nu-1}.$$

The probability distribution is the same as in the case of heterozygous advantage if a is homologized with t and b with $s + t$.

Selection Balanced by Immigration

As noted earlier, the most important sort of balance among opposing pressures from the standpoint of evolutionary theory is probably that between local selection and immigration in each deme. It may suffice to consider only that in which the selection coefficient has the form $(s + tq)$ that allows for any degree of dominance, including overdominance.

$$(13.60) \qquad \begin{aligned} \Delta q &= (s + tq)q(1 - q) - m(q - Q), \\ \varphi(q) &= Ce^{4Nsq+2Ntq^2}q^{4NmQ-1}(1 - q)^{4Nm(1-Q)-1}. \end{aligned}$$

Recurrent mutation is not included since it is usually negligible in comparison with immigration, but it may be included by interpreting Q above as $(mQ + v)/(m + u + v)$ and $(1 - Q)$ as $[m(1 - Q) + u]/(m + u + v)$.

Approximate equilibrium values were given in chapter 3 in the cases of semidominance, complete dominance, and heterozygote advantage.

Figure 13.9*a* shows the steady state distribution in cases of semidominance with three rates of immigration such that $m = 0.01, 0.001, 0.0001$, assuming that $N = 1,000, Q = 0.25, s = 0.0025$.

The figures bring out the profound change in the situation under different rates of immigration.

Figure 13.9*b* shows the distribution ($Q = 0.10, N = 1,000$) in which it is *s* that varies ($s = 0.01, 0.002, 0.001, 0.0001$) while $m = 0.001$ and $N = 1,000$ in all cases.

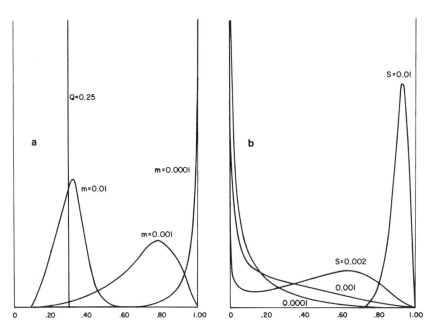

FIG. 13.9. Steady state distributions with balancing of selection and immigration, $Q = 0.25$ in populations of 1,000. In (*a*) $s = 0.0025, m = 0.0001, 0.001,$ or 0.01. In (*b*) $s = 0.0001, 0.001, 0.002,$ or 0.01; $m = 0.001$ (Wright 1942, Fig. 4; 1948, Fig. 7).

Random Fluctuations in Systematic Pressures

So far the only random process that has been considered has been that due to accidents of sampling. This section will be concerned with the effects of fluctuations in the systematic pressures and will be limited at first to systematic pressure of the form (Wright 1948).

(13.61) $\Delta q = \bar{s}q(1 - q) + (\bar{v} + \bar{m}\bar{Q})(1 - q) - [\bar{u} + \bar{m}(1 - \bar{Q})]q.$

Some simplification of the formulas can be achieved by using $\bar{m}$ in place of $(\bar{m} + \bar{u} + \bar{v})$ and $\bar{Q}$ in place of $(\bar{v} + \bar{m}\bar{Q})/(\bar{m} + \bar{u} + \bar{v})$ and thus reducing (13.61) to the form

(13.62) $\Delta q = \bar{s}q(1 - q) - \bar{m}(q - \bar{Q}).$

$$\textit{Fluctuations Only in Selection (Measured by } \sigma_s{}^2\textit{)}$$

$$\delta q = (s - \bar{s})q(1 - q),$$

$$\sigma_{\Delta q}^2 = \sigma_s{}^2 q^2 (1 - q)^2,$$

(13.63) $\varphi(q) = \dfrac{C}{q^2(1-q)^2} \left(\dfrac{q}{1-q}\right)^{(2/\sigma_s{}^2)[\bar{s}-m(1-2Q)]} \exp\left[-\dfrac{2m}{\sigma_s{}^2}\left(\dfrac{Q}{q} + \dfrac{1-Q}{1-q}\right)\right].$

$$\textit{Fluctuations Only in Amount of Immigration } (\sigma_m{}^2)$$

$$\delta q = -(m - \bar{m})(q - Q),$$

$$\sigma_{\Delta q}^2 = \sigma_m{}^2 (q - Q)^2,$$

(13.64) $\varphi(q) = C(q - Q)^{(2/\sigma_m{}^2)[s(1-2Q)-\bar{m}-\sigma_m{}^2]} \exp\{-2s[(q - Q)^2 + Q(1 - Q)]/[\sigma_m{}^2(q - Q)]\}.$

$$\textit{Fluctuations Only in Gene Frequency of Immigrants } (\sigma_Q{}^2)$$

$$\delta q = m(Q - \bar{Q}),$$

$$\sigma_{\Delta q}^2 = m^2 \sigma_Q{}^2,$$

(13.65) $\varphi(q) = C \exp\{[6m\bar{Q}q - 3q^2(m - s) - 2sq^3]/3m^2\sigma_Q{}^2\}.$

Figures 13.10a and 13.10b compare symmetrical distributions ($m = 0.01$, $Q = 0.5$) in which the variability of q is due wholly ($\sigma_s = 0$) to sampling in the former, $N = 10, 50, 100, 1{,}000$, but due wholly ($N \to \infty$) to fluctuations in selection in the latter ($\sigma_s = 0.5, 0.2, 0.1, 0.05$).

Figures 13.11a,b,c compare distributions in which the same average selection pressure, $\bar{s} = 0.01$, is balanced by the same average amount ($\bar{m} = 0.01$) and kind ($\bar{Q} = 0.25$) of immigration: $\Delta q = 0.0025 - 0.01q^2$, but with different sorts of fluctuations in gene frequency. Cases of sampling fluctuations are given in Figure 13.11a: $\sigma_{\Delta q}^2 = q(1 - q)/2N$ with $N = 10$, 100, or 1,000; of fluctuations in the selection coefficient in Figure 13.11b: $\sigma_{\Delta q}^2 = \sigma_s{}^2 q^2(1 - q)^2$ with $\sigma = 0.05, 0.10,$ or 0.20; of fluctuations in m or of Q in Figure 13.11c: $\sigma_{\Delta q}^2 = \sigma_m{}^2(q - 0.25)^2$, $\sigma_m = 0.07$ (almost the maximum) and $\sigma_{\Delta q}^2 = 0.0001\sigma_Q{}^2$, $\sigma_Q = 0.433$ (maximum).

Both fluctuations due to sampling and those in selection can bring about extensive random drift about the equilibrium point, but while the former

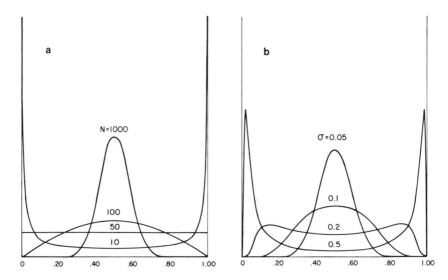

FIG. 13.10. Steady state distributions with immigration at rate 0.01, $Q = 0.50$. In (a) N varies (10, 50, 100, 1,000). In (b) the population is very large, but there is fluctuating selection, $\sigma_s = 0.05$, 0.1, 0.2, or 0.5 (Wright 1948, Figs. 1 and 2).

can in extreme cases bring about fixation or loss, the latter gives bimodal distributions which never lead by themselves to fixation or loss, as brought out by Kimura (1954, 1955c).

Fluctuations in amount, and especially in quality, of immigration bring about relatively little random drift. In the former, there can be no random drift below Q if $\hat{q} > Q$, or above if $\hat{q} < Q$. If the only pressure on gene frequency is that due to immigration, $\hat{q} = Q$, with the consequence that $\varphi(q)$ is infinitely larger at $q = Q$ than at any other value of q.

The absence of random drift in this case is an immediate consequence of the fact that $\sigma_{\Delta q}^2$ is merely a multiple of Δq.

Thus the occurrence of appreciable random drift from fluctuations in amount of immigration depends on strong opposition between the pressures of selection and immigration.

The absence of selection pressure reduces the distribution determined by fluctuation in the gene frequency of immigrants to a normal probability curve with variance $(1/2)m\sigma_Q^2$. Random drift is negligible unless m is so large that the conditions on which the equation for $\varphi(q)$ is based hold only roughly.

In this discussion, selection pressure has been treated only in the simplest case, that of semidominance. Kimura (1955c) has extended the theory of the effects of fluctuations in selection to include dominance in any degree.

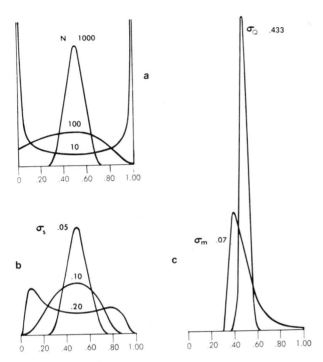

FIG. 13.11. Steady state distributions with the same local selection ($s = 0.01$) balanced by the same amount and kind of immigration ($m = 0.1$, $Q = 0.25$) but with different kinds of random drift. In (a) (upper left) $N = 10$, 100, or 1,000. In (b) (lower left) $\sigma_s = 0.05$, 0.1, or 0.2. In (c) (right) $\sigma_m = 0.07$ or $\sigma_Q = 0.433$ (Wright 1964, Figs. 5, 6, 7, reprinted by permission, Univ. of Wisconsin Press, © 1964 by The Regents of Univ. of Wisconsin).

In the case of a recessive gene and recurrent mutation in both directions:

$$\Delta q = v(1 - q) - uq - sq^2(1 - q),$$
$$\sigma_{\Delta q}^2 = \sigma_s{}^2 q^4(1 - q)^2,$$

(13.66) $$\varphi(q) = \frac{C}{q^4(1 - q)^2} \exp\left[-\frac{1}{\sigma_s{}^2} \Psi(q)\right],$$

in which

$$\psi(q) = \frac{2v}{3q^2} + \frac{v - u}{q^2} + \frac{2v - 4u - 2\bar{s}}{q} + \frac{2u}{1 - q}$$
$$+ (2v - 6u - 2\bar{s}) \log \frac{1 - q}{q}.$$

The case of heterotic loci requires consideration not only of the variances of both selective values but their covariance. It must suffice here to go into the following simple cases (Wright 1960a):

$$\Delta q = -(\bar{s} + \bar{t})q(1 - q)(q - \hat{q}), \qquad \hat{q} = \bar{t}/(\bar{s} + \bar{t}),$$

(13.67) $\qquad \delta q = q(1 - q)[(s - \bar{s})q - (t - \bar{t})(1 - q)],$

$$\sigma_{\Delta q}^2 = q^2(1 - q)^2[\sigma_s{}^2 q^2 + \sigma_t{}^2(1 - q)^2 - 2\sigma_s \sigma_t r_{st} q(1 - q)].$$

Consider first the case in which there is fluctuation merely in intensity ($r_{st} = 1$, $\hat{q}$ constant):

(13.68) $\qquad\qquad\qquad \sigma_{\Delta q}^2 = \sigma_{s+t}^2 q^2 (1 - q)^2 (q - \hat{q})^2.$

Here again, substitution in the formula for $\varphi(q)$ gives an expression in which the ordinate at $q = \hat{q}$ is always infinitely greater than at any other value of q, indicating that the distribution is confined to the equilibrium point.

If, however, s and t vary equally and in perfect negative correlation ($\sigma_s{}^2 = \sigma_t{}^2$, $r_{st} = -1$, $(s + t)$ is constant):

$$\sigma_{\Delta q}^2 = \sigma_t{}^2 q^2 (1 - q)^2,$$

(13.69) $\qquad \varphi(q) = \dfrac{\Gamma(a - 2)}{\Gamma(a\hat{q} - 1)\Gamma[a(1 - \hat{q}) - 1]} \, q^{a\hat{q} - 2}(1 - q)^{a(1 - \hat{q}) - 2},$

$$a = \frac{2(\bar{s} + \bar{t})}{\sigma_t{}^2},$$

$$\bar{q} = \frac{a\hat{q} - 1}{a - 2},$$

(13.70) $\qquad\qquad\qquad \sigma_q{}^2 = \dfrac{\hat{q}(1 - \hat{q})}{a - 1}.$

Both $\bar{s}$ and $\bar{t}$ must be positive if there is to be overdominance, on the average. Both must be small and $\sigma_t{}^2$ large for the amount of random drift to be large.

The preceding cases refer to populations so large that sampling variance may be ignored. In small populations, the effects of fluctuations in selective value are complicated by sampling errors (Kimura 1951, 1955c).

$$\Delta q = v(1 - q) - uq + \bar{s}q(1 - q),$$

$$\sigma_{\Delta q}^2 = \sigma_s{}^2 q^2 (1 - q)^2 + \frac{q(1 - q)}{2N},$$

$$\varphi(q) = Cq^{4Nv - 1}(1 - q)^{4Nu - 1}(\lambda_1 - q)^{4NA - 1}(q - \lambda_2)^{4NB - 1},$$

(13.71) $\qquad A = -\{(\bar{s}/2N\sigma_s{}^2) + u\lambda_1 - v\lambda_2\}/(\lambda_1 - \lambda_2),$

$$B = \{(\bar{s}/2N\sigma_s{}^2) - v\lambda_1 + u\lambda_2\}/(\lambda_1 - \lambda_2),$$

where λ_1 and λ_2 are the roots of the equation $\lambda^2 - \lambda - [1/(2N\sigma_s{}^2)] = 0$.

$$\lambda_1 = \frac{1}{2}\left[1 + \sqrt{\left(1 + \frac{2}{N\sigma^2}\right)}\right],$$

$$\lambda_2 = \frac{1}{2}\left[1 - \sqrt{\left(1 + \frac{2}{N\sigma^2}\right)}\right].$$

The case in which there is selection for a recessive and there are fluctuations in both the selection coefficient and sampling variance (Kimura 1951, 1955c) is still more complicated.

Whether to treat a secular change in selection, or in one of the other aspects of dispersion, as a new systematic pressure or as a random fluctuation may be a somewhat arbitrary matter. Here it is a question of the span of history with which one is concerned.

It may, indeed, sometimes be desirable to go a step further in analysis and distinguish between long-term fluctuations and those that occur in each generation (Wright 1955). The existence of long-term fluctuations is indicated by a correlation between the deviations from the mean in successive generations. Let $\delta x = b_{xx'}\,\delta x' + \delta\delta x$, where δx is the deviation of any of the coefficients from its grand average, in a given generation; $\delta x'$ that in the preceding generation; $b_{xx'}$ the regression of the former on the latter; and $\delta\delta x$ the residual deviation:

(13.72)
$$\sigma^2(\delta x) = b_{xx'}^2\sigma^2(\delta x) + \sigma^2(\delta\delta x),$$
$$\sigma^2(\Delta x) = \sigma^2(\delta x) = \sigma^2(\delta\delta x)/[1 - b_{xx'}^2].$$

Chance of Fixation of Individual Mutations

The most obvious theory of evolution under constant conditions is that it depends merely on the occasional replacement of an established gene by a more favorable mutation.

It is by no means certain that even a rather strongly favorable individual mutation will be fixed. It is indeed much more likely that it will be lost by accidents of sampling during the period in which it is carried by very few individuals. On considering a continually restored large number of such mutations in a large population, all assumed to be under the same selection pressure, the frequency distribution of mutations, treated collectively, should reach constancy. Distributions of this sort will in general be j-shaped.

Fisher (1922) discussed the chance of survival of a neutral mutation from the standpoint of the stochastic process of Watson and Galton (1874) already referred to. Haldane (1927b) extended this to advantageous mutations. He obtained $2s$ as the approximate chance of ultimate survival of a mutation with selective advantage s in heterozygotes and $\sqrt{(t/N)}$ for a recessive with selective advantage t when homozygous. Fisher (1930a) reached the same conclusion in the former case but did not consider the latter.

Let p_k be the probability of k representatives of a gene after a generation and use x^k qualitatively to indicate k representatives. The array after a generation can be written

$$f(x) = p_0 x^0 + p_1 x^1 + p_2 x^2 + \cdots.$$

For the array after two generations, x must be replaced by $f(x)$:

$$f(f(x)) = p_0 (f(x))^0 + p_1 (f(x))^1 + p_2 (f(x))^2 + \cdots.$$

This can be continued for any number of generations.

The probability for s representatives is the coefficient of x^s in the expansion of $f(f(x))$ and for the third generation in that of $f(f(f(x)))$, etc. Fisher and Haldane both assumed random (Poisson) variability:

$$(13.73) \quad f(x) = e^{-M}\left[1 + Mx + \frac{M^2 x^2}{3!} + \frac{M^3 x^3}{3!} + \cdots \right] = e^{M(x-1)},$$

where M is the mean. This can be applied to a neutral mutation in which the population number is changing in the ratio $1:M$ (Fisher) or to one with selective advantage s, and thus $M = W = 1 + s$ (Haldane).

The chance of extinction in one generation is e^{-M}. For a neutral gene in a static population ($M = 1$) this is 0.3679. For one with a selective advantage of 1%, $e^{-1.01} = 0.3642$, only slightly less. The chance of extinction in two generations is given by the first term in the expression of $f(f(x)) = e^{f(x)-1}$. For the neutral gene, $e^{0.3679-1} = 0.5315$; for one with 1% selective advantage, $e^{-1.01(1-0.3642)} = 0.5262$. In both cases more than half of the mutations are lost in two generations. Ultimately, the probability of extinction for the neutral gene is 100% in an indefinitely large population (although as noted earlier there is a chance of fixation of $1/(2N)$ in a population of size N). With selective advantage of s, there is a chance of ultimate survival of approximately 2% in this case (Haldane's $2s$).

Kojima and Kelleher (1962) considered the case of greater than random variability and used the negative binomial for $f(x)$. Their formula indicates that if the variance of family size is twice the mean instead of equal to it, as in Poisson variability, and if s is small, the chance of ultimate survival of a mutation is about two-thirds its value under Poisson variability. They note the considerably greater chance of survival of mutations that arise during expansion of a population as compared with contraction. It is indeed obvious from comparison of Fisher's and Haldane's results that a neutral or even slightly injurious mutation that arises in a period of rapid expansion may reach high absolute frequencies that persist or fall off only slowly if the population later becomes static.

The problem of survival of individual mutations can also be attacked by finding the formula for flux equilibrium of the distribution of gene frequencies.

Fixation under Flux Equilibrium

With flux equilibrium, the frequency of the class of single mutant genes is twice the frequency of new mutations, $f(1/(2N)) = 4Nv$ (equation 13.24). The frequency of the class in which all but one type of gene has been displaced, $f(1 - 1/(2N))$, is twice the frequency of fixation per generation and thus twice the flux through all heterallelic classes. The class of homallelic type genes, $f(0)$, must be treated as undepletable. The chance of fixation of an individual mutation is thus given by the ratio $f[1 - 1/(2N)]/f(1/(2N))$. It should be noted, however, that in general $f(q)/f[1/(2N)]$ has no simple relation to the chance of reaching gene frequency q. Thus heterotic mutations tend to accumulate near $\hat{q}$ in spite of flux.

This is the sort of stochastic distribution with which Fisher (1922, 1930a) was primarily concerned, in accordance with his theory of evolution. He obtained a solution in the case of semidominance from his analog of the heat diffusion equation. A suitable form of the integral equation referred to earlier (13.7, 13.29), gave a result in agreement (after reciprocal correction of errors) (Wright 1931).

As noted earlier, this method was later extended to any degree of dominance, $\Delta q = (s + tq)q(1 - q)$, $\sigma_{\Delta q}^2 = q(1 - q)/2N$ (Wright 1938b, 1942). In evaluating (13.29), it is convenient to assume that:

$$(13.74) \qquad \varphi(q) = e^{2Nsq + Ntq^2}(C_0 + C_1q + C_2q^2 + \cdots)/q(1 - q).$$

Use is made of the following approximations:

$$(13.75) \quad \begin{aligned} [1 + (s + tq)p]^{2Nq_1} &= e^{2Nq_1(s + tq)p}[1 - Nq_1(s + tq)^2p^2], \\ [1 - (s + tq)q]^{2Np_1} &= e^{-2Np_1(s + tq)q}[1 - Np_1(s + tq)^2q^2], \end{aligned}$$

$$(13.76) \quad \frac{\Gamma(2N)}{\Gamma(2Np_1)\Gamma(2Nq_1)} \int p^{2Np_1 - 1}q^{2Nq_1 - 1 + x}\, dq$$
$$= q_1{}^x + [q_1^{x-1} - q_1{}^x][x(x - 1)/4N].$$

It may be found that in a steady state (of the heterallelic classes):

$$(13.77) \quad C_m = [(4N^2s^2 + 2Nt)C_{m-2} + 8N^2stC_{m-3} + 4N^2t^2C_{m-4}]/m(m + 1),$$

ignoring terms in which the exponent of N is less than the sum of those for s and t. This leads to the following solution for (13.29) in this case:

$$(13.78) \quad \varphi(q) = 2N[Ce^{4Nsq+2Ntq^2} - 2Dqe^{2Nsq+Ntq^2}\Psi(2Nsq, 2Ntq^2)]/q(1-q),$$

where C and D are constants. For reasons apparent later, $2D$ is used. In the completely steady state, it was shown that $D = 0$, giving (13.60), after including terms for immigration and reversible mutation.

The expression $\Psi(2Nsq, 2Ntq^2)$ is a two-dimensional infinite series which was given up to terms in q^9 (Wright 1942).

$$(13.79) \quad \begin{aligned} \Psi(a, 0) &= \left[1 + \frac{a^2}{3!} + \frac{a^4}{5!} + \frac{a^6}{7!} + \cdots\right] = (e^a - e^{-a})/2a \\ \Psi(0, b) &= \left[1 + \frac{b}{3!} + \frac{7b^2}{5!} + \frac{27b^3}{7!} + \frac{321b^4}{9!} + \frac{2265b^5}{11!} + \cdots + E_m b^m\right] \end{aligned}$$

where

$$E_m = [E_{m-1} + E_{m-2}]/2m(2m+1).$$

With respect to $\Psi(2Nsq, 2Nt^2)$ it was shown later (Wright 1945b) that all of its terms are identical with those from the expansion of the two exponentials, integration of the terms of the second, and multiplication, in the expression

$$(13.80) \quad \Psi(2Nsq, 2Ntq^2) = [e^{2Nsq+Ntq^2}/q]\left[\int e^{-(4Nsq+2Ntq^2)} dq\right].$$

In the simplest case, that of neutral mutation, $\Psi(0, 0) = 1$:

$$(13.81) \quad f(q) = \varphi(q)/2N = (C - 2Dq)/q(1-q).$$

This is the same as (13.23), but we are not concerned here with the completely steady state but with that of steady flux:

$$(13.82) \quad \begin{aligned} f(1/(2N)) &= [4N^2/(2N-1)][C - 2D/(2N)] = 4Nv \quad \text{(see 13.24),} \\ f(1 - 1/(2N)) &= [4N^2/(2N-1)][C - 2D(2N-1)/(2N)] = 2 \\ &\qquad\qquad\qquad\qquad\qquad\qquad\qquad\qquad\qquad\qquad\qquad \times \text{ flux.} \end{aligned}$$

Since the number of neutral genes that reach fixation, about $(1/2)f(1 - 1/(2N))$, must be very small compared with those that start, about $(1/2)f(1/(2N)) = 2Nv$, then $f(1 - 1/(2N))$ may be put equal to zero for an approximate result, giving

$$(13.83) \quad C \approx 2v, \quad 2D \approx 2v, \quad f(q) = 2v/q.$$

From this

(13.84) $f(1 - 1/(2N)) = 2v = 2D,$

indicating a flux of v mutations, as expected, per generation. The chance of fixation of a single mutation is given by:

(13.85) $f(1 - 1/(2N))/f(1/(2N)) = 2v/4Nv = 1/(2N).$

As noted earlier (7.42), this is the rate of fixation of neutral genes in a population of effective size N.

In the case of semidominance, use is made of (13.79) in evaluating (13.78):

(13.86) $f(q) = [Ce^{4Nsq} - 2D(e^{4Nsq} - 1)/4Ns]/q(1 - q),$

(13.87)
$$f(1/(2N)) \approx 2N[C - 2D/2N] = 4Nv \qquad \text{(as before)},$$
$$f(1 - 1/(2N)) \approx 2N[Ce^{4Ns} - 2D(e^{4Ns} - 1)/4Ns].$$

It may be noted that $f(1/(2N))$ is always $4Nv$ and that the curve is always very nearly the same where there are only a few representatives of the mutant gene since selection has no appreciable effect in this region.

Again putting $f(1 - 1/(2N))$ equal to zero provisionally, the solution of equation (13.87) is

(13.88) $C = 2v, \qquad 2D = 8Nsv/(1 - e^{-4Ns}),$

(13.89) $f(q) = \dfrac{2v}{q(1 - q)} \left[\dfrac{1 - e^{-4Ns(1-q)}}{1 - e^{-4Ns}} \right].$

From this $f(1 - 1/(2N)) \approx 8Nsv/(1 - e^{-4Ns})$ and is thus the same as $2D$, showing that D is again the amount of flux.

The chance of fixation is:

(13.90) $f(1 - 1/(2N))/f(1/(2N)) = 2s/(1 - e^{-4Ns}).$

This approaches $1/(2N)$ as s approaches 0, as expected. There is a slight chance of fixation of a mutation with a selection disadvantage of s. Changing the sign of s:

$$f(1 - 1/(2N))/f(1/(2N)) = 2s/(e^{4Ns} - 1).$$

Equations (13.89) and (13.90) agree with the results obtained by Fisher (1930a). The chance that an individual semidominant mutation reaches fixation is thus about $2s$ if $4Ns$ is larger than two or three. The estimate of $2s$ for this chance was as noted earlier arrived at first by Haldane (1927b), using another method.

The next case of interest is that of recessive mutations $\Delta q = tq^2(1 - q)$ and $\sigma^2_{\Delta q} = q(1 - q)/2N$:

(13.91) $$f(q) = \frac{e^{2Ntq^2}}{q(1-q)}[C - 2Dqe^{-Ntq^2}\Psi(0, 2Ntq^2)].$$

The equations for $f(1/(2N))$ and $f(1 - 1/(2N))$ yield

(13.92) $$C = 2v, \qquad 2D = 2ve^{Nt}/\Psi(0, 2Nt).$$

Calculations of $f(q)$ were made (Wright 1942) for various values of $2Nt$ by making use of (13.79). The average chance of fixation from $f(1 - 1/(2N))/f(1/(2N))$ for values of $2Nt$ from 4 to 64 came out $1.1\sqrt{(t/2N)}$. This agreed fairly well with an earlier estimate by Haldane (1927b) as of the order of $\sqrt{(t/N)}$ and agrees well with a theoretical estimate, $\sqrt{(2t/\pi N)} = 1.128\sqrt{(t/2N)}$, made later by Kimura (1957, 1962), to which we will return. Kimura's limiting value can indeed be obtained from (13.91) and (13.92) by evaluating $\Psi(0, 2Ntq)$ from (13.80) instead of from the original series (13.79).

In the case of dominant mutations, $\Delta q = sq(1-q)^2$, $\sigma_{\Delta q}^2 = q(1-q)/2N$, $t = -s$, it is convenient to consider the distribution for the type alleles with frequency $p = 1 - q$, $\Delta p = -tp^2(1-p)$, since this permits use of the simple series $\Psi(0, -2Ntp^2)/p(1-p)$.

(13.93) $$f(p) = Ce^{-2Ntp^2} - 2Dpe^{-Ntp^2}\Psi(0, -2Ntp^2)/p(1-p).$$

In this case it is $f(1 - 1/(2N))$ that equals $4Nv$ and $f(1/(2N))$ that is very much smaller.

(13.94) $$f(1 - 1/(2N)) \approx 2N[Ce^{-2Nt} - 2De^{-Nt}\Psi(0, -2Nt)] = 4Nv,$$
$$f(1/(2N)) \approx [2NC - 2D] = 2 \times \text{flux},$$

C is negligibly small,

(13.95) $$2D \approx -2ve^{Nt}/\Psi(0, -2Nt),$$

(13.96) $$f(p) = \frac{2v}{p(1-p)}\left[pe^{Nt(1-p^2)}\frac{\Psi(0, -2Ntp^2)}{\Psi(0, -2Nt)}\right].$$

Ordinates of the curves were evaluated for values of $2Nt$ ranging from -4 to 16. The chance of fixation of favorable dominants approached $2t$ empirically, the same limit as with semidominance where the selective advantage of the heterozygotes is the same.

The case in which there is no selective difference between the homozygotes but selection favors (or opposes) the heterozygotes was also worked out: $\Delta q = s(1 - 2q)q(1-q)$, $\sigma_{\Delta q}^2 = q(1-q)/2N$. In this case, $t = -2s$.

(13.97) $$f(q) = [Ce^{4Nsq(1-q)} - 2Dqe^{2Nsq(1-q)}\Psi(2Nsq, -4Nsq^2)]/q(1-q),$$

(13.98) $$C = 2v, \qquad 2D = 2v/\Psi(2Ns, -4Ns),$$

$$(13.99) \qquad f(q) = \frac{2ve^{4Nsq(1-q)}}{q(1-q)} \left[1 - \frac{qe^{-2Nsq(1-q)}\Psi(2Nsq, -4Nsq^2)}{\Psi(2Ns, -4Ns)} \right].$$

Ordinates were evaluated for values of $2Nt$ ranging from -4 to $+4$. With stronger overdominance, there is an approach to a completely steady state (13.56).

The probabilities of fixation at various relative selective values in the four cases discussed above, as determined from the integral equation, are listed in Table 13.3. The situations are described here in terms of a parameter s that is not in all cases the same as in the preceding discussion.

TABLE 13.3. Probability of fixation of a mutation A' at various values of the parameter s, under the four sets of selective values at the top.

	Genotype	(1)	(2)	(3)	(4)
	$A'A'$	$1 + s$	$1 + s$	$1 + s$	1
	AA'	1	$1 + s/2$	$1 + s$	$1 + s$
s	AA	1	1	1	1
Large		$1.1\sqrt{(s/2N)}$	s	$2s$	0
$16/(2N)$		$4.3/(2N)$	$16/(2N)$	$31/(2N)$	—
$4/(2N)$		$2.3/(2N)$	$4.1/(2N)$	$6.6/(2N)$	$3.2/(2N)$
$1/(2N)$		$1.3/(2N)$	$1.6/(2N)$	$1.9/(2N)$	$1.4/(2N)$
0		$1/(2N)$	$1/(2N)$	$1/(2N)$	$1/(2N)$
$-1/(2N)$		$0.70/(2N)$	$0.58/(2N)$	$0.49/(2N)$	$0.71/(2N)$
$-4/(2N)$		$0.12/(2N)$	$0.075/(2N)$	$0.042/(2N)$	$0.23/(2N)$

The distributions of gene frequencies under steady flux at various sets of selective values are shown in Figures 13.12–13.15 for the four cases discussed. All ordinates are on the same scale, starting from $f(1 - 1/(2N)) = 4Nv$ (far too high to be shown if N is larger than 20), except in the case of strong heterotic selection. The first three have the same selective values of homozygotes but increasing values (plus or minus) for heterozygotes. The last two have the same selective values for heterozygotes while the second (semidominance) is here calculated for half as much differential in this respect.

The distributions for recessives, Figure 13.12, show the smallest differences in the range from $s = -4N/2N$ to $s = +16/(2N)$, and there is reversal of order at the lower gene frequencies; the unfavorable recessives reach higher frequencies than the favorable recessives at $q = 0.20$ because the flow of the former tends to be dammed up, while the latter are carried on ever more rapidly. The chance of fixation of even a strongly favorable recessive is low, however, compared with mutations with an advantageous heterozygote and a homozygote that is at least as good.

In the other three cases, the selection of the heterozygotes is naturally

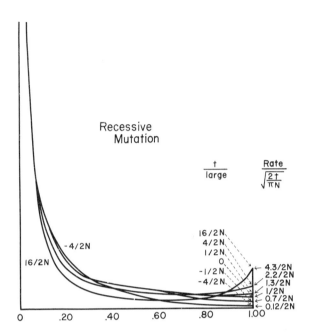

FIG. 13.12. Flux equilibrium in the case of recessive mutations with selective advantage *s* shown near the curves. The rates of fixation are shown at the right (Wright 1942, Fig. 7, reprinted by permission, The American Mathematical Society, © 1942).

the most important factor at low gene frequencies. Semidominants and dominants, with the same strong selective advantage of heterozygotes (instead of half as great in the former as in the latter as in Figures 13.13 and 13.14), show about the same rate of fixation and hence of flux. This presumably holds approximately for all degrees of dominance up to complete dominance, but there is increasing damming up at intermediate gene frequencies as complete dominance is approached. This process is naturally still more striking in heterotic mutations in which even rather weak selection favoring heterozygotes leads to an enormous accumulation at intermediate gene frequencies as the result of reduction in the flux and in rate of fixation.

Probability of Fixation by Other Methods

The method of attack on the problem of rate of fixation used above was rather cumbersome. It will be well to go briefly into two methods developed later. One of these is to start from the differential equation for a steady state, supplemented here by a constant flux through each gene frequency (represented by D) (Wright 1945b):

(13.100) $(1/2) \dfrac{d}{dq} [\sigma^2_{\Delta q} \varphi(q)] - \Delta q \varphi(q) + D = 0.$

This may be reduced to a linear equation of the first degree by the substitution $y = \sigma^2_{\Delta q} \varphi(q)$.

(13.101) $\dfrac{dy}{y} - (2\,\Delta q/\sigma^2_{\Delta q})y + 2D = 0,$

(13.102) $\varphi(q) = \left\{ \dfrac{\exp\left[2\int (\Delta q/\sigma^2_{\Delta q})\,dq\right]}{\sigma^2_{\Delta q}} \right\} \left\{ C - 2D \int \exp\left[-2\int (\Delta q/\sigma^2_{\Delta q})\,dq\right] dq \right\}.$

In the fairly general case of constant genotypic selective values (permitting any sort of interaction),

$$\Delta q = (1/2)q(1-q)\frac{\partial \log \overline{W}}{\partial q}, \qquad \sigma^2_{\Delta q} = q(1-q)/2N,$$

$$2\,\Delta q/\sigma^2_{\Delta q} = \frac{\partial \log (\overline{W})^{2N}}{\partial q}.$$

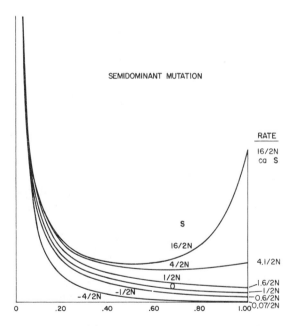

FIG. 13.13. Flux equilibrium in the case of semidominant mutations with selective advantage of homozygotes t shown near the curves (t corresponds to s in the text). The rates of fixation are shown at the right (Wright 1942, Fig. 6, reprinted by permission, The American Mathematical Society, © 1942).

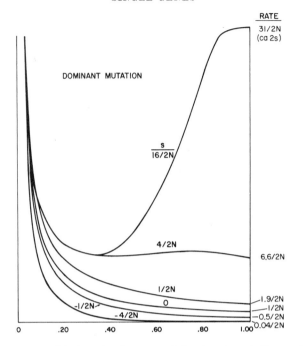

Fig. 13.14. Flux equilibrium in the case of dominant mutations with selective advantage of heterozygotes, s, shown near the curves. The rates of fixation are shown at the right (Wright 1942, Fig. 8, reprinted by permission, The American Mathematical Society, © 1942).

$$(13.103) \qquad f(q) = [\overline{W}^{2N}/q(1-q)][C - 2D \int \overline{W}^{-2N} \, dq], \quad \text{Wright (1945b)}$$

Still more generally, with frequency dependent selection where $F(w/\bar{w})$ exists, $F(w/\bar{w})$ can be substituted for $\log \overline{W}$ and $\exp[2N F(w/\bar{w})]$ for $\overline{W}^{2N}$. This equation is, however, likely to be intractable. We will consider only three simple cases, already dealt with by the integral equation.

The simplest is again that of a neutral mutation, $\overline{W} = 1$,

$$(13.104) \qquad\qquad f(q) = (C - 2Dq)/q(1-q).$$

This is the same as (13.81).

In the case of semidominance, $\overline{W} = 1 + 2sq \approx e^{2sq}$ and $\overline{W}^{2N} \approx e^{4Nsq}$.

$$(13.105) \qquad f(q) = [e^{4Nsq}/q(1-q)][C - 2D \int_0^q e^{-4Nsq} \, dq].$$

The integral is treated as definite, with limits 0 and q, so as to give (13.86) with the same C and D, and hence lead to (13.89).

In the case of a favorable recessive mutation, $\overline{W} = 1 + tq^2$ and $\overline{W}^{2N} \approx \exp(2Ntq^2)$.

$$(13.106) \qquad f(q) = \frac{\exp(2Ntq^2)}{q(1-q)} \left[C - 2D \int_0^q \exp(-2Ntq^2)\, dq \right]$$

The integral may be written

$$\sqrt{\frac{2\pi}{4Nt}} \int_0^x \frac{\exp(-0.5x^2)\, dx}{\sqrt{(2\pi)}}, \qquad \text{where} \qquad x = q\sqrt{(4Nt)}.$$

$$(13.107) \quad f(q) = \frac{\exp(2Ntq^2)}{q(1-q)} \left[C - 2D \left[\{\text{pri}\,[q\sqrt{(4Nt)}] - 0.5\} \sqrt{\frac{2\pi}{4Nt}} \right] \right]$$

$$f(1/(2N)) = 2NC = 4Nv, \qquad \text{hence} \qquad C = 2v \text{ as usual,}$$

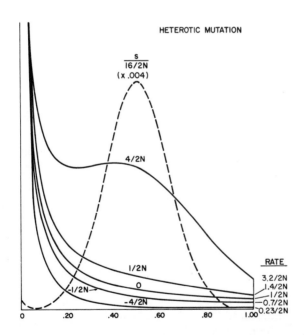

FIG. 13.15. Flux equilibrium in the case of heterotic mutations, with selective advantage s of heterozygotes over both homozygotes shown near the curves. The rates of fixation are shown at the right except in the case of $s = 16/(2N)$ (with greatly exaggerated ordinates) for which there is accumulation near $q = 0.50$ and a negligible rate of fixation (Wright 1942, Fig. 9, reprinted by permission, The American Mathematical Society, © 1942).

$$(13.108) \quad f(1 - 1/(2N)) = 2Ne^{2Nt}\left[2v - 2D\left\{[\text{pri } \sqrt{(4Nt)} - 0.5]\sqrt{\frac{2\pi}{4Nt}}\right\}\right]$$

$$= 2D,$$

$$(13.109) \qquad 2D \approx 2v\bigg/\left\{[\text{pri } \sqrt{(4Nt)} - 0.5]\sqrt{\left(\frac{2\pi}{4Nt}\right)}\right\},$$

$$(13.110) \qquad f(q) = \frac{2v \exp{(2Ntq^2)}}{q(1 - q)}\left[1 - \frac{\text{pri } [q\sqrt{(4Nt)}] - 0.5}{\text{pri } \sqrt{(4Nt)} - 0.5}\right].$$

For $Nt > 1$, pri $\sqrt{(4Nt)}$ approaches one. The rate of fixation, $2D/(4Nv)$, thus approaches $\sqrt{[2t/(\pi N)]}$, close to the value $1.1\sqrt{[t/(2N)]}$ arrived at (Wright 1942) by summation of the series involved in the integral equation (13.79) and identical with Kimura's (1957) value (and with that which could have been given if formula (13.80) (Wright 1945b) had been applied to this case).

Kimura (1962) has approached the matter in a wholly different way by considering the probability $u(q, t)$ of fixation of a gene in the time interval t, starting from gene frequency q_0, with frequencies subject to systematic pressure only from selection.

$$(13.111) \qquad u(q, t + \delta t) = \int f(q, q + \delta q; \delta t)u(q + \delta q, t)\, d(\delta q),$$

where $f(q, q + \delta q; \delta t)$ is the probability density of the change from q to $q + \delta q$ during the short time interval δt, and the integration is over all possible values of δq.

Expanding $u(q + \delta q, t)$ in terms of δq by Taylor's theorem, ignoring higher powers than $(\delta q)^2$, we have, as δt approaches zero:

$$(13.112) \qquad \frac{1}{\delta t}\int(\delta q)f(q, q + \delta q; \delta t)\, d(\delta q) = \overline{\delta q},$$

$$(13.113) \qquad \frac{1}{\delta t}\int(\delta q)^2 f(q, q + \delta q; \delta t)\, d(\delta q) = \sigma_{\delta q}^2,$$

$$(13.114) \qquad \frac{\partial u(q, t)}{\partial t} = \overline{\delta q}\,\frac{\partial u(q, t)}{\partial q} + \frac{\sigma_{\delta q}^2}{2}\frac{\partial^2 u(q, t)}{\partial q^2}.$$

The desired probability may be obtained by solving this partial differential equation (known as the Kolmogorov backward equation) with boundary conditions $u(0, t) = 0$ and $u(1, t) = 1$.

The question of greatest interest here is the ultimate probability of fixation as t becomes indefinitely large, for which

$$\frac{\partial u(q, t)}{\partial t} = 0.$$

Measuring time in generations, we may write $\overline{\delta q} = \Delta q$ and $\sigma^2_{\delta q} = \sigma^2_{\Delta q}$, in the same sense as used earlier.

(13.115) $(1/2)\sigma^2_{\Delta q} \dfrac{d^2 u(q)}{dq^2} + \Delta q \dfrac{du(q)}{dq} = 0,$ $u(0) = 0,$ $u(1) = 1.$

This yields the solution

(13.116) $u(q) = \displaystyle\int_0^q \exp\left[-2\int(\Delta q/\sigma^2_{\Delta q})\,dq\right]dq \Big/ \int_0^1 \exp\left[-2\int \Delta q/\sigma^2_{\Delta q})\,dq\right]dq.$

From its derivation, this formula holds for asexually reproducing organisms as well as for sexually reproducing ones, and in the latter case for haploids and polyploids as well as diploids.

The chance of fixation of an individual mutant gene is given by $u(1/(2N))$. In the case of one that is semidominant with respect to selection, $\Delta q = sq(1 - q)$, $\sigma^2_{\Delta q} = q(1 - q)/2N$, and

(13.117) $u(1/(2N)) = \dfrac{1 - e^{-4Nsq}}{1 - e^{-4Ns}} \approx 2s/(1 - e^{-4Ns})$

as obtained before (13.90).

In the case of one that is recessive with respect to selection, $\Delta q = tq^2(1 - q)$, $\sigma^2_{\Delta q} = q(1 - q)/2N$, and

(13.118) $u(1/(2N)) = \displaystyle\int_0^q e^{-2Ntq^2}\,dq \Big/ \int_0^1 e^{-2Ntq^2}\,dq,$

which, if t is positive and Nt large, gives $\sqrt{(2t/N\pi)} = 1.128\sqrt{(t/2N)}$, as obtained in the limiting case from (13.91) and (13.110).

Kimura considered also cases in which the sampling variance is complicated by fluctuations in the selection coefficient.

Steady Decay

We started from the consideration of probability distributions of gene frequencies in the case of inbreeding, uncomplicated by systematic pressures. It was found that the distribution spreads out from any initial gene frequency to become almost rectangular with falling off of all heterallelic frequencies at the rate $1/(2N)$ per generation as fixation proceeds. Cases that are similar except for the presence of systematic pressures are of interest in experimental studies of small populations.

With falling off at the constant proportional rate

$$k = -[1/\varphi(q, t)]\dfrac{\partial \varphi(q, t)}{dt}$$

per generation, the Fokker–Planck partial differential equation becomes an ordinary differential equation (Wright 1945b):

(13.119) $(1/2) \dfrac{d^2}{dq^2} [\sigma^2_{\Delta q} \varphi(q)] - \dfrac{d}{dq} [\Delta q \varphi(q)] + k\varphi(q) = 0,$

in which $\varphi(q)$ refers to the constant form of the heterallelic classes.

It may easily be verified that in the case of uncomplicated inbreeding ($\Delta q = 0$, $\sigma^2_{\Delta q} = q(1 - q)/2N$, $k = 1/(2N)$):

(13.120) $\varphi(q) = 1$ or $f(q, t) = C_0 e^{-t/2N}.$

In the case of irreversible mutation at an appreciable rate, $\Delta q = v(1 - q)$, $k = v$:

(13.121) $f(q) = 2v q^{4Nv-1}.$

This result was first obtained (Wright 1931) by use of the integral equation. An analogous solution applies to the effect of swamping by immigration from a population in which the gene in question is fixed, $\Delta q = m(1 - q)$:

(13.122) $f(q) = 2m q^{4Nm-1}.$

The case of semidominant selective advantage, with decay at rate k, $\Delta q = sq(1 - q)$, was also first solved by the use of the integral equation (Wright and Kerr 1954) but can also be derived from the Fokker–Planck equation:

(13.123) $\dfrac{1}{4N} \dfrac{d^2}{dq^2} [q(1 - q)\varphi(q)] - s \dfrac{d}{dq} [q(1 - q)\varphi(q)] + k\varphi(q) = 0.$

On substituting $\varphi(q) = e^{2Nsq} \chi(q)/q(1 - q)$:

(13.124) $\dfrac{\partial^2 \chi(q)}{\partial q^2} - \left[4N^2 s^2 - \dfrac{4Nk}{q(1 - q)} \right] \chi(q) = 0.$

Letting $\chi(q) = Cx[1 + C_1 x + C_2 x^2 + C_3 x^3 + \cdots]$, $x = q(1 - q)$:

$C_1 = (1 - 2Nk),$

$C_2 = (1/3)[(6 - 2Nk)C_1 + 2N^2 s^2],$

(13.125) $C_3 = (1/6)[(15 - 2Nk)C_2 + 2N^2 s^2 C_1],$

$C_n = \dfrac{2}{n(n + 1)} \{[n(2n - 1) - 2Nk]C_{n-1} + 2N^2 s^2 C_{n-2}\}.$

After $n(2n - 1)$ has become greater than $2Nk$, the coefficient of C_n has the same sign as those of C_{n-1}. The term $2N^2 s^2 C_{n-2}$ has the same sign as C_{n-2}. Thus if two successive terms after this point ever have the same sign all later ones must have the same sign and will soon begin to increase. The series of coefficients becomes either divergent positive or negative unless there is a relation of $2Nk$ to $2N^2 s^2$ at which the coefficients continue to alternate in sign and approach zero. The rapidity of divergence, one way or the other, is so great that it is easy to locate to any required number of decimal places the desired value of $2Nk$. This may be taken to be the limiting value under the assumed degree of selection.

For values of $2Ns$ much less than one, $2Nk$ is found to be closely approximated by $1 + (2Ns)^2/10$. For somewhat larger values, the term $(2Ns)^4/7000$ must be subtracted. The following was found empirically to be accurate to 11 significant figures up to $2Ns = 1$:

$$(13.126) \quad 2Nk = 1 + \frac{(2Ns)^2}{10} - \frac{(2Ns)^4}{7000} - \frac{(2Ns)^6}{1050.000}$$
$$- 0.000,000,004(2Ns)^8.$$

This is accurate to six significant figures up to $2Ns = 4$, to three significant figures up to $2Ns = 6$.

Kimura (1955c) has extended this series and given a solution that can be used for larger values of $2Ns$ based on a study of this differential equation by Stratton et al. 1941 (Table 13.4).

TABLE 13.4. Values of $2Nk$ for the indicated values of $2Ns$ (from Kimura 1955c).

$2Ns$	$2Nk$	$2Ns$	$2Nk$	$2Ns$	$2Nk$
0	1.000000	5	3.39445	10	8.753305
1	1.099855	6	4.36529	12	10.857286
2	1.397655	7	5.431835	14	12.899831
3	1.887710	8	6.54540	16	14.919894
4	2.559275	9	7.661215		

The frequencies in the subterminal classes are approximately $f(1/(2N)) = C/(2N)$ and $f(1 - 1/(2N)) = Ce^{2Ns}/(2N)$. The rates of loss and of fixation are thus $k_0 = C/(4N)$ and $k_1 = Ce^{2Ns}/(4N)$. The rate of decay of the heterallelic portion is the sum, $k = C(1 + e^{2Ns})/(4N)$ so that $C = 4Nk/(1 + e^{2Ns})$.

We will merely refer the reader to an investigation by Kimura (1957) of the more complicated case in which there is dominance in selective value.

The Approach to a Steady State

It is apparent from what has gone before that if a large number of populations of the same size N start with the same gene frequency and are subject to the same systematic and random processes, it will in general require many generations before they exhibit the steady state distribution. Such histories can be determined by the solution of the full Fokker–Planck equation for $\varphi(q, t)$ where t is time in generations. While essential for the full mathematical treatment of stochastic processes, the unavoidable complexity is rather disproportional to the biologic importance. We will therefore merely refer to Kimura's papers on this subject (esp. 1955c) and to his excellent monograph (1964), "Diffusion Models in Population Genetics." This reviews the whole field indicated by its title, from the mathematical viewpoint but also from a biologic viewpoint sufficiently close to that of the present chapter to supplement it better than would purely mathematical treatment.

CHAPTER 14

Stochastic Distributions: Multiple Alleles and Multiple Loci

Multiple Alleles

We will consider first the case of three alleles subject only to immigration pressure, $\Delta q_i = -m(q_i - Q_i)$, and accidents of sampling, $\sigma^2_{\Delta q} = q(1 - q)/2N$. Since any two may be treated as if one, the distribution of q_1 may be written:

$$(14.1) \qquad \varphi(q_1) = \frac{\Gamma(4Nm)}{\Gamma(4NmQ_1)\Gamma[4Nm(1 - Q_1)]} q_1^{4NmQ_1-1}(1 - q_1)^{4Nm(1 - Q_1)-1}.$$

The distribution of $\varphi(q_1, q_2, q_3)$ must be symmetrical in Q_1, Q_2, and Q_3. This suggests inserting $\Gamma(4NmQ_1)$ and $\Gamma(4NmQ_2)$ and removing $\Gamma(4Nm(1 - Q_1))$ in the coefficient:

$$\varphi(q_1) = \frac{\Gamma(4Nm)}{\Gamma(4NmQ_1)\Gamma(4NmQ_2)\Gamma(4NmQ_3)} \frac{\Gamma(4NmQ_2)\Gamma(4NmQ_3)}{\Gamma(4Nm(1 - Q_1))}$$
$$\times q_1^{4NmQ_1-1}(1 - q_1)^{4Nm(Q_2 + Q_3)-1}$$

$$(14.2)$$
$$= \frac{\Gamma(4Nm)}{\Gamma(4NmQ_1)\Gamma(4NmQ_2)\Gamma(4NmQ_3)} q_1^{4NmQ_1-1}(1 - q_1)^{4Nm(Q_2 + Q_3)-1}$$
$$\times \int_0^1 x^{4NmQ_2-1}(1 - x)^{4NmQ_3-1}\, dx.$$

The frequency at a given value of q_1, (q_{1a}), using C for the coefficient above is:

$$(14.3) \qquad \varphi(q_{1a}) = Cq_{1a}^{4NmQ_1-1} \int_0^1 [(1 - q_{1a})x]^{4NmQ_2-1}$$
$$\times [(1 - q_{1a})(1 - x)]^{4NmQ_3-1}(1 - q_{1a})\, dx.$$

Let $x = q_2/(1 - q_{1a})$, $1 - x = (1 - q_{1a} - q_2)/(1 - q_{1a}) = q_3/(1 - q_{1a})$, $dx = dq_2/(1 - q_{1a})$:

$$(14.4) \qquad \varphi(q_{1a}) = C \int_0^{1-q_{1a}} q_{1a}^{4NmQ_1-1}q_2^{4NmQ_2-1}(1 - q_{1a} - q_2)^{4NmQ_3-1}\, dq_2.$$

The frequency with given q_1 can also be written:

$$\varphi(q_{1a}) = \int_0^{1-q_{1a}} \varphi[q_{1a}, q_2, (1 - q_{1a} - q_2)]\, dq_2.$$

Thus the distribution with variability of q_1 as well as of q_2 and q_3 is:

$$(14.5) \quad \varphi(q_1, q_2, q_3) = \frac{\Gamma(4Nm)}{\Gamma(4NmQ_1)\Gamma(4NmQ_2)\Gamma(4NmQ_3)}$$
$$\times q_1^{4NmQ_1 - 1} q_2^{4NmQ_2 - 1} q_3^{4NmQ_3 - 1}.$$

The suggestion made above thus leads to a symmetrical expression for $\varphi(q_1, q_2, q_3)$. More generally (Wright 1949b):

$$(14.6) \quad \varphi(q_1, q_2, \ldots, q_n) = \frac{\Gamma(4Nm)}{\Gamma(4NmQ_1)\Gamma(4NmQ_2) \ldots \Gamma(4NmQ_n)} \prod q_i^{4NmQ_i - 1}.$$

Let u_{ij} be the mutation rate from A_i to A_j. In the three-allele case, $\Delta q_1 = u_{21}q_2 + u_{31}q_3 - (u_{12} + u_{13})q_1$.

If now $u_{21} = u_{31} = v_1$, $u_{12} = u_{32} = v_2$, $u_{13} = u_{23} = v_3$, then $\Delta q_x = v_x(1 - q_x) - (\sum v_i - v_x)q_x$, and v_i may be substituted for mQ_i in (14.6).

$$(14.7) \quad \varphi(q_1, q_2, \ldots, q_n) = \frac{\Gamma(4N(v_1 + v_2 + \cdots + v_n))}{\Gamma(4Nv_1)\Gamma(4Nv_2) \ldots \Gamma(4Nv_n)} \prod q_i^{4Nv_i - 1}.$$

The assumption that all alleles mutate to a given one at the same rate is not, however, very probable, so that this formula is of restricted value. No solution has been given in the general case.

If the formula for change of gene frequency involves a selection term,

$$(1/2)q_i(1 - q_i)\frac{\partial \log \overline{W}}{\partial q_i},$$

assuming the W's to be constant, the attempt to derive the formula for the distribution as above leads to unintegrable terms. The distribution for one allele as opposed to all others with any given set of relative values among the latter is:

$$(14.8) \quad \varphi(q_i) = C\overline{W}^{2N}q_i^{4NmQ_i - 1}(1 - q_i)^{4Nm(1 - Q_i) - 1}.$$

This is the cross section of the total distribution defined by the given set.

The formula

$$\varphi(q_1, q_2, \ldots, q_n) = C\overline{W}^{2N} \prod q_i^{4NmQ_i - 1}$$

is indicated since it yields any specified cross section correctly (Wright 1949b). A formal demonstration has been given by Crow and Kimura (1956) from the multidimensional Fokker–Planck differential equation. If the genotypic selective values are functions of the gene frequencies and the selection term in Δq can be expressed as $(1/2)q(1 - q)[\partial F(w/\bar{w})/\partial q]$, the term $e^{2NF(w/\bar{w})}$ may be substituted for $\overline{W}^{2N}$.

Multiple Loci

As noted earlier, the variation of a single gene frequency about its equilibrium value is important in very small populations as leading to random fixation and hence the effects of close inbreeding, but variation that does not lead to fixation is of little importance with respect to a single locus. On the other hand, variation of gene frequencies in local populations occurring simultaneously at a large number of loci that are involved in an interaction system is a process of great evolutionary importance in providing material for interlocality selection.

In the absence of interaction with respect to selective value, the multidimensional probability distribution is merely the product of the distributions for the separate loci:

$$(14.9) \quad \varphi(q_{A1} \cdots q_{Ai} \cdots ; q_{B1} \cdots q_{Bi} \cdots ; q_{I1} \cdots q_{Ii} \cdots ; \cdots) = \prod_{Ii} \varphi(q_{I1} \cdots q_{Ii} \cdots).$$

If there is selection with respect to each, the effects on total selective value may be independent (multiplicative or, if slight, practically additive). This, however, is hardly likely even in the absence of interaction effects on characters other than selective value itself, if effects are large at two or more loci, or, if not, large number of loci are under consideration. This is because reduction in population number by selection with respect to any locus tends to relax selection at the other loci.

Where there is interaction with respect to selective value, whatever its cause, the total probability distribution for all loci under consideration must be such that it reduces to that for a single locus in the subpopulation defined by any single specified genotype at each of the other loci. This condition is met only by combining the selective effects at all loci in a single factor. This factor is $\overline{W}^{2N}$ if there is constancy of the selective values of total genotypes. If there is not constancy, but a fitness function $F(w/\bar{w})$ exists, the factor is approximately $e^{2NF(w/\bar{w})}$ which reduces to $e^{2N\bar{w}}$ or, more accurately, $\overline{W}^{2N}$ if there is constancy. The formula has not been given for cases in which $F(w/\bar{w})$ does not exist.

Thus for loci with pairs of alleles and no immigration and constant genotypic selective values (Wright 1937; Crow and Kimura 1956):

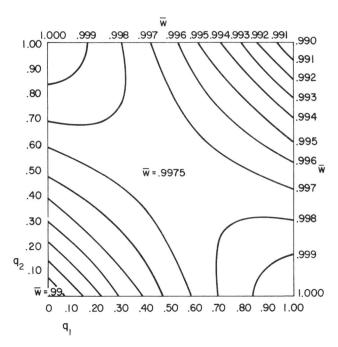

FIG. 14.1. Contours on the surface of mean selective values ($\overline{W}$) in the case of two pairs of alleles with equal and additive effects on a character on which selection acts according to the square of the deviation from the midrange. Note "peaks" at $(0, 1)$ and $(1, 0)$, "pits" at $(0, 0)$ and $(1, 1)$, and a saddle at $(0.5, 0.5)$ ($s = -0.0025$ at unit deviation).

$$(14.10) \qquad \varphi(q_A, q_B, \ldots, q_I, \ldots) = C\overline{W}^{2N} \prod_I q_I^{4Nv_I - 1}(1 - q_I)^{4Nv_I - 1}.$$

Extension to multiple alleles at loci is subject to the restrictions on the mutation rates referred to earlier.

Where the effects of mutation are overwhelmed by much more important immigration pressures, the same coefficient, m, applies to all loci, at least in the island model of structure (Wright 1949b).

$$(14.11) \quad \varphi\,(q_{A1} \cdots q_{Ai} \cdots; q_{B1} \cdots q_{Bi} \cdots; \cdots q_{Ii} \cdots q_{Ii} \cdots; \cdots)$$
$$= C\,\overline{W}^{2N} \prod_{Ii} q_{Ii}^{4NmQ_{Ii} - 1}.$$

The ordinates of such a multidimensional probability distribution tend to reflect, in enormously exaggerated degree, the surface of selective values $\overline{W}$ (or $F(w/\bar{w})$ if total selective values are not constant), modified by the effects of the other systematic pressures on the product term. Such a surface is illustrated in a case of two interacting loci in Figures 14.1 and 14.2.

Number of Alleles Maintained in Populations

The number of alleles that are maintained in a population depends, of course, on the unique properties of each one, and no general result can be obtained. The question becomes more manageable if all, or all but one, are assumed to have identical properties. This assumption may be approximated in nature in the case of self-incompatibility alleles in which selection is directed toward an intermediate frequency from both directions. This was the first case studied (Wright 1939a), but the dependence of the equilibrium frequency on the frequencies of the alleles, and especially on their number, causes complications that make it desirable to defer consideration until after discussion

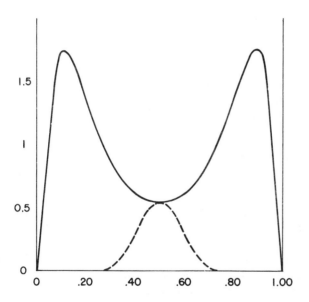

FIG. 14.2. Two cross-sections ($q_2 = 1 - q_1$ and $q_2 = q_1$) of the two-dimensional, steady state distribution based on the selective values of Figure 14.1, assuming immigration, $m = 0.001$, $Q = 0.5$, in a population of $N = 1,000$. That for the favorable diagonal, $q_2 = 1 - q_1$, is represented by a solid line; that for the unfavorable diagonal, $q_2 = q_1$, by a broken line (essentially from Wright 1937, Fig. 8).

of simpler cases. These are probably common in nature at the molecular level (Kimura 1968).

The distribution for a single allele as opposed to all others can be expressed approximately in the usual steady-state form, $\varphi(q)$. The true distribution is, of course, the step distribution with frequencies $F(q) = \varphi(q)/2N$ approximately, at intervals of $1/(2N)$. The frequency of absence from the population is such that the frequency $2NvF(0)$ of recurrence equals the frequency $(1/2)F(1/(2N))$, of loss. The same distribution, $F(q)$, applies to each allele of a set with identical properties. Since each is expected to be absent most of the time, $F(0)$ is very nearly 1. We may, however, consider the frequency distribution of the array of n alleles, present at any time, $f(q) = F(q)/[1 - F(0)]$, $\sum_{1/(2N)}^{1} f(q) = 1$, which by definition has no class at $q = 0$. The probability of an increase by mutation to $(n + 1)$ alleles is $2Nu$ while that of a decrease to $(n - 1)$ alleles in the absence of mutation is $(n/2)f(1/(2N))$. There would be a steady state only if mutation and loss always occur simultaneously. Actually a distribution of values of n must be recognized. Distributions that are in a steady state except for the possibilities of gain or loss can be determined for each value of n separately and the frequencies of the values of n can then be determined by equating the chance of gain by mutation, starting from a given number of alleles, n, with the chance of loss by accidents of sampling from the distribution for $(n + 1)$ alleles. This is rather important where q is a function of n, as with self-incompatibility alleles, but where not, it is enough for most purposes to put $2Nu = (n/2)f(1/(2N))$ in a single distribution to find $\hat{n} = 4Nu/f(1/(2N))$.

Multiple Isoalleles with No Selection

The simplest case is that in which there is no selection and all alleles mutate at the same rate u. In the first estimate (Wright 1949a) the distribution of existent alleles was expressed in discrete form $f(q) = Cq^{-1}(1 - q)^{4Nu-1}$ with $\sum_{1/(2N)}^{1} f(q) = 1$ and thus $C = 1/\sum_{1/(2N)}^{1} q^{-1}(1 - q)^{4Nv-1}$. Since $f(1/(2N)) = 2NC$ approximately, $n = 2u\sum_{1/(2N)}^{1} q^{-1}(1 - \hat{q})^{4Nu-1}$. "With $u = 10^{-6}$ a population of 250,000 may be expected to carry an average of 13.7 alleles. In larger populations, there should be a somewhat less than proportional increase, e.g., 132 alleles if N is increased tenfold."

Ewens (1964a) used the closely related continuous formula

$$n = 4Nu \int_{1/(2N)}^{1} q^{-1}(1 - q)^{4Nu-1} \, dq$$

and gave the following results:

$4Nu$	N	n	u	n
1	10^6	13.8	10^{-6}	12.4
2	2×10^6	27.0	2×10^{-6}	22.9
3	3×10^6	40.2	3×10^{-6}	32.8
4	4×10^6	55.3	4×10^{-6}	42.4

His result, $n = 12.4$ for $N = 250,000$, $u = 10^{-6}$, agrees fairly well with my estimate of 13.7.

Solution is simplified by introducing a finite rate of recurrence of each allele that is too small to affect appreciably the frequencies other than $F(0)$. The distribution of one allele opposed to all others collectively was shown to be:

$$(14.12) \quad \varphi(q) = \frac{\Gamma(4Nu + 4Nv)}{\Gamma(4Nu)\Gamma(4Nv)} q^{4Nv-1}(1-q)^{4Nu-1} \quad \text{with mean } \frac{v}{u+v}.$$

$$F\left(\frac{1}{2N}\right) = \left(\frac{1}{2N}\right)\varphi\left(\frac{1}{2N}\right) \approx \frac{\Gamma(4Nu + 4Nv)}{\Gamma(4Nu)\Gamma(4Nv)}\left(\frac{1}{2N}\right)^{4Nv},$$

$$F(0) = F(1/(2N))/4Nv.$$

Switching to the array of existent alleles:

$$(14.13) \quad \begin{aligned} \bar{q} &= \frac{v}{u+v}\left[\frac{1}{1-F(0)}\right], \\ n &= \frac{1}{\bar{q}} = \frac{4Nu + 4Nv}{4Nv}\left[1 - \frac{\Gamma(4Nu + 4Nv)}{4Nv\Gamma(4Nu)\Gamma(4Nv)}\left(\frac{1}{2N}\right)^{4Nv}\right]. \end{aligned}$$

Values of n can be calculated for each N and u, using the smallest value of $4Nv$ that the available table permits. It makes no appreciable difference whether $4Nv$ is taken as 0.0001 or 0.00001.

The results (Wright 1966) agreed fairly well with those given by Ewens (1964a) but were on the average 5.7% greater. In a later note Ewens (personal communication) has simplified (14.13):

$$(14.14) \quad n = 4Nu\{\log(2N) + \Gamma'(1) - \Gamma'(4Nu)/\Gamma(4Nu).$$

Table 14.1 gives the results from either (14.13) or (14.14) over wide ranges of N and u. If the alleles all had the same frequency, the proportion of homozygotes would be given by the inbreeding coefficient, $F = 1/[4Nu + 1]$ (essentially (12.3) in view of the relation between u and m) and this would be the reciprocal of the number of alleles present. Kimura and Crow (1964) define this as the effective number, n_e ($= 2K + 1$). It may be seen that it is much smaller than the actual number present, if this is large.

TABLE 14.1. Number of isoalleles n with no selection, maintained in populations of size N, mutation rates u. Turnover $K = 2Nu$.

N	$u = 10^{-7}$		$u = 10^{-6}$		$u = 10^{-5}$		$u = 10^{-4}$	
	K	n	K	n	K	n	K	n
10^4	0.002	1.04	0.02	1.39	0.2	4.76	2	32.3
10^5	0.02	1.49	0.2	5.68	2	41.5	20	318
10^6	0.2	6.60	2	50.7	20	410	200	3177
10^7	2	59.9	20	502	200	4098	2000	31761

In a test by computer simulation, Kimura (1966) obtained $n = 6.05$, $n_e = 2.07$ in the case $N = 50$, $u = 0.005$, as compared with theoretical 5.30 and 2.00, respectively.

Type Allele and Multiple Deleterious Mutations

Assume a type gene, A^+, and a class of equally unfavorable alleles A^i, A^j, etc., that are maintained by mutation at the rate u from all alleles, including A^+ (Wright 1966). Assume first that there is semidominance with relative selective values $(1 + 2s)$ for A^+A^+, $(1 + s)$ for A^+A^i, and 1 for A^iA^i, A^iA^j:

$$\Delta q_+ = v(1 - q_+) - uq_+ + sq_+(1 - q_+).$$

Ignoring the first term as negligible, $\hat{q}_+ = 1 - u/s$:

$$\Delta q_i = v(1 - q_i) - uq_i + (1/2)q_i(1 - q_i) \frac{\partial \bar{w}}{\partial q_i} \Big/ \bar{w},$$

The term $-uq_i$ may be ignored in this case, where

$$\bar{w} = 1 + 2sq_+ \quad \text{and} \quad \frac{\partial \bar{w}}{\partial q_i} = 2s \frac{\partial q_+}{\partial q_i} = -\frac{2sq_+}{1 - q_i}.$$

Therefore $\Delta q_i = v(1 - q_i) - uq_i - sq_+q_i$, approximately. Taking $q_+ = \hat{q}_+$, $sq_+ = s - u$, approximately: $\Delta q_i = v(1 - q_i) - sq_i$, $\sigma_{\Delta q}^2 = q_i(1 - q_i)/(2N)$,

(14.15) $$F(q_i) = \frac{1}{2N} \frac{\Gamma(4Ns + 4Nv)}{\Gamma(4Ns)\Gamma(4Nv)} q_i^{4Nv-1}(I - q_i)^{4Ns-1}.$$

This distribution excludes q_+ and thus applies only to the portion u/s of the total. Since A^i is usually absent, $F(0)$ is very nearly one. The mean for q_i is $v/(s + v)$ in this distribution. In the distribution, $f(q)$, of existent alleles, $\bar{q} = [v/(s + v)]/[1 - F(0)]$:

$$n = \frac{u}{s\bar{q}} \approx \frac{u}{v}(1 - F(0)) = \frac{u}{v}\left[1 - \frac{F(1/(2N))}{4Nv}\right],$$

(14.16)

$$n = \frac{u}{v}\left[1 - \frac{1}{4Nv}\frac{\Gamma(4Ns + 4Nv)}{\Gamma(4Ns)\,\Gamma(4Nv)}\left(\frac{1}{2N}\right)^{4Nv}\right].$$

In cases in which $(4Nu - 1)$ is an integer and $4Nv$ is much smaller, the approximation formula

$$\Gamma(c + x + 1) = c!\,c^x\left[1 + \frac{x(1 + x)}{2c}\right]$$

is convenient. The last factor is negligible if $x\,(= 4Nv)$ is very small.

(14.17) $$n = \frac{4Nu}{4Nv}\left[1 - \left(\frac{4Ns - 1}{2N}\right)^{4Nv}\frac{1}{\Gamma(1 + 4Nv)}\right].$$

A similar analysis in the case of completely recessive, noncomplementary mutations, all with selective disadvantage t to type leads to a similar formula except that the proportion of mutant alleles is $\sqrt{(u/t)}$, and $\sqrt{(ut)}$ is to be substituted for s. Both cases are illustrated in Table 14.2.

The number of deleterious alleles present at any time depends most on the rate of turnover, but with given K it decreases with the amount of selective disadvantage.

TABLE 14.2. Number of deleterious mutations in populations of size 10^5 or 10^6 maintained by mutation rates of 10^{-6} or 10^{-5}. The cases of semidominant and recessive mutations at various disadvantages are compared with neutral mutations $(s = 0)$.

N	u	K	$s = 0$	Semidominant Alleles $s = 10^{-4}$	10^{-3}	10^{-2}	Recessive Alleles $t = 10^{-3}$	10^{-2}	10^{-1}
10^5	10^{-6}	0.2	5.7	3.2	2.3	1.3	3.7	3.2	2.7
10^5	10^{-5}	2	41	32	23	13	32	27	23
10^6	10^{-6}	2	51	32	23	13	36	32	27
10^6	10^{-5}	20	410	320	226	133	320	272	226

Heterotic Loci

Consider next a system of alleles in which all homozygotes are at the same disadvantage, s, with respect to all heterozygotes (Wright 1966). It is again assumed that all alleles mutate at the same rate, u.

$$\bar{w} = 1 - s\sum q^2, \qquad \partial\bar{w}/\partial q_i = -2s[q_i - \sum q^2]/(1 - q_i),$$

$$\Delta q_i = v(1 - q_i) - uq_i - sq_i(q_i - \sum q^2)/(1 - s\sum q^2),$$

$$\Delta q_i \approx -uq_i - sq_i[q_i - \sum q^2(1 - sq_i)],$$

(14.18) $$\varphi(q) = Ce^{4Ns(1 + s\sum q^2)q}q^{-1}(1 - q)^{4Ns[1 - \sum q^2(1 - s)] + 4Nu - 1}.$$

Calculations have been made for various values of N and u, and for $s = 0.1$ or 1 (lethal homozygotes). Preliminary estimates were made of $\sum q^2$, the equilibrium frequency from selection. Relative ordinates were derived from calculations of $\log_{10} \varphi(q)$, and C was determined so as to make the sum of the frequencies excluding $F(0)$ equal to 1. This permitted empirical estimation of $\bar{q}$ and hence of $n \, (= 1/\bar{q})$, and the losses of alleles, $(n/2)f(1/(2N))$, for comparison with gains, $2Nu$. The estimate of $\sum q^2$ was revised and a second trial made. A third and usually final estimate was made by logarithmic interpolation. A check on the distribution was obtainable by empirical calculation of σ_q^2 and use of the formula $\sum q^2 = 1/n + n\sigma_q^2$. The subject has been approached from a different standpoint by Ewens (1964a).

The estimate of total number of alleles, n, may be compared with estimates reported by Kimura and Crow (1964) of effective number (n_e), taken here as the reciprocal of the equilibrium value from selection $\hat{q} \, (= \sum q^2)$ and thus the number if all frequencies were concentrated at this point. Table 14.3 gives the estimates of $\sum q^2$, $\bar{q}$, n_e, and n in the cases indicated.

A rather large number, 15, of heterotic lethal alleles is maintained in a random breeding population of one thousand, even by a mutation rate as low as 10^{-7}. The number is only doubled by a 1,000-fold increase in mutation rate. It increases rapidly, however, with increase in effective population number and becomes theoretically enormous (4,237) in one of effective population number of one million and mutation rate of 10^{-4}. The effective number of alleles in the sense used by Kimura and Crow is not much less than the actual number at low mutation rates but becomes much less at high rates, especially if the population is large.

The situation is similar with $s = 0.1$ except that the number of alleles maintained is much less unless both the population size and mutation rate are very great. This applies in exaggerated form in the limiting case of no selection and maintenance only by mutation.

The assumption that all heterozygotes have the same selective value and that all homozygotes have the same selective disadvantage are highly arbitrary. If there were important systematic differences, the number of alleles maintained in the population would be much reduced.

Self-incompatibility Alleles

It has been known for a long time that a very large number of alleles is the rule in the loci that determine self-incompatibility in many species of plants. Emerson (1939) found 37 (later 45) in Oenothera organensis, a species apparently restricted to a few moist canyons in the Organ Mountains of New Mexico. He estimated the whole species to include less than 1,000

TABLE 14.3. The quantities $\hat{q} = \sum q^2$, $\bar{q}$, n_e, and n for populations with effective numbers 10^3, 10^4, 10^5, and 10^6; mutation rates 10^{-4}, 10^{-5}, 10^{-6}, 10^{-7}, assuming equal selection against all homozygotes ($s = 0.1$, 1) relative to all heterozygotes. The actual number of alleles ($n = 1/\hat{q}$) is compared with effective number ($n_e = 1/\bar{q}$).

N	u	K	$s = 0$	$s = 0.1$				$s = 1$			
			n	$\hat{q}$	$\bar{q}$	n_e	n	$\hat{q}$	$\bar{q}$	n_e	n
10^3	10^{-7}	0.0002	1.0	0.2162	0.2006	4.6	5.0	0.0766	0.0677	13.1	14.8
	10^{-6}	0.002	1.0	.1896	.1725	5.3	5.8	.0681	.0597	14.7	16.7
	10^{-5}	0.02	1.3	.1597	.1355	6.3	7.4	.0587	.0506	17.0	19.8
	10^{-4}	0.2	3.8	.1221	.0841	11.2	11.9	.0468	.0365	21.4	27.4
10^4	10^{-7}	0.002	1.0	.0656	.0609	15.3	16.4	.0226	.0205	44.3	48.8
	10^{-6}	0.02	1.4	.0564	.0502	17.7	19.9	.0197	.0177	50.9	56.4
	10^{-5}	0.2	4.7	.0454	.0352	22.0	28.4	.0164	.0139	60.9	72.0
	10^{-4}	2	32.3	.0314	.0162	31.9	61.6	.0125	.0085	80.3	117.7
10^5	10^{-7}	0.02	1.5	.01943	.01773	51	56	.00664	.00614	151	163
	10^{-6}	0.2	5.7	.01624	.01374	62	73	.00570	.00506	175	198
	10^{-5}	2	41	.01233	.00791	81	126	.00458	.00354	218	282
	10^{-4}	20	318	.00731	.00239	137	418	.00317	.00161	315	619
10^6	10^{-7}	0.2	6.6	.00568	.00505	176	198	.00195	.00175	512	572
	10^{-6}	2	51	.00457	.00347	219	289	.00163	.00141	615	711
	10^{-5}	20	410	.00309	.00143	323	700	.00125	.00085	803	1183
	10^{-4}	200	3170	0.00145	0.00029	689	3447	0.00075	0.00024	1333	4237

individuals and very likely less than 500. He raised the question with me on how so many alleles could be present in such a small population.

It appeared to be impossible to derive an exact solution because of the peculiar mode of selection: failure of pollen tube growth on a style in which either allele is that of the pollen nucleus (chapter 5). Approximations were obtained that seemed adequate from the biological standpoint (Wright 1939a).

The consequences of the mode of selection can be illustrated in most extreme form by the case of a population that starts with only three alleles S_1, S_2, and S_3. The history of a population of 500 made up to consist of only one genotype, S_1S_2, except for one individual of genotype S_1S_3 would be as follows from the deterministic viewpoint:

Generation

Genotype	0	1	2	3	4	5	6	Later
S_1S_2	0.998	0	0.500	0.250	0.375	0.312	0.344	0.333 ± 0.0122
S_1S_3	.002	.500	.250	.375	.312	.344	.328	$.333 \pm .0122$
S_2S_3	0		0.500	0.250	0.375	0.312	0.344	$0.328 \; 0.333 \pm 0.0122$

Starting from the extreme case in which one allele, S_3, is so rare that the population would become extinct if the single individual S_1S_3 should die without reproducing, there is rapid approach to equality of the three alleles. The deviation of any allelic frequency from the equilibrium value $\hat{q} = 1/3$ is reversed in the following generation and halved in amount:

$$q - \hat{q} = -(1/2)(q' - \hat{q}),$$
$$q = (1/2)(1 - q').$$

(14.19)

The variance, disregarding accidents of sampling, becomes one-fourth of its value in the preceding generation. The frequency of seeds carrying a particular allele is $2q \,(= (1 - q'))$ because all zygotes are necessarily heterozygous. The sampling variance for N seeds: $2q(1 - 2q)/N = q'(1 - q')/N$. The sampling variance for the $2N$ representatives of this allele in the seeds is thus $q'(1 - q')/4N$ (Ewens 1964b) and thus just half its value in the absence of the self-incompatibility reaction. The population should approach a state in which the total variance remains constant.

(14.20) $$\sigma_q{}^2 = (1/4)\sigma_{q'}^2 + \int_0^{1/2} \frac{q'(1 - q')}{4N} \varphi(q') \, dq,$$

where $\varphi(q')$ is the frequency of a gene frequency. The distribution function is not known, but if N is large all gene frequencies may be expected to concentrate so closely about $q = 1/3$ that q' may be assigned this value with little error, so that the integral takes the value $1/(18N)$. Putting $\sigma_q{}^2 = \sigma_{q'}^2$, then $\sigma_q{}^2 = 2/(27N)$.

In the population of 500 of the above table, q will come to be distributed in an approximately normal distribution with mean 0.333 and standard deviation 0.0122.

Sooner or later, however, a fourth allele may be expected to appear and to be subject at once to maximum favorable selection since pollen carrying it is not inhibited by any other plant. The situation with four or more alleles is more complicated than with only three. It was shown empirically in chapter 5 that the formula (Wright 1960b)

$$\Delta q = -q(q - \hat{q})/[(1 - \hat{q})(1 - 2\hat{q})]$$

is a better approximation than a slightly different formula derived earlier (Wright 1939a), except in the case $n = 3$ in which the latter was exact. Both of these were shown to be superior to an approximation formula used by Fisher (1958).

In the above formula $\Delta q = 0$ if $\sum (q^2 - \hat{q}q) = 0$, and $\hat{q} = \sum q^2$ since $\sum q = 1$. Also $\hat{q} = (1/n) + n\sigma_q{}^2$, since $\sigma_q{}^2 = (1/n)(\sum q^2 - \bar{q} \sum q)$ and $\bar{q} = 1/n$.

The sampling variance was shown above to be $q'(1 - q')/4N$ if $n = 3$. With large n, Δq becomes so small that the sampling variance for $2N$ genes approaches the usual binomial variance $q(1 - q)/2N$ but is always somewhat smaller. Starting from N plants in which an allele has the frequency q, pollination, followed by the self-incompatibility reaction, leads to gene frequencies $q + \Delta q$ in the fertilized ova. The frequency of seeds carrying the allele is $2(q + \Delta q)$ since all are heterozygous. The sampling variance for N seeds is $2(q + \Delta q)[1 - 2(q + \Delta q)]/N$. The sampling variance for gametes carrying the allele is one-fourth of this:

(14.21) $$\sigma^2_{\Delta q} = (q + \Delta q)[1 - 2(q + \Delta q)]/2N.$$

The formula used by Fisher (1958), $\sigma^2_{\Delta q} = q(1 - 2q)/2N$, is not correct, since, as Ewens (1964b) noted, it applies to the wrong generation (yielding the obviously incorrect result $\sigma^2_{\Delta q} = 0$ if $q = 1/2$). It is, however, a better approximation than $q(1 - q)/2N$ in the neighborhood of the equilibrium frequency, and will be used here.

Terms for mutation pressure and immigration pressure must be included in the full formula for Δq if not negligible. These modify the position of the equilibrium value of q, but the symbol $\hat{q}$ will continue to be used here for that under selection alone.

(14.22) $$\Delta q = -aq(q - \hat{q}) + v(1 - q) - uq - m(q - Q),$$
$$a = 1/[(1 - \hat{q})(1 - 2\hat{q})],$$

(14.23) $\sigma^2_{\Delta q} = q(1 - 2q)/2N$,

(14.24) $\varphi(q) = Ce^{2Naq}q^{[4N(mQ + v)] - 1}(1 - 2q)^{Na(1 - 2\hat{q}) + 2N[m(1 - Q) + u] - 1}$.

In what follows m and v will be assumed to be negligible:

(14.25) $\varphi(q) = Ce^{2Naq}q^{-1}(1 - 2q)^{Na(1 - 2\hat{q}) + 2Nu - 1}$.

The corresponding discrete distribution with frequencies $F(q) \approx \varphi(q)/2N$ at intervals of $1/(2N)$ has nearly its total frequency in the class $F(0)$, but, as before, one may switch here from the distribution for a single allele to that for the array of existent alleles, all assumed to have the same statistical properties, $f(q) = F(q)/[1 - F(0)]$. This distribution applies only to periods in which there is a given number of alleles, n. If the number increases because of a mutation or decreases because of loss of an allele, the distribution changes because of change in $\hat{q}$.

The rate at which increase from n to $(n + 1)$ tends to occur is, as before, $2Nu$ per generation. The rate of loss taken in the previous cases as $(n/2)f(1/(2N))$ is modified because of the exceptionally strong selection favoring a mutation, illustrated in the case of $n = 3$ in which the rate becomes practically zero. The situation at the lower limit involves complications that make it difficult to arrive at exact estimates. Slightly different formulas have been used in various papers. We will use here the simple formula:

(14.26) $K = \frac{n - 3}{2}f(1/(2N))$

that takes cognizance of the impossibility of a value of n less than 3 in persisting populations, but that approaches the usual formulas as n increases.

As noted above and in chapter 5, my treatment has been questioned by Fisher (1958) and on different grounds by Moran (1962) and Ewens (1964b). Fisher stated that he obtained very different results from those which I had reported. Moran and Ewens held that the general mode of approach which both Fisher and I had pursued was invalid and that indeed no steady state exists. The latter point seems to have been based on failure to distinguish between the distribution $F(q)$, for a single allele which in the long run is nearly always absent and that for the array of existent alleles $f(q) = F(q)/[1 - F(0)]$ in which $f(0)$ is zero by definition. Moran was also disturbed by the non-Markovian character of the relation between generations. The dependence of selection pressures on $\hat{q}$ and the dependence of the latter on the number of alleles and on the momentary form of the distribution does, indeed, preclude a completely steady state in the usual sense, but not in an approximate sense. Moreover, if the distribution is found separately for each number of alleles and a compound distribution is constructed from these on the basis of the expected frequencies of different numbers, the difficulty from variation in number is obviated. As brought out later, the correction of the 1939a results for variation in the number of alleles has been found to be very slight. The effect of fluctuations in the form of the distribution are shown to be still less important.

Fisher (1958) did not support his statement that "the treatment of this case by S. Wright leads to results, as shown by his graphs, very different" from those that he obtained, by actual comparisons with cases that I had presented, but he instead presented two new cases. The formulas that he gave for Δq, $\sigma^2_{\Delta q}$, n, K, and (superficially) $\varphi(q)$ appeared, however, to be quite different. It was, therefore, somewhat surprising to find that when his formulas were applied to three widely different cases in my 1939a paper, the graphs were barely distinguishable. Application of my formulas to his new cases gave equally similar graphs. There were, however, great differences in the estimate of number of alleles in one of his new cases and in the required mutation rate in the other.

Table 14.4 compares estimates (Wright 1960b) for three of the cases that I had considered in 1939a (I, II, III) and the two new cases considered by Fisher (1958). Estimate A in each case is based either on my 1939a formula (W_1) for Δq or for the slight modification (W_2) that I preferred in 1960 and the customary sampling variance $\sigma^2_{\Delta q} = q(1 - q)/2N$ referred to as W. Estimate B is that which I obtained by using Fisher's formulas (F) for Δq, which differs from mine in the selection term, and in ignoring the mutation term, and for $\sigma^2_{\Delta q} = q(1 - 2q)/2N$, which I accepted in 1960. Estimate C is the same except for use of my selection terms in Δq. Estimate D differs from C in including the mutation term of Δq in the formula for $\varphi(q)$, which here and in A requires a troublesome iteration process, in order to get approximate agreement with the estimate of required u. This is wholly unnecessary where u is as small as in V, and of only slight importance, as shown by comparison of C and D in II and IV. D is, however, the preferred method before allowance for variation of n, discussed later.

The only important difference among the estimates is in the sixfold greater value of u in B of case III in comparison with A or D. This arises from the inaccuracy of Fisher's formula for Δq when n is as small as five.

Fisher himself, however, reported a considerably smaller estimate of n in IV than I obtain by use of his formulas for Δq and $\sigma^2_{\Delta q}$ (35 instead of 53). This was because he used a method that avoids the numerical integration which I used, at the expense of not being able to calculate $\bar{q}$. He used $n = 1/\hat{q}$ instead of $n = 1/\bar{q}$. These do not differ much if the distribution is compact (III, V) but may differ greatly if j-shaped (I, II, IV) and thus have

TABLE 14.4. Estimates of number of alleles (n) maintained in populations of diverse effective size (N) by specified mutation rates (u) (first three cases), or of number of alleles (n) and mutation rate (u) to give a specified equilibrium frequency $\hat{q}$ (cases IV and V) using various combinations of formulas as described in the text.

		N	$\hat{q}$	u in $\varphi(q)$	Δq	$\sigma^2_{\Delta q}$	n	u
I	A	500	0.0449	0.001	W_1	W	33.8	0.001
	D	500	.0449	.001	W_2	F	33.2	0.00097
II	A	50	.1031	0.01	W_1 or W_2	W	14.7	0.0101
	B	50	.1031	0	F	F	13.5	0.0095
	C	50	.1031	0	W_2	F	13.4	0.0083
	D	50	.1031	0.01	W_2	F	14.5	0.0104
III	A	50	.2032	10^{-6}	W_1 or W_2	W	5.1	1.2×10^{-6}
	B	50	.2032	0	F	F	5.2	8.5×10^{-6}
	D	50	.2032	10^{-6}	W_2	F	5.1	1.4×10^{-6}
IV	A	1,000	.03	10^{-3}	W_2	W	53	0.9×10^{-3}
	B	1,000	.03	0	F	F	53	0.9×10^{-3}
	C	1,000	.03	0	W_2	F	52	0.9×10^{-3}
	D	1,000	.03	10^{-3}	W_2	F	55	1.0×10^{-3}
V	A	10,000	.03	0	W_2	W	34	5×10^{-12}
	B	10,000	.03	0	F	F	34	7×10^{-12}
	C	10,000	0.03	0	W_2	F	34	4×10^{-12}

many rare alleles with rapid turnover. As I noted (1966), "A case could perhaps be made for citing the number of alleles as that for ones common enough to be likely to be found . . . if ones that appear in only 17 or less of the 1,000 zygotes are excluded about 35 are left in agreement with Fisher's estimate." Fisher, however, did not state in his criticism that he was using number of alleles in a different sense. Kimura and Crow (1964) as already noted later defined $n_e = 1/\hat{q}$ as the effective number of alleles.

Fisher also reported a 44-fold higher required mutation rate in V than I obtain by using his full formulas. This was because of his use of an erroneous approximation of his complicated full integration formula and the amplification of the erroneous factor from 4.4 to 44 by a misplaced decimal point. These errors do not, however, explain directly his statement that my graphs in the 1939a paper were very different from those that he obtained, since they relate to his two new cases. Actually, as noted above, there were no important differences in the graphs in any of the five cases, new or old.

The important conclusion emerged from these comparisons that unless the number of alleles is very small, in which case the conditions for validity of the formula for $\varphi(q)$ are met only roughly, as emphasized by Ewens (1964b), the distribution and even its subterminal class on which the rate of loss of alleles depends are not very sensitive to what superficially seem like rather important differences in the formulas.

We will consider next the effect of variations in number of alleles, the principal cause of random shifts in $\hat{q}$ and hence in the non-Markovian relation between generations which disturbed Moran.

Consider the case of a population of effective size, $N = 500$, mutation rate, $u = 10^{-6}$, from any allele to a new one:

$$\log_{10} f(q) = \log_{10} C + 2Naq \log_{10} e - \log_{10} q$$
$$+ [Na(1 - 2\hat{q}) + 2Nu - 1] \log_{10} (1 - q),$$

where $a = 1/(1 - \hat{q})(1 - 2\hat{q})$.

Calculations were made for $f(q)$ at $q = 0.001$, 0.002, 0.005, and higher values at intervals of 0.005 with rating up so that $\sum f(q) = 1$ for $\hat{q} = 0.07$, 0.08, and 0.09. The values of $\bar{q}$ and $\sigma_q{}^2$ were obtained empirically from the frequency distribution. As a check, $\sigma_q{}^2 = (1/n)[\sum q^2 - \bar{q} \sum q] = \bar{q}(\hat{q} - \bar{q})$, noting that $n = 1/\bar{q}$, $\hat{q} = \sum q^2$, $\sum q = 1$ and $k = [(n - 3)/2]f(1/(2N))$. (See Table 14.5.)

TABLE 14.5. Calculated values of $\bar{q}$, n, $1{,}000\sigma_q{}^2$, $1{,}000f(1/(2N))$ and K for values of $\hat{q}$, assuming $N = 500$, $u = 10^{-6}$.

$\hat{q}$	$\bar{q}$	n	$1{,}000\sigma_q{}^2$	$1{,}000f(1/(2N))$	K
0.07	0.06344	15.763	0.417	2.247	0.01434
.08	.07515	13.306	.364	0.2694	.001388
0.09	0.08619	11.602	0.329	0.01935	0.0000832

These, however, do not apply to integral numbers of alleles. Values of $\log_{10} K$ were estimated for each value of n from 10 to 16 by interpolation and extrapolation. The frequencies of occurrence of each of these was then estimated by the formula $2Nuf_{n-1} = Kf_n$ expressing the balance of gains and losses. Values of $(\hat{q} - \bar{q})$ were estimated by interpolation and extrapolation and $\hat{q}$ and $\sigma_q{}^2$ were calculated from these (see Table 14.6).

The mean number of alleles comes out $\bar{n} = \sum f_n n = 12.62$ with standard deviation 0.850. The mean gene frequency is $\bar{q} = 0.07957$. The variance of q can be analyzed as follows:

Variance of q:			%
With given n	$\sigma_{q.n}^2 =$	$\overline{\sigma_q{}^2} = 0.000352$	92.4
Among values of n	$\sigma_{q(n)}^2 =$	$\sigma_{\hat{q}}{}^2 = 0.000029$	7.6
Total	$\sigma_q{}^2$	$= 0.000381$	100.0

TABLE 14.6. Estimates of f_n, $\bar{q}$, $\acute{q}$, $1{,}000\sigma_q{}^2$, $1{,}000K$, and $1{,}000f(1/(2N))$ for numbers, n, of alleles, assuming $N = 500$, $u = 10^{-6}$.

n	f_n	$\bar{q}$	$\acute{q}$	$1{,}000\sigma_q{}^2$	$1{,}000K$	$1{,}000f(1/(2N))$
10	0.0017	0.10000	0.10294	0.294	0.0020	0.0006
11	.0701	.09091	.09438	.315	0.0238	0.0060
12	.3835	.08333	.08737	.337	0.1828	0.0406
13	.4082	.07692	.08157	.358	0.940	0.1879
14	.1216	.07143	.07673	.379	3.36	0.6104
15	.0140	.06667	.07267	.400	8.65	1.442
16	0.0009	0.06250	0.06925	0.422	16.67	2.565
12.62	1.0000	0.07957				

Thus only 7.6% of total variance of q is due to changes in the number of alleles. From the standpoint of the amount of error in assuming that selection is always directed toward a constant equilibrium value, $\acute{q}$ (in the derivation of the formula for $\varphi(q)$), it is more important to analyze the variance of $\acute{q}$. Its sampling variance in distributions with a given number of alleles can be derived from the formula $\acute{q} = 1/n + n\sigma_q{}^2$ leading to $\sigma_{\acute{q}.n}^2 = 2n\sigma_{q.n}^4$. The component due to changes in the number of alleles can be calculated directly from the mean expected values for the various values as given above.

Variance of $\acute{q}$		%
With given n	$\sigma_{\acute{q}.n}^2 = 3.1 \times 10^{-6}$	31.2
Among values of n	$\sigma_{\acute{q}(n)}^2 = 20.3 \times 10^{-6}$	86.8
	$\sigma_{\acute{q}}^2 = 23.4 \times 10^{-6}$	

The variance of mean $\acute{q}$ among values of n is 5.3% of the total variance of q, which is large enough to indicate the desirability of calculating distributions separately for each number of alleles. The sampling variance of q with given n is only 0.9% of the variance of q with given n, which indicates that there is little residual error after making the separate calculations.

Figure 14.3 shows the distribution of q during periods in which the number is constant (11–15).

Calculations were also made for $N = 500$ under the assumption $\sigma_{\Delta q}^2 = q(1 - q)/2N$ (Wright 1965b). For $u = 10^{-6}$, these yielded $\bar{n} = 12.50$ instead of 12.62 and $\sigma_n = 0.844$ instead of 0.850. The smallness of the differences shows again that it makes little difference which formula for $\sigma_{\Delta q}^2$ is used even if mean $\acute{q}$ is as large as 0.08.

It is of interest to compare these results (see Table 14.7) with those where new alleles are introduced into a population of the same size, a thousand

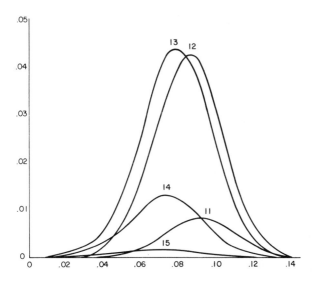

FIG. 14.3. The steady state distributions of self-incompatibility alleles maintained by a mutation rate of 10^{-6} in a population of 500 during periods in which there are 11 to 15 present, with total frequencies according to those expected for these numbers (usually 13 or 12) (essentially from Wright 1965b, Fig. 4).

times as frequently, whether by mutation or (much more probably) by immigration ($N = 500$, $u = 10^{-3}$) (case I of Table 14.4).

Estimates were made of K for each value of n from 24 to 45, of the frequencies f_n of occurrence of these numbers, and of $\hat{q}$ and of σ_q^2 as above. The mean number of alleles comes out 33.73 and the standard deviation 3.34. (See Table 14.8.)

Kimura (1965a) has made a computer study of this case involving 2,100 simulated generations in which exactly one mutation was introduced into the 1,000 gametes in each generation. The mean number of alleles from

TABLE 14.7. Calculated values of $\bar{q}$, n, $10^4\sigma_q^2$, $100f(1/(2N))$, and K for values of $\hat{q}$, assuming $N = 500$, $u = 10^{-3}$.

$\hat{q}$	$\bar{q}$	n	$10^4\sigma_q^2$	$100f(1/(2N))$	K
0.040	0.02500	40.071	3.90	8.645	1.603
.043	.02802	35.690	4.24	7.129	1.165
.045	.03023	33.083	4.46	6.171	0.928
.047	.03256	30.710	4.63	5.270	0.730
0.050	0.03627	27.573	4.83	4.046	0.497

TABLE 14.8. Estimates of f_n, $\hat{q}$, and K for numbers, n of alleles, assuming $N = 500$, $u = 10^{-3}$.

n	f_n	$\hat{q}$	K	n	f	$\hat{q}$	K
24	0.001	0.0537	0.290	35	0.107	0.0435	1.102
25	.003	.0526	0.340	36	.090	.0427	1.197
26	.007	.0516	0.396	37	.069	.0420	1.294
27	.014	.0506	0.457	38	.050	.0413	1.393
28	.027	.0496	0.522	39	.033	.0407	1.493
29	.046	.0486	0.593	40	.021	.0400	1.596
30	.068	.0477	0.668	41	.012	.0395	1.702
31	.091	.0468	0.748	42	.007	.0389	1.811
32	.110	.0459	0.832	43	.004	.0384	1.923
33	.119	.0451	0.918	44	.002	.0379	2.037
34	0.118	0.0443	1.009	45	0.001	0.0374	2.153

generation 140 at intervals of 40 generations was 36.2, with standard deviation 3.21. These agree moderately well with the theoretical values. Ewens and Ewens (1966) made a similar computer study, also introducing one mutation per generation. Their average for 800 consecutive generations after generation 200 was 32.18 and standard deviation 3.32, and agreed still better with theory, which as far as the mean is concerned was straddled by the two simulation studies.

Mayo (1966) found that in a simulation experiment 40 alleles were maintained in a population of 500 by a slightly larger mutation rate than above (about 0.0012 instead of 0.0010).

The analysis of the variance of values of q and of $\hat{q}$ are as follows:

	$\times 10^{-4}$	%	$\times 10^{-6}$	%
With given n	$\sigma^2_{q.n} = 4.390$	98.0	$\sigma^2_{\hat{q}.n} = 12.7$	64.9
Among values of n	$\sigma^2_{q(n)} = 0.090$	2.0	$\sigma^2_{\hat{q}(n)} = 6.9$	35.1
Total	$\sigma_q^2 = 4.480$	100.0	$\sigma_{\hat{q}}^2$ 19.6	100.0

In this case, the variance of $\hat{q}$ among the distributions with different values of n is only 1.5% of the total variance of q so that calculation of the values of n separately was much less important than in the preceding case. On the other hand, the sampling variance of $\hat{q}$ for given n is 2.9% of $\sigma^2_{q.n}$. The error in ignoring the variations of $\hat{q}$ that are due to fluctuations in the form of the distribution for a given number of alleles is thus appreciable though still of minor importance. This case is illustrated in Figure 14.4.

The case of a population ten times as large as the two preceding cases and with the same mutation rate as the first ($N = 5,000$, $u = 10^{-6}$) has also

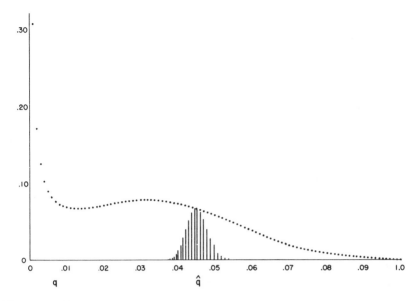

Fig. 14.4. The steady state distribution of self-incompatibility alleles maintained by a mutation rate of 10^{-3} in a population of 500 during periods in which 33 are present (dotted line). The solid lines represent the relative frequencies of numbers 24 to 45, with 33 and 34 the most common. The numbers are in inverse order on the scale q.

been worked out in the same way. Without allowing for shifting of the equilibrium point, $\hat{q}$, with changes in the number of alleles, the equilibrium frequency came out 0.027 and the mean gene frequency 0.0250, indicating that an average of 40.0 alleles were carried. The turnover was 0.0088. The number of alleles varied from about 35 to 46 with a standard deviation of 1.75. The analysis of $\sigma_q{}^2$ and $\sigma_{\hat{q}}{}^2$ gave the following results:

		$\times 10^{-5}$	%		$\times 10^{-7}$	%
With given n	$\sigma^2_{q.n}$	5.09	97.7	$\sigma^2_{\hat{q}.n}$	2.1	18.4
Among values of n	$\sigma^2_{q(n)}$	0.12	2.3	$\sigma^2_{\hat{q}(n)}$	9.3	81.6
Total	$\sigma_q{}^2$	5.21	100.0	$\sigma_{\hat{q}}{}^2$	11.4	100.0

The variance of $\hat{q}$ among the distributions is only about 1.8% of the total variance of q, so that calculation of the frequencies of values of n is again of little importance. The sampling variance of $\hat{q}$ for given n is only 0.4% of $\sigma^2_{q.n}$, so that the error in ignoring variations of q due to fluctuations in the form of the distribution for a given number of alleles is negligible. The distribution of values of n and that of q for $n = 40$ are illustrated in Figure 14.5.

The relation of number of alleles to effective size of population and mutation or immigration rate is exhibited in Figure 14.6. The case of $u = 10^0$ is that of complete replacement from an infinite population so that the number of alleles is $2N$ (all different). The lines were constructed by interpolation from a considerable number of points. For the reasons brought out above, the reliability of the distribution curves on which these are based rises with the number of alleles and the smallness of the mutation rate.

It has been assumed here that the population is homogeneous. If subdivided into small, partially isolated demes the number of alleles maintained in each deme tends to be small, but the total number for a given total size of population is larger than in a random breeding population. A number of determinations were made by Wright (1939a) (see Table 14.9). These were made with n varying and using $\sigma_{\Delta q}^2 = (1 - q)/2N$ and so are less accurate than the values discussed above, but they should be sufficiently accurate to illustrate the principle.

From the comparison of I and II it is apparent that increase in the muta-

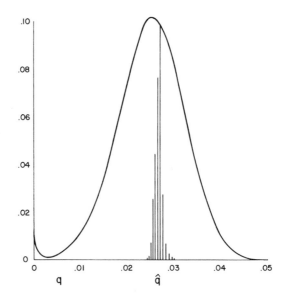

FIG. 14.5. The steady state distribution of self-incompatibility alleles maintained by a mutation rate of 10^{-6} in a population of 5,000 during periods in which 40 alleles are present. The compact distribution shows the relative frequencies of different numbers, with 40 the most common.

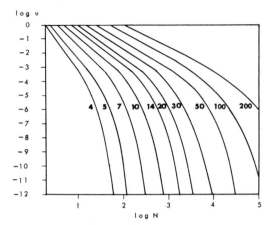

FIG. 14.6. The relation of average number of self-incompatibility alleles to log N and log u (or log m).

tion rate (or immigration from outside the total considered here) not only increases the number of alleles carried within demes and in the total but increases the latter disproportionately so that ratio of the number in the subdivided population to that in the randombred population rises from 1.14 to 1.5. The mutation rate in III is intermediate between that in I and II

TABLE 14.9. Comparison of properties of populations of effective size 500 with various mutation rates, subdivided in various ways, with a panmictic population of the same total size.

		N	m	u	n	K
	Random	500	0	0.000045	17.5	0.25
I	Deme	50	0.01	0.000045	11.6	3.6
	Total	500	0	0.000045	20.0	0.23
	Random	500	0	.001	33.8	3.0
II	Deme	50	0.01	.001	13.4	5.3
	Total	500	0	.001	50.0	2.0
	Random	500	0	.0002	22.1	0.90
III	Deme	50	0.001	.0002	8.2	1.0
	Total	500	0	.0002	50.0	0.43
	Random	500	0	.00009	19.2	0.45
IV	Deme	10	0.01	.00009	5.3	3.3
	Total	500	0	0.00009	50.0	0.18

and leads to an intermediate number in the randombred population. The much greater isolation, however, reduces the number carried by demes but increases the above ratio to 2.3. The mutation rate in IV is also intermediate between those of I and II. Because of the very small size of the demes, the number of alleles per deme is very small but because of the fivefold increase in number of demes the total population carries as many alleles as II or III and the above ratio has risen to 2.6.

It has been assumed throughout this discussion that the number of different alleles is indefinitely great and u has referred to the frequency of introduction of novel ones by mutation or immigration. If the number is finite, there is rapid approach to this as N or u is increased (Wright 1939a).

CHAPTER 15

Components of Variability: Additive Effects

Chapter 15, volume 1, was devoted to inferences on the genetics of quantitative variability that can be derived from studies of crosses. The present and following chapter will be concerned largely with inferences on the composition of such variability in populations that are either mating at random or depart from random mating in specified ways.

The general theory of components of variability has been discussed in volume 1. In the genetic case, the pertinent components are closely related to the correlations between relatives. A beginning was made by Pearson (1904) and Yule (1906). Weinberg (1909, 1910) developed the subject systematically, allowing for multiple alleles, degrees of dominance, the more familiar two-factor interactions, and environmental components. Fisher (1918) obtained similar results from a different mathematical formulation. He dealt with two-factor interactions more completely and introduced complications from assortative mating. My first paper on the subject (1917) dealt with analysis of covariance as well as variance and is discussed in volume 1. I introduced path analysis into the deduction of correlations (1920, 1921), applied the theory to threshold characters (1934), and analyzed variability and genetic correlations in the case of the optimum model (1935, 1952a). Mather (1949) reviewed and applied the theory from Fisher's mode of approach. He went especially into the complications from linkage. Comstock and Robinson (1948, 1952) have made important contributions with special reference to plant breeding. An important advance was made simultaneously by Kempthorne (1954) and Cockerham (1954) in introducing an exhaustive mode of analyzing the contribution to variance of interactions among two or more loci and relating these to the correlations between relatives. There has been an extensive development from this on such matters as associated inbreeding (Cockerham 1956, 1959, 1963; Kempthorne 1957; and Harris 1964a,b); and associated selection (Nei 1963). Hayman (1960) has developed a mode of analysis based on systematic diallel crosses which has been followed up by others.

More has been written on theory and applications in this aspect of population genetics than any other. It will not be practicable here to discuss much more than the basic concepts.

Environmental Factors

The determination of the genetic component is simple enough if it can be assumed that the effects of genes are wholly additive in relation to each other and to environmental variations. A first rough approximation may often be obtained on this hypothesis, but there may be serious complications (1) from the occurrence of dominance and of factor interactions; (2) from interactions between heredity and environment; and (3) from correlations in the occurrence of these factors.

With respect to the second of these it is not uncommon for manifestations of gene differences to be wholly restricted to particular environments. Another sort of interaction touched on in volume 1, chapter 15, is the greater susceptibility to unfavorable conditions of isogenic lines than randombred ones, which may in turn be more susceptible than first crosses between isogenic lines.

Correlations in the occurrence of genetic and environmental deviations are easily avoided in experimental populations but are not uncommon in natural populations. They are probably more frequent in plants than in animals. They are, however, usually present in a livestock population, since good management includes selection of good heredity. A sort of correlation that is fairly common, especially in mammals, is the result of effects on individuals of a character of one or both parents that has a genetic component. Correlations of this sort are almost certainly present in all human populations and provide an extremely difficult problem for disentanglement of the roles of heredity and environment.

Chapman (1946) distinguished six components of variance that are environmental with respect to direct effect on a character that he was studying (weight response of the immature rat ovary to a gonadotropic hormone):

$p_1{}^2$ permanent maternal differences with prenatal effects,
$p_2{}^2$ permanent maternal differences with postnatal effects,
$t_1{}^2$ temporary maternal differences with prenatal effects,
$t_2{}^2$ temporary maternal differences with postnatal effects,
c^2 contemporary nonmaternal environmental differences,
a^2 effects restricted to individual measurements (accidents of development or of technique).

He carried out experiments that made it possible to discriminate among these with reasonable certainty. Thus full sisters, with the same genetic components in terms of additive, dominance, and interaction effects, were obtained in four types of experiments.

Full Sisters:	Common Factors					
	p_1^2	p_2^2	t_1^2	t_2^2	c^2	a^2
Litter mates reared by their dams	1	1	1	1	1	0
Litter mates reared by different dams	1	0	1	0	1	0
Nonlitter mates reared by their dams	1	1	0	0	0	0
Nonlitter mates reared by different dams	1	0	0	0	0	0

Differences among these permitted estimation of p_2^2, t_2^2, and $(t_1^2 + c^2)$.

Comparison of maternal and paternal half-sisters, with the same genetic components, ignoring possible sex-linked factors, gave a basis for estimating $p_1^2 + p_2^2$ and thus p_1^2 in conjunction with the preceding:

Half-sisters	Common Factors					
	p_1^2	p_2^2	t_1^2	t_2^2	c^2	a^2
Paternal half-sisters reared by dam	0	0	0	0	0	0
Maternal half-sisters reared by dam	1	1	0	0	0	0

Estimates from paternal and maternal aunt-niece pairs are like the paternal half-sister pairs in having none of the environmental factors in common and in having the same autosomal genetic component. It happens that correlations with paternal aunt and with maternal half-sister have the same sex-linked component but otherwise there may be complications from sex-linkage, to be considered later.

Estimates from unrelated individuals made possible certain discriminations of environmental components.

Unrelated individuals:	Common Factors					
	p_1^2	p_2^2	t_1^2	t_2^2	c^2	a^2
Nonsibs reared by same female at same time	0	1	0	1	1	0
Nonsibs reared by same female at different times	0	1	0	0	0	0
Nonsibs reared by different females at same time (instead of different times)	0	0	0	0	1	0

These permitted estimates of p_2^2, c^2, and t_2^2. The residual variance of individuals gives a^2, thus completing the analysis of the total nongenetic variance at least in principle.

The Additive Genetic Variance

In this section, the genetic components will be assumed to be wholly additive. Genome-environment correlation and maternal influences of all sorts will be assumed to be absent, leaving only c^2 and a^2 of the above environmental components. The symbol e^2 will be used for the total environmental component and $e_1 e_2 r_{E(1)E(2)}$ for the environmental contribution to the correlation between two relatives ($= c^2$ in experiments in which the environments of the relatives may be considered identical).

Under these assumptions, the correlations between any two specified relatives, R_1 and R_2, are given at once by path analysis of the appropriate diagram (Fig. 15.1). Here H and E are used for genetic and environmental factors, respectively, and genes of gametes are indicated merely by dots.

The correlation between any two zygotes, such as H_1 and H_2, can be analyzed into contributions from all of the independent paths through common ancestors of the type H_A. Assume that there are n zygotes in such a path, including H_1 and H_2 themselves. There are $n - 2$ zygotes in the path connecting two gametes immediately back of H_1 and H_2 so that the correlation between these gametes is $\sum [(1/2)^{n-2}(1 + F_A)]$. This is to be multiplied by $a_1 a_2 \{ = 0.5/\sqrt{[(1 + F_{H1})(1 + F_{H2})]}\}$ to give the contribution through H_A. The genetic correlation between R_1 and R_2, taking account of all independent paths, is thus:

$$(15.1) \quad r_{H(1)H(2)} = \sum [0.5^{n-1}(1 + F_A)]/\sqrt{[(1 + F_{H1})(1 + F_{H2})]}$$

$$\text{(Wright 1922a).}$$

To obtain the corresponding correlation between the phenotypes of the

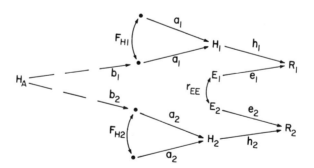

FIG. 15.1. Path diagram for correlation between two relatives R_1 and R_2, assuming only additive gene effects.

two relatives this must be multiplied by the path coefficients, h_1, h_2, describing the influence of the genetic components on their phenotypes. If there is a correlation between their environments, under the simple assumptions of this section a term $e_1 e_2 r_{E(1)E(2)}$ must be added, where $h^2 + e^2 = 1$.

The relatives that merit first consideration are parents, P, offspring, O (Wright 1921). Letting m ($= r_{H(P1)H(P2)}$) be the genetic correlation between the parental genotypes (Fig. 15.2):

$$a_1 = 1/\sqrt{[2(1 + F_{o1})]}, \qquad b_1 = \sqrt{[(1 + F_{P1})/2]}, \qquad b_2 = \sqrt{[(1 + F_{P2})/2]},$$

$$(15.2) \qquad r_{O(1)P(1)} = h_{o1} h_{P1}[a_1 b_1 + m a_1 b_2] + e_{o1} e_{P1} r_{E(O1)E(P1)}$$

In a population in a steady state, $ab = 1/2$, and subscripts may be dropped:

$$(15.3) \qquad r_{OP} = (1/2)h^2(1 + m) + e^2 r_{E(O)E(P)}.$$

If the population is in equilibrium under random mating ($m = 0$, $h_O = h_P$, all F's $= 0$) and there is no environmental correlation between parent and offspring:

$$(15.4) \qquad r_{OP} = (1/2)h^2.$$

Thus under these conditions, the heritability of the character in the population in question is given by twice the parent-offspring correlation.

The relatives that come next in interest are full sibs. It is to be noted that there is in general much more likelihood of a correlation between their

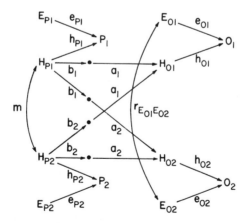

FIG. 15.2. Path diagram for correlation between offspring and parent, and between two full sibs, assuming only additive gene effects.

environments than with parent and offspring, especially if the sibs come from the same brood. Under the same assumptions as in equation (15.2) (Wright 1921):

$$(15.5) \qquad r_{O(1)O(2)} = 2h_o{}^2a^2b^2(1 + m) + e_o{}^2r_{E(O1)E(O2)}.$$

Under random mating as in equation (15.3), but assuming a correlation between the environments of the sibs:

$$(15.6) \qquad r_{O(1)O(2)} = (1/2)h^2 + e_o{}^2r_{E(O1)E(O2)}.$$

This differs from the parent-offspring correlation only in the much less frequently negligible environmental contribution.

The correlation between half-sibs is simpler to interpret than that between full sibs since there is no possibility of a correlation between dominance deviations. The genetic correlation if no parental correlation is

$$(15.7) \qquad r_{O(1)O(2)} = h^2a^2b^2 = \frac{h^2}{4}\left(\frac{1 + F_P}{1 + F_O}\right).$$

In the case of a randombreeding population this becomes

$$(15.8) \qquad r_{O(1)O(2)} = (1/4)h^2.$$

The information on possible maternal effects that may be derived from the excess of the maternal over the paternal half-sib correlation has already been noted.

The correlation between individuals and aunts or uncles, or between individuals and grandparents, can be derived similarly. In randombreeding populations, the genetic components are again $(1/4)h^2$. Environmental components may exist (for example, from herd differences in management in livestock) but are likely to be smaller than between contemporaries.

It is rarely worthwhile to use relatives with a genetic correlation of less than $(1/4)h^2$ because of usually low significance.

On the other hand, there is a special case, involving the greatest possible correlation between relatives, that is of great importance in man, that has not been considered so far—the correlation between monozygotic twins represented for simplicity by $r_{OO(M)}$. Since these have identical heredities, $r_{H(O1)H(O2)} = 1$ in this case:

$$(15.9) \qquad r_{OO(M)} = h^2 + e^2r_{E(O1)E(O2)}.$$

Calculation of Heritability

The foregoing discussion has dealt with the theoretical correlations among relatives under the assumption of additivity. The most important practical application is in determining the heritability. A great deal of attention has been paid to the most expeditious way of making estimates from various kinds of data, and extensive discussions may be found in most of the text-books on quantitative genetics (Lush 1940, 1949; Lerner 1950; Falconer 1960). We will go into this subject only briefly here. Estimates from long-continued selection experiments will be described in volume 3.

It may be well to emphasize again that heritability as the squared corre-lation between genotype and phenotype is not merely a property of the character in question but also of the population. An estimation of h^2 is valuable in planning for selection in the particular population in which it was made or in one believed to be similar. Estimates for different characters in the same or similar populations make an interesting comparison. So also do estimates for the same character in populations that differ in known ways.

Calculations may be made from correlation arrays and this has the ad-vantage that the approach to linearity is apparent on inspection. The most expeditious method, however, is by the form of analysis of variance (Lush 1940; Hazel and Terrill 1945). This may be illustrated by what is perhaps the most widely used pattern in estimating heritability in livestock. The pattern of analysis is that of (12.52), volume 1.

	Degrees of Freedom	Sum of Squares	Mean Square
Among M sires' progenies (S) in total (T)	$M-1$	$\sum\limits^{M} LK(S-T)^2$	$\sigma_3{}^2 + K\sigma_2{}^2 + KL\sigma_1{}^2$
Among L dams' progenies (D) per sire	$M(L-1)$	$\sum\limits^{M}\sum\limits^{L} K(D-S)^2$	$\sigma_3{}^2 + K\sigma_2{}^2$
Within groups of K full sibs (V)	$ML(K-1)$	$\sum\limits^{M}\sum\limits^{L}\sum\limits^{K} (V-D)^2$	$\sigma_3{}^2$
Total	$MLK-1$	$\sum\limits^{M}\sum\limits^{L}\sum\limits^{K} (V-T)^2$	

These are, of course, all estimates of the same total variance, on the hypothesis that there is no differentiation among sires or among the females with which they are mated in the heredities that they transmit. The sig-nificance of differentiation among the former, $\sigma_1{}^2$, and the latter, $\sigma_2{}^2$, may be tested by the tables of Fisher and Yates (1938).

It is desirable that L and K be constants as indicated above, and if this is not practicable they should vary as little as possible.

Let $\overline{O}$ be the theoretical mean of an indefinitely large progeny of a sire and $\sigma^2_{\overline{O}.\overline{o}}$ be the theoretical average variance within such progenies. Then $\sigma_1{}^2 = \sigma_O{}^2 - \sigma^2_{\overline{O}.\overline{o}}$ is the component of the total variance due to differentiation among sires' progenies.

Similarly, let $\bar{\bar{O}}$ be the theoretical mean of a group of full sibs and $\sigma_3{}^2 = \sigma_{O.\bar{O}}^2$ be the theoretical average variance within such groups.

The remaining component of the total variance, $\sigma_2{}^2 = \sigma_{O.\bar{O}}^2 - \sigma_{O.\bar{O}}^2$, is that due to differentiation among full sib groups within sires' progenies.

According to the usual formula, $\sigma_{x.y}^2 = \sigma_x{}^2(1 - r_{xy}^2)$:

$$(15.10)\quad \begin{aligned} \sigma_1{}^2 &= \sigma_O{}^2 - \sigma_O{}^2(1 - r_{O\bar{O}}^2) = r_{O\bar{O}}^2\sigma_O{}^2, \\ \sigma_2{}^2 &= \sigma_O{}^2(1 - r_{O\bar{O}}^2) - \sigma_O{}^2(1 - r_{O\bar{\bar{O}}}^2) = (r_{O\bar{\bar{O}}}^2 - r_{O\bar{O}}^2)\sigma_O{}^2, \\ \sigma_3{}^2 &= \sigma_{O.\bar{\bar{O}}}^2 \qquad\qquad\qquad\quad = (1 - r_{O\bar{\bar{O}}}^2)\sigma_O{}^2, \\ \sigma_1{}^2 + \sigma_2{}^2 + \sigma_3{}^2 &\qquad\qquad\qquad\qquad\quad = \sigma_O{}^2. \end{aligned}$$

Each individual of a sire's progeny may be thought of as determined by the theoretical average, a deviation due to its dam (common to full sibship) and a random deviation. The correlation between two paternal half-sibs is thus the square of the correlation with the average, $r_{OO(HS)} = r_{O\bar{O}}^2$. Similarly, an individual of a full sibship may be thought of as determined by theoretical average $\bar{\bar{O}}$ for such a group and a random deviation, and the correlation between full sibs is the square of the correlation with this average $r_{OO(FS)} = r_{O\bar{\bar{O}}}^2$. Thus:

$$(15.11)\quad \begin{aligned} \sigma_1{}^2 &= r_{OO(HS)}\sigma_O{}^2, \\ \sigma_2{}^2 &= (r_{OO(FS)} - r_{OO(HS)})\sigma_O{}^2, \\ \sigma_3{}^2 &= (1 - r_{OO(FS)})\sigma_O{}^2. \end{aligned}$$

Environmental influences, on the simple hypotheses of the preceding sections, may be divided primarily into those that are peculiar to individuals, $e_3{}^2$, common to full sibs, $e_2{}^2$, and common to paternal half-sibs, $e_1{}^2$. Assuming panmixia and additive effects:

$$(15.12)\quad \begin{aligned} \sigma_1{}^2 &= [(1/4)h^2 + e_1{}^2]\sigma_O{}^2 \\ \sigma_2{}^2 &= [(1/4)h^2 + e_2{}^2]\sigma_O{}^2 \\ \sigma_3{}^2 &= \underline{[(1/2)h^2 + e_3{}^2]\sigma_O{}^2} \\ \sigma_O{}^2 &= [h^2 + e^2]\sigma_O{}^2 \end{aligned}$$

It is evident that more information is necessary on the environmental components (unless the population is an experimental one in which $e_1{}^2$ may, perhaps, have been wholly eliminated and $e_2{}^2$ reduced to maternal effects, leaving most of the environmental components in $e_3{}^2$). The herd under common management and the individual with two or more measurements may sometimes be introduced into the analytical hierarchy to give comparisons between correlations measuring the contribution of variations in herd environment to correlations in which the variables have a minimum of common heredity or complete identity of heredity. The best procedure must be determined for each case by those thoroughly familiar with all of the circumstances and will not be discussed further at this point.

In the human case, comparison of the correlation between twins in a random collection of monozygotic and like-sexed dizygotic twins from the same population has long been an attractive method of estimating heritability. Unfortunately there is a serious complication in applying formulas (15.9) and (15.5) to man (or to cattle). There is almost certain to be a correlation between heredity and environment which requires that the terms $h_1 e_2 r_{H(1)E(2)} + h_2 e_1 r_{H(2)E(1)}$ be added to these equations. Moreover, while h^2 refers to the total heredity, including dominance and interaction in the case of monozygotic twins, h^2 of equation (15.5) must be multiplied by terms to be discussed later, if there is not additivity of all gene effects. If it is assumed that all terms involving e are the same for the two kinds of twins and that there is full additivity, and a steady state in the population so that $a^2 b^2 = (1/4)$ in (15.5), heritability can be estimated from the difference between (15.9) and (15.5) supplemented by the above environmental term, assuming that $h_1 = h_2$, $e_1 = e_2$, and $r_{H(1)E(2)} = r_{H(2)E(1)}$.

$$r_{OO(M)} = h^2 + e^2 r_{E(1)E(2)} + 2he\, r_{H(1)E(2)}$$
$$r_{OO(D)} = (1/2)h^2(1 + m) + e^2 r_{E(1)E(2)} + 2he\, r_{H(1)E(2)}$$
$$(15.13) \qquad h^2 = 2(r_{OO(M)} - r_{OO(D)})/(1 - m)$$

where (M) and (D) refer to monozygotic and dizygotic, respectively, and $m = h^2 r_{P(1)P(2)}$ if due wholly to assortative mating, making the equation quadratic in h^2.

It is likely, however, that the environments of monozygotic twins with respect to some characters are more similar to an incalculable extent than those of like-sexed dizygotic twins, a consideration which invalidates the above formula.

Correlations with respect to evaluations of temperament and personality in human twins, for example, tend to yield rather small $r_{OO(D)}$ but moderately large $r_{OO(M)}$ with the consequence that formula (15.13) may give impossible estimates of h^2, larger even than $r_{OO(M)}$ itself. Estimations of heritability from twin data are thus subject to serious uncertainties in some cases.

In such cases, estimates based on comparison of correlations involving children adopted at a very early age and natural children from the same population give more reliable results than twin correlations.

Galton (1889) proposed the use of the regression of offspring on parents as an indicator of the degree of heritability. More recently, Lush (1940, 1949) has brought out the statistical advantages in many cases over estimations based on correlations between relatives.

426   COMPONENTS OF VARIABILITY

Under random mating, the same array of environmental conditions in successive generations, and unselected and uncorrelated parents, the standard deviation of offspring is the same as that of the parents ($\sigma_O = \sigma_P$), and the regression of offspring on parent is the same as the correlation:

$$(15.14) \qquad b_{OP} = r_{OP}\sigma_O/\sigma_P = r_{OP}.$$

Since heritability is the same in both generations under these conditions:

$$(15.15) \qquad b_{OP} = (1/2)h^2.$$

Since the midparent, $\bar{P} = (1/2)(P_1 + P_2)$, is equally determined by the parents, the path coefficient x in Figure 15.3 equals $\sqrt{(1/2)}$ under the above assumptions.

$$r_{O\bar{P}} = 2xr_{OP} = r_{OP}\sqrt{2} = h^2\sqrt{(1/2)},$$
$$(15.16) \quad b_{O\bar{P}} = h^2\sigma_O\sqrt{(1/2)}/\sigma_{\bar{P}} = h^2 \quad \text{since} \quad \sigma_{\bar{P}}^2 = (1/2)\sigma_P^2.$$

It is desirable to make use of all offspring of each mating in estimating h^2. Assume that there are k offspring per mating and let y be the path coefficient relating $\bar{O}$ to O in Figure 15.4. Then $ky^2 + k(k-1)y^2r_{OO} = 1$.

$$y = \sqrt{\{(1/k)[1 + (k-1)r_{OO}]\}},$$
$$r_{\bar{O}P} = kyr_{OP} = (1/2)kyh^2,$$
$$r_{\bar{O}\bar{P}} = kyh^2\sqrt{(1/2)}.$$

These are simplified by using regressions instead of correlations:

$$(15.17) \quad b_{\bar{O}P} = r_{\bar{O}P}\sigma_{\bar{O}}/\sigma_P = (1/2)h^2 \quad \text{since} \quad \sigma_{\bar{O}} = \sigma_O/ky,$$
$$(15.18) \quad b_{\bar{O}\bar{P}} = h^2.$$

Thus the regression on midparent of the average of any number of offspring gives the heritability directly. Of still greater importance is the

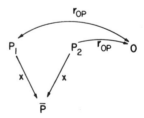

FIG. 15.3. Path diagram for correlation between offspring and midparent

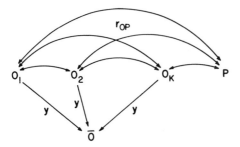

FIG. 15.4. Path diagram for correlation between parent and average offspring

relative simplicity of the formula based on regression where the parents are selected instead of being random representatives of a panmictic population, still assuming that the gene effects are additive. Selection changes the standard deviation of the parents and imposes a correlation between them, thus giving an array of offspring that are correlated with the parents in ways that have no simple relation to the correlations that would be found in the absence of selection. Nevertheless, a selection of midparents has no effect on the concrete regressions $b_{O\bar{P}}$ or $b_{\bar{O}\bar{P}}$ if there is linearity, as expected if gene effects are additive. These regressions still give h^2 directly.

It should be noted that the heritability, h^2, from these formulas pertains to the postulated unselected panmictic population, not to the selected sample with its modified variance.

In the case of livestock, calculation can be made from the intra-sire dam-offspring covariance divided by the estimate of intra-sire variance of dams (Lush 1940; Hazel and Terrill 1945).

Additive Sex-linked Factors

So far autosomal heredity has been assumed. The contribution of sex-linked genes to quantitative variability is usually small in organisms with typical numbers of chromosomes but may be important in special cases and is, of course, likely to be important in organisms with as few chromosomes as the Drosophilas.

In determining the theoretical correlations between relatives for sex-linked loci it is necessary to distinguish the cases of two female relatives, relatives of opposite sex, and two males. It is assumed that the males are heterogametic. Connecting paths that include two males in succession at any point contribute nothing, since such a succession blocks transmission of an X chromosome. Let n_f be the number of females including the propositi in a

TABLE 15.1. Theoretical correlations between relatives with respect to additive autosomal and sex-linked loci, assuming complete determination by heredity.

RELATIVE OF PROPOSITUS	AUTOSOMAL LOCI	SEX-LINKED LOCI				
		Male Propositus Relative		Female Propositus Relative		Av.
		Paternal	Maternal	Paternal	Maternal	
Parent	0.500	0	0.707	0.707	0.500	0.4786
Grandfather	.250	0	.500	0	.354	.2134
Grandmother	.250	0	.354	.500	.250	.2759
Av. grandparent	.250	0	.4268	.2500	.3018	.2447
Grandfather's father	.125	0	0	0	0	0
Grandfather's mother	.125	0	.354	0	.250	.1509
Grandmother's father	.125	0	.250	.354	.177	.1951
Grandmother's mother	.125	0	.177	.250	.125	.1380
Av. great grandparent	.125	0	.1951	.1509	.1380	.1210
Half-brother	.250	0	.500	0	.354	.2134
Half-sister	.250	0	.354	.500	.250	.2759
Av. Half-sib	.250	0	.4268	.2500	.3018	.2447
Uncle	.250	0	.250	.354	.177	.1951
Aunt	.250	0	.530	.250	.375	.2889
Av. sib of parent	.250	0	.3902	.3018	.2759	.2420
Son of uncle	.125	0	0	0	0	0
Daughter of uncle	.125	0	.177	.250	.125	.1380
Son of aunt	.125	0	.375	.177	.265	.2043
Daughter of aunt	.125	0	.265	.125	.188	.1444
Av. first cousin	.125	0	0.2043	0.1380	0.1444	.1217

		Both parents	Both parents	
Brother	.500	0.500	0.354	.4268
Sister	.500	.354	.750	.5518
Av. full sib	.500	.4268	.5518	.4893
Son of father's brother, mother's sister	.250	.375	.265	.3201
Daughter of father's brother, mother's sister	.250	.265	.438	.3514
Son of father's sister, mother's brother	.250	0	.177	.0884
Daughter of father's sister, mother's brother	.250	.177	.250	.2134
Av. double first cousin	0.250	0.2043	0.2824	0.2433

connecting path without successive males. Note that the inbreeding coefficients do not exist for males, and F_A for a male ancestor must be treated as if zero (Wright 1933a).

Two female relatives:

$$(15.19) \qquad r_{H(1)H(2)} = \frac{\sum [(1/2)^{n_f - 1}(1 + F_A)]}{\sqrt{[(1 + F_{H(1)})(1 + F_{H(2)})]}}.$$

Female (H_1) and male (H_2):

$$(15.20) \qquad r_{H(1)H(2)} = \frac{\sum [(1/2)^{n_f - 0.5}(1 + F_A)]}{\sqrt{(1 + F_{H(1)})}}.$$

Two males:

$$(15.21) \qquad r_{H(1)H(2)} = \sum (1/2)^{n_f}(1 + F_A).$$

The genetic correlations in a randombreeding stock between various sorts of relatives with respect to autosomal and sex-linked loci are compared in Table 15.1, taking account of sex in the case of sex-linkage.

It may be seen that with sex-linkage there is wide variation among relatives of the same sort except for sex, but the averages are only slightly less than for autosomal genes (Table 15.2).

TABLE 15.2. Range and average of correlations between relatives due to sex-linked heredity in comparison with those for autosomal heredity, assuming complete additivity and determination by heredity.

| RELATIVE | SEX-LINKED | | AUTOSOMAL |
	Range	Average	
Full sib	0.354–0.750	0.489	0.500
Parent	0– .707	.479	.500
Grandparent	0– .500	.245	.250
Great grandparent	0– .354	.121	.125
Half-sib	0– .500	.245	.250
Parent's sib	0– .530	.242	.250
First cousin	0– .375	.122	.125
Double first cousin	0–0.438	0.243	0.250

The effects of correlation between the genotypes of the parents may be worked out from the suitable diagrams and the appropriate path coefficients.

The phenotypic correlations in all cases require multiplication by the geometric mean of the heritabilities (h_1^2, h_2^2) and there may be supplementation by environmental contributions as in the case of autosomal heredity.

The Analysis of Variance in the Presence of Dominance

It is convenient to treat the average grade, H, of each genotype as approximated as closely as possible by a value G, in which the effect of each replacement is constant. Assuming here that the effect of loci, and of loci and environment, are additive, the difference $D = H - G$ is ascribed to dominance and is referred to as the dominance deviation. The total genetic variance σ_H^2 may then be analyzed into an additive or zygotic component σ_G^2 and a component due to dominance, making use of the method of least squares (Fisher 1918; Wright 1935) to find the best estimates.

Genotype	Frequency (f)	Average Grade		Additive Estimate		Dominance Deviation
AA	f_{AA}	H_{AA}	$=$	G_{AA}	$+$	D_{AA}
Aa	f_{Aa}	H_{Aa}	$=$	G_{Aa}	$+$	D_{Aa}
aa	f_{aa}	H_{aa}	$=$	G_{aa}	$+$	D_{aa}

Component $\sigma_D^2 (= \sum (H - G)^2 f)$ is to be minimized, noting that $G_{AA} = 2G_{Aa} - G_{aa}$.

$$(15.22) \qquad \frac{\partial \sigma_D^2}{\partial G_{Aa}} = 0, \qquad \frac{\partial \sigma_D^2}{\partial G_{aa}} = 0.$$

The solution is as follows, letting

$$(15.23) \qquad \lambda = [H_{AA} - 2H_{Aa} + H_{aa}] \Big/ \left[\frac{1}{f_{AA}} + \frac{4}{f_{Aa}} + \frac{1}{f_{aa}}\right],$$

$$(15.24) \qquad D_{AA} = \lambda/f_{AA}, \qquad D_{Aa} = -2\lambda/f_{Aa}, \qquad D_{aa} = \lambda/f_{aa},$$

$$(15.25) \qquad \sigma_D^2 = \lambda^2[1/f_{AA} + 4/f_{Aa} + 1/f_{aa}],$$

$$(15.26) \qquad \sigma_G^2 = G_A^2[f_{AA}f_{aa} + 4f_{AA}f_{aa} + f_{Aa}f_{aa}],$$

where $\qquad G_A = G_{AA} - G_{Aa} = G_{Aa} - G_{aa}.$

It is convenient to express the frequencies as deviations from those under random mating, and the average grades in terms of the contributions of the first (α_1) and second (α_2) dose of the gene in question:

Genotype	Frequency	Average Grade
AA	$q^2 + Fpq$	$\alpha_1 + \alpha_2$
Aa	$2pq - 2Fpq$	α_1
aa	$p^2 + Fpq$	0

(15.27) $\quad \lambda = -[pq(q + pF)(1 - F)(p + qF)/(1 + F)](\alpha_1 - \alpha_2).$

$$D_{AA} = -[p(p + qF)(1 - F)/(1 + F)](\alpha_1 - \alpha_2),$$

(15.28) $\quad D_{Aa} = +[(p + qF)(q + pF)/(1 + F)](\alpha_1 - \alpha_2),$

$$D_{aa} = -[q(q + pF)(1 - F)/(1 + F)](\alpha_1 - \alpha_2).$$

$$G_{AA} = \alpha_1 + \alpha_2 - D_{AA},$$

(15.29) $\quad G_{Aa} = \alpha_1 - D_{Aa},$

$$G_{aa} = -D_{aa}.$$

(15.30) $\quad G_A = [(p + qF)\alpha_1 + (q + pF)\alpha_2]/(1 + F),$

$$\sigma_D^2 = [pq(q + pF)(1 - F)(p + qF)/(1 + F)](\alpha_1 - \alpha_2)^2,$$

(15.31) $\quad \sigma_G^2 = 2pq(1 + F)G_A^2,$

$$\sigma_H^2 = \sigma_G^2 + \sigma_D^2.$$

There is considerable simplification in a randombreeding population, $F = 0$.

(15.32) $\quad \lambda = -p^2q^2(\alpha_1 - \alpha_2),$

(15.33) $\quad \begin{aligned} D_{AA} &= -p^2(\alpha_1 - \alpha_2), & G_{AA} &= \alpha_1 + \alpha_2 + p^2(\alpha_1 - \alpha_2), \\ D_{Aa} &= +pq(\alpha_1 - \alpha_2), & G_{Aa} &= \alpha_1 - pq(\alpha_1 - \alpha_2), \\ D_{aa} &= -q^2(\alpha_1 - \alpha_2), & G_{aa} &= q^2(\alpha_1 - \alpha_2). \end{aligned}$

(15.34) $\quad\quad\quad\quad\quad G_A = p\alpha_1 + q\alpha_2,$

(15.35) $\quad\quad\quad\quad\quad \begin{aligned} \sigma_D^2 &= p^2q^2(\alpha_1 - \alpha_2)^2, \\ \sigma_G^2 &= 2pqG_A^2. \end{aligned}$

The way in which the additive portion of the genetic variance, $g^2 = \sigma_G^2/\sigma_H^2$, depends on dominance as measured by $(\alpha_1 - \alpha_2)/\alpha_1$, and the frequency of the more nearly recessive allele, a, is shown in Table 15.3. Note that $(\alpha_1 - \alpha_2)/\alpha_1$ is zero if the heterozygote is exactly intermediate, is one if there is complete dominance and is two if there is pure overdominance ($H_{AA} = H_{aa}$).

It may be noted that g^2 is not much less than one even with considerable deviation from exact semidominance. For a given degree of dominance that is less than complete, g^2 is minimum for $p = \alpha_2/(\alpha_1 + \alpha_2)$, at which its value is $8\alpha_1\alpha_2/[\alpha_1^2 + 6\alpha_1\alpha_2 + \alpha_2^2]$. It also remains high if the more nearly dominant allele has a low frequency, and even though there is considerable overdominance. If, however, it is the recessive that is rare and dominance of its allele is complete, or if there is overdominance and gene frequency is close to $\alpha_2/(\alpha_2 - \alpha_1)$, g^2 is close to zero.

TABLE 15.3. Value of g^2 [$= \sigma_G{}^2/(\sigma_G{}^2 + \sigma_D{}^2)$] for various frequencies, p, and ratios $(\alpha_1 - \alpha_2)/\alpha_1$. Distribution: $(pa + qA)^2$, $\alpha_1 = (Aa) - (aa)$; $\alpha_2 = (AA) - (Aa)$, $|\alpha_1| \geq |\alpha_2|$ (Wright 1952a).

p	$(\alpha_1 - \alpha_2)/\alpha_1$								
	0	0.25	0.50	0.75	1	1.25	1.50	1.75	2
0	(1)	(1)	(1)	(1)	(0)	(1)	(1)	(1)	(1)
.10	1	0.995	0.964	0.807	0.182	0.182	0.547	0.706	0.780
.20	1	.992	.947	.780	.333	.000	.182	.395	.529
.30	1	.990	.942	.793	.462	.087	.010	.136	.276
.40	1	.990	.942	.818	.571	.250	.036	.007	.077
.50	1	.990	.947	.847	.667	.419	.182	.039	.000
.60	1	.991	.955	.879	.750	.571	.372	.197	.077
.70	1	.992	.965	.910	.824	.704	.561	.412	.276
.80	1	.994	.976	.941	.889	.818	.731	.633	.529
.90	1	0.997	0.988	0.971	0.947	0.916	0.877	0.832	0.780
1.00	(1)	(1)	(1)	(1)	(1)	(1)	(1)	(1)	(1)

Correlations between Relatives in the Presence of Dominance

Since the application of path analysis to systems in which there is departure from linearity because of dominance is rather limited, it will be well to begin with the direct method used by most authors beginning with Pearson (1904): the construction of the actual correlation array for the relatives under consideration.

The correlation array for parent and offspring, assuming gene frequency array $(pa + qA)$ and random mating, is shown in Table 15.4.

$$(15.36) \qquad \overline{H}_O = \overline{H}_P = (1 - p^2)\alpha_1 + q^2\alpha_2,$$

$$(15.37) \qquad \sigma_{H(O)}^2 = \sigma_{H(P)}^2 = pq[(p\alpha_1 + q\alpha_2)^2 + (p\alpha_1{}^2 + q\alpha_2{}^2)] = \sigma_G{}^2 + \sigma_D{}^2,$$

$$(15.38) \quad r_{H(O)H(P)} = (p\alpha_1 + q\alpha_2)^2/[(p\alpha_1 + q\alpha_2)^2 + (p\alpha_1{}^2 + q\alpha_2{}^2)]$$
$$= (1/2)\sigma_G{}^2/(\sigma_G{}^2 + \sigma_D{}^2) = (1/2)g^2,$$

$$(15.39) \qquad r_{OP} = (1/2)g^2h^2$$

(disregarding possible environmental contributions).

TABLE 15.4. Correlation array for parent and offspring

PARENT	OFFSPRING			TOTAL	H
	aa	Aa	AA		
AA	0	pq^2	q^3	q^2	$\alpha_1 + \alpha_2$
Aa	p^2q	pq	pq^2	$2pq$	α_1
aa	p^3	p^2q	0	p^2	0
Total	p^2	$2pq$	q^2	1	

In the case of semidominance ($\alpha_2 = \alpha_1$): $\bar{H} = 2q\alpha_1$, $\sigma^2 = 2pq\alpha_1{}^2$, and $r_{OP} = (1/2)h^2$ as expected.

In the case of complete dominance ($\alpha_2 = 0$): $\bar{H} = (1 - p^2)\alpha_1$, $\sigma_H{}^2 = p^2(1 - p^2)\alpha_1{}^2$, $g^2 = 2p(1 + p)$, $d^2 = (1 - p)/(1 + p)$, and $r_{OP} = h^2p/(1 + p)$. This reduces to $(1/3)h^2$ if $p = q = 1/2$, the case considered by Pearson.

From the standpoint of path analysis (Fig. 15.5), there is a correlation of 1/2 between genotypes of parent and offspring in a panmictic population. The correlation between genotype and genetic component of the phenotype or heredity H is $g = \sigma_G/\sigma_H$. This relation is nonlinear but this does not affect the contribution to $r_{H(O)H(P)}$ through the genotypes. There is no possibility of a correlation between the dominance deviations, $r_{D(O)D(P)} = 0$, since these are connected through only one gamete and the dominance deviation is a property of the association of two gametes. The correlation between the heredities need merely be multiplied by the heritability to give the correlation between the phenotypes of offspring and parent, $r_{OP} = (1/2)g^2h^2$, in agreement with the result from the parent-offspring array. The derivation by path analysis is more general since it applies irrespective of the number of alleles, their frequencies, or values. Possible contributions from environmental correlations are here ignored.

This sort of analysis can be applied to any case in which the relatives in question are connected through only one gamete of one of them. Thus the

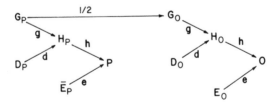

FIG. 15.5. Path diagram for correlation between offspring and parent on allowing for dominance deviations.

correlations between offspring and grandparent, between two half-sibs, or between propositus and uncle or aunt are all $(1/4)g^2h^2$ in a panmictic population. That between single first cousins is $(1/8)g^2h^2$.

The situation is more complicated if there is a possibility that the genotypes of the two relatives may be identical since this indicates a correlation between the dominance deviations as well as between the additive genotypes. The correlation array for full sibs in a panmictic population is shown in Table 15.5. The mean and variance are as before.

TABLE 15.5. Correlation array for two offspring of the same parents

	aa	Aa	AA		H
AA	$(1/4)p^2q^2$	$(1/2)q^2(1-q^2)$	$(1/4)q^2(1+q)^2$	p^2	$\alpha_1 + \alpha_2$
Aa	$(1/2)p^2q(2-q)$	$pq(1+q-q^2)$	$(1/2)q^2(1-q^2)$	$2pq$	α_1
aa	$(1/4)p^2(2-q)^2$	$(1/2)p^2q(2-q)$	$(1/4)p^2q^2$	q^2	0
Total	p^2	$2pq$	q^2	1	

The correlation between the dominance deviations $r_{D(1)D(2)}$ is readily found to be $1/4$. Since $r_{G(1)G(2)} = 1/2$, the correlation between heredities is $(1/2)g^2 + (1/4)d^2$, which merely needs to be multiplied by h^2 to give that between the phenotypes of two full sibs, assuming that there is no environmental contribution. There is, however, very likely to be such a contribution $(e^2 r_{E(1)E(2)})$:

$$(15.40) \qquad r_{O(1)O(2)} = (1/2)g^2h^2 + (1/4)d^2h^2 + e^2 r_{E(1)E(2)}.$$

Pearson considered the case of complete dominance and $p = q = 0.5$, in which case $g^2 = 2p/(1 + p) = 2/3$, $d^2 = (1 - p)/(1 + p) = 1/3$, and $r_{O(1)O(2)} = (1 + 3p)/[4(1 + p)] = 5/12$. The more general result was obtained by Weinberg (1909, 1910).

Malécot (1948) pointed out that the correlation between dominance deviations of noninbred individuals is given by the probability of identity by origin of the genotypes of the two relatives. Since the probability of identity of the genes derived from the mother is $1/2$ and that of genes derived from the father is also $1/2$, and these are independent, the probability of identity of the genotypes is the product or $1/4$, in agreement with the value derived from the actual correlation array of dominance deviations of full sibs.

From the standpoint of path coefficients (Fig. 15.6), the dominance deviations may be looked upon as connected by a joint path, the contribution of which is the product of all elementary path coefficients in both paths connecting gametes $r_{D(1)D(2)} = b^4 = 1/4$, since $b = \sqrt{(1/2)}$ in a panmictic population.

This extension of path analysis can be applied to cases in which the connecting paths are longer or there are two or more independent joint paths,

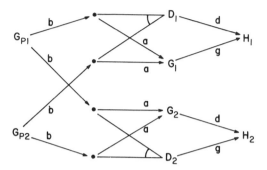

Fig. 15.6. Path diagram for correlation between genotypes of two full sibs on allowing for dominance deviations.

and it obviously agrees with Malécot's probability of identity by origin in all cases. It is subject to the same restriction that neither of the individuals in question be inbred ($F_1 = F_2 = 0$) since in this case the correlation between dominance deviations cannot be identified with the probability of identity by origin.

In the case of double first cousins (Fig. 15.7) the dominance deviations are

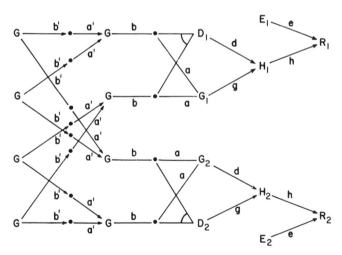

Fig. 15.7. Path diagram for correlation between double first cousins R_1 and R_2, on allowing for dominance deviations.

connected by four independent joint paths each with value 1/64. The correlation between genotypes being 1/4, the phenotypic correlation is

$$(15.41) \qquad r_{R(1)R(2)} = (1/4)g^2h^2 + (1/16)d^2h^2.$$

The contribution of a correlation between dominance deviations is rather small in this case. It is evident that it can play little role in the correlation between more remote relatives in populations in which there is little departure from random mating.

The estimation of the correlations from analysis of variance in the pattern considered earlier takes the following form on allowing for dominance:

	DF	Mean Square	Components
Among M sires' progenies	$M - 1$	$\sigma_3^2 + K\sigma_2^2 + KL\sigma_1^2$	$\sigma_1^2 = [(1/4)g^2h^2 \qquad\qquad + e_1^2]\sigma_0^2$
Among L dams' progenies per sire	$M(L - 1)$	$\sigma_3^2 + K\sigma_2^2$	$\sigma_2^2 = [(1/4)g^2h^2 + (1/4)d^2h^2 + e_2^2]\sigma_0^2$
Within groups of K full sibs	$ML(K - 1)$	σ_3^2	$\sigma_3^2 = [(1/2)g^2h^2 + (3/4)d^2h^2 + e_3^2]\sigma_0^2$
	$MLK - 1$	σ_0^2	$\sigma_0^2 = \quad[g^2h^2 + \quad d^2h^2 + e^2]\sigma_0^2$

As before it is necessary to obtain more information on the nongenetic components. If this can be done it may be possible to estimate d^2. As noted, however, it is g^2, heritability in the narrow sense, given as before by $4\sigma_1^2$ under favorable conditions (negligible common environment, e_1^2, of paternal half-sibs) that is most important practically.

The regression of offspring on midparent or, better, the intrasire regression of offspring on dam (Lush 1940) has the advantage (in a panmictic population) of giving g^2h^2 directly without complication from d^2h^2.

This regression is affected by dominance, however, if the parents are selected, since the relation between heredities of successive generations is not linear in this case. In the examples in Table 15.6 and Figure 15.8, there are four completely dominant independent pairs of alleles making equal and additive contributions to the character. All gene frequency arrays are of the type $(1/2)a + (1/2)A$. In case 1, the dominant genes act in the plus direction (mean = 3). In case 2, two of them act positively and two negatively (mean = 2). $\overline{O}_L$ is the best linear estimate.

In both cases $g^2 = 2/3$ and $h^2 = 1$, so that $b_{\overline{O}\overline{P}}$ in the total distributions is 2/3. If two matings with different values of $\overline{P}$ are selected from case 1, the regression rises from 0.444 near the upper end of the scale to 1.333 near the lower end. If two matings are selected similarly from case 2, the regression varies between 0.584 near the middle to 1.244 near the ends.

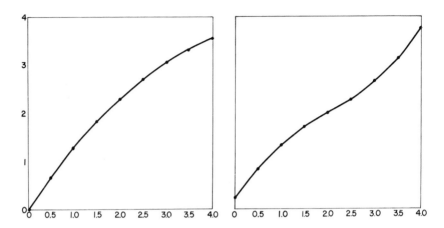

FIG. 15.8. Curvilinear regression lines relating offspring (ordinates) to midparent (abscissas) in the case of four equivalent completely dominant genes: (*a*) (left) all four dominants act in the same direction; (*b*) (right) two act in one direction, two in the other.

Under sex-linkage (males heterogametic) the correlation between dominance deviations of sisters is $1/2$, recalling that the path coefficients relating X-bearing sperm to father's genotype is one. There is no such correlation in

TABLE 15.6. Frequencies of offspring means $\bar{O}$ and best linear approximation $\bar{O}_L$ for each grade of midparent in two cases of quantitative variability due to four loci with complete dominance.

	Case 1			Case 2		
	$[(1/4)aa + (3/4)A-]^4$			$[(1/4)aa + (3/4)A-]^2[(3/4)M- + (1/4)mm]^2$		
$\bar{P}$	Weight	$\bar{O}$	$\bar{O}_L$	Weight	$\bar{O}$	$\bar{O}_L$
4	6561	3.556	3.667	81	3.778	3.333
3.5	17496	3.333	3.333	1080	3.156	3.000
3	20412	3.048	3.000	5724	2.665	2.667
2.5	13608	2.698	2.667	15240	2.292	2.333
2	5670	2.286	2.333	21286	2.000	2.000
1.5	1512	1.810	2.000	15240	1.708	1.667
1	252	1.270	1.667	5724	1.335	1.333
0.5	24	0.667	1.333	1080	0.844	1.000
0	1	0	1.000	81	0.222	0.667
	65536			65536		

the case of mother and daughter, nor between half-sisters, nor, of course, in any case involving a male.

In cases in which either parent is inbred, the correlation between dominance deviations cannot be calculated as above. Moreover, the total genetic correlation cannot in general be analyzed into components due to additive effects and to dominance deviations. The reader may be referred to Kempthorne (1957) for detailed discussion of this matter. There seems to be no other method than the actual construction of the correlation array for the two relatives. Kempthorne (1955c, 1957) has derived the rather complicated formula for full sibs, and for propositus with parent and more remote ancestors in populations in which there is exclusively self-fertilization.

Multiple Factors

With multiple loci, the total additive genetic variance is the sum of the contribution from each locus, and similarly with the variance of dominance deviations.

The contributions of loci to the total genetic variance depends on the gene frequency and degree of dominance $((\alpha_1 - \alpha_2)/\alpha_1)$. Values are shown in Table 15.7, taking $\alpha_1 = 1$ (Wright 1952a).

TABLE 15.7. Values of $\sigma_H{}^2$ ($= (\sigma_G{}^2 + \sigma_D{}^2)$) if $\alpha_1 = 1$ and p is the frequency of the more nearly recessive allele (Wright 1952a).

	$(\alpha_1 - \alpha_2)/\alpha_1$								
p	0	0.25	0.50	0.75	1	1.25	1.50	1.75	2
0	0	0	0	0	0	0	0	0	0
0.10	0.180	0.109	0.056	0.024	0.010	0.015	0.040	0.084	0.148
0.20	.320	.206	.122	.066	.038	.040	.070	.130	.218
0.30	.420	.289	.188	.120	.082	.075	.100	.156	.244
0.40	.480	.350	.250	.178	.134	.120	.134	.178	.250
0.50	.500	.387	.297	.230	.188	.168	.172	.199	.250
0.60	.480	.392	.322	.268	.230	.210	.206	.220	.250
0.70	.420	.362	.314	.277	.250	.233	.226	.230	.244
0.80	.320	.290	.266	.246	.230	.220	.214	.214	.218
0.90	0.180	0.172	0.164	0.159	0.154	0.150	0.148	0.147	0.148
1.00	0	0	0	0	0	0	0	0	0

The contribution approaches zero if either allele—but especially the more nearly recessive one—is rare. It is maximum if there is exact semidominance and $p = 0.5$. The maximum contribution in the case of complete dominance is reached if $p = \sqrt{(1/2)}$ and in the case of pure overdominance again if $p = 0.5$.

The contributions of loci to the correlation between relatives must be weighted by their contributions to variance (as illustrated in Table 15.8). It is theoretically possible, if there is complete dominance at all loci, that the parent-offspring correlation be nearly zero, even though all variability is genetic. This occurs when all recessives are rare. A value less than $(1/3)h^2$ is not likely, however, because of the much greater contribution of the loci with the higher frequencies of recessives. Table 15.8 shows the values of r_{OP} and r_{OO} for certain distributions of gene frequencies $(\varphi(p))$ and for equivalent single gene frequencies assuming complete dominance (Wright 1952a).

TABLE 15.8. Additive (g^2) and dominance (d^2) portions of the genetic variance, and autosomal correlations between parent and offspring (r_{OP}) and between full sibs (r_{OO}) for certain distributions of gene frequencies $(\varphi(p))$ or equivalent single gene frequency (p) on the hypothesis of complete dominance but no interaction between loci and no interaction or correlation between heredity and environment, in a randombreeding population (Wright 1952a).

$\varphi(p)$	Equivalent p	g^2	d^2	r_{OP}	r_{OO}
—	$0+$	$0+$	$1-$	$0+$	$0.250h^2+$
C/p	$1/2$	$2/3$	$1/3$	$0.333h^2$	$.417h^2$
C	$3/5$	$3/4$	$1/4$	$.375h^2$	$.438h^2$
$C/p(1-p)$	$2/3$	$4/5$	$1/5$	$.400h^2$	$.450h^2$
$C/(1-p)$	$3/4$	$6/7$	$1/7$	$.429h^2$	$.464h^2$
—	$1-$	$1-$	$0+$	$0.500h^2(-)$	$0.500h^2(-)$

With appreciable intermediacy of the heterozygotes, the above correlations rise rapidly toward the value $0.500h^2$ of exact intermediacy. Very low values of r_{OP}, on the other hand, may easily occur if there is overdominance at all loci. In the former case, estimates of heritability based on the parent-offspring correlation as if dominance were absent are likely to be only slightly in defect. If, however, there is much overdominance, such estimates are almost worthless.

It is possible to estimate g^2 and d^2 from comparisons of r_{OP} and r_{OO} (as attempted by Fisher (1918) in the case of Pearson's data on human stature and other measurements), but only if environmental correlations can be determined (not the case in this data). The fraternal correlation may exceed the parent-offspring correlation either because of dominance or because of a higher environmental correlation, or both, making evaluation difficult in natural populations.

Other complications arise if there is assortative mating or selection of parents. It was noted that these could be obviated by using the regression of offspring on midparent as the measure of heritability, if it could be assumed that gene effects are additive and not complicated by environmental effects. With dominance in any degree this regression is not linear and thus is affected by selection of parents. Assortative mating introduces a correlation between dominance deviations of parents and offspring and between dominance deviations of either and additive deviations of the other. Accurate deduction of heritability thus becomes practically impossible if there is appreciable assortative mating in the presence of dominance. In making experiments aimed at estimation of heritability from correlations or regressions it is thus important to avoid, as far as possible, assortative mating, selection of parents, and environmental correlations between relatives.

Assortative Mating

The relations among two full sibs (O_1, O_2) and their parents (P_1, P_2) under assortative mating, assuming additive gene effects and no correlation between

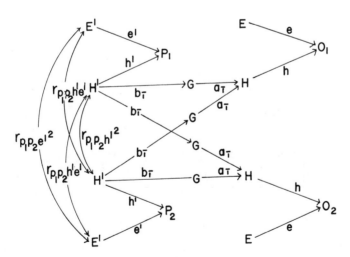

Fig. 15.9. Path diagram for correlations between offspring and parent, and between two full sibs under assortative mating.

environments of parent and offspring, in terms of the path coefficients shown in Figure 15.9 and defined in chapter 11, lead at once (Wright 1921) to the equations:

$$
\begin{aligned}
r_{OP} &= ha_T b_T [h'(1 + r_{PP} h'^2) + e' r_{PP} h' e'] \\
&= hh' a_T b_T (1 + r_{PP}),
\end{aligned}
$$

(15.42)

(15.43) $r_{OO} = 2h^2 a_T^2 b_T^2 (1 + r_{PP} h'^2).$

Tables 15.9 and 15.10 show values of the correlations between parent and offspring (r_{OP}) and between full sibs, respectively, under various degrees of assortative mating and various numbers of equivalent loci, assuming semidominance and gene frequencies all 0.50, as in Tables 11.2 and 11.3. In the foundation stock (generation 0) $r_{PP} = 0$.

TABLE 15.9. Correlation between parent and offspring by generation of assortative mating $(r_{PP} = 1, h_0^2 = 1$ or $0.5; r_{PP} = 0.5, h_0^2 = 1; r_{PP} = -1, h_0^2 = 1)$, assuming various numbers of equivalent loci, semidominance, and gene frequency 0.5, as in Tables 11.2 and 11.3.

| GENERA-TION | PERFECT ASSORTATIVE MATING $r_{PP} = 1$ $h_0^2 = 1$ | | | | IMPERFECT ASSORTATIVE MATING | | | | PERFECT DISASSOR-TATIVE MATING $r_{PP} = -1$ $h_0^2 = 1$ | |
| | | | | | $r_{PP} = 1$ $h_0^2 = 0.5$ | | $r_{PP} = 0.5$ $h_0^2 = 1$ | | | |
	$n = 1$	$n = 2$	$n = 4$	$n = 10$	$n = 1$	$n = 4$	$n = 1$	$n = 4$	$n = 1$	$n = 4$
0	0.500	0.500	0.500	0.500	0.250	0.250	0.500	0.500	0.500	0.500
1	0.816	0.816	0.816	0.816	.471	.471	.671	.671	0	0
2	0.926	0.894	0.880	0.872	.544	.533	.732	.707	0	0
3	0.966	0.926	0.909	0.900	.569	.572	.745	.722	0	0
4	0.984	0.945	0.928	0.919	.579	.600	.749	.732	0	0
5	0.992	0.957	0.941	0.932	.583	.622	.750	.737	0	0
10	1.000	0.985	0.972	0.963	.586	.682	.750	.748	0	0
15	1.000	0.995	0.984	0.976	.586	.708	.750	.750	0	0
∞	1.000	1.000	1.000	1.000	0.586	0.739	0.750	0.750	0	0

Correlation between Characters

Two characters may be correlated because of common environmental factors or common genetic factors or both. The formulas for the correlations in each respect were given by Hazel (1943). Figure 15.10 shows the relation of an

TABLE 15.10. Correlation between full sibs by generation of assortative mating ($r_{PP} = 1$, $h_0{}^2 = 1$ or 0.5; $r_{PP} = 0.5$, $h_0{}^2 = 1$; $r_{PP} = -1$, $h_0{}^2 = 1$), assuming various numbers of equivalent loci, semidominance, and gene frequency 0.5, as in Tables 11.2 and 11.3.

GENERA-TION	PERFECT ASSORTATIVE MATING				IMPERFECT ASSORTATIVE MATING				PERFECT DISASSOR-TATIVE MATING	
	$r_{PP} = 1$ $h_0{}^2 = 1$				$r_{PP} = 1$ $h_0{}^2 = 0.5$		$r_{PP} = 0.5$ $h_0{}^2 = 1$		$r_{PP} = -1$ $h_0{}^2 = 1$	
	$n = 1$	$n = 2$	$n = 4$	$n = 10$	$n = 1$	$n = 4$	$n = 1$	$n = 4$	$n = 1$	$n = 4$
0	0.500	0.500	0.500	0.500	0.250	0.250	0.500	0.500	0.500	0.500
1	0.667	0.667	0.667	0.667	.333	.333	.600	.600	0	0
2	0.857	0.800	0.774	0.760	.414	.398	.714	.667	0	0
3	0.933	0.857	0.827	0.810	.444	.440	.741	.696	0	0
4	0.968	0.892	0.861	0.844	.456	.472	.748	.714	0	0
5	0.984	0.915	0.885	0.868	.461	.497	.749	.725	0	0
10	1.000	0.970	0.945	0.928	.464	.570	.750	.746	0	0
15	1.000	0.988	0.968	0.953	.464	.603	.750	.749	0	0
∞	1.000	1.000	1.000	1.000	0.464	0.642	0.750	0.750	0	0

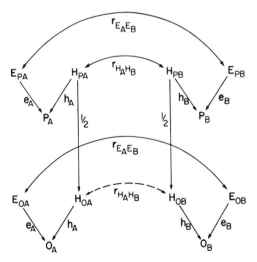

FIG. 15.10. Path diagram for correlation between two characters, A and B, of offspring and parent, and of two offspring.

offspring (O) to one of its parents (P) relative to two characters A and B. It is assumed that there are random mating and similar conditions in successive generations. It is further assumed that A and B are affected by common environmental factors, causing a correlation $r_{E(A)E(B)}$, and common genetic factors causing a correlation $r_{H(A)H(B)}$ in the parental generation.

There is one feature of the diagram that may require clarification. The correlation between H_{OA} and H_{OB} would seem to be only $(1/4)r_{H(A)H(B)}$ unless there are connections that are not shown. One such connection is obvious since only one parent is shown, but on taking account of the other parent this correlation is raised only to $(1/2)r_{H(A)H(B)}$. Nevertheless, $r_{H(A)H(B)}$ should be the same in both generations. On constructing a diagram (Fig. 15.11) in which the parental heredity is represented as determined by two gametes, each with two effects (A, B), it is evident that the correlation between these effects in either gamete must be $r_{H(A)H(B)}$. But any gamete produced by the parent is identical with one or other of the two that united to produce it with respect to the locus in question, so that the correlation between the two effects must also be $r_{H(A)H(B)}$. The diagram can be made consistent only by introducing a residual path (value $(1/2)r_{H(A)H(B)}$). This is justified by the fact that the gametes considered here do not represent independent segregations but refer in fact to two aspects of the same gamete. The gamete may be considered as determined half by derivation for the parental zygote and the other half by chance at segregation; in this case, the chance factor is the same for both.

Returning to Figure 15.10, the following are among the equations that can be written:

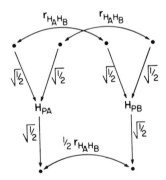

FIG. 15.11. Auxiliary path diagram for Fig. 15.10

$$r_{O(A)P(A)} = (1/2)h_A{}^2; \qquad r_{O(B)P(B)} = (1/2)h_B{}^2;$$

$$r_{O(A)P(B)} = r_{O(B)P(A)} = (1/2)h_A h_B r_{H(A)H(B)};$$

(15.44)
$$r_{H(A)H(B)} = \frac{r_{O(A)P(B)}}{\sqrt{(r_{O(A)P(A)}r_{O(B)P(B)})}} = \frac{r_{O(B)P(A)}}{\sqrt{(r_{O(A)P(A)}r_{O(B)P(B)})}}$$

$$= \sqrt{\left(\frac{r_{O(A)P(B)}r_{O(B)P(A)}}{r_{O(A)P(A)}r_{O(B)P(B)}}\right)}.$$

The last form is preferable since it makes equal use of both of the observed correlations $r_{O(A)P(B)}$ and $r_{O(B)P(A)}$ and thus minimizes sampling errors.

If the diagram is complicated by including both parents and their average, $\bar{P}$:

$$r_{O(A)\bar{P}(A)} = h_A{}^2\sqrt{(1/2)}; \qquad r_{O(B)\bar{P}(B)} = h_B{}^2\sqrt{(1/2)};$$

$$r_{O(A)\bar{P}(B)} = r_{O(B)\bar{P}(A)} = h_A h_B r_{H(A)H(B)}\sqrt{(1/2)};$$

(15.45)
$$r_{H(A)H(B)} = \sqrt{\left(\frac{r_{O(A)\bar{P}(B)}r_{O(B)\bar{P}(A)}}{r_{O(A)\bar{P}(A)}r_{O(B)\bar{P}(B)}}\right)}.$$

It is desirable to replace the correlations on the right side by the corresponding regression coefficients to take advantage of the invariance of the latter to selection of parents. The factor $\sqrt{(1/2)}$ in the equations disappears in the regression coefficients because $\sigma_{\bar{P}} = \sigma_P\sqrt{(1/2)}$.

(15.46)
$$r_{H(A)H(B)} = \sqrt{\left(\frac{b_{O(A)\bar{P}(B)}b_{O(B)\bar{P}(A)}}{b_{O(A)\bar{P}(A)}b_{O(B)\bar{P}(B)}}\right)}.$$

Finally the correlation between the environmental effects can be found from the equations:

$$h_A{}^2 + e_A{}^2 = 1; \qquad h_B{}^2 + e_B{}^2 = 1;$$

$$r_{O(A)O(B)} = h_A h_B r_{H(A)H(B)} + e_A e_B r_{E(A)E(B)};$$

$$r_{E(A)E(B)} = \frac{r_{O(A)O(B)} - \sqrt{(2r_{O(A)\bar{P}(B)}r_{O(B)\bar{P}(A)})}}{\sqrt{[(1 - r_{O(A)\bar{P}(A)}\sqrt{2})(1 - r_{O(B)\bar{P}(B)}\sqrt{2})]}}$$

(15.47)
$$= \frac{r_{O(A)O(B)} - \sqrt{(b_{O(A)\bar{P}(B)}b_{O(B)\bar{P}(A)})}}{\sqrt{[(1 - b_{O(A)\bar{P}(A)})(1 - b_{O(B)\bar{P}(B)})]}}.$$

It should again be emphasized that these coefficients all refer to the values in the unselected panmictic population even though the regressions are calculated from selected parents and offspring. Formulas are not given for offspring averages, $\bar{O}$, since to do this would require assumptions with respect to the correlations between the environments of different offspring.

The relations between the two characters and their heredities may, however, be more complex, and these formulas should not be applied blindly.

Properties of Subdivided Populations

The structures of populations were described in chapter 12 in terms of inbreeding coefficients. Structure has effects on the statistics of characters which will be considered here (cf. Wright, 1943b, 1951, 1965c).

It will be assumed that the effects of loci and of environment on a quantitatively varying character are additive. The array of zygotic frequencies for n alleles of type A_i, gene frequency q_i, has been given as

$$(15.48) \qquad (1 - F)\left[\sum_{i}^{n} q_i(A_i)\right]^2 + F\left[\sum q_i A_i A_i\right].$$

Let c_{ij} represent the contribution of $A_i A_j$ to the character. Let $M_{(F)}$ be the mean and $\sigma^2_{(F)}$ the genetic component of the variance under the system of mating characterized by coefficient F. Then $M_{(0)}$ and $\sigma^2_{(0)}$ are the corresponding statistics under random mating ($F = 0$), and $M_{(1)}$ and $\sigma^2_{(1)}$ those of an array of completely fixed lines ($F = 1$), arrived at without selection (Wright 1922b, 1951).

$$
\begin{aligned}
M_{(F)} &= (1 - F) \sum_{j=1}^{n} \sum_{i=1}^{n} (q_i q_j c_{ij}) + F \sum_{i=1}^{n} (q_i c_{ii}) \\
(15.49) \qquad &= (1 - F)M_{(0)} + FM_{(1)} \\
&= M_{(0)} + F[M_{(1)} - M_{(0)}].
\end{aligned}
$$

Thus if complete fixation without change of gene frequency affects the mean, as it would unless the effects of alleles are additive, the effect of any intermediate degree of inbreeding of the population is proportional to F, under the above assumptions.

$$
\begin{aligned}
\sigma^2_{(F)} &= (1 - F)\sum\sum(q_i q_j c_{ij}^2) + F\sum(q_i c_{ii}^2) - M_{(F)}^2 \\
(15.50) \qquad &= (1 - F)(\sigma^2_{(0)} + M^2_{(0)}) + F(\sigma^2_{(1)} + M^2_{(1)}) \\
&\quad - [(1 - F)M_{(0)} + FM_{(1)}]^2 \\
&= (1 - F)\sigma^2_{(0)} + F\sigma^2_{(1)} + F(1 - F)[M_{(1)} - M_{(0)}]^2.
\end{aligned}
$$

The change in total variance due to the system of mating is thus a quadratic function of F.

The case of semidominance at all pertinent loci is of special interest. Letting c_i be the contribution of allele A_i, then the contribution of zygote $A_i A_j$ is $(c_i + c_j)$. The mean is unaffected by the system of mating in this case.

$$(15.51) \qquad M_{(F)} = M_{(0)} = M_{(1)} = 2 \sum_{i}^{n} q_i c_i.$$

With respect to the variance:

$$
\begin{aligned}
(15.52) \qquad \sigma_{(0)}^2 &= \sum_i \sum_i \left[q_i q_j (c_i + c_j)^2 - 4 \left(\sum q_i c_i \right)^2 \right] \\
&= 2 \sum q_i c_i{}^2 + 2 \left(\sum q_i c_i \right)^2 - 4 \left(\sum q_i c_i \right)^2 \\
&= 2 \left[\sum q_i c_i{}^2 - \left(\sum q_i c_i \right)^2 \right] = 2 \sigma_{c(i)}^2,
\end{aligned}
$$

$$(15.53) \qquad \sigma_{(1)}^2 = 4 \sum q_i c_i{}^2 - 4 \left(\sum c_i q_i \right)^2 = 4 \sigma_{c(i)}^2,$$

$$(15.54) \qquad \sigma_{(F)}^2 = (1 - F)\sigma_{(0)}^2 + F\sigma_{(1)}^2 = (1 + F)\sigma_0{}^2.$$

This variance and the inbreeding coefficient both here refer to individuals relative to the total population. The formula can be written more explicitly in the case of a subdivided population:

$$(15.55) \qquad \sigma_{IT(F)}^2 = (1 + F_{IT})\sigma_{IT(0)}^2.$$

It is of interest to find the average variance, $\overline{\sigma_{IS}^2}$, of individuals within strains that are themselves inbred (F_{IS}), and the variance of strain means within the total, σ_{ST}^2, the corresponding inbreeding coefficient being F_{ST}.

If random mating is initiated within the strains, without changing gene frequencies $(F_{IS} = 0)$, there is no change in F_{ST} since this is in any case the correlation between random gametes within strains relative to the unchanged total array of gametes. There is, however, change in F_{IT} which becomes the same as F_{ST}. The variance of individuals within the total, if the strains are randombred, is thus:

$$(15.56) \qquad \sigma_{IT}^2 \mid (F_{IS} = 0) = (1 + F_{ST})\sigma_{IT(0)}^2.$$

The mean variance within the randombred strains is

$$(15.57) \qquad \overline{\sigma_{IS}^2} \mid (F_{IS} = 0) = (1 - F_{ST})\sigma_{IT(0)}^2.$$

Since the total variance is the sum of the components, σ_{ST}^2 is the difference between (15.56) and (15.57):

$$(15.58) \qquad \sigma_{ST}^2 = (1 + F_{ST})\sigma_{IT(0)}^2 - (1 - F_{ST})\sigma_{IT(0)}^2 = 2F_{ST}\sigma_{IT(0)}^2.$$

As expected, this is the same whether the strains are inbred or not, since the means of the strains are unchanged.

The average variance within strains if inbred is

$$(15.59) \qquad \overline{\sigma_{IS}^2} = \sigma_{IT}^2 - \sigma_{ST}^2 = (1 + F_{IT} - 2F_{ST})\sigma_{IT(0)}^2.$$

Summing up:

	Strains Inbred		Strains Randombred
	$(F_{IT} = F_{IS} + F_{ST} - F_{IS}F_{IT})$		$(F_{IS} = 0, \quad F_{IT} = F_{ST})$
σ_{IS}^2	$(1 + F_{IT} - 2F_{ST})\sigma_{IT(0)}^2$		$(1 - F_{ST})\sigma_{IT(0)}^2$
σ_{ST}^2	$2F_{ST}\,\sigma_{IT(0)}^2$		$2F_{ST}\,\sigma_{IT(0)}^2$
σ_{IT}^2	$(1 + F_{IT})$	$\sigma_{IT(0)}^2$	$(1 + F_{ST})\sigma_{IT(0)}^2$

(15.60)

$$\sigma_{IT(0)}^2 = 2\sigma_{c(i)}^2$$

This analysis is restricted to the case of complete additivity of gene effects. If there is departure from semidominance, no unique analysis of σ_{IT}^2 can be made into σ_{IS}^2 and σ_{ST}^2. It becomes necessary to have information on the probability distribution of gene frequencies under the breeding structure in question.

Alan Robertson (1952) carried through the analysis in the case of completely isolated strains of given size, tending toward fixation without interference from mutation or selection. The distribution of gene frequencies was found to take a succession of forms that depended wholly on the successive values of F_{IT} which are known. The mathematical formulas for the distribution of gene frequencies was not then known and is very complicated but as Robertson showed, it is only necessary to find the law of change of the first four moments. This was done, and it was shown that there are almost qualitative differences from the results with semidominance. Robertson found a considerable *reduction* in the total variance, as inbreeding increases, in the case in which the gene frequency of the recessive allele is sufficiently high, and a very considerable *increase* in the variance within strains with increasing F, up to a certain point, in the case in which the gene frequency of the recessive is sufficiently low.

The results are not very different in the simpler case in which a steady state has been reached in a population divided into partially isolated strains, the tendency toward fixation being balanced by occasional outcrossing. The analysis is simple, since the form of the distribution of gene frequencies is relatively simple (Wright 1952b).

The strains are assumed to be alike in effective size (N) and other conditions. The following four equations are merely definitions, that for $F\,(=\,F_{IT})$ being here based on proportional approach to homozygosis:

$$\int_0^1 \varphi(q)\,dq = 1,$$

$$\int_0^1 q\varphi(q)\,dq = \bar{q},$$

(15.61)

$$\int_0^1 (q - \bar{q})^2\varphi(q)\,dq = \sigma_q{}^2,$$

$$2\int_0^1 q(1 - q)\varphi(q)\,dq = 2\bar{q}(1 - \bar{q})(1 - F).$$

From these:

(15.62) $$\int_0^1 q^2\varphi(q)\,dq = \bar{q}^2 + \sigma_q{}^2 = \bar{q}^2 + \bar{q}(1 - \bar{q})F.$$

The mode of analysis may be illustrated simply, in the case of semidominance, with character values 0, α, and 2α assigned to genotypes aa, Aa, and AA, respectively. For a strain with zygotic array $[pa + qA]^2$ the mean and variance of the character are $M = 2q\alpha$ and $\sigma_{IS}^2 = 2pq\alpha^2$.

(15.63) $$\bar{M} = \int_0^1 M\varphi(q)\,dq = 2\bar{q}\alpha,$$

(15.64) $$\bar{\sigma}_{IS}^2 = \int_0^1 \sigma_{IS}^2\varphi(q)\,dq = 2\alpha^2 \int_0^1 q(1 - q)\varphi(q)\,dq = 2\bar{p}\bar{q}(1 - F)\alpha^2,$$

(15.65) $$\sigma_{ST}^2 = \int_0^1 (M - \bar{M})^2\varphi(q)\,dq = 4\alpha^2 \int_0^1 q^2\varphi(q)\,dq - \bar{M}^2$$
$$= 4\bar{p}\bar{q}F\alpha^2,$$

(15.66) $$\sigma_{IT}^2 = \bar{\sigma}_{IS}^2 + \sigma_{ST}^2$$
$$= 2\bar{p}\bar{q}(1 + F)\alpha^2.$$

These agree with the previous results.

Consider now the case of complete dominance, letting q be the frequency of the recessive allele in a strain and α be the differential effect of aa. For the mean and variance in the phenotypic array $[(1 - q^2)A + q^2aa]$ within a strain we have $M = q^2\alpha$ and $\sigma_{IS}^2 = q^2(1 - q^2)\alpha^2$.

(15.67) $$\bar{M} = \alpha \int_0^1 q^2\varphi(q)\,dq = (\bar{q}^2 + \bar{p}\bar{q}F)\alpha,$$

$$(15.68) \quad \bar{\sigma}_{IS}^2 = \alpha^2 \left[\int_0^1 q^2 \varphi(q) \, dq - \int_0^1 q^4 \varphi(q) \, dq \right],$$

$$(15.69) \quad \sigma_{ST}^2 = \alpha^2 \int_0^1 q^4 \varphi(q) \, dq - \bar{M}^2,$$

$$(15.70) \quad \sigma_{IT}^2 = \alpha^2 \int_0^1 q^2 \varphi(q) \, dq - \bar{M}^2 = [\bar{q}^2 + \bar{p}\bar{q}F][1 - (\bar{q}^2 + \bar{p}\bar{q}F)]\alpha^2.$$

Thus the total variance can be evaluated in terms of $\bar{q}$, F, and α irrespective of the form of $\varphi(q)$. The value agrees with that obtained by substituting $M_{(0)} = \bar{q}^2\alpha$, $\sigma_{(0)}^2 = \bar{q}^2(1 - \bar{q}^2)\alpha^2$, $M_1 = \bar{q}\alpha$, and $\sigma_{(1)}^2 = \bar{q}(1 - \bar{q})\alpha^2$ in the more general formula.

Apportionment of this total variance into $\bar{\sigma}_{IS}^2$ and σ_{ST}^2 requires evaluation of $\int_0^1 q^4 \varphi(q) \, dq$.

Letting m represent the effective amount of replacement of each strain by immigrants, representative of the total, the systematic tendency toward change in gene frequency is $\Delta q = -m(q - \bar{q})$. The equation for $\varphi(q)$ is thus (13.48):

$$(15.71) \quad \varphi(q) = \frac{\Gamma(4Nm)}{\Gamma(4Nm\bar{q})(4Nm(1 - \bar{q}))} q^{4Nm\bar{q} - 1}(1 - q)^{4Nm(1 - \bar{q}) - 1}.$$

The moments about zero are easily evaluated:

$$(15.72) \qquad\qquad \int_0^1 \varphi(q) \, dq = 1,$$

$$(15.73) \qquad\qquad \mu_1{}^1 = \int_0^1 q\varphi(q) \, dq = \bar{q}.$$

$$(15.74) \qquad\qquad \mu_2{}^1 = \int_0^1 q^2 \varphi(q) \, dq = \frac{\bar{q}(4Nm\bar{q} + 1)}{4Nm + 1}.$$

On equating to (15.62) and solving, $F = 1/(4Nm + 1)$ as before (12.3).

$$(15.75) \quad \begin{aligned} \mu_3{}^1 = \int_0^1 q^3 \varphi(q) \, dq &= \frac{\bar{q}(4Nm\bar{q} + 1)(4Nm\bar{q} + 2)}{(4Nm + 1)(4Nm + 2)} \\ &= (\bar{q}^2 + \bar{p}\bar{q}F)\left(\bar{q} + \frac{2F\bar{p}}{1 + F}\right), \end{aligned}$$

$$(15.76) \quad \begin{aligned} \mu_4{}^1 = \int_0^1 q^4 \varphi(q) \, dq &= \frac{\bar{q}(4Nm\bar{q} + 1)(4Nm\bar{q} + 2)(4Nm\bar{q} + 3)}{(4Nm + 1)(4Nm + 2)(4Nm + 3)} \\ &= (\bar{q}^2 + \bar{p}\bar{q}F)\left[\left(\bar{q} + \frac{2F\bar{p}}{1 + F}\right)\left(\bar{q} + \frac{3F\bar{p}}{1 + 2F}\right)\right]. \end{aligned}$$

From (15.68), (15.69), (15.74), and (15.76):

$$(15.77) \quad \bar{\sigma}_{IS}^2 = (\bar{q}^2 + \bar{p}\bar{q}F)\left[1 - \left[\left(\bar{q} + \frac{2F\bar{p}}{1+F}\right)\left(\bar{q} + \frac{3F\bar{p}}{1+2F}\right)\right]\right]\alpha^2,$$

$$(15.78) \quad \sigma_{ST}^2 = (\bar{q}^2 + \bar{p}\bar{q}F)\left[\left(\bar{q} + \frac{2F\bar{p}}{1+F}\right)\left(\bar{q} + \frac{3F\bar{p}}{1+2F}\right) - (\bar{q}^2 + \bar{p}\bar{q}F)\right]\alpha^2.$$

These add up to (15.70) as expected.

Table 15.11 shows values of σ_{IT}^2 for various values of $\bar{q}$ and F letting $\sigma = 1$. The decrease in total variance with increased F, where the recessive allele is relatively abundant, referred to earlier, is shown in this table. This holds for $q > \{\sqrt{[2(1-F) + F^2]} - F\}/2(1-F)$ and thus for $q > 0.707$ if F is close to zero and for $q > 0.50$ if F is close to one.

The increase in average intra-strain variance $\bar{\sigma}_{IS}^2$ with increased F, where the recessive allele is relatively rare and F not too large, is shown in Table 15.12. It depends largely on the increase in the mean with increase in F. There is no increase in the mean under semidominance, but a pronounced increase in the case of dominance and small $\bar{q}$. For very small $\bar{q}$, the intra-strain variance approaches $\bar{q}F(1-F)(1+4F)/(1+F)(1+2F)$ with maximum at 0.46.

Robertson's formula for $\bar{\sigma}_{IS}^2$ under progressive inbreeding was

$$(15.79) \quad \bar{\sigma}_{IS}^2 = \bar{p}\bar{q}[0.8(1-F) - (1-2\bar{q})(1-F)^3 + (0.2 - \bar{p}\bar{q})(1-F)^6]\alpha^2.$$

This appears to be very different from (15.77), but the ratios of the values under this formula to those in Table 15.12, shown in Table 15.13, do not for the most part differ much from one.

The effects of intermediate degrees of dominance and of overdominance in a system of partially isolated strains in a steady state, can be analyzed similarly, using the first four moments, but they are considerably more cumbersome.

TABLE 15.11. The variance (σ_{TT}^2) of a total population characterized by inbreeding coefficient F in the case of a dominant-recessive pair of alleles with unit difference in grade. In this table $\bar{q}$ is the frequency of the recessive allele (Wright 1952b).

$\bar{q}$	0	0.10	0.20	0.30	0.40	0.50	0.60	0.70	0.80	0.90	1.00
						F					
0.05	0.0025	0.0072	0.0119	0.0165	0.0210	0.0256	0.0300	0.0345	0.0398	0.0432	0.0475
0.10	.0099	.0186	.0272	.0356	.0439	.0520	.0599	.0677	.0753	.0827	0.900
0.20	.0384	.0529	.0668	.0803	.0932	.1056	.1175	.1289	.1398	.1501	.1600
0.30	.0819	.0957	.1146	.1296	.1437	.1570	.1693	.1808	.1914	.2012	.2100
0.40	.1344	.1501	.1647	.1782	.1905	.2016	.2116	.2204	.2281	.2346	.2400
0.50	.1875	.1994	.2100	.2194	.2275	.2344	.2400	.2444	.2475	.2494	.2500
0.60	.2304	.2365	.2415	.2454	.2481	.2496	.2500	.2492	.2473	.2442	.2400
0.70	.2499	.2499	.2490	.2472	.2445	.2410	.2365	.2312	.2250	.2180	.2100
0.80	.2304	.2257	.2204	.2147	.2084	.2016	.1943	.1865	.1782	.1693	.1600
0.90	.1539	.1482	.1424	.1364	.1303	.1240	.1176	.1109	.1041	.0971	.0900
0.95	0.0880	0.0841	0.0803	0.0763	0.0723	0.0683	0.0642	0.0601	0.0560	0.0518	0.0475
1.00	0	0	0	0	0	0	0	0	0	0	0

TABLE 15.12. The average variance (σ^2_{IS}) within partially isolated subdivisions of a population in which a steady state (constant F) has been reached between the tendency toward fixation due to inbreeding and the opposed effect of occasional crossbreeding, for the same character, as in Table 15.1. The variance of the means of the subdivisions is the difference between corresponding entries in Tables 15.11 and 15.12. In this table $\bar{q}$ is the frequency of the recessive allele (Wright 1952b).

$\bar{q}$	F (Steady State)										
	0	0.10	0.20	0.30	0.40	0.50	0.60	0.70	0.80	0.90	1.00
0.05	0.0025	0.0068	0.0100	0.0120	0.0128	0.0126	0.0114	0.0095	0.0069	0.0037	0
0.10	.0099	.0174	.0226	.0254	.0262	.0252	.0225	.0185	.0133	.0071	0
0.20	.0384	.0483	.0538	.0554	.0539	.0496	.0430	.0345	.0244	.0128	0
0.30	.0819	.0885	.0898	.0869	.0806	.0717	.0605	.0475	.0329	.0170	0
0.40	.1344	.1325	.1260	.1162	.1039	.0896	.0738	.0567	.0386	.0197	0
0.50	.1875	.1734	.1571	.1395	.1208	.1016	.0818	.0617	.0413	.0208	0
0.60	.2304	.2032	.1772	.1524	.1285	.1056	.0834	.0618	.0408	.0202	0
0.70	.2499	.2122	.1793	.1502	.1238	.0997	.0773	.0563	.0366	.0179	0
0.80	.2304	.1896	.1562	.1279	.1033	.0816	.0622	.0447	.0286	.0138	0
0.90	.1539	.1234	.0994	.0797	.0632	.0492	.0369	.0261	.0165	.0079	0
0.95	0.0880	0.0697	0.0556	0.0442	0.0348	0.0268	0.0200	0.0141	0.0088	0.0042	0
1.00	0	0	0	0	0	0	0	0	0	0	0

TABLE 15.13. The ratio of the average variance within completely isolated strains with unimpeded progress toward complete fixation, measured by successive values of F (Robertson's case) to the average variance within strains under conditions which yield the same values of F in steady states (of Table 15.12). In this table, $\bar{q}$ is the frequency of the recessive allele (Wright 1952b).

$\bar{q}$	F									
	0	0.10	0.20	0.30	0.40	0.50	0.60	0.70	0.80	0.90
0.05	1.000	1.015	1.042	1.069	1.087	1.095	1.092	1.076	1.049	1.010
.10	1.000	1.012	1.034	1.056	1.072	1.079	1.076	1.063	1.039	1.004
.20	1.000	1.007	1.022	1.036	1.046	1.050	1.048	1.038	1.020	0.994
.30	1.000	1.004	1.012	1.019	1.024	1.025	1.022	1.014	1.002	0.984
.40	1.000	1.002	1.004	1.005	1.005	1.003	0.999	0.993	0.984	0.973
.50	1.000	1.000	0.997	0.993	0.988	0.983	0.977	0.972	0.967	0.963
.60	1.000	0.998	0.991	0.983	0.973	0.965	0.957	0.953	0.951	0.954
.70	1.000	0.996	0.986	0.973	0.960	0.948	0.939	0.935	0.936	0.944
.80	1.000	0.994	0.981	0.964	0.948	0.933	0.922	0.918	0.921	0.935
.90	1.000	0.993	0.977	0.957	0.936	0.919	0.906	0.902	0.907	0.926
0.95	1.000	0.992	0.975	0.953	0.931	0.912	0.899	0.894	0.900	0.921

CHAPTER 16

Effect of Factor Interaction on Variance

In the preceding chapter, the variance of populations was treated as the sum of effects of separate loci and of environmental factors. While this is probably adequate to a first approximation for most ordinary quantitative variability, there are probably always some nonadditive interactions which must be considered in a complete analysis. They are unfortunately much more difficult to deal with. Yet it is important to understand the sorts of complications that may occur. The first papers on the subject were by Weinberg (1910) and Fisher (1918).

Two Pairs of Alleles with Dominance

Assume that the average grade (H) of each genotype is approximated as closely as possible by a value, J, to which the contribution of each locus is constant. The difference, $H - J$, is ascribed to interaction (I). The values of J in turn are approximated as closely as possible by the total of additive gene effects (G) and the total of dominance deviations (D) (Wright 1935, 1952a).
Thus

$$H_{AABbcc} = J_{AABbcc} + I_{AABbcc} = (G_{AABbcc} + D_{AABbcc}) + I_{AABbcc},$$

$$(16.1) \quad H_{AABbcc} = (G_{aabbcc} + 2G_A + G_B) + (D_{AA} + D_{Bb} + D_{cc}) + I_{AABbcc},$$

where G_A, G_B, and G_C are the best additive values of A, B, and C, respectively, taking the values of $aabbcc$ as the base, and the D's are the dominance deviations.

The total hereditary variance, σ_H^2, may then be analyzed into components due to additive gene effects (σ_G^2), dominance deviations (σ_D^2), and interaction deviations, $\sigma_I^2 (= \sum (H - J)^2 f)$.

The simplest case is that for two pairs of alleles, assuming complete dominance of one allele in each $(J_{A-B-} = J_{A-bb} + J_{aaB-} - J_{aabb})$:

$$(16.2) \quad \frac{\partial \sigma_I^2}{\partial J_{Abb}} = 0, \quad \frac{\partial \sigma_I^2}{\partial J_{aaB}} = 0, \quad \frac{\partial \sigma_I^2}{\partial J_{aabb}} = 0.$$

The solution is as follows, letting $K = H_{A-B-} - H_{A-bb} - H_{aaB-} + H_{aabb}$:

$$
\begin{aligned}
I_{A-B-} &= K/[f_{A-B-} \sum (1/f)], \\
I_{A-bb} &= -K/[f_{A-bb} \sum (1/f)], \\
I_{aaB-} &= -K/[f_{aaB-} \sum (1/f)], \\
I_{aabb} &= K/[f_{aabb} \sum (1/f)],
\end{aligned}
$$

(16.3)

(16.4) $$\sigma_I^2 = K^2/\sum (1/f).$$

Under random combination which will now be assumed:

$$
\begin{aligned}
f_{A-B-} &= (1 - p_a^2)(1 - p_b^2), \\
f_{A-bb} &= (1 - p_a^2)p_b^2, \\
f_{aaB-} &= p_a^2(1 - p_b^2), \\
f_{aabb} &= p_a^2 p_b^2.
\end{aligned}
$$

(16.5)

$$
\begin{aligned}
I_{A-B-} &= K p_a^2 p_b^2, \\
I_{A-bb} &= -K p_a^2 (1 - p_b^2), \\
I_{aaB-} &= -K(1 - p_a^2)p_b^2, \\
I_{aabb} &= K(1 - p_a^2)(1 - p_b^2).
\end{aligned}
$$

(16.6)

$$
\begin{aligned}
D_{AA} &= -p_a^2(H_{A-} - H_{aa}), \\
D_{Aa} &= +p_a(1 - p_a)(H_{A-} - H_{aa}), \\
D_{aa} &= -(1 - p_a)^2(H_{A-} - H_{aa}),
\end{aligned}
$$

(16.7)

where

$$H_{A-} = (1 - p_b^2)H_{A-B-} + p_b^2 H_{A-bb}$$

$$H_{aa} = (1 - p_b^2)H_{aaB-} + p_b^2 H_{aabb}$$

H_{B-}, H_{bb}; D_{BB}, D_{Bb}, and D_{bb} are analogous.

(16.8) $G_A = p_a(H_{A-} - H_{aa})$, $G_B = p_b(H_{B-} - H_{bb})$,

(16.9) $\sigma_G^2 = 2p_a(1 - p_a)G_A^2 + 2p_b(1 - p_b)G_B^2$ (total genotype),

(16.10) $\sigma_D^2 = [p_a(1 - p_a)(H_{A-} - H_{aa})]^2 + [p_b(1 - p_b)(H_{B-} - H_{bb})]^2$,

(16.11) $\sigma_I^2 = p_a^2 p_b^2(1 - p_a^2)(1 - p_b^2)K^2$,

(16.12) $\sigma_H^2 = \sigma_G^2 + \sigma_D^2 + \sigma_I^2$.

The correlations between the interaction effects of two gene pairs in two relatives can be calculated directly from the products of the I's for each two-factor genotype of each relative weighted by the joint frequencies for each locus. With dominance, the joint frequencies given in Table 15.4 for offspring-parent and in Table 15.5 for two full sibs reduce to a 2×2 table for each locus and thus give 16 entries in joint array of I's.

$$(16.13) \quad r_{I(o)I(P)} = \sum_{}^{16} [I_o I_p f_{(op)_A} f_{(op)_B}]/\sigma_I^2 = p_a p_b/[(1 + p_a)(1 + p_b)],$$

$$(16.14) \quad r_{op} = h^2 \left[\frac{1}{2} \frac{\sigma_G^2}{\sigma_H^2} + \frac{p_a p_b}{(1 + p_a)(1 + p_b)} \frac{\sigma_I^2}{\sigma_H^2} \right],$$

$$(16.15) \quad \begin{aligned} r_{I(o)I(o')} &= \sum_{}^{16} [I_o I_{o'} f_{(oo')_A} f_{(oo')_B}]/\sigma_I^2 \\ &= (1 + 3p_a)(1 + 3p_b)/[16(1 + p_a)(1 + p_b)], \end{aligned}$$

$$(16.16) \quad r_{oo'} = h^2 \left[\frac{1}{2} \frac{\sigma_G^2}{\sigma_H^2} + \frac{1}{4} \frac{\sigma_D^2}{\sigma_H^2} + \frac{1}{16} \frac{(1 + 3p_a)(1 + 3p_b)}{(1 + p_a)(1 + p_b)} \frac{\sigma_I^2}{\sigma_H^2} \right].$$

Table 16.1 gives an analysis of the variability in the two-factor F_2's with dominance in which the 9:3:3:1 ratio is modified in various ways. It is assumed that the successive terms in the ratio differ phenotypically by 16 units. In all cases h^2 is taken as one and $d^2 = (\sigma_D^2/\sigma_H^2) = (1/2)g^2$. The genetic correlations (with $p = 1/2$) are:

$$(16.17) \qquad\qquad r_{op} = (1/2)g^2 + (1/9)i^2,$$

$$(16.18) \qquad\qquad r_{oo} = (1/2)g^2 + (1/4)d^2 + (25/144)i^2.$$

The effects of the loci are additive in the first four cases ($i^2 = 0$). The rest are arranged in the order of increasing determination by interaction (where there is a difference). In the first four of these, one locus behaves as a specific modifier of one of the alleles at the other locus. Interaction determines only from 5% to 10% of the variance and the correlations are not much less than with no interaction. Among the four cases in which three of the classes are indistinguishable, the interaction variance constitutes only 14% in the 9:7 case, 23% in the 3:13 case, but 60% in cases 15:1 and 10:6. In all of the remaining cases (as well as in the 10:6 case) genes act in different directions in different combinations. The degree of determination by interaction ranges from only 10% in the case 9:3:1:3 to 93% in the case of 6:9:1. In the last case r_{op} is only 0.126 and r_{oo} only 0.190.

The Optimum Model of Interaction

We will consider next a type of multifactorial case that is of special importance in the theory of evolution. This is the case in which a secondary

TABLE 16.1. Analysis of variability in two-factor F_2 populations with complete dominance, and correlations between parent and offspring (r_{op}) and sibling (r_{oo}), assuming complete determination by heredity. If heritability is not complete these figures are to be multiplied by h^2 (Wright 1952a).

	H				G_{aabb}	G		D		I				σ_H^2	g^2	d^2	i^2	r_{op}	r_{oo}
	A–B–	A–bb	aaB–	aabb		A	B	AA*/aa	BB*/bb	A–B–	A–bb	aaB–	aabb						
9:3:3:1	48	32	16	0	12	16	8	−8	−4	0	0	0	0	240	0.667	0.333	0	0.333	0.417
9:6:1	32	16	16	0	8	8	8	−4	−4	0	0	0	0	96	.667	.333	0	.333	.417
3:9:1:3	32	48	0	16	20	16	−8	−8	4	0	0	0	0	240	.667	.333	0	.333	.417
3:10:3	16	32	0	16	16	8	−8	−4	4	0	0	0	0	96	.667	.333	0	.333	.417
9:3:4	32	16	0	0	1	14	6	−7	−3	1	−3	−3	9	183	.634	.317	.049	.322	.405
12:1:3	32	32	0	16	13	14	−2	−7	1	1	−3	−3	9	159	.629	.314	.057	.321	.403
3:9:4	16	32	0	0	11	10	−6	−5	3	−1	3	3	−9	111	.613	.306	.081	.315	.397
12:3:1	32	32	16	0	15	10	2	−5	−1	−1	3	3	−9	87	.598	.299	.103	.310	.392
9:3:1:3	48	32	32	16	10	20	4	10	−2	2	−6	−6	18	348	.598	.299	.103	.310	.392
9:7	16	0	0	0	−3	6	6	−3	−3	1	−3	−3	9	63	.571	.286	.143	.301	.382
3:13	0	16	16	16	7	2	−6	−1	3	−1	3	3	−9	39	.513	.256	.231	.282	.361
9:4:3	32	16	0	0	6	12	4	−6	−2	2	−6	−6	18	156	.513	.256	.231	.282	.361
3:9:3:1	32	48	16	0	22	12	−4	−6	2	−2	6	6	−18	156	.513	.256	.231	.282	.361
9:1:6	32	0	0	16	−1	10	10	−5	−5	3	−9	−9	27	231	.433	.216	.351	.255	.331
9:1:3:3	48	16	0	32	8	16	8	−8	−4	4	−12	−12	36	384	.417	.208	.375	.250	.326
10:3:3	32	16	16	0	11	10	2	−5	−1	3	−9	−9	27	159	.327	.164	.509	.220	.293
15:1	16	16	16	0	11	2	2	−1	−1	−1	3	3	−9	15	.267	.133	.600	.200	.271
3:12:1	16	32	16	0	18	4	−4	−2	2	−2	6	6	−18	60	.267	.133	.600	.200	.271
10:6	16	0	0	16	2	4	4	−2	−2	2	−6	−6	18	60	.267	.133	.600	.200	.271
3:3:9:1	16	48	32	0	32	0	−8	0	4	−4	12	12	−36	192	.167	.083	.750	.167	.234
6:9:1	16	32	32	0	25	−2	−2	1	1	−3	9	9	−27	87	.046	.023	.931	.126	.190

* Dominance deviations of heterozygotes have the same numerical value but opposite sign.

character (H) falls off relatively to quantitative variability determined by multiple independent additive factors (primary character, V) according to the square of the deviation of the latter from an optimum ($\hat{V}$) (Wright 1935), discussed at length in chapter 4. It is assumed that there is random combination.

It is probable that selective value in nature is usually related to quantitative variability in roughly this way.

$$(16.19) \quad H = 1 - s(V - \hat{V})^2 = 1 - s[(V - \bar{V}) + (\bar{V} - \hat{V})]^2,$$

$$(16.20) \quad \bar{H} = 1 - s[\mu_2(V) + (\bar{V} - \hat{V})^2],$$

$$\sigma_H^2 = s^2(\sum H_0^2 f - \bar{H}^2),$$

$$(16.21) \quad \sigma_H^2 = s^2\{\mu_4(V) - [\mu_2(V)]^2 + 4(\bar{V} - \hat{V})\mu_3(V) + 4(\bar{V} - \hat{V})^2\mu_2(V)\}.$$

The Case of Complete Dominance

We will consider first the relatively simple case of complete dominance at all loci with frequency array $p^2aa + (1 - p^2)A-$ at a typical locus. It is assumed the selection coefficient s is so small in comparison with the amount of recombination that loci may be assumed to be combined at random in the population without appreciable error. The moments on the primary scale are as follows taking α as the effect of the dominant genotype:

$$(16.22) \quad \bar{V} = \sum \alpha(1 - p^2),$$

$$(16.23) \quad \mu_{2(V)} = \sum \alpha^2 p^2(1 - p^2),$$

$$(16.24) \quad \mu_{3(V)} = \sum \alpha^3 p^2(1 - p^2)(2p^2 - 1),$$

$$(16.25) \quad \mu_{4(V)} = \{\sum \alpha^4 p^2(1 - p^2)[1 - 6p^2(1 - p^2)] + 3[\sum \alpha^2 p^2(1 - p^2)]^2\}.$$

The various statistics of the secondary scale can be calculated:

$$(16.26) \quad K = -2s\alpha_1\alpha_2,$$

$$(16.27) \quad \bar{H} = 1 - s[\sum \alpha^2 p^2(1 - p^2) + (\bar{V} - \hat{V})^2],$$

$$(16.28) \quad G_A = -s\alpha_1 p_1[\alpha_1(2p^2 - 1) + 2(\bar{V} - \hat{V})^2],$$

$$(16.29) \quad \sigma_G^2 = 2s^2 \sum G_A^2 p(1 - p),$$

$$(16.30) \quad \sigma_D^2 = s^2 \sum G_A^2(1 - p)^2,$$

$$(16.31) \quad \sigma_{I(A_1A_2)}^2 = 4s^2\alpha_1^2\alpha_2^2 p_1^2 p_2^2(1 - p_1^2)(1 - p_2^2).$$

With n gene pairs the sum of $n(n - 1)/2$ contributions of this type is

$$(16.32) \quad \sigma_I^2 = 2s^2\{[\sum \alpha^2 p^2(1 - p^2)]^2 - \sum \alpha^4 p^4(1 - p^2)^2\}.$$

It may be found that $(\sigma_G{}^2 + \sigma_D{}^2 + \sigma_I{}^2)$ as given above agrees with $\sigma_H{}^2$ as calculated by substitution of the moments in (16.21). Thus there can be no contributions from interactions involving more than two loci in this case.

If the mean and optimum coincide and variability is due to n pairs of alleles, all with the same frequency (p) of the recessive and all with an equal effect, α, in one direction or the other, on the primary scale:

(16.33) $\qquad \sigma_G{}^2 = 2ns^2p^3(1 - p)(1 - 2p^2)^2\alpha^4$

(16.34) $\qquad \sigma_D{}^2 = ns^2p^2(1 - p)^2(1 - 2p^2)^2\alpha^4$

(16.35) $\qquad \sigma_I{}^2 = 2n(n - 1)s^2p^4(1 - p^2)^2\alpha^4$

(16.36) $\qquad \sigma_H{}^2 = ns^2p^2(1 - p^2)[1 + (2n - 6)p^2(1 - p^2)]\alpha^4$

It may be seen that the portion of the variability due to interaction tends to predominate if a large number of loci are involved, unless p is very small. With very small p, the dominance variance tends to be most important. Formulas (16.14) for r_{op} and (16.16) for $r_{oo'}$ apply (with $h^2 = 1$).

The Case of Semidominance

The case of semidominance on the primary scale is probably more important as a rule, since the complete dominance seems to be unusual for loci involved in quantitative variability and there is little departure from the results of exact semidominance even with considerable deviations (Table 15.3). Taking $[(1 - q_i)a_i + q_iA_i]^2$ as the genotypic array at a locus and α_i as the effect on the primary additive scale (S) of gene A_i, the moments on this scale are as follows:

(16.37) $\quad \overline{V} = 2 \sum \alpha q,$

(16.38) $\quad \mu_{2(V)} = 2 \sum \alpha^2 q(1 - q),$

(16.39) $\quad \mu_{3(V)} = 2 \sum \alpha^3 q(1 - q)(1 - 2q),$

(16.40) $\quad \mu_{4(V)} = 2 \sum \alpha^4 q(1 - q) + 12[\sum \alpha^2 q(1 - q)]^2 - 12 \sum \alpha^4 q^2(1 - q)^2.$

Substitution in (16.19) and (16.21) gives:

(16.41) $\quad \overline{H} = 1 - s[2 \sum \alpha^2 q(1 - q) + (\overline{V} - \hat{V})^2],$

(16.42) $\quad \sigma_H{}^2 = s^2\{8[\sum \alpha^2 q(1 - q)]^2 + 2 \sum \alpha^4 q(1 - q) - 12 \sum \alpha^4 q^2(1 - q)^2$
$\qquad\qquad + 8(\overline{V} - \hat{V}) \sum \alpha^3 q(1 - q)(1 - 2q) + 8(\overline{V} - \hat{V})^2 \sum \alpha^2 q(1 - q)\}.$

The momentary change in gene frequency is given approximately by

$$\Delta q_i = G_i q_i(1 - q_i) \quad \text{in which} \quad G_i = (1/2)\frac{\partial \overline{H}}{\partial q_i}.$$

(16.43) $G_i = -s\alpha_i[\alpha_i(1 - 2q_i) + 2(\bar{V} - \hat{V})],$

$\sigma_G{}^2 = 2s^2 \sum G_i{}^2 q_i(1 - q_i),$

(16.44) $\sigma_G{}^2 = s^2[2 \sum \alpha^4 q(1 - q)(1 - 2q)^2 + 8(\bar{V} - \hat{V}) \sum \alpha^3 q(1 - q)(1 - 2q)$

$+ 8(\bar{V} - \hat{V})^2 \sum \alpha^2 q(1 - q)].$

Next let V' be the deviation on the primary scale of the optimum from the grade of $a_1 a_1$ when associated with a particular complex of the other genes. The grades of $A_1 A_1$, $A_1 a_1$, and $a_1 a_1$ on the scale of selective values are then $1 - s(2\alpha_1 - V')^2$, $1 - s(\alpha_1 - V')^2$, and $(1 - sV'^2)$, respectively.

The value of λ can now be found from (15.32):

(16.45) $$\lambda_1 = -2s\alpha_1{}^2 q_1{}^2 (1 - q_1)^2.$$

But this is independent of V' and is therefore the same for all associated gene complexes. Thus with a given gene frequency and gene effect, the gene pair $A_1 a_1$ makes a constant contribution

(16.46) $$\sigma_{D_1}^2 = 4s^2 \alpha_1{}^4 q_1{}^2 (1 - q_1)^2$$

to the portion of the total variance due to dominance deviation:

(16.47) $$\sigma_D{}^2 = 4s^2 \sum \alpha^4 q^2 (1 - q)^2.$$

The contribution of interaction deviations may now be found by subtracting (16.44) and (16.47) from (16.42):

(16.48) $$\sigma_I{}^2 = 8s^2 \{[\sum \alpha^2 q(1 - q)]^2 - \sum \alpha^4 q^2 (1 - q)^2\}.$$

In the case of only two loci, this contribution may easily be found directly. The interaction deviation in this case may be found by subtracting the deviations from the mean due to each locus separately from the effect due to the combination, e.g.:

(16.49) $I_{A_1 A_1 A_2 A_2} = (\bar{H}_{A_1 A_1 A_2 A_2} - \bar{H}) - (\bar{H}_{A_1 A_1} - \bar{H}) - (\bar{H}_{A_2 A_2} - \bar{H}).$

Genotype	I	f
$A_1 A_1 A_2 A_2$	$-8s\alpha_1\alpha_2(1 - q_1)(1 - q_2)$	$q_1{}^2 q_2{}^2$
$A_2 a_2$	$-4s\alpha_1\alpha_2(1 - q_1)(1 - 2q_2)$	$2q_1{}^2 q_2(1 - q_2)$
$a_2 a_2$	$+8s\alpha_1\alpha_2(1 - q_1)q_2$	$q_1{}^2(1 - q_2)^2$
$A_1 a_1 A_2 A_2$	$-4s\alpha_1\alpha_2(1 - 2q_1)(1 - q_2)$	$2q_1(1 - q_1)q_2{}^2$
$A_2 a_2$	$-2s\alpha_1\alpha_2(1 - 2q_1)(1 - 2q_2)$	$4q_1(1 - q_1)q_2(1 - q_2)$
$a_2 a_2$	$+4s\alpha_1\alpha_2(1 - 2q_1)q_2$	$2q_1(1 - q_1)(1 - q_2)^2$
$a_1 a_1 A_2 A_2$	$+8s\alpha_1\alpha_2 q_1(1 - q_2)$	$(1 - q_1)^2 q_2{}^2$
$A_2 a_2$	$+4s\alpha_1\alpha_2 q_1(1 - 2q_2)$	$2(1 - q_1)^2 q_2(1 - q_2)$
$a_2 a_2$	$-8s\alpha_1\alpha_2 q_1 q_2$	$(1 - q_1)^2(1 - q_2)^2$

(16.50) $\bar{I} = 0,$

(16.51) $\sigma_I^2 = 16s^2\alpha_1^2\alpha_2^2q_1(1 - q_1)q_2(1 - q_2).$

With n gene pairs, the sum of $n(n - 1)/2$ contributions of the above type comes out the same as total σ_I^2 of equation (16.48). Thus, as in the case of complete dominance, there are no interactions involving simultaneously more than two loci.

The correlations between interaction deviations of parent and offspring can again be determined directly from the two-factor interaction deviations and the joint frequencies as given in Table 15.4. There are 81 terms each consisting of the joint frequency $f_{(OP)_1}$ for A_1, a_1; the joint frequency $f_{(OP)_2}$ for A_2, a_2; the interaction deviation of offspring $I_{12(O)}$; and that of parent $I_{12(P)}$. After much reduction,

(16.52) $r_{I_{12(O)}I_{12(P)}} = (1/\sigma_{I_{12}}^2) \sum^{81} I_{12(O)}I_{12(P)}f_{(OP)_1}f_{(OP)_2} = 1/4.$

Since this is constant, it applies to the total interaction effect of all loci. The total correlation is:

(16.53) $r_{OP} = \dfrac{1}{2}\dfrac{\sigma_G^2}{\sigma_H^2} + \dfrac{1}{4}\dfrac{\sigma_I^2}{\sigma_H^2}.$

In the case of two offspring, the joint frequencies of Table 15.5 may be used. The 81 terms again yield the value 1/4 for each pair of loci and hence for all loci. The total correlation is:

(16.54) $r_{OO'} = \dfrac{1}{2}\dfrac{\sigma_G^2}{\sigma_H^2} + \dfrac{1}{4}\dfrac{\sigma_D^2}{\sigma_H^2} + \dfrac{1}{4}\dfrac{\sigma_I^2}{\sigma_H^2}.$

It is again of interest to consider the contributions of additive effects, dominance, and interaction from given number (n) of loci with the same gene frequency q, equal effects on the primary scale, and optimum at the mean:

(16.55) $\sigma_G^2 = 2ns^2q(1 - q)(1 - 2q)^2\alpha^4$

(16.56) $\sigma_D^2 = 4ns^2q^2(1 - q)^2\alpha^4$

(16.57) $\sigma_I^2 = 8n(n - 1)s^2q^2(1 - q)^2\alpha^4$

(16.58) $\sigma_H^2 = 2ns^2q(1 - q)[1 + (4n - 6)q(1 - q)]\alpha^4.$

The interaction effects always contribute more than the dominance deviation in the ratio $2(n - 1):1$.

The additive effects contribute most if gene frequency is low and the number of loci small, but the interaction deviation becomes increasingly important as the number of loci increases. Table 16.2 compares the cases of semidominance and complete dominance for n equivalent loci with gene frequencies all $1/2$.

TABLE 16.2. Variance components in cases discussed in text

	Semidominance on Primary Scale	Complete Dominance on Primary Scale
σ_G^2	0	$(1/32)ns^2\alpha^4$
σ_D^2	$(1/4)ns^2\alpha^4$	$(1/64)ns^2\alpha^4$
σ_I^2	$(1/2)n(n-1)s^2\alpha^4$	$(9/128)n(n-1)s^2\alpha^4$
σ_H^2	$(1/4)n(2n-1)s^2\alpha^4$	$(3/128)n(3n-1)s^2\alpha^4$

Even in the two-factor case, i^2 is $2/3$ with semidominance and 0.60 (case of 10:6 ratio in Table 16.1) with complete dominance. With numerous factors, almost the entire variance is due to interaction and the correlations between relatives approach 0.25 in both cases.

The General Case of the Optimum Model

The interaction deviations in the optimum model and the correlations between them in relatives can easily be determined on a much broader basis than in the preceding discussion, i.e., for any number of alleles at each of any number of loci, with any set of postulated gene effects and of degrees of dominance on the primary scale, which as before is assumed to be additive with respect to locus effects. It must suffice here to represent three loci: A, B, and C. It will be convenient in this section to take the mean as the origin on the primary scale ($\bar{V} = 0$) and thus to use V with a subscript for the *deviation* from the mean of the indicated genotype. The subscripts 1 and 2 will designate specific alleles (not necessarily different) at each locus, and subscripts i and j (also not necessarily different, and applying independently at each locus), will be used where there is to be averaging over all alleles. It is assumed as before that there is random mating and that the selection coefficient is so small in comparison with the amount of recombination that loci may be assumed to be combined at random. Here M is used for the mean of an array of genotypes (weighted by their frequencies) indicated by the following parenthesis. Thus $M(V_{A_iA_j}) = 0$ by definition and $M(V_{A_iA_j}^2) = \mu_2(V_{AA})$.

(16.59) $M(V_{A_iA_jB_iB_jC_iC_j}) = 0,$

(16.60) $M(V_{A_1A_2B_iB_jC_iC_j}) = V_{A_1A_2},$ etc.,

(16.61) $V_{A_1A_2B_1B_2C_1C_2} = V_{A_1A_2} + V_{B_1B_2} + V_{C_1C_2},$

(16.62) $$M(V_{A_iB_j})^2 = \mu_2(V_{AA}), \text{ etc.,}$$

(16.63) $$H_{A_1A_2B_1B_2C_1C_2} = 1 - s[V_{A_1A_2B_1B_2C_1C_2} - \hat{V}]^2,$$

Noting that $\bar{V} = 0$ in (16.20):

(16.64) $$\bar{H} = M[H_{A_iA_jB_iB_jC_iC_j}] = 1 - s[\mu_2(V_{AA}) + \mu_2(V_{BB})$$
$$+ \mu_2(V_{CC}) + \hat{V}^2],$$

(16.65) $$\bar{H}_{A_1A_2} = M[H_{A_1A_2B_iB_jC_iC_j}] = 1 - s[V^2_{A_1A_2} + \mu_2(V_{BB}) + \mu_2(V_{CC})$$
$$- 2\hat{V}V_{A_1A_2} + \hat{V}^2], \text{ etc.,}$$

$$I_{A_1A_2B_1B_2C_1C_2} = (H - \bar{H}) - (\bar{H}_{A_1A_2} - \bar{H}) - (\bar{H}_{B_1B_2} - \bar{H})$$
$$- (\bar{H}_{C_1C_2} - \bar{H}),$$

(16.66) $$= H - \bar{H}_{A_1A_2} - \bar{H}_{B_1B_2} - \bar{H}_{C_1C_2} + 2\bar{H},$$
$$= -2s[V_{A_1A_2}V_{B_1B_2} + V_{A_1A_2}V_{C_1C_2} + V_{B_1B_2}V_{C_1C_2}].$$

The interaction effects are independent of the position of the optimum and are made up of similar contributions from each pair of loci and none from interaction of more than two loci. It is obvious from the derivation that these conclusions would apply to systems involving any greater number of loci. It may readily be confirmed that the results for complete dominance and for semidominance, two alleles at each locus, derived by the method of least squares, are merely special cases of the above formula.

The variance of interaction deviations is given by the sum of contributions from the 2-factor interactions. The value of the first of the latter is $\sigma^2_{I(AB)} = 4s^2\mu_2(V_{AABB}) = 4s^2\mu_2(V_{AA})\mu_2(V_{BB})$.

The correlation between interaction deviations of two relatives drawn from a panmictic population can be deduced much more easily by using the extension of path analysis to joint paths, valid in such populations, than from the actual correlation arrays used above in the special cases. Let I_1 and I_2 be the total interaction deviations of the two relatives, each the sum of $(1/2)n(n-1)$ contributions if n loci, each contribution being determined jointly by the effects on the primary scale of a pair of loci $(2V_{A_1A_2}V_{B_1B_2})$. In Figure 16.1 there are three loci and hence three contributions. The latter are represented by I_{AB}, I_{AC}, and I_{BC}. It is to be noted that these refer to the total contributions from the pairs in question and must be carefully distinguished from contributions from interactions between single genes of the two loci used later in a more detailed analysis. The correlation between the additive locus effects of the two relatives (e.g., $V_{AA(1)}$ and $V_{AA(2)}$) are represented by $r_{12(A)}$, $r_{12(B)}$, and $r_{12(C)}$ for simplicity. Thus

(16.67) $$r_{I_1I_2} = \frac{\sigma^2_{I(AB)}}{\sigma_I^2} r_{12(A)}r_{12(B)} + \frac{\sigma^2_{I(AC)}}{\sigma_I^2} r_{12(A)}r_{12(C)} + \frac{\sigma^2_{I(BC)}}{\sigma_I^2} r_{12(B)}r_{12(C)},$$

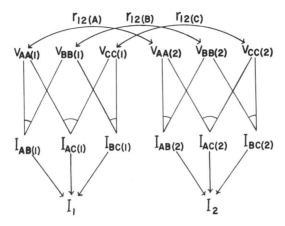

FIG. 16.1. Path diagram for the correlation between interaction deviations of two relatives.

noting that $V_{A_iA_j} = G_i + G_j^{'} + D_{A_iA_j}$, the correlation between $V_{AA(1)}$ and $V_{AA(2)}$, is simply the genotypic correlation between the relatives in question with respect to the A locus. For parent and offspring this is (1/2) if semidominance, $p/(1 + p)$, if complete dominance and p the frequency of the recessive allele. For two offspring, this is again (1/2) if semidominance, but $(1 + 3p)/[4(1 + p)]$ if complete dominance (15.40). The formulas for $r_{I_1I_2}$ derived from the correlation arrays are in agreement.

The contributions of the additive locus effects and the dominance deviations to the total variance and to the correlation between relatives are in general considerably more complicated than those from the interaction effects.

We will follow essentially the analytic approach of Kempthorne (1954, 1955a) and of Cockerham (1954) in their general treatments of interaction systems for a more detailed analysis of the optimum model. It is only necessary to consider a single pair of loci. The selection coefficient, s, will be omitted for simplicity. Note that, as before, $V_{A_iA_j}$ is the deviation of the primary locus effect from the mean, so that $M(V_{A_iA_j}) = 0$, and similarly that the means of its components are each zero, $M[G_{V(A_i)}] = M[G_{V(A_j)}] = 0$ and $M[D_{V(A_iA_j)}] = 0$, and that also $M(V^2_{A_iA_j}) = \mu_2(A_iA_j)$. On the secondary scale, δ will be used for deviation from the mean:

$$(16.68) \quad \delta H_{A_1A_2B_1B_2} = V^2_{A_1A_2} + V^2_{B_1B_2} + 2V_{A_1A_2}V_{B_1B_2} - \mu_2(V_{AA})$$
$$- \mu_2(V_{BB}) - 2\hat{V}[V_{A_1A_2} + V_{B_1B_2}].$$

Replace B_2 by B_j and average $\delta H_{A_1A_2B_1B_j}$ for all B_j's, and similarly with other replacements by variable alleles. The symbols for the variable alleles may be omitted on the H scale without ambiguity.

$$(16.69) \quad M[\delta H_{A_1A_2B_1}] = V^2_{A_1A_2} + M[V^2_{B_1B_j}] + 2V_{A_1A_2}M(V_{B_1B_j})$$
$$- \mu_2(V_{AA}) - \mu_2(V_{BB}) - 2\hat{V}[V_{A_1A_2} + M(V_{B_1B_j})],$$

$$(16.70) \quad M[\delta H_{A_1B_1}] = M(V^2_{A_1A_i}) + M(V^2_{B_1B_j}) + 2M(V_{A_1A_i})M(V_{B_1B_j})$$
$$- \mu_2(V_{AA}) - \mu_2(V_{BB}) - 2\hat{V}[M(V_{A_1A_i}) + M(V_{B_1B_j})],$$

$$(16.71) \quad M[\delta H_{A_1A_2}] = V^2_{A_1A_2} - \mu_2(V_{AA}) - 2\hat{V}V_{A_1A_2},$$

$$(16.72) \quad M[\delta H_{A_1}] = M(V^2_{A_1A_j}) - \mu_2(V_{AA}) - 2\hat{V}M(V_{A_1A_j}) = G_{H(A_1)}.$$

The last expression gives $G_{H(A_1)}$, the additive contribution of A_1 to $\delta H_{A_1A_2B_1B_2}$. The contribution for dominance can be calculated from the relation $M[\delta H_{A_1A_2}] = G_{H(A_1)} + G_{H(A_2)} + D_{H(A_1A_2)}$.

$$(16.73) \quad \begin{aligned} D_{H(A_1A_2)} = V^2_{A_1A_2} &- M(V^2_{A_1A_j}) - M(V^2_{A_iA_2}) + \mu_2(V_{AA}) \\ &- 2\hat{V}\{V_{A_1A_2} - M[V(A_1A_j)] - M[V(A_iA_2)]\}. \end{aligned}$$

The various kinds of interaction components can be calculated similarly by subtracting from each of the above mean differences the contributions from component genes.

$$(16.74) \quad \begin{aligned} I_{H(A_1B_1)} &= M(\delta H_{A_1B_1}) - G_{H(A_1)} - G_{H(B_1)}, \\ &= 2M(V_{A_1A_j})M(V_{B_1B_j}). \end{aligned}$$

$$(16.75) \quad \begin{aligned} I_{H(A_1A_2B_1)} &= M(\delta H_{A_1A_2B_1}) - G_{H(A_1)} - G_{H(A_2)} - G_{H(B_1)} \\ &\qquad - D_{H(A_1A_2)} - I_{H(A_1B_1)} - I_{H(A_2B_1)}, \\ &= 2[V_{A_1A_2} - M(V_{A_1A_j}) - M(V_{A_2A_i})]M(V_{B_1B_j}). \end{aligned}$$

Finally, $I_{H(A_1A_2B_1B_2)}$ the component of the total interaction deviation $(I_{A_1A_2B_1B_2})$ involving all genes can be obtained by subtracting from $M(\delta H_{A_1A_2B_1B_2})$ the four G_H's, both D_H's, the four two-factor interactions, and the four three-factor interactions:

$$(16.76) \quad \begin{aligned} I_{H(A_1A_2B_1B_2)} = 2[V_{A_1A_2} &- M(V_{A_1A_j}) - M(V_{A_2A_i})][V_{B_1B_2} \\ &- M(V_{B_1B_j}) - M(V_{B_2B_i})]. \end{aligned}$$

These contributions from interaction can be simplified by evaluating the terms of the type $M(V_{A_1A_j})$:

$$(16.77) \quad M(V_{A_1A_j}) = \sum q_j[G_{V(A_1)} + G_{V(A_j)} + D_{V(A_1A_j)}].$$

The term $\sum q_j D_{V(A_1A_j)} = 0$ if there are only two alleles.

Genotype	f	D
A_1A_1	q_1	$-(1 - q_1)^2(\alpha_1 - \alpha_2) = D_{V(A_1A_1)}$
A_1A_2	$(1 - q_1)$	$q_1(1 - q_1)(\alpha_1 - \alpha_2) = -\dfrac{q_1}{1 - q_1} D_{V(A_1A_1)}$

If there are multiple alleles, one allele (such as A_1) may be opposed to all the others as if the latter group were a single allele.

$$
(16.78) \quad
\begin{aligned}
M(D_{V(A_1A_j)}) &= \sum [q_j D_{V(A_1A_j)}] \\
&= q_1 D_{V(A_1A_1)} + (1 - q_1)\left(-\frac{q_1}{1 - q_1}\right) D_{V(A_1A_1)} = 0.
\end{aligned}
$$

Next, since $\sum [q_i G_{V(A_1)}] = G_{V(A_1)}$ and $\sum [q_j G_{V(A_j)}] = 0$:

$$(16.79) \qquad M(V_{A_1A_j}) = G_{V(A_1)},$$

$$(16.80) \qquad I_{H(A_1B_1)} = 2G_{V(A_1)}G_{V(B_1)},$$

$$(16.81) \qquad I_{H(A_1A_2B_1)} = 2D_{V(A_1A_2)}G_{V(B_1)},$$

$$(16.82) \qquad I_{H(A_1A_2B_1B_2)} = 2D_{V(A_1A_2)}D_{V(B_1B_2)}.$$

The sum of all nine contributions is, as indicated by 16.66.

$$
(16.83) \quad
\begin{aligned}
I_{A_1A_2B_1B_2} &= 2[G_{V(A_1)} + G_{V(A_2)} + D_{V(A_1A_2)}][G_{V(B_1)} + G_{V(B_2)} + D_{V(B_1B_2)}] \\
&= 2V_{A_1A_2}V_{B_1B_2}.
\end{aligned}
$$

These expressions bring out the appropriateness of the terms used by Kempthorne (1954) and Cockerham (1954): additive-additive (or AA) for those of type $I_{H(A_1B_1)}$, dominant-additive (or DA) for those of type $I_{H(A_1A_2B_1)}$, additive-dominant (or AD) for those of type $I_{H(A_1B_1B_2)}$, and dominant-dominant (or DD) for those of type $I_{H(A_1A_2B_1B_2)}$.

It may be noted that the total contribution from interaction (16.83) is simpler than any of its components (16.80 to 16.82), in the case of the optimum model.

It is also of interest that if there is semidominance on the primary scale (all D_V's zero), the total interaction is additive-additive.

The variance components due to interaction are very simple:

$$(16.84) \qquad \mu_2(I_{H(AB)}) = 2\mu_2[G_{V(A)}]\mu_2[G_{V(B)}],$$

$$(16.85) \qquad \mu_2(I_{H(AAB)}) = 2\mu_2[D_{V(AB)}]\mu_2[G_{V(B)}],$$

$$(16.86) \qquad \mu_2(I_{H(ABB)}) = 2\mu_2[G_{V(A)}]\mu_2[D_{V(AB)}],$$

$$(16.87) \qquad \mu_2(I_{H(AABB)}) = 2\mu_2[D_{V(AA)}]\mu_2[D_{V(BB)}].$$

The additive and dominance contributions to $\mu_2(H_{A_1A_2B_1B_2})$ are not as simple as the interaction contributions. They consist of the variances of the following quantities and the analogous ones for the other genes.

(16.88) $G_{H(A_1)} = M(V_{A_1A_j}^2) - \mu_2(V_{AA}) - 2\hat{V}G_{V(A_1)},$

(16.89) $D_{H(A_1A_2)} = V_{A_1A_2}^2 - M(V_{A_1A_j}^2) - M(V_{A_2A_l}^2) + \mu_2(V_{AA})$
$$- 2\hat{V}[D_{V(A_1A_2)}].$$

These can, however, be calculated for each allele and each zygote, and the variance components for all loci can be calculated. The total variance (secondary scale) is given by $\sigma_H{}^2 = \sum f(\delta H)^2$:

(16.90) $\sigma_H{}^2 = \sum \mu_4(V) + 2[\sum \mu_2(V)]^2 - 3\sum[\mu_2(V)]^2 - 4\hat{V}\sum\mu_3(V)$
$$+ 4\hat{V}^2[\sum\mu_2(V)].$$

The correlation between relatives can be calculated as usual from knowledge of the portions of the total variance determined by its various components —additive, dominance, and interaction—and the correlations between relatives with respect to each.

Environmental Effects

So far it has been assumed that the primary character is completely determined by heredity. Most quantitatively varying characters are, however, affected by variable environmental factors. This inevitably introduces interaction with respect to the secondary character, selective value, which will be represented by W instead of H in this section. To bring out the nature of this complication in as simple a case as possible, it will be assumed that the genetic and environmental effects on the character, V_G and V_E respectively, are additive and uncorrelated and that both of their distributions and that of their sum, V, are normal. This implies that there are numerous more or less equivalent loci and thus that most of the genetic contribution is due to gene interactions. (16.36), (16.58). As in the preceding section, the mean is taken as the origin on the primary scale ($\bar{V} = 0$) (Wright 1935).

With normality on the primary scale:

(16.91) $\mu_2(V) = \mu_2(V_G) + \mu_2(V_E),$

(16.92) $\mu_3(V) = 0,$

(16.93) $\mu_4(V) = 3[\mu_2(V)]^2.$

On the scale of selective values

(16.94) $W = 1 - s[V_G + V_E - \hat{V}]^2$ from (16.19)
$$= 1 - s[(V_G{}^2 - 2\hat{V}V_G) + (V_E{}^2 - 2\hat{V}V_E) + 2V_GV_E + \hat{V}^2].$$

The factors of W thus consist of second and first powers of V_G and V_E and a joint or interaction term.

(16.95) $\overline{W} = 1 - s[\mu_2(V_G) + \mu_2(V_E) + \hat{V}^2]$,

(16.96) $\sigma_W{}^2 = s^2[2[\mu(V)]^2 + 4\hat{V}^2\mu_2(V)]$

$= 2s^2\{\sigma_{V(G)}^2[\sigma_{V(G)}^2 + 2\hat{V}^2] + \sigma_{V(E)}^2(\sigma_{V(E)}^2 + 2\hat{V}^2) + 2\sigma_{V(G)}^2\sigma_{V(E)}^2\}.$

The last term is the interaction variance.

If now the optimum is at the mean ($\hat{V} = 0$)

(16.97) $\sigma_W{}^2 = 2s^2(\sigma_{V(G)}^2 + \sigma_{V(E)}^2)^2 = 2s^2\sigma_V{}^4.$

The squared path coefficients, relating W to its factors, are:

(16.98)
$$p_{WW(G)}^2 = \sigma_{V(G)}^4/\sigma_V{}^4$$
$$p_{WW(E)}^2 = \sigma_{V(E)}^4/\sigma_V{}^4$$
$$p_{WW(GE)}^2 = 2\sigma_{V(G)}^2\sigma_{V(E)}^2/\sigma_V{}^4$$

As noted earlier, the correlation between the interaction deviations of two relatives, R_1 and R_2, is the product of the compound path coefficients for their factors, provided that these factors are not correlated, as is here assumed.

(16.99) $r_{W(1)W(2)} = p_{WW(G)}^2 r_{W(G1)W(G2)} + p_{WW(E)W(E1)W(E2)}^2$

$+ p_{WW(GE)}^2 r_{W(G1)W(G2)} r_{W(E1)W(E2)}.$

If there is no environmental correlation between the relatives,

(16.100) $r_{W(1)W(2)} = (\sigma_{V(G)}^4/\sigma_V{}^4) r_{W(G1)W(G2)}.$

This contrasts with the correlation between the relatives with respect to the character, $r_{V(1)V(2)} = (\sigma_{V(G)}^2/\sigma_V{}^2) r_{V(G1)V(G2)}.$

As noted above, the assumption of normal variability of the character implies that $r_{W(G1)W(G2)}$ is due largely to the genetic interaction. This has been given for two dominant genes, frequencies p_a and p_b, as $[p_a/(1 + p_a)] \times [p_b/(1 + p_b)]$ in the case of parent and offspring (16.13) and as $[(1 + 3p_a)/4(1 + p_a)][(1 + 3p_b)/4(1 + p_b)]$ in the case of full sibs (16.15). These are the locus products of the genotypic correlations between these relatives on the primary scale (15.39, 15.40). If gene frequencies are all the same, the genotypic correlations between these relatives with respect to a multifactorial character are $[p/(1 + p)]^2$ and $[(1 + 3p)/4(1 + p)]^2$, respectively, and the phenotypic correlations are given by multiplying by h^2 ($= \sigma_{V(G)}^4/\sigma_V{}^4$). Thus under these assumptions the phenotypic correlations with respect to selective value are the squares of those with respect to the character. A similar situation holds in the case of semidominance in which the correlation between interaction deviations is 1/4 for parent and offspring (16.52) and full sibs (16.54) in comparison with the genotypic correlations, 1/2, in both cases.

In all of these cases

(16.101) $$r_{W(1)W(2)} = (r_{V(1)V(2)})^2.$$

This principle is generalized in the next section.

Limiting Case of the Optimum Model

The values of the correlations between any relatives in a panmictic population with respect to selective value (W) are related very simply to those on the underlying scale if it is assumed that the optimum is at the mean of the underlying character ($\hat{V} = 0$) (Wright 1952a) and there is normal variability on the latter because of there being a large number of independent minor additive factors, environmental as well as genetic.

(16.102) $$W = \overline{W} - V^2,$$

(16.103) $$\overline{W} = \overline{\overline{W}} - \sigma_V^2,$$

(16.104) $$W - \overline{W} = \sigma_V^2 - V^2,$$

(16.105) $$\sigma_W^2 = M[\sigma_V^2 - V^2]^2 = \mu_4(V) - \sigma_V^4.$$

Let $W_1 = (\overline{W} - V_1^2)$ and $W_2 = (\overline{W} - V_2^2)$ be the grades in pairs of relatives in the population in question. These relatives are equally variable (σ_V^2) under the assumption of panmixia.

(16.106) $$\begin{aligned} r_{W_1W_2} &= M[(\sigma_V^2 - V_1^2)(\sigma_V^2 - V_2^2)]/\sigma_W^2, \\ &= M(V_1^2V_2^2 - \sigma_V^4)/[\mu_4(V) - \sigma_V^4]. \end{aligned}$$

Let $V_2 = b_{V_2V_1}V_1 + y_2 = r_{V_1V_2}V_1 + y_2$ where $b_{V_2V_1}$ is the regression of V_2 on V_1, and y_2 is independent of V_1. Then

(16.107) $$\begin{aligned} M[V_1^2V_2^2] &= M\{V_1^2[r_{V_1V_2}^2V_1^2 + 2V_1y_2r_{V_1V_2} + y_2^2]\}, \\ &= r_{V_1V_2}^2\mu_4(V) + \sigma_V^2\sigma_{y_2}^2. \end{aligned}$$

But $\sigma_{y_2}^2 = \sigma_V^2(1 - r_{V_1V_2}^2)$. Thus:

(16.108) $$M[V_1^2V_2^2] = r_{V_1V_2}^2\mu_4(V) + \sigma_V^4 - \sigma^4 r_{V_1V_2}^2,$$

(16.109) $$r_{W_1W_2} = r_{V_1V_2}^2.$$

Thus the correlation between any relatives with respect to selective value (or other secondary character), under the assumptions that have been made, is the square of its correlation with respect to the underlying character. This is irrespective of degrees of dominance or effects of environmental factors.

The distribution of the secondary character would be extremely asymmetrical (χ^2 distribution with one degree of freedom). If, however, the secondary character is the sum of equal independent contributions, each of which is of the above sort, the observed distribution becomes a χ^2 distribution with a corresponding number of degrees of freedom, and thus less asymmetrical. More generally let

$$(16.110) \qquad W = \overline{W} - \sum_{i}^{n} k_i V_i^2$$

where the k's are weights for n independent normal variables. By steps analogous to those preceding:

$$(16.111) \qquad r_{W_1 W_2} = \sum_{i}^{n} [k_i' r_{V_1 V_2}^2] / \sum_{i}^{n} [k_i']$$

where $k_i' = k_i^2 \sigma_V^4$.

The correlation for the secondary character is thus a weighted average of the squared correlations with respect to the underlying character.

If the optima do not coincide with the means, the correlations in general involve portions due to additive and dominance deviation and are intermediate between the first and second powers of the underlying correlation.

Interaction in General

The discussion of specific interaction systems so far has been restricted to that present in two-factor F_2 ratios involving complete dominance and that found in secondary characters that fall off as the square of the deviation of a primary additive character from its optimum, as representative of the type of character (selective value) that is most important in evolutionary theory. There are, of course, a virtually infinite number of other interaction patterns that might be considered. The method of Kempthorne and Cockerham is generally applicable, provided that the individuals are drawn from a panmictic population.

There may be interactions involving three or more variables simultaneously. The contributions of additive effects (A), dominance effects (D), and interactions of all sorts AA, AD, DA, AAA, AAD, etc., may be determined step by step as indicated for the optimum model and the variance components determined from these. The correlations between these contributions in relatives of any sort can be found as the products of those pertaining to the components of a joint path. For the type of interaction, AAD, this correlation is the product of correlations between additive effects at the first locus, between additive effects for the second locus, and between dominance effects at the third locus.

Kempthorne (1955b) has extended the analysis to polyploids.

CHAPTER 17

Conclusions

This volume has been concerned with the theory of the genetic composition of populations in terms of gene frequencies, and of the immediate changes to be expected under various conditions. The applications to actual populations, experimental and natural, and to long-time evolutionary changes, are deferred to volume 3.

At one time, natural populations were often thought of as being essentially homallelic at all loci with qualification only because of the occasional occurrence of mutations, soon eliminated if, as usual, unfavorable. Favorable mutations appear very rarely and fixation of one was considered a typical step in evolution. The basic viewpoint of population genetics is, on the contrary, that large populations tend to be heterallelic at all loci and strongly so at many. Mathematically, the species is thought of as located at a point in a gene frequency space with $\sum (k_i - 1)$ dimensions, k_i being the number of alleles at the ith locus and summation being over all loci. Evolution consists of movement in this space.

The first chapter recalls briefly the conclusions of volume 1 concerning which principles of genetics and biometry should be given most attention, in the development of population genetics. The first new topic (chapter 2) is the genetic situation to be expected in a large population, in the absence of any disturbing factors. Not surprisingly, it appears that the combinations both of alleles within loci and of nonalleles among loci tend to be at random or to become so if a deviation has been imposed. With a diploid organism, random combination of autosomal alleles is attained in the first generation after the frequencies have become the same in the male and female gametes, giving the Hardy–Weinberg distribution $[\sum_i q_i A_i]^2$ at each locus, where A_i is the ith allele, and q_i is its frequency. In the case of a $2k$-somic, random combination $[\sum q_i A_i]^{2k}$ is approached at rate $1 - \lambda = [k + (k - 1)e]/(2k - 1)$ per generation, where e is the rate of double reduction. It is approached in oscillatory fashion in the case of sex-linked genes, with the deviation of the frequencies of eggs (q_e) and of sperms (q_s) from their weighted average,

$\bar{q} = [(2/3)q_e + (1/3)q_s]$—if males are heterogametic—being reversed in direction and halved in each generation.

Random combination of genes in different loci is attained only gradually even in the case of autosomal diploids (rate $\bar{c}$ per generation where $\bar{c}$ is the average recombination percentage in eggs and sperm). The rate is approximately $\bar{c}$ in the case of two closely linked polysomic loci and approximately $2c/3$ in the case of two sex-linked loci. The exact values in these cases are rather complicated.

The most elementary evolutionary process is taken to be change of gene frequency. Directed changes, Δq, are distinguished from random changes, measured by the variance $\sigma^2_{\Delta q}$. Very rare or unique events may also be important in evolution, but since they do not lend themselves to mathematical treatment they are not discussed in this volume.

Directed changes (chaps. 3–5) are of three sorts—those due to recurrent mutation, to recurrent immigration, and to selection. The last is a wastebasket category that includes all causes of directed change that do not involve change of the genetic material or introduction from without. Thus it includes changes due to differential viability at any stage, differential emigration, differential mating, differential fecundity, and systematic asymmetry at segregation (meiotic drive).

The basic formula for the pressure of recurrent mutation on a particular gene frequency, in the presence of multiple alleles, is $\Delta q_x = (\sum u_{ix}q_i) - (\sum u_{xi})q_x$, where u_{ix} and u_{xi} are the rates per generation from A_i to A_x and A_x to A_i, respectively. The total rate of mutation of the gene in question may, however, be assumed to be constant under given conditions and represented by u_x. or merely u. The total rate to it from all of its alleles may be represented by a single symbol $v = u_{.x}$, but unless there is only a pair of alleles, the value of v may be expected to change with the changes in frequency of the alleles. If there is only a pair of alleles, then $\Delta q = v(1 - q) - uq$.

Immigration pressure is given by $\Delta q = -m(q - Q)$ where Q is the frequency of the gene in question in the immigrants and m is the amount of replacement of the population by the immigrants. Both Q and m are likely to be variable, but it is the deterministic aspect that is under consideration here.

The absolute selective value of a genotype is represented by W with appropriate subscript. It is the average ratio of the effective population number to that in the preceding generation under the given array of other genotypes and the given environment. It is often more convenient, however, to use w, the selective value relative to that of a specified standard.

The basic formula for the selection pressure in terms of the net relative selective value of the gene itself is $\Delta q = q(w - \bar{w})/\bar{w}$ but it is more useful in most cases to express this in terms of the relative selective values of the locus genotypes and their frequencies with average $\bar{w} = \sum wf$ and $\Delta q = q(1 - q)(d\bar{w}/dq)/2\bar{w}$ for one of a pair of alleles in a diploid population. In the $2k$-somic case the denominator is $2k\bar{w}$ and for a sex-linked gene approximately $1.5\,\bar{w}$. With multiple alleles, total differentiation of the mean selective value must be replaced by partial differentiation

$$\Delta q_x = q_x(1 - q_x) \frac{\partial \bar{w}}{\partial q_x} \bigg/ 2\bar{w},$$

in evaluating which,

$$\frac{\partial q_i}{\partial q_x} = -q_i/(1 - q_x).$$

In all of these cases, $\bar{w}$ in the denominator may be treated as one with little error if the selective differences are slight.

The most important special cases in diploid populations are those for a semidominant gene, $\Delta q_A = s q_A(1 - q_A)$, where the selective values of AA, Aa, and aa are as $(1 + 2s):(1 + s):1$, respectively; for a recessive gene $\Delta q_a = s q_a^2(1 - q_a)$, where the selective values of $A-$ and aa are as $1:(1 + s)$, respectively; and for a heterotic pair, $\Delta q_A = q_A(1 - q_A)[t - (s + t)q_A]$, where the selective values of AA, Aa, and aa are as $(1 - s):1:(1 - t)$, respectively.

Some more complicated modes of selection of pairs of alleles are discussed. There are often different values in males and females. If the differences are small, the effect is approximately that for the average, but if the differences are great, the course of selection can only be worked out generation by generation. There may be different values in haploid and diploid phases of the reproductive cycle or with respect to maternal influence and the individual, or in early and late phases of the same life cycle. Wholly different modes of selection may be involved here, as in viability and fecundity. In the case of successive effects, the overall selective value of a genotype is the product of the components. Finally, the somewhat complicated effects of meiotic drive are considered.

The simpler formulas permit estimation of the course of change over many generations by integration (treating Δq as dq/dt) if the selective differences are slight, but only step-by-step estimates can be made otherwise.

Typically, all kinds of pressures are operating simultaneously. If the partial pressures are small, the total may be taken as the sum without regard to order. Thus for one of a pair of alleles in a diploid:

$$\Delta q = v(1 - q) - uq - m(q - Q) + q(1 - q) \frac{d\bar{w}}{dq} \bigg/ 2\bar{w}.$$

Gene frequency changes until $\Delta q = 0$, whether because the gene has become fixed ($q = 1$) or has been lost ($q = 0$) or has come to a stable equilibrium ($q = \hat{q}$). There may be equilibrium from mutation alone, $\hat{q} = v/(u + v)$, in the case of a pair of alleles, but a set of equations, $\Delta q_i = 0$, must be solved for all q_i's with multiple alleles, and there is no equilibrium if indefinitely many alleles are possible.

Immigration brings the population to the immigrant average, $\hat{q} = Q$, if this is constant, in the absence of other pressures.

There can be near-equilibrium from selection alone where the heterozygote has a not too unequal advantage over both homozygotes, $\hat{q}_A = t/(s + t)$. If all heterozygotes of multiple alleles have the same selective value and this is superior to that of all homozygotes ($1:1 - s_i$) there is near-equilibrium at $\hat{q}_x = (1/s_x)/\sum (1/s_i)$. There are other cases. There may be net selective advantage of heterozygotes in any of the sorts of compound selection merely because of some tendency toward dominance of different genes with respect to different components. In none of these cases involving only selection is there stable equilibrium in an absolute sense, since there is always some chance that an allele may be lost and selection alone cannot bring about recovery.

In all of these cases, there is also a possibility of unstable equilibrium as a result of net heterozygous disadvantage. These are the simplest cases of two selective peaks, or more if there are multiple alleles.

Other kinds of equilibrium result from joint action of two of the kinds of pressures. Perhaps the commonest is that from recurrent mutations of a deleterious gene. If recessive, $\hat{q} = \sqrt{(r/s)}$; if more or less dominant, $\hat{q} = r/s$. The mean relative selective value at equilibrium in these cases is independent of the severity of the selection, $\hat{w} = 1 - v$ in the case of a deleterious recessive; $\bar{w} = 1 - 2v$ for grades of dominance up to complete dominance (Haldane's principle). The rate at which equilibrium is approached is, however, very much dependent on the severity.

Especially important for the theory of evolution is the balance between recurrent immigration and local selection. Taking the case of a locally unfavorable semidominant gene, there is near loss if $s \gg m$, ($\hat{q} \approx mQ/s$); near-swamping by immigration if $s \ll m$, ($\hat{q} \approx Q[1 - (s/m)(1 - Q)]$); and an intermediate frequency if s and m are about equal, $\hat{q} \approx 1 - \sqrt{(1 - Q)}$ (or $\hat{q} = \sqrt{Q}$ in the case of a locally favorable gene).

Selection formulas for single loci can never be more than momentary approximations because of the practical universality of interactions with the other loci and the universal dependence of selective values on gene frequencies. Interaction effects, assuming constant selective values for the pertinent multifactorial genotypes, are discussed in chapter 4. It is convenient to distinguish two major types of interaction. First are the physiological and developmental interactions. The characters with which an organism responds to its environment are not in general immediate products of gene action but the resultants of a network of processes. The effects of any one gene are thus affected by the situation at many other loci. The ultimate character, however, to which the mathematical formulation must apply is selective value itself, and interaction among genes is very likely to be introduced at this level even if effects on observable characters happen to be almost additive on the most appropriate scale. This occurs if, as must usually be the case in nature, the optimal grade of the character is intermediate. In this case, each gene that contributes to the character in the positive direction is favorable if the effect is added to a total from others that is some distance below the optimum, but unfavorable otherwise, and conversely with genes that contribute in the negative direction.

Whether interaction is physiological or is imposed by intermediacy of the optimal grade, it usually tends to bring about a deviation from random combination in balance with the restitutive tendency of meiosis. This complicates the mathematical treatment enormously. If, however, interactive selection is slight in ratio to the amount of recombination, as is usually the case if many genes are involved and are in different chromosomes or are only loosely linked, the deviation from random combination may be shown to be slight and a useful approximation may be obtained by assuming random combination:

$$\Delta q_x = q_x(1 - q_x) \frac{\partial \bar{w}}{\partial q_x} \Big/ 2\bar{w}, \qquad \frac{\partial q_i}{\partial q_x} = -q_i/(1 - q_x).$$

This is formally the same as for multiple alleles at a single locus, but in this case the w's refer to the multifactorial genotypes of the interaction system. Their frequencies, f's, involved in $\bar{w}\, (= \sum f w_i)$, are taken as the products of the frequencies of the locus genotypes under the assumption of random combination.

A number of interactions among two pairs of loci are considered on this basis. An important case is that of specific modifiers of the degree of dominance of type over a deleterious mutation. It is brought out that the selection pressure from this cause is so exceedingly minute (of the order of the mutation rate or less) that any appreciable effect of the modifier in homozygous wild-type would take precedence in determining fixation or loss. Known modifiers of dominance have, in general, effects of their own. This situation was used to illustrate the concept of a pleiotropic threshold among the partial selection pressures, acting on any gene.

Especial attention is devoted to deviations from random combination in the case of an intermediate optimum. In the case of two pairs of loci with optimum at the mean, there are a saddle and two selective peaks. Taking s as the selective disadvantage at a single step from the mean and c as the amount of recombination, it is shown that if s is of lower order than c the deviations from random combination are unimportant for most purposes. If, however, s is of higher order than c, coupling linkages become fairly rare. This applies also to the terminal pair of a succession of four or six such linked loci and also seems to be the case with the middle pair in a succession of six. Otherwise, coupling linkages, though lower in frequency than repulsion linkages, are not rare unless s/c is unusually large. Unbalanced gametes as wholes are strongly reduced in frequency if s/c is large, but alternating sequences of plus and minus factors are not maintained to an important extent.

The general equations for change of gene frequency in the case of two pairs of alleles, allowing for deviation from random combination, are discussed. Kimura's principle that the ratio $R = f_{AB}f_{ab}/f_{Ab}f_{aB}$ tends to "quasi equilibrium" under widely occurring conditions leads to consideration of the "surface" of selective values in the field of gamete frequencies which the point representing the population approaches and on which it moves toward the selective peak on the slope of which it lies. In the case of two pairs, the "surface" is approximated very closely under the assumption of random combination if the index $k = \bar{s}_I/cw_{AaBb}$, where $\bar{s}_I$ measures the average interactive selection, is less than 0.05, and it is roughly approximated even if k is as large as 0.5.

This is taken to justify investigation of centripetal selection, under the assumption of random combination, with respect to such matters as inequality of gene effects, degrees of dominance (reinforcing or oppositional) in the two factor case, and the number of selective peaks where there are many loci and multiple alleles. The number mounts rapidly with number of either loci or alleles.

The preceding conclusions are all under the assumption of constancy of the selective values of the total genotypes in the interaction system. The effects of frequency dependence of the selective value are taken up in chapter 5. The approximate formulas where the assumption of random combination is adequate are, in the diploid case:

$$\Delta q_x = (1/2)q_x(1 - q_x) \sum \left[(W/\overline{W}) \frac{\partial f}{\partial q_x} \right], \qquad \frac{\partial q_i}{\partial q_x} = -q_i/(1 - q_x).$$

The surface of mean selective values, $\overline{W}$, is not in general that on which the population tends to move. This is, instead, the fitness function where it exists.

$$F(W/\overline{W}) = \int \sum \left[(W/\overline{W}) \frac{\partial f}{\partial q_x} \right] dq_x$$

$$\Delta q_x = (1/2)q_x(1 - q_x) \frac{\partial F(W/\overline{W})}{\partial q_x}.$$

The peaks in the fitness surface are the points at which

$$\frac{\partial F(W/\overline{W})}{\partial q_x} = 0$$

or at which the gene is fixed ($q_x = 1$) or lost ($q_x = 0$).

As implied, the fitness peaks are not, in general, the same as those on the surface of mean selective values, $\overline{W}$. Both surfaces are important in evolutionary theory—the fitness peaks for selection within demes, the mean selective values for that among demes.

The fitness function always exists in the case of a character determined by a single pair of alleles. A number of cases are discussed in which selective value is a specified function of the frequency of the gene in question. Some of these are simplified models for a population that lives in a heterogeneous environment in which one genotype is at an advantage in some places, others elsewhere, and individuals can search out favorable environments while avoiding overcrowding. This implies a selective disadvantage to a gene from overabundance and leads to another sort of equilibrium than those considered before. Conversely, a selective disadvantage to a gene from rarity, which may occur under certain conditions, gives a point of unstable equilibrium and two selective peaks.

The fitness function exists only in certain special cases where there are multiple alleles or multiple loci. One of those includes the cases in which the selection among individuals is of such a nature that the size of population is not affected while the relative selective values are constant. Competition among males is an example. This implies frequency dependence among the absolute selective values, $W_i = kw_i/\bar{w}$, so that $\overline{W} = k$, a constant. The fitness function $F(W/\overline{W})$, however, is not constant, and the population moves toward one of its peak values, which in this case is a peak value of $\bar{w}$.

If the absolute selective values are all multiples of some function ψ of certain gene frequencies, this is not involved in the relative selective values, $W_i = \psi w_i$ and $\overline{W} = \psi\bar{w}$. Again the population reaches stability at a peak value of $F(W/\overline{W})$ (or of $\bar{w}$), but the rate of population growth ($\overline{W} - 1$) is greatest at a peak value of $\overline{W}$ which may be very different. It is quite possible for "fitness" to keep increasing while the population is tending to extinction because $\overline{W} < 1$. An example is that of a genotype that derives superior individual fitness by preying on its own species and brings the latter to destruction on passing a certain relative frequency. Conversely, a genotype that contributes to the success of the species, as measured by $\overline{W}$, will tend to be eliminated if it does so to its own detriment. The effect of selection among populations is not here considered.

A genotype may have some effects that are reflected in growth of the population and others that are not. Again the peaks in the controlling surface $F(W/\overline{W})$ may be very different from those in mean selective value, $\overline{W}$.

If selective values of genotypes vary solely as functions of their own frequencies, an approximate fitness function exists irrespective of number of loci or of alleles at each. Thus, if $W_i = \chi(f_i)$ and $\overline{W} = \sum f_i \chi(f_i)$, then $F(W/\overline{W}) \approx \int \chi(f_i)\, df_i$. Examples are given of multiple alleles and of multiple loci, involving selective advantage of rarity.

A number of cases are considered in which the fitness function, as defined, does not exist. In some of these, the point representing the species in the gene frequency space moves in a spiral fashion toward a position at which it comes to rest which may or may not be a peak value of $\overline{W}$. These are selective "goals," if not strictly selective peaks of a definable fitness surface. A two-factor case, $[pA + (1 - p)a][qB + (1 - q)b]$, is discussed in which $F(w/\bar{w})$ as defined does not exist but another fitness function, $F'(w/\bar{w})$, can be devised in which

$$\Delta p = p(1 - p)q(1 - q)\, \frac{\partial F'(w/\bar{w})}{\partial p}\bigg/ \bar{w},$$

and Δq is analogous. The slope determines the movement of the population toward a peak, qualified by the positive factor $p(1 - p)q(1 - q)$ instead of by the usual $q(1 - q)$. In general there are multiple selective goals which may or may not be the same as the peaks in the surface $\overline{W}$, which always exist.

A number of special cases of frequency dependent selection are considered. One of these is intrabrood selection. The rate of change of gene frequency comes out the same (if selective differentials are small) as if there were constant selective differentials of half the assigned values, applied to competition in the panmictic population as a whole instead of merely within broods. Another system that is considered is that of the self-incompatibility mechanism of many flowering plants, failure of pollen tube growth on a style in which either of the alleles is that of the pollen grain. Selection always favors a new mutant allele because of the absence of inhibition. Only an approximate formula for selection pressure can be obtained in this case. Other cases are maternal-fetal interaction with respect to blood group genes and the very important case of selective mating.

The treatment of selection, where multiple loci are involved, by assuming constant selective values is never strictly accurate. The excess reproductive capacity of organisms is limited. Increased selection of one locus necessarily reduces the intensity at other loci. This is brought out in the case of uni-directional selection of quantitative variability, dependent on multiple additive genes. The formula can be written $\Delta q = q(1 - q)(z/p)(\alpha/\sigma)$ in the case of semidominance where z is the ordinate of the unit normal curve that bounds the selected portion p, α is the contribution of the gene in question, and σ is the standard deviation of the character. The term z/p can be re-placed by $\Delta M_p/\sigma$ where ΔM_p is the deviation of the mean of the selected portion from the mean of the total population. The selection coefficient of the gene in question, $s = (z/p)(\alpha/\sigma)$, is dependent on the frequencies of all of the genes and on the environmental variability, because of the presence of the total standard deviation in the formula. The presence of variation in a given locus, by increasing σ, reduces the selection intensity at all other loci as compared with a situation which is the same except for the absence of variation in the given locus. This consideration prevents the simultaneous presence of many strong selection pressures. The great majority of selection pressures must be small.

The dependence of selective value on population density has a regulatory effect that keeps total selection pressure within bounds.

The dynamics of selection of cytoplasmic differences is discussed briefly in chapter 6. It is noted that strictly maternal transmission gives results essentially similar to those in an array of clones except that there is often extreme instability of the character. This instability has suggested non-equational apportionment of multiple entities at each cell division.

The most important class of cytoplasmic differences, from the evolutionary standpoint, seems to be that involved in the nucleocytoplasmic incom-patibilities, which probably play an important role in genetic isolation. The rather common case of pollen sterility from conjunction of a maternally transmitted entity and a particular genome, however, turns out to be in-capable of initiating such isolation. Such a possibility is, on the other hand, indicated in the case of the inviability of one or both reciprocal crosses of a sort described in races of mosquitoes.

The analysis of the determinative aspects of genetic composition needs to be supplemented by the consideration of random changes in gene frequencies. Where the latter are sufficiently common and regular to be describable by a variance, $\sigma^2_{\Delta q}$, the joint effect is a probability distribution of gene frequencies, $\varphi(q)$, centered in the equilibrium value, $\hat{q}$, from the determinative processes.

This topic is discussed in chapters 13 and 14 and will be taken up here before topics concerned with population structure.

The random processes that can most easily be associated with the determinative processes in mathematical treatment are those due to accidents of sampling in a population of limited effective size, N, or to fluctuations in selective intensity, σ_s^2, or in amount of immigration, σ_m^2, or in the gene frequency of immigrants, σ_Q^2. Under the simplest mode of selection (semidominance), the total variance of random changes in gene frequency in a diploid population is $\sigma_{\Delta q}^2 = (1/2N)q(1 - q) + \sigma_s^2 q^2(1 - q)^2 + \sigma_m^2(q - Q)^2 + m^2\sigma_Q^2$.

It is shown that with a total mean rate of directed change, Δq, and total variance of random changes, $\sigma_{\Delta q}^2$, the resulting probability distribution for a single gene is

$$\varphi(q) = (C/\sigma_{\nabla q}^2) \exp \left[2 \int (\Delta q/\sigma_{\Delta q}^2) \, dq\right], \qquad \int_0^1 \varphi(q) \, dq = 1.$$

This gives the expected distribution of the gene frequency in a single population over a very long period of time, or the distribution of an array of gene frequencies with the same parameters in a single population at any one time, or the distribution of the gene frequency in question in an array of isolated similar populations at any time.

These are all conditions that are very unlikely to be realized exactly in nature, but the theoretical probability distribution gives an indication of the amounts of deviation from theoretical equilibrium frequencies that are reasonable.

As an example, if

$$\Delta q = \left[q(1 - q) \frac{\partial \bar{w}}{\partial q}\bigg/ 2w\right] - m[q - Q] \qquad \text{and} \qquad \sigma_{\Delta q}^2 = q(1 - q)/2N,$$

then $\varphi(q) = C\overline{W}^{2N}q^{4NmQ - 1}(1 - q)^{4Nm(1 - Q) - 1}$. The distribution $\varphi(q)$ ranges from near restriction to the equilibrium value $\hat{q}$ if N and hence both of the exponents are large; to a u-shaped distribution if Nm is so small that the exponents of q and $(1 - q)$ are both close to -1. The formulas of the distributions where the random changes are due to fluctuation in selection or in amount or kind of immigration are more complicated.

On starting from a given gene frequency in a large number of similar populations, there would be a succession of transition distributions before a steady state is reached. The rather complicated formulas of such transition states have been worked out but are not discussed here except in special cases in which constancy of form is attained while all frequency classes are decreasing at a uniform rate, the end result being complete fixation or loss because of the absence of recurrent mutation or immigration.

In the absence of all directed processes, this form is rectangular, $\varphi(q) = 1$, with decay at the rate $1/(2N)$ per generation since fixation and loss both proceed at the rate $1/(4N)$. In the case of a single favorable mutation and selection, the probability distribution for frequencies reaches a steady form which permits determination of the chance of fixation from the ratio of the terminal frequencies. This chance can also be determined in other ways. A more or less dominant mutation with heterozygous selective advantage s has an approximate chance $2s$ of being fixed. For a favorable recessive mutation the chance is $\sqrt{(2s/\pi N)}$, or $1.13\sqrt{(s/2N)}$. These, however, postulate a persistence of the selective advantage over such enormous periods of time that they are probably rather unrealistic. Associated genes and environment are almost certain to change.

The number of alleles, similar with respect to selection and mutation rate, which tend to be maintained in a population of given size can be estimated from the balance between origin of alleles by mutation and their loss by accidents of sampling in the steady state distribution for the array of similar existent alleles. It may be very great. The cases of neutral isoalleles, of similarly deleterious ones, of heterotic ones, and of self-incompatibility alleles are discussed.

The probability distribution for a single gene is of little evolutionary significance in itself. What is of primary significance is the existence of a joint distribution for all of the loci involved in an interaction system. The distribution for any single gene may, however, be thought of as a cross-section of the total for a given set of frequencies at all other loci. Chapter 14 deals with the steady state formulas for multiple alleles and for multiple loci. While no completely general formula has been obtained, the formulas representing the balance at each locus between local selection and immigration,

$$\Delta q = (1/2)q(1 - q) \frac{\partial F(W/\overline{W})}{\partial q} - m(q - Q),$$

and the effects of accidents of sampling ($\sigma^2_{\Delta q} = q(1 - q)/2N$) as the simplest representative of the random processes, lead to a multilocus formula of considerable evolutionary significance:

$$\varphi(q_1 \cdots q_i \cdots q_n) = Ce^{2NF(W/\overline{W})} \prod q^{4NmQ-1}.$$

The gene frequencies here include in one list all alleles at all of the loci under consideration. The selection term shows that the distribution reflects in enormously exaggerated form the surface of fitness values, qualified by the product of the immigration terms for each gene. If the genotypic selective values can be considered constant to an adequate approximation, so that log $\overline{W}$ may be substituted for $F(w/\bar{w})$, the selection term becomes $\overline{W}^{2N}$, which brings out more clearly the way in which the surface of mean selective values (in this case) in exaggerated form is a factor in the joint probability distribution.

The frequencies clustered about a single selective peak of the distribution indicate the amount of multidimensional random drift in this portion of the total. The occasional passage across a two-factor saddle on the fitness surface (or surface of mean selective values), to control by a new peak, marks an elementary evolutionary step in the population in question. Such a step has, as indicated, only an extremely small probability of occurring in a single population under the conditions represented by the formula. The latter, however, includes only one form of random process, and the probability may be greater under a broader concept of such processes, a subject to be discussed at length in volume 3. More important, however, are the consequences of subdivision of a large population into numerous partially isolated demes. The subject of population structure is considered in chapters 7–12.

The first question here is the analysis of the theoretical consequences of inbreeding. Since the outcome is different in different inbred lines, the best model is that of a large array of completely isolated lines derived from the same panmictic population. It turns out that the single most useful parameter is the fixation index F (in this case the inbreeding coefficient) defined as the correlation, relative to the gene array of the foundation stock, between the representatives of a locus that are brought together by fertilization. As derived by path analysis, this is independent of the number of alleles, the values assigned them, or their frequencies, but differs for autosomal and sex-linked diploid loci and for polysomic loci. In the diploid case, path analysis at once gives the general formula $F = \sum [(1/2)^n(1 + F_A)]$ which involves the summation of all different paths by which one may pass through the pedigree from one of the uniting gametes to the other, without passing through an individual twice; n is the number of individuals along the path; and F_A is the inbreeding coefficient of the common ancestor to which the paths back of the two gametes trace. Alternatively, this formula can be derived from the fact that the probability of identity of the uniting alleles by descent from the foundation stock is the same as the correlation in all cases in which this correlation is positive. The fixation index F must be positive for the inbreeding coefficient as defined above, but it may be negative in such cases as disassortative mating and in the correlation between uniting alleles relative to the *current* array within the line (instead of to the foundation stock), where there is avoidance of consanguinity.

In regular systems of mating, the value of F in any generation can readily be expressed in terms of values in a number of preceding generations. The final expressions take on a somewhat simpler form in terms of the complement of F, called the panmictic index, $P = 1 - F$. The average ratio of P to its value in the preceding generation in a given system of mating in a population of constant size is easily obtained. The simplest example is that of continued self-fertilization. Using a prime to indicate the preceding generation, $P = (1/2)P'$. Under sib mating, $P = 0.809P'$. Under double first cousin mating, $P = 0.920P'$. With completely random union of gametes in a population of N monoecious individuals, $P = [1 - 1/(2N)]P'$. The difference is slight if self-fertilization is avoided,

$$P \approx \left(1 - \frac{1}{2N + 1}\right)P',$$

and is the same as the last under random mating in a population of N, equally divided between males and females. More generally, in a population of N_m males and N_f females,

$$P \approx \left(1 - \frac{4N_fN_f}{N_m + M}\right)P',$$

of which an important case is that of a herd with one male and many females ($P = 0.890P'$). There is an interesting contrast between systems of a given size in which consanguinity is avoided as much as possible (multiple cousins) and in which it is maximized (half-sib circle). If each parent produces just two offspring, avoidance delays the onset of inbreeding but ultimately leads to a more rapid decline,

$$P \approx \left[1 - \frac{1}{4N - (m + 1)}\right]P',$$

in a population of size 2^m in contrast with

$$P \approx \left[1 - \left(\frac{\pi}{2N + 4}\right)^2\right]P'.$$

With random mating among $N/2$ males, $N/2$ females, but selection of just two offspring from each individual, the ultimate rate is

$$P \approx \left(1 - \frac{1}{4N - 3}\right)P'.$$

Index F gives the amount of decrease in heterozygosis relative to the foundation stock, and in a regular system $(\Delta P)/P'$ is the rate of decrease per generation. The deviation of a population from panmixia can readily be described, the frequencies of homozygotes A_iA_i being of the type $(1 - F)q_i^2 + Fq_i$ and of heterozygotes, A_iA_j being $2(1 - F)q_iq_j$ instead of q_i^2 and $2q_iq_j$, respectively, for $F = 0$.

The effective size of a population, N_e (chap. 8), may be quite different from the number of mature individuals. This can be considered from two viewpoints: the decrease of the panmictic index, $P = [1 - 1/(2N)]P'$, in the simplest case, and the sampling variance, $\sigma_q^2 = q(1 - q)/2N$. Fortunately the number that should replace N in these two cases (if random gametic union in a monoecious population is taken as standard) is the same in a static population (but not in one of changing size). The population may have an unequal sex ratio. If so,

$$N_e = \frac{4N_mN_f}{N_m + N_f},$$

approaching $4N_m$ if N_f is much greater than N_m. There may be differential productivity,

$$N_e \approx \frac{4N}{2 + \sigma_K^2},$$

where σ_K^2 is the variance of number of offspring per parent giving $N_e = N$ with random (Poisson) variability $\sigma_K^2 = 2$; giving $N_e = 2N$ if just two offspring are chosen from each parent $(\sigma_K^2 = 0)$, as above; but giving $N_e < N$ if there is variability in excess of random. The most important reason for N_e being much less than apparent N is probably, however, great variation in numbers over a small number (n) generations, in which case

$$N_e = 1 \Big/ \left\{ \frac{1}{n} \left[\sum^n \frac{1}{n} \right] \right\} = H_N$$

where H_N is the harmonic mean.

Chapter 9 goes into the consequence of inbreeding where there is not random combination among loci in the foundation stock (such as a stock that is a cross between two inbred lines or in a mixture). With close inbreeding and strong linkage, recombination does not go far before it is brought to an end by fixation, but with only moderate inbreeding and loose, if any, linkage, recombination is largely complete. A wholly different question is the amount of joint fixation of two or more loci on starting from a panmictic population. For loci that are in different chromosomes and no self-fertilization, this is merely the joint probability of independent events but is a complicated matter with respect to linked genes.

Selection, especially if favoring heterozygotes, and enforced heterozygosis at a linked locus interfere with the progress of inbreeding in ways described in chapter 10.

Assortative mating without change of gene frequency, is discussed in chapter 11. With respect to a character determined by multiple semidominant factors, there is fixation of the extreme genotypes if there is complete determination by heredity and perfect assortative mating, but not otherwise. With a given correlation between genotypes, $m = h^2 r_{PP}$, where h^2 is the heritability and r_{PP} the phenotypic assortative mating, there is considerably more fixation with high r_{PP}, low h^2 than the converse. A correlation between genotype and the environment in which the offspring develops has the effect of increasing the apparent heritability and thus the apparent genotypic assortative mating for a given phenotypic assortative mating.

The construction of models of natural population structures which permit determination of the genetic consequences is of great importance in evolutionary theory. The use of various forms of the fixation index F in this connection is the subject of chapter 12.

In the island model, local populations of effective size N are assumed to derive the portion m from immigrants representative of the species as a whole in which the frequency of the gene under consideration is Q. Effective m here is usually much less than the actual proportion of immigrants, which may be expected to come from neighboring populations which largely agree in their differences from the species as a whole. In this case, F is approximately $1/(4Nm + 1)$, which is in general much larger—in terms of effective N and m—than if these had their observed values. The variance of the values of q of the "islands" is $\sigma_q{}^2 = Q(1 - Q)F$.

There may be hierarchic subdivision of the total species through a number of categories before reaching the random breeding "deme." It is convenient to use a number of F-statistics: F_{IT} is the correlation between mating gametes relative to the total, F_{IS} is the average correlation within subdivisions, and F_{ST} is the average correlation between random gametes of the same subdivision relative to the total. These are connected by the formula $F_{IT} = F_{IS} + F_{ST} - F_{IS}F_{ST}$ or more simply in terms of panmictic indexes, $P_{IT} = P_{IS}P_{ST}$. This can be extended if there is further subdivision, to $P_{IT} = P_{IR}P_{RS}P_{ST}$, etc.

Correlation F_{ST} can also be defined as the ratio of the variance of gene frequencies of subdivisions to its limiting value, irrespective of their own structure: $F_{ST} = \sigma_{q(ST)}^2/q_T(1 - q_T)$. If there is no inbreeding within the substrains this is the same as the formula $F = \sigma_q{}^2Q(1 - Q)$ implied above, since q_T is the same as Q.

The formula for F_{ST} is applicable whatever the nature of the differentiation among substrains. If this is due to local differences in selection, however, the value of F_{ST} pertains to each locus separately instead of applying to many loci (all that are neutral), as is the case where the differentiation is the automatic consequence of inbreeding. Index F_{ST} is necessarily positive, but F_{IS} calculated from $(F_{IT} - F_{ST})/(1 - F_{ST})$ may be negative if consanquineous matings are avoided within substrains.

At the opposite extreme from the island model is that of isolation merely by distance in a continuum. Differentiation arises from the balance between the tendency toward local fixation by inbreeding and the swamping effect of dispersion. The most important unit is the "neighborhood," with an effective size, N_1, which is that of the population from which the parents of an individual may be considered as if drawn at random. If birthplaces of parents are distributed normally, with standard deviation σ in relation to that of the individual in the case of a linear continuum, N_1 is equivalent to the effective number of individuals along a strip of length $2\sigma\sqrt{\pi} = 3.5\sigma$. In a continuous area, N_1 is equivalent to the effective number in a circle of radius 2σ. These are modified somewhat if the immediate distribution of dispersion is leptokurtic, especially in the case of the linear continuum.

The differentiation of neighborhoods automatically carries with it, in the course of time, differentiation of larger regions up to a limit imposed by the rate of mutation or by a mechanism of rare long-range dispersal. There may be very great random differentiation even with N_1 of many thousands in the case of a linear continuum, but there is virtual panmixia if N_1 is greater than 1,000 in an area continuum. There is appreciable differentiation if N is as small as 200 and much if of the order of 20. A pattern of randomly distributed clusters of high density but only slight dispersal between clusters results in differentiation of larger areas largely in accordance with the small N_1 implied by this dispersal rather than in accordance with the size of the clusters.

Differentiation from local inbreeding and restricted dispersion is a much slower process than that from differential local selection, but it has special significance because of its completely random character. That for local selection may, however, be considered random from the standpoint of the evolution of the species as a whole, even though directed from the standpoint of the locality. As noted above, a coefficient F_{ST} can be determined for each gene frequency that can be observed. The value of F_{ST} for a cline does not fall off with the size of the area (S) under consideration as rapidly as does that from local inbreeding and in fact remains nearly constant up to large fractions of the total.

Throughout this volume, the genetic compositions of populations have been discussed almost wholly in terms of gene frequencies. The conclusions can be applied to natural and experimental populations insofar as the frequencies of genes are determinable. Unfortunately, many of the most important characters in either sort of population are continuously varying

ones in which gene frequencies cannot be determined. The first step in
bridging the gap is the analysis of the phenotypic variability of such characters into components that are of genetic significance (chaps. 15 and 16).

The primary cleavage is between the genetic and nongenetic variances.
There may be cleavage of the latter that is of interest (components due to
tangible environmental factors, to developmental accident, etc.). The most
important cleavage of the genetic variance is into a completely additive
component, a component that is due to dominance deviations, and components due to interaction. The latter can be analyzed in a very detailed
way: the additive-additive, the additive-dominant, and the dominant-
dominant "interactions" between pairs of loci, and the various kinds among
three loci, and so on. In the optimum model the total interaction is as
simple as the components which are wholly two-factor ones.

The correlations between parent and offspring, between sibs, and between
other relatives are properties of populations that are determinable and
closely related to the analysis of variance into components. Theoretical
values are presented for autosomal and sex-linked genes, with and without
dominance and, in principle at least, for kinds of interactions. Again there is
too much detail for brief summary. One interesting property of the case in
which the character depends on the squared deviation of an underlying
variable from the mean as its optimal value may be noted. In this case, the
correlation between any pair of relatives is approximately the square of its
correlation on the underlying scale.

A related topic is the correlation between relatives under assortative
mating.

Finally, an analysis of the genetic variance of quantitatively varying
characters can be made with respect to hierarchic population structures. If
the effects of genes are completely additive, the mean of the character in the
total population or its subdivisions depends only on the gene frequencies
but the variances depend on the F-statistics. The variance of individuals in
the total, σ_{IT}^2, is analyzed below into the variance of subdivision means,
σ_{ST}^2, and the mean of the variances within subdivisions σ_{IS}^2. The variance that
would be found with the same gene frequencies but random mating through-
out is represented by $\sigma_{IT(0)}^2$.

General	Randombred Subdivisions
	$(F_{IS} = 0, \quad F_{ST} = F_{IT})$
$\sigma_{ST}^2 \quad 2F_{ST}\sigma_{IT(0)}^2$	$2F_{IT}\sigma_{IT(0)}^2$
$\sigma_{IS}^2 \quad (1 + F_{IT} - 2F_{ST})\sigma_{IT(0)}^2$	$(1 - F_{IT})\sigma_{IT(0)}^2$
$\sigma_{IT}^2 \quad (1 + F_{IT})\sigma_{IT(0)}^2$	$(1 + F_{IT})\sigma_{IT(0)}^2$

If there is other than semidominance, the mean is affected in a way that is responsible for the usual inbreeding decline. At a given gene frequency, the mean with a given value of F_{IT}, represented by $M(F_{IT})$, is related to the means under random mating $M(0)$, and under complete fixation of subdivisions $M(1)$ by the formula $M(F_{IT}) = M(0) + F_{IT}[M(1) - M(0)]$. This applies to subgroups, on replacing F_{IT} by F_{IS}.

The total genetic variance under inbreeding, $\sigma^2_{IT(F)}$, is related to those under random mating and complete fixation by the formula

$$\sigma^2_{IT(F)} = (1 - F_{IT})\sigma^2_{IT(0)} + F_{IT}\sigma^2_{IT(1)} + F_{IT}(1 - F_{IT})[M(1) - M(0)]^2.$$

The analysis of this quantity into components $\sigma^2_{ST(F)}$ and $\sigma^2_{IS(F)}$ requires third and fourth moments of the distribution of gene frequencies among subdivisions. The somewhat surprising results under progressive inbreeding or in a steady state because of balancing of inbreeding and immigration are discussed.

REFERENCES

Bartlett, M. S., and Haldane, J. B. S. 1934. The theory of inbreeding in auto-tetraploids. *Jour. Genet.* 29:175–80.

———. 1935. The theory of inbreeding with forced heterozygosis. *J. Genet.* 31:327–40.

Bateman, A. J. 1947. Contamination of seed crops. III. Relation with isolation distance. *Heredity* 1:303–36.

Bennett, J. H. 1953. Linkage in hexasomic inheritance. *Heredity* 7:265–83.

———. 1954. Panmixia with tetrasomic and hexasomic inheritance. *Genetics* 39:150–58.

Bennett, J. H., and Binet, F. E. 1956. Association between Mendelian factors with mixed selfing and random mating. *Heredity* 10:51–55.

Bernstein, F. 1930. Fortgesetzte Untersuchungen aus der Theorie der Blutgruppen. *Zeit. ind. Abst. Ver.* 56:233–73.

Bodmer, W. F., and Parsons, P. A. 1960. The initial progress of new genes with various genetic systems. *Heredity* 15:283–99.

———. 1962. Linkage and recombination in evolution. *Adv. Genetics* 11:1–100.

Breese, E. L. 1956. The genetical consequences of assortative mating. *Heredity* 10:323–43.

Bruck, D. 1957. Male segregation ratio advantage as a factor in maintaining lethal alleles in wild populations of house mice. *Proc. Nat. Acad. Sci.* 43:152–58.

Carmon, J. L., Stewart, H. A., Cockerham, C. C., and Comstock, R. E. 1956. Prediction equations for rotational crossbreeding. *Jour. Animal Sci.* 15:920–36.

Caspari, E., and Watson, G. S. 1959. On the evolutionary importance of cytoplasmic sterility in mosquitoes. *Evolution* 13:568–70.

Caspari, E., Watson, G. S., and Smith, Woolcott. 1966. The influence of cytoplasmic pollen sterility on gene exchange between populations. *Genetics* 53:741–46.

Castle, W. E. 1903. The laws of heredity of Galton and Mendel and some laws governing race improvement by selection. *Proc. Amer. Acad. Sci.* 39:233–42.

Chapman, A. B. 1946. Genetic and nongenetic sources of variation in the weight response of the immature rat ovary to a gonadotropic hormone. *Genetics* 31:494–507.

Clarke, B., and O'Donald, P. 1964. Frequency dependent selection. *Heredity* 19:201–6.

Cockerham, C. C. 1954. An extension of the concept of partitioning hereditary variance for analysis of covariances among relatives when epistasis is present. *Genetics* 39:859–82.

———. 1956. Effects of linkage on covariances between relatives. *Genetics* 41:138–41.

———. 1959. Partitions of hereditary variance for various genetic models. *Genetics* 44:1141–48.

———. 1963. Estimates of genetic variances. *Statistical Genetics and Plant Breeding*, Edited by W. D. Hanson and H. F. Robinson. Nat. Acad. Sci.–Nat. Res. Council Publ. No. 982:53–93.

Comstock, R. E., and Robinson, H. F. 1948. The components of genetic variance in populations of biparental progenies and their use in estimating the average degree of dominance. *Biometrics* 4:254–66.

———. 1952. Estimation of average dominance of genes. In *Heterosis*, pp. 494–516. Edited by J. W. Gowen. Ames, Ia.: Iowa State College Press.

Correns, C. 1937. Nichtmendelnde Vererbung. *Handbuch der Vererb. Wiss.* 12:1–159. Edited by F. von Wettstein. Berlin: Gebrüder Borntraeger.

Crow, J. F. 1954a. Breeding structure of populations. II. Effective population number. In *Statistics and mathematics in biology*, pp. 543–56. Edited by O. Kempthorne, T. A. Bancroft, J. W. Gowen, and J. L. Lush. Ames, Ia.: Iowa State Univ. Press.

———. 1954b. Random mating with linkage in polysomics. *Amer. Nat.* 88:431–34.

Crow, J. F., and Kimura, M. 1956. Some genetic problems in natural populations. *Proc. Third Berkeley Symp. on Math. Stat. and Prob.* 4:1–22.

Crow, J. F., and Morton, N. E. 1955. Measurement of gene frequency drift in small populations. *Evolution* 9:202–14.

Dobzhansky, Th., and Wallace, B. 1953. The genetics of homeostasis in Drosophila. *Proc. Nat. Acad. Sci.* 39:162–71.

Dobzhansky, Th., and Wright, S. 1941. Genetics of natural populations. V. Relations between mutation rate and accumulation of lethals in populations of Drosophila pseudoobscura. *Genetics* 26:23–51.

Dunn, L. C. 1957. Evidences of evolutionary forces leading to the spread of lethal genes in wild populations of house mice. *Proc. Nat. Acad. Sci.* 43:158–63.

East, E. M. 1936. Heterosis. *Genetics* 21:375–97.

Emerson, S. 1939. A preliminary survey of the Oenothera organensis population. *Genetics* 24:524–37.

Ephrussi, B. 1953. *Nucleo-cytoplasmic relations in microorganisms.* Oxford: Clarendon Press.

Ewens, W. J. 1964a. The maintenance of alleles by mutation. *Genetics* 50:891–98.

———. 1964b. On the problem of self-sterility alleles. *Genetics* 50:1433–38.

———. 1965a. A note on Fisher's theory of the evolution of dominance. *Ann. Human Genet.* 29:85–88.

————. 1965b. Further notes on the evolution of dominance. *Heredity* 20:443–50.

Ewens, W. J., and Ewens, P. M. 1966. The maintenance of alleles by mutation. Monte Carlo results for normal and self-sterility alleles. *Heredity* 21:371–78.

Falconer, D. S. 1960. *Introduction to quantitative genetics.* New York: Ronald Press Co.

Feller, W. 1955. Diffusion processes in genetics. *Proc. Second Berkeley Symp. on Math. Stat. and Prob.*, pp. 227–46.

————. 1966. On the influence of natural selection on population size. *Proc. Nat. Acad. Sci.* 55:733–38.

Felsenstein, J. 1965. The effect of linkage on directional selection. *Genetics* 52:349–63.

Fish, H. D. 1914. On the progressive increase of homozygosis in brother-sister matings. *Amer. Nat.* 48:759–61.

Fisher, R. A. 1918. The correlation between relatives on the supposition of Mendelian inheritance. *Trans. Roy. Soc. Edinburgh* 52:399–433.

————. 1922. On the dominance ratio. *Proc. Roy. Soc. Edinburgh* 42:321–41.

————. 1928. The possible modification of the response of the wild-type to recurrent mutations. *Amer. Nat.* 62:115–26.

————. 1929. The evolution of dominance: A reply to Professor Sewall Wright. *Amer. Nat.* 63:563–56.

————. 1930a. *The genetical theory of natural selection.* Oxford: Clarendon Press.

————. 1930b. The distribution of gene ratios for rare mutations. *Proc. Roy. Soc. Edinburgh* 50:205–20.

————. 1934. Professor Wright on the theory of dominance. *Amer. Nat.* 68:370–74.

————. 1937. The wave of advance of advantageous genes. *Ann. Eugen.* 7:355–69.

————. 1941. Average excess and average effect of a gene substitution. *Ann. Eugen.* 11:53–63.

————. 1947. The theory of linkage in polysomic inheritance. *Phil. Trans. Roy. Soc.* B233:55–87.

————. 1949. *The theory of inbreeding.* Edinburgh: Oliver & Boyd.

————. 1958. *The genetical theory of natural selection.* 2d edition. New York: Dover Publ.

Fisher, R. A., and Mather, K. 1943. The inheritance of style length in Lythrum salicaria. *Ann. Eugen.* 12:1–23.

Fisher, R. A., and Yates, F. 1938. *Statistical tables for biological, agricultural and medical research.* Edinburgh: Oliver & Boyd.

Fraser, A. S. 1958. Simulation of genetic systems by automatic digital computers. 5-linkage, dominance and epistasis. *Biometrical Genetics*, pp. 70–83. London: Pergamon Press.

————. 1960. Simulation of genetic systems by automatic digital computers. *Austr. Jour. Biol. Sci.* 13:150–62.

Fraser, A. S., and Burnell, D. 1967. Simulation of genetic systems. XII. Models of inversion polymorphism. *Genetics* 57:267–82.

Gairdner, A. E. 1929. Male sterility in flax. II. A case of reciprocal crosses differing in F_2. *Jour. Genet.* 21:117–24.

Galton, F. 1889. *Natural inheritance.* London: Macmillan & Co.

Geiringer, H. 1944. On the probability theory of linkage in Mendelian heredity. *Ann. Math. Stat.* 15:25–57.

——. 1948a. On the mathematics of random mating in case of different recombination values for males and females. *Genetics* 33:548–64.

——. 1948b. Contribution to the heredity theory of multivalents. *Jour. Math. Physics* 26:246–78.

——. 1949a. Contribution to the linkage theory of autopolyploids. *Bull. Math. Biophysics* 11:59–82, 197–219.

——. 1949b. Chromatid segregation of tetraploids and hexaploids. *Genetics* 34:665–84.

Gilmour, J. S. L., and Gregor, J. W. 1939. Demes: A suggested new terminology. *Nature* 144:333.

Green, E. L., and Doolittle, D. P. 1963. Systems of mating used in mammalian genetics. In *Methodology in mammalian genetics*, pp. 3–41. Edited by W. J. Burdette. San Francisco: Holden-Day.

Gregory, R. P. 1915. On variegation in Primula sinensis. *Jour. Genet.* 4:305–21.

Griffing, B. 1960a. Theoretical consequences of truncation selection based on the individual phenotype. *Austr. Jour. Biol. Sci.* 13:307–43.

——. 1960b. Accommodation of linkage to mass selection theory. *Austr. Jour. Biol. Sci.* 13:501–26.

——. 1962. Consequences of truncation selection based on combination of individual performance and general combining ability. *Austr. Jour. Biol. Sci.* 15:333–51.

Grun, D., and Aubertin, M. P. 1965. Evolutionary pathways of cytoplasmic male sterility in Solanum. *Genetics* 51:399–409.

Haldane, J. B. S. 1924a. A mathematical theory of natural and artificial selection. Part I. *Trans. Camb. Phil. Soc.* 23:19–41.

——. 1924b. A mathematical theory of natural and artificial selection. Part II. The influence of partial self-fertilisation, inbreeding, assortative mating and selective fertilisation on the composition of Mendelian populations and on natural selection. *Proc. Camb. Phil. Soc., Biol. Sci.* 1:158–63.

——. 1926. A mathematical theory of natural and artificial selection. Part III. *Proc. Camb. Phil. Soc.* 23:363–72.

——. 1927a. A mathematical theory of natural and artificial selection. Part IV. *Proc. Camb. Phil. Soc.* 23:607–15.

——. 1927b. A mathematical theory of natural and artificial selection. Part V. Selection and mutation. *Proc. Camb. Phil. Soc.* 23:838–44.

——. 1930a. A mathematical theory of natural and artificial selection. Part VI. Isolation. *Proc. Camb. Phil. Soc.* 26:220–30.

———. 1930b. A note on Fisher's theory of the origin of dominance and on a correlation between dominance and linkage. *Amer. Nat.* 64:87–90.

———. 1930c. Theoretical genetics of autopolyploids. *Jour. Genet.* 22:359–72.

———. 1931a. A mathematical theory of natural and artificial selection. Part VII. Selection intensity as a function of mortality rate. *Proc. Camb. Phil. Soc.* 27:131–36.

———. 1931b. A mathematical theory of natural and artificial selection. Part VIII. Metastable populations. *Proc. Camb. Phil. Soc.* 27:137–42.

———. 1932a. A mathematical theory of natural and artificial selection. Part IX. Rapid selection. *Proc. Camb. Phil. Soc.* 28:244–48.

———. 1932b. *The causes of evolution.* London: Longmans, Green & Co.

———. 1934. A mathematical theory of natural and artificial selection. Part X. Some theorems on artificial selection. *Genetics* 19:412–29.

———. 1937a. Some theoretical results of continued brother-sister mating. *Jour. Genet.* 34:265–74.

———. 1937b. The effect of variation on fitness. *Amer. Nat.* 71:337–49.

———. 1942. Selection against heterozygosis in man. *Ann. Eugen.* 11:333–43.

———. 1955. The complete matrices for brother-sister and alternate parent-offspring mating involving one locus. *Jour. Genet.* 53:315–24.

———. 1956. The conflict between inbreeding and selection. I. Self-fertilization. *Jour. Genet.* 54:56–63.

———. 1957. The cost of natural selection. *Jour. Genet.* 55:511–24.

———. 1961. Conditions for stable polymorphism at an autosomal locus. *Nature* 193:1108.

Haldane, J. B. S., and Jayakar, S. D. 1963. Polymorphism due to selection depending on the composition of a population. *Jour. Genet.* 58:318–23.

———. 1964. Equilibrium under natural selection at a sex-linked locus. *Jour. Genet.* 59:29–36.

Haldane, J. B. S., and Moschinsky, P. 1939. Inbreeding in Mendelian populations with special reference to human cousin marriage. *Ann. Eugen.* 9:321–40.

Haldane, J. B. S., and Waddington, C. H. 1931. Inbreeding and linkage. *Genetics* 16:357–74.

Hardy, G. H. 1908. Mendelian proportions in a mixed population. *Science* 28:49–50.

Harris, D. L. 1964a. Biometrical parameters of self-fertilizing diploid populations. *Genetics* 50:931–56.

———. 1964b. Genotypic covariances between inbred relatives. *Genetics* 50:1319–48.

Harris, T. E. 1963. *The theory of branching processes.* Englewood Cliffs, N.J.: Prentice-Hall.

Hayman, B. I. 1960. The theory and analysis of diallel crosses. III. *Genetics* 45:155–72.

Hayman, B. I., and Mather, K. 1953. The progress of inbreeding when homozygotes are at a disadvantage. *Heredity* 7:165–83.

————. 1956. Inbreeding when homozygotes are at a disadvantage: A reply. *Heredity* 10:271–74.

Hazel, L. N. 1943. The genetic basis for constructing selection indexes. *Genetics* 28:476–90.

Hazel, L. N., and Terrill, C. E. 1945. Heritability of weaning weight and staple length in range Rambouillet lambs. *Jour. Animal Sci.* 4:347–58.

Hiraizumi, Y., Sandler, L., and Crow, J. F. 1960. Meiotic drive in natural populations of Drosophila melanogaster. III. Populational implications of the segregation-distorter locus. *Evolution* 14:433–44.

Jain, S. K., and Allard, R. W. 1965. The nature and stability of equilibria under optimizing selection. *Proc. Nat. Acad. Sci.* 54:1436–43.

————. 1966. The effects of linkage, epistasis, and inbreeding on population changes under selection. *Genetics* 53:633–59.

Jain, S. K., and Workman, P. L. 1967. Generalized *F*-statistics and the theory of inbreeding and selection. *Nature* 214:674–78.

Jennings, H. S. 1914. Formulae for the results of inbreeding. *Amer. Nat.* 48:693–96.

————. 1916. Numerical results of diverse systems of breeding. *Genetics* 1:53–89.

————. 1917. The numerical results of diverse systems of breeding with respect to two pairs of characters, linked or independent, with special relation to the effects of linkage. *Genetics* 2:97–154.

Jones, D. F. 1917. Dominance of linked factors as a means of accounting for heterosis. *Proc. Nat. Acad. Sci.* 3:310–12.

————. 1918. The effects of inbreeding and crossbreeding upon development. *Conn. Agric. Exp. Sta., Bull. 207.*

Kempthorne, O. 1954. The correlation between relatives in a random mating population. *Proc. Roy. Soc. B*143:103–13.

————. 1955*a*. The theoretical values of the correlation between relatives in random mating populations. *Genetics* 40:153–67.

————. 1955*b*. The correlation between relatives in a simple autotetraploid population. *Genetics* 40:168–74.

————. 1955*c*. The correlations between relatives in inbred populations. *Genetics* 40:681–91.

————. 1957. *An introduction to genetic statistics.* New York: John Wiley & Sons.

Kimura, M. 1951. Effect of random fluctuation of selective value on the distribution of gene frequencies in natural populations. *Ann. Rept. Nat. Inst. Genet. Japan* 1:45–51.

————. 1953. "Stepping stone" model of population. *Ann. Rept. Nat. Inst. Genet. Japan* 3:62–63.

————. 1954. Process leading to quasi-fixation of genes in natural populations due to random fluctuation of selection intensities. *Genetics* 39:280–95.

————. 1955*a*. Solution of a process of random genetic drift with a continuous model. *Proc. Nat. Acad. Sci.* 41:144–50.

————. 1955*b*. Random genetic drift in a multiallelic locus. *Evolution* 9:419–35.

————. 1955c. Stochastic processes and distribution of gene frequencies under natural selection. *Cold Spring Harbor Symp. Quant. Biol.* 20:33–53.

————. 1956a. Random genetic drift in a triallelic locus: Exact solution with a continuous model. *Biometrics* 12:57–66.

————. 1956b. Rules for testing stability of a selection polymorphism. *Proc. Nat. Acad. Sci.* 42:336–40.

————. 1956c. A model of a genetic system which leads to closer linkage by natural selection. *Evolution* 10:278–87.

————. 1957. Some problems of stochastic processes in genetics. *Ann. Math. Stat.* 28:882–901.

————. 1958. On the change of population fitness by natural selection. *Heredity* 12:145–67.

————. 1962. On the probability of fixation of mutant genes in a population. *Genetics* 47:713–19.

————. 1963. A probability method for treating inbreeding systems especially with linked genes. *Biometrics* 19:1–17.

————. 1964. Diffusion models in population genetics. *Jour. Applied Prob.* 1:177–232 (and Methuen's Review Series in Applied Probability, 2:1–57. Edited by M. S. Bartlett and J. Gani).

————. 1965a. Simulation studies on the number of self-sterility alleles maintained in a small population. *Ann. Rept. Nat. Inst. Genet. Japan* 16:86–88.

————. 1965b. Attainment of quasi-linkage equilibrium when gene frequencies are changing by natural selection. *Genetics* 52:875–90.

————. 1966. Simulation studies on the number of neutral alleles maintained in a finite population by mutation. *Ann. Rept. Nat. Inst. Japan* 17:64–65.

————. 1968. Evolutionary rate at the molecular level. *Nature* 144:333.

Kimura, M., and Crow, J. F. 1963a. The measurement of effective population number. *Evolution* 17:279–88.

————. 1963b. On the maximum avoidance of inbreeding. *Genet. Rev. Cambridge* 4:399–415.

————. 1964. The number of alleles that can be maintained in a finite population. *Genetics* 49:725–38.

Kimura, M., and Weiss, G. H. 1964. The stepping stone model of population structure and decrease of genetic correlation with distance. *Genetics* 49:561–76.

Kojima, K. 1959a. Role of epistasis and overdominance in stability of equilibria with selection. *Proc. Nat. Acad. Sci.* 45:984–89.

————. 1959b. Stable equilibria for the optimum model. *Proc. Nat. Acad. Sci.* 45:989–93.

————. 1965. The evolutionary dynamics of two gene systems: *Computers in biomedical research*, 1:197–220. New York: Academic Press.

Kojima, K., and Kelleher, T. M. 1961. Changes of mean fitness in a random mating population when epistasis and linkage are present. *Genetics* 46:527–40.

————. 1962. Survival of mutant genes. *Amer. Nat.* 96:329–46.

Kolmogorov, A. 1935. Deviations from Hardy's formula in partial isolation. *C. R. de l'Acad. des Sciences de l'URSS* 3:129–32.

Latter, B. D. H. 1959. Natural selection for an intermediate optimum. *Aust. Jour. Biol. Sci.* 13:30–35.

Laven, H. 1959. Speciation by cytoplasmic isolation in the Culex pipiens complex. *Cold Spring Harbor Symp. Quant. Biol.* 24:166–73.

Lerner, I. M. 1950. *Population genetics and animal improvement.* Cambridge: At the University Press.

———. 1954. *Genetic homeostasis.* New York: John Wiley & Sons.

Levene, H. 1953. Genetic equilibrium when more than one ecological niche is available. *Amer. Nat.* 87:331–33.

Lewontin, R. C. 1958. A general method for investigating the equilibrium of gene frequencies in a population. *Genetics* 43:419–34.

———. 1963. The role of linkage in natural selection: *Genetics today. Proc. XI Internat. Congress of Genetics,* pp. 517–24. Oxford: Pergamon Press.

———. 1964a. The interaction of selection and linkage. I. General considerations: Heterotic models. *Genetics* 49:49–67.

———. 1964b. The interaction of selection and linkage. II. Optimum models. *Genetics* 50:757–82.

Lewontin, R. C., and Kojima, K. 1960. The evolutionary dynamics of complex polymorphisms. *Evolution.* 14:458–72.

Li, C. C. 1955a. *Population Genetics.* Chicago: Univ. of Chicago Press.

———. 1955b. The stability of an equilibrium and the average fitness of a population. *Amer. Nat.* 89:281–95.

———. 1963. Equilibrium under differential selection of the sexes. *Evolution* 17:482–96.

———. 1967. Genetic equilibrium under selection. *Biometrics* 23:397–484.

Lotka, A. J. 1925. *Elements of physical biology.* Baltimore: Williams & Wilkins Co.

Lush, J. L. 1940. Intrasire correlations or regressions of offspring on dam as a method of estimating heritability of characteristics. *Proc. Am. Soc. Animal Prod.* 1940:293–301.

———. 1949. Heritability of quantitative characteristics in farm animals. *Proc. 8th Internat. Congr. of Genetics. Hereditas Suppl.* (1949): 356–75.

———. 1950. The theory of inbreeding. By Ronald A. Fisher. *Amer. Jour. Human Genet.* 2:97–100.

Malécot, G. 1948. *Les mathématiques de l'hérédité.* Paris: Masson, et Cie.

Mandel, S. P. H. 1959. The stability of a multiple allelic system. *Heredity* 13:289–302.

Martin, F. G., and Cockerham, C. C. 1960. High speed selection studies. In *Biometrical genetics,* pp. 35–45. Edited by O. Kempthorne. New York: Pergamon Press.

Mather, K. 1941. Variation and selection of polygenic characters. *Jour. Genet.* 41:159–93.

————. 1943. Polygenic inheritance and natural selection. *Biol. Rev.* 18:32–64.

————. 1949. *Biometrical genetics.* New York: Dover Publications.

————. 1954. The genetical units of continuous variation. *Proc. 9th Internat. Genet. Congress. Caryologia Suppl.* 6:100–123.

Mayo, O. 1966. On the problem of self-incompatibility alleles. *Biometrics* 22:111–20.

Mendel, G. 1866. Versuche über Pflanzen Hybriden. *Verh. Naturforsch. Ver in Brünn* 4:3–47. Translation in *Mendel's principles of heredity* by W. Bateson, 1909. Cambridge: At the University Press.

Michaelis, P. 1955. Über Gesetzmässigkeiten der Plasmon-Umkombination und über eine Methode zur Trennung einer Plastiden-Chondriosomenresp-Sphaerosomen (Mikrosomen)-und einer Zytoplasmavererbung. *Cytologia* 20:318–38.

————. 1959. Cytoplasmic inheritance and the segregation of plasma genes. *Proc. X Intern. Genetics Congress* 1:375–85.

Moran, P. A. P. 1962. *The statistical processes of evolutionary theory.* Oxford: Clarendon Press.

————. 1964. On the nonexistence of adaptive topographies. *Ann. Human Genet.* 27:383–93.

Morton, N. E., Crow, J. F., and Muller, H. J. 1956. An estimate of the mutational damage in man from data on consanguineous marriages. *Proc. Nat. Acad. Sci.* 42:855–63.

Muller, H. J. 1932. Further studies on the nature and causes of gene mutation. *Proc. 6th Intern. Congress Genet.* 1:213–55.

————. 1950. Our load of mutations. *Amer. Jour. Human Genet.* 2:111–76.

Nanney, D. L., and Allen, S. L. 1959. Intranuclear coordination in Tetrahymena. *Physiol. Zool.* 32:221–29.

Narain, P. 1965. Homozygosity in a selfed population with an arbitrary number of linked loci. *Jour. Genet.* 59:254–66.

————. 1966. Effect of linkage on homozygosity of a population under mixed selfing and random mating. *Genetics* 54:303–14.

Nei, M. 1963. Effect of selection on the components of genetic variance. In *Statistical genetics and plant breeding.* Edited by W. D. Hanson and H. F. Robinson. Nat. Acad. Sci.–Nat. Res. Council Publ. No. 982:501–14.

————. 1968. The frequency distribution of lethal chromosomes in finite populations. *Proc. Nat. Acad. Sci.* 60:517–24.

Nei, M., and Murata, M. 1966. Effective population size when fertility is inherited. *Gen. Res. Cambridge* 8:257–60.

O'Donald, P. 1960. Assortative mating in a population in which two alleles are segregating. *Heredity* 14:389–96.

Parsons, P. A. 1963a. Polymorphism and the balanced polygenic combination. *Evolution* 17:564–74.

————. 1963b. Complex polymorphism where the coupling and repulsion heterozygotes differ. *Heredity* 18:369–74.

Pearl, R. 1913. A contribution towards an analysis of the problem of inbreeding. *Amer. Nat.* 47:577–614.

———. 1914. On the results of inbreeding a Mendelian population: A correction and extension of previous conclusions. *Amer. Nat.* 48:57–62.

———. 1917. Studies on inbreeding. *Amer. Nat.* 51:545–59, 636–39.

Pearson, K. 1904. On a generalized theory of alternative inheritance with special reference to Mendel's laws. *Phil. Trans. Roy. Soc.* A203:53–86.

Penrose, L. S., Smith, S. M., and Sprott, D. A. 1956. On the stability of allelic systems with special reference to haemoglobins A, S and C. *Ann. Human Genet.* 21:90–93.

Plunkett, C. R. 1932. Temperature as a tool of research in phenogenetics: Methods and results. *Proc. 6th Intern. Congress of Genetics* 2:158–60.

Preer, J. P. 1950. Microscopically visible bodies in the cytoplasm of the "killer" strains of Paramecium aurelia. *Genetics* 35:344–62.

Punnett, R. C. 1915. *Mimicry in butterflies.* Cambridge: At the University Press.

Reeve, E. C. R. 1955. Inbreeding with the homozygotes at a disadvantage. *Ann. Human Genetics* 19:332–46.

———. 1957. Inbreeding with selection and linkage. I. Selfing. *Ann. Human Genet.* 21:277–88.

Reeve, E. C. R., and Gower, J. C. 1958. Inbreeding with selection and linkage. II. Sib-mating. *Ann. Human Genet.* 23:36–49.

Rhoades, M. M. 1943. Genic induction of an inherited cytoplasmic difference. *Proc. Nat. Acad. Sci.* 29:327–29.

———. 1946. Plastid mutations. *Cold Spring Harbor Symp. Quant. Biol.* 11:202–7.

Robbins, R. B. 1918. Application of mathematics to breeding problems. II. *Genetics* 3:73–92.

Robertson, A. 1952. The effect of inbreeding on the variation due to recessive genes. *Genetics* 37:189–207.

———. 1956. The effect of selection against extreme deviants based on deviation or on homozygosis. *Jour. Genet.* 54:236–48.

———. 1962. Selection for heterozygotes in small populations. *Genetics* 47:1291–1300.

———. 1964. The effect of nonrandom mating within inbred lines on the rate of inbreeding. *Genet. Res. Comb.* 5:164–67.

Sandler, L., and Novitski, E. 1957. Meiotic drive as an evolutionary force. *Amer. Nat.* 91:105–10.

Schäfer, W. 1936. Über die Zunahme der Isozygotie (Gleicherbigkeit) bei fortgesetzter Bruder-Schwester-Inzucht. *Zeit. ind. Abst. Ver.* 72:50–79.

Schnell, F. W. 1961. Some general formulations of linkage effects in inbreeding. *Genetics* 46:947–57.

Shull, G. H. 1908. The composition of a field of maize. *Amer. Breeders Assoc.* 4:296–301.

Singh, M., and Lewontin, R. C. 1966. Stable equilibria under optimizing selection. *Proc. Nat. Acad. Sci.* 56:1345–48.

Sonneborn, T. M. 1943. Genes and cytoplasm. I. The determination and inheritance of the killer character in variety 4 of Paramecium aurelia. *Proc. Nat. Acad. Sci.* 29:329–38.

Stratton, J. A., Morse, P. M., Chu, L. J., and Hutner, P. A. 1941. *Elliptical, cylinder and spheroidal wave functions.* New York: John Wiley & Sons.

Wahlund, S. 1928. Zusammensetzung von Population und Korrelationserscheinung vom Standpunkt der Vererbungslehre aus Betrachtet. *Hereditas* 11:65–105.

Watson, G. S., and Caspari, E. 1960. The behavior of cytoplasmic pollen sterility in populations. *Evolution* 14:56–63.

Watson, H. W., and Galton, F. 1874. On the probability of the extinction of families. *Jour. Anthrop. Inst. Great Britain and Ireland* 4:138–44.

Weinberg, W. 1908. Über den Nachweis der Vererbung beim Menschen. Jahreshaft Ver. vaterlandisch. *Naturkunde Württemberg.* 64:368–82.

———. 1909. Über Vererbungsgesetze beim Menschen. *Zeit. ind Abst. Ver.* 1:277–330.

———. 1910. Weitere Beiträge zur Theorie der Vererbung. *Arch. Rass. Gesellsch. Biol.* 7:35–49.

Wentworth, E. N., and Remick, B. L. 1916. Some breeding properties of the generalized Mendelian population. *Genetics* 1:608–16.

Winters, L. M. 1952. Rotational crossbreeding and heterosis. In *Heterosis*, pp. 371–77. Edited by J. W. Gowen. Ames, Iowa: Ames State College Press.

Workman, P. L. 1964. The maintenance of heterozygosity by partial negative assortative mating. *Genetics* 50:1369–82.

Workman, P. L., and Jain, S. K. 1966. Zygotic selection under mixed random mating and self-fertilization: Theory and problems of estimation. *Genetics* 54:159–71.

Wright, J. W. 1952. Pollen dispersion of some forest trees. U.S. Forest Service Northeast Forest Exper. Sta. Paper No. 46.

Wright, S. 1917. The average correlation within subgroups of a population. *Jour. Washington Acad. Sci.* 7:532–35.

———. 1920. The relative importance of heredity and environment in determining the piebald pattern of guinea pigs. *Proc. Nat. Acad. Sci.* 6:320–32.

———. 1921. Systems of mating. *Genetics* 6:111–78.

———. 1922a. Coefficients of inbreeding and relationship. *Amer. Nat.* 56:330–38.

———. 1922b. The effects of inbreeding and crossbreeding on guinea pigs. III. Crosses between highly inbred families. Bull. 1121, U.S. Department Agric., pp. 1–60.

———. 1929a. Fisher's theory of dominance. *Amer. Nat.* 63:274–79.

———. 1929b. The evolution of dominance. *Amer. Nat.* 63:556–61.

———. 1929c. Evolution in a Mendelian population. *Anat. Rec.* 44:287.

———. 1931. Evolution in Mendelian populations. *Genetics* 16:97–159.

———. 1932. The roles of mutation, inbreeding, crossbreeding and selection in evolution. *Proc. 6th Intern. Congress of Genetics* 1:356–66.

———. 1933a. Inbreeding and homozygosis. *Proc. Nat. Acad. Sci.* 19:411–20.

———. 1933b. Inbreeding and recombination. *Proc. Nat. Acad. Sci.* 19:420–33.

———. 1934. The results of crosses between inbred strains of guinea pigs, differing in number of digits. *Genetics* 19:537–51.

———. 1935. The analysis of variance and the correlations between relatives with respect to deviations from an optimum. *Jour. Genet.* 30:243–56.

———. 1937. The distribution of gene frequencies in populations. *Proc. Nat. Acad. Sci.* 23:307–20.

———. 1938a. Size of population and breeding structure in relation to evolution. *Science* 87:430–31.

———. 1938b. The distribution of gene frequencies under irreversible mutation. *Proc. Nat. Acad. Sci.* 24:253–59.

———. 1938c. The distribution of gene frequencies in populations of polyploids. *Proc. Nat. Acad. Sci.* 24:372–77.

———. 1939a. The distribution of self-fertility alleles in populations. *Genetics* 24:538–52.

———. 1939b. Statistical genetics in relation to evolution. In *Actualités scientifiques et industrielles*. No. 802, pp. 5–64. Exposés de Biométrie et de la statistique biologique XIII. Paris: Hermann et Cie.

———. 1940a. Breeding structure of populations in relation to speciation. *Amer. Nat.* 74:232–48.

———. 1940b. The statistical consequences of Mendelian heredity in relation to speciation. *The New Systematics*, pp. 161–83. Edited by J. S. Huxley. Oxford: Clarendon Press.

———. 1942. Statistical genetics and evolution. *Bull. Amer. Math. Soc* 48:223–46.

———. 1943a. Isolation by distance. *Genetics* 28:114–38.

———. 1943b. An analysis of local variability of flower color in Linanthus parryae. *Genetics* 28:139–56.

———. 1945a. Tempo and mode in evolution: A critical review. *Ecology* 26:415–19.

———. 1945b. The differential equation of the distribution of gene frequencies. *Proc. Nat. Acad. Sci.* 31:383–89.

———. 1946. Isolation by distance under diverse systems of mating. *Genetics* 31:39–59.

———. 1948. On the roles of directed and random changes in gene frequency in the genetics of populations. *Evolution* 2:279–94.

———. 1949a. Genetics of populations. *Encyclopaedia Britannica*, 14th ed., 10:111–12.

———. 1949b. Adaptation and selection. In *Genetics, paleontology and evolution*, pp. 365–89. Edited by G. L. Jepson, G. G. Simpson, and E. Mayr. Princeton, N.J.: Princeton Univ. Press.

———. 1951. The genetical structure of populations. *Ann. Eugenics* 15:323–54.

———. 1952a. The genetics of quantitative variability. In *Quantitative inheritance*, pp. 5–41. Edited by E. C. R. Reeve and C. H. Waddington. Agric. Res. Council. London: Her Majesty's Stationery Office.

———. 1952b. The theoretical variance within and among subdivisions of a population that is in a steady state. *Genetics* 37:312–21.

———. 1955. Classification of the factors of evolution. *Cold Spring Harbor Symp. Quant. Biol.* 20:16–24D.

———. 1956. Modes of selection. *Amer. Nat.* 50:5–24.

———. 1960a. Physiological genetics, ecology of populations and natural selection. In *Evolution after Darwin*, 1:429–75. Edited by Sol Tax. Chicago: Univ. of Chicago Press. Also 1959, *Perspectives in Biol. and Med.* 3:107–51.

———. 1960b. On the number of self-incompatibility alleles maintained in equilibrium by a given mutation rate in a population of a given size: A re-examination. *Biometrics* 16:61–85.

———. 1963. Discussion of "Systems of mating in mammalian genetics" by E. L. Green and D. P. Doolittle. In *Methodology in mammalian genetics*, pp. 42–53. Edited by W. J. Burdette. San Francisco: Holden-Day.

———. 1964. Stochastic process in evolution. In *Stochastic models in medicine and biology*, pp. 199–241. Edited by J. Gurland. Madison, Wis.: Univ. of Wisconsin Press.

———. 1965a. Factor interaction and linkage in evolution. *Proc. Roy. Soc. London* B162:80–104.

———. 1965b. The distribution of self-incompatibility alleles in populations. *Evolution* 18:609–19.

———. 1965c. The interpretation of population structure by F-statistics with special regard to systems of mating. *Evolution* 19:395–420.

———. 1966. Polyallelic random drift in relation to evolution. *Proc. Nat. Acad. Sci.* 55:1074–81.

———. 1967. "Surfaces" of selective value. *Proc. Nat. Acad. Sci.* 58:165–72.

Wright, S., and Chase, H. B. 1936. On the genetics of the spotted pattern of the guinea pig. *Genetics* 21:758–87.

Wright, S., and Dobzhansky, Th. 1946. Genetics of natural populations. XII. Experimental reproduction of some of the changes caused by natural selection in certain populations of *Drosophila pseudoobscura*. *Genetics* 31:125–56.

Wright, S., and Kerr, W. E. 1954. Experimental studies of the distribution of gene frequencies in very small populations of Drosophila melanogaster. II. Bar. *Evolution* 8:225–40.

Yule, G. U. 1902. Mendel's laws and their probable relation to intra-racial heredity. *New Phytol.* 1:192–207, 222–38.

———. 1906. On the theory of inheritance of quantitative compound characters and the basis of Mendel's law: A preliminary note. *Rept. 3rd Intern. Congr. Genet.*, pp. 140–42.

AUTHOR INDEX

SUBJECT INDEX

DATE DUE